D0282717

Springer Series on Social Work

Albert R. Roberts, PhD, Series Editor
Graduate School of Social Work, Rutgers
The State University of New Jersey

Advisory Board: Gloria Bonilla-Santiago, PhD, Barbara Berkman, PhD, Elaine P. Congress, DSW, Gilbert J. Greene, PhD, Jesse Harris, DSW, C. Aaron McNeece, DSW

2007 Theoretical Perspectives for Direct Social Work Practice:
A Generalist-Eclectic Approach
Nick Coady, PhD, and Peter Lehmann, PhD, LCSW

2007 Handbook of Forensic Mental Health With Victims and Offenders:
Assessment, Treatment, and Research
David W. Springer, PhD, and Albert R. Roberts, PhD

2006 Cognitive Behavior Therapy in Clinical Social Work Practice
Tammie Ronen, PhD, and Arthur Freeman, EdD, ABPP

2005 Multicultural Perspectives in Working With Families, Second Edition
Elaine P. Congress, ACSW, DSW, and Manny Gonzalez, DSW

2004 Dilemmas in Human Services Management: Illustrative Case Studies
Raymond Sanchez Mayers, PhD, Federico Souflee, Jr, PhD, and Dick J. Schoech, PhD

2004 The Changing Face of Health Care Social Work: Professional Practice in
Managed Behavioral Health Care, Second Edition
Sophia F. Dziegielewski, PhD, LCSW

2003 Adolescent Pregnancy: Policy and Prevention Services
Naomi Farber, PhD, MSW

2002 Human Behavior and the Social Environment:
Integrating Theory and Evidence-Based Practice
John S. Wodarski, PhD, and Sophia F. Dziegielewski, PhD, LCSW, Editors

2002 A Guide for Nursing Home Social Workers
Elise M. Beaulieu, MSW, ACSW, LICSW

2002 New Routes to Human Services: Information and Referral
Risha W. Levinson, DSW

2001 Social Work Practice and Psychopharmacology
Sophia F. Dziegielewski, PhD, LCSW, and Ana Leon, PhD, LCSW

2001 Understanding Narrative Therapy: A Guidebook for the Social Worker
Paul Abels, MSW, PhD, and Sonia L. Abels, MSW

2001 Law and Social Work Practice, Second Edition
Raymond Albert, MSW, JD

2000 Evidence-Based Social Work Practice With Families: A Lifespan Approach
Jacqueline Corcoran, PhD

Nick Coady, PhD, is Professor, Faculty of Social Work (FSW), and Associate Dean, Faculty of Graduate Studies, Wilfrid Laurier University (WLU), Waterloo, Ontario, Canada. Dr. Coady has been with the FSW/WLU since 1994, and prior to that he taught in the FSW at the University of Calgary for 5 years. He teaches direct practice, and his practice background includes residential child welfare work, individual and family counseling with high-risk adolescents, and group work with abusive men. Dr. Coady's research, teaching, and publications have focused on the importance of relationship and other common factors in direct practice. His recent research has involved an exploration of good helping relationships in child welfare and men's experiences of child welfare involvement.

Peter Lehmann, PhD, LCSW, is Associate Professor, School of Social Work, The University of Texas at Arlington. His research interests include evaluating men and women charged with domestic violence as well as fidelity development with solution-focused therapy. Dr. Lehmann divides his time between teaching direct practice and codirecting the Community Services Center at the School of Social Work.

Theoretical Perspectives for Direct Social Work Practice

A Generalist-Eclectic Approach

Second Edition

Nick Coady, PhD

Peter Lehmann, PhD, LCSW

Editors

SPRINGER PUBLISHING COMPANY

New York

Springer Publishing Company, LLC
11 West 42nd Street
New York, NY 10036
www.springerpub.com

Acquisitions Editor: Jennifer Perillo
Project Manager: Carol Cain
Cover Design: Joanne E. Honigman
Composition: Apex Publishing, LLC

07 08 09 10/ 5 4 3 2 1

Library of Congress Cataloging-in-Publication Data

Theoretical perspectives for direct social work practice : a
generalist-eclectic approach / [edited by] Nick Coady, Peter Lehmann.—2nd ed.
    p. cm.
  Includes bibliographical references and index.
  ISBN-13: 978-0-8261-0286-7 (alk. paper)
  ISBN-10: 0-8261-0286-7 (alk. paper)
  1. Social case work. I. Coady, Nick. II. Lehmann, Peter, Ph. D.

HV43.T42 2008
361.3'2—dc22   2007022456

Printed in the United States of America by Bang Printing.

To my best friends: my partner, Laurie, and my daughters,
Devyn and Blaire (with honorable mention to the members
of the Wednesday night poker club, including my father, Matt;
members of Thursday night pool; and the amigos golf foursome).

Nick Coady

To Delphine, Daley, and Rory, my forever and loving family,
and to the best and really smart student interns who learn about
practice at the Community Service Center, you keep me focused
on "building what's strong not just fixing what's wrong."

Peter Lehmann

Contents

PART III: MID-LEVEL THEORIES FOR DIRECT SOCIAL WORK PRACTICE

PART IV: SERVICE MODELS FOR HIGH-RISK POPULATIONS

PART V: SUMMARY AND CONCLUSION

About the Contributors

Rudy Buckman, PhD, is an assistant professor of counseling at Southern Arkansas University. From 1991 to 2004, Dr. Buckman was a therapist/clinical coordinator and cofounder of the Reunion Institute at the Salesmanship Club Youth and Family Centers, Inc. He has published several articles and has presented to over thirty professional conferences.

Cheryl-Anne Cait, PhD, is an associate professor at the Lyle S. Hallman Faculty of Social Work, Wilfrid Laurier University, where she teaches practice with individuals as well as research methods. Her research and writing focuses on adolescent bereavement, mentoring in Aboriginal communities, and clinical social work using relational and intersubjectivity theories. Dr. Cait practice specialization is children, adolescents, and families.

Scottye J. Cash, PhD, is an associate professor of social work at Ohio State University. She is the principal investigator on an evaluation project to determine the reliability and predictive validity of Ohio's new safety and risk assessment systems. Dr. Cash has completed numerous research projects in child welfare and has worked to bring these findings into the classroom. Dr. Cash teaches practice, policy, statistics, and research at the BSW, MSW, and PhD levels.

Norman H. Cobb, PhD, is an associate professor in the School of Social Work at the University of Texas at Arlington. He was the director of the School of Social Work's mental health clinic for 7 years. He currently teaches classes in mental health treatment, couples counseling, and human behavior. He maintains a small clinical practice with adults and adolescents.

Elaine P. Congress, PhD, is a professor and associate dean at Fordham University's Graduate School of Social Service. She has lectured and published extensively in the areas of cultural diversity, social work ethics, and social work education. Her most recent book, *Multicultural Perspectives in Working With Families* (Springer Publishing, 2005), includes the *culturagram*, a family assessment tool for working with culturally diverse families. Before entering academia she worked as a practitioner, supervisor, and administrator in a community mental health clinic serving immigrant families.

Jacqueline Corcoran, PhD, is an associate professor at Virginia Commonwealth University's School of Social Work. She was previously on the faculty at the University of Texas at Arlington School of Social Work from 1996 to 2000, where she also served as codirector of the Community Service Clinic at the School of Social Work. She received her PhD from the University of Texas at Austin in 1996.

Theresa J. Early, PhD, is an associate professor and the doctoral program director at Ohio State University. She has managed mental health programs for adults, been a trainer for children's mental health case managers, developed a training curriculum for crisis intervention with children with serious emotional disorders and their families, and conducted research about families with children with serious emotional disorders. Her current work centers on recovery-oriented organizational change in mental health settings.

Donald K. Granvold, PhD, is a professor of social work at the University of Texas at Arlington. Dr. Granvold has been a leader in the advancement of cognitive-behavioral and constructivist treatment methods. He has authored numerous book chapters and articles in social work and allied helping profession journals, and he is editor of the volume *Cognitive and Behavioral Treatment: Methods and Applications*. Dr. Granvold is a Founding Fellow in the Academy of Cognitive Therapy.

Rosemary Hazelton, PhD, is currently a practicing psychotherapist in Toronto, working with children and adolescents as well as adults and couples. She has a clinical background in child and family mental health. Her research has examined the influence of early attachment relationships on the effects of parental separation, and she is trained in the classification and scoring system of the Adult Attachment Interview.

Delane Kinney, PhD, is the associate executive director of the Salesmanship Club Youth and Family Centers, Dallas. She has served in an advisory capacity to nonprofit agencies and is a past president of the Dallas Psychological Association. Dr. Kinney maintains a small but active private practice. She is interested in the reciprocal relationship of mental health and culture, politics, and power and is committed to facilitating more responsive and respectful mental health services.

Karen S. Knox, PhD, is an associate professor for the School of Social Work at Texas State University. She has been a social work practitioner since 1982, specializing in the fields of child abuse, sexual assault, sex offenders, and victims of violent crimes. Her direct practice experience includes working with Child Protective Services, the Austin Police Department Victim Services Division, the Travis County District Attorney's Office, and the Travis County Juvenile Court Adolescent Sex Offender Program.

James I. Martin, PhD, is an associate professor and the director of the doctoral program at New York University's School of Social Work. His scholarship focuses on HIV prevention, the relationship between sexuality and spirituality, clinical practice, GLBT identities, and other issues related to sexual orientation and gender identity. His writing appears in numerous social work and interdisciplinary journals and in several anthologies on clinical practice and research methods.

Christine Mello, PhD, has been a practicing school psychologist for 22 years. She has been trained by Dr. Kathleen Nader to screen and treat traumatized children. Her work has included treatment and ongoing consultation following school disasters as well as training mental health professionals in the use of PTSD screening instruments.

Kathleen Nader, PhD, is known nationally and internationally for her work in the field of posttraumatic stress. Dr. Nader served as a director for a UCLA trauma program. Her work has included scale development, assessments, consultation, training, and specialized interventions for children and adults following catastrophic events in the United States and abroad. Dr. Nader has written and coauthored a variety of publications, screening instruments, and videotapes regarding the assessment and treatment of trauma in youth and regarding school interventions. She was among the first researchers to conduct rigorous study of childhood PTSD and has coauthored widely used childhood trauma and exposure assessment instruments.

Blanca M. Ramos, PhD, is an associate professor at the School of Social Welfare, State University of New York at Albany, where she teaches clinical social work, cultural diversity, and task-centered practice. Her scholarly activities focus on task-centered practice, health disparities, domestic violence, and mental health with a focus on multicultural social work and Latino populations.

Elizabeth Randall, PhD, is an associate professor of social work at West Virginia University. She has 21 years of direct practice experience in the field of behavioral health, including inpatient and outpatient work with children, youth, adults, families, and groups. She is a member of Phi Kappa Phi, the president of the West Virginia State Chapter of the National Association of Social Workers, and a member of the West Virginia Comprehensive Behavioral Health Advisory Board.

Ann Reese, MSW, PhD, has been a clinician and trainer with Salesmanship Club Youth and Family Centers since 1988. Dr. Reese serves as the agency's codirector of Family Therapy. She is a licensed clinical social worker and a licensed marriage and family therapist. During her career, Dr. Reese has gained extensive experience with families in which sexual and physical abuse has occurred. Dr. Reese has coauthored journal articles, has consulted with several nonprofit organizations, has taught and mentored many future clinicians, and maintains a private practice.

Albert R. Roberts, PhD, is a professor of criminal justice and social work in the Faculty of Arts and Sciences at Rutgers, the State University of New Jersey, Livingston College Campus. He is the author or editor of nearly 30 books and the author of numerous journal articles. He is the editor of the Springer Series on Family Violence and the Springer Series on Social Work. He edited *The Social Workers' Desk Reference*, which has become a standard reference in the field since it was published in 2002, and he coedited, with David W. Springer, the *Handbook of Forensic Mental Health With Victims and Offenders* (Springer Publishing, 2007).

Michael Rothery, PhD, is a professor at the University of Calgary in Canada. He teaches social work theory and practice, and he is active in the community as a volunteer and scholar. His publications include books on clinical practice, family violence, and research methods. Throughout his professional and academic career, Dr. Rothery has studied services to vulnerable families, with violence in adult intimate relationships having been an especially strong interest for many years.

Christine Flynn Saulnier, PhD, is the author of numerous articles on feminist practice and other social justice issues. She is coeditor of *Affilia: Journal of Women and Social Work*. She has practiced in school, health, community, and higher education settings. A professor and former dean of social work at Simmons College in Boston, Dr. Saulnier wrote *Feminist Theories and Social Work: Approaches and Applications*.

Carol A. Stalker, PhD, is a professor in the Faculty of Social Work at Wilfrid Laurier University. She has 20 years of practice experience in mental health settings and teaches clinical social work practice courses. Her publications include an examination of attachment organization in women sexually abused as children and the study of insecure attachment as a predictor of outcome following inpatient treatment for trauma associated with child abuse.

Eleanor Reardon Tolson, PhD, is an associate professor emeritus at Jane Addams College of Social Work, University of Illinois at Chicago, where she taught practice, research, and human behavior. Her authored and edited books include *Generalist Practice: A Task-Centered Approach*, *The Metamodel and Clinical Social Work*, *Perspectives on Direct Practice Evaluation*, and *Models of Family Treatment*.

Leslie Tutty, PhD, is a professor with the Faculty of Social Work at the University of Calgary where she teaches courses in both clinical social work methods and research. Over the past 19 years, her research has focused on services for family violence including a number of evaluations of shelter and post-shelter programs for abused women, support groups for abused women, treatment for adult and child victims of sexual abuse, and groups for men who abuse their partners. Since 1999, Dr. Tutty has served as the academic research coordinator of RESOLVE Alberta, a tri-provincial research institute on family violence. RESOLVE is one of Canada's centers of excellence in research on violence against women and children. As such, Dr. Tutty has collaborated with a number of the leading researchers in family violence across the country. Her extensive body of research on domestic violence spans the perspectives of social services, justice, health, and mental health and addresses prevention, intervention, and policy.

Preface

The primary purpose of the second edition of our book continues to be to provide an overview of theories for direct social work practice and a framework for integrating the use of theory with central social work principles and values, as well as with the artistic elements of practice. It is intended primarily for graduate-level social work students and practitioners. This book has similarities to other books that provide surveys of clinical theories; however, we think it has a number of distinctive and useful features. In brief, these features include (a) grounding direct practice specialization firmly in the generalist perspective of social work practice; (b) documenting the trend toward and rationale and empirical support for eclecticism in the broad field of counseling/psychotherapy, and reviewing various approaches to eclecticism; (c) bringing order to and demystifying theories by differentiating among levels of theory, organizing direct practice theories into like groupings, and providing an overview of the central characteristics of each grouping of theories; (d) providing a critical perspective on the dominant, scientific paradigm of direct practice that centers the use of theory and technique, and putting equal emphasis on the artistic elements of practice; and (e) proposing the problem-solving model as a useful structure for facilitating the integration of the artistic and scientific elements of practice.

The contents of all of the chapters in this second edition have been revised and updated to reflect developments in theory, practice, and research since the first edition was published. There is a new chapter on relational theory that replaces the earlier chapter on interpersonal theory, and there are new authors of the chapters on cognitive-behavioral theory, existential theory, and wraparound services. We have updated information on the movement toward eclecticism in counseling/psychotherapy, and we have added a critique of the movement toward empirically supported treatments. We have also refined our conceptualization of the generalist-eclectic approach and our particular approach to eclecticism.

Similar to the first edition, the book is divided into five parts with a total of 21 chapters.

The first three chapters constitute Part I of this book, which focuses on explicating our generalist-eclectic approach to direct social work practice. The next three parts of the book review various theories, models, and therapies for direct practice, categorized according to level of abstraction. In Part II, high-level/meta-theories for direct practice are presented. The two chapters in this part focus on ecological systems theory and individual and family development theory. Part III is divided into four sections of three chapters each and focuses on theories, models, and therapies for direct practice that are at a mid-level of abstraction. The four sections contain chapters on psychodynamic, cognitive-behavioral, humanistic and feminist, and postmodern theories. In Part IV, three chapters on models and therapies that have been developed for specific populations, particularly those who are disadvantaged and/or at high risk, are presented. Part V consists of a summary chapter that considers the similarities and differences between the theories, models, and therapies that are reviewed in the book and the principles and values that are integral to our generalist-eclectic approach. The issue of integrating the use of theory with the artistic elements of practice via the problem-solving model is also revisited in this final chapter, and implications for research and practice are discussed.

We are very grateful to all of the contributing authors for taking time from their busy schedules and lives to write the original chapters contained herein. Their willingness to follow the structural guidelines for the chapters, the clarity of their writing, and their being amenable to editorial suggestions made our work that much easier. We feel privileged to have collaborated with a group of very gifted and personable professionals. Special thanks go to Dr. Al Roberts, editor of the Springer Series on Social Work and contributor to this book, for his continuing support. We would also like to thank Jennifer Perillo, acquisitions editor at Springer, for her support and patience. Finally, thanks go to Jenn Bowler, who provided very helpful editorial assistance from the perspective of a social work student.

N. C.
Waterloo, ON
P. L.
Arlington, TX

PART I

The Generalist-Eclectic Approach

An Overview of and Rationale for a Generalist-Eclectic Approach to Direct Social Work Practice

Nick Coady and Peter Lehmann

The focus of this book is on theories for direct (or clinical, micro) social work practice. More specifically, the book focuses on theories for practice with individuals, although the relevance of these theories for practice with families and groups is also considered. Beyond simply offering a survey of clinical theories, we promote what we call "a generalist-eclectic approach" for the use of theory in direct practice.

Including the word "generalist" in the name of our approach might seem odd because one of the generally accepted hallmarks of generalist social work practice is that it spans direct and indirect (or macro) practice methods, whereas our approach focuses only on direct practice. By using the word "generalist" to describe our approach to direct practice, we want to emphasize our belief that specialization in direct practice must be firmly grounded in the generalist perspective of social work practice. Simply put, we believe that the values, principles, generic processes, and holistic perspective that are integral to generalist social work practice are a necessary foundation for direct practice specialization. Although this might be taken for granted by some, we think this sometimes gets lost in the rush to specialization.

One reason it is important to ensure that direct practice is grounded explicitly within the generalist perspective is because most theories that clinical social workers use have been developed outside of the profession and aspects of such theories may not fit well with some social work principles. When this is the case, we think that modifications to these aspects of theories are necessary. For example, theories that place the worker in the role of expert should be used in a more egalitarian, collaborative fashion, and theories that have a specific and narrow conception of human problems should be broadened to include consideration of a wide range of factors (e.g., environmental and sociocultural factors need to be considered along with biological, intrapsychic, and interpersonal factors).

A second reason for embedding direct practice within the generalist perspective is that the latter can function to broaden the mandate and role of direct practitioners beyond narrow clinical confines. For instance, we think it is important that the focus of clinical social work should include helping clients to meet basic needs by providing them with or linking them to resources and services as well as engaging in social advocacy for clients. The generalist perspective reminds us of the importance of such helping strategies.

This chapter provides an overview to our generalist-eclectic approach to direct practice. First, we review the major elements of the generalist social work perspective that are central to our practice framework. Then, we provide an overview of the distinctive aspects of our generalist-eclectic approach. Finally, we discuss in some detail the issue of eclecticism, primarily with regard to the trend toward eclecticism over the last 30 years in the broad field of counseling/psychotherapy. The latter discussion includes (a) an overview of eclecticism that documents historical resistance to eclecticism, the fact of and reasons for the trend toward the eclectic use of theory and technique, and continuing resistance to eclecticism (particularly in the form of the empirically supported treatment movement); (b) a review of the four major approaches to eclecticism in the literature and some of the specific eclectic models within each of the approaches; and (c) a delineation of our approach to eclecticism.

ELEMENTS OF THE GENERALIST PERSPECTIVE THAT ARE CENTRAL TO OUR GENERALIST-ECLECTIC APPROACH

There are many characteristics that are common to the various descriptions of the generalist perspective in the literature. The major elements of generalist social work practice that we have adopted for our generalist-eclectic approach to direct social work practice have been drawn from a range of literature (Derezotes, 2000; Hepworth, Rooney, & Larsen, 2002; Johnson & Yanca, 2004; Kirst-Ashman & Hull, 2002; Landon, 1995, 1999; Locke, Garrison, & Winship, 1998; Miley, O'Melia, & DuBois, 2007; Shatz, Jenkins, & Sheafor, 1990; Sheafor & Horejsi, 2006; Sheafor & Landon, 1987; Timberlake, Farber, & Sabatino, 2002; Tolson, Reid, & Garvin, 2003). These elements are summarized in Table 1.1 and are described below.

A Person-in-Environment Perspective Informed by Ecological Systems Theory

"The central focus of social work traditionally seems to have been on people in their life situation complex—a simultaneous dual focus on individuals and environment" (Gordon, as cited in Compton & Galaway, 1994, p. 6). A generalist approach embraces this traditional person-in-environment perspective of social work practice. This perspective emphasizes the need to view the interdependence and mutual influence of people and their social and physical environments. Also, it recognizes the link between private troubles (i.e., individual problems) and public issues (i.e., social problems; Mills, 1959). The person-in-environment perspective has been one of the primary factors that has distinguished direct social work practice from the practice of other helping/counseling professions (i.e., psychology, marriage and family therapy, psychiatry).

Ecological systems theory (see chapter 4) is a conceptual framework for the person-in-environment perspective "that has achieved nearly universal acceptance in the profession" (Mattaini, Lowery, & Meyer, 1998, p. 12). This theory "recognizes an interrelatedness of human problems, life situations, and social conditions" (Shatz et al., 1990, p. 223). As explained in chapter 2, it is a high-level or meta-theory that is particularly

TABLE 1.1   Elements of the Generalist Perspective That Are Central to Our Generalist-Eclectic Approach

- A person-in-environment perspective that is informed by ecological systems theory

- An emphasis on the development of a good helping relationship that fosters empowerment

- The flexible use of a problem-solving model to provide structure and guidelines for work with clients

- A holistic, multilevel assessment that includes a focus on issues of diversity and oppression and on strengths

- The flexible and eclectic use of a wide range of theories and techniques that are selected on the basis of their relevance to each unique client situation

useful for helping workers to see the big picture in terms of the reciprocal influence of people and the various systems (e.g., family, work, community) with which they interact. As such, it "provides an organizing theoretical framework for the generalist practice approach" (Miley, O'Melia, & DuBois, 1998, p. 23).

The Development of a Good Helping Relationship That Fosters Empowerment

Historically, social work has led the helping professions in advocating the importance of a collaborative, warm, empathic, supportive worker–client relationship. Social workers have described this type of relationship as the "soul" (Biestek, 1957), "heart" (Perlman, 1979), and "major determinant" (Hollis, 1970) of the helping endeavor. Although clinical social work has drifted away from such an emphasis over the last few decades in favor of attention to the theoretical/technical/scientific aspects of practice (Coady, 1993b; Perlman, 1979), the generalist perspective has reemphasized the importance of the helping relationship.

Along with a reaffirmation of the importance of a good helping relationship, the generalist perspective has promoted a focus on empowerment. A number of authors of generalist textbooks (e.g., Landon, 1999; Locke et al., 1998; Miley et al., 2007) have combined a consideration of empowerment and the strengths perspective (Saleebey, 2006). For example, Miley and colleagues (2007) argued that "an orientation toward strengths and empowerment compels social workers to redefine their relationships to embrace the notion of collaboration and partnership" (p. 95). Gutiérrez (as cited in Miley et al., 2007) noted that this involves basing the helping relationship on "collaboration, trust, and shared power; accepting the client's definition of the problem; identifying and building upon the client's strengths; actively involving the client in the change process; [and] experiencing a sense of personal power within the helping relationship" (p. 130).

The Flexible Use of a Problem-Solving Model

Since Perlman's (1957) formulation of the problem-solving model for social casework, problem solving has been an integral part of social work practice. Most generalist approaches to social work practice include some version of the problem-solving model, and although there are various conceptualizations of the stages or phases of problem solving, all versions include guidelines for the entire helping process, from initial engagement to termination.

Some generalist approaches, in an effort to emphasize a strengths focus versus a problem focus, have renamed the problem-solving model.

For example, Locke and colleagues (1998) called their version of the problem-solving model a "phase model," and Miley and colleagues (2007) called their version "phases and processes of empowering practice." We agree, however, with McMillen, Morris, and Sherraden (2004), who contended that the recent "grudge match" within social work that pits strengths-based against problem-focused approaches represents a false and destructive dichotomy. Thus, our use of the term "problem solving model" does not denote a deficit or pathology orientation to practice. As is generally the case within social work, we construe problem-solving as a collaborative process between workers and clients that has the ultimate goal of capacity building and empowering clients (see chapter 3 for a more detailed discussion of problem solving).

A Holistic, Multilevel Assessment

The person-in-environment perspective and ecological systems theory suggest the necessity of a holistic, multilevel assessment. The term "holistic" refers to a "totality in perspective, with sensitivity to all the parts or levels that constitute the whole and to their interdependence and relatedness" (McMahon, 1996, p. 2). This represents a focus on the whole person (i.e., the physical, emotional, spiritual) in the context of his or her surroundings. Multilevel assessment goes hand in hand with a holistic focus because this means considering the entire range of factors, from micro to macro, that could be impacting a client. Thus, in conducting an assessment, the generalist direct practitioner should consider the potential influence of biophysical, intrapsychic, interpersonal/familial, environmental, and sociocultural factors. With regard to the latter class of factors, a generalist approach to direct practice assessment includes particular sensitivity to issues of diversity (e.g., gender, race, culture, class, sexual orientation, disability, age, religion) and oppression (Shatz et al., 1990). A generalist approach also demands that the assessment process include a focus on clients' strengths, resources, and competencies.

The Flexible and Eclectic Use of a Wide Range of Theories and Techniques

The commitment to a holistic, multilevel assessment precludes a rigid adherence to narrow theories of human problems. A generalist approach should be "unencumbered by any particular practice approach into which the client(s) might be expected to fit" (Sheafor & Landon, 1987, p. 666). Theories can be useful in the assessment process if they are considered tentatively as potential explanations for clients' problems; however, theories represent preconceived ideas about human problems and can blind one to alternative explanations.

Just as the assessment process must avoid rigid adherence to narrow theoretical perspectives, the same is true for the intervention process: "The generalist perspective requires that the social worker be *eclectic* (i.e., draw ideas and techniques from many sources)" (Sheafor & Horejsi, 2006, p. 87). Generalists are open to using theories and techniques that seem most relevant to the understanding of the unique client situation: "Single model practitioners do a disservice to themselves and their clients by attempting to fit all clients and problems into their chosen model" (Hepworth et al., 2002, p. 17). Guidelines for selecting theories and techniques for particular types of clients and problems are reviewed later in this chapter in the discussion of approaches to eclecticism, as well as in chapter 3.

DISTINCTIVE ASPECTS OF OUR GENERALIST-ECLECTIC APPROACH

A Differentiated Understanding and Demystification of Theory

One distinctive aspect to our approach of using theory in practice is differentiating between types and levels of theory and classifying clinical theories in like groupings. Our approach to understanding theory differentiates between (a) high-level or meta-theories (ecological systems and human development theories; see Part II, chapters 4–5); (b) mid-level practice theories (see Part III, chapters 6–17); and (c) low-level models for specific populations and problems (see Part IV, chapters 18–20). Meta-theories provide general guidance for holistic assessment and the generation of ideas for intervention; mid-level practice theories provide more specific ideas and directions for assessment and intervention for a range of presenting concerns; and low-level models provide more specific guidelines for work with specific populations and problems.

Furthermore, in an effort to demystify the vast array of practice theories that exist, we classify these theories in like groupings: psychodynamic (chapters 6–8), cognitive-behavioral (chapters 9–11), humanistic (chapters 12–13), feminist (chapter 14), and postmodern (chapters 15–17). We provide a brief overview of the distinguishing characteristics of each of these larger classifications of theory in chapter 2.

A Critical Perspective on the Use of Theory and Valuing the Artistic Elements in Practice

Perhaps the most distinctive feature of our generalist-eclectic approach is that it includes a critical perspective on the scientific view of practice, which contends that use of theory and technique reflects the essence and is the sole cornerstone of effective, professional direct social work practice. We certainly do not deny the value of this scientific approach to practice (after all, this book does focus on the use of theory in practice), although we clearly favor an eclectic use of theory and technique over adherence to a single theory and its techniques. Still, a key element of our framework is the recognition and valuing of the artistic elements of practice (Coady, 1995; Goldstein, 1990; Schon, 1983).

An artistic approach to practice includes the use of intuition, gut instincts, empathic listening, and inductive reasoning to collaboratively build with the client a theory that fits his or her unique case and to problem-solve creatively. We believe that practice is at least as much art as science, and is based at least as much on intuition, inductive reasoning, theory building, and general interpersonal/relationship skill as on the deductive application of theoretical knowledge and technical skill. Theory and research that pertain to this issue are reviewed both later in this chapter and in the second part of chapter 2, where the artistic, intuitive-inductive approach to practice is discussed. Our stance is that the best social work practice integrates scientific (i.e., theoretical/technical) and artistic (i.e., intuitive-inductive) elements.

Use of the Problem-Solving Model to Integrate the Art and Science of Practice

One of the main difficulties with both theoretically eclectic and artistic, intuitive-inductive approaches to practice is a lack of structure and guidelines for practice. For example, workers who are theoretically eclectic are sometimes overwhelmed by the sheer number of theories from which to choose. Also, practice can lack coherence and direction when one moves back and forth between theories, and sometimes workers can become preoccupied with, or distracted by, theoretical considerations. When this happens, the worker's understanding of and relationship with the client can suffer.

On the other hand, workers who prefer a more artistic, humanistic approach to practice that is based on intuition and inductive reasoning sometimes feel as if they are flying by the seat of their pants. Their practice can similarly lack coherence and direction. This is a major reason why some practitioners prefer to adhere to a single theoretical orientation in their practice—a single theory approach provides clear structure and guidelines. The cost of adherence to a single theory is too large, however—there is no one theory that is comprehensive enough to fit for all clients, and clients should not be forced into theoretical boxes.

We believe that the problem-solving model offers a solution to the lack of structure and guidelines for practice that are commonly experienced by workers who prefer theoretically eclectic and/or intuitive-inductive approaches to practice. The general strategies for the various phases of helping (from engagement to termination) that constitute the problem-solving model provide useful and flexible structure and guidelines for both the scientific and artistic approaches to practice and enable workers to integrate these two approaches in their work. The generality and flexibility of the guidelines in each phase of the problem-solving process provide sufficient structure and direction for practice while also allowing workers to integrate theory and use intuition and inductive reasoning. This issue is discussed briefly later in this chapter, and in more depth in chapter 3.

AN OVERVIEW OF ECLECTICISM

As is evident from the discussion above, eclecticism is an inherent orientation in generalist practice and is endorsed by most authors of generalist practice (e.g., Locke et al., 1998; Sheafor & Horejsi, 2006; Tolson et al., 2003) and direct practice (Derezotes, 2000; Hepworth et al., 2002) social work textbooks. For example, Hepworth and colleagues (2002) argued that "because human beings present a broad array of problems of living, no single approach or practice model is sufficiently comprehensive to adequately address them all" (p. 17). Also, a survey (Jensen, Bergin, & Greaves, 1990) of a wide variety of mental health professionals revealed that the majority (68%) of social workers consider themselves eclectic, although this was the second lowest percentage among the four professional groups surveyed (corresponding figures for marriage and family therapists, psychologists, and psychiatrists were 72%, 70%, and 59%, respectively). Despite clear and logical arguments for eclecticism and its prevalence in practice, it is still a contentious issue in the helping professions—and we think this is particularly so in clinical social work (see discussion in Historical Resistance to Eclecticism, below).

We would like to alert readers to the fact that our consideration of eclecticism in much of the rest of this chapter relies heavily on literature in clinical psychology because this is where most of the theory and research on eclecticism has been generated. Because of the reliance on literature from outside our profession, terms other than what we would normally use appear frequently (e.g., *therapist* instead of *worker*, *patient* instead of *client*, *therapy* instead of *direct practice* or *counseling*). We emphasize that we do not endorse the use of such terms and that our approach to eclecticism in direct practice is firmly rooted in social work values.

Historical Resistance to Eclecticism

A historical perspective is necessary to understand the contentiousness of eclecticism. For most of the 20th century the helping professions were marked by rigid adherence to narrow theories. Up until the 1960s, psychodynamic theory remained relatively unchallenged as the dominant theory in the helping professions (Lambert, Bergin, & Garfield, 2004). As humanistic and behavioral theories gained increasing prominence in the 1960s, they began to challenge the dominance of psychodynamic theory, and this initiated the era of the "competing schools of psychotherapy." For the most part, the next 25 years were marked by rigid adherence to one or another of an increasing number of theoretical camps, rancorous debate about which theory was right, and extensive research focused on proving which therapeutic approach was the most effective. Although there were some efforts to bridge the differences among the numerous competing schools of therapy, eclecticism was clearly a dirty word. As Norcross (1997) has commented, "You have all heard the classic refrains: eclectics are undisciplined subjectivists, jacks of all trades and masters of none, products of educational incompetency, muddle-headed, indiscriminate nihilists, fadmeisters, and people straddling the fence with both feet planted firmly in the air" (p. 87).

Unfortunately, such negative views of eclecticism are still prevalent within the field of counseling, particularly within clinical social work. Despite the endorsement of eclecticism by the generalist perspective, many social workers do not seem aware of or at least have not embraced the movement toward eclecticism that has been sweeping the larger field of psychotherapy. Also, despite the prevalence of eclecticism in practice, many social workers seem loath to admit this publicly because they know that eclecticism is still a dirty word in some circles. We have encountered many clinical social workers (academics and practitioners) who have disdain for eclecticism. One of the social work academics we approached to write a chapter for the first edition of this book declined to contribute because of our endorsement of both a generalist perspective and eclecticism. Unfortunately, such traditional negative views of eclecticism are difficult to change, and they quickly filter down to students. We have had students tell us that their field instructors counsel them to never admit to an eclectic orientation in a job interview because it would count against them.

It is not surprising that adherence to one theoretical orientation is most prevalent for those who were trained in an older, more traditional theory. The Jensen et al. (1990) survey found that the most common exclusive theoretical orientation was psychodynamic. Furthermore, to bolster our contention about the conservative streak in clinical social work, this survey found that "of individuals endorsing an exclusively psychodynamic approach, 74% were either psychiatrists or social workers" (p. 127) (25% of social workers and 36% of psychiatrists identified themselves as exclusively psychodynamic, whereas less than 10% of the other professional groups did so).

It should also be pointed out, however, that this phenomenon of adherence to one theoretical perspective also seems to be common for social workers who embrace the newer, fashionable therapeutic approaches—for example, in the 1990s, solution-focused therapy (see Stalker, Levene, & Coady, 1999), and in the 1980s, family systems therapy (see Coady, 1993a). Thus, we felt that it was important to emphasize our endorsement of eclecticism in the title of the book and to review the fact of and rationale for the trend toward eclecticism.

Documenting the Trend Toward Eclecticism in Counseling/Psychotherapy

Two decades ago, with regard to the broad field of counseling/psychotherapy, Garfield and Bergin (1986) concluded that the era of the competing schools of psychotherapy was over:

> A decisive shift in opinion has quietly occurred; and it has created an irreversible change in professional attitudes about psychotherapy and behavior change. The new view is that the long-term dominance of the major theories is over and that an eclectic position has taken precedence. (p. 7)

The trend toward eclecticism is evidenced in a number of ways. First, the precedence of eclecticism has been demonstrated by surveys. The Jensen et al. (1990) survey found that the majority of practitioners in each of the four groups of helping professionals were eclectic (68% overall). Furthermore, Lambert, Bergin, and Garfield (2004) have noted that such surveys repeatedly indicate that one-half to two-thirds of practitioners in North America prefer some type of eclecticism.

Second, an international professional organization, the Society for the Exploration of Psychotherapy Integration (SEPI), which has been in existence for over 15 years, has been influential in furthering the study of eclecticism in psychotherapy. SEPI has published the *Journal of Psychotherapy Integration* since 1991, holds annual conferences, and has created a Web site (www.cyberpsych.org/sepi). We should clarify that the term "integration" is often used together with or instead of the term eclecticism in the literature. In brief, the difference between these approaches is that integration focuses on blending theories together to arrive at a new, more comprehensive theory, while eclecticism simply draws on different theories and their techniques. The difference between eclectic and integrative models will be revisited in our discussion of approaches to eclecticism; however, for the most part, we use the term eclecticism to encompass both approaches.

Third, there has been a proliferation of literature on eclecticism. The number of journal articles focused on eclecticism continues to increase annually. This is also true for books on this topic. *Psychoanalysis and Behavior Therapy* (Wachtel, 1977), *Systems of Psychotherapy: A Transtheoretical Analysis* (Prochaska, 1979), and *Psychotherapy: An Eclectic Approach* (Garfield, 1980) were three of the first books that presented arguments for eclecticism and/or integration. Some of the more recent editions of such books include Dryden (1992), Stricker and Gold (1993), Garfield (1995), Gold (1996), Prochaska and Norcross (2003), Beutler and Harwood (2000), Lebow (2002), and Norcross and Goldfried (2005).

Reasons for the Trend Toward Eclecticism: Key Conclusions From Cumulative Research

Although various writers have argued for eclecticism (e.g., Thorne, 1950) or have promoted the integration of various theories (e.g., Dollard & Miller, 1950) in the more distant past, it is only in the last 30 years that a definite trend toward eclecticism has emerged in the broad field of counseling/psychotherapy. The trend toward eclecticism has been fueled primarily by two interrelated sets of research findings, discussed below.

The Equal Outcomes/Dodo Bird Phenomenon

The era of the competing schools of psychotherapy spawned an immense volume of research that overall has failed to demonstrate the superiority of one type of psychotherapy over another. Two recent, comprehensive reviews of research (Lambert & Ogles, 2004; Wampold, 2001) examined both numerous meta-analyses (a quantitative method that aggregates the findings of numerous studies in order to test hypotheses; e.g., Smith & Glass, 1977; Wampold et al., 1997) and exemplary studies (large, well-designed studies; e.g., the National Institute of Mental Health Treatment of Depression Collaborative Research Program [NIMH TDCRP; Elkin, 1994]) of the comparative outcomes of different therapy models.

These comprehensive reviews of the research have both reinforced what is commonly referred to as the "equal outcomes" or "Dodo bird effect" conclusion. That is, overall, studies have indicated that the various types of therapy (psychodynamic, cognitive-behavioral, humanistic, etc.) have roughly equal effectiveness and therefore, in the words of the Dodo bird from Alice in Wonderland, "Everybody has won, and all must have prizes" (Carroll, as cited in Wampold et al., 1997, p. 203).

Although the equal outcomes conclusion has been generally accepted, there are those who continue to question its legitimacy. Beutler (1991) has surmised that in the future, more sophisticated research designs may yield superior outcomes for specific therapy/client problem combinations. On this same issue, from within social work, Reid (1997) concluded from his own review of meta-analyses that cognitive-behavioral approaches may have an edge in treatment effectiveness over other approaches with regard to certain specific problems such as panic-agoraphobia and juvenile delinquency. Furthermore, Reid contended that the equal outcomes conclusion may not be valid (a) when studies of specific interventions for specific problems are focused upon and (b) for the range of problems of concern to social workers. We believe, however, that these contentions are not supported by empirical evidence to date. Lambert and Ogles (2004) have also pointed out tentative evidence that cognitive-behavioral approaches may yield superior outcomes for a few specific, difficult problems (e.g., panic, phobic, and compulsive disorders); however, they still accept the general validity of the equal outcomes conclusion. Furthermore, Wampold's (2001) thorough, meticulous review of the research concluded that the equal outcomes result has held even in studies that have focused on specific treatments for depression and anxiety. These are two problems for which cognitive-behavioral treatments were thought to be particularly appropriate, and these are among the most common client problems for clinical social workers.

Thus, we agree with Wampold's (2001) conclusion that "the Dodo bird conjecture has survived many tests and must be considered 'true' until such time as sufficient evidence for its rejection are produced" (p. 118). The acceptance of this conclusion does not lead directly to an argument for eclecticism; however, it does promote acceptance of the validity of alternative approaches. This, along with the recognition that "no single school can provide all theoretical and practical answers for our psychological woes . . . [makes it seem sensible] to cross boundaries, to venture beyond one's borders in search of nuggets that may be deposited among the hills and dales of other camps" (Lazarus, 1996, p. 59).

The Importance of Relationship and Other Common Factors

The cumulative results of psychotherapy research have stimulated interest in what have come to be known as "common factors." The findings of nonsignificant outcome differences among the variety of different therapies (the equal outcomes phenomenon) led many researchers to latch onto the ideas promoted earlier by Rosenzweig (1936) and Frank (1961) that factors specific to the various therapies (i.e., distinctive theory and techniques) had less impact on outcomes than factors that were common across therapies—particularly worker–client relationship factors. Early research on the client-centered core conditions of empathy, warmth, and genuineness, and later research on the related concept of the therapeutic alliance, have established that relationship factors are the most powerful predictors of client outcome and that a good helping relationship is necessary for good outcome regardless of the approach to therapy (Horvath & Symonds, 1991; Lambert & Barley, 2001; Wampold, 2001).

Cumulative research suggests that "factors common across treatments are accounting for a substantial amount of improvement . . . [and] common factors may even account for most of the gains that result from psychological intervention" (Lambert & Ogles, 2004, p. 172). Wampold's (2001) book, entitled *The Great Psychotherapy Debate: Models, Methods, and Findings*, focused on reviewing research related to the controversial question of whether therapy effectiveness is related more to common factors (e.g., therapeutic relationship) or specific factors (e.g., theory and technique). Wampold concluded that the research evidence provides overwhelming support for the importance of common versus specific factors. He found that "at least 70% of the psychotherapeutic effects are general effects (i.e., due to common factors)" (p. 207), whereas therapy techniques (or "specific ingredients") account for at most 8% of such effects.

Although a variety of factors that are common across therapies have been conceptualized, and there is empirical support for the importance of a number of such factors (e.g., encouragement of facing problems/fears, support of efforts to master problems/fears, affective experiencing/catharsis; Lambert & Ogles, 2004), the therapeutic relationship or alliance "is the most frequently mentioned common factor in the psychotherapy literature" (Grencavage & Norcross, 1990) and it has been called the "quintessential integrative variable" (Wolfe & Goldfried, as cited in Wampold, 2001, p. 150) in counseling. Wampold notes that the therapeutic relationship "accounts for dramatically more of the variability in outcomes than does the totality of specific ingredients" (p. 158). Again, although the research on common factors does not lead directly to an argument for eclecticism with regard to theory and technique, it does promote openness to crossing therapeutic boundaries (see Approaches to Eclecticism, below, for further discussion of common factors).

Summary

Although there have been long-standing and persuasive arguments for eclecticism, the trend toward eclecticism has been fueled largely by research findings—both the equal outcomes phenomenon and the importance of relationship and other common factors relative to specific (i.e., theory and technique) factors. As Lambert and Ogles (2004) have noted, the trend toward eclecticism "appears to reflect a healthy response to empirical evidence" (p. 180). This has led practitioners to "increasingly acknowledge the inadequacies of any one school and the potential value of others" (Norcross, 1997, p. 86).

Pockets of Resistance to Eclecticism

Acceptance of the research findings that have fueled the trend toward eclecticism has not been easy for many mental health practitioners. Over three decades ago, Frank (as cited in Lambert & Ogles, 2004) anticipated resistance to his hypotheses about equal outcomes across therapies and the importance of common factors when he noted that "little glory derives from showing that the particular method one has mastered with so much effort may be indistinguishable from other models in its effects" (p. 175). Similarly, as Glass suggested in the Foreword to Wampold's (2001) book, giving up the idea that one's cherished theory and associated techniques are no more effective than another approach to therapy and that effectiveness is due largely to factors that are common across therapies "carries a threat of narcissistic injury" (p. x).

Even more dramatically, Parloff (as cited in Wampold, 2001) contended that, in some practitioners' minds, if the conclusion about the primary importance of common factors is accepted, "then the credibility of psychotherapy as a profession is automatically impugned" (p. 29). With regard to this last point, we would argue that acceptance of these research findings does not impugn the credibility of psychotherapy, but it does change the general conceptualization of psychotherapy from a primarily scientific, theoretical/technique-oriented enterprise to one that is more humanistic and artistic. Wampold (2001) has called for such a shift in advocating for what he calls a "contextual meta-model" of therapy, in which common factors are emphasized, to replace the current "medical meta-model." Still, there is "tremendous resistance" (Lambert, Garfield, & Bergin, 2004, p. 809) to accepting these research findings and this reconceptualization of psychotherapy/clinical practice.

The Challenge of the Empirically Supported Treatment (EST) Movement

The research findings on equal outcomes across different types of therapy, the importance of relationship and other common factors to outcomes, and the weak effect of specific techniques on outcomes stand in stark contrast to the rise of the EST movement in psychology in the 1990s. As part of the broader movement toward evidence-based practice in psychology (Barlow, 2000) and social work (Gambrill, 1999; Gibbs & Gambrill, 2002; Howard, McMillen, & Pollio, 2003; Magill, 2006; Rubin & Parrish, 2007), the EST movement was spurred by the Division of Clinical Psychology of the American Psychological Association, which created criteria for the empirical support of therapies.

It is clear that the implicit assumption of the EST movement is that specific ingredients (i.e., therapeutic techniques and their underlying theory) are the important curative factors in psychotherapy (Messer, 2001). The EST movement has pushed for using specific treatments with specific disorders and using only treatments that have been "proven" effective in randomized clinical trial research that includes a formal diagnosis of the client's problem, a specific treatment that is delivered in accordance with a treatment manual, and outcome measures related to the diagnosis. The result has been to develop a list of empirically supported treatments, the vast majority of which are cognitive-behavioral in orientation. ESTs have become widely advocated by managed care, insurance companies, and government (Messer, 2001). In this regard, Wampold (2001) has lamented that "doctoral level psychologists and other psychotherapy practitioners (e.g., social workers, marriage and family therapists) are economically coerced to practice a form of therapy different from what they were trained and different from how they would prefer to practice" (p. 2).

Critique of the EST Movement

Critics have pointed out that the predominance of cognitive-behavioral treatments (CBTs) in the EST list is due to the fact that other more process-oriented therapies do not readily fit the research protocol requirements for manualized treatment and focus on specific symptoms with associated specific outcome measures, and that these requirements are biased toward CBTs (Messer, 2001). The use of treatment manuals has also been criticized. Wampold's (2001) review of research found that adherence to treatment manuals is generally not associated with outcomes, and Messer (2001) noted that some studies have found that overly close adherence to treatment manuals can have a negative effect on outcomes, presumably because this stifles "artistry, flexibility, reflection, and imagination" (p. 8).

More generally, Lambert and Ogles (2004) argued that decades of research that have confirmed the equal outcomes phenomenon "argue against the current trend of identifying empirically supported therapies that purport to be uniquely effective" (p. 167). Similarly, Lambert, Bregin, and Garfield (2004) pointed out that "the success of treatment appears to be largely dependent on the client and the therapist, not on the use of 'proven' empirically based treatments" (p. 9). Lambert, Garfield and Bregin concluded that "the generation of lists of empirically supported therapies appears to be misguided and overvalued" (p. 808). Henry (1998) has summarized the argument against ESTs:

> The largest chunk of outcome variance not attributable to pre-existing patient characteristics involves individual therapist differences and the emergent interpersonal relationship between patient and therapist, regardless of technique or school of therapy. This is the main thrust of three decades of empirical psychotherapy research. (p. 128)

We agree with those who contend that the focus of EST research is misplaced and that the results are misleading. Cumulative research on psychotherapy (i.e., the equal outcomes phenomenon) suggests that most treatment approaches (including eclectic approaches) would be empirically supported if they could be and were subjected to the EST research protocol, but research also suggests that treatment approaches might be made less effective by being made to conform to such research protocol (e.g., a treatment manual) because the quality of the therapeutic relationship might suffer. Wampold (2001) pointed out that there has never been a direct comparison of the same therapy practiced in a clinical research trial context (with the research protocols of ESTs such as training in the use of a treatment manual) and practiced naturally in a clinical practice setting. He also pointed out that there has never been a comparison of an EST and an eclectic therapy in a clinical practice context. Although Wampold does not specifically predict the results of such research, it is clear that he (and we) would bet that the EST would not prove superior.

We concur with Wampold's (2001) conclusion that "designated empirically supported treatments should not be used to mandate services, reimburse service providers, or restrict or guide the training of therapists" (p. 225). As should be evident from the emphasis we have placed on reviewing research, we are not against the general concept of evidence-based practice; however, we think that psychologists and social workers who align themselves with the assumptions and principles of the EST movement are barking up the wrong tree in searching for empirically supported theories and techniques. Instead, we think that funders, researchers, and practitioners should shift to more productive research foci.

One example of a more productive research focus is that of the Division 29 APA Task Force (Norcross, 2001, 2002), which was established to explore empirically supported (therapy) relationships (ESRs). This task force was established to counter or at least balance the EST movement. Among the general elements of the therapy relationship that this task force found "demonstrably effective" were the overall quality of the therapeutic relationship/alliance, empathy, and goal consensus and collaboration. Other elements found to be "promising and probably effective" were positive regard, genuineness, self-disclosure, and addressing/repairing problems in the therapy relationship (Ackerman et al., 2001). The two task force members who reviewed research on the therapeutic relationship concluded that "improvement of psychotherapy may be best accomplished by learning to improve one's ability to relate to clients and tailoring that relationship to individual clients" (Lambert & Barley, 2001, p. 357).

As alluded to in the quote by Henry (1998) above, another example of a potentially productive focus for research is individual therapist differences. Although research has established equal outcomes across different types of therapy, it has also established that there are significant differences in effectiveness among therapists within each approach to therapy. There are clearly some very effective therapists and some therapists who are not very effective. Even when treatment manuals are used in efforts to control for individual therapist differences, studies have still found significant differences in effectiveness among therapists (Messer, 2001). From his review of research on this issue, Wampold (2001) concluded that "clearly, the person of the therapist is a critical factor in the success of therapy" (p. 202), yet "very little is known about the qualities and actions of therapists who are eminently successful" (p. 211). On this issue, Lambert and Ogles (2004) have called for "research focused on the 'empirically validated psychotherapist' rather than on empirically supported treatment" (p. 169).

It is likely that differences in effectiveness among practitioners have much to do with the ability to establish good interpersonal relationships with clients, particularly difficult clients, and to use such relationships therapeutically (Asay & Lambert, 2001). Thus, promising foci for research on therapist differences include relationship and general interpersonal skills, interpersonal style, emotional well-being, and attitudes toward clients. Although we do not know how widespread it has become, Messer (2001) noted it was encouraging that some "managed care companies are moving to a system of evaluating therapists and referring cases to the successful ones, rather than requiring the use of ESTs" (p. 9).

APPROACHES TO ECLECTICISM

Despite pockets of strong resistance such as the EST movement, the trend toward eclecticism and integration is clear in the broad field of counseling/psychotherapy and the profession of clinical psychology. As we have argued, however, despite the endorsement of eclecticism in the generalist perspective, this trend is less clear in direct social work practice. We think it is important for social workers to become familiar with the literature on eclecticism and integration in psychotherapy. Many of the ideas and principles in this literature (e.g., the valuing of multiple perspectives for understanding and intervening, the centrality of the helping relationship) are consistent with and can inform social work practice.

Four broad approaches to eclecticism are commonly identified in the literature: technical eclecticism, theoretical integration, assimilative integration, and common factors (Castonguay, Reid, Halperin, & Goldfried, 2003; Lampropoulos, 2001; Norcross, 2005). A recent survey (Norcross, Karpiak, & Santoro, as cited in Norcross, 2005) of psychologists who self-identified as eclectics and integrationists found that each of these four approaches to eclecticism is subscribed to by a sizable proportion of therapists (19%–28% each).

Each of the general approaches to eclecticism subsumes a number of more specific models of eclectic/integrative practice; however, not surprisingly, there are differences in the literature with regard to classifying some models. Table 1.2 presents an overview of the characteristics of the four general approaches to eclecticism, along with examples of therapy

TABLE 1.2   Approaches to Eclecticism/Integration

Broad Approaches	Examples of Therapies	General Characteristics of Approaches
Technical Eclecticism	Multimodal Behavior Therapy (MMT; Lazarus, 1981, 2005) Systematic Treatment Selection (STS; Beutler, 1983; Beutler & Clarkin, 1990; Beutler, Consoli, & Lane, 2005)	Using techniques from different theories based on their proven effectiveness with similar client problems/characteristics, without necessarily subscribing to any of the theories
Theoretical Integration	Integrative Relational Therapy (Wachtel, 1977; Wachtel, Kruk, & McKinney, 2005) The Transtheoretical Model (TTM; Prochaska & DiClemente, 1984, 2005; Prochaska & Norcross, 2003)	Integrating/synthesizing the strengths of two or more theories to create a more comprehensive theory to explain and guide intervention with human problems
Assimilative Integration	Assimilative Psychodynamic Psychotherapy (Gold & Stricker, 2001; Stricker & Gold, 2005) Widening the Scope of Cognitive Therapy (Safran, 1990a, 1990b, 1998)	Incorporating other theories and techniques into one's primary theoretical orientation
Common Factors	Common Factors/Contextual Meta-Model (Frank & Frank, 1991; Wampold, 2001) Eclectic-Integrative Approach (Garfield, 1995) Outcome-Informed Clinical Work (Hubble, Duncan, & Miller, 1999; Miller, Duncan, & Hubble, 2005)	Focusing on factors that are shared by all types of therapy and that are central to therapeutic effectiveness (e.g., a good helping relationship)

models for each approach. Although it is beyond the scope of this book to review specific eclectic/integrative models in detail, the discussion of each of the four general approaches below provides brief explanation of some of the specific models that fall under their domain. Following this, we elaborate on the type of eclecticism we endorse for our generalist-eclectic approach.

Technical Eclecticism

Technical eclecticism, which is sometimes referred to as systematic eclecticism or prescriptive matching, "refers to the relatively atheoretical selection of clinical treatments on the basis of predicted efficacy rather than theoretical considerations" (Alford, 1995, p. 147). Thus, those who ascribe to technical eclecticism use knowledge about what has worked best with clients with similar characteristics or problems to draw techniques from different therapy models, without necessarily subscribing to any of the theories (Norcross, 2005). Lazarus (1996) differentiated this type of eclecticism from "the ragtag importation of techniques from anywhere or everywhere without a sound rationale" (p. 61). Technical eclecticism attempts to address the specificity question posed by Paul (as cited in Lampropoulos, 2001): "*What* treatment, by *whom*, is most effective for *this* individual with *that* specific problem, and under *which* set of circumstances?" (p. 7).

Multimodal Behavior Therapy (MMT)

Lazarus's (1981, 2005) MMT is one of the most prominent examples of technical eclecticism. MMT is based on assessment that specifies the client's problem and his or her primary aspects, or modalities, of functioning (i.e., behavior, affect, sensation, imagery, cognition, interpersonal relationships, and drugs/biological functioning [BASIC I.D.]). Lazarus contended that different techniques should be selected to address the client's various prominent modalities and that these should be addressed sequentially according to their "firing order" (e.g., if client affect leads to behavior and then cognition, these modalities should be treated in this order). He also argued that therapy should address as many modalities as possible. MMT uses techniques from a variety of theories, including humanistic, psychodynamic, and family systems theories, but there is an emphasis on cognitive-behavioral techniques (Lazarus, 2005).

Systematic Treatment Selection (STS)

A second prominent example of technical eclecticism is the STS therapy of Beutler (1983; Beutler & Clarkin, 1990; Beutler, Consoli, & Lane,

2005; Beutler & Harwood, 1995). In this approach, techniques from a wide variety of theories are selected on the basis of "empirical evidence of usefulness rather than by a theory of personality or of change" (Beutler & Harwood, 1995, p. 89). STS focuses on matching treatment strategies and techniques to client characteristics (client–treatment matching) and is one of the most ambitious and thorough models of eclecticism. In this model, a thorough assessment of client variables (e.g., demographic qualities, coping style, level of distress, level of resistance, expectations of therapy, social supports, diagnosis) and a consideration of empirical evidence related to such variables lead to decisions about (a) treatment contexts (individual, group, marital, family therapy), (b) choice of therapist (e.g., based on interpersonal compatibility and demographic similarity), (c) goal of therapy (i.e., focus on symptoms or underlying themes), (d) primary level of experience to be addressed (affect, cognition, or behavior), (e) style of therapist (e.g., degree of directiveness, support, confrontation), and (f) therapeutic techniques (Beutler & Harwood, 1995).

The STS model has been researched extensively, and the most promising results are related to matching treatment to client coping style and reactance/resistance level. With regard to coping style, it has been found that clients who externalize (e.g., blame others) do better in structured treatments such as CBT, whereas clients who internalize (e.g., blame themselves) do better in more process-oriented treatment (e.g., insight or relationship-oriented therapy). With regard to resistance, it has been found that clients who are highly resistant do better in less directive therapy (e.g., client centered), whereas clients low in resistance do better in more directive therapy (e.g., CBT; Schottenbauer, Glass, & Arnkoff, 2005).

Theoretical Integration

In this second category of approaches "there is an emphasis on integrating the underlying theories of psychotherapy along with therapy techniques from each" (Prochaska & Norcross, 2003, p. 485). The goal is to produce a more comprehensive, overarching theoretical framework that synthesizes the strengths of individual theories. Norcross (2005) has referred to theoretical integration as "theory smushing" (p. 8). The ultimate form of theoretical integration would incorporate all of the various theories of therapy (i.e., those subsumed under psychodynamic, cognitive-behavioral, humanistic/feminist, and postmodern classifications, as well as biological and family systems approaches) into a synthesized/unified whole. Leaving aside the question of whether such a lofty goal is viable or not, to date "psychotherapy integration has not succeeded in that grand attempt, . . . the leading current approaches usually incorporate two, or at most three, of these perspectives" (Stricker, 1994, p. 6). As

Lampropoulos (2001) noted, theoretical integration is "the ideal, optimistic, but utopian view" (p. 6).

Integrative Relational Therapy

Wachtel's (1977, 1997; Wachtel, Kruk, & McKinney, 2005) integration of psychodynamic and behavioral theories is the most commonly cited example of an integrative approach. Building on the earlier work of Dollard and Miller (1950), Wachtel integrated the strengths of the social-learning model of behavioral theory with his interpersonal type of psychodynamic theory to create integrative relational therapy (Wachtel et al., 2005). This integrative theory posits that unconscious conflicts/anxieties and interpersonal interactions are mutually influencing and create vicious cycles (e.g., anxiety about dependency needs results in keeping people at arm's length, which heightens the anxiety). In this model, intervention involves integrating a psychodynamic focus on insight with a behavioral focus on action (e.g., skills training).

The Transtheoretical Model (TTM)

The TTM (Prochaska & DiClemente, 1984, 2005; Prochaska & Norcross, 2003) is another influential integrative model. In the TTM, the selection of interventions, or change processes as they are called, is based on the assessment of two factors. First, consideration is given to the *stages of change* through which people progress. Thus, the worker needs to assess which of the five stages of change a client is in:

1. precontemplation (relatively unaware of problems with no intention to change),
2. contemplation (aware of a problem and considering but not committed to change),
3. preparation (intending and beginning to take initial steps toward change),
4. action (investment of considerable time and energy to successfully alter a problem behavior), or
5. maintenance (working to consolidate gains and prevent relapse).

Second, the *level/depth of change* required needs to be assessed. Thus, the worker and client need to mutually determine which of five problem levels to focus on:

1. symptom/situational problems,
2. maladaptive cognitions,

3. current interpersonal conflicts,
4. family/systems conflicts, or
5. intrapersonal conflicts.

After an assessment of the client's stage of change and the level of change required, the TTM suggests that available empirical evidence of effectiveness be considered, as much as possible, to determine which interventions from different theoretical perspectives to use. In general, with regard to stages of change, techniques from cognitive, psychodynamic, and humanistic therapies are thought to be most useful in the precontemplation and contemplation stages, whereas "change processes traditionally associated with the existential and behavioral traditions . . . are most useful during the action and maintenance stages" (Prochaska & Norcross, 2003, p. 528). More specifically, when the level of change required is considered in the action stage, behavioral techniques would usually be chosen for the symptom/situational level, cognitive techniques would be employed at the level of maladaptive cognitions, and psychodynamic interventions would be used at the intrapersonal conflict level. The general principle in this model is to focus intervention initially at the symptom/situational level and then to proceed to deeper levels only if necessary.

Assimilative Integration

This approach to eclectic/integrative practice, proposed initially by Messer (1992), maintains that it is important to keep a firm grounding in one theory of therapy while incorporating ideas and techniques from other theories. Lampropoulos (2001) explained how assimilative integration can be seen as a bridge between technical eclecticism and theoretical integration:

> When techniques from different theoretical approaches are incorporated into one's main theoretical orientation, their meaning interacts with the meaning of the "host" theory, and both the imported technique and the pre-existing theory are mutually transformed and shaped into the final product, namely the new assimilative, integrative model. (p. 9)

Assimilative Psychodynamic Psychotherapy

One example of assimilative integration is assimilative psychodynamic psychotherapy (Gold & Stricker, 2001; Stricker & Gold, 2005). As its name indicates, this is clearly a psychodynamic therapy, but one which allows for the incorporation of more active/directive interventions from other therapies. Gold and Stricker (2001) acknowledged that psychodynamic therapy "is very good at answering the 'why' and 'how did this happen' questions . . . but it is not as effective at answering questions such as 'so now what do I do' or 'how do I change this' " (p. 55). As a result, they are open to using the entire spectrum of therapeutic techniques, "from cognitive-behavioral methods such as assertiveness training to experientially oriented chair work to systemic and strategic interventions" (p. 47).

Widening the Scope of Cognitive Therapy

Another example of this approach is Safran's (1990a, 1990b, 1998; Safran & Segal, 1990) attempt to widen the scope of cognitive therapy by incorporating aspects of psychodynamic (psychoanalytic and interpersonal) and humanistic theories. Beyond the cognitive and behavioral dimensions of human functioning that are the sole foci of most CBTs, Safran's model also considers emotional, developmental, interpersonal, and conflictual dimensions. Techniques from other theoretical orientations are incorporated to address issues associated with these additional aspects of human experience.

Common Factors

In this last category of approaches to eclecticism, there is an attempt to identify and utilize the "effective aspects of treatment shared by the diverse forms of psychotherapy" (Weinberger, 1993, p. 43). This approach has been influenced largely by the extensive work of Jerome Frank, particularly his classic book entitled *Persuasion and Healing* (1961, 1973, and coauthored with his daughter, Julia Frank, 1991). Frank's writing on common factors amounted to a meta-model of psychotherapy, rather than a specific approach to therapy. Wampold (2001) has adopted Frank's broad common factors conceptualization of psychotherapy, calling it a contextual meta-model of psychotherapy, and contrasting it to the medical meta-model, which purports that theory and technique (i.e., specific factors) are the keys to therapeutic effectiveness.

As we have noted earlier, Wampold's (2001) thorough analysis of psychotherapy research provides compelling empirical support for the common factors/contextual meta-model of psychotherapy. Although Wampold (2001) clearly attributed the meta-model discussed in his book to Frank, because of Wampold's contributions to the conceptual development and empirical validation of the model, we see this model as a joint product of both authors' work. We will review the common factors/contextual meta-model of Frank and Wampold in some depth before considering more specific common factors therapy models.

Common Factors/Contextual Meta-Model

Building on the earlier ideas of Rosenzweig (1936), Frank developed the demoralization hypothesis, which proposes that most of the distress suffered by clients stems from being demoralized and that "features shared by all therapies that combat demoralization account for much of their effectiveness" (Frank, 1982, p. 32). Frank (1982; Frank & Frank, 1991) suggested there are four factors that are shared by all forms of psychotherapy, as well as by religious and other secular types of healing, that represent means of directly or indirectly combating demoralization and that are primarily responsible for the effectiveness of any approach to healing.

First, and foremost, is an "emotionally supportive, confiding relationship with a helping person" (Frank, 1982, p. 19). If helpers can convince clients that they care and want to help, then this decreases clients' sense of alienation, increases expectations of improvement, and boosts morale.

Second is a "healing setting" that heightens the helper's prestige, thereby increasing the client's expectation of help, and provides safety. In psychotherapy, the healing setting is usually an office or clinic that carries the aura of science; in religious healing, it is usually a temple or sacred grove.

Third is a theoretical rationale or "myth" that provides a believable explanation for clients' difficulties. Frank uses the word "myth" to underscore the contention that the accuracy of the explanation is less important than its plausibility in the eyes of the client. Any explanation of their difficulties that clients can accept alleviates some distress and engenders hope for change.

Fourth is a set of therapeutic procedures or a "ritual" that involves the participation of helper and client in activities that both believe will help the client to overcome the presenting difficulties. With regard to the fourth common factor, on the basis of empirical studies of therapy, Frank and Frank (1991) contended that therapeutic procedures will be optimally effective if they

1. provide new learning experiences for clients (these enhance morale by helping clients to develop more positive views of themselves and their problems);
2. arouse clients' emotions (this helps clients to tolerate and accept their emotions and allows them to confront and cope more successfully with feared issues and situations—thus strengthening self-confidence, sense of mastery, and morale); and
3. provide opportunities for clients to practice what they have learned both within therapy and in their everyday lives (thus reinforcing therapeutic gains, a sense of mastery, and morale).

Lambert and Ogles (2004) and Wampold (2001) concurred with Frank that there is substantial empirical support for these therapeutic procedures that are common across therapies.

Although there is extensive empirical support for the first (therapeutic relationship) and fourth (common therapeutic procedures) of Frank's common factors, there is little research on the healing setting or on the theoretical rationale/myth. There is indirect support, however, for the latter factor. Frank's hypothesis about the importance of a theoretical rationale/myth that provides a believable explanation to clients of their problems is linked to "goal consensus and collaboration," which is one of the aspects of the therapeutic alliance for which there is strong empirical support (Ackerman et al., 2001). Clearly, in order to establish goal consensus and collaboration, clients must believe in workers' explanation for their difficulties and strategies for ameliorating problems. Frank and Frank (1991) maintained that in order to maximize the sense and quality of an alliance with clients,

> therapists should select for each patient the therapy that accords, or can be brought to accord, with the patient's personal characteristics and view of the problem. Also implied is that therapists should seek to learn as many approaches as they find congenial and convincing. Creating a good therapeutic match may involve both educating the patient about the therapist's conceptual scheme and, if necessary, modifying the scheme to take into account the concepts the patient brings to therapy. (p. xv)

Following Frank and Frank's line of argument, and based on his review of research, Wampold (2001) has suggested that therapists should choose an approach to counseling that accords with the client's worldview: "The therapist needs to realize that the client's belief in the explanation for their [sic] disorder, problem, or complaint is paramount" (p. 218).

Eclectic-Integrative Approach

A more specific approach to therapy that has been classified as a common factors model is the eclectic-integrative approach of Garfield (1995). Garfield contended that despite the many apparent differences among the various therapeutic approaches and the fact that these schools of therapy tend to emphasize the importance of their specific techniques, factors that are common across therapies account for much of their success. Garfield's (1995) model places a strong "emphasis on the therapeutic relationship and on the common factors in psychotherapy" (p. 167), while also supporting the eclectic use of interventions from different theoretical approaches. Echoing Frank, Garfield (1995) contended that "being given some explanation for one's problems by an interested expert in the role of healer, may be the important common aspect of these divergent therapies" (p. 34). Garfield (1995) rationalized the theoretical openness of his approach:

> Although the absence of a unifying and guiding theory has its drawbacks, an awareness of one's limitations and of the gaps in our current knowledge is, in the long run, a positive thing—even though it may make for uncertainties. It is better to see the situation for what it really is than to have what may be an incorrect or biased orientation. (p. 216)

Garfield's model does, however, provide some structure for practitioners by presenting general guidelines for the various stages of therapy (beginning, middle, later, and termination). This is very similar to the use of the problem-solving model in the generalist-eclectic approach. Also, Garfield's approach has elements of technical eclecticism in that therapists are advised, where possible, to choose techniques "which on the basis of empirical evidence seem to be most effective for the specific problems presented by the client" (p. 218).

Outcome-Informed Clinical Work

Another, more recent, common factors approach is the outcome-informed clinical work model (Hubble, Duncan, & Miller, 1999; Miller, Duncan, & Hubble, 2005). This model focuses on the importance of the therapeutic relationship. It emphasizes three core ingredients of the alliance: (a) shared goals for counseling, (b) consensus on the approach to counseling (means, methods, tasks), and (c) the emotional bond between worker and client. It is proposed that one key to developing a strong alliance is to adopt the client's theory of change; that is, "the client's frame of reference regarding the presenting problem, its causes, and potential remedies" (Miller et al., 2005, p. 87).

A second important key is to solicit and respond to, on an ongoing basis, client feedback regarding the therapeutic alliance. This is the "outcome-informed" element of the model. If the client voices concern about any aspect of the alliance, then "every effort should be made to accommodate the client" (p. 94).

Summary

It needs to be emphasized that these four broad approaches to eclecticism are not mutually exclusive and "the distinctions may be largely semantic and conceptual, not particularly functional, in practice" (Norcross, 2005, p. 10). For example, it is unlikely that models within technical eclecticism and common factors approaches totally ignore theory, and it is quite likely that all of the approaches to eclecticism incorporate an emphasis on common factors.

We should note that there is another trend within the overall trend toward eclecticism, which is the development of eclectic/integrative therapies for specific populations and problems. Prominent examples of these include Linehan's (1993; Heard & Linehan, 2005) dialectical behavior therapy (DBT) for borderline personality disorder, McCullough's (2000) cognitive behavioral analysis system of psychotherapy (CBASP) for chronic depression, and Wolfe's (2005) integrative psychotherapy for anxiety disorders.

We do not count these eclectic/integrative therapies for specific populations and problems as a fifth classification of approaches to eclecticism because each of these more specific therapies can be subsumed under one of the four broader approaches to eclecticism. For example, DBT and CBASP can be classified as assimilative integration models because although they integrate a number of different theories, their primary theoretical base is cognitive-behavioral. Wolfe's therapy for anxiety, however, can be classified as a theoretical integration model because it blends psychodynamic and cognitive-behavioral views of and treatment strategies for anxiety.

Finally, we would like to note that research on eclectic/integrative models has increased substantially over the last few years, although it still lags behind research on single theory approaches. In a recent review of research on eclectic/integrative therapies, Schottenbauer et al. (2005) concluded that there is substantial empirical support (i.e., 4 or more randomized controlled studies) for 7 such therapies, some empirical support (i.e., 1–4 randomized controlled studies) for another 13, and preliminary empirical support (i.e., studies with nonrandomized control group or no control group) for another 7. In 1992, Lambert predicted, "To the extent that eclectic therapies provide treatment that includes substantial overlap with traditional methods that have been developed and tested, they rest on a firm empirical base, and they should prove to be at least as effective as traditional school-based therapies" (p. 121). It would seem that Lambert was right. Still, we agree with those researchers who contend that it would be more productive to focus research on exploring common factors and therapist factors that impact on outcome than continuing to focus on validating individual models of therapy, whether these are single theory or eclectic models.

THEORETICAL ECLECTICISM: OUR APPROACH

Given our commitment to the spirit of eclecticism, as well as the obvious overlap among the various approaches to eclecticism, we believe there is value in all four approaches discussed above. Although our approach to eclecticism incorporates some aspects of all of the approaches identified in the literature, it is closest to the common factors approaches, especially the common factors/contextual meta-model of Frank and Frank (1991) and Wampold (2001) and Garfield's (1995) eclectic-integrative approach. We think, however, that our approach to eclecticism does not fit neatly into the common factors category of approaches because the use of theory is not a central feature for most models in this category. Although the common factors/contextual meta-model (Frank & Frank, 1991; Wampold, 2001) and Garfield's (1995) model support the use of multiple theoretical perspectives, as we do, the use of theory in our approach differs in some important ways from these approaches (see Comparison below). We think that our approach to eclecticism is distinct enough from the four approaches currently identified in the literature, and that it has enough merits, to warrant a fifth classification of eclectic practice, which we call "theoretical eclecticism."

Our theoretically eclectic approach values the potential relevance of all theories and promotes the use of multiple theories and their associated techniques with individual clients. The essence of theoretical eclecticism is to consider the relevance of multiple theoretical frameworks to each client's problem situation in order to develop, collaboratively with the client, a more complex, comprehensive understanding that fits for the client, and then to choose intervention strategies or techniques that fit with this in-depth understanding. It is important to remind the reader that our generalist-eclectic approach to practice does not rely solely on the use of theory to develop in-depth understanding and choose intervention strategies, however. The eclectic use of theory is complemented by artistic, intuitive-inductive processes, and both of these are guided by the problem-solving model.

Comparison of Theoretical Eclecticism to the Four Major Approaches to Eclecticism

Theoretical eclecticism is different from technical eclecticism in that it emphasizes the use of multiple theoretical perspectives, rather than focusing primarily on the techniques that are derived from theories and matching these to client characteristics or problems. It is different from theoretical integration because it does not attempt to synthesize or "smush" theories. Theoretical eclecticism is different from assimilative integration in that it does not promote primary reliance on one theory of practice. Similar to these three approaches to eclecticism, however, our approach supports the idea of drawing techniques from a wide variety of theories, depending on their fit for particular clients. In contrast to some models in these approaches, however, our approach to matching techniques to client variables (e.g., coping style, level of resistance, stage of change) relies at least as much on worker judgment as on empirical evidence.

There are two reasons why we do not favor an exclusive reliance on empirical evidence for choosing techniques. First, we agree with Stiles, Shapiro, and Barkham (1995) and Wampold (2001), who contended that there is not enough empirical evidence to warrant firm decisions about such matching of techniques to client variables. Second, we do not like the mechanistic flavor of some prescriptive matching models because individual clients are too unique to rely on formulaic decisions about a certain type of intervention for a certain type of client or problem.

For these reasons, we favor what has been called "responsive matching" (Stiles et al., 1995). "Responsive matching is often done intuitively, we suspect, as practitioners draw techniques from their repertoire to fit their momentary understanding of a client's needs" (Stiles et al., 1995, p. 265). This type of matching should draw on theory and empirical findings but is more tentative and open to modification based on sensitivity to the client's response: "It is grounded in both theory and observation of the individual case" (Stiles et al., 1995, p. 265). In the same vein, Garfield (1995) has argued the following:

> In the absence of research data, the therapist has to rely on his own clinical experience and evaluations, or on his best clinical judgment . . . and make whatever modifications seem to be necessary in order to facilitate positive movement in therapy. (p. 218)

Such an approach fits well with our valuing of the artistic, intuitive-inductive aspects of practice.

As mentioned, our approach to eclecticism has the most similarities with common factors approaches, particularly with regard to the emphasis placed on the worker–client relationship. Similar to all common factor approaches, and supported by a vast body of research, we emphasize the importance of a trusting, collaborative, supportive, warm, empathic helping relationship that is focused on instilling hope, boosting morale, and empowering the client. Other common factors that have received strong empirical support, and that we endorse, include addressing and resolving problems in the worker–client relationship, achieving consensus on problem formulation and goals (Ackerman et al., 2001), soliciting and responding supportively to client feedback (Miller et al., 2005), supporting emotional expression/catharsis, providing the client with mastery experiences (Lambert & Ogles, 2004), and helping clients attribute change to their own efforts (Weinberger, 1993). Also, we agree with Wampold's (2001) recommendation that, at least in parity with the emphasis placed on learning theory and technique, clinical practitioners should be trained to "appreciate and be skilled in the common . . . core therapeutic skills, including empathic listening and responding, developing a working alliance, working through one's own issues, . . . and learning to be self-reflective about one's work" (pp. 229–230).

Theoretical eclecticism differs, however, from most common factor approaches in that the latter tend not to emphasize the use of theory. Although Garfield's (1995) model does support the eclectic use of theory, this is largely with regard to choosing techniques and procedures for intervention. Curiously, in Garfield's (1995) book, there is virtually no discussion of using various theoretical perspectives in the assessment process to develop understanding of the client's situation, which is a central feature of our theoretical eclecticism.

Although the common factors/contextual meta-model of Frank and Frank (1991) and Wampold (2001) espouses the value of multiple theoretical perspectives, there are important differences between their use of theory and ours. Wampold (2001) and Frank and Frank (1991) argued that practitioners should learn as many therapy models as possible so that they can better match or modify a model to fit clients' worldview or understanding of their problems. This follows from Frank's (1961; Frank & Frank, 1991) use of the word "myth" to underscore his contention that the accuracy of a theoretical rationale for the client's problem is less important than its plausibility in the eyes of the client. He argued that any explanation of their difficulties that clients can accept alleviates distress and engenders hope. Thus, Frank allowed for the therapist to persuade the client that his or her theoretical rationale makes sense or to modify his or her preferred theoretical understanding to fit better with the client's understanding.

What is missing from the common factors/contextual meta-model is the emphasis our theoretical eclecticism places on an open, holistic assessment that is conducted collaboratively with the client. In this process, the views of both worker and client are considered together with multiple theoretical perspectives in an effort to build a comprehensive and shared understanding of the client's situation. This process allows for the development of understanding by both worker and client that may be different from and/or more comprehensive than either of their initial understandings of the problem. A more comprehensive understanding of the problem situation can lead to formulation of strategies for intervention that have a higher likelihood of success. We agree that it is necessary to eventually arrive at an understanding of the problem that fits for the client, but we think that an open, collaborative exploration/assessment can not only expand awareness of the problem and potential solutions but can also foster the development of a strong therapeutic alliance and a sense of empowerment for the client, all of which help to overcome demoralization and instill hope.

One of the most important distinguishing features of our approach to eclecticism, which stems from its grounding in social work's generalist perspective, is that it is broader in focus and scope of intervention than most of the approaches to eclecticism that are in the clinical psychology literature. The generalist perspective of social work demands a holistic, person-in-environment focus that is sensitive to issues of diversity, oppression, and empowerment. It necessitates that direct practice be viewed broadly. Thus, as mentioned earlier, we think that the mandate and role of clinical social work includes helping clients to meet basic needs by providing them with or linking them to resources and services and engaging in social advocacy.

It is heartening and worth noting that some of the leaders of the movement toward eclecticism in clinical psychology are also beginning to attend to a traditional social work holistic focus. In a consideration of the future of psychotherapy integration in the concluding chapter of Norcross and Goldfried's (2005) *Handbook of Psychotherapy Integration*, it is suggested that "in order to understand and effectively meet clients' needs, therapists should attend more to the broader social context of clients' lives, including social values . . . , economic realities . . . , and cultural differences" (Eubanks-Carter, Burckell, & Goldfried, 2005, pp. 506–507). Also, in the introductory chapter to this same volume, Norcross (2005) noted that recent thrusts in psychotherapy integration include focus on multicultural theory, spirituality, and social advocacy. Furthermore, in elaborating upon the necessity for therapists to align their theoretical views with the client's worldview, Wampold (2001) noted,

> Clients from populations of historically oppressed persons will benefit particularly from therapists who understand this dynamic, who are credible to the client, who can build an alliance with a client who may mistrust therapists representing institutional authority, [and] who are multiculturally competent. (p. 226)

Although some might view these recent trends in eclecticism as an incursion by psychologists into the domain of social work, we welcome this broadened understanding of eclecticism in direct practice by an allied helping profession, with the hope that all helping professionals can move together in such a direction.

One potential drawback to theoretical eclecticism, which is also shared by the common factors and technical eclecticism approaches, is that without a primary theoretical base (as in assimilative integration), or a synthesis of two or three theoretical bases (as in theoretical integration), there can be a lack of structure and guidelines for practice. In our approach to theoretical eclecticism, however, this is remedied by the use of social work's general problem-solving model. As explained earlier, the problem-solving model provides structure and guidelines for practice across all the phases of helping (from engagement to termination), but these are general and flexible enough to allow for an eclectic use of theory and techniques. We think that the use of the problem-solving model to guide practice in our theoretically eclectic approach is better than using a primary theoretical base, as in assimilative integration, or using a synthesis of theories, as in theoretical integration. The latter approaches are less theoretically open and have more theoretical biases than a theoretically eclectic approach that uses a problem-solving model. Our use of the problem-solving model has parallels to Garfield's (1995) common factors approach, which provides general guidelines for what he calls the stages of the therapeutic process (beginning, middle, later, and termination stages).

SUMMARY

This chapter has provided an overview of our generalist-eclectic approach to direct practice. It has included a description of the elements of a generalist social work perspective that are central to our approach, a delineation of the distinctive aspects of our generalist-eclectic approach, an overview of the rationale for and trend toward eclecticism in direct practice, a review of the major approaches to eclecticism in the literature, and a discussion of theoretical eclecticism—our particular approach to eclecticism. It was beyond the scope of this chapter to discuss many of the topics in the depth that they deserve. Readers are directed to the literature cited in our discussions for a more detailed review of topics that are of interest to them. In the next chapter, the types, levels, and classifications of theories for direct practice are discussed in an effort to demystify theory and facilitate its use in practice. In addition, a critical examination of how and the extent to which theory is used in practice is presented, and a complementary, intuitive-inductive approach that represents the art of practice is considered.

REFERENCES

Ackerman, S. J., Benjamin, L. S., Beutler, L. E., Gelso, C. J., Goldfried, M. R., Hill, C., et al. (2001). Empirically supported therapy relationships: Conclusions and recommendations of the Division 29 Task Force. *Psychotherapy, 38,* 495–497.

Alford, B. A. (1995). Introduction to the special issue: "Psychotherapy integration" and cognitive psychotherapy. *Journal of Cognitive Psychotherapy, 9,* 147–151.

Asay, T. P., & Lambert, M. J. (2001). Therapist relational variables. In D. J. Cain & J. Seeman (Eds.), *Humanistic psychotherapies: Handbook of research and practice* (pp. 531–558). Washington, DC: American Psychological Association.

Barlow, D. H. (2000). Evidence-based practice: A world view. *Clinical Psychology: Science and Practice, 7*, 241–242.

Beutler, L. E. (1983). *Eclectic psychotherapy: A systematic approach.* Elmsford, NY: Pergamon Press.

Beutler, L. E. (1991). Have all won and must all have prizes? Revisiting Luborsky et al.'s verdict. *Journal of Consulting and Clinical Psychology, 59*, 226–232.

Beutler, L. E., & Clarkin, J. (1990). *Systematic treatment selection: Toward targeted therapeutic interventions.* New York: Brunner/Mazel.

Beutler, L. E., Consoli, A. J., & Lane, G. (2005). Systematic treatment selection and prescriptive psychotherapy. In J. C. Norcross & M. R. Goldfried (Eds.), *Handbook of psychotherapy integration* (2nd ed., pp. 121–146). New York: Oxford University Press.

Beutler, L. E., & Harwood, T. M. (1995). Prescriptive psychotherapies. *Applied and Preventive Psychology, 4*, 89–100.

Beutler, L. E., & Harwood, T. M. (2000). *Prescriptive psychotherapy.* New York: Oxford University Press.

Biestek, F. (1957). *The casework relationship.* Chicago: Loyola University Press.

Castonguay, L. G., Reid, J. J., Halperin, G. S., & Goldfried, M. R. (2003). Psychotherapy integration. In G. Stricker & T. A. Widiger (Eds.), *Handbook of psychology: Vol. 8. Clinical psychology* (pp. 327–345). New York: Wiley.

Coady, N. F. (1993a). An argument for generalist social work practice with families versus family systems therapy. *Canadian Social Work Review, 10*, 27–42.

Coady, N. F. (1993b). The worker-client relationship revisited. *Families in Society, 74*, 291–298.

Coady, N. F. (1995). A reflective/inductive model of practice: Emphasizing theory building for unique cases versus applying theory to practice. In G. Rogers (Ed.), *Social work field education: Views and visions* (pp. 139–151). Dubuque, IA: Kendall/Hunt.

Compton, B. R., & Galaway, B. (1994). *Social work processes* (5th ed.). Pacific Grove, CA: Brooks/Cole.

Derezotes, D. S. (2000). *Advanced generalist social work practice.* Thousand Oaks, CA: Sage.

Dollard, J., & Miller, N. E. (1950). *Personality and psychotherapy: An analysis in terms of learning, thinking, and culture.* New York: McGraw-Hill.

Dryden, W. (Ed.). (1992). *Integrative and eclectic therapy: A handbook.* Buckingham, England: Open University Press.

Elkin, I. (1994). The NIMH Treatment of Depression Collaborative Research Program: Where we began and where we are. In A. E. Bergin & S. L. Garfield (Eds.), *Handbook of psychotherapy and behavior change* (4th ed., pp. 114–139). New York: Wiley.

Eubanks-Carter, C., Burckell, L. A., & Goldfried, M. R. (2005). Future directions in psychotherapy integration. In J. C. Norcross & M. R. Goldfried (Eds.), *Handbook of psychotherapy integration* (2nd ed., pp. 503–520). New York: Oxford University Press.

Frank, J. D. (1961). *Persuasion and healing: A comparative study of psychotherapy.* Baltimore: Johns Hopkins University Press.

Frank, J. D. (1973). *Persuasion and healing: A comparative study of psychotherapy* (2nd ed.). Baltimore: Johns Hopkins University Press.

Frank, J. D. (1982). Therapeutic components shared by all psychotherapies. In J. H. Harvey & M. M. Parks (Eds.), *The master lecture series: Vol. 1. Psychotherapy research and behavior change* (pp. 9–37). Washington, DC: American Psychological Association.

Frank, J. D., & Frank, J. B. (1991). *Persuasion and healing: A comparative study of psychotherapy* (3rd ed.). Baltimore: Johns Hopkins University Press.

Gambrill, E. (1999). Evidence-based practice: An alternative to authority-based practice. *Families in Society, 80*, 341–350.

Garfield, S. L. (1980). *Psychotherapy: An eclectic approach.* New York: Wiley.

Garfield, S. L. (1995). *Psychotherapy: An eclectic-integrative approach* (2nd ed.). New York: Wiley.

Garfield, S. L., & Bergin, A. E. (1986). Introduction and historical overview. In S. L. Garfield & A. E. Bergin (Eds.), *Handbook of psychotherapy and behavior change* (3rd ed., pp. 3–22). New York: Wiley.

Gibbs, L., & Gambrill, E. (2002). Evidence-based practice: Counterarguments to objections. *Research on Social Work Practice, 12,* 452–476.

Gold, J. R. (1996). *Key concepts in psychotherapy integration.* New York: Plenum Press.

Gold, J. R., & Stricker, G. (2001). A relational psychodynamic perspective on assimilative integration. *Journal of Psychotherapy Integration, 11,* 43–58.

Goldstein, H. (1990). The knowledge base of social work practice: Theory, wisdom, analogue, or art? *Families in Society, 71,* 32–43.

Grencavage, L. M., & Norcross, J. C. (1990). Where are the commonalities among the therapeutic common factors? *Professional Psychology: Research and Practice, 21,* 372–378.

Heard, H. H., & Linehan, M. M. (2005). Integrative therapy for borderline personality disorder. In J. C. Norcross & M. R. Goldfried (Eds.), *Handbook of psychotherapy integration* (2nd ed., pp. 299–320). New York: Oxford University Press.

Henry, W. P. (1998). Science, politics, and the politics of science: The use and misuse of empirically validated treatment research. *Psychotherapy Research, 8,* 126–140.

Hepworth, D. H., Rooney, R. H., & Larsen, J. A. (2002). *Direct social work practice: Theory and skills* (6th ed.). Pacific Grove, CA: Brooks/Cole.

Hollis, F. (1970). The psychosocial approach to the practice of casework. In R. Roberts & R. Nee (Eds.), *Theories of social casework* (pp. 33–75). Chicago: University of Chicago Press.

Horvath, A. O., & Symonds, B. D. (1991). Relation between working alliance and outcome in psychotherapy. *Journal of Counseling Psychology, 38,* 139–149.

Howard, M. O., McMillen, C. J., & Pollio, D. E. (2003). Teaching evidence-based practice: Toward a new paradigm for social work education. *Research on Social Work Practice, 13,* 234–259.

Hubble, M. A., Duncan, B. L., & Miller, S. D. (Eds.). (1999). *The heart & soul of change: What works in therapy.* Washington, DC: American Psychological Association.

Jensen, J. P., Bergin, A. E., & Greaves, D. W. (1990). The meaning of eclecticism: New survey and analysis of components. *Professional Psychology: Research and Practice, 21,* 124–130.

Johnson, L. C., & Yanca, S. J. (2004). *Social work practice: A generalist approach* (8th ed.). Boston: Pearson.

Kirst-Ashman, K. K., & Hull, G. H. (2002). *Understanding generalist practice* (3rd ed.). Pacific Grove, CA: Brooks/Cole.

Lambert, M. J. (1992). Psychotherapy outcome research: Implications for integrative and eclectic therapists. In J. C. Norcross & M. R. Goldfried (Eds.), *Handbook of psychotherapy integration* (pp. 94–129). New York: Basic Books.

Lambert, M. J., & Barley, D. E. (2001). Research summary on the therapeutic relationship and psychotherapy outcome. *Psychotherapy: Theory, Research, Practice, Training, 38,* 357–361.

Lambert, M. J., Bergin, A. E., & Garfield, S. L. (2004). Introduction and historical overview. In M. J. Lambert (Ed.), *Bergin and Garfield's handbook of psychotherapy and behavior change* (5th ed., pp. 3–15). New York: Wiley.

Lambert, M. J., Garfield, S. L., & Bergin, A. E. (2004). Overview, trends, and future issues. In M. J. Lambert (Ed.), *Bergin and Garfield's handbook of psychotherapy and behavior change* (5th ed., pp. 805–822). New York: Wiley.

Lambert, M. J., & Ogles, B. M. (2004). The efficacy and effectiveness of psychotherapy. In M. J. Lambert (Ed.), *Bergin and Garfield's handbook of psychotherapy and behavior change* (5th ed., pp. 139–193). New York: Wiley.

Lampropoulos, G. K. (2001). Bridging technical eclecticism and theoretical integration: Assimilative integration. *Journal of Psychotherapy Integration, 11,* 5–19.

Landon, P. S. (1995). Generalist and advanced generalist practice. In *Encyclopedia of social work* (19th ed., Vol. 2, pp. 1101–1108). Washington, DC: NASW Press.

Landon, P. S. (1999). *Generalist social work practice.* Dubuque, IA: Eddie Bowers.

Lazarus, A. A. (1981). *The practice of multimodal therapy.* New York: McGraw-Hill.

Lazarus, A. A. (1996). The utility and futility of combining treatments in psychotherapy. *Clinical Psychology: Science and Practice, 3,* 59–68.

Lazarus, A. A. (2005). Multimodal therapy. In J. C. Norcross & M. R. Goldfried (Eds.), *Handbook of psychotherapy integration* (2nd ed., pp. 105–120). New York: Oxford University Press.

Lebow, J. (2002). Integrative and eclectic therapies at the beginning of the twenty-first century. In J. Lebow (Ed.), *Comprehensive handbook of psychotherapy: Vol. 4. Integrative/eclectic* (pp. 1–10). New York: Wiley.

Linehan, M. M. (1993). *Cognitive-behavioral treatment of borderline personality disorder.* New York: Guilford Press.

Locke, B., Garrison, R., & Winship, J. (1998). *Generalist social work practice: Context, story, and partnerships.* Pacific Grove, CA: Brooks/Cole.

Magill, M. (2006). The future of evidence in evidence-based practice: Who will answer the call for clinical relevance? *Journal of Social Work, 6,* 101–115.

Mattaini, M. A., Lowery, C. T., & Meyer, C. H. (Eds.). (1998). *The foundations of social work practice: A graduate text* (2nd ed.). Washington, DC: NASW Press.

McCullough, J. P., Jr. (2000). *Treatment for chronic depression: Cognitive behavioral analysis system of psychotherapy (CBASP).* New York: Guilford Press.

McMahon, M. O. (1996). *The general method of social work practice: A problem-solving approach* (3rd ed.). Englewood Cliffs, NJ: Prentice Hall.

McMillen, J. C., Morris, L., & Sherraden, M. (2004). Ending social work's grudge match: Problems versus strengths. *Families in Society, 85,* 317–325.

Messer, S. B. (1992). A critical examination of belief structures in integrative and eclectic psychotherapy. In J. C. Norcross & M. R. Goldfried (Eds.), *Handbook of psychotherapy integration* (pp. 130–165). New York: Basic Books.

Messer, S. B. (2001). Empirically supported treatments: What's a nonbehaviorist to do? In B. D. Slife, R. N. Williams, & S. H. Barlow (Eds.), *Critical issues in psychotherapy: Translating new ideas into practice* (pp. 3–25). Thousand Oaks, CA: Sage.

Miley, K. K., O'Melia, M., & DuBois, B. (1998). *Generalist social work practice: An empowering approach.* Boston: Allyn & Bacon.

Miley, K. K., O'Melia, M., & DuBois, B. (2007). *Generalist social work practice: An empowering approach* (5th ed.). Boston: Pearson.

Miller, S. D., Duncan, B. L., & Hubble, M. A. (2005). Outcome-informed clinical work. In J. C. Norcross & M. R. Goldfried (Eds.), *Handbook of psychotherapy integration* (2nd ed., pp. 84–104). New York: Oxford University Press.

Mills, C. W. (1959). *The sociological imagination.* New York: Oxford University Press.

Norcross, J. C. (1997). Emerging breakthroughs in psychotherapy integration: Three predictions and one fantasy. *Psychotherapy, 34,* 86–90.

Norcross, J. C. (2001). Purposes, process, and products of the Task Force on Empirically Supported Treatment Relationships. *Psychotherapy: Theory, Research, Practice, Training, 38,* 345–356.

Norcross, J. C. (Ed.). (2002). *Psychotherapy relationships that work*. New York: Oxford University Press.

Norcross, J. C. (2005). A primer on psychotherapy integration. In J. C. Norcross & M. R. Goldfried (Eds.), *Handbook of psychotherapy integration* (2nd ed., pp. 3–23). New York: Oxford University Press.

Norcross, J. C., & Goldfried, M. R. (Eds.). (2005). *Handbook of psychotherapy integration* (2nd ed.). New York: Oxford University Press.

Perlman, H. H. (1957). *Social casework: A problem-solving process*. Chicago: University of Chicago Press.

Perlman, H. H. (1979). *Relationship: The heart of helping people*. Chicago: University of Chicago Press.

Prochaska, J. O. (1979). *Systems of psychotherapy: A transtheoretical analysis*. Homewood, IL: Dorsey Press.

Prochaska, J. O., & DiClemente, C. C. (1984). *The transtheoretical approach: Crossing the traditional boundaries of therapy*. Homewood, IL: Dow Jones-Irwin.

Prochaska, J. O., & DiClemente, C. C. (2005). The transtheoretical approach. In J. C. Norcross & M. R. Goldfried (Eds.), *Handbook of psychotherapy integration* (2nd ed., pp. 147–171). New York: Oxford University Press.

Prochaska, J. O., & Norcross, J. C. (2003). *Systems of psychotherapy: A transtheoretical analysis* (5th ed.). Pacific Grove, CA: Brooks/Cole.

Reid, W. J. (1997). Evaluating the dodo bird's verdict: Do all interventions have equivalent outcomes? *Social Work Research, 21,* 5–16.

Rosenzweig, S. (1936). Some implicit common factors in diverse methods of psychotherapy. *American Journal of Orthopsychiatry, 6,* 412–415.

Rubin, A., & Parrish, D. (2007). Views of evidence-based practice among faculty in master of social work programs: A national survey. *Research on Social Work Practice, 17,* 110–122.

Safran, J. D. (1990a). Towards a refinement of cognitive therapy in light of interpersonal theory: I. Theory. *Clinical Psychology Review, 10,* 87–105.

Safran, J. D. (1990b). Towards a refinement of cognitive therapy in light of interpersonal theory: II. Practice. *Clinical Psychology Review, 10,* 107–121.

Safran, J. D. (1998). *Widening the scope of cognitive therapy*. Northvale, NJ: Jason Aronson.

Safran, J. D., & Segal, Z. V. (1990). *Interpersonal processes in cognitive therapy*. New York: Basic Books.

Saleebey, D. (Ed.). (2006). *The strengths perspective in social work practice* (4th ed.). New York: Longman.

Schon, D. A. (1983). *The reflective practitioner: How professionals think in action*. New York: Basic Books.

Schottenbauer, M. A., Glass, C. R., & Arnkoff, D. B. (2005). Outcome research on psychotherapy integration. In J. C. Norcross & M. R. Goldfried (Eds.), *Handbook of psychotherapy integration* (2nd ed., pp. 459–493). New York: Oxford University Press.

Shatz, M. S., Jenkins, M. E., & Sheafor, B. W. (1990). Milford redefined: A model of initial and advanced generalist social work. *Journal of Social Work Education, 26,* 217–231.

Sheafor, B. W., & Horejsi, C. R. (2006). *Techniques and guidelines for social work practice* (7th ed.). Boston: Pearson.

Sheafor, B. W., & Landon, P. S. (1987). The generalist perspective. In *Encyclopedia of social work* (18th ed., Vol. 1, pp. 660–669). Silver Spring, MD: NASW Press.

Smith, M. L., & Glass, G. V. (1977). Meta-analysis of psychotherapy outcome studies. *American Psychologist, 32,* 752–760.

Stalker, C. A., Levene, J. E., & Coady, N. F. (1999). Solution-focused brief therapy—One model fits all? *Families in Society, 80*, 468–477.

Stiles, W. B., Shapiro, D. A., & Barkham, M. (1995). Technical eclecticism. In J. C. Norcross (Ed.), A roundtable on psychotherapy integration: Common factors, technical eclecticism, and psychotherapy research. *Grand Rounds, 4*, 248–271.

Stricker, G. (1994). Reflections on psychotherapy integration. *Clinical Psychology: Science and Practice, 1*, 3–12.

Stricker, G., & Gold, J. R. (Eds.). (1993). *Comprehensive handbook of psychotherapy integration*. New York: Plenum Press.

Stricker, G., & Gold, J. R. (2005). Assimilative psychodynamic psychotherapy. In J. C. Norcross & M. R. Goldfried (Eds.), *Handbook of psychotherapy integration* (2nd ed., pp. 221–240). New York: Oxford University Press.

Thorne, F. C. (1950). *Principles of personality counseling: An eclectic view*. Brandon, VT: Journal of Clinical Psychology.

Timberlake, E. M., Farber, M. Z., & Sabatino, C. A. (2002). *The general method of social work practice: McMahon's generalist perspective*. Boston: Allyn & Bacon.

Tolson, E. R., Reid, W. J., & Garvin, C. D. (2003). *Generalist practice: A task-centered approach* (2nd ed.). New York: Columbia University Press.

Wachtel, P. L. (1977). *Psychoanalysis and behavior therapy: Toward an integration*. New York: Basic Books.

Wachtel, P. L. (1997). *Psychoanalysis, behavior therapy, and the relational world*. Washington, DC: American Psychological Association.

Wachtel, P. L., Kruk, J. C., & McKinney, M. K. (2005). Cyclical psychodynamics and integrative relational psychotherapy. In J. C. Norcross & M. R. Goldfried (Eds.), *Handbook of psychotherapy integration* (2nd ed., pp. 172–195). New York: Oxford University Press.

Wampold, B. E. (2001). *The great psychotherapy debate: Models, methods, and findings*. Mahwah, NJ: Lawrence Erlbaum.

Wampold, B. E., Mondin, G. W., Moody, M., Stich, F., Benson, K., & Ahn, H. (1997). A meta-analysis of outcome studies comparing bona fide psychotherapies: Empirically, "All must have prizes." *Psychological Bulletin, 122*, 203–215.

Weinberger, J. (1993). Common factors in psychotherapy. In G. Stricker & J. R. Gold (Eds.), *Comprehensive handbook of psychotherapy integration* (pp. 43–56). New York: Plenum Press.

Wolfe, B. E. (2005). Integrative psychotherapy of the anxiety disorders. In J. C. Norcross & M. R. Goldfried (Eds.), *Handbook of psychotherapy integration* (2nd ed., pp. 263–280). New York: Oxford University Press.

CHAPTER 2

The Science and Art of Direct Practice: *An Overview of Theory and an Intuitive-Inductive Approach to Practice*

Nick Coady

This chapter provides an overview of two complementary approaches to direct practice: (a) the predominant "scientific" approach of the deductive use of theory to understand clients and their life situations and to facilitate change; and (b) the less accepted "artistic," humanistic approach, which emphasizes the use of intuitive processes and inductive reasoning to build a theory that fits the unique circumstances of each client and to develop individualized change strategies.

This chapter is divided into three parts. In the first part, theories for direct practice are considered with regard to two key dimensions (function and level of abstraction) and definitions of key terms (perspective, theory, model, and therapy) are provided and linked to these dimensions. Second, the major classifications of direct practice theories (i.e., psychodynamic, cognitive-behavioral, humanistic, feminist, and postmodern) are described. A critical examination of the scientific understanding of practice and a discussion of the complementary, artistic approach to practice are presented in the third part of the chapter.

GENERAL FUNCTIONS AND LEVELS OF ABSTRACTION OF THEORY

It is useful to compare and classify theories for direct social work practice on two general dimensions. One dimension has to do with the function of theory. With regard to function, it is useful to consider the extent to which a theory focuses on (a) describing and explaining human behavior, or (b) facilitating changes in human behavior.

The other dimension has to do with the level of abstraction of theory. Theories at higher levels of abstraction provide general ideas for understanding and/or intervening with a wide range of human behavior (e.g., human development theory provides a broad lens for understanding human behavior across the life span and provides general ideas for intervention). Theories at lower levels of abstraction provide more specific ideas for understanding and/or intervening with a more circumscribed range of human behavior (e.g., the theory of interactive trauma/grief-focused therapy provides specific ways to understand and intervene with childhood trauma). A simultaneous consideration of the function and the level of abstraction of theory provides a useful way of conceptualizing the multitude of theories that inform direct social work practice (see Figure 2.1).

In Figure 2.1, the vertical axis relates to the function of theory (degree of focus on explanation or facilitation of change) and the horizontal axis relates to the level of abstraction. The right-hand column of the figure represents the artistic, intuitive-inductive approach to practice. This will be discussed later in this chapter, and for the time being it is enough to say that this approach is at the lowest level of abstraction because the focus is on the individual, unique client and it is equally concerned with explanation and facilitation of change. For the present, the focus will be on the rest of the figure, which conceptualizes how the theories that are reviewed in this book can be classified with regard to their general function and level of abstraction. (Note: The theories in Figure 2.1 are those reviewed in this book and are only examples of theories at the various levels of abstraction.)

One issue that becomes apparent in looking at the figure is the need to define some commonly used terms: *perspectives, theories, models,* and *therapies.* In most of this book, the term *theory* is used in a general sense to encompass all of these terms; however, more specific definitions are helpful. These terms are bandied about a great deal in the social work literature, and there are many different definitions for them. In presenting a particular understanding of these terms, it is acknowledged that there are alternate conceptualizations and that the boundaries around them are often fuzzy. In discussing these terms, an understanding of the functions and levels of abstraction of theory is elaborated upon.

Perspective denotes the highest level of generality among these terms and is referred to only at the highest level of abstraction in Figure 2.1. A

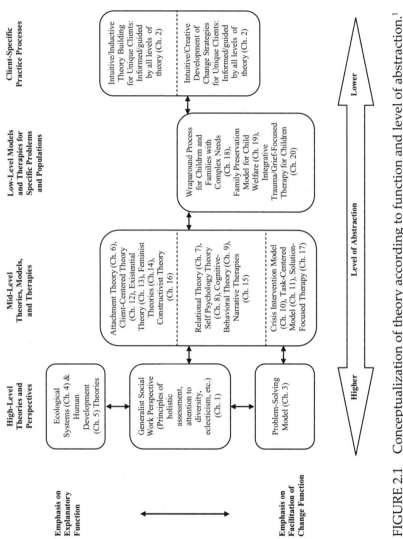

FIGURE 2.1   Conceptualization of theory according to function and level of abstraction.[1]

[1]The authors would like to thank Michael Rothery for allowing us to adapt a version of this figure that he had prepared for chapter 4 of this book.

perspective is a broad, general way of viewing human behavior and social work practice. Thus, as described in chapter 1, a generalist perspective provides a broad conceptual lens for viewing human behavior in that it reminds us to focus holistically on person–environment interactions, human strengths and resiliency, and issues of diversity and oppression, and to be eclectic in the use of theory. Because the generalist perspective neither focuses on explanations for human behavior nor on guidelines for facilitating change, it is placed in the middle of this continuum.

An example of another commonly referred to perspective for social work practice is the "strengths perspective" (Saleebey, 2006), which is conceptualized as part of the broader generalist perspective. Although ecological systems "theory" and a problem-solving "model" are included as elements of the generalist "perspective," these are depicted as separate from but linked to this perspective in Figure 2.1 to clarify distinctions among these terms (i.e., theory, model, and perspective).

The term *theory* is reserved for a conceptual framework that offers an explanation of human behavior. Many theories also provide guidelines for facilitating behavior change. For example, psychodynamic theory offers both an explanation of human problems and guidelines for helping people overcome problems. All theories are placed in the top half of Figure 2.1 because they focus at least as much on explanation as on facilitation of change. At the highest level of abstraction are ecological systems and human development theories (see Part II of this book). Although these two theories provide a general way of understanding a broad range of human behavior, they provide only general ideas and few guidelines for intervention. Theories at the highest level of abstraction are commonly referred to as *meta-theories*.

At a mid-level of abstraction are theories that provide more specific understanding of a broad range of human behavior, as well as guidelines for facilitating behavior change. These are typically what social workers think of when they think of *practice theories*, and most of this book (i.e., Part III) is devoted to reviewing theories (as well as models and therapies) at this level of abstraction. Although all theories at this mid-level of abstraction offer both explanations for human behavior and guidelines for facilitating behavior change, some theories place more emphasis on one than the other. In Figure 2.1, the placement of theories, models, and therapies in three groupings in the mid-level box (divided by the dotted lines) reflects our assessment of the degree to which emphasis is placed on explanation or guidelines for change (e.g., attachment theory is in the top grouping because it emphasizes explanation, whereas solution-focused therapy is in the bottom grouping because it emphasizes prescriptions for the change process).

Models and *therapies* are distinguished from theories by the fact that they do not focus as much on theoretical explanations of human behavior.

Models and therapies are focused more on providing guidelines to facilitate change, and thus are placed in the lower half of Figure 2.1 (e.g., the problem-solving model at the highest level of abstraction and solution-focused therapy at the mid-level of abstraction). There are many models and therapies at a low level of abstraction that have been developed for intervening with specific populations (e.g., the family preservation model for child welfare families at risk of child placement) or problems. The only important distinction between these terms is that models can be at a high level of abstraction (e.g., the problem-solving model) whereas therapies are restricted to mid levels and low levels of abstraction.

Whether one accepts the definitions of the terms (i.e., perspective, theory, model, and therapy) that are provided in this chapter or one prefers alternate conceptualizations, in order to avoid confusion it should be acknowledged that in common usage (and often in the professional literature) many of these terms are used interchangeably. Thus, for example, one will find the therapeutic approach of Carl Rogers referred to variously as client-centered theory, client-centered therapy, or the client-centered model of practice. Correct terminology is much less important than understanding how theories can be understood and classified according to their general function and level of abstraction.

In addition to bringing some order to the vast array of theories that inform direct social work practice, consideration of the general function and the level of abstraction of theories aids in understanding their strengths and limitations. For example, it is evident that it is important to use ecological systems and human development theories to understand clients' behavior, but that if one wants more specific guidelines for intervention, it is necessary to consider mid-level theories, models, or therapies. Furthermore, if a worker has a client with a very specific problem and the worker prefers very specific guidelines for helping with the identified problem, then he or she would be best to use a low-level model or therapy for the specific problem (e.g., interactive trauma/grief-focused therapy for a child who has been traumatized). Alternatively, if a worker prefers a more theoretically open, individualized approach to working with clients, he or she could rely primarily on an intuitive-inductive approach to theory building and developing change strategies for the unique case, while using the problem-solving model to provide general guidelines to the helping process and drawing eclectically on various theories if they seem to fit the client's situation.

MAJOR CLASSIFICATIONS OF MID-LEVEL DIRECT PRACTICE THEORIES

Most theories for direct practice exist at or are linked closely to the mid-level of abstraction denoted in Figure 2.1, and most of this book is devoted to reviewing mid-level theories. Although there has been a recent trend toward the development of many low-level models and therapies for specific problems and populations, many of these have a primary allegiance to one of the mid-level practice theories (e.g., the family preservation model for child welfare draws primarily from cognitive-behavioral theory).

Estimates of the overall number of theories for direct practice have ranged from 200 to 400 (Lambert, Bergin, & Garfield, 2004). Because of the overwhelming and confusing array of direct practice theories from which to choose, another useful strategy for conceptualizing and understanding these theories is to organize the mid-level practice theories in like groupings. Mid-level direct practice theories can be divided into five major classifications: (a) psychodynamic theories, (b) cognitive-behavioral theories, (c) humanistic theories, (d) feminist theories, and (e) postmodern theories. Table 2.1 provides a broad characterization of these five major classifications of direct practice theories. After a brief discussion of the usefulness of this broad characterization of the major classifications of theory, each of the five classifications will be discussed in more detail.

The broad characterization of the major classifications of direct practice theory found in Table 2.1 allows for identifying the commonalities among theories in each of the five groups, as well as for pointing out differences across groups. This description helps to bring order and clarity to the overwhelming number of theories within the field and allows for the identification of the strengths and weaknesses of the various classes of theory, both of which facilitate the eclectic use of theory.

The concepts in the left-hand column of the table represent some of the important dimensions by which to compare theoretical perspectives. It should be emphasized that the characterizations of the classes of theory with regard to these dimensions are very general and should be construed as descriptions of central tendencies. For example, although the primary focus in most cognitive-behavioral and humanistic therapies is on the present, this is not to say that such therapies do not focus at all on the past. The same caution applies to the characterization of the classes of theory with regard to focus on affect, cognition, and behavior; focus on symptoms or general growth/development; and degree of structure and directiveness. The dangers of such broad characterizations include the potential to minimize differences within groups of theory and to overlook similarities across groups.

An example of the danger of minimizing differences within groups of theory is found in some of the major differences between solution-focused therapy and the other types of postmodern theory. As pointed out in the discussion of postmodern theories (see below), solution-focused therapy concentrates more on specific symptoms and behaviors and is more directive, compared to narrative and constructivist theories. With regard to the danger of exaggerating differences across groups of theory, integrative theorists have demonstrated how seemingly antithetical theories are not as different and incompatible as one might suppose (e.g., see discussion in chapter 1 of Wachtel, Kruk, & McKinney's [2005] integrative relational therapy, which combines psychodynamic and behavioral theories).

With these limitations in mind, a general consideration of how the concepts in the left-hand column of Table 2.1 are construed by or manifested in each class of theory can help the practitioner to consider which class of theory might best suit particular clients at particular points in the counseling process, as well as to consider which classes of theory might be used simultaneously to address clients' concerns more holistically. For instance, a client who wants to focus on specific symptoms in current day-to-day functioning, to avoid exploration of painful feelings, and to have a high degree of structure and direction in counseling may be best served, at least initially, by a cognitive-behavioral approach. Once this client learns to cope more effectively with presenting symptoms, however, he or she and the worker may decide that a focus on feelings (i.e., affect) may be helpful to consolidate and further gains. If client issues seem to be connected to early problematic relationships with caregivers, a psychodynamic approach might then be used to explore the link between affective difficulties in the present and the past and to work through such feelings. If a connection to earlier intimate relationships is not apparent, or if the client is averse to exploring such connections, a humanistic approach may be more appropriate for dealing with affective issues. If the client is a woman whose issues seem to be connected to a history of abuse or oppression, it would be important to integrate a feminist approach with any of these other approaches. Also, a postmodern approach could be integrated with any of the other theoretical approaches or used as a follow-up to other approaches in order to integrate changes into more empowering views of one's self and one's life story.

Psychodynamic Theories

A broad conceptualization of psychodynamic theories includes all those that have evolved from Freud's theory of human psychological development. In general, psychodynamic approaches postulate that the root causes of most problems are painful, frightening, or unsupportive experiences in childhood. These theories hold that unconscious internal conflicts or developmental deficits underlie problematic behaviors, thoughts, and feelings. The goal of most psychodynamic therapies is to make the unconscious conscious. This is done primarily through the use of *interpretations* to help the client develop *insight* (cognitive and emotional understanding) into how the deprivations and/or frustrations suffered early in life have

TABLE 2.1 Characterization of Classes of Direct Practice Theories

	Psychodynamic	Cognitive-Behavioral	Humanistic	Feminist	Postmodern
View of Causation of Human Problems	Traumatic experiences or inadequate nurturance in childhood lead to unconscious internalization of conflict or developmental deficits	Maladaptive behaviors and/or cognitions are learned through conditioning, reinforcement, and/or modeling	Defenses against painful aspects of experience lead to losing touch with authentic experiencing in the present	Institutionalized system of male privilege results in exploitation and oppression of women and other marginalized groups	Negative interpretation of self and of life experience and/or internalization of toxic cultural narratives result in oppression and marginalization
Goal of Intervention	Develop emotional/cognitive understanding of connection between early and current problems	Learn more adaptive thoughts and behaviors	Develop new awareness and meaning of experiences in the present	Raise consciousness of oppression, and empower for personal and social change	Develop more positive views of self and of life experience and/or develop freedom from oppressive cultural assumptions

Primary Focus on Past or Present	Past and Present	Present	Present	Present and Past	Present and Past
Primary Focus on Affect, Cognition, or Behavior	Affect and Cognition	Cognition and Behavior	Affect	Affect, Cognition, and Behavior	Cognition
Primary Focus on Specific Symptoms or General Growth/Development	General Growth/Development	Specific Symptoms	General Growth/Development	General Growth/Development	General Growth/Development
Degree of Structure and Directiveness (Low, Medium, High)	Low-Medium	Medium-High	Low-Medium	Low-Medium	Low-Medium

Note. The characterizations in this table are broad generalizations that do not hold for all of the more specific approaches within these classes (see discussion in this chapter).

caused misperceptions and distortions of experience in the present (Gelso & Carter, 1985). It is noteworthy that psychodynamic theory remained the dominant influence in psychotherapy, including clinical social work, for more than half of the 20th century (Lambert, Bergin, et al., 2004).

Although classical psychoanalysis, which is sometimes referred to as id (or drive) psychology (Strean, 1996), is no longer the most common type of psychodynamic therapy, some still consider it as the most thorough and powerful of these therapies (Gelso & Carter, 1985). Classical psychoanalytic theory holds that there are universal, biologically determined drives that are associated with psychosexual stages (oral, anal, phallic, oedipal, latency, and genital) through which personality develops. Problems represent unresolved conflicts that result in fixation at or regression to one or more of these stages. Classical psychoanalysis is a long-term (often lasting years), intensive therapy (four to five sessions weekly). The client is encouraged to free associate (i.e., to talk about whatever comes to mind). The therapist is generally neutral and passive (acting like a blank screen) so that the client projects thoughts and feelings about early authority figures (especially parents) onto the therapist. This leads to the development of a transference neurosis, whereby the client confuses (on an unconscious level) the therapist with such early authority figures. The therapist then gradually interprets this transference to help the client develop insight into how his or her reactions to the therapist and other authority figures in the present are inappropriate and influenced by unresolved conflicts from childhood. Insight involves becoming aware of all aspects of the unresolved conflict—the childhood wish, fantasy, or memory; the anxiety or fear that was associated with this; and the defense mechanisms that were used to keep it from becoming conscious (Gold, 1996).

Many different types of psychodynamic therapies have evolved from classical psychoanalysis. Most therapies based on more recent psychodynamic theories are of shorter duration than classical psychoanalysis, and most have incorporated a greater recognition of the importance of social and interpersonal factors, as well as of the need for the practitioner to be more active, personal, and warm. Ego psychology was an important development within the psychodynamic school and was influential in placing more emphasis on social factors and the adaptive ability of the rational part of the mind (the ego). Erikson (1950) formulated the psychosocial (as opposed to psychosexual) stages of development across the life span (see chapter 5), and Hartmann (1958) elaborated on ego adaptation and mastery.

Another important development in psychodynamic theory has involved a number of separate schools of psychodynamic thought that focused their attention on the importance of primary relationships to the developing individual. These theories, sometimes referred to collectively as the *relational structure model* (Greenberg & Mitchell, as cited in Gold, 1996), include interpersonal psychoanalysis (Sullivan, 1953), object relations theories (e.g., Winnicott, 1965), self psychology (Kohut, 1977; see chapter 8), attachment theory (Bowlby, 1980; see chapter 6), and relational theory (Aron, 1996; see chapter 7). Each of these theories focuses in some way on how children internalize experiences of self, other, and relationships, and how these largely unconscious internalizations affect subsequent cognition, affect, and interpersonal behavior (Gold, 1996). These theories incorporated Alexander and French's (1946) idea of therapy as a "corrective emotional experience" to explain how a good relationship with a caring therapist could help clients to develop more positive internal images of self, other, and relationships, which in turn could lead to a healthier sense of self and more adaptive interpersonal functioning.

The primary focus of psychodynamic therapies is on personality development and growth toward emotional maturity—resolution of specific symptoms and problems is expected to occur as the client "overcomes general difficulties such as internal conflicts, faulty assumptive systems, or emotional blocks" (Frank & Frank, 1991, p. 188). The focus on insight suggests a primary focus on cognition in psychodynamic therapies; however, affect is also emphasized with regard to the need for emotional understanding and for working through issues from the past. In more traditional forms of psychodynamic therapy, the practitioner's role is that of a rather passive, neutral expert. More recent models (particularly the ones included in this book), however, place much more emphasis on collaboration, worker empathy, and the importance of a good therapeutic relationship. With regard to the latter issue, it should be noted that the large body of conceptual and empirical work on the therapeutic alliance originated within psychodynamic psychotherapy, although this now spans other theoretical approaches.

Over the last few decades, there has been a proliferation of psychodynamic approaches to brief therapy, which is defined generally as having an upper limit of 25 sessions (Koss & Shiang, 1994). Most of these approaches maintain some focus on the development of insight into the origins of one's problems; however, interpretations "focus on present circumstances, not on childhood experiences" (Koss & Shiang, 1994, p. 666). Some of the more prominent examples of brief psychodynamic therapies are interpersonal therapy (Klerman & Weissman, 1993; Klerman, Weissman, Rounsaville, & Chevron, 1984; Schwartz, 2001), supportive-expressive therapy (Luborsky, 1984), and time-limited dynamic therapy (Strupp & Binder, 1984). More recent trends in psychodynamic psychotherapy include a move toward eclecticism and the development of treatment models that target specific problems (e.g., depression, substance abuse; Lambert, Garfield, & Bergin, 2004). The chapters in this book on psychodynamic approaches include (a) attachment theory (chapter 6), (b) relational theory (chapter 7), and (c) self psychology theory (chapter 8). These approaches are part of the relational structure model group of psychodynamic therapies (discussed above) and are among the psychodynamic approaches that have the most in common with generalist-eclectic social work principles and values.

Cognitive-Behavioral Theories

It used to be common for behavioral and cognitive theories to be classified separately. Early behavior therapies were based on classical (i.e., Pavlovian) and/or operant (i.e., Skinnerian) conditioning paradigms and focused on overt behavior only. Social learning theory (e.g., Bandura & Walters, 1963) broadened behavioral theory to include consideration of observational learning and modeling of social behavior. Cognitive theories (e.g., Beck, 1976) extended the application of learning theory principles to thoughts and beliefs, although some behaviorists were slow to accept this. Currently, although there is still friction between advocates of the behavioral and cognitive traditions, it is common to group together, under a cognitive-behavioral classification, therapies that are based on a learning model of human functioning (Lambert, Garfield, et al., 2004). "To separate procedures that are truly behavioral from procedures that are purely cognitive is rather artificial. Most cognitive procedures have clear behavioral techniques in them, and though less obvious, most behavioral procedures also contain cognitive elements" (Emmelkamp, 2004, p. 393).

As mentioned above, cognitive-behavioral approaches adhere to a learning model of human behavior. Thus, the basic premise of these theories is that maladaptive human behaviors and cognitions are learned. The corollary is that therapy involves the unlearning of problematic behaviors and thoughts and/or the learning of more adaptive ones. Furthermore, although it is acknowledged that such problematic behaviors and thoughts may have been learned in the past, cognitive-behavioral approaches focus on change in the present. Specific symptoms are the focus of the change effort, and specific procedures are used to help the client make changes, both within the counseling session and in daily life, between sessions. For instance, more behaviorally oriented therapies for depression often focus on social skills training to increase positive reinforcements for social interactions. More cognitively oriented therapies for depression focus on identifying and modifying covert self-statements and cognitive patterns (schemas) that support negative thinking (Emmelkamp, 2004).

There are a great number of cognitive-behavioral therapies. A primary reason for this is because so many of these therapies have been developed for very specific problems (e.g., panic attacks, phobias, insomnia, and depression). These therapies can be placed at various points on a continuum of relative focus on behavior or cognition. On the behavioral end of the continuum, therapies can be divided into two main groups: counterconditioning (e.g., Wolpe's [1958, 1990] systematic desensitization therapy) and reinforcement (e.g., Paul & Lentz's [1977] token economy for clients with chronic mental health problems). Prominent therapies on the cognitive end of the continuum include Ellis's (1962) rational emotive therapy (RET) and Beck's (1976, 1991) cognitive therapy for depression. Other cognitive-behavioral therapies that can be placed somewhere in the middle of the continuum include Meichenbaum's (1985) stress inoculation training (SIT), D'Zurilla and Goldfried's (1971) problem-solving training (PST), Barlow and Cerny's (1988) panic control treatment (PCT), and Marlatt and Gordon's (1985) relapse prevention (RP).

The goal of cognitive-behavioral therapies is to alleviate specific symptoms or solve specific problems—it is assumed that general improvement in personal functioning will follow from such changes (Frank & Frank, 1991). These therapies are much more focused and directive than psychodynamic therapies. Although early behavioral approaches did not emphasize the importance of the helping relationship, all cognitive-behavioral approaches now recognize the importance of collaboration and worker warmth as facilitating factors in therapeutic change. It is evident that the primary focus of such therapies is on behavior and cognitions; however, many approaches have integrated a focus on affect as well. A recent trend has been for cognitive-behavioral therapies to incorporate aspects of psychodynamic and humanistic theories (Hollon & Beck, 2004; Lambert, Garfield, et al., 2004), as illustrated by the focus on changing self-schemas (McCullough, 2000).

Due to the multiplicity of cognitive-behavioral theories, it was difficult to choose which ones to include in this book. We decided to include one chapter (chapter 9) that provided a more detailed overview of cognitive-behavioral theory than what could be provided in this thumbnail sketch. For the other two chapters, we chose models that are prominent within social work practice and, although not usually classified narrowly as cognitive-behavioral, that are largely consistent with this theory base. Thus, chapters 10 and 11 focus on the crisis intervention and task-centered models of practice, respectively. It is acknowledged that the task-centered model is construed as an atheoretical structure for eclectic practice; however, it is most consistent with and has borrowed most frequently from cognitive-behavioral theory (Tolson, Reid, & Garvin, 2003). Similarly, although the crisis intervention model is an eclectic model that has roots in psychodynamic ego psychology, most of its principles (e.g., focus on the present, emphasis on structured/directive intervention, use of contracts) have strong similarities to those of cognitive-behavioral theory, as well as to the task-centered model (Payne, 1991).

Humanistic Theories

Cain (2001) traced the origin of humanistic psychotherapies to Carl Rogers and his development of client-centered therapy, beginning in the 1940s. The foundational influence of Rogers's theory on all humanistic therapy is one reason that client-centered theory (chapter 12) was one of the two humanistic theories chosen for inclusion in this book, the other being existential theory (chapter 13). Another reason for choosing client-centered theory is its close historical connection to social work. As Rothery and Tutty explain in chapter 12, Rogers worked closely with social workers, and the Functional school of social work and client-centered theory had common roots in the ideas of Otto Rank and a common belief in the importance of the therapeutic relationship.

Humanistic theories share an optimistic view of people as having an inherent drive toward growth, health, and self-actualization. In general, humanistic approaches hold that individuals' problems stem from developing defenses against painful or traumatic aspects of experience and then losing touch with authentic experiencing in the present. Thus, the key therapeutic task is to help clients to develop new awareness of and new meaning about their ongoing states of experience (Elliott, Greenberg, & Lietaer, 2004). In client-centered therapy, this involves overcoming "conditions of worth" that have been imposed by others and coming to know and accept oneself more completely and authentically. In existential therapy, this involves getting in touch with the painful realities of personal responsibility and free choice and developing new meaning in one's life.

All humanistic therapies promote an egalitarian, authentic worker–client relationship characterized by warmth, respect, genuine concern, trust, and empathy—and this type of relationship is seen as key to therapeutic effectiveness. Korchin (as cited in Williams, 1997) has described the essence of humanistic approaches as follows: "Above all else, therapy involves an authentic encounter between two real individuals, free of sham and role-playing, rather than technical acts of an interpretive, advising, or conditioning sort" (p. 242). Humanistic therapies are also "united by the general principle that people are wiser than their intellect alone" (Elliott et al., 2004, p. 494). Thus, there is a belief in "the adaptive nature of emotion in effective decision-making and effective functioning" (Cain, 2001, p. 10) and an emphasis on helping clients to get in touch with their emotional experiencing. Focus on the present (or here and now) versus the past and on general personality growth (self-actualization) versus specific symptom alleviation are also hallmarks of humanistic approaches.

Although all humanistic therapies are nondirective with regard to the content of therapy, some are more directive with regard to process (i.e., encouraging and directing clients to explore emotions more deeply). Examples of the latter include Gestalt therapy (Perls, 1969), experiential psychotherapy (Mahrer, 1983), focusing-oriented psychotherapy (Gendlin, 1996), and process-experiential (PE) therapy (Greenberg, Rice, & Elliott, 1993).

Feminist Theories

"Feminist therapy grew out of the women's movement during the late 1960s and early 1970s . . . and has its foundations in feminist analyses of social problems" (Funderburk & Fukuyama, 2001, pp. 4–5). As stressed in chapter 14, there is a diverse group of feminist theories that differ from one another in a variety of respects. Thus, the reader should keep in mind that the broad characterization of feminist theories presented here does not do justice to the theoretical and practical diversity within this category.

In general, feminist theories construe the root cause of individual and social problems as the institutionalized system of male privilege (i.e., the patriarchy) that relies on the domination and exploitation of people. Although some feminist theories focus primarily on the power and privilege of men over women, many feminist theories include a broader focus on the damage that patriarchal systems do to all groups of people (including men), as well as to the natural environment (Bricker-Jenkins & Hooyman, 1986). The code of ethics of the Feminist Therapy Institute (as cited in Funderburk & Fukuyama, 2001) states, "A feminist analysis addresses the effects of sexism on the development of females and males and the relationship of sexism to other forms of oppression, including, but not limited to, racism, classism, homophobia, ageism, and anti-Semitism" (p. 4).

Some of the common principles of feminist practice are (a) to minimize the power differential between worker and client and to establish a collaborative partnership that is marked by mutuality and informality and is respectful of self-determination; (b) to raise consciousness about how the institutionalized system of male privilege results in the domination, exploitation, and abuse of women; (c) to explore the link between personal and political/social issues so that personal issues are contextualized and depathologized; (d) to validate the client's subjective experience and feelings and to highlight resiliency and strength; (e) to connect clients with each other and with community resources in order to facilitate empowerment, growth, and self-actualization; (f) to engage in social and political action to change conditions and beliefs that support the patriarchy;

and (g) to value diversity and promote awareness of how all forms of oppression are linked and harmful to human well-being (Bricker-Jenkins & Hooyman, 1986; Funderburk & Fukuyama, 2001; Marecek, 2001).

The range of feminist approaches to practice is immense. On one end of the continuum are feminist approaches that eschew a therapeutic focus because this is seen as a distraction from, or even an undermining of, social justice work. On the other end of the continuum are feminist approaches that focus primarily on individual healing and change. In the middle of the continuum are feminist approaches that see a therapeutic focus as a necessary prerequisite for effective social and political action. Also, feminist approaches that emphasize a therapeutic focus run the gamut with regard to theoretical orientation. There are feminist approaches that are predominantly psychodynamic (e.g., Luepnitz, 1988), cognitive-behavioral (e.g., Russell, 1984), experiential/humanistic (e.g., Laidlaw, Malmo, & Associates, 1990), and postmodern (e.g., Gottlieb & Gottlieb, 1996; Van Den Bergh, 1995). The common thread that holds all feminist approaches together, however, is the focus on the damage done by a patriarchal system that uses power and privilege to oppress women and other marginalized groups.

Postmodern Theories

Postmodern philosophy challenges the modernist viewpoint that truth can be discovered via objective scientific observation and measurement. As opposed to the modernist quest to discover universal principles and large-scale theories that underlie all human behavior, the postmodernist holds that there is no absolute truth, only points of view. Two central tenets of postmodernism are that "human experience is language-based and socially constructed" (Guterman & Rudes, 2005, p. 2). Postmodern critiques have been applied to many fields (e.g., literature, political science, education) to challenge the objective basis of accepted knowledge and to point out that such knowledge has been socially constructed (Nichols & Schwartz, 2004). A number of related postmodern philosophies have influenced the field of counseling. Two of the more dominant philosophies are constructivism and social constructionism. Constructivism (see chapter 16) holds that there is no objective reality and that either individuals mentally construct their own truths (radical constructivism) or realities are created through the process of coevolution with others (Maturana & Varela, 1987). Social constructionism focuses on the power of social interaction and culturally shared assumptions for shaping knowledge and meaning. Of particular interest is the intersection among power, social discourse, and culture, which is seen as engendering meaning for people (Gergen, 1985).

A variety of postmodern approaches to counseling have emerged since the 1990s. Although there are variations across postmodern therapies, in general these approaches are characterized by (a) a collaborative, egalitarian worker stance that recognizes clients as the experts on their experiences; (b) avoiding presumptions or theoretical ideas in order to concentrate on understanding clients' worlds from their perspective; and (c) a view of therapy that emphasizes the important role of language in a mutual search for new, more empowering understanding of clients' stories.

Postmodern approaches to counseling contend that problems stem from the way people construe their experience and/or from the internalization of toxic cultural narratives. As a result, there is optimism that people can overcome problems by developing more positive and empowering views of their lives. The goal of most postmodern therapies is to bring about overall improvement or general well-being (only solution-focused therapy focuses on solutions to specific problems). These therapies are typically unstructured and nondirective (except for solution-focused therapy, which is more prescriptive), and the worker's role is one of empathic listener and collaborator. The focus on the construction of meaning places the emphasis of these therapies more on cognition; however, some postmodern approaches are beginning to attend to affect. Only the solution-focused model places much emphasis on behaviors.

The postmodern approaches to counseling reviewed in this book are (a) narrative therapies, including White and Epston's (1990) narrative deconstruction therapy and Anderson and Goolishian's (1988) collaborative language systems therapy (see chapter 15); (b) constructivist therapy (chapter 16); and (c) solution-focused therapy (chapter 17). These were chosen because they are among the most dominant postmodern approaches in social work practice. Other postmodern approaches can be found in the work of Andersen (1991), Cecchin, Lane, and Ray (1993), Hoffman (1988), and Tomm (1987).

AN ARTISTIC, INTUITIVE-INDUCTIVE APPROACH TO PRACTICE

As mentioned in chapter 1, because this book is largely a survey of theories for direct practice and our framework for practice stresses the eclectic use of theory in practice, we feel it is necessary to be explicit about the importance we attach to the artistic side of practice and how this is an integral part of our generalist-eclectic approach. There has been a long-standing debate within all of the helping professions about whether effective counseling consists primarily of (a) an objective, rational, scientific, deductive application of theoretical knowledge and technical skill;

or (b) a subjective, humanistic, artistic, intuitive-inductive process. Klein and Bloom (1995) have noted that, within social work, this debate continues to be confrontational and couched in either/or terms. We agree with Klein and Bloom's argument that good practice integrates "both of these two sources of knowledge rather than excluding one or the other" (p. 799). In this section of the chapter, an argument for the importance of the artistic elements of practice is presented.[1]

Historical Predominance of a Scientific View of Practice

There is no doubt that the scientific view of practice held sway within the helping professions, as well as many other professions, for most of the 20th century and continues to do so (Schon, 1983). Schon argued that this view began to dominate professions as they gradually became ensconced in universities in the early part of the 20th century. He contended that universities have adhered, for the most part, to a positivistic, technical-rational view of knowledge that "fosters selective inattention to practical competence and professional artistry" (Schon, 1983, p. vii).

Goldstein (1986) noted that social casework began to move away from its idealistic, pragmatic, and humanistic roots in the 1920s, with the adoption of Freudian theory. In the 1930s and 1940s the Functional school of social work reasserted the importance of the humanistic and artistic elements of practice; however, this influence gradually faded out over the next couple of decades. In the 1970s, "the increasing demand for empirical testing and validation of our knowledge and practice" (Hartman, 1990b, p. 3), as well as the acceleration of the shift in power from the profession to the university (Hartman, 1990a), led to a heightened predominance of the technical-rational outlook. Prominent pronouncements such as "Science makes knowledge, practice uses it" (Rein & White, 1981, p. 36) and "If you cannot measure the client's problem, you cannot treat it" (Hudson, 1978, p. 65) reflected the positivistic position that the essence of good practice was the deductive application of empirically generated theory (Scott, 1990).

The predominance of the technical-rational outlook within social work has had a number of negative consequences. Hartman (1990a) has noted that this has led to the academizing of schools of social work, whereby fewer instructors have "authentic knowledge about practice grounded not only in research and theory but in experience as well" (p. 48). This trend may be related to Gitterman's (1988) lament that professional social work education sometimes "formalizes our work and stiffens our approach" (p. 36) and can result in practitioners hiding "behind professional masks" (p. 37). This sort of professional stiffness is unfortunate but understandable given the fact that within a technical-rational outlook, "uncertainty is a threat; its admission is a sign of weakness" (Schon, 1983, p. 69). Mahoney (1986) has commented on how the reliance on conceptual knowledge in training counselors has led to the unfortunate "unconscious search for a 'secret handbook' of practical 'how-to-do-it' knowledge and explicit techniques for achieving specified ends" (pp. 169–170). This point echoes Perlman's (1957) earlier observation that

> the more individualized and creative a process is, the more skill eludes being captured and held in the small snares of prefabricated kinds of behavior; and the paradox is that the less susceptible skill is to being caught and mastered by ready-made formulas, the more anxiously are formulas sought. (pp. 157–158)

The artistic, intuitive-inductive approach to practice recognizes the limits to the scientific, technical-rational approach to practice and values the subjective, humanistic, and creative elements of practice.

The Resurgence of Interest in Intuitive-Inductive Practice

Fortunately, in the last 25 years, numerous challenges to the predominance of the technical-rational outlook in the helping professions have resurfaced and there has been a resurgence of interest in the artistic elements of practice. Schon's (1983) study of five professions (engineering, architecture, management, town planning, and psychotherapy) led to his challenging the idea that the essence of effective professional practice consists of the application of established theory and technique. He proposed that two complementary and largely intuitive processes were at the heart of much of professional practice. First, "knowing in action" represents the "spontaneous behavior of skilful practice . . . which does not stem from a prior intellectual operation" (Schon, 1983, p. 51). Although he acknowledged that some knowing in action may be based on knowledge that has become internalized, Schon maintained that much of this develops naturally as "knowing how" and was never dependent on "knowing that."

Second, and most important, "reflection in action" involves improvising or thinking on one's feet when faced with a unique or uncertain situation. Schon (1983) described this as reasoning inductively to "construct a new theory of the unique case" (p. 68). In a later publication, Schon (1987) argued persuasively that "professional education should be redesigned to combine the teaching of applied science with coaching in the artistry of reflection-in-action" (p. xii).

A number of social workers have linked Schon's ideas to earlier social work emphases on the art of practice and have called for social workers to re-embrace this heritage. Papell and Skolnik (1992) identified

Bertha Reynolds and Virginia Robinson, among other social workers of the Functional school, as social workers who emphasized the artistic and creative elements of practice. Referring to social work education, Reynolds (as cited in Papell & Skolnik, 1992) stressed that "learning an art . . . cannot be carried on solely as an intellectual process" (p. 21). Similarly, Robinson (as cited in Papell & Skolnik, 1992) contended that the goal of professional development should be "wisdom that goes beyond knowledge" (p. 21). Noting the modern-day emphasis on theory and technique, Papell and Skolnik (1992) argued for the "elevation of art, intuition, creativity, and practice wisdom to essential places in professional functioning" (p. 20). Goldstein (1990) has challenged the "insistent pursuit of a scientific image for social work" (p. 38) and has argued that "effective practice is less a technical enterprise than it is a creative, reflective, and, to a considerable extent, an artistic and dramatic event" (p. 38). As mentioned earlier, Klein and Bloom (1995) have argued for integrating a " 'subjective,' or intuitive-phenomenological, practice model" with the dominant " 'objective,' or empirical, practice model" (p. 799). An attempt was made to depict this integration in Figure 2.1 by including client-specific, intuitive-inductive processes (the right-hand column of the figure) along with the various levels of theory for practice.

It is ironic that a number of findings from research in the positivistic, technical-rational tradition have also fueled interest in and provided support for the artistic, intuitive-inductive aspects of practice. As detailed in chapter 1, there are two widely accepted conclusions derived from cumulative research on psychotherapy that have fueled the movement toward eclecticism—and these same two conclusions provide support for the importance of the artistic elements of practice. First is the equal outcomes/Dodo bird conclusion that the various theoretical approaches to counseling are generally equivalent in effectiveness (Lambert & Ogles, 2004; Wampold, 2001). Second is the related conclusion that factors that are common across the various theoretical approaches (i.e., common factors, particularly the therapeutic relationship) have much stronger associations with effectiveness than do the specific factors of theory and technique (Lambert & Ogles, 2004; Wampold, 2001). Wampold (2001) concluded that the empirical evidence to date supports an artistic/humanistic (what he refers to as the contextual meta-model) rather than a scientific (what he refers to as a medical meta-model) model of psychotherapy/counseling.

One other body of research that was not reviewed in chapter 1 provides further support for the importance of the humanistic/artistic elements of practice. Christensen and Jacobson (1994) concluded that research evidence "strongly suggests that under many if not most conditions, paraprofessionals or professionals with limited experience perform as well as or better than professionally trained psychotherapists" (p. 10). Similarly, Lambert, Bergin, et al. (2004) concluded that research has established "the proven effectiveness of paraprofessionals in a variety of roles . . . [and] few studies can be found that show superiority for the highly trained professional" (p. 5). Clearly, if paraprofessional counselors can be as effective as highly trained mental health professionals, then this provides further support for an approach to direct practice that values the humanistic, artistic, intuitive-inductive elements of practice.

As stated previously, it is important to avoid pitting the artistic, intuitive-inductive approach to practice against the scientific approach to practice that emphasizes the use of theory and technique. Nevertheless, it is important to emphasize the research support for the artistic, intuitive-inductive approach, because, despite the results of research, it is still the less accepted and less dominant paradigm of direct practice (Wampold, 2001). We believe that this is as true in social work as it is in psychology. As Derezotes (2000) has noted, "social work practice continues to hold a dualistic position related to art and science in which the importance of art is deemphasized" (p. 19).

It is instructive to consider the parallels between the scientific and artistic paradigms of direct practice and the quantitative and qualitative approaches to research, respectively. In quantitative research terms, the scientific approach to direct practice applies established theory deductively to formulate hypotheses about the client's problem, which are then confirmed or disconfirmed by collecting and examining data. If the hypotheses are confirmed, the theory's empirically validated techniques for dealing with such problems are applied.

In qualitative research terms, the artistic, intuitive-inductive approach "attempts to make sense of the situation without imposing preexisting expectations" (Patton, 1990, p. 44) and endeavors to build a theory that is grounded in the client's unique experience. Once a mutual, felt understanding of the client's unique situation is arrived at, together the worker and client use this understanding and their reflective abilities to develop and enact change strategies. Similar to artistic, intuitive-inductive practice, qualitative research has struggled to achieve credibility in the scientific community. In the struggle to achieve credibility, it is understandable but unfortunate that proponents of artistic practice and qualitative research have sometimes taken the extreme position of totally rejecting the scientific approach to practice and research, respectively.

In sum, the generalist-eclectic approach contends that both quantitative and qualitative approaches to research, and both the scientific and artistic approaches to practice, are legitimate, valuable, and complementary. The generalist-eclectic approach has a firm commitment to integrating the eclectic use of theory and technique with an artistic, intuitive-inductive approach to practice. Klein and Bloom (1995) argued that "practice wisdom responds to the limitations of the practice knowledge base by supporting a qualitative and inductive inquiry into the . . . specific case" (p. 804). They were careful to point out, however, that "if it is truly wise, practice wisdom incorporates information from a wide variety of sources, including those that are empirically based" (p. 806). Similarly, Goldstein (1990) has argued persuasively that "In a profession like social work that is concerned with personal meanings, ethical dilemmas—in general, all that it means to be human—artistry and theory are not polarities but resonating aspects of the same continuum" (p. 38).

SUMMARY

This chapter has provided an overview of direct practice theory and an artistic, intuitive-inductive approach to practice. The discussion of theory included a consideration of how theories can be understood and organized according to function (the degree to which they focus on providing explanations for, or facilitating changes in, human behavior) and level of abstraction (from highly abstract meta-theories that provide general understanding of a broad range of human behavior to highly specific models for understanding and intervening with specific problems or populations).

The chapter also discussed how organizing practice theories at the mid-level of abstraction into like groupings (psychodynamic, cognitive-behavioral, humanistic, feminist, and postmodern) can facilitate understanding of the vast array of such theories. These discussions of theory included consideration of how all theories can be used eclectically in practice.

The review of an artistic, intuitive-inductive approach to practice included a critical examination of the predominant belief that effective practice is primarily a scientific enterprise characterized by a deductive application of empirically validated theory and technique. It was argued that practice is at least as much art as science and that intuition, inductive reasoning, and practice wisdom are key elements of practice.

Finally, it was summarized that the generalist-eclectic approach endorses an integration of the scientific and artistic approaches to practice. The next chapter will examine how the problem-solving model can provide flexible structure and guidelines for practice that allow for an integration of the scientific and artistic approaches.

NOTE

1. The section of this chapter on an artistic, intuitive-inductive approach to practice has been adapted, in part, from an earlier chapter by Coady: "A Reflective/Inductive Model

of Practice: Emphasizing Theory Building for Unique Cases Versus Applying Theory to Practice," by N. F. Coady, 1993. In G. Rogers (Ed.), *Social Work Field Education: Views and Visions* (pp. 139–151). Dubuque, IA: Kendall/Hunt.

REFERENCES

Alexander, F., & French, T. (1946). *Psychoanalytic therapy*. New York: Ronald Press.

Andersen, T. (1991). *The reflecting team*. New York: W. W. Norton.

Anderson, H., & Goolishian, H. A. (1988). Human systems as linguistic systems: Preliminary and evolving ideas about the implications for clinical theory. *Family Process, 27*, 371–393.

Aron, L. (1996). *A meeting of minds: Mutuality in psychoanalysis*. Hillsdale, NJ: The Analytic Press.

Bandura, A., & Walters, R. (1963). *Social learning and personality development*. New York: Holt, Rinehart and Winston.

Barlow, D. H., & Cerny, J. A. (1988). *Psychological treatment of panic*. New York: Guilford Press.

Beck, A. T. (1976). *Cognitive therapy and the emotional disorders*. New York: International Universities Press.

Beck, A. T. (1991). Cognitive therapy: A 30-year retrospective. *American Psychologist, 46*, 368–375.

Bowlby, J. (1980). *Attachment and loss (Vol. 3): Loss: Sadness and depression*. New York: Basic Books.

Bricker-Jenkins, M., & Hooyman, N. (Eds.). (1986). *Not for women only: Social work practice for a feminist future*. Silver Spring, MD: NASW Press.

Cain, D. J. (2001). Defining characteristics, history, and evolution of humanistic psychotherapies. In D. J. Cain & J. Seeman (Eds.), *Humanistic psychotherapies: Handbook of research and practice* (pp. 3–54). Washington, DC: American Psychological Association.

Cecchin, G., Lane, G., & Ray, W. (1993). From strategizing to nonintervention: Toward irreverence in systemic practice. *Journal of Marital and Family Therapy, 19*, 125–136.

Christensen, A., & Jacobson, N. S. (1994). Who (or what) can do psychotherapy: The status and challenge of nonprofessional therapies. *Psychological Science, 5*, 8–14.

Derezotes, D. S. (2000). *Advanced generalist social work practice*. Thousand Oaks, CA: Sage.

D'Zurilla, T. J., & Goldfried, M. R. (1971). Problem-solving and behavior modification. *Journal of Abnormal Psychology, 78*, 107–126.

Elliott, R., Greenberg, L. S., & Lietaer, G. (2004). Research on experiential psychotherapies. In M. J. Lambert (Ed.), *Bergin and Garfield's handbook of psychotherapy and behavior change* (5th ed., pp. 493–539). New York: Wiley.

Ellis, A. (1962). *Reason and emotion in psychotherapy*. New York: Lyle Stuart.

Emmelkamp, P. M. (2004). Behavior therapy with adults. In M. J. Lambert (Ed.), *Bergin and Garfield's handbook of psychotherapy and behavior change* (5th ed., pp. 393–446). New York: Wiley.

Erikson, E. (1950). *Childhood and society*. New York: W. W. Norton.

Frank, J. D., & Frank, J. B. (1991). *Persuasion and healing: A comparative study of psychotherapy* (3rd ed.). Baltimore: Johns Hopkins University Press.

Funderburk, J. R., & Fukuyama, M. A. (2001). Feminism, multiculturalism, and spirituality: Convergent and divergent forces in psychotherapy. *Women & Therapy, 24*, 1–18.

Gelso, C., & Carter, J. (1985). The relationship in counseling and psychotherapy: Components, consequences, and theoretical antecedents. *The Counseling Psychologist, 13*, 155–243.

Gendlin, G. T. (1996). *Focusing-oriented psychotherapy: A manual of the experiential method.* New York: Guilford Press.

Gergen, K. (1985). The social constructionist movement in modern psychology. *American Psychologist, 40,* 266–275.

Gitterman, A. (1988). Teaching students to connect theory and practice. *Social Work With Groups, 11,* 33–41.

Gold, J. R. (1996). *Key concepts in psychotherapy integration.* New York: Plenum Press.

Goldstein, H. (1986). Toward the integration of theory and practice: A humanistic approach. *Social Work, 31,* 352–357.

Goldstein, H. (1990). The knowledge base of social work practice: Theory, wisdom, analogue, or art? *Families in Society, 71,* 32–43.

Gottlieb, D., & Gottlieb, C. (1996). The narrative/collaborative process in couples therapy: A post-modern perspective. In M. Hill & E. Rothblum (Eds.), *Couples therapy: Feminist perspectives* (pp. 37–48). Binghamton, NY: Haworth Press.

Greenberg, L. S., Rice, L. N., & Elliott, R. (1993). *Facilitating emotional change: The moment-by-moment process.* New York: Guilford Press.

Guterman, J. T., & Rudes, J. (2005). A narrative approach to strategic eclecticism. *Journal of Mental Health Counseling, 27,* 1–12.

Hartman, A. (1990a). Education for direct practice. *Families in Society, 71,* 44–50.

Hartman, A. (1990b). Many ways of knowing. *Families in Society, 71,* 3–4.

Hartmann, H. (1958). *Ego psychology and the problem of adaptation* (D. Rappaport, Trans.). New York: International Universities Press. (Original work published in 1939)

Hoffman, L. (1988). A constructivist position for family therapy. *The Irish Journal of Psychology, 9,* 110–129.

Hollon, S. D., & Beck, A. T. (2004). Cognitive and cognitive behavioral therapies. In M. J. Lambert (Ed.), *Bergin and Garfield's handbook of psychotherapy and behavior change* (5th ed., pp. 447–492). New York: Wiley.

Hudson, W. W. (1978). First axioms of treatment. *Social Work, 23,* 65–66.

Klein, W. C., & Bloom, M. (1995). Practice wisdom. *Social Work, 40,* 799–807.

Klerman, G. L., & Weissman, M. M. (Eds.). (1993). *New applications of interpersonal psychotherapy.* Washington, DC: American Psychiatric Press.

Klerman, G. L., Weissman, M. M., Rounsaville, B. J., & Chevron, E. S. (1984). *Interpersonal psychotherapy of depression.* New York: Basic Books.

Kohut, H. (1977). *The restoration of the self.* New York: International Universities Press.

Koss, M. P., & Shiang, J. (1994). Research on brief psychotherapy. In A. E. Bergin & S. L. Garfield (Eds.), *Handbook of psychotherapy and behavior change* (4th ed., pp. 664–700). New York: Wiley.

Laidlaw, T., Malmo, C., & Associates. (1990). *Healing voices: Feminist approaches to therapy with women.* San Francisco: Jossey-Bass.

Lambert, M. J., Bergin, A. E., & Garfield, S. L. (2004). Introduction and historical overview. In M. J. Lambert (Ed.), *Bergin and Garfield's handbook of psychotherapy and behavior change* (5th ed., pp. 3–15). New York: Wiley.

Lambert, M. J., Garfield, S. L., & Bergin, A. E. (2004). Overview, trends, and future issues. In M. J. Lambert (Ed.), *Bergin and Garfield's handbook of psychotherapy and behavior change* (5th ed., pp. 805–822). New York: Wiley.

Lambert, M. J., & Ogles, B. M. (2004). The efficacy and effectiveness of psychotherapy. In M. J. Lambert (Ed.), *Bergin and Garfield's handbook of psychotherapy and behavior change* (5th ed., pp. 139–193). New York: Wiley.

Luborsky, L. (1984). *Principles of psychoanalytic psychotherapy: A manual for supportive-expressive treatment.* New York: Basic Books.

Luepnitz, D. A. (1988). *The family interpreted: Psychoanalysis, feminism, and family therapy.* New York: Basic Books.

Mahoney, M. J. (1986). The tyranny of technique. *Counseling and Values, 30,* 169–174.

Mahrer, A. R. (1983). *Experiential psychotherapy: Basic practices.* New York: Brunner/ Mazel.

Marecek, J. (2001). Bringing feminist issues to therapy. In B. D. Slife, R. N. Williams, & S. H. Barlow (Eds.), *Critical issues in psychotherapy: Translating new ideas into practice* (pp. 305–319). Thousand Oaks, CA: Sage.

Marlatt, A., & Gordon, J. (1985). *Relapse prevention: Maintenance strategies in the treatment of addictive behaviors.* New York: Guilford Press.

Maturana, H., & Varela, F. J. (1987). *The tree of knowledge: The biological roots of human understanding.* Boston: New Science Library.

McCullough, J. P., Jr. (2000). *Treatment for chronic depression: Cognitive behavioral analysis system of psychotherapy (CBASP).* New York: Guilford Press.

Meichenbaum, D. (1985). *Stress inoculation training.* New York: Pergamon Press.

Nichols, M. P., & Schwartz, R. C. (2004). *Family therapy: Concepts and methods* (6th ed.). Boston: Pearson.

Papell, C. P., & Skolnik, L. (1992). The reflective practitioner: A contemporary paradigm's relevance for social work education. *Journal of Social Work Education, 28,* 18–26.

Patton, M. Q. (1990). *Qualitative evaluation and research methods* (2nd ed.). Newbury Park, CA: Sage.

Paul, G. L., & Lentz, R. J. (1977). *Psychosocial treatment of chronic mental patients.* Cambridge, MA: Harvard University Press.

Payne, M. (1991). *Modern social work theory: A critical introduction.* London: Macmillan.

Perlman, H. H. (1957). *Social casework: A problem-solving process.* Chicago: University of Chicago Press.

Perls, F. (1969). *Gestalt therapy verbatim.* Lafayette, CA: Real People Press.

Rein, M., & White, S. (1981). Knowledge for practice. *Social Service Review, 55,* 1–41.

Russell, M. (1984). *Skills in counseling women—The feminist approach.* Springfield, IL: Charles C Thomas.

Saleebey, D. (Ed.). (2006). *The strengths perspective in social work practice* (4th ed.). New York: Longman.

Schon, D. A. (1983). *The reflective practitioner: How professionals think in action.* New York: Basic Books.

Schon, D. A. (1987). *Educating the reflective practitioner.* San Francisco: Jossey-Bass.

Schwartz, A. (2001). Interpersonal therapy. In P. Lehmann & N. Coady (Eds.), *Theoretical perspectives for direct social work practice: A generalist-eclectic approach* (pp. 128–144). New York: Springer Publishing Company.

Scott, D. (1990). Practice wisdom: The neglected source of practice research. *Social Work, 35,* 564–568.

Strean, H. S. (1996). Psychoanalytic theory and social work treatment. In F. J. Turner (Ed.), *Social work treatment: Interlocking theoretical approaches* (4th ed., pp. 523–554). New York: Free Press.

Strupp, H. H., & Binder, J. L. (1984). *Psychotherapy in a new key: A guide to time-limited dynamic psychotherapy.* New York: Basic Books.

Sullivan, H. S. (1953). *The interpersonal theory of psychiatry.* New York: W. W. Norton.

Tolson, E. R., Reid, W. J., & Garvin, C. D. (2003). *Generalist practice: A task-centered approach* (2nd ed.). New York: Columbia University Press.

Tomm, K. (1987). Interventive interviewing: Part II. Reflexive questioning as a means to enable self-healing. *Family Process, 25,* 167–184.

Van Den Bergh, N. (Ed.). (1995). *Feminist practice in the 21st century.* Washington, DC: NASW Press.

Wachtel, P. L., Kruk, J. C., & McKinney, M. K. (2005). Cyclical psychodynamics and integrative relational psychotherapy. In J. C. Norcross & M. R. Goldfried (Eds.), *Handbook of psychotherapy integration* (2nd ed., pp. 172–195). New York: Oxford University Press.

Wampold, B. E. (2001). *The great psychotherapy debate: Models, methods, and findings.* Mahwah, NJ: Lawrence Erlbaum.

White, M., & Epston, D. (1990). *Narrative means to therapeutic ends.* New York: W. W. Norton.

Williams, M. H. (1997). Boundary violations: Do some contended standards of care fail to encompass commonplace procedures of humanistic, behavioral, and eclectic psychotherapies? *Psychotherapy, 34,* 238–249.

Winnicott, D. W. (1965). *The maturational processes and the facilitating environment.* New York: International Universities Press.

Wolpe, J. (1958). *Psychotherapy through reciprocal inhibition.* Stanford, CA: Stanford University Press.

Wolpe, J. (1990). *The practice of behavior therapy* (4th ed.). Elmsford, NY: Pergamon Press.

CHAPTER 3

The Problem-Solving Model: *A Framework for Integrating the Science and Art of Practice*

Nick Coady and Peter Lehmann

Since Perlman (1957) promoted a problem-solving process for social casework (i.e., direct social work practice), the problem-solving model has developed into a cornerstone of social work practice. The problem-solving model has been called the *general method* of social work because it "may be utilized with individuals, groups, families, or communities" (McMahon, 1996, p. 35). The problem-solving model is a critically important element in our generalist-eclectic approach to direct practice because its flexible structure and general guidelines for practice facilitate an eclectic use of theory and technique (the science of practice) and the use of reflective, intuitive-inductive processes (the art of practice).

In this chapter we (a) review the early development of the problem-solving model for social work practice; (b) discuss the later development of the problem-solving model in terms of its extension to and further elaboration by generalist models of social work practice; (c) provide an overview of how the problem-solving model allows for the integration of the scientific and artistic elements of practice; and (d) discuss the phases of the problem-solving model (i.e., engagement; data collection and assessment; planning, contracting, and intervention; and evaluation and termination) with attention to how theoretical and intuitive-inductive processes interact in problem solving.

EARLY DEVELOPMENT: PERLMAN'S PROBLEM-SOLVING MODEL

The application of the problem-solving model to social work practice was first suggested by Perlman (1957) in her book *Social Casework: A Problem-Solving Process*. Perlman was influenced by John Dewey's (1933) description of learning as a problem-solving process. She believed that "the operations of casework are essentially those of the process of problem-solving" (Perlman, 1957, p. v).

Perlman's problem-solving model represented an attempt to integrate or at least bridge the differences between the two dominant schools of social casework of the time. Perlman had been trained in the scientifically oriented Freudian or Diagnostic school of social casework, but was attracted to many of the ideas of the humanistically oriented Functional or Rankian school of social casework. She blended the Diagnostic school's emphasis on applying psychodynamic theory through the scientific process of study, diagnosis, and treatment, with the Functional school's emphasis on starting where the client is in the present, partializing problems into manageable pieces, and developing a genuinely supportive relationship that serves to motivate clients and free their potential for growth (Perlman, 1986). Perlman (1986) has identified the problem-solving model as an eclectic construct, with theoretical roots in psychodynamic ego psychology and selected ideas from existential, learning, and ecological systems theories.

Perlman's model "stands firmly upon the recognition that life is an ongoing, problem-encountering, problem-solving process" (Perlman, 1970, p. 139). Perlman pointed out that effective problem-solving, whether in everyday life or in professional helping, consists of similar processes. In professional helping, these processes include (a) identifying the problem, (b) identifying the person's subjective experience of the problem, (c) examining the causes and effects of the problem in the person's life, (d) considering the pros and cons of various courses of action, (e) choosing and enacting a course of action, and (f) assessing the effectiveness of the action (Perlman, 1970). These problem-solving processes or stages that were outlined by Perlman are the basis of most current problem-solving models in social work.

Perlman (1970) stressed that the problem-solving process does not always take place as a linear, logical progression and that "in the spontaneity of action" (p. 158) the steps or phases can blend together, occur out of order, and repeat in a cyclical fashion. She pointed out that guiding people through a problem-solving process not only can help them cope more effectively with their presenting problems but also can help them cope more effectively with future difficulties. Most important, Perlman

(1970) emphasized that problem-solving is not just a cognitive, rational process and that the development of a good relationship with clients is intertwined with the problem-solving process: "Relationship is the continuous context within which problem-solving takes place. It is, at the same time, the emerging product of mutual problem-solving efforts; and simultaneously it is the catalytic agent" (p. 151).

LATER DEVELOPMENT: THE EXTENSION OF THE PROBLEM-SOLVING MODEL TO GENERALIST SOCIAL WORK PRACTICE

Perlman (1957) noted that her application of the problem-solving process to casework stemmed from "a conception of human life as being in itself a problem-solving process" (p. 53). This foreshadowed generalist models of social work practice extending the use of a problem-solving process, by one name or another, to work with all levels of client systems (groups, families, organizations, and communities). As Sheafor and Horejsi (2006) have noted, subsequent to Perlman's description of the phases of the problem-solving process, "various authors divided these phases into more discrete units, described them in more detail, and demonstrated their application in a range of helping approaches and in work with client systems of various sizes" (p. 125).

Perlman's conceptualization of and central ideas about the problem-solving process are part of most current generalist models; however, a couple of common changes in emphasis should be noted. First, as noted in the quote above from Sheafor and Horejsi (2006), most contemporary models have delineated the stages in the problem-solving process in more detail and have been more specific in identifying the goals and activities in each stage. Second, current models of problem-solving place greater emphasis on collaboration and partnership between the worker and the client in all phases of the process—in Perlman's model there was more of an emphasis on the worker's primary responsibility for assessment and treatment planning (Compton & Galaway, 1999). We think these changes in emphasis are positive, and they are reflected in our conception of the problem-solving process.

One change that some generalist models have instituted, which we do not agree with, is to move away from the term *problem-solving*. Authors who have done this have been influenced by critiques from proponents of the strengths-based and empowerment-based approaches that contend the problem-solving model is part of the profession's heritage of focusing on pathology, disease, and disorder (e.g., Saleebey, 2006). Thus, for example, Locke, Garrison, and Winship (1998) simply called their version of the helping process a "phase model," and Miley, O'Melia, and DuBois (2007) called their model of the helping process "phases and processes of empowering practice" (p. 107). As McMillen, Morris, and Sherraden (2004) noted somewhat wryly,

> In the past 15 years, social workers have been encouraged to refashion themselves into strengths-based, solution-focused, capacity building, asset creating, motivation enhancing, empowerment specialists. And somewhere along the line, it became an insult to be problem-focused. (p. 317)

We agree with McMillen et al.'s (2004) argument that the dichotomy between a problem focus and a strengths focus is false and that the "grudge match" between these perspectives is damaging for the profession. Based on a sound historical analysis of this issue, these authors pointed out,

> Throughout our history, those who championed a problem-oriented practice also emphasized strengths and growing client capacity, and today's strength-based, capacity-oriented practitioners typically advocate for the solving of consumer's presenting problems. (p. 317)

We understand and support the trend toward depathologizing the concerns that clients typically bring to counseling—and it should be noted that Perlman was a pioneer in this regard. Rather than to deny the existence of problems and the utility of a problem-solving process, however, we prefer to promote the understanding that problems are a normal part of life. We agree with Compton and Galaway's (1994) contention that "describing a change process as a problem-solving model is quite different from characterizing it as a problem-focus model. . . . The model might well be called problem solving but strength-focused" (p. 7).

PROBLEM-SOLVING: A FRAMEWORK FOR INTEGRATING THE SCIENTIFIC AND ARTISTIC ELEMENTS OF PRACTICE

As discussed in chapters 1 and 2, the scientific aspect of social work practice is usually conceptualized as the deductive application of theory and technique to understanding and intervening with human problems. Our generalist-eclectic approach values the scientific aspect of practice but eschews rigid adherence to narrow theories and advocates for a flexible and eclectic use of a wide range of theories and techniques. One of the primary dangers of theoretical and technical eclecticism, however, is that it can be haphazard and directionless. Eclectic practice does not enjoy the clear structure and explicit guidelines for practice that are afforded by following a single theory.

We propose the use of a problem-solving model to help remedy the difficulties of eclectic practice. The phases of the problem-solving model (from engagement to termination) provide a flexible structure and general guidelines for practice while allowing for the eclectic application of theories and techniques. The problem-solving approach contains no assumptions about the causes of and solutions to client problems. The general guidelines that the problem-solving process provides for assessment allow for the tentative application of multiple theoretical perspectives to help develop understanding of each unique client situation. Similarly, the general guidelines for intervention in the problem-solving model allow for the eclectic use of techniques from different theories to help clients overcome or cope more effectively with problems.

Also discussed in chapters 1 and 2 is the fact that an appreciation for the artistic elements of practice is a central feature of our generalist-eclectic approach. We agree with Derezotes' (2000) contention that "social workers currently underutilize and undervalue the art of practice" (p. 19). Similar to a theoretically and technically eclectic approach to practice, one of the main difficulties in an intuitive-inductive approach to practice is a lack of focus and direction. When workers rely on inductive reasoning in an effort to build a theory that fits the unique client situation and on reflective and creative abilities to develop and enact change strategies, they can sometimes feel lost and uneasy about flying by the seat of their pants. In the same fashion that the problem-solving model can provide a flexible structure and general guidelines that facilitate an eclectic use of theory and technique, it can do the same for the artistic, intuitive-inductive aspects of practice. Perlman (1957) believed that the problem-solving model met the need

> for some dependable structure to provide the inner organization of the [casework] process. . . . In no sense is such a structure a stamped-out routine. It is rather an underlying guide, a pattern for action which gives general form to the caseworker's inventiveness or creativity. (p. vi)

The guidelines for practice of the various phases of the problem-solving process provide focus and direction for the worker while being general enough to allow for the use of intuition and creative, inductive reasoning.

The essence of effective problem-solving of any kind might be construed as the judicious blending of knowledge and skill with imagination and creativity. Following this line of thinking, we believe that the effectiveness of a problem-solving approach will depend upon blending the scientific (theoretical/technical) and artistic (intuitive-inductive) aspects of practice. Of course, this is easier said than done. Our review of the stages in the problem-solving process will incorporate more specific discussion of combining the artistic and scientific elements of practice, and our final chapter will revisit this issue.

THE PHASES OF THE PROBLEM-SOLVING MODEL

Different conceptualizations of the phases in the problem-solving process proliferate in the social work literature. Although there are many differences with regard to the number of phases that are specified and in the language that is used to describe the phases, these differences represent only minor variations on the same themes. We have divided the problem-solving process into four phases for the purposes of our discussion. These phases are (a) engagement; (b) data collection and assessment; (c) planning, contracting, and intervention; and (d) evaluation and termination. Below, each phase is reviewed briefly with regard to general goals and strategies for achieving them.

Engagement

We agree with Perlman's (1979) contention that the social work relationship is the heart of the helping process, and we believe that the engagement phase is crucial to creating the conditions from which a good helping relationship can grow. We see engagement as a complex process that may begin prior to meeting the client for the first time. Workers will often have some information (e.g., via a referral letter or intake assessment) that allows them to do some preliminary "tuning in," which "involves the worker's effort to get in touch with potential feelings and concerns that the client may bring to the helping encounter" (Shulman, 1999, p. 44). This should include a tentative ecological assessment of the particular problems and life circumstances of clients. Tuning in amounts to the old social work dictum of "putting oneself in the client's shoes" or to the development of preparatory empathy.

At the same time, it is important for workers to tune in to themselves; that is, to become more aware of how they are feeling with regard to what they know about the client (e.g., presenting problem, cultural background, voluntary versus involuntary status). It is particularly important for workers to prepare themselves to work with clients who are involuntary and who may present as resistant or unwilling participants in the helping process. Understandably, workers are often leery of dealing directly with such issues; however, if these issues are not discussed openly and worked through, engagement can remain superficial. In tuning in to how one might engage with such clients, it is necessary to prepare for responding empathically versus defensively and to consider, in addition to any mandated goals, goals that might appeal to the client. The intent of the tuning-in process prior to initial contact with clients is for workers to establish a positive internal condition that can facilitate the engagement process.

The first session with clients is important for setting the tone, the focus, and the parameters for the helping process. Wherever the first meeting may take place, it is important for the worker to attend to basic issues such as privacy and comfort. If the meeting is in the worker's agency, it is appropriate for the worker to play host and attend to social amenities. For example, a handshake with the initial introduction is usually appropriate, as is some brief social chitchat (e.g., commenting on the weather or asking clients if they had any trouble finding the agency) to break the ice.

Following this, a number of basic issues need to be attended to. Workers need to clarify their role and purpose and reach for client feedback about these issues (Shulman, 1999). Clients' problem situations need to be explored in more depth, and it is often helpful to establish some tentative goals. Then, a preliminary agreement (subject to change) about working together (e.g., general goals and time frame) needs to be achieved.

In attending to these engagement tasks, it is imperative that the worker's manner reflects warmth, empathy, and respect for the client. Workers need to normalize clients' problems appropriately, communicate empathy and support for clients' struggles, highlight clients' strengths and coping abilities, credit them for reaching out for help, express a desire to work together, and promote a realistic hopefulness about the outcome of working together. Where appropriate, engagement can be deepened by the worker's sensitive exploration of how issues of diversity (e.g., race, culture, class, gender, sexual orientation, physical capacity, age, religion/spirituality) may be related to the presenting problem or to concerns about engaging in counseling.

There is no reason to think that all of these tasks must be accomplished in a first session. We see engagement as an ongoing process that blends together with initial data collection and assessment. In fact, aspects of later phases of problem-solving are also evident in the engagement phase. For example, the provision of empathy and support is a type of *intervention* that can have an important impact even as early as the first session. Initial *planning and contracting* are evident in arriving at a tentative agreement to work together. *Evaluation* should be attended to with respect to eliciting client feedback about the first session, including how it fit with the client's expectations and whether he or she has any questions or concerns. Also, it is important to address the issue of *termination* in the first session with respect to the anticipated time frame for working together.

Although relationship building is ongoing throughout all phases of the helping process, the important foundations are laid in the engagement phase. There are a number of general strategies that can be helpful in initiating a positive helping relationship. The value of tuning-in has already been discussed as a way of developing preparatory empathy and readying oneself psychologically to be supportive and nondefensive. Another related strategy is to explore in the first session the client's thoughts, feelings, and expectations about coming for counseling. As part of this exploration it is often helpful to acknowledge and normalize the common difficulty many people have in coming for counseling and to ask about any negative preconceptions or fears about counseling that the client may have. It is also important to ask the client about any prior experience with counseling and what he or she did or did not like about it. The goal of such discussions is to identify any fears of or resistance to counseling, to show understanding of and empathy for such issues, and to develop a mutual agreement about a preferred way of working together (e.g., that counseling will be a collaborative problem-solving process).

A similar process should be used on an ongoing basis to assess the quality of the helping relationship with a client and to identify and work through any problems. Research has found that problems in helping relationships are rarely identified and discussed, and that unless this happens, the relationship does not improve and the outcome is likely to be poor (Safran, McMain, Crocker, & Murray, 1990). Safran et al. (1990) developed helpful guidelines for addressing and ameliorating "ruptures" in the helping relationship. They suggested that workers should (a) continually watch for and be sensitive to signs of negative reactions from clients, (b) encourage clients to express any negative feelings and show understanding and empathy, (c) validate clients' views and experiences, and (d) take responsibility and apologize for one's contributions to the difficulties. Their research showed that when workers followed these guidelines, initially poor helping relationships could be improved dramatically (see Safran & Muran, 2000, for a more in-depth consideration of repairing relationship ruptures). In a similar vein, a key element in Miller, Duncan, and Hubble's (2005) outcome-informed model is to solicit and respond supportively to client feedback about the therapeutic relationship on an ongoing basis.

Data Collection and Assessment

Data collection involves fact gathering with regard to issues that are most critical to the client's problem situation, and should include a focus on strengths and resources, as well as on vulnerabilities and stressors. As-sessment is the culmination of data collection and involves distilling the facts that are most central to the client's concern and developing these into a succinct, coherent summary that reflects an overall understanding of the client's problem situation. As mentioned above, initial data collec-tion often begins even before the first meeting with a client and it is inter-twined with the engagement process. In fact, as Perlman (1970) pointed out, ideally, relationship development and data collection deepen each other. Data collection and assessment blend together and in some sense continue to evolve throughout the problem-solving process. An assess-ment leads to an intervention plan, but carrying out the intervention plan provides new data that may build on or alter the original assessment.

Our generalist-eclectic approach to practice adheres to a person-in-environment (or ecological systems) view that emphasizes the need to con-sider the entire range of factors, from micro (e.g., biological and intrapsy-chic) to macro (e.g., environmental and sociocultural), that could impact positively or negatively on a client's problem situation. The eclectic nature of our approach also necessitates the consideration of multiple theoretical perspectives to help develop understanding of clients' problem situations.

In addition, in order to arrive at a comprehensive assessment, it is usually important to consider client history and factors that may have impacted on the development of the problem situation over time. The four Ps—predisposing, precipitating, perpetuating, and protective factors (Weerasekera, 1993)—offer a useful framework for data collection and assessment that integrates the historical dimension as well as a consider-ation of strengths (i.e., protective factors).

Table 3.1 offers a conceptual framework that combines a consider-ation of (a) the broad person-in-environment perspective; (b) the range of theoretical perspectives covered in this book; and (c) predisposing, precipitating, perpetuating, and protective factors. Although a grid such as this could prove useful as a tool for organizing data collection, its pri-mary utility is in providing a way of conceptualizing the range of data and perspectives that could be important to understanding any given client's problem situation.

The factors listed in Table 3.1 are only examples of the types of factors that could be considered in data collection and assessment. Obvi-ously, the scope of information that could be relevant to any given client's problem situation is enormous. Although this may conjure the intimidat-ing prospect of a long process of detailed, structured data collection and analysis, in practice most data collection usually flows naturally from allowing and encouraging clients to tell their stories. Aided by sensitive questions and probes that flow from the natural curiosity of the worker and his or her desire to more fully understand, clients' accounts often

TABLE 3.1 Holistic/Eclectic Grid for Data Collection and Assessment

	Factors Related to General Person-in-Environment Perspective					Factors Related to Theoretical Perspectives					
	Biological	Environmental	Sociocultural	Ecological Systems	Individual/Family Life Cycle	Psychodynamic	Cognitive-Behavioral	Humanistic	Feminist	Post-modern	Couple/Family
Predisposing Factors	Genetic vulnerability	Raised in poverty	Member of oppressed group	Social isolation	Problems in earlier stages	Early attachment problems	Poor parental role modeling	Conditions of worth imposed by parent	Patriarchal society	Oppressive cultural story	Enmeshment in family of origin
Precipitating Factors	Onset of illness	Loss of job	Experience of discrimination	Loss of social support network	Current developmental crisis	Relationship loss or problems	Classical conditioning leading to phobia	Conditions of worth imposed by adult partner	Battering incident	Problem-saturated story	Separation

Perpetuating Factors	Chronic mental illness	Inadequate income	Institutional racism	Social isolation	Developmental crises of other family members	Maladaptive interpersonal patterns	Irrational beliefs	Low self-esteem	Internalizing blame	Oppressive internalized view of self	Poor communication
Protective Factors	Good health	Adequate income	Connected to/proud of cultural heritage	Strong social support network	Earlier developmental successes	Corrective emotional experience	Positive reinforcement from career	Unconditional positive regard from parent	Relationship with positive female role model	Small victories, unique outcomes	Good couple relationship

Note. Adapted from "Formulation: A Multiperspective Model," by P. Weeresekera, 1993, *Canadian Journal of Psychiatry, 38*, 351–358.

provide detailed information about the who, what, when, why, where, and how of their problem situations. As the worker and client collaboratively review and summarize their developing understanding of the issues, further questions usually emerge to clarify and deepen understanding.

Table 3.1 suggests how workers might use professional knowledge to guide data collection and assessment. First, in exploring the possible predisposing, precipitating, perpetuating, and protective factors related to clients' problem situations, workers should employ a person-in-environment perspective and be cognizant of the possible influence of micro (e.g., biological) and macro (e.g., environmental and sociocultural) factors.

Second, workers should also use their knowledge of various theoretical perspectives to explore the possible impact of a wide variety of factors. This is not to say that workers should explicitly check with clients about every conceivable theoretical explanation for their difficulties. Workers need to use their developing understanding of the client's story in order to ascertain whether certain lines of inquiry seem relevant. For example, if it becomes apparent that there is a clearly identifiable, recent precipitating factor for a client's difficulties and that the client had a high level of social functioning prior to this, then it would make no sense to pursue an exploration of predisposing psychodynamic factors. Thus, workers need to exercise their judgment in order to keep the data collection process focused and pertinent.

The issue of worker judgment is related to the fact that data collection and assessment are also guided by intuitive-inductive processes. As Derezotes (2000) has noted, "Of all the artistic factors in social work assessment, probably the most used, yet least recognized, is intuition" (p. 24). Workers often develop intuitive hunches about various aspects of clients' problem situations as they tell their stories. If these hunches or "gut instincts" are shared tentatively and checked out with clients, this can often lead to deeper understanding. For example, if a client is talking about an intimate relationship in glowing terms but a worker develops a sense that this is masking some underlying ambivalence about the relationship, this thought should be shared tentatively and empathically (e.g., "From how you describe your relationship, it sounds like you and your partner care very much about each other, but I am also hearing that you might have some concerns about the relationship").

Furthermore, as workers hear more and more of clients' stories they often begin to put pieces together or make links in their minds. This type of inductive theory building should also be checked with clients in a tentative fashion. For example, in hearing a client describe a number of different relationships, if a worker develops a sense that there may be an underlying theme of discomfort with intimacy, this idea should also be shared tentatively and empathically (e.g., "Intimacy can be very uncomfortable for many people, and I get the impression you may have struggled with this issue in a number of different relationships").

Deductive theory application and intuitive-inductive theory building in data collection and assessment should be construed as complementary processes. In the example cited above, if the worker's hunch about a pervasive, underlying discomfort with intimacy were confirmed by the client, the worker's knowledge of psychodynamic theory might be used to explore the potential connection with early experiences of intimate relationships as undependable or unsatisfactory. In turn, this theoretically informed exploration might lead to other hunches or theory building and so forth.

Oftentimes the data collection and assessment process may involve more than client verbal reports and direct observation of the client. It might include, with client consent, the gathering of information and viewpoints from family members or other professionals who know the client, or referral for psychological (e.g., measures of anxiety or depression) or medical (e.g., neurological) testing. Decisions about how much information to collect from the variety of sources available should be based on the joint judgment of worker and client as to the potential benefits and costs.

There are also a number of potentially valuable tools that can be employed to facilitate data collection and assessment. Two such tools commonly used by social workers are the ecomap and the genogram. The ecomap (Hartman, 1978, 1994) depicts clients in their social environment, with attention to identifying supports and stressors (see chapters 4 and 5). The genogram (McGoldrick & Gerson, 1985; McGoldrick, Gerson, & Shellenberger, 1999) depicts relationships within a family over two or three generations (see chapter 5). Another more recently developed tool is the culturagram (Congress, 1994; Congress & Kung, 2005), which helps to understand clients within their cultural context (see chapter 5).

Although data collection and assessment processes continue to some extent throughout the problem-solving process, this phase culminates in the development of an understanding shared by worker and client about the client's problem situation. This understanding needs to include not only an identification of the predisposing, precipitating, and perpetuating stressors (micro and macro), but also of the client's strengths and other protective factors. The shared nature of this understanding is crucial and can only evolve from a truly collaborative exploration that is grounded in a relationship characterized by mutual trust, liking, and respect. Even when such a strong relationship seems to exist, it is important to check with the client that the general understanding of the problem situation fits for him or her (Barnard & Kuehl, 1995). Thus, it is helpful to ask questions such as "Does this understanding of your situation fit for you?" or "Is there anything that doesn't fit for you or that I've missed?"

It is usually helpful, and usually required by agencies, that an assessment be summarized in a structured, written report. There is no definitive structure for an assessment report, but an example of a fairly comprehensive structure is provided in Table 3.2. Again, worker judgment should be used to decide how much detail should be afforded to the various issues that are included in an assessment format. The complexity of human life prevents any client assessment from being definitive and fully comprehensive. To a large degree, however, the effectiveness of the helping process depends on the quality of the assessment because it leads directly to ideas for intervention.

TABLE 3.2   Sample Format for an Assessment Report

Identifying Information (name, age, family constellation, employment, etc.)
Referral Source and Information
Presenting Problem(s)
History of:
Current and previous difficulties and coping
Family of origin and individual development
Family Development
Personal Functioning (strengths and difficulties)
Physical Functioning and Health
Emotional Functioning
Cognitive Functioning
Interpersonal Functioning
Spirituality
Sociocultural Factors (culture, ethnicity, class, gender, sexual orientation, etc.)
Motivation
Life-Cycle Stage Issues
Family Functioning (strengths and difficulties)
Functioning of Various Subsystems
Communication Patterns
Affective Expression and Involvement
Role Performance
Values and Norms
Spirituality
Sociocultural Factors
Life Cycle Stage Issues
Environmental Stressors and Supports (strengths and difficulties)
Social Supports
Social Stressors

(Continued)

TABLE 3.2   (Continued)

Economic Situation
Housing and Transportation
Sociocultural Factors
Summary/Formulation (understanding of presenting problem[s] with regard to
  predisposing, precipitating, perpetuating, and protective factors)
Goals and Intervention Plan

Planning, Contracting, and Intervention

Once the worker and client arrive at a shared understanding of the client's problem situation, they need to plan and contract with each other about a course of action or intervention and then implement the plan. Again, collaboration is key in these processes. The more clients are involved in and take ownership for the plan of action, the more likely it is that they will be motivated to implement the plan. Planning and contracting involve (a) clarifying and prioritizing the problems to be worked on; (b) identifying realistic goals that are concrete, specific, and achievable; (c) considering the pros and cons of various strategies for achieving goals; (d) deciding on a course of action; and (e) specifying the roles and responsibilities of the worker and client and the anticipated time lines for working together. Intervention involves carrying out the plan.

A client's need and preference, as opposed to a worker's theoretical orientation, should determine the goals and the action strategies, as well as the degree to which the plan and contract are specific and explicit. This is not to say that the worker is a silent and passive partner in such determinations. Workers have a right, and in fact a responsibility, to share their viewpoints on goals and action strategies. Ideally, decisions on these issues are consensual; however, where there are differences in opinion, workers should follow client preferences (unless of course these are illegal or involve threat of harm to self or others). As with assessment, planning and contracting should be construed as flexible and open to revision, with the worker always being mindful of client input. Clients should be asked questions such as "Do these ideas for addressing your difficulties make sense to you" and "Do you have any other ideas of how to make the changes you want?"

Planning, contracting, and intervention should be guided by the assessment. Sometimes the determination of problems, goals, and action strategies is relatively straightforward. For example, if it has been determined that a client's most pressing problem is having been evicted and having no money, then there is an obvious need to find shelter and financial assistance. Most times problems are not so easy to specify and prioritize and solutions are not so clear. Still, the assessment provides a good place to start, and the specification of problems to work on and the exploration of courses of action should be guided by both deductive/ eclectic theory application and intuitive-inductive processes.

The systematic treatment selection (STS) approach of Beutler, Consoli, and Lane (2005) and the transtheoretical model (TTM) of Prochaska and DiClemente (2005), both of which were discussed in chapter 1, offer examples of a deductive theory application approach to the process of intervention (see chapter 1). Although empirical support has not been firmly established for any of the attempts to match client or problem characteristics with therapeutic approaches, there are a number of promising ideas with intuitive appeal in this regard. A client's natural coping style is one variable to consider in choosing a therapeutic approach. Thus, for example, the STS model suggests that clients who tend to cope by externalizing blame and punishing others are best suited to cognitive-behavioral approaches, whereas clients who tend to cope by internalizing blame and punishing themselves are best suited to psychodynamic approaches. Weerasekera (1993) suggested that a more general assessment of clients' coping style might also be used to select a therapeutic approach. Thus, a client who is action oriented and copes by "doing something" may do best with a behavioral approach, whereas a client who is motivated toward self-understanding and uses introspection to cope may be more amenable to a psychodynamic approach. Another variable to consider in choosing a theory to guide intervention is the level/depth of the client problem. Thus, the TTM model contends that problems at the symptom/situational level are best suited to cognitive-behavioral approaches, whereas problems at the intrapersonal conflict level would be best suited to psychodynamic approaches.

It should be kept in mind that an eclectic use of theory might involve the sequential use and/or the simultaneous application of different theoretical perspectives. With regard to sequencing approaches, although a problem at the level of intrapersonal conflict might suggest a psychodynamic approach, a particular client may not be stable enough to tolerate painful introspection and revisiting difficult childhood issues. A cognitive-behavioral approach to building interpersonal skills and changing irrational beliefs might be a necessary step for preparing a client to do more emotional, insight-oriented work.

With regard to simultaneous application of different theoretical perspectives, any combination of approaches may be appropriate to address different aspects of a client's problem situation. For example, as cognitive-behavioral techniques are used to help a client become aware of irrational thoughts, psychodynamic techniques may be used to help the client identify the origins of and work through the feelings associated with such thoughts. The holistic/eclectic grid presented in Table 3.1 provides useful guidance to workers in choosing intervention approaches. This type of grid can function to remind workers of the range of theoretical perspectives to choose from, as well as of the possibilities for biological, environmental, and sociocultural intervention.

Inductive-intuitive processes should continue to interact with a deductive application of theory in planning, contracting, and intervention. The helping process is never a straightforward application of theory and technique. Workers need to be reminded that a rigid or formula-like approach to using theory and technique in practice will take away from the collaborative process and that the quality of the relationship with the client is the best predictor of outcome. The complexity of human life precludes certainty in the helping process and necessitates that workers combine their intuition and inductive reasoning with an eclectic use of theory. Thus, throughout the intervention process, workers need to continue to listen, to provide empathy and support, to instill hope, and to use their intuition and commonsense reasoning to help clients achieve their goals. If it becomes apparent that the intervention is not achieving the desired outcome, the plan and contract, as well as the assessment, should be revisited.

Evaluation and Termination

Evaluation is an ongoing process that should begin in the early phases of helping and continue as work progresses. Evaluation should address the process and outcome of helping. Workers need to constantly check with clients about their satisfaction with the helping process (e.g., "Are you getting what you need here?" or "How do you feel about our work together thus far?"), and they should use client feedback to make adjustments (this is often referred to as formative evaluation). Evaluation of outcome relates to assessing the effectiveness of the interventions in relation to client goals (referred to as summative evaluation).

Evaluation of outcomes may be more or less formal and comprehensive, and as with all aspects of the helping process, clients' needs and preferences should take precedence in such decisions. Outcome evaluation can be as simple as client self-reports and worker judgment. On the other hand, it has become increasingly common to use more formal tools, including standardized rating scales, task achievement scaling, goal attainment scaling, outcome checklists, individualized rating scales, and client satisfaction questionnaires (see Sheafor & Horejsi, 2006, for examples). In some situations, particularly where a client's presenting problems involve risk of harm to self or others, standardized scales and reports from others in the client's social milieu can add valuable information to client self-reports and worker evaluation. Some clients, however, find the use of more formal measurement unnecessary and alienating.

As progress toward achieving client goals becomes evident, and/or as any prescribed time limitations on the helping process approach, the worker and client should begin to discuss and negotiate the end of their work together. As mentioned previously, termination should be addressed at the beginning of the helping process with regard to contracting about the time period of work together. It should also be addressed regularly throughout the helping process by way of periodic discussions about progress toward goals and time limitations (e.g., "Given that we have three sessions left in our contract, how are you feeling about your progress and our work together coming to an end?").

Client reactions toward termination vary widely. Although some clients are more than happy to leave counseling, others may be hesitant or fearful. The quality of the helping relationship and clients' previous experiences with endings may provide some indication of clients' probable reactions to termination. To maximize the likelihood of a positive experience with termination it is usually helpful to (a) discuss termination well in advance, (b) anticipate and explore feelings (the worker's as well as the client's feelings) about termination, (c) review the process and content of the work that was done together, (d) articulate the gains made and credit the client for achievements, and (e) discuss potential future difficulties and develop coping strategies and supports.

SUMMARY

This chapter has provided an overview of the problem-solving model and its usefulness for direct practice. We discussed how the flexible structure and the general guidelines for practice of the problem-solving model facilitate an integration of the eclectic use of theory with artistic, intuitive-inductive processes. To reiterate Perlman's (1957) provisos, the reader should keep in mind that, in practice, the phases of the problem-solving process are not as distinct as they are presented here, and that the helping endeavor rarely proceeds in a linear, orderly fashion. The reader is referred to other social practice texts (e.g., Hepworth, Rooney, & Larsen, 2002; Sheafor & Horejsi, 2006) that provide a more detailed review of the problem-solving phases.

REFERENCES

Barnard, C. P., & Kuehl, B. P. (1995). Ongoing evaluation: In-session procedures for enhancing the working alliance and therapy effectiveness. *American Journal of Family Therapy, 23,* 161–172.

Beutler, L. E., Consoli, A. J., & Lane, G. (2005). Systematic treatment selection and prescriptive psychotherapy. In J. C. Norcross & M. R. Goldfried (Eds.), *Handbook of psychotherapy integration* (2nd ed., pp. 121–146). New York: Oxford University Press.

Compton, B. R., & Galaway, B. (1994). *Social work processes* (5th ed.). Pacific Grove, CA: Brooks/Cole.

Compton, B. R., & Galaway, B. (1999). *Social work processes* (6th ed.). Pacific Grove, CA: Brooks/Cole.

Congress, E. P. (1994). The use of culturagrams to assess and empower culturally diverse families. *Families in Society, 75,* 531–540.

Congress, E. P., & Kung, W. (2005). Using the culturagram to assess and empower culturally diverse families. In E. P. Congress & M. Gonzalez (Eds.), *Multicultural perspectives in working with families* (2nd ed., pp. 3–21). New York: Springer Publishing Company.

Derezotes, D. S. (2000). *Advanced generalist social work practice.* Thousand Oaks, CA: Sage.

Dewey, J. (1933). *How we think* (Rev. ed.). New York: D.C. Heath.

Hartman, A. (1978). Diagrammatic assessment of family relationships. *Social Casework, 59,* 465–476.

Hartman, A. (1994). Diagrammatic assessment of family relationships. In B. R. Compton & B. Galaway (Eds.), *Social work processes* (5th ed., pp. 154–165). Pacific Grove, CA: Brooks/Cole.

Hepworth, D. H., Rooney, R. H., & Larsen, J. A. (2002). *Direct social work practice: Theory and skills* (6th ed.). Pacific Grove, CA: Brooks/Cole.

Locke, B., Garrison, R., & Winship, J. (1998). *Generalist social work practice: Context, story, and partnerships.* Pacific Grove, CA: Brooks/Cole.

McGoldrick, M., & Gerson, R. (1985). *Genograms in family assessment.* New York: W. W. Norton.

McGoldrick, M., Gerson, R., & Shellenberger, S. (1999). *Genograms: Assessment and intervention.* New York: W. W. Norton.

McMahon, M. O. (1996). *The general method of social work practice: A problem-solving approach* (3rd ed.). Englewood Cliffs, NJ: Prentice Hall.

McMillen, J. C., Morris, L., & Sherraden, M. (2004). Ending social work's grudge match: Problems versus strengths. *Families in Society: The Journal of Contemporary Social Services, 85,* 317–325.

Miley, K. K., O'Melia, M., & DuBois, B. (2007). *Generalist social work practice: An empowering approach* (5th ed.). Boston: Pearson.

Miller, S. D., Duncan, B. L., & Hubble, M. A. (2005). Outcome-informed clinical work. In J. C. Norcross & M. R. Goldfried (Eds.), *Handbook of psychotherapy integration* (2nd ed., pp. 84–104). New York: Oxford University Press.

Perlman, H. H. (1957). *Social casework: A problem-solving process.* Chicago: University of Chicago Press.

Perlman, H. H. (1970). The problem-solving model in social case work. In R. W. Roberts & R. H. Nee (Eds.), *Theories of social casework* (pp. 131–179). Chicago: University of Chicago Press.

Perlman, H. H. (1979). *Relationship: The heart of helping people.* Chicago: University of Chicago Press.

Perlman, H. H. (1986). The problem-solving model. In F. J. Turner (Ed.), *Social work treatment: Interlocking theoretical approaches* (3rd ed., pp. 245–266). New York: Free Press.

Prochaska, J. O., & DiClemente, C. C. (2005). The transtheoretical approach. In J. C. Norcross & M. R. Goldfried (Eds.), *Handbook of psychotherapy integration* (2nd ed., pp. 147–171). New York: Oxford University Press.

Safran, J. D., McMain, S., Crocker, P., & Murray, P. (1990). Therapeutic alliance rupture as a therapy event for empirical investigation. *Psychotherapy, 27,* 154–165.

Safran, J. D., & Muran, J. C. (2000). *Negotiating the therapeutic alliance: A relational treatment guide.* New York: Guilford Press.

Saleebey, D. (2006). *The strengths perspective in social work practice* (4th ed.). Boston: Allyn & Bacon.

Sheafor, B. W., & Horejsi, C. R. (2006). *Techniques and guidelines for social work practice* (7th ed.). Boston: Pearson.

Shulman, L. (1999). *The skills of helping: Individuals, families, and groups* (4th ed.). Itasca, IL: Peacock.

Weerasekera, P. (1993). Formulation: A multiperspective model. *Canadian Journal of Psychiatry, 38,* 351–358.

PART II

Meta-Theories for Direct Social Work Practice

CHAPTER 4

Critical Ecological Systems Theory

Michael Rothery

In this chapter, an exploration of ecological systems theory as a model for generalist social work practice begins with the historical development of core concepts and ends by considering how this evolving, robust perspective will continue to serve our profession in the future. The term *critical* has been added to the perspective's designation to highlight recent developments in our thinking about it, a conceptual step that will be explored below. A single case study, the Macdonnell family, is used throughout the discussion in order to make abstract ideas concrete and to demonstrate their considerable practical importance.

ECOLOGICAL SYSTEMS THEORY AS A LONG-STANDING PERSPECTIVE FOR SOCIAL WORK

"The first social work course ever taught," wrote Wood and Geismar (1989), "was on 'The Treatment of Needy Families in Their Own Homes,' at the New York Charity Organization Society's Summer School of Applied Philanthropy (later the Columbia University Graduate School of Social Work)" (pp. 48–49; see also Axinn & Levin, 1992). This was well over 100 years ago, when psychiatry (the other prominent helping profession) was firmly focused on the person, on individual subjectivity and dynamics (Ellenberger, 1970). In contrast, even then social work's focus was on families as much as individuals and it was seen as important to work with people in their social contexts rather than in the artificial world of the professional's office. From very early days, the rough beginnings of an ecological, person-in-environment perspective were apparent.

In 1949, Swithun Bowers published a review of everything he could find in the professional literature to that point exploring the definition and meaning of social casework (direct practice), concluding thus:

> Social casework is an art in which knowledge of the science of human relations and skill in relationship are used to mobilize capacities in the individual and resources in the community appropriate for better adjustment between the client and all or any part of his total environment. (Bowers, 1949, p. 417)

Further, Bowers found no argument for giving priority to a focus on either individuals or their ecological context:

> This mobilization of inner and outer resources is in varying circumstances variously emphasized; in some instances it will be a primary mobilization of the individual's strengths; in others, mainly placing community resources on an active footing in regard to the client. (Bowers, 1949, pp. 416–417)

Decades after Bowers published his work, ecological systems (or ecosystems) theory has emerged as a contemporary effort to conceptualize social work practice (for the *whole* profession) in a way that gives equal weight to the individuality of our clients as people *and* to the social (even physical) environments that do so much to determine their well-being. However, as the discussion above indicates, it is not in any deep sense a departure from what we have always understood our job to be, and in this social work is special.

As social work is slow to properly respect its own history, we should pause to appreciate this surprising accomplishment. The discovery of the *systemic* nature of families and other social units is often credited to people like Bateson (1972), von Bertalanffy (1968), Ackerman (1958, 1966), and Minuchin (Minuchin, Montalvo, Guerney, Rosman, & Schumer, 1967). The truth, however, is that the basic insights on which these authors drew came from social workers in child and family guidance agencies (Wood & Geismar, 1989; Ackerman, for one, recognized this), and some of the early important theoretical work came from social work scholars (Hern, 1958). As important as their work is, psychologists such as Kurt Lewin (1935, 1951) and Urie Bronfenbrenner (1979) did not on their own pioneer ecological thinking as an important perspective for understanding healthy human development—responsible as they were for important foundational theory and research, their basic insights were also part of contemporaneous professional conversations in social work agencies.

The point is not meant to be territorial, as the work of the people just identified represents a richness we would not wish to be without. The hope is simply to support a pride in the work that our professional ancestors accomplished, and to establish that the eco-systems perspective has been (despite shifts in language) a hallmark of social work since it emerged as a discipline (Rothery, 2005).

What *is* relatively new about ecological systems theory is the conceptual frame with which it attempts to describe people's embeddedness in their environments. We are thoroughly dependent on our social and physical world: without the resources it provides from moment to moment we would instantly perish. This is an obvious fact whose importance is easily lost, especially in a culture that overvalues ideals of individuality and autonomy.

Ecological systems theory is above all a *relational* perspective, pressing us always to take a surprisingly difficult conceptual step. The person and the environment are unceasingly, intricately, thoroughly (and more or less successfully) reciprocally sustaining and shaping one another. When we try to understand ourselves, our clients, or our work by focusing on one at the expense of the other we become reductionistic and prone to mistakes. Properly employed, an eco-systems focus is on the *mutual* contribution and response of each to an unending transactional process on which both are altogether dependent.

BASIC CONCERNS ABOUT ECOLOGICAL SYSTEMS THEORY

Although ecological systems thinking is seen as a framework capable of integrating (and extending) our traditional perspectives (e.g., Gilgun, 1996a, 1996b), the profession's growing interest in this perspective has not been unanimously applauded. Wakefield (1996a, 1996b) and others have worried that the eco-systems perspective is so abstract or "metaphorical" that it cannot reliably be operationalized. Social work is an applied profession, it is argued, and needs concepts that inform its efforts to ameliorate practical problems—"domain specific" knowledge about such areas as addictions, child welfare, or mental health. The search for a general theory that can inform all practice risks a serious loss of credibility respecting the delivery of concrete services. We are reduced to expounding general principles and philosophy, while other less lofty disciplines do the real work of helping people.

Another concern has to do with the perspective's open-endedness, which can be both good and bad news. As a strength, this openness encourages a broad understanding of the issues clients bring to us; instead of a narrow focus on the private lives and troubles of people seen as isolated individuals, we look also at the social context within which those troubles occur and to which they are inevitably bound. The potential bad news is that too broad a scope can be paralyzing: in principle, there is no end to the avenues that can be explored if the goal is a holistic understanding of someone's life. This elasticity of focus is illustrated when writers argue that a "deep" eco-systems perspective must expand to include concern for all of the natural environment or even an apparently spiritual appreciation of the unifying interrelatedness of all things (Ungar, 2002, discusses examples). While accepting the real importance of such matters, this chapter's necessary boundaries restrict it to a focus on traditional social work concerns more narrowly understood—people in their sociocultural environments.

A further concern with the eco-systems perspective has to do with time. People and their social environments have a history and future, expressing the past and making choices about perceived possibilities. An eco-systems perspective need not be exclusively present oriented but tends in practice to have such an emphasis, which can appear as a limitation to practitioners for whom the past roots and future solutions of problems are critical. This is a long-standing issue:

> Having sought to persuade the reader of the superiority of the process-person-context model over its contemporaries, I shall now, perversely, point to a major lacuna in this powerful design. The missing element is the same one that was omitted in Lewin's original formula—the dimension of *time*. This dimension has been given short shrift in most empirical work as well. (Bronfenbrenner, 2005b, p. 119)

A very important additional criticism is that the ecological perspective emphasizes adaptation; as such it can easily become a model through which practitioners encourage clients to accommodate to oppressive circumstances. It is for this reason that in the discussion that follows an emphasis is placed on the fact that social realities such as oppression and injustice are part of the environment that must be considered in an ecological analysis. An ecological systems approach can be misused if it is employed in the absence of articulated social values; thus, social work's traditional concern for social justice is a necessary complement to the model. An integration of values like social justice with ecological thinking is altogether possible, fortunately. They are not antagonistic ideas, which is why the word *critical* in the term *critical ecological systems theory* is being recommended.

The word *critical* is not intended to imply "negative" so much as a questioning, self-reflective use of theory within the context of a firm commitment to social justice. A thorough discussion of social justice theory is beyond the scope of this chapter (see McGrath Morris, 2002; McLaughlin, 2006; Miller, 1999; Nussbaum, 2001), and for our present purposes it is enough to say that just societies provide members with the essentials they need to flourish, such as food, comfort, safety, opportunities to grow, freedom, respect, and dignity. Some social justice theorists prefer to focus on the question of social recognition (Fraser, 1996; Young, 2000), emphasizing the need we all have for validation from the people around us. We are all happiest when we are welcome in our communities and are recognized as competent and credible—as having something of value to offer. The denial of such recognition through racism, sexism, or other forms of discrimination is what is usually implied by terms such as *disempowerment*, *marginalization*, or *oppression*.

As we explore the details of the critical eco-systems perspective, it should be apparent that it is a framework that easily accommodates social justice considerations. We will discuss how the ecological niche that people inhabit comprises a balance of demands and resources; it is not difficult to bring the fair distribution of essential social justice "goods" into that equation. We will note the ecological systems belief that everyone needs access to meaningful social roles, and this is in effect an argument for adequate social recognition—which allows us to keep social work's anti-oppressive agenda high on our list of professional priorities.

Thus, useful concerns have been raised about the ecological systems perspective, but it seems the model is open and robust enough to accommodate them. Having made this case, the remainder of this chapter is an effort to present critical eco-systems thinking in a way that highlights its practical possibilities. Practicality is hopefully enhanced by proposing a framework that draws upon social support concepts regarding resources (Cameron & Vanderwoerd, 1997; Rothery & Cameron, 1985), the "stress and coping" models' emphasis on demands and competence (Lazarus, 1993; Lazarus & Folkman, 1984), and elements of cognitive theory in our discussion of beliefs (cf. Brower & Nurius, 1993).

Still, the model remains a deliberately somewhat abstract "metaphor" that provides a basic orientation to clients and their problems but does not prescribe interventions (Germain & Gitterman, 1996; Meyer, 1988). Offered as a conceptualization within which eclecticism with respect to models and methods can be organized, it provides a useful map and ideas about desirable destinations but is silent on the question of how, concretely, we and our clients can travel from points A to B.

CASE EXAMPLE

Before exploring the critical eco-systems perspective in detail, there is a family to introduce. The Macdonnells have agreed to allow information about their experience to be used in this chapter, suitably altered to protect their anonymity.

Fifteen-year-old Colin Macdonnell attracted attention at his school as his grades dropped precipitously. When this was commented on in the staff coffee room, his English teacher added another concern: He had submitted an essay that was severely depressed in tone (well beyond normal adolescent angst), in which he devoted considerable space to the question of suicide.

Colin was interviewed by the school social worker, who subsequently invited his parents to come with him for a family meeting. Colin's mother, Dawn, accepted the invitation, but his father, Eric, did not.

Both Colin and his mother were troubled and knew they had serious issues to address. Each was therefore motivated to talk, and because they were also articulate, the initial interviews provided considerable information. Dawn's assessment was that Colin had begun "losing it" when his older brother, Sean, was charged with selling drugs to other students in their high school. Two days after he was charged, Sean came to class inebriated and was promptly suspended.

Sean was 2 years older than Colin and they were students in the same school. Sean's troubles were, of course, highly public. For weeks, it seemed to Colin that the various student grapevines talked of nothing else. He felt humiliated and helpless, and he withdrew from friends and his school activities, wishing he could somehow simply "disappear."

With very little prompting, Dawn also discussed deepening tensions in her marriage to Eric. In her view, Eric was alcoholic, though he rejected the label, preferring to see himself as a hard-living bon vivant, determined to live life to the full and contemptuous of sensible people and their lives of banal moderation. Dawn considered that his drinking had cost the family dearly financially and that he had often neglected and occasionally embarrassed them.

Another important tension concerned religious commitments. Dawn was devoutly Roman Catholic. Eric professed to be committed spiritually to the values of the church but was strongly anticlerical, for which reason he refused to participate in services or other church activities. Once, when he was very drunk, he accused his wife (in the presence of both sons) of having an affair with a young priest with whom she had been fund-raising for their parish.

Annoyed with his wife and son for talking about their family to a social worker, and wanting to correct any inaccuracies they might have put forth, Eric joined them for the third interview (and, sporadically, a number of sessions after that). He came across as a loquacious man with modest accomplishments and a romanticized view of himself. He was not overtly hostile toward the worker, but he did communicate a degree of amused superiority respecting the helping enterprise, with frequent references to "psychobabble" and "wet shoulders for hire."

Eric worked as a journalist. Well into middle age, he was earning an adequate income, and he enjoyed a certain local reputation based on his willingness to put forth conventional opinions in a flamboyant style. When he talked of his work, one could easily imagine him running with the likes of Hemingway and Mailer, battling the perniciousness of the powerful and struggling, against all odds, to expand the awareness of ordinary people. "Against human stupidity," he liked to recite, "the gods themselves contend in vain."

Eric was perplexed, he said, by his wife's unhappiness. He had no detailed analysis of what could explain it but was attracted by the general idea that it implied a lack of understanding, or an unwillingness to be realistic on her part. Respecting his sons, he often declared that they were "wonderful" kids, dismissing Sean's difficulties as ordinary adolescent rebellion, perhaps even admirable in some ways. He thought Colin might be simply confronting some of his limitations, having done well in an educational system with low standards until he reached grade 10 and the sudden expectation that he should perform.

Eric acknowledged that his alcohol consumption was well above average. Harboring a certain fear of being "average," he was, at least at one level, proud of this. He could reference many accomplished people who did not bother to contain similar appetites. Sir Winston Churchill was an example, as were many famous writers and heroic figures in the journalism trade. He stressed that he was not a "wino" but a person of discriminating taste—pointing out that he was an active member of the Opimian Society, a group that exists to celebrate the good life, especially as it is enhanced by fine wines and spirits. He also invoked the requirements of his profession, arguing that many important story ideas and leads were traded among his journalistic colleagues over drinks after work.

In an earlier time, a psychodynamically oriented social worker might focus very strongly on Eric's denial and narcissism, recognizing how frustrating such a father can be to his children. This alone helps explain the strength of Sean's acting out and the depth of Colin's hopeless despair. An eco-systems analysis does not prohibit such considerations (Meyer, 1988), although it does require that we not stop with them. There is a broader view available to us, with a more complex understanding of the sources of this family's pain and options for ameliorating it.

OVERVIEW OF CRITICAL ECO-SYSTEMS THEORY WITH REFERENCE TO THE CASE

As its somewhat clumsy name suggests, critical eco-systems theory draws on two related schools of thought originating in the life sciences: general system theory and ecological theory (Meyer, 1995). Introduced to social work in the 1950s (Hern, 1958), general system theory has been enormously important in highlighting how interconnected we are as people embedded in various social systems. Colin Macdonnell's problems are not simply adolescent depression. Rather, his experience is better understood as the consequence of a much larger set of interacting factors: his family situation, his relationships to peers, the impact of the school, the school's treatment of his older brother (and the vicarious effect of that on him), and so on. How such elements interact, reciprocally influencing each other, is the purview of systems theory.

Ecological theory was wedded to systems theory in the 1970s, enhancing it in important ways. "Ecology," according to Meyer (1995), "is the science that is concerned with the adaptive fit of organisms and their environments. . . . Ecological ideas denote the transactional processes that exist in nature and thus serve as a metaphor for human relatedness through mutual adaptation" (p. 19). When systems concepts are used to understand better how people like Colin achieve (or fail to achieve) a *goodness of fit* with the various aspects of their environment, eco-systems thinking is the result. We are not simply interested in Colin's symptoms, or in how they might be explained as the actions of complex systems of which he is a part. We also attend to the vital question of how well Colin and those systems are adapting to *each other*, and the implications of that adaptation for his ability to meet his needs.

CENTRAL CONCEPTS FROM GENERAL SYSTEM THEORY

Key ideas from general system theory that inform the eco-systems perspective are:

1. All people or groups of people in a system share a reciprocal influence on one another. "When a gnat blinks," said Constance Nissen-Weber (1923), "the universe adjusts itself" (p. 244), which is the extreme statement of the systems theory recognition that everything in a system is constantly influencing everything else (however intangibly).
2. In systems, causes are considered to be *circular* rather than *linear*. Colin Macdonnell's depression and withdrawal are a consequence of a complex set of interactions between different people in the systems of which he is a part. When his brother comes to school drunk, he initiates events that lead to Colin withdrawing. If Colin's friends feel abandoned and become angry, they may in turn distance themselves from him. This distancing confirms

Colin's belief that he is an outcast, and he withdraws further, becoming more acutely unhappy. When systems theorists talk about circular causality, they have such reciprocal transactions in mind, as opposed to simpler arguments—attributing Colin's depression to a neurotransmitter deficiency (and nothing else) would be an example of a nonsystemic, linear causal model.

3. Systems possess structure, consisting of predictable patterns of behavior and boundaries. Boundaries are always somewhat arbitrary, but not entirely so. Given the impossibility of relating effectively to the whole of creation, we arbitrarily draw boundaries around a more manageable unit for analysis and intervention. We might decide, for example, to focus on the Macdonnell nuclear family, or more broadly on the family plus its proximal community, including the school, the church, and Sean's friends. This illustrates the idea of boundaries in the arbitrary sense. It is also the case that the school, the church, or the Macdonnell nuclear family possess boundaries in a nonarbitrary sense, which means that there is a flow of information *within* a given system that is different (quantitatively and qualitatively) from the information exchanged with people or groups outside itself. The Macdonnell family members know things about each other that others do not know, for example, and this represents a boundary. Dawn and Eric, as parents (or, more ponderously, a *parental subsystem*), share information with each other that their children (the *sibling subsystem*) know nothing of, and vice versa. Thus, there are boundaries within the family defining its parts, just as there are boundaries that separate it from other elements of its environment.

4. Boundaries are qualitatively different, in that the type and amount of information they restrict varies. Systems that exchange information relatively freely are considered *open*, whereas systems that rigidly restrict the flow of information are relatively *closed*. Social systems like families are never completely impervious to influence from outside, so they are always to some extent open, and can only be *relatively* closed. Excessive openness leads to a loss of identity and other risks, while excessive closedness results in deprivation. A balance is what is desirable, with systems like families being open enough to access the resources they need to thrive, but closed enough that undesirable influences can be screened out and identity maintained. Some authors use the term *permeability* to describe ideal boundaries that are well defined but sufficiently open (Nichols & Schwartz, 2004).

5. Because everything affects everything else in a circular, reciprocal fashion, it can be observed that different interventions can

have similar impacts. Colin might experience relief if his father and mother reduce the conflict in their relationship, or if Sean is provided effective treatment for his substance abuse, or if the teachers in his school find a way to rally to his support. A corollary is that very similar interventions can have rather different outcomes, depending on how the system responds to them. In terms of the case, a prescription of antidepressant medications could help Colin feel better, decreasing his social withdrawal, and signaling his father that the situation is serious and revisions to their relationship are in order. On the other hand, if such an intervention results in scapegoating—dismissal as an emotional weakling, for example—then Colin's symptoms may be made worse. This unpredictability is referred to by the terms *equifinality* (to indicate similar outcomes evolving from different beginnings) and *multifinality* (to indicate that similar beginnings can lead to multiple consequences).

CENTRAL CONCEPTS FROM ECOLOGICAL THEORY

As a complement to general systems thinking, ecological theory adds an important new dimension to the foregoing concepts. This is, as noted earlier, the emphasis on "goodness of fit," or the adequacy of the many relationships that link clients to their social (and physical) environments (Brower & Nurius, 1993; Germain & Gitterman, 1996; Gitterman, 1996; Meyer, 1988; Rothery, 2001).

The ecological perspective is complex, as are our lives. Perhaps the best way to present it properly is step by step, "building" the overall model in manageable pieces. Using Colin as an example, we will start with him as a person and work our way up to a more comprehensive view of him as a person in a complex environment.

The Person

To understand Colin's suicidal despair, we need to understand a singular person in a particular place and time. Colin's experience is the unique creative result of an interaction between himself (the person) and the circumstances life has handed him (his environment).

Needs

It is a given that most people who consult a social worker do so because they have *needs* that are not being adequately met. There is something they do not have that is necessary if they are to live well. Determining what our clients' needs are—what change could make their lives more successful and gratifying—is the basic purpose of the ecological perspective. It helps us help our clients to answer fundamental questions: "What do you need?" "What do you want?" "What will make the necessary difference in your life?"

Biology

Years ago, an earlier social work framework had an awkward name: the *biopsychosocial* model. Although this term is not currently in vogue, it did serve a purpose, emphasizing that people and their problems are understood holistically if we remember they have bodies (biology), minds (psychology), and a social context.

All people's physical bodies are obviously basic to who they are. Our gender, temperament, skin color, height, and a host of other things help define us, and are largely inherited. Other important physical attributes are acquired as we live, with nutritional practices, disease and accidents, and lifestyle choices making their mark.

Strengths-based approaches like critical ecological systems thinking are often presented as antithetical to medical or disease models, and these different perspectives are seen as alternatives between which one must choose. Concerns about biological approaches to human problems applied reductionistically are perfectly valid, of course. However, it can also be unhelpfully simplistic to dismiss biology and biological interventions as unpalatable irrelevancies. For this reason, a more inclusive *bioecological* perspective has recently been proposed for its theoretical (Bronfenbrenner, 2005a) and practical (Taylor, 2003, 2006) value. How the biological fact of illness interacts with ecosystemic events is also, understandably, an issue that has attracted scholars in the specialized field of family systems nursing (Wright, Watson, & Bell, 1996).

Creativity and Choice

A vitally important point to keep in mind is that while our environments are, obviously, very powerful in determining our health, happiness, and opportunities, we also have power; we are not passively becoming whatever our environment demands, but we are shaping it as it shapes us. Colin, like everyone else, is engaged in a two-way relationship with his environment, and we would be disrespectful if we failed to recognize how he changes that environment through his creative choices and behaviors, at the same time as *it* affects *him*. The fact that our circumstances have a large effect on our health and happiness should not blind us to our capacities for creativity (Runco, 2004) and choice—capacities that we use to decide which paths to follow and that enable us to have a positive impact on our world (Rothery & Enns, 2001).

Effective social workers know how improved circumstances can be essential to a client's healing but also take care to recognize their client's ability to make creative choices. In working with Colin, who is feeling hopeless and alone, our skill at connecting with his creative self will do much to determine whether we are helpful to him or not.

Beliefs

We all have a habitual way of interpreting our lives, which affects how we feel about what happens to us. The result is beliefs that shape our feelings and behaviors, and this is something we listen for carefully when we talk to our clients.

Sustaining beliefs are seen when clients can be helped to feel hopeful and optimistic and their motivation to change is enhanced. *Hope* is the belief that problems can be managed or solved and that something meaningful can come from painful, difficult times (Rothery & Enns, 2001). A client like Colin may not easily express hope, but if he can be helped to find and strengthen his capacity for optimism, he will benefit greatly from doing so.

Another critical sustaining belief is *self-esteem*. Our relationship to ourselves is complicated, and very few people would say they like everything about who they are and how they have lived their lives. But those of us who generally believe we have value and our lives are meaningful are very fortunate compared to people who lack that sense of themselves.

We also all have different *beliefs about the world* we live in. A person like Colin who has become depressed will typically struggle with *constraining* beliefs of this sort, and it is easy to see how this will affect our efforts to help. How easy will it be for Colin to work with us to do something about his problems if he believes his world is empty of resources that mean anything to him? "My situation is hopeless," he seems to think, and this is an impediment—a very difficult base from which to attempt positive changes.

Another important category of beliefs has to do with *how we see other people* and our relationship to them. If there are people in your life whom you trust and admire, and with whom you feel you belong, that set of beliefs will be enormously supportive to you. If you are convinced that all or most other people are untrustworthy, selfish, or stupid—dangerous to be close to and not worth the effort in any event—you will likely be isolated and fearful. Given his recent history, Colin may well have difficulty believing other people can be trusted, and he might consequently cut himself off from the emotional support he needs.

The importance of values to helping professionals is widely discussed. Our commitment to beliefs in people's rights to dignity, justice, and equitable access to resources is a large part of what defines us—these values tell us and the world what we are about. The same is true individually: Values are basic and powerful beliefs that determine who we are and how we will respond to situations. Many social workers work long hours in very stressful circumstances, and they are able to do this because of a strong belief that their work is important—it has a personal and social value for them. Similarly, Colin's mother Dawn believes in the rightness and importance of her commitment and obligation to her children, and she regularly puts their needs ahead of her own. This is part of the reason why, knowing Colin is at risk, Dawn is strongly motivated to find a way to make things better.

Dawn is also someone with strong spiritual commitments, and if she were asked what keeps her going in very difficult times, she would invariably give her church and faith a full measure of credit. Her religion comprises a very powerful set of sustaining beliefs, and this is true for large numbers of people. *Spirituality*, for many clients (and helpers), is a critical source of meaning and values, which is why it can be such an essential dimension in people's lives (Folkman & Moskowitz, 2004). As social work and other professions have confronted the importance of cultural diversity, they have also come to accept the variety and often surprising power of the spiritual traditions in which our clients may be embedded. For this reason, the literature on spiritual diversity in social work and other helping professions has grown enormously in recent years (for example, see two special themes on spiritual diversity in *Currents: New Scholarship in the Human Services* at http://fsw.ucalgary. ca/currents).

Strengths and Competencies

To relate to Colin effectively, his social worker will empathize respectfully with his painful experiences but will carefully balance that conversation with recognition of his strengths and competencies and his capacity for making effective, creative choices. Our clients' strengths and competencies are critical to their ability to change. If Colin seeks help for his depression and is told that his life is a disaster and it is high time he gets it back on track, he might agree with the assessment but he will not feel hopeful. If, in contrast, he is told that he has many strengths and successes to draw on as he figures out what to do about a situation that has had him stymied, he will approach the need to change in an entirely different frame of mind. First, he will feel more optimistic and therefore motivated; second, he will have ideas about what he has done in other situations that he could apply to the present problem.

Exploring clients' strengths is not always easy. Colin is feeling like a failure, regarding himself as worthless and incompetent, and he therefore might not find a discussion of what is right with his life very convincing. However, it is part of our professional skill and discipline to systematically and patiently look for the good news buried in the bad. One way to accomplish this is by thinking about roles.

Roles. Each of us occupies a number of social "spaces" that carry with them a set of expectations and prerogatives. Being a child in your family of origin is a role, a space you occupy in which your parents and siblings (and you yourself) expect certain things from you and in which you have certain rights and responsibilities. If Colin goes for help with his depression, he will occupy a client role with the agency that serves him. He is also a son, a student, and a friend to others in his social network. In discussion it emerges that he is a very good writer (like his father), and that until recently he was editor of his school's student newspaper.

Take a moment to reflect: Does the last item of information we have just presented change your mental image of Colin in any significant way? Until now, we have focused on his pain, and, as a result, it is likely you developed a mental image of him based on that aspect of his life. Hearing about one of his successes suggests a somewhat different picture—perhaps a more hopeful one.

We do not always hear about our clients' successes unless we ask, and if we don't ask, we miss an opportunity to learn about their strengths and competencies. We then are at risk of treating people reductionistically, as *nothing but* another depressed teenager, alcoholic, or parent lacking essential skills.

A necessary part of our assessment with clients, therefore, is not simply to discuss their problems but to develop an understanding of the roles they occupy and to explore with them the success and competencies they bring to each. This can be admittedly difficult—it is a discipline and skill that we can spend a lifetime perfecting.

We have now discussed the first element in our ecological model, which is drawn as a simple circle (see Figure 4.1). The circle will overlap with others to be added soon, and it is drawn using a dotted rather than a solid line. This is because we as people are not isolated entities, cut off from our environments; rather, we are always in communication with our surroundings and the people in them, influencing and being influenced on an ongoing basis.

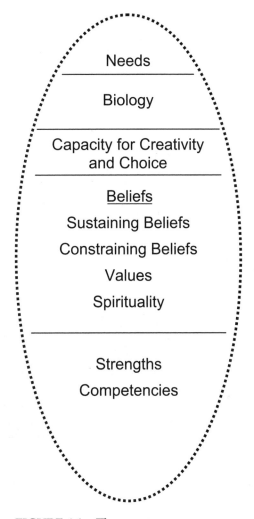

FIGURE 4.1   The person.

The Immediate Environment: The Ecological Niche

Ecological theorists tend to differentiate aspects of our environment that have an immediate impact on our ability to cope from those that are less directly influential, aspects that are *micro* (relatively small) versus *macro* (larger and broader), or *proximal* (close) versus *distal* (further away). These terms are usefully suggestive but imprecise. Metaphors having to do with size and distance can mislead when applied to social phenomena, and might inappropriately suggest that some environmental aspects are more important than others when, in actuality, importance varies from circumstance to circumstance.

There are environmental influences we can consider immediate, however, because they are commonly obvious contributors to clients' problems and targets for change. Other influences are no less important but tend to be less immediate, often less apparent, and less amenable to change in the short term. For purposes of discussion we will address these types of influence separately, recognizing that the distinction can be fuzzy. Following a discussion of more immediate environmental influences, the less immediate aspects of the environment will be considered.

If Colin were helped by a psychiatrist or a clinical psychologist wishing to alleviate his depression, the helper would likely focus primarily on him as a person, addressing possible medical needs and one or two of the other variables listed in Figure 4.1 (problematic beliefs are a likely example). Working with him from social work's ecological perspective, there is more to take into account. Not only does our profession insist that the *whole* person is important—all the elements in Figure 4.1 deserve our attention—but we also know we cannot adequately understand Colin without considering his environment.

The pressures Colin faces and the help that is there for him combine to make an immediate environment that is or is not adequate. Given his unique capacities and needs, is Colin's immediate environment one in which he is likely to be successful? To answer this question, we need to explore the *goodness of fit* between him and his environment.

The social and physical space that Colin occupies is, to use the technical term, an *ecological niche* (Bronfenbrenner, 2005a; Brower & Nurius, 1993; Rothery, 2002). We all are given (and create) such a space for ourselves, and it has two aspects that are important for understanding how well we "fit" with our environments. The first of these aspects is *demands*, which means the things in our lives that require our attention for some reason: problems we have to attend to, fires to put out, people to care for, jobs to perform, a dog demanding a walk, and so on. The second aspect is *resources*, which means the sources of help and support that we rely on as we cope with life's demands. Let's have a close look at each of these aspects in turn.

Demands

Demands, as we just indicated, are events or situations in our lives that we have to respond to (Lazarus & Folkman, 1984). We have to adapt to these events or situations, which can be trivial (your nose itches and you adapt by scratching it) or vitally important (your car goes out of control on a slippery road and you have a second or two to determine what action to take). Most are easily managed, and a minority present varying degrees of challenge.

Demands are with us from the cradle to the grave, as a constant part of living. For the most part, they are positive; by responding adaptively we learn and grow, and our sense of mastery and interest in life are sustained—we are all familiar with the pleasures of successfully solving problems or surmounting challenges. Under some circumstances, however, the demands in our lives have negative impacts.

A final general note has to do with time, an issue with ecological systems thinking that was identified earlier. The demands that affect us are not necessarily in the present. If you are a student who aced an exam a month ago, the memory of that triumph may still give you pleasure. If you anticipate that finding a job when you are finished with your training is going to be difficult, you may well feel anxious *now* even though the event is still just an expectation.

Resources

In order to cope with the demands in his life, responding adaptively and creatively, Colin will rely on his own creative competence. However, he will depend on something else as well, and that is the resources in his environment. Of course, all of us do likewise—to take good enough care of ourselves we need tools, skills, and help from our friends and loved ones. The resources we all need to live well are described in different ways by different authors, but the four categories we suggest are consistent with what other scholars and researchers have concluded (Cameron, 1990; Cameron & Rothery, 1985). Here is what you have available to you when your world is as it should be:

1. *Emotional supports* are relationships that provide opportunities to discuss how you feel about the demands in your life, especially when you are feeling somehow vulnerable. Further, you can have those discussions expecting an empathic response (your confidant is understanding and is a safe person to talk to). Colin will go for help with his depression if he is supported in doing so by someone who understands his distress and responds to it compassionately.
2. *Information supports* are sources of the knowledge we need to effectively deal with particular demands. Dawn will be able to parent Colin more successfully if she has the best possible information about teenagers and depression and about how other families have dealt with adolescent suicide risk.
3. *Concrete, instrumental supports* are help in the form of goods and services. The Macdonnells are a middle-class family, more economically privileged than many clients. Still, they have needs for services that are effective and affordable, and the availability

of such help in a timely manner matters enormously in determining the eventual outcomes of their troubles. Unfortunately, given Sean's criminal involvements, even legal services may well be an example of this type of support for this family.

4. *Affiliational supports* are the roles in which we feel competent and valued. If Colin feels like his family is failing him, his role as a son may not be providing him with a sense of importance and belonging. The same can be said of his role as a student and friend—roles from which he has withdrawn as they became, in his perception, more stressful than supportive.

Goodness of Fit: Demands and Resources in Balance

In any situation where we have to mobilize our resources to meet life's demands, we perform a balancing act, more or less like that diagrammed in Figure 4.2. The weight of the demand(s) and strength of the resources available to us are something we to try to fit together: We draw on our strengths and competencies to access resources and use them effectively to deal with the demands we face.

If, *in our perception*, the demands are manageable, our resources are sufficient, and we are able to rise to the challenge, our experience will be positive. We will take care of the situation and enjoy a gratifying outcome. If, unlike in Figure 4.2, we perceive that the weight of the demands we face is great and the resources at our disposal are inadequate, the consequence will be distress.

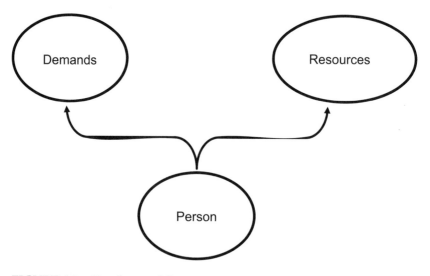

FIGURE 4.2   Goodness of fit.

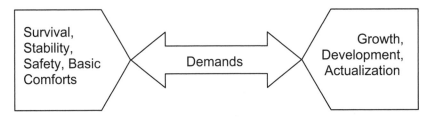

FIGURE 4.3   Continuum of types of demands.

A Continuum of Responses to Demands

Dawn has a son who has thought about killing himself and another who has been suspended from school for criminal activities. These are not the same thing as more common issues, such as having a child whose math grades are slipping, for example, and such qualitatively different types of experience demand a different sort of response from a social worker.

Figure 4.3 suggests that we experience demands on a continuum, with our place on the continuum determined by our perception of what is at stake. On one side are those demands that we believe represent a threat to our survival, stability, safety, or basic comforts. On the other side are demands that have implications for our quality of life, our growth as people, our ability to pursue a life that we find gratifying and meaningful (see also Rothery, 1990).

Dawn sees Colin's depression as a survival issue; given his suicidal ideation, we would not wish to argue with her. This, then, is a very different type of demand than Colin's slipping grades, which, although important, have to do with long-term success in life, but not survival. Similarly, we could make a serious mistake by attempting to get Dawn to learn to communicate more effectively with her husband if we don't *first* help her find ways to contain the threat of her son harming himself.

This understanding of demands is a very important piece of social work's ecological perspective. More than other professions, we have insisted on considering how services should be appropriate to our clients' needs—to the demands they confront. We "start where the client is." When we face demands we respond in different ways, and those differences can again be described as a continuum (see Figure 4.4).

The information summarized in Figure 4.4 has extremely important implications. It helps us respond appropriately (and avoid serious mistakes) with clients like Colin and his family. We cope adaptively and comfortably when we perceive that the resources available to us and our competencies exceed (or are at least equal) to the weight of the demands we face.

When demands are more than we feel we can bear, we tend to become rigid, or even disorganized or immobilized—the demands' weight has us

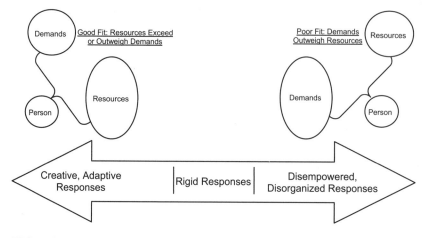

FIGURE 4.4   A continuum of responses to demands.

feeling defeated. This can be partly due to the *number* of things we have to cope with: Sometimes there is simply too much going on. However, it can also be a result of the *quality* of those demands. Demands that we perceive as relevant to our safety, survival, or basic comforts are heavier than other demands, and they lead us to feeling defeated and overwhelmed more easily because of their strong and immediate importance.

We set out to build our ecological perspective step by step. Figure 4.5 summarizes what we have considered so far: the person, dealing with life's demands on one hand, utilizing the resources in his or her environment on the other.

Note that we continue to use dotted lines, to symbolize the fact ecological thinking emphasizes how our selves, demands, and resources overlap and constantly interact, influencing each other. They are not as easily separable as we sometimes seem to suggest when we divide them up for purposes of analysis.

Also note that the circle for the person has new information added— the tendency to react in adaptive, rigid, or disorganized ways. This would not have made sense at the point where we introduced Figure 4.1, but its meaning and importance have been established in the material that has been covered since.

The Environment: Less Immediate Aspects

Demands and resources obviously constitute a significant part of Colin's environment and do much to determine the quality of his life. However, understanding the context with which he or any other client must cope requires attention to other, broader issues. We cannot offer an exhaustive list, but we will suggest a few that are universally important:

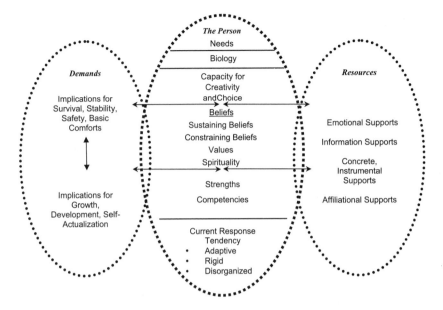

FIGURE 4.5   The person and the environment.

1. As with all of us, Colin's culture provides him with language
    and ways of interpreting reality that work, minute by minute, to
    shape the way he relates to demands and resources, and provide
    him with preferred ways of interacting with his world and the
    people in it.
2. Gender also matters enormously. Imagine if we had taken all
    the elements of this example but written about a young woman
    instead of Colin. The story would be similar in some respects but
    it would also have many important differences.
3. Everything changes as we age. The fact that Colin is a teenager
    with depression means he is having feelings that are somewhat
    similar to an elderly person with the same condition—but his
    experience, its consequences for him, the help he will receive,
    and what he needs to do to cope are all different as well.

Culture, gender, and development work together to set a somewhat
broader context than simply thinking about environment in terms of demands and resources, and they are contextual variables that modern
social work treats with considerable respect (see Figure 4.6).

There is in Figure 4.6 one more circle of environmental elements to
discuss in our effort to understand our clients' contexts—at which point
we will declare our model finished for now (though it is an open model

and therefore never complete). The elements that social work theory tends to highlight, which we have placed in our outer circle, are these:

1. Our societies determine what our lives are like in myriad ways, because they are made up of arrangements and rules about who has power, status, and economic privilege.
2. As an extension of the previous point, the idea of *oppression* refers to social arrangements that systematically disadvantage some groups of people, impeding their ability to lead safe, comfortable, and rewarding lives. Familiar examples of oppression

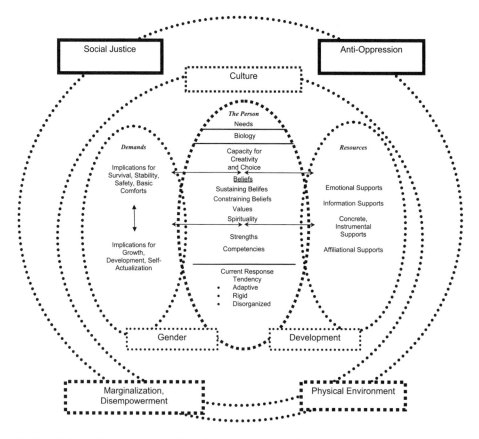

FIGURE 4.6   The "complete" ecological perspective.

are racism and sexism—social norms and practices whereby people with a particular skin color (or other visible attributes) or gender consistently face dangers and limitations that more privileged members of society do not.

3. A related social reality that affects many of our clients is *marginalization*. This is a term (another is *disempowerment*) that recognizes how some groups are socially defined as powerless and unimportant.

THE ECOMAP: A TOOL FOR ANALYSIS

Not surprisingly, eco-systems theorists have experimented with various ways of diagramming the complex person-in-environment systems that they see as being the focus for social work practice. Genograms (see chapter 5) are a popular tool for helping us understand nuclear and extended families, looking for the patterns that have affected the people with whom we work. From sociology and anthropology, approaches to diagramming social networks (in addition to kinship systems) have also been adapted.

The ecomap (Hartman, 1978, 1994) is a flexible tool that has been widely used and is employed here to expand our understanding of Colin Macdonnell and his difficulties. It should be noted that there is not a standard approach to drawing ecomaps; rather, different authors suggest different formulae. Some approaches are very simple (Meyer, 1995), and some attempt to capture the full complexity of clients' contexts (Lachiusa, 1996).

The degree of complexity to be observed in constructing an ecomap is a practical matter. Such diagrams cannot be complete; indeed, they are useful *because* they are somewhat reductionistic. The more we include, the more complicated and difficult-to-understand the diagram will become; on the other hand, we need to include enough information so that we and our clients achieve a practical awareness of important contextual aspects of their problems and opportunities. A middle-of-the road approach, similar to Johnson and Yanca's (2003), will be used here.

To begin, a simple genogram of the Macdonnell nuclear family is drawn and enclosed in a circle, representing a boundary (see Figure 4.7). Then, more circles are used to represent systems outside the family that are important (or potentially important) influences, impinging on the Macdonnells.

One immediate advantage to this exercise in visualization is that it can direct our attention to systems that may have been neglected in the preliminary discussions. For example, where are Eric and Dawn's extended families in the above picture?

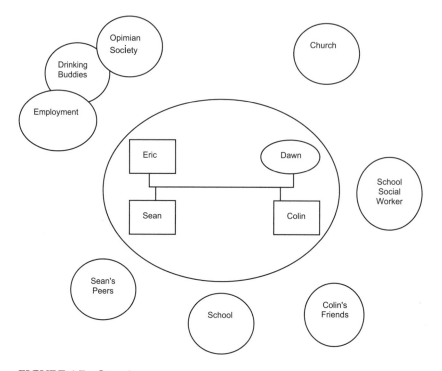

FIGURE 4.7   Step 1 ecomap.

When this is inquired into, further information is acquired. Dawn's father is dead, and her mother is a rather depressed person, distant geographically and emotionally. While they keep in touch, Dawn considers that her mother (and her siblings) have had a steadily waning influence on her since she left home as a young adult.

Eric's extended family is another matter. Dawn is ambivalent toward them, mixing admiration with misgivings. Eric likes to talk about them and, not surprisingly, describes his father and brothers (he had no sisters) as larger than life, and as models for his relentless pursuit of good times. All live at a distance, but there are annual stereotypically male reunions at his parents' mountain cabin, described by Eric as a convivial (if exhausting) few days of skiing, drinking, telling stories, and "smoking our brains out." Eric's mother is presented as a genteel person, who does not participate in such events, and who, as Eric describes her, does not possess the color or presence of the men in the family.

Once the major systems have been identified, the next step is to diagram relationships between them. There are no standard formulae for doing this—the example in Figure 4.8 incorporates suggestions by

Hartman (1978, 1994) and Johnson and Yanca (2003), somewhat modi-fied. Different social workers and agencies evolve similar adaptations of the basic idea, in the service of their varying priorities and focuses.

The completed ecomap is a rich stimulus for thinking about Colin and his family. Once the legend becomes familiar, the visual representation of their situation suggests numerous avenues for further exploration. In most cases, it is desirable to include the client(s) in such discussions, because a picture such as the above can be both illuminating and emotionally impactful for the people featured in it.

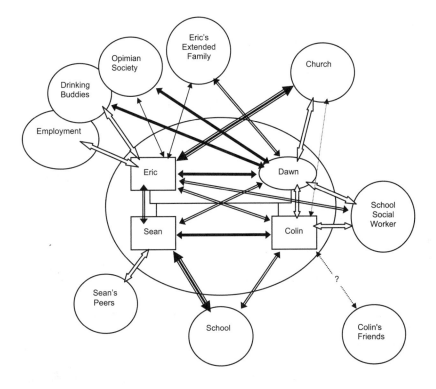

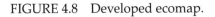

FIGURE 4.8   Developed ecomap.

Ecomaps are snapshots, frozen in time. Thus, they represent a piece of a client's reality at one point—they are necessarily incomplete and only temporarily valid. In fact, they are often redrawn at selected intervals as an aid in identifying and emphasizing changes as they occur.

At the time when the map in Figure 4.8 was drawn, Colin's isolation was made painfully clear: The only positive relationships he identified were with his mother and school social worker. Relations with his father and brother (and the school) were mixed at best, and although he attended church with his mother, he was uncertain about its importance to him as a support. He had been actively avoiding his friends for weeks, and did not know what, if any, relationships still existed (or could be retrieved).

At the same time as the diagram highlights Colin's plight, it identifies opportunities for change—positive relationships that can be used and valued, tenuous relationships that could be strengthened, and resources (his friends, for example) that have been unavailable to him but with which reconnections could be attempted.

Consider Colin's older brother Sean. With his relations to his parents mixed and connection to the school highly acrimonious, the only clearly positive relationships he has are with his friends. This makes these relationships very powerful in his life, and, because his friends are implicated in his substance abuse problems, that aspect of the ecomap is ominous.

Similarly, Eric's inducements to continue abusing alcohol are very powerful. His family is not as comfortable a place for him as one might wish, and his positive relationships to work and his drinking friends (which overlap), along with the Opimian Society and his extended family, all encourage his overuse of alcohol. Like his son Sean, if he were to give up abusing, he would also risk losing very important sources of social support.

The fact that Dawn's only positive extrafamilial involvement (aside from the school social worker) is with the church makes it extremely important to her. Eric's very negative relationship to the clergy therefore also represents a distancing factor in their marriage for which there is no existing antidote. A striking, more general feature of the ecomap is the extent to which these marital partners are being pulled in different directions. Since their own relationship has become hostile, the fact that they have no shared positive relations elsewhere suggests that the marriage will not likely last, unless corrective measures are undertaken.

Interestingly, it was through the drawing of the ecomap that Eric eventually began to contemplate the need for change, to recognize how serious his marital difficulties were, and to acknowledge (grudgingly) that his alcohol use was a contributing factor—and to see his sons' difficulties with more concern.

A final aspect to think about is the position of the social worker in this picture. The reader who empathically tries to imagine being in her place will immediately sense the difficulty one has maintaining balance when trying to engage helpfully with different people who are at odds with one another. The opportunities to become unhelpfully triangulated in this situation are many, and the worker will need to exercise considerable sensitivity and skill to sidestep such risks.

SUMMARY

In ancient Greek mythology, the goddess Harmonia represented concordance, or the value of things working well together—her name comes from the word *harmos*, which means *joint*, or the place where things are made to fit. Thus, the conviction that the healthy life is one of balance and *goodness of fit* is ancient, and it appears to have an impressive shelf life. As a contemporary expression of that belief, critical ecological systems theory is rooted in the same basic insight: If people are to flourish, they require relationships that work, fitting them adequately well with the families and societies on which their lives depend.

Social workers are practical people, usually more given to action than philosophy, and it is hoped that the discussion that is about to end has shown how some admittedly abstract, grand ideas have very real practical value. Hopefully, we have also fully recognized that, like any ideas with power, it is possible for this theory to be misused if we are not careful to continuously ask challenging questions—a critical intelligence will always be an important asset in our profession.

Necessarily, a critical ecological systems perspective will always be a draft, a work in progress. The model's own basic premises require that it be kept open and can never be considered complete. In a world that is infinitely complex and restlessly changing, there can be no final word. For this reason, our work requires a certain humility and cautiousness, and in part that means accepting that whatever models we employ can never do justice to the rich complexity of our clients and their social lives.

There is a competitive narrative characterizing the helping professions, in which models or schools of helping tend to define themselves *against* the practice wisdom that has gone before, and to market themselves as uniquely effective. One of the virtues of a critical ecosystems perspective is that it does not encourage this; it is, instead, essentially *integrative*. New approaches and techniques and new professional challenges that come with social and cultural change prompt us to respond creatively with innovative suggestions about how to help. Not all new approaches will prove equally good, but progress does benefit from our experimental spirit, and the theory featured in this chapter is a useful frame within which to evaluate next month's bright idea: How congruent is it with our core commitments to social justice? How good is it for assisting us in understanding what our clients need so they can flourish once more in areas of their lives that have been going wrong? What are its strengths and deficiencies vis-à-vis our commitment to developing arrangements that enhance our clients' competence and opportunities to live lives they find rich and meaningful?

When schools of helping are promoted competitively, clients often pay a price: If we believe one model (*our* model) is the one most worth knowing, we can easily expect that our clients should benefit from it and that there is something wrong with them if they do not—this is a distressingly frequent occurrence. One size does not fit all, and another value in the ecological systems approach is that it discourages us from ever imagining that it should. Indeed, the perspective suggests that many different interventions may well be helpful, and even that, as often as not, *service packages* will make much more sense than a singular intervention, however sophisticated (see Rothery, 1990).

The psychologist Kurt Lewin's famous dictum that there is nothing more practical than good theory is an apt conclusion. Social workers are, we said above, practical people, and they strive to respond usefully to a daunting array of complex challenges. The hope is that the critical ecological systems theory as developed for this chapter will help, not by prescribing particular interventions but by encouraging us to keep asking pertinent, useful questions.

REFERENCES

Ackerman, N. W. (1958). *The psychodynamics of family life.* New York: Basic Books.

Ackerman, N. W. (1966). *Treating the troubled family.* New York: Basic Books.

Axinn, J., & Levin, H. (1992). *Social welfare: A history of the American response to need.* White Plains, NY: Longman.

Bateson, G. (1972). *Steps to an ecology of mind.* New York: Ballantine.

Bowers, S. (1949). The nature and definition of social casework: Part III. *Social Casework, 30*(10), 412–417.

Bronfenbrenner, U. (1979). *The ecology of human development: Experiments by nature and design.* Cambridge, MA: Harvard University Press.

Bronfenbrenner, U. (2005a). The bioecological theory of human development. In U. Bronfenbrenner (Ed.), *Making human beings human: Bioecological perspectives on human development* (pp. 3–15). Thousand Oaks, CA: Sage.

Bronfenbrenner, U. (2005b). Ecological systems theory. In U. Bronfenbrenner (Ed.), *Making human beings human: Bioecological perspectives on human development* (pp. 106–173). Thousand Oaks, CA: Sage.

Brower, A., & Nurius, P. (1993). *Social cognition and individual change: Current theory and counseling guidelines.* Newbury Park, CA: Sage.

Cameron, G. (1990). The potential of informal social support strategies in child welfare. In M. Rothery & G. Cameron (Eds.), *Child maltreatment: Expanding our concept of helping* (pp. 145–167). Hillsdale, NJ: Lawrence Erlbaum.

Cameron, G., & Rothery, M. (1985). *An exploratory study of the nature and effectiveness of family support measures in child welfare.* Toronto, Ontario, Canada: Ontario Ministry of Community and Social Services.

Cameron, G., & Vanderwoerd, J. (1997). *Protecting children and supporting families: Promising programs and organizational realities.* New York: Aldine de Gruyter.

Ellenberger, H. F. (1970). *The discovery of the unconscious: The history and evolution of dynamic psychiatry.* New York: Basic Books.

Folkman, S., & Moskowitz, J. T. (2004). Coping: Pitfalls and promise. *Annual Review of Psychology, 55*, 745–774.

Fraser, N. (1996). *Social justice in the age of identity politics: Redistribution, recognition, participation.* Retrieved June 25, 2006, from http://www.tannerlectures.utah.edu/lectures/Fraser98.pdf

Germain, C., & Gitterman, A. (1996). *The life model of social work practice: Advances in theory and practice* (2nd ed.). New York: Columbia University Press.

Gilgun, J. F. (1996a). Human development and adversity in ecological perspective, Part 1: A conceptual framework. *Families in Society, 77*, 395–402.

Gilgun, J. F. (1996b). Human development and adversity in ecological perspective, Part 2: Three patterns. *Families in Society, 77*, 459–476.

Gitterman, A. (1996). Ecological perspective: Response to Professor Jerry Wakefield. *Social Service Review, 70*, 472–476.

Hartman, A. (1978). Diagrammatic assessment of family relationships. *Social Casework, 59*, 465–476.

Hartman, A. (1994). Diagrammatic assessment of family relationships. In B. R. Compton & B. Galaway (Eds.), *Social work processes* (5th ed., pp. 154–165). Pacific Grove, CA: Brooks/Cole.

Hern, G. (1958). *Theory building in social work.* Toronto, Ontario, Canada: University of Toronto Press.

Johnson, L. C., & Yanca, S. J. (2003). *Social work practice: A generalist approach* (8th ed.). Boston: Allyn & Bacon.

Lachiusa, T. A. (1996). Development of the graphic social network measure. *Journal of Social Service Research, 21*(4), 1–35.

Lazarus, R. S. (1993). Coping theory and research: Past, present, and future. *Psychosomatic Medicine, 55*, 234–247.

Lazarus, R. S., & Folkman, S. (1984). *Stress, appraisal, and coping.* New York: Springer Publishing Company.

Lewin, K. (1935). *A dynamic theory of personality.* New York: McGraw-Hill.

Lewin, K. (1951). *Field theory in social science.* New York: Harper & Brothers.

McGrath Morris, P. (2002). The capabilities perspective: A framework for social justice. *Families in Society, 83*, 365–373.

McLaughlin, A. (2006). Liberal interpretations of social justice for social work. *Currents: New Scholarship in the Human Services.* Retrieved October 20, 2006, from http://fsw.ucalgary.ca/currents

Meyer, C. (1988). The eco-systems perspective. In R. Dorfman (Ed.), *Paradigms of clinical social work* (pp. 275–295). New York: Brunner/Mazel.

Meyer, C. (1995). The eco-systems perspective: Implications for practice. In C. Meyer & M. Mattaini (Eds.), *The foundations of social work practice* (pp. 16–27). Washington, DC: NASW Press.

Miller, D. (1999). *Principles of social justice.* Cambridge, MA: Harvard University Press.

Minuchin, S., Montalvo, B., Guerney, B., Rosman, B., & Schumer, F. (1967). *Families of the slums.* New York: Basic Books.

Nichols, M. P., & Schwartz, R. C. (2004). *Family therapy: Concepts and methods* (6th ed.). Boston: Pearson.

Nissen-Weber, C. (1923). *Essays and aphorisms* (W. Streicher, Trans.). Berlin, Germany: Steinalter Koenig-Kohl Press.

Nussbaum, M. (2001). *Upheavals of thought: The intelligence of emotions.* Cambridge, England: Cambridge University Press.

Rothery, M. (1990). Family therapy with multiproblem families. In M. Rothery & G. Cameron (Eds.), *Child maltreatment: Expanding our concept of helping* (pp. 1–9). Hillsdale, NJ: Lawrence Erlbaum.

Rothery, M. (2001). Ecological systems theory. In P. Lehmann & N. Coady (Eds.), *Theoretical perspectives for direct social work practice: A generalist-eclectic approach* (pp. 65–82). New York: Springer Publishing Company.

Rothery, M. (2002). The resources of intervention. In F. J. Turner (Ed.), *Social work practice: A Canadian perspective* (2nd ed., pp. 241–254). Toronto, Ontario, Canada: Prentice Hall.

Rothery, M. (2005). Ecological theory. In F. J. Turner (Ed.), *Encyclopedia of Canadian social work* (pp. 111–112). Waterloo, Ontario, Canada: Wilfrid Laurier University Press.

Rothery, M., & Cameron, G. (1985). *Understanding family support in child welfare: A summary report.* Toronto, Ontario, Canada: Ontario Ministry of Community and Social Services.

Rothery, M., & Enns, G. (2001). *Clinical practice with families: Supporting creativity and competence.* New York: Haworth Press.

Runco, M. A. (2004). Creativity. *Annual Review of Psychology, 55,* 657–687.

Taylor, E. H. (2003). Practice methods for working with children who have biologically based mental disorders: A bioecological model. *Families in Society, 84,* 39–50.

Taylor, E. H. (2006). The weaknesses of the strengths model: Mental illness as a case in point. *Best Practices in Mental Health, 2*(1), 1–30.

von Bertalanffy, L. (1968). *General system theory: Foundations, development, applications.* New York: George Braziller.

Ungar, M. (2002). A deeper, more social ecological social work practice. *Social Service Review, 76,* 480–499.

Wakefield, J. C. (1996a). Does social work need the eco-systems perspective? Part 1. Is the perspective clinically useful? *Social Service Review, 70,* 2–32.

Wakefield, J. C. (1996b). Does social work need the eco-systems perspective? Part 2. Does the perspective save social work from incoherence? *Social Service Review, 70,* 184–213.

Wood, K. M., & Geismar, L. L. (1989). *Families at risk: Treating the multiproblem family.* New York: Human Sciences Press.

Wright, L. M., Watson, W. L., & Bell, J. M. (1996). *Beliefs: The heart of healing in families and illness.* New York: Basic Books.

Young, I. M. (2000). *Inclusion and democracy.* Oxford, England: Oxford University Press.

CHAPTER 5

Individual and Family Development Theory

Elaine P. Congress

Theories of individual and family development provide an important knowledge base for direct social work practice. These theories are particularly helpful in the data collection and assessment phases of helping because they direct the practitioner to explore the potential significance of issues that individuals and families commonly face at different stages of development. Although individual and family development theories are primarily explanatory, they often provide general ideas for intervention.

Individual and family development theories are best studied together, as families are made up of individuals and 69% of individuals live within families (U.S. Bureau of Census, 2000). This chapter will focus specifically on the individual development theory of Erikson (1980, 1997) and the family life cycle theory of Carter and McGoldrick (2004) within a changed and continually changing social context. There will also be discussion of Kohlberg's (1981) moral stages of development and Gilligan's (1982) feminist perspective on moral development.

Because the United States is increasingly culturally diverse, these developmental theories will be viewed through a cultural lens. Family assessment tools including the ecomap (Hartman & Laird, 1983), genogram (McGoldrick, Gerson, & Shellenberger, 1999), and culturagram (Congress, 2002) that can help clinicians apply development theories to their work with individuals and families will be presented.

INDIVIDUAL DEVELOPMENT THEORY

The developmental theory of Erikson corresponds well with the biopsychosocial orientation of social work. Departing from Freud's psychoanalytic approach, Erikson acknowledged the importance of social variables such as the family, community, and culture shaping the individual (Greene, 2000). His theory is an optimistic one, as he believed all individuals have the capacity to successfully master their environment. This theme is echoed in the strengths perspective in which clients are seen as having inherent capabilities for succeeding in life's activities (Saleebey, 2006). Unlike Freud, whose development stages stopped at adolescence, Erikson formulated eight life stages, starting with the infant at birth and ending with old age and death (Greene, 2000). Each life stage provided an opportunity for the individual to learn new skills for progressing to the next stage.

Using the strengths perspective as an underlying framework, each individual is seen as having the inherent capacity to master successfully the developmental challenges presented by that stage. Each stage is characterized by two contradictory extremes that produce a psychosocial crisis. Developmental crisis has been defined as an internal event that upsets the usual psychological equilibrium of the individual. Although providing a challenge, each crisis produces an opportunity for the individual to change and grow in a positive way (Roberts, 2005). These crises are normative, universal experiences, and the expectation is that individuals will be able to integrate conflicting themes and move on to the next developmental stage.

The biopsychosocial development of individuals also includes moral development. How do children learn to make decisions about right and wrong behavior? Kohlberg (1981) has postulated six stages of moral development that can be condensed into three levels. The first level includes the premoral stage (0–4 years) and the preconventional stage (4–10 years). The child follows rules, but primarily to avoid punishment by a powerful person or to satisfy one's own needs.

The second level is that of conventional/role conformity and includes a good boy/good girl orientation (stage 3) and an authority and social order maintaining orientation (stage 4). This level implies that doing right is primarily related to either the desire to meet the approval of others or be seen as a good citizen. Kohlberg believed that level 2 was obtained by the majority of people.

The third level is characterized by postconventional/self-accepted moral principles and includes a contractual/legalistic orientation (stage 5) and the morality of individual principles of conscience (stage 6). At this level individuals do what is right because it is legal and following laws is the most rational choice or because of their own moral sense of right and wrong. Kohlberg believed that one progressed through each stage sequentially and saw education as essential in promoting moral development.

Gilligan (1982) in her early work took issue with Kohlberg's stages of moral development and stated that they were primarily male oriented. She questioned whether the ideal of moral development could be found only within one's self and proposed that women follow a different course of moral development. Through her research she learned that women always considered the interpersonal and a relational perspective in making moral decisions. This reflected a different, but not an inferior, foundation for ethical decision making.

To understand more about different stages of development, the nine stages of development described by Erikson (1980, 1997) can be used as a framework. Information from Levinson (1978, 1996) in terms of adult development and the feminist critique of Erikson and Levinson (Gilligan, 1982; Miller, 1991; Surrey, 1991) is also helpful in understanding different stages of development.

Trust Versus Mistrust (0–2 years)

Occurring between birth and 2 years of age, Erikson's first stage parallels Freud's oral phase. The main issues for the infant relate to conflicts about trust and mistrust. Ideally, the infant learns about trust—the mother will be there to meet the dependent baby's needs. Early infancy provides a learning environment about trust and mistrust. If this stage is successfully mastered, the end result is hope; that is, the individual emerges with the belief that one can attain one's goal. This early developmental stage is universal throughout cultures. External social factors, however, including poverty, social dislocation, and physical and emotional neglect, can detrimentally affect the development of trust. If not successfully mastered, emotional and social detachment will be the result. An adult manifestation might be the individual who has difficulty in making a commitment to any close, interpersonal relationship. Although it is important to achieve this goal in order to move successfully to the next stage of development, failure to achieve this goal is not irreversible. Erikson believed that teachers, clergy members, therapists, and other supportive people might help individuals revisit and resolve this psychosocial crisis in a positive way (Greene, 2000).

Autonomy Versus Shame (2–4 years)

Erikson's second stage, which corresponds to Freud's anal stage, is described as early childhood. Between the ages of 2 and 4, the struggle is between autonomy and shame. During this stage children first learn to act independently without a loss of self-esteem. They struggle with overcoming a sense of shame and doubt. The positive outcome is will; that is, the promotion of autonomous behavior. A failure during this stage can lead to compulsion and guilt-ridden behavior in adults.

Initiative Versus Guilt (4–6 years)

This third stage corresponds to Freud's genital phase. In contrast to Freud, however, Erikson focused primarily on social interaction rather than individual psychosexual development. Described as the play stage, children face the crisis of initiative versus guilt. Ideally, children learn to initiate and take pride in their activities; they also develop a sense of what is right and wrong. The goal for this stage is the development of purpose, in which the child learns to formulate and pursue goals (Newman & Newman, 2005). The problem is inhibition, and one sees adult manifestations of failure to pass successfully through this stage in the adult who procrastinates and avoids and is fearful of initiating any new project.

Industry Versus Inferiority (6–12 years)

Erikson (1980) described this period of a child's life as characterized by industry versus inferiority. At this time the child first goes to school and learns to use knowledge and skills in a structured way. Children are interested in learning in the classroom, in the community, and from peers. However, because of external or internal factors, a child may have difficulty moving successfully through this period. There may be factors in the external environment of the community or school that detrimentally affect mastery at this level. For example, the child may live in a dangerous neighborhood and going to school may be a threatening experience. The school itself may not be a receptive environment, with a deteriorating building, lack of supplies, and an overburdened, unresponsive teacher. The family may not provide support, which is essential in mastering this stage. For example, the mother may be overwhelmed by psychosocial-economic problems to the point that she is neglectful and abusive. Children may also have learning difficulties such as hyperactivity, developmental disabilities, or health problems that impede the development of competence during the latency years.

Although the latency years mark a school-related separation from family for all children, these years may be especially traumatic for immigrant children. Attending school marks the entrance into an environment that is very different from the home environment. The child may be uncomfortable with English as the primary language or with the policies of American schools (Hendricks, 2005). In an earlier article (Congress & Lynn, 1994), the authors presented the case example of an 8-year-old immigrant child who was extremely upset after assignment to a classroom apart from his sibling who was 11 months younger. American schools focus on the individual development of children, and for that reason even identical twins are usually placed in separate classes, if possible. Yet this child had always been with his younger sibling, and his unhappiness caused by the school's policy of separating siblings impeded his learning and achieving mastery within the school environment.

Identity Versus Identity Confusion (12–22 years)

The period of adolescence, between the ages of 12 and 22, is characterized by the psychosocial crisis of identity versus identity confusion (Erikson, 1980). The adolescent becomes more independent of the parents and may look more to the peer group for support and guidance. This period is often rife with struggle and conflict, both intrapsychic and interpersonal, within the family. Much attention has been given to the adolescent's attempts at separation—wanting one's own private space, extended curfew, and dress and behaviors that differ markedly from the family. This period, however, is best characterized by ambivalence. The teenager who fought so hard for an extended curfew may call home several times to see how everything is. There is a need for parents to provide structure in order to promote the establishment of identity. It should be noted that adolescence may begin prior to 12 years of age, as children often develop physically and socially at an earlier age than at the time that Erikson first developed his theory. Also, for some youth, adolescence may end prior to the late teens, as they start families of their own. For others, this adolescent phase may extend well into their 20s as they pursue graduate and postgraduate education.

Many immigrants may come from backgrounds in which the adolescence stage of development did not exist or was extremely curtailed. For families in which children married young and/or left school in early adolescence to begin working, identity formation occurs at a much younger age. There may be much conflict within families in which the parents' adolescence was limited, while their adolescent children seek the lengthy American adolescent experience of their peers.

Intimacy Versus Isolation (22–34 years)

Erikson characterized the young adult era by the psychosocial crisis of intimacy versus isolation. Successful achievement during this period is measured by finding a love object, as well as satisfying work (Erikson,

1980). The age parameters for this stage should be viewed as very flexible. Many young adults are so involved in developing their careers during their young adult years that the development of an intimate relationship does not occur. For others, developing an intimate relationship may have occurred at a younger age. Also, in a society in which the divorce rate approaches 50%, developing a permanent love relationship in the early 20s is not a desirable goal for many young people. Although Erikson did not address the gay and lesbian population, it should be noted that the love object can be a person of the same sex. Finally, some adults choose never to find an individual person for a love relationship.

Levinson (1978) divided early adulthood into the following stages: early adult transition (17–22), entering the adult world (22–28), transition (28–33), and settling down (33–40). Important tasks included beginning careers and families. Many individuals, especially in developed countries, are completing their education during the early transition years. It should be noted that the age at which individuals get married and have children has been steadily increasing (U.S. Bureau of Census, 2000). The focus for many in their 20s is to complete their education and begin careers. Thus, settling down with partners and beginning families is often postponed until individuals are in their 30s. Crisis often occurs for individuals at times of transition, as for example when adolescents transit to adulthood in their late teens.

Generativity Versus Stagnation (34–60 years)

The seventh Erikson stage occurs between 34 and 60 years and involves the psychosocial crisis of generativity versus stagnation. This period involves learning to care for others and may include having a family and/ or pursuing a career. Initially it was thought that the midlife period presented a time of crisis for men with the realization of failure to achieve previous goals, whereas for women the crisis involved children leaving the home. More recently, the midlife crisis period has been considered a myth, as both men and women tend to make positive career changes during the midlife years (Hunter & Sundel, 1989). Also, as most women now work outside the home, the end of their role of child caretaker has declined in importance. Furthermore, one can question if this stage in truth ends at 60, as many continue to work much longer.

Levinson (1978) pointed to the crisis of transition periods during the adult middle years. He characterized this middle adulthood period as occurring between 40 and 65 and divided these years into the following periods: midlife transition (40–45), entering middle adulthood (45–50), age 50 transition (50–55), and the culmination of middle adulthood (55–60). Middle age often is perceived as a crisis period as individuals realize career and personal limitations. There is a growing realization that they may never achieve the personal and professional goals set for themselves during the adult beginning years. This may result in major life changes, such as becoming involved with a younger woman or leaving a successful career to undertake a new, simpler lifestyle. Peck (1968) has postulated four major steps that are crucial to psychological adjustment during the middle years. They are socializing rather than sexualizing human relationships, valuing wisdom rather that physical powers, emotional flexibility rather than fixation, and mental flexibility instead of rigidity.

A concern about Levinson's early (1978) research was that it focused primarily on men. Research on women (Papalia & Olds, 1995) has indicated major differences between age-linked developmental changes of men and women. Women were seen as less likely to have mentors and more likely to have dreams that were split between relationships and achievement. Levinson (1996) studied women and concluded that women did go through predictable periods, but transitions between periods were likely to be more turbulent than for men. He noted that women who pursued traditional roles as well as those who pursued careers often struggled with integrating the two.

Integrity Versus Despair (age 60–death)

Erikson (1980) described the final stage of old age as characterized by the psychosocial crisis of integrity versus despair. The psychologically healthy older person is seen as one who has come to terms with past successes and failures, one who has few regrets, and one who has accepted death. Those who do not resolve this crisis experience despair at impending death and lost opportunities. Erikson's eighth stage did not include the recent phenomenon of many older adults who now assume caretaking roles for their grandchildren. It could be argued that these grandparents may experience the generativity of an earlier stage of development. Also, as mentioned earlier, as life expectancy increases, many older people continue to work well past the age of 60.

A Ninth Stage (80 years and beyond)

Since Erikson's theory was last published in 1994, life expectancy has increased to 71.8 and 78.8 years for men and women, respectively (U.S. Bureau of Census, 2000). The number of older people in our society is rapidly increasing, and the fastest growing group of older people are the "old old" who are defined as 85 and older (American Association of Retired People [AARP], 1997). To address this phenomenon, a ninth stage of development was formulated for those who live into their 80s and 90s (Erikson, 1997). This stage is characterized ideally by gerotranscendence. An older person achieves this stage by mastering each previous stage, as well as transcending the physical and social losses associated with old age.

Feminist Critique of Traditional Theories of Individual Human Development

Traditional theories of individual development, such as those proposed by Erikson (1980) and Levinson (1978), have been recognized as being based largely on a male, middle-class, White, Western European model. The discussion of Erikson's theory in this chapter attempted to include considerations of various types of diversity (e.g., culture, class, sexual orientation). It is also important, however, to consider the feminist critique of traditional theories of individual development.

Feminists have argued that Erikson's and Levinson's theories of human development for the most part ignore women's developmental experiences. Gilligan (1982) proposed that traditional theories of development represent the male experience of self-development through separation and ignore the female experience of progression toward interdependence through relationships and attachments. Similarly, Miller (1991) has pointed out that women's sense of self develops through emotional connections with and caring for others and that such experiences are ignored and undervalued by traditional theories, thus undermining the development of self-esteem for women. Surrey (1991) has explicated the self-in-relation theory of women's development, with the dual goals of "response-ability" to others and the ability to care for oneself. Feminist critiques have argued convincingly that theories of development that undervalue the importance of emotional connections are detrimental to both men and women. These critiques have made an important contribution to broadening theories of individual development so that attachment, affiliation, and relationship are valued as much as separation and self-development.

FAMILY DEVELOPMENT THEORY

Families are made up of individuals of different ages and at different stages of development. Although early family literature focused primarily on the nuclear family in which members ranged in age from infancy to adulthood, many families now are intergenerational and may have members of all ages. In order to work effectively with individuals and families, the clinician must have an awareness of the developmental stage of each family member, as well as the stage of the family life cycle.

Carter and McGoldrick (2004) have developed a family life cycle model that delineates predictable stages in family development. Similar to Erikson's model of individual development, families experience a crisis when they pass from one life cycle stage to another. If not resolved, a family developmental crisis can lead to family conflict and breakup (Congress, 1996). The six stages of the traditional middle-class family life cycle delineated by Carter and McGoldrick (1980, 1989) are (a) Between Families—The Unattached Young Adult; (b) The Joining of Families Through Marriage—The Newly Married Couple; (c) The Family With Young Children; (d) The Family With Adolescents; (e) Launching Children and Moving On; and (f) The Family in Later Life.

New roles for women, social and economic trends, an increasing divorce rate, and class differences have all contributed to diverse forms of the family life cycle (Carter & McGoldrick, 2004). Approximately one out of every two marriages in the United States ends in divorce (U.S. Bureau of Census, 2000). Also, most of the divorced remarry within a few years (Congress, 1996). To address these phenomena, Carter and McGoldrick (2004) have identified family life cycle stages for divorced and remarried families. Also, approximately 22% of people choose never to marry, which represents a dramatic increase over the last 2 decades (U.S. Bureau of Census, 2000). Some of the unmarried are lesbian and gay couples involved in long-term intimate relationships. Although the literature has focused primarily on the family life cycle as heterosexual, the family life cycle for lesbians and gay men has also been discussed (Appleby & Anastas, 1998; Mallon, 2005). In addition, it is also important to note that approximately 50% of couples choose to remain childless (U.S. Bureau of Census, 2000); therefore, alternate conceptions of stages 3, 4, and 5 in Carter and McGoldrick's family life cycle are needed for this population.

Unfortunately, it is beyond the scope of this chapter to consider the many population-specific variations of the family life cycle—the reader is referred elsewhere for this important information. The following discussion pertains to Carter and McGoldrick's (2004) formulation of the traditional middle-class family life cycle. Attempts are made to acknowledge how issues of diversity limit the generalization of these stages, and to relate these stages to those in individual development theory.

Stage 1: Between Families—The Unattached Young Adult

This first stage of family development usually occurs in late adolescence and early adulthood. Developmental tasks for this period have traditionally included emotional and physical separation from the family of origin, developing peer relationships, and establishing oneself in work (Carter &

McGoldrick, 2004). It should be noted that this period may span the late part of Erikson's adolescence stage and the early part of the adult stage. Both the young adult and the parents must participate in this separation process. Ambivalence about separating may produce a family crisis. Separation involves more than physical separation. Often young adults who do not successfully complete this process of emotional separation may have difficulties establishing their own independent family.

The age at which individuals marry for the first time is increasing; therefore, the stage of the young, unattached adult may be extended. Economic factors may contribute to young adults remaining physically and financially dependent on their parents for housing and financial support. Parents may also apply adolescent rules to young adults still living in their house, which can precipitate family crises and conflict.

It should be noted that a lengthy stage of young, unattached adulthood may be increasing for both middle-class Anglo families as well as poor, culturally diverse families. America has become increasingly culturally diverse, and it is estimated that by the mid-21st century the majority of the population will be from backgrounds other than Western European (U.S. Bureau of Census, 2000). According to the 2000 U.S. census, already a third of U.S. citizens are immigrants or children of immigrants (U.S. Bureau of Census, 2000). Many cultures continue to have an expectation that young adults remain at home until married, thus keeping offspring emotionally connected and dependent on their families. Furthermore, with adolescent single parenthood, this stage leading to marriage may not exist. Young, unattached adolescents/adults may not choose to establish their own home, but rather continue to live in an intergenerational family. Although mothers and grandmothers involved in raising adolescents'/adults' children may provide needed emotional and concrete support, family conflict often occurs with regard to parental roles and power.

Serious romantic involvements during this stage pave the way for young adults to leave home and form their own families. Again, there may be family conflict when parents and adult children disagree about a future marriage partner. An increasing number of young adults choose to live together before marriage (U.S. Bureau of Census, 2000).

Stage 2: The Joining of Families Through Marriage — The Newly Married Couple

The second family life cycle stage identified by Carter and McGoldrick (2004), that of the newly married couple, is often challenging for young people. Each partner must learn that the other may have differing expectations, choices, and goals (Congress, 1996), and together the couple must learn to compromise in making both major and minor decisions. Although one might assume that this stage would be less challenging for couples who have lived together before marriage, relating to in-laws as a married couple is still apt to produce conflict (Carter & McGoldrick, 2004). The increasing rate of divorce among couples, especially in the first few years of marriage, is often the outcome of family crisis and conflict during this stage.

It should be noted that marriages occur not only among young adults but at different ages along the individual life cycle. Whereas marriage in adolescence is decreasing, an increasing number marry and remarry in their 30s, 40s, and 50s. Marriage also occurs among people in Erikson's eighth stage, that of old age. Although the developmental tasks around establishing an intimate relationship may be similar, other psychosocial tasks related to work issues may impact differently on newly married couples. For example, when young adults marry, they may be struggling to establish careers. When middle-aged adults with existing careers marry, however, they may be faced with the demands of finding time for their new marriage partners, relocating for one partner's career, as well as the familial stress of stepchildren. Older adults who marry or remarry may face conflict around retirement and shrinking financial resources.

Stage 3: The Family With Young Children

The third family life cycle stage has been described as the "pressure cooker" phase in that the majority of divorces occur within this time period (Carter & McGoldrick, 1989). The major developmental task is faced when the couple must begin to think of themselves as a triad rather than a dyad. An infant is extremely demanding of time and attention. While the family is in this developmental phase, the child is in the first stage of individual development during which trust is so important. There are many occasions for conflict to arise during this period.

Current social trends may contribute to the stress of this period. Women are usually older and working while children are young, which produces additional stress. Also, the increase in the number of single-parent households often means role overload for the primary caretaker. Furthermore, remarriages and blended families may result in the need to negotiate complicated relationships with stepparents and stepchildren (Carter & McGoldrick, 2004).

Having children of one's own often reenacts and reawakens old unresolved issues in individual members. For example, a spouse who has not been able to successfully resolve the developmental psychosocial crisis of establishing trust may be especially threatened by the birth of a baby who now receives special attention.

Another complicating factor is that in most families children are often at different stages of individual development. For example, a multichild family may be challenged by having a new infant who is very demanding of time and attention and also a latency age child who needs help to develop peer relationships. Families may also experience a crisis in handling sibling conflict, especially for siblings of different ages with differing psychosocial needs.

Stage 4: The Family With Adolescents

This fourth phase has been identified as a major family crisis point (Carter & McGoldrick, 2004). While adolescents are struggling with identity and separation issues, their parents may be coping with their own issues around employment and health. Parents often have difficulty in granting adolescents any independence and may wish for a return to latency years when their children were more connected with the family. Although adolescents may seem to want more independence, there still continues to be a need for structure, and parents may alternate between being too restrictive and too lenient. Intrafamilial differences also impact on culturally diverse families during this period, as adolescents often want to associate only with their American peers, while parents prefer the family relationship patterns they have learned in their country of origin.

Stage 5: Launching Children and Moving On

Although this stage has been referred to in the past as the "empty nest phase," this term may not accurately reflect what actually occurs in families. First, because of economic factors, many young adults do not leave home until they are much older, and even then they frequently return to the parental home. Second, two factors mitigate the impact of the empty nest syndrome. The majority of women with children work outside the home, and many women in mid-life actively pursue new careers and higher education. This family life cycle stage may be linked to individual development issues. Parents may be struggling with midlife concerns around career changes, while their offspring are only beginning to pursue their work objectives. Difficulties may arise when parents try to enforce their unrealized career wishes on their children, as for example when a middle-aged father who worked in a clerical social service position insisted that his son attend law school after graduating from college.

During this phase the family changes from being a small group with one or more offspring to a dyad again. For couples who have spent most of their married years raising a family, relating as a dyad again may be challenging. Many couples, however, look forward to this phase and welcome the opportunity to be relieved of demanding child care responsibilities. Time can be spent on advancing careers, pursuing education, and travel. For these couples who were looking forward to being a dyad again, adult children who do not want to leave home or who thrust child caring responsibilities on their parents may be perceived as challenging.

Stage 6: The Family in Later Life

The final stage of the family life cycle, the family in later life, occurs when children have left home. With increasing life expectancies, this phase may span over 30 years. Although the number of older people in our population is rapidly increasing, especially as the baby boomers hit 60, the increase of the old (85 or older) is especially striking (AARP, 1997). The transitions and tasks in later life include issues of retirement, grandparenthood, illness and dependency, and loss and death. One common challenge for individuals and couples in this period, especially for those with failing health, is the experience of role reversal with their children.

As life expectancies increase and women continue to live longer than men, the number of widowed women has increased and will continue to increase (U.S. Bureau of Census, 2000). The majority of older people live alone in the community, not in institutional care or with their families (AARP, 1997). Although elders living with families has been the pattern for many American cultural minorities, there is some evidence that this is changing (Congress & Johns, 1994). Regardless of where they live, many culturally diverse grandmothers do not "retire" from the family in old age, but rather are called upon to serve as parents to grandchildren whose parents have died or are unable to care for their children.

Does the family cease when there is one remaining member, often an elderly woman whose husband has died and whose children have developed their own families? The interest in reminiscence groups, both in nursing homes as well as senior centers, attests to the continuing importance of family throughout the life cycle.

Loss may be an especially difficult issue for lesbian and gay families during the later years. The loss of a partner may be even more traumatic for the remaining person, because he or she may not be comfortable sharing with others about the loss in what is yet largely a homophobic society (Humphries & Quam, 1998).

IMPLICATIONS AND TOOLS FOR PRACTICE

The social worker must be cognizant of developmental theory in work with individuals and families. Making an assessment about what the current stage of development is for each individual, as well as for the total family, is particularly helpful, as there are certain needs and tasks of individuals and families at different stages.

For example, a young, newly married couple in their 20s is very different from a recently divorced single-parent family with two adolescent children. In the former, each member must work on establishing a commitment to each other and the marriage; they must be able to work out issues of appropriate emotional separation from their family of origin, yet realign relationships with extended families and friends to include the spouse. In the latter situation, the family must work out financial and familial relationships with the departing spouse/parent. Unless contraindicated by issues of safety, contact with the absent spouse must be maintained and a visitation plan developed. Also, it should be noted that, according to individual development theory, adolescents are in the process of establishing their own identity apart from their parents and families. They often turn to their peers for support and guidance during this phase rather than their parents, which may cause increased conflict within a family that has already endured the crisis of separation and divorce.

Even when couples seem to be in the same family life cycle stage, there may be important differences based on their individual ages. A young couple in their 20s who are engaged may be struggling with issues of separation from their family of origin, whereas a middle-aged couple engaged to be married may have to work out issues of separation and connection with previous spouses and children.

There are a number of family assessment tools that can help the practitioner identify and understand individual and family development issues. Below, a brief overview is provided of three such tools: (a) the ecomap, (b) the genogram, and (c) the culturagram.

Ecomap

The ecomap (Hartman & Laird, 1983) is built on an ecological approach to practice and outlines the relationship of the family as a whole, and its individual members, with the outside world. It provides a snapshot of the family at a certain point in time. By looking at the ecomap the clinician can assess to what extent the developmental needs of the family and its individual members are being met. For example, the previously discussed newly divorced family with two adolescents should show some connection with the absent parent. If this link is missing or conflictual, family problems can be addressed in treatment. Also, the ecomap demonstrates connection with different resources in the community. It would be of concern if the ecomap illustrated that an adolescent had no connection with peers for recreational activities. The reader is referred to chapter 4 for a more detailed discussion and an example of an ecomap.

Genogram

The genogram (McGoldrick et al., 1999) is another family assessment tool that examines the intergenerational relationships within a family. The genogram maps out family constellations, relationships, and events over three generations. This tool allows the social worker to become aware of the current and past connections in the immediate family, as well as connections with extended family. The clinician is able to assess the individual and family development stages when therapeutic work begins. Also, the clinician can gain an understanding of historical issues in individual and family development.

Figure 5.1 is a genogram of the recently divorced family with two adolescent children that has been referred to previously. The genogram allows the clinician to examine the connection of parents and children with extended family, as well as the absent parent. Also, it is possible to look at what was happening at key points in the family history; for example, at the time of the divorce, at the time of the children's birth, and at the time of the parents' marriages. Key events such as births, separations, divorces, death, serious health problems, employment reversals, relocations, and other crisis events all impact on individual and family development.

The genogram can help to clarify when these events occurred and their impact on family development. For example, an examination of Figure 5.1 indicates that the Jamison/Hernandez family has experienced many crises this year. John Jamison Jr. and Juanita Hernandez were recently divorced, and shortly afterward John remarried. Also, we are aware John's new wife is in her 20s, only 10–12 years older than her new stepsons. The two adolescent boys live with their mother, and there is indication that both have experienced academic and behavioral problems around the time of the divorce. Although Juanita has continued as the custodial parent, the social worker would want to explore what arrangements have been made for the adolescent sons to visit their father.

In terms of important historic facts we note that John III was born only 6 months after his parents were married, which may suggest that the couple had little time to adjust to living together as a couple before they were married. Also, there is the possibility that John Jr. and Juanita "had to get married" and that John III was not planned. The Jamison family experienced a major crisis when John III was an infant when John Jr.'s brother was in a fatal accident. There may be pressure on the oldest male child, John Jr., and now John III to carry on the family tradition.

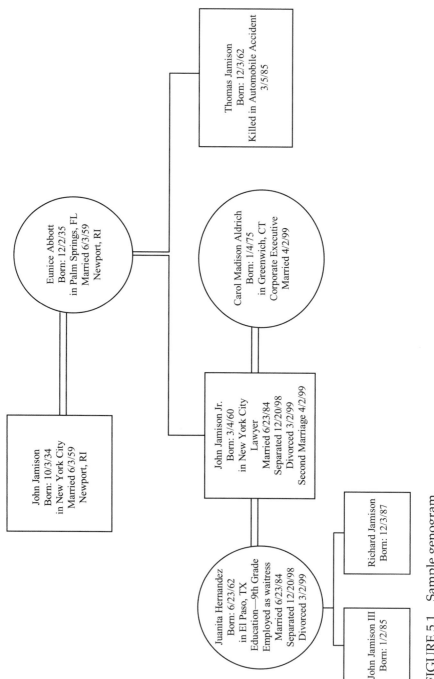

FIGURE 5.1 Sample genogram.

Also we note ethnic, geographic, and class differences between the Jamison and the Hernandez side of the family. The Jamisons and the new wife, Carol Madison Aldrich, come from the Northeast, whereas Juanita was born in Texas. The Jamisons appear to be from a White, Anglo-Saxon background, whereas Juanita is Mexican American. John Jr. has completed graduate education, while Juanita did not graduate from high school. Both sons are in the adolescent phase of development during which children strive to become more independent of their parents. Yet parental roles and values are very important in shaping adolescent and adult identity. Because both parents come from such different backgrounds, the social worker would want to explore the impact this has had on the family in the past as well as the present.

Culturagram

The ecomap and genogram are useful tools in assessing the development of the family, as well as the developmental stages of its members. These tools, however, neglect the important role of culture in assessing and understanding the family. To increase understanding of the impact of culture on the family, the culturagram (Congress, 1994, 1997; Congress & Kung, 2005) has been developed and applied to work with people of color (Lum, 2003), battered women (Brownell & Congress, 1998), children (Webb, 2003), immigrants (Congress, 2004), people with health problems (Congress, 2004), and older people (Brownell, 1997). The culturagram grew out of the recognition that families are becoming increasingly culturally diverse. It is estimated that over 25% of those living in the United States are either immigrants or children of immigrants (Potocky-Tripodi, 2002). Although earlier immigrants to the United States were primarily men, recent waves of immigration have been mostly women and children (Foner, 2005).The presence of families from 125 nations in one zip code attests to the increasing diversity of our country (National Geographic, 1998).

Practitioners demonstrate varied degrees of cultural competence in working with individuals and families from different cultures. Schools, agencies, and governmental organizations are frequently rooted in a Western European background. Individual and family development theories were originally based on practice with traditional White American middle-class families. Cultural differences often have a major impact on individual and family development. For example, individuals and families from other cultures are often more familial and communal than their White Anglo-Saxon American counterparts. Class also may be an important factor. Middle-class families from other cultures may be more assimilated and may follow Carter and McGoldrick's family development patterns more closely than poor families.

The clinician must guard against judging individuals or families as pathological because they do not follow traditional individual and family development patterns. The adolescent who chooses not to separate from his parents to attend a distant college despite a full scholarship is not pathological, but perhaps heeds a cultural norm that maintaining familial connection is more important than individual achievement. The culturally diverse family in the launching stage in which adult children choose not to move out and live independent of their parents may believe that ongoing connection with family provides essential lifetime support.

Many culturally diverse families exhibit much strength in handling the crisis of each developmental stage. Some examples of this include the single adolescent mother who struggles to receive a General Equivalency Diploma, while working full-time to support her child; the working-class family in which the father, as a janitor, and mother, as a housekeeper, manage to provide for and raise a large family; and the grandmother who, despite serious health problems, cares for her grandchildren.

When attempting to understand culturally diverse families in terms of individual and family development theory, it is important to assess the family within a cultural context. Some authors have written about the unique characteristics of different cultures (Ho, 2004; McGoldrick, Pearce, & Giordano, 1996). Considering a family only in terms of a specific culture, however, may lead to overgeneralization and stereotyping (Congress & Kung, 2005). For example, a Puerto Rican family who has lived in the United States for 40 years is very different from a Mexican family that emigrated last month, although both families are Hispanic. Also, one cannot assume even within a particular cultural group that all families are similar.

The culturagram (see Figure 5.2) is a family assessment tool that represents an attempt to individualize culturally diverse families (Congress & Kung, 2005). Completing a culturagram with a family can help a practitioner develop a better understanding of the family in terms of individual and family development theory. The culturagram can be a powerful tool for better assessment, treatment planning, and intervention in work with culturally diverse families.

As is apparent in Figure 5.2, the culturagram consists of 10 major areas that are important to consider in order to understand culturally diverse families. They are (a) reasons for immigration; (b) length of time in the community; (c) legal status; (d) language spoken at home and in the community; (e) health beliefs; (f) impact of crisis events; (g) holidays and special events; (h) contact with cultural and religious institutions; (i) values about education and work; and (j) values about family, including structure and roles.

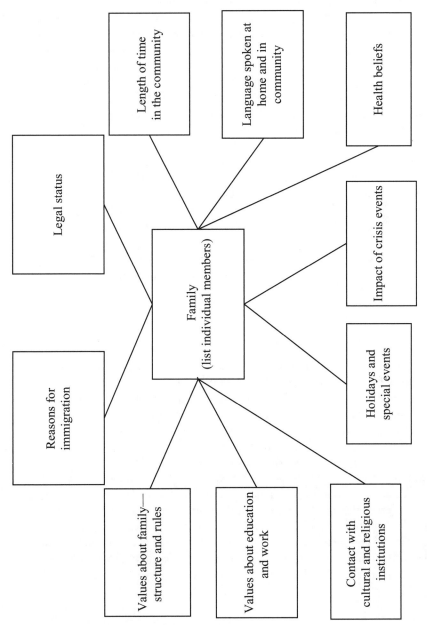

FIGURE 5.2 Culturagram.

Reasons for Immigration

Reasons for immigration vary among families. Many families come because of economic opportunities in America, whereas others relocate because of political and religious discrimination in their country of origin. For some it is possible to return home again and they often travel back and forth for holidays and special occasions. Others know that they can never go home again. Economic and social differences between the country of origin and America can affect immigrant families. For example, in America, latency age children often attend large schools far from their communities and begin to develop peer relationships apart from their families. For culturally diverse families that come from backgrounds in which education is not easily accessible, and even young children are supposed to work and care for younger siblings, the American school system—with its focus on individual academic achievement and peer relationships—may seem strange. Furthermore, immigrant children who bring a history of individual or family oppression may feel very isolated and lonely in their new environments.

Individual development theory for latency aged children, as well as family development theory for families with young children, needs to be understood in the context of immigration issues involving loss, change, and assimilation.

Length of Time in the Community

This area of the culturagram assessment provides an important context for understanding culturally diverse families. Usually the family members who have arrived earlier are more assimilated than other members. Also, because of attending American schools and developing peer relationships, children are often more quickly assimilated than their parents. This may lead to conflictual role reversals in which children assume a leadership role. A current phenomenon involves mothers first immigrating to the United States and then sending for their children. These circumstances can certainly impact on individual and family development. A young infant left in the care of relatives in the homeland may have difficulties in developing trust because of the lack of continuity in parenting during this crucial development period. Also, the family with young children that is disrupted when the mother emigrates to America may face challenges in reuniting as a family after several years hiatus.

Legal Status

The legal status of a family may have an effect on both individual and family development. Often families consist of both documented and undocumented members. In families affected by domestic violence, often a husband with legal status may threaten his undocumented wife with reporting her undocumented status to immigration authorities. If a family is undocumented and fears deportation, individual members, as well as the family as a whole, may become secretive and socially isolated. Latency age children and adolescents may be discouraged from developing peer relationships because of the fears of others knowing their immigration secret.

Language

Language is the mechanism by which families communicate with each other. Often families may use their own native language at home, but speak English in contacts with the outside community. Sometimes children begin to prefer English as they see knowledge of this language as most helpful for survival in their newly adopted country. This may lead to conflict in families. A most literal communication problem may develop when parents speak no English and children speak only minimally their native tongue.

Health Beliefs

Families from different cultures have varying beliefs about health, disease, and treatment (Congress, 2004; Congress & Lyons, 1992). Often health issues impact on individual and family development, as for example when the primary wage earner with a serious illness is no longer able to work, a family member has HIV/AIDS, or a child has a chronic health condition such as asthma or diabetes. The children of immigrants may be at greater risk for certain chronic adult diseases (Santora, 2006), and the access to care and care they receive is very important. Also, mental health problems can impact negatively on individual and family development. Families from different cultures may encounter barriers in accessing medical treatment, or may prefer alternative resources for diagnosing and treating physical and mental health conditions (Congress, 2004). Many immigrants may use health care methods other than traditional Western European medical care involving diagnosis, pharmacology, x-rays, and surgery (Congress, 2004). The social worker who wishes to understand families must study their unique health care beliefs.

Crisis Events

Families can encounter developmental crises as well as "bolts from the blue" crises (Congress, 1996). As discussed previously, developmental crises may occur when a family moves from one life cycle stage to another. Life cycle stages for culturally diverse families may be quite different from those for traditional middle-class families. For example, for many culturally diverse families, the "launching children" stage may not occur at all, as single and even married children may continue to live in close proximity to the parents. If separation is forced, this developmental crisis might be especially traumatic.

Families also deal with "bolts from the blue" crises in different ways. A family's reaction to crisis events is often related to their cultural values. For example, a father's accident and subsequent inability to work may be especially traumatic for an immigrant family in which the father's providing for the family is an important family value. While rape is certainly traumatic for any family, the rape of a teenage girl may be especially traumatic for a family who values virginity before marriage. Families from different cultures who suffered a loss as a result of the 9/11 tragedy may demonstrate a variety of crisis-related symptoms (Congress & Lynn, 2005).

Holidays and Special Events

Each family has particular holidays and special events. Some events mark transitions from one developmental stage to another; for example, a christening, a bar mitzvah, a wedding, or a funeral. It is important for the social worker to learn the cultural significance of important holidays for the family, as they are indicative of what families see as major transition points in their family development.

Contact With Cultural and Religious Institutions

Contact with cultural and religious institutions often provides support to an immigrant family. Family members may use cultural institutions differently. For example, a father may belong to a social club, a mother may attend a church where her native language is spoken, and adolescent children may refuse to participate in either because they wish to become more Americanized. The clinician also needs to explore the role of spirituality within the immigrant family.

Values About Education and Work

All families have differing values about work and education, and culture is an important influence on such values. Social workers must explore what these values are in order to understand the family. For example, employment in a high-status position may be very important to the male breadwinner. Often it is especially traumatic for the immigrant family when the father cannot find any work or only work of a menial nature. Sometimes there may be a conflict in values. This occurred when an adolescent son was accepted with a full scholarship to a prestigious university 1,000 miles away from home. Although the family had always believed in the importance of education, the parents believed that the family needed to stay together and that they did not want to have their only child leave home even to pursue education.

Values About Family

Many families from culturally diverse backgrounds may have differing views about family structure and roles, based on gender and age. Often American families are more egalitarian, with women and children having equal voices within the families. This may be very different for many families from cultures in which males were considered the most dominant, women were subservient, and children had limited voices. Also, some cultures have much respect for older people and depend on their input for decision making, while in America there is often more of a youth orientation. Because of language differences, however, often a role reversal occurs with children assuming greater power because of their greater fluency in English. In working with culturally diverse families, clinicians need to be aware of family values that are different from those of themselves or other American families.

SUMMARY

Social workers need to integrate knowledge of individual and family development theory in their work. Such knowledge can help workers identify and normalize individual and family problems. The stages of individual and family development should not, however, be applied rigidly. There is a risk of characterizing individuals or families as pathological if they do not follow the expected guidelines for the stage. Any attempt to describe "normal" development runs the risk of pathologizing those who do not fit the theoretical descriptions. It is important to recognize that theories of individual and family development have been based largely on a White, male, middle-class model. These theories must continue to be expanded to take into account various types of diversity and changing social trends.

With regard to individual development, for example, more recognition must be afforded to women's experience, and affiliation and connection need to be valued as much as separation and self-development.

With regard to family development theory, the need for flexibility and multiple conceptions of normal development is necessitated by phenomena such as single-parent, blended, gay and lesbian, and culturally diverse families. Even when changing social trends and diversity are given due recognition, individual and family development theories provide only broad guidelines in work with clients. Social workers must apply these theories in the context of the specific, unique individuals and families with whom they are working. Using the tools of the ecomap, genogram, and culturagram helps in understanding families from diverse class and cultural backgrounds.

REFERENCES

American Association of Retired People. (1997). *Profile of retired persons: 1997*. Washington, DC: Author.

Appleby, G., & Anastas, J. (Eds.). (1998). *Not just a passing phase: Social work with gay, lesbian, and bisexual people*. New York: Columbia University Press.

Brownell, P. (1997). The application of the culturagram in cross cultural practice with elder abuse victims. *Journal of Elder Abuse and Neglect, 9*(2), 19–33.

Brownell, P., & Congress, E. P. (1998). Application of the culturagram to assess and empower culturally and ethnically diverse battered women. In A. R. Roberts (Ed.), *Battered women and their families: Intervention and treatment strategies* (pp. 387–404). New York: Springer Publishing Company.

Carter, B., & McGoldrick, M. (1980). *The family life cycle: A framework for family therapy*. New York: Gardner Press.

Carter, B., & McGoldrick, M. (1989). *The changing family life cycle: A framework for family therapy* (2nd ed.). Boston: Allyn and Bacon.

Carter, B., & McGoldrick, M. (2004). *The expanded family life cycle: Individual, family, and social perspectives* (3rd ed.). Boston: Allyn & Bacon.

Congress, E. P. (1994). The use of culturagrams to assess and empower culturally diverse families. *Families in Society, 75*, 531–540.

Congress, E. P. (1996). Family crisis—Life cycle and bolts from the blue: Assessment and treatment. In A. R. Roberts (Ed.), *Crisis management and brief treatment: Theory, technique, and applications* (pp. 142–159). Chicago: Nelson-Hall.

Congress, E. P. (1997). Using the culturagram to assess and empower culturally diverse families. In E. P. Congress (Ed.), *Multicultural perspectives in working with families* (pp. 3–16). New York: Springer Publishing Company.

Congress, E. P. (2002). Using culturagrams with culturally diverse families. In A. R. Roberts & G. J. Greene (Eds.), *Social workers' desk reference* (pp. 57–61). New York: Oxford University Press.

Congress, E. P. (2004). Cultural and ethnic issues in working with culturally diverse patients and their families: Use of the culturagram to promote cultural competency in health care settings. *Social Work in Health Care, 39*, 249–262.

Congress, E. P., & Johns, M. (1994). Cultural diversity and practice with older people. In I. Gutheil (Ed.), *Work with older people: Challenges and opportunities* (pp. 65–84). New York: Fordham University Press.

Congress, E. P., & Kung, W. (2005). Using the culturagram to assess and empower culturally diverse families. In E. P. Congress & M. Gonzalez (Eds.), *Multicultural perspectives in working with families* (2nd ed., pp. 3–21). New York: Springer Publishing Company.

Congress, E. P., & Lynn, M. (1994). Group work programs in public schools: Ethical dilemmas and cultural diversity. *Social Work in Education, 16*(2), 107–114.

Congress, E. P., & Lynn, M. (2005). Family and group approaches with culturally diverse families: A dialogue to increase collaboration. In E. P. Congress & M. Gonzalez (Eds.), *Multicultural perspectives in working with families* (2nd ed., pp. 22–37). New York: Springer Publishing Company.

Congress, E. P., & Lyons, B. (1992). Ethnic differences in health beliefs: Implications for social workers in health care settings. *Social Work in Health Care, 17,* 81–96.

Erikson, E. H. (1980). *Identity and the life cycle* (2nd ed.). New York: W. W. Norton.

Erikson, E. H. (1997). *The life cycle completed.* New York: W. W. Norton.

Foner, N. (2005). *In a new land: A comparative view of immigration.* New York: New York Press.

Gilligan, C. (1982). *In a different voice: Psychological theory and women's development.* Cambridge, MA: Harvard University Press.

Greene, R. (2000). *Human behavior theory and social work practice (Modern applications of social work).* New York: Aldine de Gruyter.

Hartman, A., & Laird, J. (1983). *Family oriented treatment.* New York: Free Press.

Hendricks, C. O. (2005). The multicultural triangle of the child, the family, and the school: Culturally competent approaches. In E. P. Congress & M. Gonzalez (Eds.), *Multicultural perspectives in working with families* (2nd ed., pp. 71–92). New York: Springer Publishing Company.

Ho, M. K. (2004). *Family therapy with ethnic minorities.* Newbury Park, CA: Sage.

Humphries, N., & Quam, J. (1998). Middle-aged and old gay, lesbian, and bisexual adults. In G. Appleby & J. Anastas (Eds.), *Not just a passing phase: Social work with gay, lesbian, and bisexual people* (pp. 245–267). New York: Columbia University Press.

Hunter, S., & Sundel, M. (1989). *Midlife myths.* Newbury Park, CA: Sage.

Kohlberg, L. (1981). *The philosophy of moral development.* New York: Harper & Row.

Levinson, D. J. (1978). *The seasons of a man's life.* New York: Knopf.

Levinson, D. J. (1996). *The seasons of a woman's life.* New York: Knopf.

Lum, D. (2003). *Social work practice and people of color: A process-stage approach* (5th ed.). Belmont, CA: Wadsworth.

Mallon, G. (2005). Practice with families where sexual orientation is an issue: Lesbian and gay individuals and their families. In E. P. Congress & M. Gonzalez (Eds.), *Multicultural perspectives in working with families* (2nd ed., pp. 199–227). New York: Springer Publishing Company.

McGoldrick, M., Gerson, R., & Shellenberger, S. (1999). *Genograms: Assessment and intervention.* New York: W. W. Norton.

McGoldrick, M., Pearce, J., & Giordano, J. (1996). *Ethnicity and family therapy* (2nd ed.). New York: Guilford Press.

Miller, J. B. (1991). The development of women's sense of self. In J. V. Jordan, A. G. Kaplan, J. B. Miller, I. P. Stiver, & J. L. Surrey (Eds.), *Women's growth in connection: Writings from the Stone Center* (pp. 11–26). New York: Guilford Press.

National Geographic (September, 1998). *All the world comes to Queens.*

Newman, B., & Newman, P. (2005). *Development through life: A psychosocial approach* (9th ed.). Belmont, CA: Wadsworth.

Papalia, D. E., & Olds, S. W. (1995). *Human development* (6th ed.). New York: McGraw-Hill.

Peck, R. (1968). Psychological development in the second half of life. In B. Neugarten (Ed.), *Middle age and aging* (pp. 88–92). Chicago: University of Chicago Press.

Potocky-Tripodi, M. (2002). *Best practices with refugees and immigrants.* New York: Columbia University Press.

Roberts, A. R. (2005). *Crisis intervention handbook: Assessment, treatment, and research* (3rd ed.). New York: Oxford University Press.

Saleebey, D. (2006). *Strengths perspective in social work practice* (4th ed.). New York: Allyn & Bacon.

Santora, M. (2006, January 12). East meets west: Adding pounds and peril. *The New York Times*, p. A1.

Surrey, J. L. (1991). The self-in-relation: A theory of women's development. In J. V. Jordan, A. G. Kaplan, J. B. Miller, I. P. Stiver, & J. L. Surrey (Eds.), *Women's growth in connection: Writings from the Stone Center* (pp. 51–66). New York: Guilford Press.

U.S. Bureau of Census. (2000). *Statistical analysis of the United States 2000*. Austin, TX: Reference Press.

Webb, N. B. (2003). *Social work practice with children* (2nd ed.). New York: Guilford Press.

PART III

Mid-Level Theories for Direct Social Work Practice

Section A
Psychodynamic Theories

CHAPTER 6

Attachment Theory

Carol A. Stalker and Rosemary Hazelton

John Bowlby, a British child psychiatrist and psychoanalyst, developed attachment theory in response to his observations of the effects on young children of separations from and losses of caregivers. In particular, during the 1930s and 1940s, he studied the effects of lengthy institutional care and frequent changes in the primary caregiver. His writing came to have a significant impact on child care policies; in 1951, in a report commissioned by the World Health Organization, he argued that children's mental health was severely compromised by early separation from their mothers. As a result, hospitals throughout the world, reversing earlier policies, began to permit parents to visit their sick children, and the prevalence of large institutional orphanages with multiple rotating caregivers declined dramatically (Rutter, 1995). Attachment theory and research continues to have very important implications for work with children (Rutter & O'Connor, 1999).

The theory developed as a variant of the object relations school of psychoanalytic theory (Bowlby, 1988). It initially focused on the quality of affectional ties between infants and caregivers, but it has evolved into an explanation of the role of attachment across the life span, the transmission of attachment patterns across generations, and the influence of attachment in both healthy development and emotional disturbance. Recently it has been described as unique among psychoanalytic theories in bridging the gap between general psychology and clinical psychoanalytic theory (Fonagy, 2001; Fonagy & Target, 2003). The theory has attracted much interest, primarily because of the considerable empirical research that supports it.

AN OVERVIEW OF THE THEORY

Understanding of Human Problems

Attachment theory holds that psychological problems derive from disturbances, deprivations, or disruptions in early caregiving relationships and from resulting distortions or limitations in internal representations of self, others, and relationships. These internal representations are believed to guide feelings, thoughts, and expectations in later relationships. Bowlby's (1958) view was that all human infants are predisposed to become attached to their caregivers because they provide a source of emotional security, comfort, and protection. He emphasized the infant's biological proclivity to initiate, maintain, and terminate interaction with the caregiver, and to use this person as a "secure base" for exploration and self-enhancement (Fonagy & Target, 2003).

Reconceptualizing earlier perspectives that described emotional dependence on others in adulthood as unhealthy, attachment theory stresses the human propensity to be close to others across the life span. It recognizes that the concepts of dependence and independence are not mutually exclusive but complementary, and that relative independence or interdependence develops from positive relationship experiences early in life when caregivers are consistently reliable and responsive to emotional needs (Bowlby, 1979).

Conception of Therapeutic Intervention

Following Bowlby's ideas, therapeutic change is believed to occur within the context of an emotionally significant relationship that provides a secure, caring, and safe environment. Within the safety of this relationship, clients are helped to challenge and disconfirm beliefs and assumptions about self and others that derive from difficulties in past experiences and negatively influence current functioning. Effective psychotherapy has also been described as a "corrective attachment experience" (Lieberman, as cited in Erickson, Korfmacher, & Egeland, 1992, p. 501).

A range of approaches to the clinical application of attachment theory has been articulated (e.g., Holmes, 1996, 2001; Lyons-Ruth, Melnick, Bronfman, Sherry, & Llanas, 2003; Lyons-Ruth & Spielman, 2004; Slade, 1999a, 2000). Slade (1999a) suggested that attachment theory has the potential to change the way clinicians listen to, think about, and respond to their clients; that is, the theory informs rather than defines clinical understanding and intervention. Holmes (2001), on the other hand, placed attachment theory at the heart of psychotherapy and has developed a model of attachment-based practice. In addition, there is an inherent affinity between attachment theory and infant–parent psychotherapy, reflecting attachment theory's view that the foundation of healthy emotional development is the parent–child relationship (Lieberman & Zeanah, 1999). Attachment theory has also made substantial contributions to clinical practice in the children's mental health field (Baradon, 2003; Cicchetti & Toth, 1995; Lieberman, 1991, 1999; Slade, 1999b).

HISTORICAL DEVELOPMENT

Bowlby trained as a psychoanalyst at a time when there was much turmoil in psychoanalytic circles in Britain. He did not hold the classical view that the child's tie to a primary caregiver was based on the gratification of physical needs, and he rejected the minimization of the role of the environment in much of psychoanalytic theory of the time. Bowlby's (1958) ideas were, however, in agreement with the Hungarian school of psychoanalysis (Balint, as cited in Bowlby, 1969) and other British theorists (Fairbairn, 1956; Suttie, 1935), both of whom viewed the infant's need for a caregiver as a primary social need, independent of bodily needs.

Although initially rejected by classical psychoanalysis, Bowlby's theory was embraced by developmental psychologists, apparently because of its inclusion of concepts from biology, ethology, and cognitive psychology. Over the past 3 decades, numerous researchers including Ainsworth (1989), Fonagy (Fonagy, Steele, & Steele, 1991), Lyons-Ruth (Lyons-Ruth, Bronfman, & Atwood, 1999), Main (1996), Slade (2005), and Sroufe (2005) have contributed to an "explosion in mother-infant research" (Holmes, 1994, p. 65). As a result of the empirical support for attachment theory that this research has provided, all fields of study concerned with human development have been forced to take notice.

At the same time, the rift between attachment theory and psychoanalytic thinking has been closing. This rapprochement has been helped by the evolution of psychoanalytic theories to their contemporary relational and interpersonal focus, the strengthening of empirical research in psychoanalysis, and the increasing recognition of the effects of abusive and other traumatic experiences on psychological development (Fonagy, 2001; Holmes 2000).

Of current significance is the interface between attachment and neuroscience (Perry, 2001; Schore, 2003). It is now understood that the earliest emotional relationships are a major factor qualitatively influencing the developing brain, and that whether or not certain brain developments take place depends on the nature of early caregiving experiences (Green,

2003). The fostering of optimal brain development requires sensitive and calming responses from caregivers when infants and children are distressed (LeDoux, 2000).

Hypotheses about the place of attachment with respect to genetic influences on psychological development have also been advanced (Fonagy, 2003). It is postulated that whether or not genetic inheritance or risk becomes manifest depends at least in part on the quality of the relationship environment that the child experiences. Thus, attachment is viewed as providing an experiential filter and critical mediator in relation to genetic potential. Further understanding of the interaction between experience and the expression of genetic disposition will be the task of researchers and clinicians in the coming decades (Fonagy, 2003).

CENTRAL THEORETICAL CONSTRUCTS

Attachment as a Behavioral System

Attachment behavior is defined as "any form of behavior that results in a person attaining or maintaining proximity to some other clearly identified individual who is conceived as better able to cope with the world" (Bowlby, 1988, p. 27). It is most apparent during childhood, but it can be observed throughout the life cycle, and especially when an individual, whether young or old, is frightened, injured, distressed, fatigued, or ill. Bowlby (1969) emphasized the survival value of attachment in its provision of protection and safety, and he viewed this as the biological function of attachment behavior. When attachment behavior is adequately responded to, the individual's subjective experience is one of emotional security. Attachment behaviors were considered by Bowlby to be part of a behavioral system, a concept that he drew from ethology. A behavioral system involves inherent motivation and is distinct from any other motivation or need. It explains why feeding is not causally linked to attachment, and also why children become attached to their abusive caregivers (Bowlby, as cited in Cassidy, 1999; Fonagy, 2001).

During the first years of life, attachment behaviors become directed toward a specific person or a small number of persons (attachment figures) who care for the child, usually parents. Attachment behaviors in infants and young children include clinging to caregivers when frightened, protesting caregivers' departure, and greeting and following caregivers after an absence. Thus, any behaviors that increase the probability of caregivers' proximity and availability are deemed attachment behaviors. When children's attachment behaviors are adequately responded to, they move freely away from caregivers and explore the environment, suggesting that the attachment behavior system operates in balance and interdependently with the exploratory behavioral system (Bowlby, 1988; Grossmann, Grossmann, & Zimmermann, 1999).

Adults, especially when ill, fatigued, or overwhelmed by life events or adverse circumstances, also seek proximity to an attachment figure, a person who is often a sexual partner as well (West & Sheldon-Keller, 1994). However, their motivation or goal is the same as that of children, to attain or reestablish a sense of emotional security.

Secure Base

A central premise is that sensitive, responsive caregivers provide emotionally nurturing relationship experiences that establish for infants and small children a secure base from which they can explore both the material and interpersonal world, and from which they can expand their mastery of the environment and freely apply their abilities. In time, the child is no longer wholly dependent on the physical presence of caregivers but can be reassured and comforted by the thought or memory of them, the child's internal representation of himself or herself in relation to a caregiver, or what Bowlby referred to as an internal working model.

Developmental Pathways

Bowlby did not view the developmental process as a sequence or progression of stages suggested by some theorists (Mahler, Pine, & Bergman, 1975, for example), but viewed early attachment as initiating pathways that increase the probability of certain developmental outcomes (Sroufe, 1997). Thus, infants are seen as having a variety of possible ways of developing, depending on the interactions between them and their caregivers and other aspects of the environment. The implication is that there are many pathways that lead to mental health and adaptive functioning, as well as many routes to maladaptive outcomes. Development, then, is the joint product of developmental history and current circumstances and experiences, not either alone (Sroufe, Carlson, Levy, & Egeland, 1999).

Internal Working Models: A Representational System Underlying Attachment

Bowlby noted that patterns of attachment, once formed, tend to endure (Ainsworth, 1989; Bowlby, 1980; Bretherton & Munholland, 1999; Sable, 1992). Integrating ideas from psychoanalysis and cognitive psychology, he postulated that, based on their subjective interactive experiences with parents or caregivers, children develop inner representational models of themselves and others that include both cognitive and affective aspects. These models then guide feelings about self and others, expectations of self and others, and behavior in relationships with others. These inner models, reflecting the quality of early attachment experiences, are largely unconscious and consequently do not change easily, but can be revised and updated in response to experiences that do not support a current working model. Both positive and negative experiences can result in change, with adverse experience, if severe or cumulative enough, resulting in an insecure working model despite earlier experiences that were generally positive and generated a sense of security (Steele, 2003). However, longitudinal research has shown that an early secure working model of attachment is a protective factor with respect to later difficulties; that is, individuals assessed as securely attached to caregivers in the first 2 years of life demonstrate more resilience and are less vulnerable to the effects of later stressful experience (Sroufe, 2005).

Attachment Classification: Children

Bowlby (1969) emphasized that caregiver behavior and response determines the development of predictable patterns of attachment in the child. The earliest observable patterns are behavioral, and are the first manifestations of what will become representations or internal working models of attachment that will guide the individual's feelings, thoughts, and expectations in later relationships (Bretherton & Munholland, 1999). These different patterns of attachment also reflect differences in an individual's degree of access to or awareness of thoughts, feelings, and memories, and access is based on the thoughts, feelings, and experiences that are recognized and allowed expression within the child–caregiver relationship (Slade, 1999a).

Three decades of empirical research has yielded both measures and classification systems for these patterns of attachment that reflect the quality of early caregiving experiences. A pioneer in attachment research, Mary Ainsworth, a Canadian-born psychologist who worked with Bowlby, developed the Strange Situation Protocol, which has been referred to as the "Rosetta stone" of infancy research (Karen, 1990). It is a laboratory procedure designed originally to assess the effect of maternal absence on 12-month-old infant exploration, but the focus of attention shifted to the infant's reunion behaviors following brief separations from the mother as these behaviors seemed to best reflect the quality of the relationship. Employing close study of videotapes of the child's behavior in the Strange Situation, Ainsworth and her colleagues identified three patterns of attachment: secure, insecure-avoidant, and insecure-ambivalent (Ainsworth, Blehar, Waters, & Wall, 1978). In further research, Mary Main and her colleagues identified a fourth pattern and classification group called disorganized (Main & Solomon, 1990). The separations and reunions between infant and parent in the Strange Situation have been described as a procedure for observing infants' internal working models in action (Fonagy & Target, 2003).

The infants and toddlers assessed in the Strange Situation as securely attached typically explore the unfamiliar playroom in the presence of the caregiver but become distressed during the caregiver's brief absence and anxious in the presence of a stranger during the separation. However, they immediately seek contact with the parent at the point of reunion, are easily reassured and comforted by the contact, and quickly return to their exploration.

Those children who explore the new environment without checking to be certain of their mother's presence, and who appear not to be affected when their parent leaves the room, are classified as insecure-avoidant. They do not seek proximity and often avoid looking at the parent following the separation, and appear not to prefer her/him any more than the stranger. Avoidant children are thought to minimize the expression of their attachment needs and suppress their emotions and feelings of distress as a coping strategy or adaptation to caregiving patterns that involve rejection, or a lack of recognition or dismissal of affective signals.

The third group of children, assessed as insecure-ambivalent, tend to cling to their parents, seem to be afraid to explore the room, are usually highly distressed and agitated by the separation, and are not reassured and comforted by the reunion. These children tend to be hypervigilant, displaying heightened or exaggerated expressions of attachment need and emotion that reflect an adaptation to inconsistent or unpredictable parenting, and a strategy to elicit more responsive care (Ainsworth & Eichberg, 1991).

A fourth group displays disorganized/disoriented behavior and was identified following the study of children who were originally considered "unclassifiable" in the original three-pattern classification. Main (1996) noted that most of these infants

> exhibited a diverse array of anomalous or conflicted or contradictory behaviors in the parent's presence, as evidenced, for example, in rocking on hands and knees with face averted after an abortive approach; freezing all movement, arms in the air, with a trance-like expression; moving away from the parent to lean on the wall when frightened; and rising to meet the parent then falling prone. (p. 239)

Research suggests that for these children, the caregiver appears frightened or her behavior is frightening to the child as in situations of parental abuse or dissociated behavior, for example. Thus, the caregiver is at the same time a source of both fear and safety, and the arousal of attachment needs and behaviors evokes strong conflicting motivations and feelings for the child (Main, 1995; Main & Hesse, 1990). Disorganization in children has also been associated with disturbances or disruptions in parental affective communications such as withdrawal, role-confused and negative-intrusive responses, as well as failures to respond to the child's clear emotional signals, particularly fear and high levels of distress (Lyons-Ruth et al., 1999; Lyons-Ruth et al., 2003).

These patterns of attachment tend to be stable, with secure children at 12 months tending to be secure when assessed years later, and insecure children tending to remain insecure. However, the research evidence concerning long-term stability is mixed, with continuity or change over time likely depending on important family circumstances that have a mediating influence (Thompson, 1999). In general, stability has been found to be lower in high-risk populations where major changes in family functioning are more common (Solomon & George, 1999). At the same time, stability in the disorganized classification has been relatively high (Lyons-Ruth, Repacholi, McLeod, & Silver, 1991).

Attachment patterns are associated with later social and emotional development and mental health indicators. Children classified as secure in the Strange Situation have been found several years later to be more socially competent, more empathic, and happier than children rated in one of the insecure categories (Main & Weston, 1981). Support for Bowlby's (1973) hypothesis that secure attachment was the basis for self-reliance has been found in longitudinal research, with children having avoidant and ambivalent histories exhibiting more dependent behaviors and responses (Sroufe, 1996). Similar findings with respect to the capacity for emotion regulation will be discussed later in the chapter. It is important to note that the organized patterns of avoidant and ambivalent insecure attachment are not viewed as problematic in themselves, but as a significant core of early development that is a risk factor for later problems. On the other hand, early attachment disorganization by itself is considered a strong predictor of later disturbance (Sroufe, 2005).

Attachment Classification: Adults

Taking this research further, Mary Main and her colleagues developed the Adult Attachment Interview (AAI; George, Kaplan, & Main, 1996), a measure of adult attachment considered the gold standard among measures. The AAI, also used with adolescents in modified forms, assesses an individual's "state of mind in respect to attachment," a concept that is synonymous with that of the internal working model of attachment. The AAI is an audiotaped, semistructured interview that asks the individual to describe childhood relationships with parents and to provide specific biographical episodes that support more general descriptions. The interviewer asks directly about experiences of rejection; being upset, ill, and hurt; and experiences of loss, abuse, and separation. The individual is also asked to reflect on and evaluate the effects of early experiences on his or her development. The interview protocol and technique has been described by the authors as "surprising the unconscious" as it quickly taps into sensitive issues. Verbatim transcriptions of the interview are studied carefully and rated on a number of variables, of which the coherence of the discourse and narrative is the most significant.

Main and others (see van IJzendoorn, 1995) have found that parents of securely attached children tend to value attachment relationships, acknowledge their need for close connections to others, and are able to discuss their experiences in a thoughtful, reflective, and coherent way. Even when their childhood experiences were painful and abusive, these parents demonstrate that they have been able to think about what happened, make some sense or meaning of their experiences, and talk about them coherently. In addition, their portrayal of negative experiences in relation to their parents is often implicitly forgiving (Hesse, 1999). The AAI classification system labels such adults as "autonomous" (free to evaluate attachment relationships).

Parents of children judged "insecure-avoidant" in the Strange Situation tend to have difficulty recalling the events of childhood and/or they dismiss or devalue childhood events in terms of their current impact on their personalities. The narratives produced by these parents usually reflect a claim to strength, normalcy, and independence, and lack coherence because biographical details do not support or may actually contradict these claims. They are classified as "dismissing" of attachment. This classification is assigned to individuals whose state of mind seems to indicate an attempt to limit the influence of attachment relationships on thought, feeling, or daily life (Hesse, 1999).

Parents of "insecure-ambivalent" children tend to produce long, confusing narratives that reflect mental entanglement, passivity of thought and overtly vague expressions and descriptions of experience, or unresolved anger with their own parents and/or difficulty in coherently describing attachment-related experiences. Their discussion of experiences does not seem fruitful, objective, or incisive. These adults are classified as "preoccupied" with or by early attachments.

Finally, the AAIs of parents of children judged "disorganized" in the Strange Situation are significantly more likely than other parents to be classified as "unresolved" with respect to loss or trauma because of "lapses in the monitoring of reasoning or discourse, or reports of extreme reactions during discussion of these events" (Main, personal communication, 1994). These discourse/reasoning lapses are considered to be suggestive of temporary lapses in consciousness or memory, apparent disruption by normally dissociated memory or beliefs, or absorptions that involve memory evoked by the discussion of traumatic experiences (Hesse, 1999; Hesse & Main, 1999).

Early attachment research with both children and adults focused primarily on nonclinical samples, but samples are increasingly being drawn from clinical populations. This broader focus has led to more attention to the disorganized infant category and the unresolved adult category. Children classified as disorganized have the highest risk for later mental disorder (Lyons-Ruth, 1996; Main, 1996; Ogawa, Sroufe, Weinfield, Carlson, & Egeland, 1997), and in adult clinical samples, the unresolved (in terms of loss or trauma) category is much more highly represented than in nonclinical samples. Some studies have also suggested that a subgroup of the preoccupied category is associated with the diagnosis of borderline personality disorder (Fonagy et al., 1996; Patrick, Hobson, Castle, Howard, & Maughan, 1994).

Intergenerational Transmission of Attachment Patterns

Studies using the Strange Situation and the Adult Attachment Interview have provided support for the intergenerational transmission of attachment patterns. These studies have also supported Bowlby's concept of internal working models of self, other, and attachment relationships as the means by which attachment experiences are internalized and come to guide feelings, expectations, and behavior in significant relationships, including parents' relationships with their children. Several studies have shown that the attachment classification of a child at 12 months can be reliably predicted from the assessment of the mother's attachment pattern prior to the child's birth (Hesse, 1999).

Attachment theory and research has emphasized the role of caregiver sensitivity in the intergenerational transmission of attachment patterns, and evidence has been provided for links between classification on the AAI in parents and ratings of sensitive and responsive behavior in relation to their infants or children (Crowell & Feldman, 1988; Grossmann, Grossmann, Spangler, Suess, & Unzar, 1985; Ward & Carlson, 1995). At the same time, researchers have noted that concordance found in studies between parent and child attachment has been modest. It has been found predominantly for parents classified as secure, but has been much lower for dyads when the child is judged insecure, particularly if the parent has been assessed as unresolved for loss (George & Solomon, 1999).

In an analysis of a number of studies investigating concordance (van IJzendoorn, 1995), the existence of a "transmission gap" was suggested, indicating that full understanding of the mechanisms involved in the intergenerational transmission process was lacking. This finding was based on evidence that behavioral measures of sensitivity in parents did not account adequately for the strong link between the AAI and the Strange Situation (Grienenberger, Kelly, & Slade, 2005; Hesse, 1999). However, more recent research has found evidence that the "transmission gap" may be closing. These findings will be discussed in the next section.

Mentalization, Reflective Function, and Affect Regulation

In the past decade, Fonagy and his colleagues have advanced attachment theory with the introduction of the constructs of mentalization and reflective function, and with hypotheses about how these constructs relate to the development of affect regulation (Fonagy, Gergely, Jurist, & Target, 2002; Fonagy et al., 1995; Fonagy & Target, 1997). Mentalization refers to the capacity to understand one's own behavior and that of others in terms of underlying mental states (thoughts, feelings, intentions, desires, beliefs), a capacity that is usually acquired in the context of the earliest attachment relationships. This same capacity is operationalized for research as reflective function, a term that refers to the manifestation of the capacity to mentalize in speech and conversation (Fonagy & Target, 2003).

Mentalization is believed to begin with the infant's awareness of emotions by means of the caregiver's responses. Both clinical and research evidence demonstrate that infants' experiences of themselves as having a mind, a psychological self, and emotions is not a genetic given. It is a development that evolves from infancy through childhood and depends on an interactive process between caregiver(s) and child that is described as natural, mundane, not conscious, and exercised by parents in different ways. Children's perceptions of their own mental states develop from observation of the mental world of their caregivers. It is caregivers' abilities to hold in their own minds a representation of their child as having feelings, desires, and intentions that allows the child to discover his or her own mental states; that is, when a child observes that his or her parents' gestures, responses, and words indicate that the parents view the child as having feelings, desires, and intentions, this allows the child to begin to recognize them in him or herself.

This is the beginning of self-organization and self-understanding, as well as an understanding of others as having internal experiences. In healthy development, it leads to the recognition that one's own ideas and feelings do not define those of another, and what is subjectively real for oneself is not necessarily the subjective experience of someone else (Slade, 2005).

The capacity to mentalize also includes parents' abilities to mirror the affect of their child, using facial expressions and voice tones to represent the feelings that the parents assume the child is experiencing (Fonagy et al., 2002). This affective mirroring has the effect of calming and soothing the child (i.e., it regulates the child's affect). Over the course of repeated mirroring interactions, children learn that they can stimulate a predictable affect-regulating response from their caregivers, and in time come to experience themselves as "self-regulating agents." This experience with external affect regulation in combination with maturation ultimately enables children to represent their own emotions, understand them, and modulate them without external assistance.

Fonagy and colleagues (2002) also report evidence suggesting that after the child has developed the capacity to mentalize, a more sophisticated form of affect regulation is available, one that involves being able to think about the causes and consequences of one's own emotional states and to also make sense of others' emotional states. The theory suggests that when caregivers, for whatever reason, are not able to adequately engage with the child in this affective mirroring, the child's ability to understand and regulate his or her own affective experience will be compromised. In addition, the developing child's ability to understand what others might be feeling or to make sense of his or her feelings is restricted.

Research has supported the link between quality of attachment and affect regulation. In preschool and summer camp contexts, teachers who were blind to children's attachment classifications were more likely to rate secure children (compared to insecure children) as "exuberant on the playground but contained and attentive during classroom structured activities" (Sroufe, 2005, p. 357). Secure children were also more likely to be perceived as flexible, curious, and able to bounce back after stress, and less likely to become anxious when the environment was unpredictable (Sroufe, 2005).

Research also supports the idea that the capacity to mentalize is a crucial mechanism in the intergenerational transmission of attachment organization. A conceptual framework that puts mentalization at the center of intergenerational transmission promises better explanation than one that posits sensitive caregiving behavior as the means of transmission. A study assessing the quality of parent–infant affective communication, which is believed to be an observable expression of mentalizing capacity, provided evidence for its mediating role in the relation between a measure of parents' reflective functioning and infant attachment (Grienenberger et al., 2005). In addition, there has been evidence for a significant relationship between adult attachment assessed on the AAI and parental reflective functioning, as well as for parental reflective functioning and infant attachment (Slade, Grienenberger, Bernbach, Levy, & Locker, 2005). Our knowledge, therefore, of what constitutes secure (and insecure) attachment and how it is transmitted from one generation to the next has been expanded and refined by the development of the constructs of mentalization and reflective function and the empirical support for their critical role in development.

PHASES OF HELPING

The development of the Adult Attachment Interview with its emphasis on the structure and coherence of the narrative has been credited with providing an essential link between attachment research and psychotherapy (Holmes, 2001; Slade, 1999a). It is argued that this emphasis is similar to what clinicians have always understood good clinical listening to require: "listening for changes in voice; for contradictions, lapses, irrelevancies, and breakdowns in meaning; and for the subtle ongoing disruptions and fluctuations in the structure and organization of discourse" (Slade, 1999a, p. 582). In addition, the identification of reflective function has greatly facilitated clinicians' recognition of the usefulness of attachment theory for psychotherapy. Holmes (2001) argued that the empirical support for the association of secure attachment and reflective function is an endorsement of psychotherapy, because increasing reflective function or capacity to mentalize is one of the main functions of psychotherapy.

Although attachment organization does not explain all aspects of human experience, it offers a way of thinking about clients and a way of understanding the dynamics of the therapeutic relationship that can guide the therapist's interventions (Slade, 1999a). Holmes (2001) argued that attachment theory provides a theoretical base for "the story-telling, story-listening and story-understanding that form the heart of psychotherapy sessions" (p. 16).

Engagement

The task for therapists in the engagement phase is to establish themselves as a secure base from which clients can explore painful aspects of their lives and find new ways of understanding themselves and others. If therapists are not able to provide clients with some sense of security, therapy cannot even begin (Bowlby, 1988).

Attachment theory guides therapists to use different strategies to engage clients with different attachment styles. Clients who primarily use avoidant/dismissing strategies will be cautious, and therapists need to respect this and allow such clients to develop trust at their own pace (Holmes, 2001; Slade 1999a). Clients with a primarily ambivalent/

preoccupied strategy readily communicate that they value the therapy, but the "inability to collaborate with and thus take in the therapist's words and support is what makes therapy with such individuals so difficult" (Slade, 1999a, p. 587). Progress with these clients often requires emotional availability over a long period of time and the ability to tolerate clients' attempts to have the therapist take care of them. These are individuals whose experiences have taught them that attachment needs must be expressed strongly to make certain that caregivers will respond (Slade, 1999a).

Disorganized/unresolved clients may miss sessions or stop attending. Holmes (2001) argued that therapists should reach out to such clients by writing, telephoning, or even visiting them in their homes. With very disturbed clients, including those with personality disorders, therapists need to work very hard at establishing the therapeutic alliance. He also advocates the use of extended assessment, pretherapy preparation, clear boundaries, and therapeutic contracts when working with these clients.

Data Collection/Assessment and Intervention

In attachment-informed treatment, assessment and intervention are not easily separated. Initial sessions are normally used to gather information about the presenting problem and the client's history, but assessment is ongoing and continually informs the therapist's interventions. During the first and subsequent interviews, attachment-informed therapists will attend as much to the style used by clients to tell their stories as to the content of the story; therapists will also pay attention to their own emotional responses to the way clients present (Holmes, 2001). This information, in combination with knowledge of attachment patterns, will guide therapists' formulations of clients' experiences and their intervention strategies.

It should be noted that in clinical practice, clients do not always fall neatly into the categories defined by the AAI coding procedure. Attachment patterns or representations can be viewed as being on a continuum. At one end are styles that involve "deactivating" attachment strategies associated with the avoidant/dismissing classifications, and at the other end are styles associated with the "hyperactivating" strategies associated with ambivalent/preoccupied classifications. In the middle are styles that reflect a balance in the use of attachment strategies and that are associated with the secure classification (Slade, 1999a). The categories that are defined by the AAI can be seen as prototypes that serve to guide one's thinking but should not be expected to always translate exactly to clients seen in clinical practice.

Clients who display avoidant/dismissing forms of attachment are seen to have rigid, inflexible stories that function to restrict emotional expression because experience has taught them such expression leads to rejection. These stories lack coherence in that events that would be expected to evoke pain are minimized, or relationships are described as "good" or "fine" when the evidence is not convincing. Attachment theory guides the therapist "to find ways into the patient's affective experience and memory" (Slade, 1999a, p. 586) and to encourage the client to deconstruct the rigid story and find a narrative that allows for a greater range of emotional expression and a more complex perspective.

Clients with ambivalent/preoccupied attachment organization seem overwhelmed by intense feelings, their discourse tends to be rambling and unstructured, and they may have difficulty coming to the point. The therapist's task with these clients is to help them modulate their intense affect and construct narratives that provide structure and organization to their ways of thinking about themselves and others.

Clients who are disorganized/unresolved with respect to loss or trauma can be particularly challenging. As noted earlier, this classification is much more highly represented in clinical samples than in nonclinical samples. Holmes (2001) stressed the importance of timing and sequencing with these clients and the importance of first establishing a secure base and strong alliance before any form of interpretation, challenge, or confrontation.

Holmes (2001) argued that attachment research's identification of the importance of metacognitive monitoring and mentalization or "thinking about thinking" for secure attachment can guide clinical work with disorganized clients. The therapist, he advised, must introduce a "conversation about conversation" (Holmes, 2004, p. 188) to help the client become aware of "the possibility of a shared language of intimacy" (p. 189). Talking about talking also helps the therapist involve the client in a discussion of the dilemma that the therapist frequently experiences when working with the disorganized client. This dilemma has to do with the fact that talking about trauma and abuse usually reduces symptoms and distress in the long run, but the process of talking about trauma also involves much fear and shame and may be experienced by the client as once again being abused and retraumatized.

Here again, for therapists, a well-developed capacity to reflect on their own emotional responses is crucial because the client's anguished discourse and clinging or angry behavior evokes emotional states in therapists similar to those experienced by clients. Skilled therapists use their awareness of their own feelings and their own reflective function to understand at a deep level what the client is experiencing. This capacity to reflect on one's own and others' mental states allows the therapist to more accurately appreciate the client's dilemma and communicate with the client more empathically.

In general, the goal for attachment-informed psychotherapy is to help clients establish a secure base as an internal representation, and in the form of satisfying relationships. When the therapist is able to provide the responsiveness, attunement, and the "holding" of the painful emotions that tend to overwhelm the client, the client experiences this essential "secure base" and over time internalizes it. The old and formerly unconscious perceptions and expectations of self and others are modified, and clients begin to think, feel, and act in more adaptive ways, suggesting healthy changes in their internal working models of attachment.

Termination

Attachment theory's focus on the damaging effects of unresolved losses and separations means that an attachment-informed therapist encourages the client to express thoughts and feelings about the ending of the therapy and encourages the client to recognize that the responses evoked by this ending may shed light on his or her reactions to earlier losses and separations.

Attachment theory alerts therapists to be skeptical of models that advocate brief interventions with clients who present with pervasive and long-standing difficulties in interpersonal relationships. The theory implies that brief interventions can be helpful for many individuals, especially those who have experienced secure attachment relationships and who are dealing with situational and life transitional issues. But, with clients who have experienced significant losses in early life, rejection of attachment behaviors by primary caretakers, and experiences of abuse and neglect and other traumatic experiences that preclude the construction of secure working models of relationships, attachment theory would predict that longer term therapy, or at least the availability of a therapist or an agency over an extended period, would almost always be required. Slade (1999a) stated, "The brief psychotherapies are unlikely to result in the 'reworking' of representational models, or in changing the quality of attachment representations" (p. 590).

On the other hand, Holmes (2001) has developed Brief Attachment-Based Intervention (BABI), which is described as integrating Rogerian, dynamic, and cognitive-behavioral techniques. It was developed to provide a therapy that is explicitly based on attachment theory and to contribute to the demand for more evidence-based treatments. Holmes characterized BABI as time limited, collaborative, and having a strong emphasis on formulation. Therapists using this approach have a structured plan for each session (to which the client has agreed), provide opportunities for the client to express spontaneous themes, and assign homework between sessions. The general principle is that the therapist follows the client's lead because the goal is to be responsive to the client. To increase their ability to be responsive to the client, therapists using BABI receive regular supervision.

APPLICATION TO FAMILY AND GROUP WORK

Family Work

Attachment theory can be seen as providing a framework that can integrate a number of ways of working with families. Byng-Hall (1991) argued that attachment theory suggests the concept of a secure family base, which can be seen as an overall aim or superordinate goal of family therapy. Once achieved, this allows the family to explore new solutions to family problems both during and after therapy. An attachment framework allows for a variety of techniques to be used in the pursuit of more specific goals, but the family therapist is required to model and reinforce behavior and attitudes that increase the sense of security in the family for all family members. Knowledge of insecure attachment dynamics can also help family therapists to positively reframe behavior that on the surface appears to be hostile or controlling (Byng-Hall, 1995).

A variety of family therapists and family researchers have been working toward integration of attachment theory and family systems theory (Erdman & Caffery, 2003). For example, Johnson and Best (2003) described Emotionally Focused Couples Therapy (EFT), a brief, empirically validated intervention that "views close relationships from the perspective of attachment theory and integrates systemic and experiential interventions" (p. 165). They argued that attachment theory extends the systemic perspective and leads couples therapists to understand interactional patterns "in the context of needs for contact, comfort and security that have been laid down in the process of evolution and have protected men and women from the dangers and trauma of isolation" (p. 168).

Group Work

An excellent example of group work based on attachment theory is provided by Egeland and Erikson (1993) and Erikson et al. (1992). These authors described a group in which young, high-risk mothers were brought together for biweekly group sessions from the time their babies were born until the children were 1 year old. This group work approach assumed that therapy can affect internal working models in two ways: (a) through insight, in which the parent becomes conscious of thoughts and attitudes that were previously unconscious; and (b) through the therapeutic relationship itself, in which the "therapist maintains a healthy, supportive alliance with the parent, proving to the parent that such relationships are possible" (Erickson et al., 1992, p. 501).

Flores (2001) argued that attachment theory can be used in combination with self psychology and perspectives from the 12-step abstinence-based models to understand why individuals with substance abuse disorders usually respond well to group treatment. He suggested that addiction is a kind of attachment disorder and that individuals use substances as a substitute for satisfying relationships with others. The highs provided by the substance come to compensate for the pain associated with unmet attachment needs. Flores explained that an ongoing therapy group provided at the optimal time in the treatment of addiction can create the capacity for reciprocal attachment and mutually satisfying relationships, which the individual must achieve in order to give up the substances that have become his or her "secure base." The group must become an "attachment object" so that the group therapy can be "a way of eliciting, exploring, integrating, and modifying attachment styles represented within a person's internal working model" (p. 75). He wrote that group treatment is more effective than individual treatment because the group dilutes the intensity of the shame, hostility, and ambivalence that often floods the client in a one-to-one setting. Here again, the response of the group leader is critical to the development of a group that can serve the secure base function. Furthermore, therapists who can reflect on their own affect and "absorb anger" without expressing hostility are essential.

COMPATIBILITY WITH THE GENERALIST-ECLECTIC APPROACH

The reader will recognize that attachment theory is very compatible with the generalist-eclectic framework for direct social work practice. Holmes (1993b) wrote that attachment theory should not be seen as simply another form of psychotherapy, but rather as having "*defining features that are relevant to therapy generally* [italics added]—individual, group, family . . ." (p. 151). With its conceptualization of the therapist as a "trusted companion" (Bowlby, 1988) who provides a secure base from which to explore problems, attachment theory shares with the generalist-eclectic framework a strong emphasis on the development and maintenance of the worker–client relationship. Also, attachment theorists recognize that there are many ways to provide a secure base; however, recent advances in attachment theory involving the concepts of mentalization and reflective function imply that therapists need to have well-developed abilities to reflect on their own mental/emotional states and those of others in order to help clients develop this capacity.

Bowlby (1988) explicitly stated that the therapeutic stance he advocated was "You know, you tell me" rather than "I know, I'll tell you" (p. 151). This defines his approach as collaborative rather than expert oriented. Holmes (2001) stressed the need for the therapist to allow the client to lead, noting that responsiveness is essential to providing a secure base. The therapist's role is to use his or her own feelings and perceptions to help the client create a more coherent narrative and to stimulate consideration of new ways of understanding his or her life story. The concept of potentially innumerable developmental pathways also supports a view of individuals that recognizes the uniqueness, potential resilience, and strengths of each.

Attachment theory is also compatible with a systemic perspective and a holistic, multilevel assessment. It was Bowlby's criticism of previous theories' rigidity, and lack of attention to environmental factors, that spurred the development of the theory. Sable (1995b) has been a strong advocate of the usefulness of attachment theory in social work practice and its compatibility with the biopsychosocial perspective of systems thinking. Similarly, Egeland (1998), whose longitudinal studies of high-risk families have supported the tenets of attachment theory, argued for the use of a comprehensive ecological model that recognizes that poverty and other social stressors have a significant impact on parents' ability to provide a secure base for their children. Following this line of thinking, Holmes (2004) has argued that borderline personality disorder is best viewed as a social/psychological construct related to failures of society to care for its members:

> Social configurations such as endemic racism create fear in victimized minorities, and that fear transmits itself via attachment relationships to oppressed people's children. Similarly, the salience of absent or abusive fathers in the life-histories of people diagnosed as suffering from BPD cannot, and should not, be seen merely at the level of individual psychology. The social seedbed for these negative male roles—colonialism and consequent immigration, educational disadvantage, the move from manufacturing to a service economy—needs also to be acknowledged, and ultimately, worked with in increasing reflexive function of BPD sufferers not just in their own psychology, but consciousness of choices and dilemmas faced by their progenitors in previous generations. (p. 184)

With regard to eclecticism, many clinicians have recognized that attachment theory can be integrated with concepts from other models of therapy. As noted previously, attachment theory is being integrated with systems theory in the field of family therapy, and Holmes's Brief Attachment-Based Intervention integrates techniques from other models. McMillen (1992) noted that attachment theory "can easily be integrated into several approaches to clinical [social work] practice" (p. 211), and he identified these as psychosocial therapy, self psychology, cognitive therapy, and family therapy. Many writers (Holmes, 1993a; McMillen, 1992; Rutter, 1995) have commented on the compatibility of attachment theory with cognitive-behavioral techniques in view of the similarities in the concepts of internal working models, basic assumptions, and cognitive schemata.

Attachment and narrative theories can also be productively integrated (Fish, 1996; Holmes, 1993b; Holmes, 2001). Holmes (1993b) conceptualized psychotherapy as a process where the therapist and client work together on a "tentative and disjointed" story brought by the client until a more "coherent and satisfying narrative emerges" (p. 158). He explained, "Out of narrative comes meaning—the 'broken line' of insecure attachment is replaced by a sense of continuity, an inner story which enables new experience to be explored, with the confidence that it can be coped with and assimilated" (Holmes, 1993b, p. 158).

CRITIQUE

Strengths

The greatest strength of attachment theory is the growing empirical support for its tenets (Holmes, 2001; McMillen, 1992; Paterson & Moran, 1988). The ideas that the ability to be an adequate parent and the ability to relate to others in satisfying ways are transmitted from one generation to another through experiences beginning in early life is no longer just a hypothesis; it has reached the status of a well-supported proposition. Furthermore, we have clearer understandings of the mechanisms for this transmission, and therefore more specific ideas about how to intervene with high-risk families.

A second strength is that attachment theory has made clearer the relationship between certain kinds of early experiences with caregivers and attachment strategies commonly seen in adult clients. This knowledge can also help our ability to understand and respond empathically to difficult clients whose behaviors are often confusing, upsetting, and distancing.

A third strength is the accessibility of attachment theory. "Ideas are expressed simply and directly, in everyday language and without traditional jargon" (Sable, 1995b, p. 34). Attachment theory retains many of the strengths of other relational theories (e.g., viewing relationship as the crucial factor and recognizing the power of the unconscious and internalized ideas) without the difficult terminology. Such accessibility in language reflects the "experience-near" quality of the concepts of attachment theory, which likely contributes to workers' comfort with the theory and their ability to be responsive to the client (Sable, 1992). Other strengths of this theory referred to earlier include a focus on normalcy versus pathology, an acknowledgment of the influence of environmental factors, and recognition of the prime importance of the worker-client relationship.

Weaknesses

Attachment theory has been criticized for insufficiently acknowledging the role in human development of temperament, racism, poverty, social class, and other environmental conditions; it has also been argued that the theory puts too much importance on the relationship between mother and child and consequently supports "mother blaming" ideologies (Birns, 1999). In response to studies reporting different distributions of attachment classifications across cultures using the Strange Situation Protocol, some authors (e.g., Levene & Miller, as cited in Bolen, 2000) have also questioned whether the Strange Situation Protocol is a valid measure of attachment in cultures markedly different from the middle-class American experience.

We believe that many of these criticisms focus on a narrow view of the theory and fail to take into account the evolution of the theory since Bowlby first articulated it. Current attachment researchers recognize that there is some overlap across behavioral domains associated with attachment and temperament, but they argue that the two domains reflect distinct constructs, and that the existing evidence does not support strong conclusions about the relationship between the two (Vaughn & Bost, 1999). Attachment researchers also recognize that fathers and other caregivers can be as important as mothers in the role of attachment figure and that a wide variety of environmental conditions that affect the well-being of caregivers affect the quality of attachment between caregivers and children in important ways. Van IJzendoorn and Sagi (1999) reviewed attachment studies conducted in non-Western cultures including Africa, China, Japan, and Israel and concluded that the three major attachment classifications have been found in every culture, and, in all of the studies, the majority of infants were classified as securely attached. The evidence suggests that attachment behavior interacts with cultural context to produce "culture-specific behavioral markers of a universal and normative phenomenon" (van IJzendoorn & Sagi, 1999, p. 727). Future research needs to focus more on this interaction and on the specific ways in which secure and insecure attachment are manifested across cultures (Bolen, 2000).

In terms of application to social work practice, a decade ago one might have argued that attachment theory lacked specific guidelines and techniques for therapy (Holmes, 1993a). This situation has changed in recent years, and Holmes's Brief Attachment-Based Intervention is only one example of clearer guidelines for the application of the theory to practice. The relative lack of structured techniques can also be construed as a strength of attachment-informed clinical practice. Like a good parent, it provides a firm enough framework to help therapists feel secure in the basic assumptions and approach to clients, but permits autonomy and flexibility in the specific implementation of therapy with different clients.

Populations Most Suited to Attachment Theory

Attachment theory has something to contribute to the understanding of all clients. The most obvious populations to which attachment theory can be applied are those of all ages dealing with bereavement and loss, and children who, for whatever reason, have been separated from parents, or have experienced maltreatment (Howe, Brandon, Hinings, & Schofield, 1999; McMillen, 1992). Recent research has led to increasingly sophisticated assessment models for intervening with children who display controlling attachment behavior, which is believed to develop in response to unresolved/disorganized attachment in their parents (e.g., Vallance, 2005).

Attachment theory has also been recognized as useful in working with adults coping with the negative sequelae of childhood abuse, including posttraumatic stress disorder (PTSD; Sable, 1995a), complex PTSD (Herman, 1992), and dissociative disorders. Examples include the development of an attachment framework for working with complex trauma (Pearlman & Courtois, 2005) and a model based on the hypothesis that therapy for this population should focus on developing internal working models of protection (Thomas, 2003). Sable, a social worker, has also described the application of attachment theory to borderline personality disorder (Sable, 1997) and anxiety and agoraphobia (Sable, 1991).

CASE EXAMPLE

The following case example illustrates how attachment theory helps the therapist to challenge the tendency of many adult clients to label as weakness or pathology their human need to have supportive and nurturing relationships. It is also an example of how the therapist allows the client to use her or him as a secure base so that the client can explore her or his feelings, thoughts, and attitudes, both present and past, and modify those ways of thinking and perceiving that are interfering with positive feelings about self and others.

Virginia was a 25-year-old married woman with no children who sought therapy because of a history of periodic depressive episodes for which she had received short-term cognitive-behavioral treatment on three previous occasions. When depressed, she had suicidal thoughts, had difficulty getting up in the morning, had difficulty concentrating, had little appetite, and felt worthless. When not depressed, she had much energy, worked very hard, and had aspirations to have a successful career in a demanding field. She had always been a good student and had completed a university degree.

Virginia was the second of three children. Her father had worked hard from difficult beginnings to become a successful executive. He was very critical of coworkers and acquaintances that never seemed to meet his high expectations. He was also very disparaging of his wife's "weakness." The client's mother had suffered a number of illnesses during Virginia's childhood, and Virginia felt that her mother had been frustrated by her own inability to pursue a career. She described a good relationship between herself and her father, whom she felt was less demanding with her than with her brothers. She also felt she had a positive relationship with her mother, which she described as one in which they took turns looking after one another.

Virginia acknowledged in the first session that it was hard for her to seek help because she wanted to be independent, and she felt she had failed when she could not pull herself out of the depression. She indicated that her husband was very supportive and understanding. In fact, they had met at a time when she was quite depressed, and he had been very sympathetic and helpful to her whenever she had been "down." Virginia knew that especially when she was depressed, she was very self-critical and that her negative self-statements were irrational. Still, she had not been able to change them.

The therapist pointed out the strength and determination that Virginia was showing by coming for help and by continuing to look for ways to overcome her depression. She also acknowledged how hard it is to get up and go to work when one is depressed and praised Virginia for her efforts to do the things that were likely to help herself, such as seeing her family doctor about antidepressant medication, forcing herself to eat, and getting some exercise. She contracted to see Virginia initially for 10 weekly sessions with the plan to reevaluate the need to continue at that point. She indicated that Virginia could call her between sessions if she felt overwhelmed and needed additional support. The therapist's capacity to reflect on the client's cognitive and emotional experience led her to believe that Virginia would be very reluctant to ask about availability between sessions but would feel reassured if the therapist stated this explicitly. The therapist also explained that her approach was to work with her clients to understand better what past and current experiences had led to thoughts and feelings that were hindering optimal functioning in the present. She encouraged Virginia to talk about whatever was important to her in the sessions.

Early in the treatment, the therapist encouraged Virginia to talk more about her expectations of herself and how she had come to be so critical of herself when she felt her performance was less than stellar. In thinking about this, the client recognized that she had, as a child, decided that she would not be like her mother, and that she would be more like her father—a strong, independent, and successful person. She also identified her mixed feelings about being like her father. She felt sorry for her mother when she thought about her father's attitude toward her, and thought that he had not been fair to her.

Over time, as the therapy conversation went back and forth between current feelings and behavior and past feelings and experiences, Virginia became aware of anger toward both of her parents for what she came to recognize as unrealistic and inappropriate expectations. She recalled that at age 7, when she complained of being picked on at school by older children, her parents asked Virginia to consider how she had contributed to the problem, and told her that she could solve the problem herself. She recognized that she interpreted this as meaning that she was the cause of the problem, and there was something wrong with her if she could not solve it. This insight evoked memories of feelings of great despair in the face of what she now recognized was cruel bullying by bigger and stronger children.

Virginia came to recognize that she only felt acceptable when she perceived herself as solving her own problems and needing no one. This idea had come from many experiences but certainly from both parents, who, with positive intentions, had been trying to encourage self-sufficient behavior in their daughter. The therapist reminded Virginia that all humans need support and care from others, and that this was not a sign of weakness or "dependence." Virginia began to postulate that some part of her rebelled at the internal pressure to constantly be strong and self-sufficient, and the depression might be an unconscious attempt to receive care and nurture from others without consciously acknowledging her need for support. Over time, she began to perceive that in her current life, she actually received very little support when she was not depressed, as her husband's behavior seemed to change to a more critical stance when she was feeling good and being more assertive in her work and home life.

After 3 months of therapy, Virginia was no longer depressed; however, she chose to continue therapy in order to better understand how ways of coping that were adaptive in the past were interfering with healthy and satisfying choices in the present. The therapist saw Virginia on a weekly basis for 10 months, and once monthly for 3 more months. The therapist believed that the support and safety afforded by the therapeutic relationship allowed Virginia over time to modify internal models of self, other, and relationships so that she could more comfortably accept her needs for nurturing and achieve greater intimacy in a reciprocal and respectful relationship with her husband.

SUMMARY

Attachment theory provides the theoretical framework for enormous amounts of research into a wide range of human experiences. This research continues to both support and amplify the basic tenets of the theory and to grow at a phenomenal rate. The theory provides a way of understanding human relationships that is very compatible with the best of social work practice. Attachment theory can be integrated with other perspectives and can guide the use of techniques from a variety of therapeutic models. It is applicable to individual, family, and group interventions. It also has much to offer policies and interventions that aim to prevent mental health problems in future generations.

REFERENCES

Ainsworth, M. D. S. (1989). Attachments beyond infancy. *American Psychologist, 44,* 709–716.

Ainsworth, M. D. S., Blehar, M. C., Waters, E., & Wall, S. (1978). *Patterns of attachment: A psychological study of the Strange Situation.* Hillsdale, NJ: Lawrence Erlbaum.

Ainsworth, M. D. S., & Eichberg, C. G. (1991). Effects on infant-mother attachment of mother's unresolved loss of an attachment figure or other traumatic experience. In P. Marris, J. C. Stevenson-Hinde, & C. Parkes (Eds.), *Attachment across the life cycle* (pp. 160–183). New York: Routledge.

Baradon, T. (2003). Psychotherapeutic work with parents and infants. In V. Green (Ed.), *Emotional development in psychoanalysis, attachment theory and neuroscience* (pp. 129–143). New York: Brunner-Routledge.

Birns, B. (1999). Attachment theory revisited: Challenging conceptual and methodological sacred cows. *Feminism & Psychology, 9,* 10–21.

Bolen, R. M. (2000). Validity of attachment theory. *Trauma, Violence, & Abuse, 1,* 128–153.

Bowlby, J. (1958). The nature of the child's tie to his mother. *Journal of Psycho-Analysis, 39,* 350–373.

Bowlby, J. (1969). *Attachment and loss: Vol. 1. Attachment.* London: Hogarth.

Bowlby, J. (1973). *Attachment and loss: Vol. 2. Separation: Anxiety and anger.* London: Hogarth.

Bowlby, J. (1979). *The making and breaking of affectional bonds.* London: Tavistock.

Bowlby, J. (1980). *Attachment and loss: Vol. 3. Loss: Sadness and depression.* New York: Basic Books.

Bowlby, J. (1988). *A secure base.* New York: Basic Books.

Bretherton, I., & Munholland, K. A. (1999). Internal working models in attachment relationships: A construct revisited. In J. Cassidy & P. R. Shaver (Eds.), *Handbook of attachment: Theory, research, and clinical applications* (pp. 89–111). New York: Guilford.

Byng-Hall, J. (1991). An appreciation of John Bowlby: His significance for family therapy. *Journal of Family Therapy, 13,* 5–16.

Byng-Hall, J. (1995). Creating a secure family base: Some implications of attachment theory for family therapy. *Family Process, 34,* 45–58.

Cassidy, J. (1999). The nature of the child's ties. In J. Cassidy & P. R. Shaver (Eds.), *Handbook of attachment: Theory, research, and clinical applications* (pp. 3–20). New York: Guilford.

Cicchetti, D., & Toth, S. (1995). Child maltreatment and attachment organization: Implications for intervention. In S. Goldberg., R. Muir, & J. Kerr (Eds.), *Attachment theory: Social, developmental, and clinical perspectives* (pp. 279–308). Hillsdale, NJ: The Analytic Press.

Crowell, J. A., & Feldman, S. S. (1988). Mothers' internal models of relationships and children's behavioral and developmental status: A study of mother-child interaction. *Child Development, 59,* 1273–1285.

Egeland, B. R. (1998, October). *The longitudinal study of attachment and psychopathology.* Paper presented at the Second International Conference on Attachment and Psychopathology, Toronto, Ontario, Canada.

Egeland, B. R., & Erickson, M. F. (1993). Attachment theory and findings: Implications for prevention and intervention. In S. Kramer & H. Parens (Eds.), *Prevention in mental health: Now, tomorrow, ever?* (pp. 21–50). Northvale, NJ: Jason Aronson.

Erdman, P., & Caffery, T. (2003). *Attachment and family systems: Conceptual, empirical, and therapeutic relatedness.* New York: Brunner-Routledge.

Erickson, M. F., Korfmacher, J., & Egeland, B. R. (1992). Attachments past and present: Implications for therapeutic intervention with mother-infant dyads. *Development and Psychopathology, 4,* 495–507.

Fairbairn, W. R. D. (1956). A critical evaluation of certain basic psychoanalytical conceptions. *British Journal of Philosophy and Science, 7,* 49–60.

Fish, B. (1996). Clinical implications of attachment narratives. *Clinical Social Work Journal, 24,* 239–253.

Flores, P. J. (2001). Addiction as an attachment disorder: Implications for group therapy. *International Journal of Group Psychotherapy, 51,* 63–81.

Fonagy, P. (2001). *Attachment theory and psychoanalysis.* New York: Other Press.

Fonagy, P. (2003). The interpersonal interpretive mechanism: The confluence of genetics and attachment theory in development. In V. Green (Ed.), *Emotional development in psychoanalysis, attachment theory and neuroscience* (pp. 107–126). New York: Brunner-Routledge.

Fonagy, P., Gergely, G., Jurist, E., & Target, M. (2002). *Affect regulation, mentalization, and the development of the self.* New York: Other Press.

Fonagy, P., Leigh, T., Steele, M., Steele, H., Kennedy, R., Mattoon, G., et al. (1996). The relation of attachment status, psychiatric classification, and response to psychotherapy. *Journal of Consulting and Clinical Psychology, 64,* 22–31.

Fonagy, P., Steele, M., & Steele, H. (1991). Maternal representations of attachment during pregnancy predict the organization of infant-mother attachment at one year of age. *Child Development, 62,* 880–893.

Fonagy, P., Steele, M., Steele, H., Leigh, T., Kennedy, R., Mattoon, G., et al. (1995). Attachment, the reflective self, and borderline states: The predictive specificity of the Adult Attachment Interview and pathological emotional development. In S. Goldberg, R. Muir, & J. Kerr (Eds.), *Attachment theory: Social, developmental, and clinical perspectives* (pp. 233–278). Hillsdale, NJ: The Analytic Press.

Fonagy, P., & Target, M. (1997). Attachment and reflective function: Their role in self-organization. *Development and Psychopathology, 9,* 679–700.

Fonagy, P., & Target, M. (2003). *Psychoanalytic theories: Perspectives from developmental psychopathology.* New York: Brunner-Routledge.

George, C., Kaplan, N., & Main, M. (1996). *Adult Attachment Interview* (3rd ed.). Unpublished manuscript, Department of Psychology, University of California, Berkeley.

George, C., & Solomon, J. (1999). Attachment and caregiving: The caregiving behavioral system. In J. Cassidy & P. R. Shaver (Eds.), *Handbook of attachment: Theory, research, and clinical applications* (pp. 649–670). New York: Guilford.

Green, V. (2003). Emotional development—biological and clinical approaches—towards an integration. In V. Green (Ed.), *Emotional development in psychoanalysis, attachment theory and neuroscience* (pp. 1–20). New York: Brunner-Routledge.

Grienenberger, J., Kelly, K., & Slade, A. (2005). Maternal reflective functioning, mother-infant affective communication, and infant attachment: Exploring the link between mental states and observed caregiving behavior in the intergenerational transmission of attachment. *Attachment & Human Development, 7,* 299–311.

Grossman, K., Grossman, K. E., Spangler, G., Suess, G., & Unzar, L. (1985). Maternal sensitivity and newborn's orientation response as related to quality of attachment in Northern Germany. In I. Bretherton & E. Waters (Eds.), Growing points of attachment theory and research. *Monographs of the Society of Research in Child Development, 50*(1–2, Serial No. 209). Chicago: University of Chicago Press.

Grossman, K. E., Grossman, K., & Zimmerman, P. (1999). A wider view of attachment and exploration: Stability and change during the years of immaturity. In J. Cassidy & P. R. Shaver (Eds.), *Handbook of attachment: Theory, research, and clinical applications* (pp. 760–786). New York: Guilford.

Herman, J. (1992). *Trauma and recovery.* New York: Basic Books.

Hesse, E. (1999). The Adult Attachment Interview: Historical and current perspectives. In J. Cassidy & P. R. Shaver (Eds.), *Handbook of attachment: Theory, research, and clinical applications* (pp. 395–433). New York: Guilford.

Hesse, E., & Main, M. (1999). Second-generation effects of unresolved trauma in nonmaltreating parents: Dissociated, frightened, and threatening parental behavior. *Psychoanalytic Inquiry, 19,* 481–540.

Holmes, J. (1993a). Attachment theory: A biological basis for psychotherapy? *British Journal of Psychiatry, 163,* 430–438.

Holmes, J. (1993b). *John Bowlby and attachment theory.* London: Routledge.

Holmes, J. (1994). The clinical implications of attachment theory. *British Journal of Psychotherapy, 11,* 62–76.

Holmes, J. (1996). *Attachment intimacy, autonomy: Using attachment theory in adult psychotherapy.* Northvale, NJ: Jason Aronson.

Holmes, J. (2000). Attachment theory and psychoanalysis: A rapprochement. *British Journal of Psychotherapy, 17,* 157–180.

Holmes, J. (2001). *The search for the secure base.* Philadelphia: Taylor & Francis.

Holmes, J. (2004). Disorganized attachment and borderline personality disorder: A clinical perspective. *Attachment & Human Development, 6,* 181–190.

Howe, D., Brandon, M., Hinings, D., & Schofield, G. (1999). *Attachment theory, child maltreatment, and family support.* Basingstoke, England: Palgrave.

Johnson, S. M., & Best, M. (2003). A systemic approach to restructuring adult attachment: The EFT model of couple's therapy. In P. Erdman & T. Caffery (Eds.), *Attachment and family systems: Conceptual, empirical, and therapeutic relatedness* (pp. 165–189). New York: Brunner-Routledge.

Karen, R. (1990, Feb.). Becoming attached. *The Atlantic Monthly,* 35–70.

LeDoux, J. (2000). *Synaptic self: How our brains become who we are.* New York: Viking.

Lieberman, A. (1991). Attachment theory and infant-parent psychotherapy: Some conceptual, clinical and research issues. In D. Cicchetti, & S. Toth (Eds.), *Rochester Symposium on Developmental Psychopathology: Vol. 3. Models and integrations* (pp. 261–288). Hillsdale, NJ: Lawrence Erlbaum.

Lieberman, A. (1999). Negative maternal attributions: Effects on toddlers' sense of self. *Psychoanalytic Inquiry, 19,* 737–756.

Lieberman, A., & Zeanah, C. (1999). Contributions of attachment theory to infant-parent psychotherapy and other interventions with infants and young children. In J. Cassidy & P. Shaver (Eds.), *Handbook of attachment: Theory, research, and clinical applications* (pp. 555–574). New York: Guilford.

Lyons-Ruth, K. (1996). Attachment relationships among children with aggressive behavior problems: The role of disorganized early patterns. *Journal of Consulting and Clinical Psychology, 64,* 32–40.

Lyons-Ruth, K., Bronfman, E., & Atwood, G. (1999). A relational diathesis model of hostile-helpless states of mind: Expressions in mother-infant interaction. In J. Solomon & C. George (Eds.), *Attachment disorganization* (pp. 33–70). New York: Guilford.

Lyons-Ruth, K., Melnick, S., Bronfman, E., Sherry, S., & Llanas, L. (2003). Hostile-helpless relational models and disorganized attachment patterns between parents and their young children: Review of research and implications for clinical work. In L. Aitkinson, & S. Goldberg (Eds.), *Attachment issues in psychopathology and intervention* (pp. 65–94). Mahwah, NJ: Lawrence Erlbaum.

Lyons-Ruth, K., Repacholi, B., McLeod, S., & Silver, E. (1991). Disorganized attachment behavior in infancy: Short-term stability, maternal and infant correlates, and risk-related sub-types. *Development and Psychopathology, 3,* 377–396.

Lyons-Ruth, K., & Spielman, E. (2004). Disorganized infant attachment strategies and helpless-fearful profiles of parenting: Integrating attachment research with clinical intervention. *Infant Mental Health Journal, 25,* 318–335.

Mahler, M. S., Pine, F., & Bergman, A. (1975). *The psychological birth of the human infant.* New York: Basic Books.

Main, M. (1995). Recent studies in attachment: Overview, with selected implications for clinical work. In S. Goldberg, R. Muir, & J. Kerr, (Eds.), *Attachment theory: Social, developmental, and clinical perspectives* (pp. 407–474). Hillsdale, NJ: The Analytic Press.

Main, M. (1996). Introduction to the special section on attachment and psychopathology: 2. Overview of the field of attachment. *Journal of Consulting and Clinical Psychology, 64,* 237–243.

Main, M., & Hesse, E. (1990). Parents' unresolved traumatic experiences are related to infant disorganized attachment status: Is frightened or frightening parental behavior the linking mechanism? In M. T. Greenberg, D. C. Cicchetti, & E. M. Cummings (Eds.), *Attachment in the preschool years: Theory, research, and intervention* (pp. 161–182). Chicago: University of Chicago Press.

Main, M., & Solomon, J. (1990). Procedures for identifying infants as disorganized/disoriented during the Ainsworth Strange Situation. In M. T. Greenberg, D. C. Cicchetti, & E. M. Cummings (Eds.), *Attachment in the preschool years: Theory, research, and intervention* (pp. 121–160). Chicago: University of Chicago Press.

Main, M., & Weston, D. R. (1981). The quality of the toddler's relationship to mother and to father: Related to conflict behavior and the readiness to establish new relationships. *Child Development, 52,* 932–940.

McMillen, J. C. (1992). Attachment theory and clinical social work. *Clinical Social Work Journal, 20,* 205–218.

Ogawa, J., Sroufe, L. A., Weinfield, N., Carlson, E., & Egeland, B. (1997). Development and the fragmented self: A longitudinal study of dissociative symptomatology in a nonclinical sample. *Development and Psychopathology, 9,* 855–879.

Paterson, R. J., & Moran, G. (1988). Attachment theory, personality development, and psychotherapy. *Clinical Psychology Review, 8,* 611–636.

Patrick, M., Hobson, P., Castle, P., Howard, R., & Maughan, B. (1994). Personality disorder and the mental representation of early social experience. *Development and Psychopathology, 94,* 375–388.

Pearlman, L. A., & Courtois, C. A. (2005). Clinical applications of the attachment framework: Relational treatment of complex trauma. *Journal of Traumatic Stress, 18,* 449–459.

Perry, B. (2001). Violence and childhood: How persisting fear can alter the child's developing brain. In D. Schetky & E. Benedek (Eds.), *Textbook of child and adolescent forensic psychiatry* (pp. 221–238). Washington, DC: American Psychiatric Press.

Rutter, M. (1995). Clinical implications of attachment concepts: Retrospect and prospect. *Journal of Child Psychology and Psychiatry, 4,* 549–571.

Rutter, M., & O'Connor, T. (1999). Implications of attachment theory for child care policies. In J. Cassidy & P. Shaver (Eds.), *Handbook of attachment: Theory, research, and clinical applications* (pp. 823–844). New York: Guilford.

Sable, P. (1991). Attachment, anxiety, and agoraphobia. *Women & Therapy, 11,* 55–69.

Sable, P. (1992). Attachment theory: Application to clinical practice with adults. *Clinical Social Work Journal, 20,* 271–283.

Sable, P. (1995a). Attachment theory and post-traumatic stress disorder. *Journal of Analytic Social Work, 2,* 89–109.

Sable, P. (1995b). Attachment theory and social work education. *Journal of Teaching in Social Work, 12,* 19–38.

Sable, P. (1997). Attachment, detachment, and borderline personality disorder. *Psychotherapy, 43,* 171–181.

Schore, A. (2003). The human unconscious: The development of the right brain and its role in early emotional life. In V. Green (Ed.), *Emotional development in psychoanalysis, attachment theory and neuroscience* (pp. 23–54). New York: Brunner-Routledge.

Slade, A. (1999a). Attachment theory and research: Implications for the theory and practice of individual psychotherapy with adults. In J. Cassidy & P. R. Shaver (Eds.), *Handbook of attachment: Theory, research, and clinical applications* (pp. 575–594). New York: Guilford.

Slade, A. (1999b). Representation, symbolization, and affect regulation in the concomitant treatment of a mother and child: Attachment theory and child psychotherapy. *Psychoanalytic Inquiry, 19,* 797–830.

Slade, A. (2000). The development and organization of attachment: Implication for psychoanalysis. *Journal of the American Psychoanalytic Association, 48,* 1147–1174.

Slade, A. (2005). Parental reflective functioning: An introduction. *Attachment & Human Development, 7,* 269–281.

Slade, A., Grienenberger, J., Bernbach, E., Levy, D., & Locker, A. (2005). Maternal reflective functioning, attachment, and the transmission gap: A preliminary study. *Attachment & Human Development, 7*, 283–298.

Solomon, J., & George, C. (1999). The measurement of attachment security in infancy and childhood. In J. Cassidy & P. R. Shaver (Eds.), *Handbook of attachment: Theory, research, and clinical applications* (pp. 287–316). New York: Guilford.

Sroufe, L. A. (1996). *Emotional development: The organization of emotional life in the early years.* New York: Cambridge University Press.

Sroufe, L. A. (1997). Psychopathology as an outcome of development. *Development and Psychopathology, 9*, 251–268.

Sroufe, L. A. (2005). Attachment and development: A prospective, longitudinal study from birth to adulthood. *Attachment & Human Development, 7*, 349–367.

Sroufe, L. A., Carlson, E., Levy, A., & Egeland, B. (1999). Implications of attachment theory for developmental psychopathology. *Development and Psychopathology, 11*, 1–13.

Steele, M. (2003). Attachment, actual experience, and mental representation. In V. Green (Ed.), *Emotional development in psychoanalysis, attachment theory and neuroscience* (pp. 86–106). New York: Brunner-Routledge.

Suttie, I. (1935). *The origins of love and hate.* London: Kegan Paul.

Thomas, P. M. (2003). Protection, dissociation, and internal roles: Modeling and treating the effects of child abuse. *Review of General Psychology, 7*, 364–380.

Thompson, R. A. (1999). Early attachment and later development. In J. Cassidy & P. R. Shaver (Eds.), *Handbook of attachment: Theory, research, and clinical applications* (pp. 265–286). New York: Guilford.

Vallance, D. (2005). Assessment of controlling attachments in preschool children. *IMPrint: The Newsletter of Infant Mental Health Promotion, 43*, 2–5.

van IJzendoorn, M. H. (1995). Adult attachment representation, parental responsiveness, and infant attachment: A meta-analysis on the predictive validity of the Adult Attachment Interview. *Psychological Bulletin, 117*, 387–403.

van IJzendoorn, M. H., & Sagi, A. (1999). Cross-cultural patterns of attachment: Universal and contextual dimensions. In J. Cassidy & P. R. Shaver (Eds.), *Handbook of attachment: Theory, research, and clinical applications* (pp. 713–734). New York: Guilford.

Vaughn, B. E., & Bost, K. K. (1999). Attachment and temperament: Redundant, independent, or interacting influences on interpersonal adaptation and personality development? In J. Cassidy & P. R. Shaver (Eds.), *Handbook of attachment: Theory, research, and clinical applications* (pp. 198–225). New York: Guilford.

Ward, M., & Carlson, E. (1995). The predictive validity of the Adult Attachment Interview for adolescent mothers. *Child Development, 66*, 69–79.

West, M. L., & Sheldon-Keller, A. E. (1994). *Patterns of relating: An adult attachment perspective.* New York: Guilford.

CHAPTER 7

Relational Theory

Cheryl-Anne Cait

Social work training promotes and emphasizes context when learning about people. Learning about ecosystems is a fundamental part of the learning process: how organizations, institutions, and other important bodies create a web around individuals and influence behavior (Hartman & Laird, 1983). Relational theory offers an inclusive theoretical approach to practice in a variety of contexts. Borden (2000) suggested the "relational paradigm provides contexts of understanding for social workers in ongoing efforts to connect biological, psychological, and social domains of concern, to enlarge conceptions of person and environment, and to deepen appreciation of interactive processes at multiple systems levels" (p. 367).

Relational psychoanalytic theory is a broad umbrella term for different theoretical orientations that, in part, consider how the self develops in relationship to other selves and how the self is based on patterns from this interactive process (Atwood & Stolorow, 1984; Benjamin, 1988; Mitchell, 1988; Sullivan, 1953). "Relational theory is essentially a contemporary eclectic theory anchored in the idea that it is relationships (internal and external, real and imagined) that are central" (Aron, 1996, p. 18).

Relational theory encompasses the merger of intrapsychic and interpersonal perspectives. The intrapsychic largely consists of the "internalization of interpersonal experience" (Ghent, as cited in Aron, 1996, p. 16). Relational theory does not necessarily create narrow boundaries when focusing on the interactive process. It is interested in the relationship between the external environment and internal world (Altman, Briggs, Frankel, Gensler, & Pantine, 2002).

179

OVERVIEW OF RELATIONAL THEORY

Understanding of Human Problems

Human problems through a relational lens can connect to both biology (constitutional factors) and environment (including interpersonal factors); even when problems are biologically connected they are always influenced and mediated by environment. Problems exist on a continuum of normal development. How problems come to be defined can, in part, depend on the sociocultural and subjective values of the viewer (Altman et al., 2002)

From a relational perspective, psychological difficulties are understood in three distinctive ways: "patterns of attachment and relatedness" (Altman et al., 2002, p. 133), "patterns of subjective experience" (Altman et al., 2002, p. 144), and self-regulation (Beebe & Lachmann, 1988). All of these concepts contain interpersonal and intrapsychic dimensions. Patterns of attachment and relatedness focus on how our early important relationships are internalized and create the blueprint for our future interactions with people in everyday life. Our relationships are influenced by our subjective sense of self, how we experience others, and our expectations of these interactions. Problems are conceived as difficulties in interpersonal relations (Mitchell, 1988). Patterns of subjective experience focus on dissociation and the various ways it manifests itself. Dissociation, while initially providing relief from the problem, merely staves off its reoccurrence. Self-regulation refers to problems regulating both inner experience and behavior.

Conception of Therapeutic Intervention

From a relational perspective, "what is most important is that the patient have a new experience rooted in a new relationship" (Aron, 1996, p. 214). The interactive process, in and of itself, is significant and can lead to change. The client and therapist co-construct ways of being with each other, facilitating healthy relationships for the client. This contrasts with more traditional psychoanalytic theory, often referred to as a "one-person" psychology, where treatment focuses on the client's intrapsychic world. Therapy from a relational psychoanalytic perspective is based on a two-person model of intervention. This means the therapist is an active participant in therapy and that his or her subjectivity is critical in the interactive dynamics. Because personality development is based on transactional patterns in our interpersonal relationships (both internal and external), intervention can be based on shifting internalized patterns (as has been done traditionally) and/or shifting a person's day-to-day interactive patterns (Frank, 2002).

The relationship between therapist and client serves important purposes deemed as curative factors in treatment: a safe, reliable space; empathic understanding; recognition; the development of interpersonal skills; improvement of social functioning; and experiential learning through interpersonal interaction (Borden, 2000; Kohut, 1977, 1984; Reid, 1992; Winnicott, 1965). Therapeutic intervention is no longer only based on interpretation and insight, as in earlier psychodynamic models. Relational theory holds that changing ways of interacting directly in the therapeutic relationship can be more helpful: "The combination of insight and new forms of interpersonal engagement works synergistically to produce change" (Aron, 1996, p. 214).

Countertransference and enactment are very important for intervention (Mills, 2005). In relational theory, understanding countertransference calls upon the therapist to be vigilant and aware of his or her own thoughts, feelings, subjectivity, history, and experiences and how these play out in the therapeutic interaction. Enactment involves the process of enacting patterns with the therapist based on earlier interactions. Enactment brings to life our expectancies through interaction with the therapist. Enactments are two-person processes based on therapist and client (McLaughlin, 1991). Therapists can improve intervention by focusing on enactments and discussing them as they emerge (Frank, 2002).

HISTORICAL DEVELOPMENT

Psychoanalytic theory has gradually shifted from focusing on the individual to focusing on the interactive nature of development (Aron, 1996; Borden, 2000; Mitchell, 1988). For the most part, prior to 1960, psychoanalysis was dominated by the classical emphasis on structural theory (the mind divided into id, ego, and superego) and the view that people were motivated by libidinal and aggressive drives. In the 1960s and 1970s, relational perspectives (even some from ego-psychology) developed; theories highlighted that people were motivated through the subjective experience of interactions and not through drives. Relational psychoanalytic theory has its roots in similar, though distinct, schools of thought, including object relations, British and American interpersonal theory, self psychology, and feminist-psychoanalysis. Relational perspectives were developed in opposition to classical psychoanalytic theory.

In 1983, Greenberg and Mitchell solidified the relational perspective in their book *Object Relations in Psychoanalytic Theory*, in which they outlined two distinct branches of theory: the drive-structural model and the relational model. For them, theory in psychoanalysis is entrenched in "social, political, and moral contexts" (Aron, 1996, p. 10). This was diametrically opposed to drive theory, which saw human development as primarily an individual endeavor. Relational theory maintains an integrative emphasis and provides a link between the Interpersonal school and contemporary British theorizing on object relations. "The relational approach is an attempt to bridge theories that have traditionally emphasized either internal object relations or external interpersonal relations, the intrapsychic or the interpersonal, constitutional factors or environmental factors, one-person psychology versus two-person psychologies" (Aron, 1996, p. 17). In the 1980s and 1990s, relational concepts and perspectives consolidated under the term relational theory. In the 1990s, theories such as feminism, constructivism, hermeneutics, and gender studies influenced current relational theory (Aron, 1996; Mills, 2005; Mitchell & Aron, 1999).

Central concepts for social work, namely, the importance of the therapeutic relationship and of understanding the person as embedded in his or her environment, are also highlighted in relational theory. Saari (2005) explained how the relational consideration of the internal world can be linked to the external world. According to Saari, our individual identities rely on the context of our environments. Citing the research of Nelson, she explained that toddlers attempt to understand their surroundings in order to understand themselves. Important concepts linking the inner world and outer worlds are event representations (Nelson, 1986) and social participation (Nelson, 1988). Saari (2005) explained that children make sense of the people in their worlds not as individuals but as individuals who are part of an event; "context or culture, the environment, is always a part of that global whole which is initially experienced" (p. 7). Nelson (1988) discussed the importance of social participation for learning. She conducted a study of 5-year-olds who went to a museum with their mothers. When the children were asked a week later what they remembered, only that which was discussed with their mothers was remembered. All of this recognizes that what we take in, in terms of our experiences and people, is done in the context of relationships with the environment and people in our environment. This provides a bridge between social work and relational theory (Saari, 2005).

CENTRAL THEORETICAL CONSTRUCTS

Many different theorists and clinicians identify themselves and write under the umbrella of relational theory, creating a rich, textured model of views both convergent and discordant. Although each person connected with relational theory might emphasize particular assumptions and concepts,

I will outline three main tenets of relational theory, as discussed by Mills (2005), that represent the shared ideas in this area.

Relatedness

Indisputably, the primary concepts threaded through all relational thinking are

> the centrality of interactions with others, forming relationships, interpersonally mediated experience, human attachment, the impact of others on psychic development, reciprocal dyadic communication, contextually based social influence, and the recognition of competing subjectivities. (Mills, 2005, p. 158)

Mills argued that this focus on relatedness is not unique to relational theory, and in fact, that Freud, in *Totem and Taboo* and *Group Psychology and the Analysis of the Ego*, discussed human relatedness in social and cultural terms, from a drive/structural lens. Relational theory, however, represents for the most part a turn away from classical theory that focuses on drives as central to human development. "Mind has been redefined from a set of predetermined structures emerging from inside an individual organism to transactional patterns and internal structures derived from an interactive, interpersonal field" (Mitchell, 1988, p. 17). It is important to note, however, that relational theory's emphasis on human relations does not denigrate the importance of the biological:

> Relational theorists have in common an interest in the intrapsychic as well as the interpersonal, but the intrapsychic is seen as constituted largely by the internalization of interpersonal experience mediated by the constraints imposed by biologically organized templates and delimiters. . . . Relational theorists do not substitute a naïve environmentalism for drive theory. Due weight is given to what the individual brings to the interaction: temperament, bodily events, physiological responsivity, distinctive patterns of regulation and sensitivity. Unlike earlier critics of drive theory, relational theorists do not minimize the importance of the body or of sexuality in human development. (Ghent, as cited in Aron, 1996, p. 16)

Intersubjectivity

Intersubjectivity is a term originally used by Jurgen Habermas, a German philosopher whose work was based in social theory (Habermas, 1970). Benjamin (1988) and Stolorow, Brandchaft, and Atwood (1987) have been credited with bringing this concept to psychoanalytic theory. Intersubjectivity focuses on the psychic world of individuals, as they interact with each other. Intersubjectivity says the self develops in relation and connection to "other selves" (Oarnge, Atwood, & Stolorow, 1997). The intersubjective process "describes the unequal power distributions between servitude and lordship culminating in a developmental, historical, and ethical transformation of recognizing the subjectivity of the other" (Mills, 2005, p. 159). Relational theorists highlight the importance of intersubjectivity, without negating the existence of individual subjectivity or external reality (Mills, 2005).

Benjamin (1988, 1999), writing from a developmental perspective, explained how traditional psychoanalytic theory can be enriched through an intersubjective lens. Benjamin (1988), discussing Mahler's (1963) theory of separation-individuation (emphasizing how the individual separates from another "object"), suggested that the other "object" is another "self" and has its own experiences and history and interacts from that position. By acknowledging the other "object" as a subject in and of itself, the focus shifts to the interactive dynamics of two people, rather than only the relationship the self only has with the internalized object. Through this lens, intersubjectivity depicts a developmental theory along a continuum where people shift in their ability to recognize the subjectivity of others (Benjamin, 1999). Benjamin (1988) stressed the tension in how we relate to others as distinct, autonomous selves and our need to negate this and relate to others as objects of our own needs. She argued separation and individuation, connection and mutuality happen at the same time, because we rely on others to recognize who we are. This insinuates we have the need and desire to be recognized and the aptitude "to recognize others in return—mutual recognition" (Benjamin, 1999, p. 186).

Intersubjectivity recognizes that while the therapy is for the client, "the emotional history and psychological organization of patient and analyst are equally important to the understanding of any clinical exchange" (Oarnge et al., 1997, p. 9). The therapist is no longer neutral, and his or her subjectivity contributes to shaping the therapeutic dialogue and to the understanding of the client's struggles (Berman, 1997; McLaughlin, 1991).

The Contribution of Social Constructionism

Relational theorists generally adhere to social constructionism. This means that knowledge and meaning are created linguistically through dialogue and through social institutions constituted in part through interpersonal negotiations. In the therapeutic relationship, this meaning is created through interaction between therapist and client and is intertwined with context.

PHASES OF HELPING

Engagement, Data Collection, and Assessment

A unifying feature for relational theorists is the emphasis on mutuality and reciprocity in the therapeutic process. Although relational therapists acknowledge the differences in the relationship between therapist and client, including issues of power and responsibility, the "real relationship" is favored over a hierarchical relationship (Altman et al., 2002). Assessment, for the entire therapeutic process, is mutually negotiated between therapist and client. This also means agreement for therapy must be mutual and the therapy becomes a joint venture. In traditional psychoanalytic work, it is the client who provides the information (data) for the therapy. In relational theory, what is important is the "mutual generation of data" (Aron, 1996, p. 124). This means the therapist becomes part of the field to be explored and the therapist influences the information that is collected. The therapist is participant and observer with an emphasis on the first. This minimizes the distance between client and therapist; commonalities between the two are highlighted, not their differences (Aron, 1996).

For relational theorists and clinicians, assessment is an evolving process of discovery. The process of collecting information is adapted to the comfort level of the client. Information about the individual, interpersonal patterns and interactive dynamics of the therapist and client is collected. Particularly important for relational theory is that the therapist not only pay attention to content of what is said but also to the nonverbal enactments in the therapeutic process. The therapist must constantly be aware of his or her reactions and shifts in self throughout the therapy. The assessment process involves looking at the whole individual and his or her environment. If the client is a child, a decision needs to be made about the combinations in which the child would be seen; that is, individually, with parents, or parents alone. Over the course of therapy with a child it is likely a combination of all of the above will be used; however, it is important that decisions around this are made in consultation with the client. From a relational perspective, the work is partly systemic, and when working with children this can mean bringing in and/or working with people involved in the child's life.

Planning/Contracting and Intervention

Instead of making definitive decisions about the therapy from the beginning, treatment planning is provisional and continuous (Altman et al., 2002). Mutuality and negotiation play an important role in the planning and action of the therapy. As is the case for assessment, goals for therapy are jointly negotiated as client and therapist influence each other. Because mutual influence plays an important part in the therapy process, the person of the therapist and how he or she participates in the therapy is very important. Interpretation is no longer seen as something done by the therapist but is part of the reciprocal process between therapist and client.

Transference and countertransference are also important for therapy, although they are not conceived in the same way by relational therapists and some argue for the importance of developing new terms (Aron, 1996; McLaughlin, 1981). From the relational perspective, transference is something constructed by therapist and client; the therapist's behavior influences the client's transference. Understanding the transference as interpersonally created provides a new way of intervening with the client. That is, material based on the interaction between therapist and client leads the exploration in therapy. Countertransference encourages us to consider how the therapist's unconscious and/or conscious reaction to the client might impact on the therapy. It necessitates that we look at the therapist's thoughts and feelings; however, reaction is the operative word. Aron (1996) suggested that the client's subjectivity, his or her history and experiences, is not primary, because it is the patient's subjectivity to which the therapist responds. For Aron, countertransference fails to address what can happen and be learned through ongoing therapist and client interaction. Countertransference does not happen episodically throughout therapy; it is central to the process.

The concept of enactment is also critical for intervention in relational therapy. In relational theory, enactments are an inevitable part of the therapeutic process. For Bromberg (1999), enactment is "an externalization of the patient's internal communication with his own subjective phenomenon in the form of an enactment with his analyst's reality" (p. 386). Clients come to play out old expectancies in their lives within the therapeutic relationship. The therapist allows the enactments to happen, and to be within the enactment with the client to understand and experience it. Bromberg argued that "the personal narrative cannot be edited simply by more accurate verbal input. . . . [The therapy] must provide an experience that is perceivably (not just conceptually) different from the patient's narrative memory" (p. 391). By providing a different way of being in and engaging in relationships, a client's approach is challenged. Therapy then "breaks down the old narrative frame (the patient's 'story') by evoking, through a process of negotiation, perceptual experience that doesn't fit it; enactment is the primary perceptual medium that allows narrative change to take place" (Bromberg, 1999, p. 391). For Bromberg, what is important is "the immediacy of a discrepant, external perception of oneself as seen by another" (p. 394). Equally important is that this comes through dialogue; that it is a relational act and not an isolated struggle for a person. A therapist must respect and believe in the reality presented by a client while simultaneously negotiating and constructing an alternative perspective. It is not enough to assimilate the new language and words describing an alternative reality; it is the relational experience of constructing a new understanding that must be assimilated to be effective.

From a relational perspective, the therapeutic process and negotiated interaction between therapist and client can help change the client's "internal dialogue" (Bromberg, 1999, p. 393). It is through interaction with another who sees and offers a discrepant perception of the client that one's self-narrative can change. But before this can happen, the therapist "both accepts the validity of the patient's inner reality and participates in the here-and-now act of constructing a negotiated reality discrepant with it" (Bromberg, 1999, p. 395).

Intervention in relational theory can be based on a variety of modalities that are seamlessly integrated (Frank, 2002) and is described by Wachtel (1993) as "a mode of working that is at once psychoanalytic and active, that aims to explore and understand and to help the patient give shape to his yearnings in ways that render them more realizable" (p. 600). This means the work of therapy not only happens within therapy but also outside therapy.

Termination

Ending therapy from a relational perspective is negotiated between therapist and client. The therapist can offer his or her perspective on ending within a relational frame; however, the process needs to be collaborative. Therapists working from a traditional analytic perspective would not believe in tapering sessions or maintaining an open door with clients once the therapy was over because this might mean a denial of the loss and possible mourning that is important in termination. Therapists working from a relational perspective would not adhere as strictly to these rules (Wachtel, 2002).

APPLICATION TO FAMILY AND GROUP WORK

Relational theory's focus on interpersonal dynamics, as well as a systemic process, makes it well suited for both family and group work; however, this theory is most often discussed around work with individuals. Cohen and Schermer (2001), writing from a self psychological and intersubjective perspective, discussed self-disclosure in group psychotherapy. In relational theory, there is an emphasis on the subjectivity of the therapist. Cohen and Schermer acknowledged self-disclosure between therapist and group members is not asymmetrical; that is, while there must be limits to a therapist's disclosure, the contribution of therapist and group members allows for transformation in relationships. When group members and therapist, through their participation, recognize the subjectivity of each other, they have more flexibility from rigidly prescribed roles and relationships. Self-disclosure can act as an "intersubjective bridge" and vehicle for communication to group members about the therapist and recognition of his or her fallibility. This models a way of being open and sharing about one's intimate world while remaining psychologically stable. It also helps deconstruct the "therapist as an authority figure with an exclusive claim on the strengths and powers essential to members' well-being" (p. 51–52).

Altman and colleagues' (2002) work on relational child psychotherapy discussed family work as a very important part of the process. They saw their work method as a field model and drew on Stern's (1995) "field-theoretical model." They also suggested that their model is similar to a family systems approach although differing in many respects. Altman and colleagues (2002) acknowledged that "systemic patterns have enormous shaping power on each individual" (p. 14). At the same time, they recognized the importance of individuals (clients and therapists) and their "representational worlds" (i.e., how relational experiences of people are represented in the memory and shape expectations for interactions). This model acknowledges that individuals within the family can be perceived differently by each other depending on the person's position in the family and his or her representational world. Each member of the family system can influence another member of the system. This relational model recognizes the complexities of child and family work by not only looking at the family system and systemic patterns, but also the representational worlds of the individuals. Family interventions involve changing systemic patterns and family dynamics. By doing this, the child no longer needs to be the symptom in the family. Parents can be helped to become more empathic and attuned to their children's feelings and moods, and this includes focus on "parental projections and misunderstandings of the child's affective states" (Altman et al., 2002, p. 341).

COMPATIBILITY WITH GENERALIST-ECLECTIC FRAMEWORK

Relational theory is compatible with the generalist-eclectic framework in most respects. First, relational theory is eclectic because it recognizes the complexity of people and situations in social work practice and attempts to bridge theoretical systems to account for this complexity. It has much in common with and can be integrated with other psychodynamic approaches (e.g., object relations, self psychology, and attachment theories). It has also been integrated with other therapy models (Frank, 2002). Frank (2002) integrated a cognitive-behavioral approach with relational theory; Hoffman (1998) and Bromberg (1999) integrated constructivism. Narrative therapy would also be compatible with relational theory's underlying emphasis on relational and interactive dynamics.

Second, relational theory is also consistent with the person-in-environment perspective of the generalist-eclectic framework. Relational theorists recognize the importance of an individual's interdependence and relatedness to his or her environment, including the biological, physiological, psychological (intrapsychic and interpersonal), and, for some, the spiritual, and they use this understanding in assessment (Aron, 1996). Relational theorists suggest the individual is entrenched in his or her environment and cannot be understood apart from his or her interactions. How individuals identify, for example, racially, culturally, economically, and by sexual orientation, influences their interpersonal relationships. Issues of diversity cannot be separated from understanding relational dynamics. Altman (1995) used a systems and ecological approach in his relational perspective and encourages clinical acknowledgment of the influence of institutions and community in practice, research, and theory.

Third, for relational theorists a good helping relationship is central; in fact, all relationships, internal and external, are central to the theory. The helping relationship is seen as a main vehicle for change. In this theory, the helping relationship is always contributed to by both client and therapist, with an equal emphasis on the latter. Aron (1990) explained that the "implication of a two-person psychology is that who the analyst is, not only how he or she works, but his or her very character, makes a real difference" (p. 479). An important role of the therapist is to validate the client's reality, and this can be empowering in and of itself. Also, that the client's perspective is a welcomed view and used in the therapeutic process speaks to the collaborative negotiated process (Bromberg, 1999; Renik, 1999). People feel empowered when their view is considered both important and helpful and therapist and client can learn from it. A relational emphasis on the cyclical and ongoing nature of development, life span development, instead of linear conceptions of development, inherently widens the focus on health and strengths. Some relational theorists (Bromberg, 1998; Mitchell, 1993) speak about the multiple selves that make up an individual. This way of understanding provides greater latitude in understanding an individual's strengths and ways of being. It also recognizes that we act differently depending on those with whom we are interacting.

CRITIQUE OF THEORY

Strengths

Relationships are understood as a central part of mental health (Surber, 1994). The relationship has long been recognized as important to growth, and change in therapy and empirical evidence complements this view (Binder, Strupp, & Henry, 1995; Bordin, 1979; Catty, 2004; Clarkson, 1990; Elkin, 1999; Luborsky, 1996). Another strength of the theory is its broad integrative emphasis and its ability to hold the tension of a both/and perspective. It encompasses the intersubjective and intrasubjective, biology and the sociocultural environment, kinship systems and societal systems. To believe in the importance of the relationship for therapeutic change yet ignore the subjectivity of the therapist would be negligent; relational theory allows us to understand the therapist's importance and how this plays a role in the therapeutic process.

Limitations

Although relational concepts, in theory, allow for the acknowledgment and integration of race, ethnicity, class, gender, and sexual orientation, people suggest real attention to these issues is just beginning (Altman, 1995; Borden, 2000). A greater emphasis needs to be placed on the sociocultural and political in all areas, including theory, research, and practice. Feminist writers (Benjamin, 1988, 1995; Flax, 1990, 1993; Goldner, 1991) have started to address issues of power and gender inequity in the theory. For example, it has been pointed out that aspects of female identity other than motherhood have been ignored and that differential access to resources has been overlooked (Burack, 1998). Goldner (1991) argued relational theory needs to move beyond a two-person psychology when understanding gender. Gender is constructed amongst more than two people, in interactions with parents and siblings.

Finally, Borden (2000) suggested that "many relational concepts remain global and poorly defined. The failure to operationalize key constructs has limited the development of systematic research and practice models" (p. 370).

Populations Most and Least Suited To

For adherents to relational theory, the interactive nature of the relationship between client and therapist acts as a vehicle for change. For this reason, I would argue this model is suited to most populations and can be used in case management as well. Relational theory can hold the complexity of case management by allowing for multifocus interventions. In fact, the Canadian Mental Health Association (CMHA), Elgin Branch, provides case management services based on a perspective that integrates relational and systemic theories. Their model consists of three parts: assessing the "client's capacity for relationships" (or core problem), assessing needs for environmental structure (structural plan), and the relationship (interactive plan) that promotes client aptitude (Cait & Koplowitz, 2006, p. 68).

CASE EXAMPLE

I met with Helen, a 21-year-old senior, at a college counseling service, once a week throughout her final year at the college. Helen came for counseling to deal with issues in her relationship with her partner, Cassandra. Helen also felt, as the year became more stressful, that she might have difficulty with her eating, a previous problematic area. Helen had a history of an eating disorder, and was hospitalized in her first year of college, when she lost 15 pounds. At that point she was put on medical leave and was diagnosed with Eating Disorder Not Otherwise Specified. During the first semester of her final year, Helen learned that her aunt, her mother's twin, with whom she was very close, was diagnosed with ovarian cancer and given 12 to 15 months to live. Helen also wished her parents could see her pain and be able to deal with the intensity of her feelings. She said that feelings were not discussed in the family and there was the expectation that family members would keep their "chins up" and "deal with and get over" any problems.

At first it was difficult to create an alliance with Helen. The therapeutic relationship changed, however, when I began to recognize Helen's subjectivity; her assertion of self. That is, to recognize that while she still had difficulty with eating, she was no longer "anorexic." She was attempting to assert this in both our therapy and with health services. I believe Helen also recognized the shift in my understanding of her and our alliance strengthened. Although it was at times difficult to believe in Helen's improvement and there was pressure from outside influences to do otherwise, recognizing this aspect of Helen was critical for the therapy. Benjamin (1999) states, "The other must be recognized as another subject in order for the self to fully experience his or her subjectivity in the other's presence" (p. 186).

In therapy, Helen commented she thought she was losing weight because her clothes were looser. She said that she was not restricting her food intake but had missed a meal a couple of times. She felt she was hypermetabolic; her metabolism was increasing, as was her anxiety and stress level, which affected her appetite. Helen planned to increase her caloric intake by using a nutritional supplement.

Concerned about her own risk for cancer, Helen made an appointment for a pap smear at medical services. At medical services, it was determined that she weighed less than she had during her first year at college. She was placed on a strict regimen of weekly weigh-ins, with the threat of having to go on medical leave or go to day treatment during spring break if she did not gain weight. Although Helen's weight was down, she was not medically at risk. Helen, however, made creative use of the intervention by the medical services. She set a meal plan for herself with a high caloric value and gained the required weight.

In her second semester, as Helen began the process of separating from Cassandra, she moved into a new residence to leave behind a dorm, where she had shared many memories with Cassandra. At the same time, Helen realized she could no longer take care of her parents or Cassandra and started to plan for graduation and a move to a new city.

Intersubjectivity theory highlights the complexity of the case and its multiple layers. In the language of more traditional "second individuation" theory (Blos, 1967), Helen's process of separation and individuation moved along a continuum of development where regression was a necessary precondition for future growth. The tension was between a regressive-pull and progressive position. Benjamin's (1988) translation of traditional theory through an intersubjective lens holds that as Helen strives for autonomy she also endeavors to be recognized as separate from her mother and Cassandra. This striving for recognition and autonomy, paradoxically, comes through connection and engagement with others. Helen wanted to be recognized as someone other than "anorexic," and different from her girlfriend, Cassandra.

From a relational intersubjective perspective, Helen needed to be recognized as herself, not as her mother's daughter and caregiver, not as Cassandra's girlfriend and caregiver, and not as "anorexic Helen." It is through this new recognition and connection in therapy that Helen could experience her separateness from a former "self" and experience herself more fully. This happened through her move to a new residence and her attempts to reveal a new self-determination with health services. The tension became that of feeling connected with self and others while also asserting an individuated self.

Recognition of another's subjectivity can be imperfect and clouded by one's own subjectivity. As the therapist, I had my own story of loss: a deceased father and a mother who had recently suffered a stroke. I was also facilitating a bereavement group at the college, largely attended by young women whose mothers had died. As the therapist, my own unconscious fears of death, particularly maternal death, prevented me from truly bearing witness to and recognizing Helen's concern for her aunt's impending death and other issues of loss in her life. Although issues of death and loss were glaringly present in both my personal and professional life, I was unable to fully see how they influenced the therapeutic process. The unconscious fear of death, the unbearable pain it can bring and the helplessness it instills, perpetuates our inability to give people a full hearing around their loss.

Although Helen's story could be conceptualized as her difficulties with separation and differentiation, it was truly a story of loss. Interestingly, with separation and differentiation inevitably comes loss. Helen's life was plagued with it: loss of her girlfriend and the relationship; the imminent loss of her academic life (school) when she graduated, and the structure it provided for her; and the possible future loss of her aunt. Helen's aunt's diagnosis with ovarian cancer must have intensified her fears for her own life and for the life of her mother.

Helen's parents expected her to take care of herself with the paradoxical expectation that she would come to them with her problems. Is it any surprise that this exact scenario was reenacted in the therapy? Helen was expected to come and talk to me about her difficulties; however, sadness and grief were only allowed into treatment in small amounts and the focus was quickly shifted to Helen's strength, resiliency, and her ability to make it through the muck. Helen's feelings, which were tightly sealed away, were rarely given a full hearing.

The strands of the enactment were slowly being woven in the therapy. As McLaughlin (1991) explained, enactment is a two-person process:

> Whether analyst or patient, our deepest hopes for what we may find the world to be, as well as our worst fears of what it will be, reflect our transference expectancies as shaped by our developmental past. We busy ourselves through life with words and actions aimed at obtaining some response in self and other, in keeping with these expectancies. (p. 599)

Everyone's development, client and therapist alike, is evolving. This means the partially resolved issues and old conflicts of a therapist could be stirred and "given fresh and specific intensities by the particular qualities of the patient's dynamics and transference concerns" (McLaughlin, 1991, p. 600). McLaughlin (1991) referred to these as a therapist's "blind spots." Since my mother's illness, issues of maternal loss resonated with me. My lapse around acknowledging the powerful emotional impact Helen's aunt's diagnosis must have had on her, and her own fears of her mother's mortality, was almost inevitable.

As my recognition of Helen's full subjectivity was inconsistent, so was Helen's recognition of and response to me. As previously mentioned, there was a shift in therapy as Helen recognized my belief in her ability to get better. It seems that Helen was struggling, as Benjamin (1999) asserted, with the "constant tension between recognizing the other and asserting the self" (p. 191). Helen's transference to me was maternal. With that came the expectation that Helen could come to me and that I would support her; however, strength was almost a precondition for support and so some of her feelings remained locked deep inside. For Helen, in the process of attempting to assert herself, dependence (as it could be seen) on another could negate her assertion of independence. "In its encounter with the other, the self wishes to affirm its absolute independence, even though its need for the other and the other's similar wish give the lie to it" (Benjamin, 1999, p. 190).

The progress and limitations in this case stem from similar areas. From a relational, intersubjective perspective it was critical that Helen be recognized for herself and not as "anorexic" and not as her mother's or Cassandra's caregiver. It was through our connection and engagement in therapy that I was able to recognize Helen's subjectivity, her autonomous self. By doing this Helen was able to recognize and assert her healthy self with health services and in her relationships. Helen demonstrated to health services that she could manage her eating. She also started to make plans for her future: graduation and her move to a new city. The shift in my ability to recognize the varied aspects of Helen's subjectivity in the therapeutic process allowed Helen to experience herself differently; more fully, with depth and texture. My recognition, however, of Helen's subjectivity was imprecise. From a relational perspective, this happens through a counselor's blind spots and reenactments in the therapeutic process, both of which are regular occurrences in counseling. Helen's self, the self that kept painful feelings of loss locked deep inside, did not receive a full hearing.

SUMMARY

Relational theory emphasizes the relational matrix, with relational having a broad integrative emphasis. This means relationships include our external relationships, our internalized patterns of relating, and relationships with the sociocultural environment. It does this without ignoring our biological roots. Intersubjectivity, an important part of the theory, highlights our developmental recognition of each other's unique subjectivities and the systemic characteristics of the relational milieu. A constructivist interpretation is also central to the theory. The theory mirrors central concepts in social work (Borden, 2000; Saari, 2005), with its focus on relationships and environmental context. The theory needs to further delineate focal concepts in order to facilitate future research on efficacy of this model.

REFERENCES

Altman, N. (1995). *The analyst in the inner city.* Hillsdale, NJ: The Analytic Press.

Altman, N., Briggs, R., Frankel, J., Gensler, D., & Pantine, P. (2002). *Relational child psychotherapy.* New York: Other Press.

Aron, L. (1990). One person and two person psychologies and the method of psychoanalysis. *Psychoanalytic Psychology, 7,* 475–485.

Aron, L. (1996). *A meeting of minds: Mutuality in psychoanalysis.* Hillsdale, NJ: The Analytic Press.

Atwood, G., & Stolorow, R. (1984). *Structures of subjectivity.* Hillsdale, NJ: The Analytic Press.

Beebe, B., & Lachmann, F. (1988). The contribution of mother-infant mutual influence to the origins of self- and object-representations. *Psychoanalytic Psychology, 5,* 305–337.

Benjamin, J. (1988). *The bonds of love.* New York: Pantheon Books.

Benjamin, J. (1995). *Like subjects, love objects.* New Haven: Yale University Press.

Benjamin, J. (1999). Recognition and destruction: An outline of intersubjectivity. In S. T. Mitchell & L. Aron (Eds.), *Relational psychoanalysis: The emergence of a tradition* (pp. 181–210). Hillsdale, NJ: The Analytic Press.

Berman, E. (1997). Psychoanalytic supervision as the crossroads of a relational matrix. In M. H. Rock (Ed.), *Psychodynamic supervision: Perspectives of the supervisor and supervisee* (pp. 161–185). Northvale, NJ: Jason Aronson.

Binder, J., Strupp, H., & Henry, W. (1995). Psychodynamic therapies in practice: Time-limited dynamic psychotherapy. In B. Bonger & L. E. Beutler (Eds.), *Comprehensive textbook of psychotherapy* (pp. 48–63). New York: Oxford University Press

Blos, P. (1967). The second individuation process of adolescence. *The Psychoanalytic Study of the Child, 22,* 162–186. New York: International Universities Press.

Borden, W. (2000). The relational paradigm in contemporary psychoanalysis: Toward a psychodynamically informed social work perspective. *Social Service Review, 74,* 352–373.

Bordin E. S. (1979). The generalizability of the psychoanalytic concept of the working alliance. *Psychotherapy, 16,* 252–260.

Bromberg, P. M. (1998). *Standing in the spaces: Essays on clinical process, trauma, and dissociation.* Hillsdale, NJ: The Analytic Press.

Bromberg, P. M. (1999). Shadow and substance: A relational perspective on clinical process. In S. T. Mitchell & L. Aron (Eds.), *Relational psychoanalysis: The emergence of a tradition* (pp. 379–406). Hillsdale, NJ: The Analytic Press.

Burack, C. (1998). Feminist psychoanalysis: The uneasy intimacy of feminism and psychoanalysis. In P. Marcus & A. Rosenberg (Eds.), *Psychoanalytic versions of the human condition* (pp. 392–411). New York: New York University Press.

Cait, C., & Koplowitz, K. (2006). A relational psychoanalytic model for case management: A literature review. *Psychoanalytic Social Work, 13*(1), 67–83.

Catty, J. (2004). "The vehicle of success": Theoretical and empirical perspectives on the therapeutic alliance in psychotherapy and psychiatry. *Psychology and Psychotherapy: Theory, Research, and Practice, 77,* 255–272.

Clarkson, P. (1990). A multiplicity of therapeutic relationships. *British Journal of Psychotherapy, 7,* 148–163.

Cohen, B., & Schermer, V. (2001). Therapist self-disclosure in group psychotherapy from an intersubjective and self psychology standpoint. *Group, 25*(1/2), 41–57.

Elkin, I. (1999). A major dilemma in psychotherapy outcome research: Disentangling therapists from therapies. *Clinical Psychology, 6,* 10–32.

Flax, J. (1990). *Thinking fragments.* Berkeley: University of California Press.

Flax, J. (1993). *Disputed subjects: Essays on psychoanalysis, politics, and philosophy.* New York: Routledge.

Frank, K. A. (2002). The "ins and outs" of enactment: A relational bridge for psychotherapy integration. *Journal of Psychotherapy Integration, 12,* 267–286.

Goldner, V. (1991). Toward a critical relational theory of gender. *Psychoanalytic Dialogues, 1,* 249–272.

Greenberg, J., & Mitchell, S. (1983). *Object relations in psychoanalytic theory.* Cambridge, MA: Harvard University Press.

Habermas, J. (1970). A theory of communicative competence. In H. P. Dreitzel (Ed.), *Recent sociology no. 2* (pp. 114–148). New York: Macmillan.

Hartman, A., & Laird, J. (1983). *Family-centered social work practice.* New York: Free Press.

Hoffman, I. Z. (1998). *Ritual and spontaneity in the psychoanalytic process.* Hillsdale, NJ: The Analytic Press.

Kohut, H. (1977). *The restoration of the self.* New York: International Universities Press.

Kohut, H. (1984). *How does analysis cure?* Chicago: University of Chicago Press.

Luborsky, L. (1996). Theories of cure in psychoanalytic psychotherapies and the evidence for them. *Psychoanalytic Inquiry, 16,* 257–264.

Mahler, M. (1963). Thoughts about development and individuation. *The Psychoanalytic Study of the Child, 18,* 307–324.

McLaughlin, J. T. (1981). Transference, psychic reality, and countertransference. *Psychoanalytic Quarterly, 50,* 639–664.

McLaughlin, J. T. (1991). Clinical and theoretical aspects of enactment. *Journal of American Psychoanalytic Association, 39,* 595–614.

Mills, J. (2005). A critique of relational psychoanalysis. *Psychoanalytic Psychology, 22,* 155–188.

Mitchell, S. (1988). *Relational concepts in psychoanalysis.* Cambridge, MA: Harvard University Press.

Mitchell, S. (1993). *Hope and dread in psychoanalysis.* New York: Basic Books.

Mitchell, S., & Aron, L. (1999). *Relational psychoanalysis: The emergence of a tradition.* Hillsdale, NJ: The Analytic Press.

Nelson, K. (1986). *Event knowledge: Structure and function in development.* Hillsdale, NJ: Lawrence Erlbaum.

Nelson, K. (1988). The ontogeny of memory for real events. In U. Neisser & E. Winograd (Eds.), *Remembering reconsidered: Ecological and traditional approaches to memory* (pp. 244–276). New York: Cambridge University Press.

Oarnge D. M., Atwood, G. E., & Stolorow, R. D. (1997). *Working intersubjectively: Contextualism in psychoanalytic practice.* Hillsdale, NJ: The Analytic Press.

Reid, W. J. (1992). *Task strategies: An empirical approach to social work practice.* New York: Columbia University Press.

Renik, O. (1999). Analytic interaction: Conceptualizing technique in light of the analyst's irreducible subjectivity. In S. T. Mitchell & L. Aron (Eds.), *Relational psychoanalysis: The emergence of a tradition* (pp. 407–424). Hillsdale, NJ: The Analytic Press.

Saari, C. (2005). The contribution of relational theory to social work practice. *Smith College Studies in Social Work, 75*(3), 3–14.

Stern, D. (1995). *The motherhood constellation: A unified view of parent-infant psychotherapy.* New York: Basic Books.

Stolorow, R. D., Brandchaft, B., & Atwood, G. (1987). *Psychoanalytic treatment: An intersubjective approach.* Hillsdale, NJ: The Analytic Press.

Sullivan, H. S. (1953). *The interpersonal theory of psychiatry.* New York: W. W. Norton.

Surber, R. W. (1994). An approach to care. In R. W. Surber (Ed.), *Clinical case management: A guide to comprehensive treatment of serious mental illness* (pp. 3–20). London: Sage.

Wachtel, P. L. (1993). Active intervention, psychic structure, and the analysis of transference: Commentary on Frank's "Action, Insight, and Working Through." *Psychoanalytic Dialogues, 3,* 589–603.

Wachtel, P. L. (2002). Termination of therapy: An effort at integration. *Journal of Psychotherapy Integration, 12,* 373–383.

Winnicott, D. W. (1965). *The maturational process and the facilitating environment.* New York: International Universities Press.

CHAPTER 8

Self Psychology Theory

James I. Martin

Self psychology is a psychodynamic theory that originated in the United States only in the last 35 years. Although it was first conceived as a theory of psychoanalysis, self psychology is applicable to a wide variety of practice contexts and client populations. It is primarily used in clinical work with individuals, but it is increasingly being applied to other modalities.

According to this theory, people require an empathically responsive interpersonal environment to fuel their development and sustain their adaptive functioning. Many problems experienced by people today derive from an insufficiently responsive interpersonal environment. Practitioners using self psychology restore clients' adaptive functioning by meeting their needs for empathic understanding. To enhance adaptive functioning, practitioners help clients to influence their interpersonal environment more effectively so that it is more responsive to their psychological needs. Clients whose developmental process is stalled because of a chronic lack of responsiveness in their interpersonal environment may need long-term intervention in order to build missing psychic structure.

HISTORICAL DEVELOPMENT

Self psychology originated with Heinz Kohut who, as a young psycho-analyst, escaped the Nazi Holocaust and settled in the United States in 1942. Kohut eventually became president of the American Psychoanalytic Association. As a result of his clinical experience in postwar America, Kohut began to modify Freudian psychoanalytic theory (Lessem, 2005). Increasingly, he found that psychoanalysis based on Freudian theory was not effective with the "narcissistic" problems of his clients (Cushman,

1995). He gradually developed a new theory that fit within the framework of ego psychology at first (see Kohut, 1971), but which eventually abandoned many existing psychoanalytic assumptions (see Kohut, 1984). This new theory, which he called "the psychology of the self," ultimately grew well beyond its initial attempt to explain clinical narcissism (Lessem, 2005). Kohut died in 1981, after which the development of self psychology continued on several different paths.

Self psychology had its roots in British object relations theories and ego psychology (Bacal & Newman, 1990). Unlike classical psychoanalytic theory, which maintained that personality development resulted from the resolution of intrapsychic conflicts associated with biological drives, object relations theory asserted that development resulted from experiences in interpersonal relationships. Similarly, ego psychology theory minimized the importance of both the drives and intrapsychic conflict, instead stressing the development of "conflict-free" adaptive abilities. All three theories focused on early childhood as the boilerplate for adult psychopathology, for which the recommended treatment was psychoanalysis. Preceding Kohut, ego psychology theorist Hartmann (1939) and object relations theorist Winnicott (1965) expressed interest in both the self as the core of the personality and the important role of an average expectable environment for normal development.

Since Kohut's death, self psychology's influence has gone far beyond the domain of psychoanalysis. Writers in several fields have continued to develop the theory in a variety of ways. Some theorists continue to examine the theory within the context of psychoanalysis and long-term psychoanalytic psychotherapy, although among them there are different perspectives on important clinical and theoretical issues (e.g., Fosshage, 1998; Stolorow, Brandchaft, & Atwood, 1987; Wolf, 1988). New developments are continuing in the application of self psychology theory to interventions with couples (O'Connor, 1993), families (Pinsof, 1995), and groups (e.g., Harwood, 1998; Livingston, 1999; Phillips, 2005; Shapiro, 1997), and to short-term interventions with individuals (e.g., Basch, 1995; Gardner, 1991; Martin, 1993). The theory is increasingly used to understand and treat people's problems across the life span (e.g., Goldmeier & Fandetti, 1992; Miller, 1996; Shreve & Kunkel, 1991). The variety of problems to which self psychology has been applied include substance abuse (Chernus, 2005; Robinson, 1996), intimate partner violence (Brown, 2004), phobias (Jenkins, 2002), and end of life (Koppel, 2004).

In an even greater departure from its psychoanalytic origins, some writers have examined the theory's relevance to practice in child welfare settings (Goldmeier & Fandetti, 1991), in supervision of clinical trainees (Gardner, 1995), and for understanding health risk behaviors (Martin & Knox, 1995, 1997).

Social workers have been exposed to self psychology theory since its early development. In 1970, the University of Chicago Student Mental Health Clinic's chief psychiatric social worker, Miriam Elson, invited Kohut to lead a yearlong multidisciplinary seminar on the treatment of young adults. Elson (1987) compiled the case vignettes that were presented in the seminar along with Kohut's discussion and analysis of them. Since Kohut's death, numerous social workers have continued to interpret and expand the theory and its application to direct practice (e.g., Chenot, 1998; Elson, 1986; Goldstein, 1997; Martin, 1993; Mishne, 1993; Paradis, 1993; Young, 1994).

CENTRAL THEORETICAL CONSTRUCTS

Self-Cohesiveness and Self-Fragmentation

Self psychology concerns itself with the relative cohesiveness of the human *self*, the enduring core of the personality and center of one's experience and initiative. However, Kohut believed that the self could only be understood within its subjective context (Lessem, 2005). The self may be evaluated, as both a long-term characteristic and a short-term state, on a continuum from *cohesive* to *fragmented*. Thus, even a person with a relatively cohesive self may experience states of *self-fragmentation*. An individual's ability to regulate self-esteem, monitor and regulate stress, and pursue realistic goals indicates *self-cohesiveness*. In states of self-cohesiveness people may feel energized, self-efficacious, focused, and whole. They may function relatively well in their social and occupational roles. Conversely, unstable self-esteem, inability to self-soothe, and problems with goal attainment indicate self-fragmentation. In states of self-fragmentation people may feel weakened, hopeless, confused, and scattered. They may experience difficulties in role performance. Addictive behaviors, depression, insomnia, suicide, panic, somatic preoccupations, social withdrawal, and nonorganic cognitive impairments may indicate a state of self-fragmentation.

Basic Structure of the Self

Most contemporary theorists consider the self to be a tripolar structure. The three poles, which Kohut named the *pole of ambitions*, the *pole of ideals*, and the *pole of twinship*, are actually major themes of self-related experience that develop over a lifetime. The pole of ambitions consists of experiences of uniqueness, vigor, and greatness. The pole of ideals consists of experiences of calm, support, and uplift. The pole of twinship consists of experiences of essential belonging and likeness to others.

Kohut (1977) theorized that people are born with a primitive *virtual self* that contains the seeds from which the three poles of self-structure grow. These poles consist of needs for admiration, praise, and confirmation (*mirroring needs*); calming, supportive, and uplifting responses from others (*idealizing needs*); and acceptance and kinship responses (*twinship needs*). Self-structure develops in the three poles as a result of interactions between the virtual self (and later, the developing self) and the interpersonal environment. To the extent that any of these needs are understood and met with appropriate responses from significant others over time, self-structure is built in each of the poles. But to the extent that any of these needs are repeatedly misunderstood or disregarded, self-structure fails to develop.

Selfobject Needs and Functions

Self psychology calls mirroring, idealizing, and twinship *selfobject needs*; appropriate responses to them *selfobject functions*; and the sources of those responses *selfobjects*. Selfobjects are one's subjective experiences of people as they respond in ways that enhance one's self-cohesiveness. Selfobjects that respond empathically to mirroring needs are mirroring selfobjects, and selfobjects that respond to idealizing or twinship needs are, respectively, idealizing and twinship selfobjects. When parents provide what they believe to be reassurance and calming responses to their child's distress, they are not themselves idealizing selfobjects. Rather, the selfobjects are simply those dimensions of the parents that the child experiences as providing reassurance and calm. In addition, though a parent might provide reassurance and calm, it might not be quite the response that the child needs at that moment. In other words, people's subjective experiences of having their selfobject needs met are far more important than any outsider's view of the interaction. Therefore, the only way to know whether an interpersonal response provided a selfobject function for a person is to examine whether that response resulted in enhancement of the person's self-cohesion.

Self psychology views the development of the adult self as the result of innumerable experiences of empathic responsiveness to an individual's selfobject needs. Gradually, selfobject functions provided externally become internalized as self-functions through a process called *transmuting internalization*. Self psychology theorists have debated the process by which transmuting internalization results in the building of self-structure. Kohut (1977) proposed that development of self-structure requires some frustration of selfobject needs (*optimal frustration*). According to this formulation, children whose selfobject needs are understood and met perfectly have no reason to internalize the selfobject functions, so they will remain dependent on external sources. However, occasional lapses in empathic responsiveness provide children with the motivation to take over a bit of the mirroring, idealizing, or twinship functions for themselves. As long as the lapses are not too frequent or severe, they will result in the gradual building of self-structure. Later theorists (Bacal, 1985; Stolorow, 1983) argued that the inevitable lapses in empathic responsiveness during development are incidental to the development of self-structure. Rather, self-structure develops as a result of the gradual accumulation of experiences of empathic responsiveness (*optimal responsiveness*).

Although self psychology considers the process of development as one in which individuals gradually increase their ability to meet their own selfobject needs, it also asserts that people never become completely independent of selfobjects (Elson, 1986). Especially during periods of severe stress, disappointment, loss, or illness, adults who have cohesive self-structures can still experience heightened needs for externally provided selfobject functions in order to restore or maintain their self-cohesiveness. Kohut and Wolf (1978) called such episodes *secondary disorders of the self*, or temporary self-fragmentation states that occur in a person who has a cohesive self-structure. They called problems associated with deficits in self-structure *primary disorders of the self*. These disorders exist because of chronic lapses in empathic responsiveness to selfobject needs associated with at least two of the three poles during the course of development. Although people can usually compensate for deficits in one pole of self-structure with strengths in another pole, they are unlikely to overcome deficits in two or more poles in this way (Kohut, 1977). People with primary disorders of the self are highly vulnerable to experiencing self-fragmentation states. They may experience emotional distress and cognitive or behavioral symptoms in reaction to a much wider variety of stressors than people who have more cohesive self-structures (Martin & Knox, 1995).

Children and adults alike cue others to respond to their selfobject needs through *transference*. In traditional psychoanalytic theory, transference is considered to derive from unresolved developmental conflicts. However, self psychology views transference as a normal component of interpersonal relationships, consisting of a set of expectations (Elson, 1986) that are not always related to developmental issues. For example, people with a secondary disorder of the self may express strong needs for mirroring or idealizing through transference even though they have a cohesive self.

Role of Defenses

Although most people develop defenses to protect themselves from fragmentation, people with primary disorders of the self are especially likely to use primitive defenses to protect their fragile self-structure. *Withdrawal* and *disavowal* are two noteworthy defenses described by Basch (1988). Withdrawal is the most primitive defense against experiencing painful affect. Infants may withdraw either by turning attention away from the source of displeasure or by falling asleep. Similarly, adults may withdraw behaviorally from social interaction in order to prevent expected injuries to their self. People utilizing disavowal unconsciously block the formation of a link between their perception of a threatening event and the development of painful affect that would likely be associated with it. As a result, they have no awareness of unpleasant feelings associated with the event.

In addition to these defenses, people with primary disorders of the self are likely to have defensive structures consisting of frequent behaviors and/or fantasies used to cover over their self-structure deficits (Elson, 1987) and prevent fragmentation. One example is a combination of social withdrawal and retreat into wish-fulfillment fantasies, and another is the abuse of chemicals and the use of compulsive sex. In both examples, the use of these defensive structures may lessen the frequency or severity of self-fragmentation episodes through behavioral, cognitive, and/or affective avoidance of threatening stimuli.

A Hopeful View of Development

Even though self psychology regards childhood to be the most critical period of time for the development of self-structure, it considers development to be a never-ending process. Kohut believed that maladaptive patterns are only "way stations on the path to health" (Elson, 1987, p. 36). In other words, disorders of the self should not be considered permanent. In a sufficiently responsive interpersonal environment, people with such disorders may progress along a developmental spiral of increasing self-esteem and competence to establish a new equilibrium (Basch, 1988).

PHASES OF HELPING

Although Kohut's theories about the self and its development have become increasingly popular, his theory of treatment is perhaps even more significant (Chernus, 1988). The concept of the *empathic mode of listening* is particularly important. Practitioners who use self psychology seek to understand clients' subjective experience of reality throughout the helping process, and they intervene from the perspective of that knowledge (Livingston, 1999). They attempt to understand how and why clients feel and think the way they do, assuming that at some level even the most maladaptive and troublesome behavior must make sense. The empathic mode of listening distinguishes self psychology from other clinical models in which practitioners strive for objectivity as external observers of clients and their problems. For example, the concept of cognitive distortions, as used in cognitive therapy, is incompatible with the empathic mode because it presumes the practitioner understands objective reality better than the client.

The following description of self psychology in the social work helping process focuses on short-term interventions. Because Kohut's original theory of treatment was a theory of psychoanalysis, it must be modified in several ways in order to be used in short-term practice. According to Martin (1993), these modifications include selection of limited treatment goals and a decrease in emphasis on transference material.

Engagement

Because self psychology places great emphasis on developing an empathic understanding of clients, practitioners do not challenge a client's interpretation of events during the engagement phase of the helping process. Instead, they focus on understanding how the client experiences events, and the affect and meaning associated with them. Practitioners attempt to support the client's subjective experience, although they may not necessarily agree with it. Attention to affect is a critical component of engaging clients for two reasons. First, affect is considered to provide the primary motivation for all behavior. Second, self psychology considers the acceptance and understanding of one's feelings a fundamental human need (Basch, 1988).

Assessment

The primary focus of assessment in self psychology is clients' relative self-cohesiveness. Thus, practitioners must determine whether their clients are experiencing a state of self-fragmentation. Here, examining clients' recent history is critical. Clients who report numerous episodes of self-fragmentation may have a primary disorder of the self and/or they may live in an extraordinarily stressful environment. By contrast, clients experiencing isolated episodes of self-fragmentation are likely to have a secondary disorder of the self. In either case, practitioners must determine clients' particular selfobject needs in order to help them restore self-cohesiveness.

Kohut (1959/1978) emphasized the importance of empathy as a scientific tool used for collecting data about clients' subjective reality. Although empathy is most likely to be used this way in intensive, long-term clinical practice, it remains a component of the assessment process in short-term practice. Basch (1988) explained how practitioners obtain and use data through introspection and empathy. The first step is to focus one's awareness on the affects that are stimulated in oneself through interactions with the client. Second, practitioners attempt to view their affective reaction from an objective perspective, rather than simply experiencing it. Third, practitioners examine whether their affective reaction is related to the client's behavior and verbal message. In the fourth step, practitioners attempt to determine how the information gained through their own introspection may enhance understanding of the client's behavior and verbal message.

The most important information about clients' selfobject needs is expressed through their transference to the practitioner. The use of introspection and empathy is especially important for obtaining this information. Expressions of transference are most likely to emerge in the course of longer term, intensive intervention. Because of self psychology's view of transference as a normal component of interpersonal relationships, practitioners should also look for it in even the briefest professional contacts with clients. In the course of short-term intervention, practitioners may also obtain information about clients' selfobject needs and defensive strategies by examining their interpersonal relationship patterns. For this reason, data concerning clients' current and past interpersonal relationships are extremely important for assessment.

Intervention

When clients have a secondary disorder of the self, intervention must be oriented toward restoring self-cohesiveness so that they can return to their previous level of functioning. In some cases, a practitioner's focused empathic understanding may be sufficient for this purpose. Thus, some clients feel restored after only a single session or two, even before any formal interventions begin. In other cases, directly providing selfobject functions in response to clients' mirroring, idealizing, and/or twinship needs acts to restore their self-cohesiveness (Elson, 1986; Lazarus, 1991; Paradis, 1993).

In order to accomplish significant improvement in primary disorders of the self, practitioners must help clients to internalize the self-structure they currently lack through long-term, insight-oriented intervention. In the short term, practitioners can be helpful to such clients by focusing intervention on bolstering self-cohesiveness. However, this strategy will not resolve the underlying primary disorder. To the extent that limited time and resources allow, practitioners should also help to enhance self-cohesiveness so the frequency or severity of future fragmentation episodes may be reduced. Martin (1993) described some ways in which practitioners can do so, including raising clients' consciousness about their needs for particular selfobject functions and building better strategies for getting those needs met.

When raising clients' consciousness about their selfobject needs, practitioners should avoid psychotherapeutic terminology. They can reduce client shame associated with needing other people by universalizing these needs. Adult clients may be surprised and relieved to learn that no one is entirely independent, and that we all need others to praise or support us from time to time. By using examples from clients' reported patterns of interpersonal relationships, along with appropriate use of transference, practitioners can help clients identify the selfobject functions they appear to need most in order to maintain their self-cohesiveness (Martin, 1993; Young, 1994). Practitioners should also help clients analyze the extent to which the members of their current support system are responsive to their needs.

When helping clients strategize better ways to get their needs met in relationships with others, a number of options should be considered. In some cases, clients might need help in changing patterns of communication in order to express their needs more clearly or assertively. In other cases, they might need help in both accepting the limitations of significant others and identifying new sources of needed selfobject functions. As described by Young (1994), practitioners might also need to intervene in the interpersonal environment in order to improve its responsiveness, especially when clients are children or adolescents. For example, they could educate parents about more effective ways of responding to their child's needs, or they could provide the opportunity for exposure to new selfobjects by drawing on appropriate community resources.

Termination

Consistent with the use of the empathic mode, practitioners should focus on understanding clients' subjective experience of impending termination. When clients experience termination as a positive transition, practitioners should not insist that they are denying negative feelings. When clients experience mild self-fragmentation as the termination date nears, practitioners should explore clients' feelings about terminating. The practitioner's focused empathic attention should help to restore cohesiveness. The longer the length of intervention, the more time practitioners should allow clients to prepare for termination. A single session might be sufficient for brief interventions, but as many as three or four sessions might be needed when the clinical work lasts more than 6 months.

As part of termination, practitioners should always review the extent to which clients feel they attained the goals set at the beginning of the helping process, even if objective measures were used to monitor progress. Especially when intervention is short-term, practitioners should help clients identify the extent to which they have remaining problems and strategize ways for them to work toward managing those problems in the future. Such strategies might lead to referrals for other services, including support, self-help, or therapy groups. At minimum, practitioners should encourage clients to maintain awareness of those situations or behaviors that precipitated the most recent fragmentation episode, and to seek interactions with others that help enhance their self-cohesiveness.

APPLICATION TO FAMILY AND GROUP WORK

Pinsof (1995) conceptualized self psychology as the deepest of the theoretical orientations that may guide practitioners' understanding of families and their problems because the self is "the most fundamental layer of human existence" (p. 20). When practitioners find that the fragile self-structure of a family member presents significant constraints on a family's ability to resolve its problems, they should consider referring that member for individual treatment. Solomon (1988) made similar recommendations for practitioners treating "narcissistically vulnerable" couples. Ungar and Levene (1994) described how viewing a family as a matrix of selfobjects can enhance practitioners' understanding of the family. In other words, the family, as a "supraordinate selfobject" (p. 307), may collectively function to satisfy its members' needs for mirroring, idealizing, and/or twinship. This view adds to an understanding of dyadic relationships between family members, and it may help self psychology-informed practitioners engaged in family treatment to maintain a systemic paradigm. According to O'Dell (2000), self psychology–informed clinical work may be especially helpful for validating the experiences of gay and lesbian families.

Several authors (Harwood & Pines, 1998; Livingston, 1999; Phillips, 2005; Shapiro, 1991; Stone, 1992) have examined the application of self psychology to group work. For example, Phillips (2005) described how a self psychology-informed bereavement group can provide an opportunity for both restoring and enhancing members' self-cohesiveness. In such groups, members and leaders are potential sources of selfobject functions. In addition, the group as a whole—the *group self*—may serve as a source of selfobject functions for its members. Thus, a group member experiencing an episode of self-fragmentation might regain cohesiveness through participation with the group as a whole, as opposed to interactions with a particularly significant member of the group (Phillips, 2005). According to Harwood (1998), self psychology may be particularly useful in group work when treating clients with narcissistic and borderline problems.

COMPATIBILITY WITH GENERALIST-ECLECTIC FRAMEWORK

The use of self psychology in direct social work practice is certainly compatible with a generalist-eclectic framework. Because self psychology is really three theories in one—a theory of development, a theory of psychopathology, and a theory of treatment—it may provide a metaframework for both understanding and treating clients while allowing for a variety of intervention techniques and strategies. In fact, self psychology de-emphasizes specific techniques in its focus on empathic immersion in clients' subjective experience (Livingston, 1999). In addition, practitioners using the empathic mode avoid limiting assessments to narrow theoretical preconceptions because they must subordinate any theoretical formulations to clients' subjective reality.

Finally, self psychology emphasizes the importance of client-practitioner relationships characterized by warmth, genuineness, respect, and collaboration. It puts the highest value on the practitioner's use of empathy. At the center of the theory is the assertion that empathic responsiveness resolves client problems associated with self-fragmentation (Chenot, 1998). In addition, the disciplined use of empathy is a part of the assessment process. Because self psychology emphasizes clients' subjective reality over objective reality, it is well suited for respecting and supporting client uniqueness. Because it asserts that people naturally progress toward maturity and health (Chenot, 1998), self psychology–informed treatment empowers clients by supporting and adding to their strengths and removing obstacles to progress.

CRITIQUE OF THE THEORY

As conceptualized by Kohut (1977, 1984), self psychology was intended to guide long-term, intensive interventions with individuals. Practitioners limited to brief or short-term interventions with individuals, families, or groups are likely to find self psychology unhelpful without significant modifications to the theory, such as those indicated in this chapter.

Cushman (1995) warned that clinical practitioners who ignore the political, social, and economic forces that fuel the growth of "narcissistic" clinical problems in contemporary society might unknowingly contribute to them. According to Cushman, the dominant construction of the self in contemporary American society is the "empty self," of which the feeling of existential emptiness is a primary characteristic. A main reason for this feeling is the extreme emphasis on self-contained individuality by society's institutions and the consequent destruction of family and interpersonal relationships. Today's consumerist economy contributes to this feeling of emptiness because people must purchase more and more products (including psychotherapy) in order for the economy to function well. However, people's existential emptiness cannot be relieved by a product alone, and so both the emptiness and the promotion of products to relieve it continue endlessly. Cushman argued that relying on self psychology to understand and treat people's problems might contribute to society's overemphasis on self-contained individuality and result in existential emptiness. Thus, practitioners must maintain awareness of the political, social, and economic forces impacting clients, and expand their repertoire of intervention strategies beyond those designed to resolve intrapsychic problems.

The extent to which self psychology is applicable across cultural groups is not clear. By its very focus on the individual self, the theory expresses Western cultural traditions. As noted by Steele (1998), these traditions place great value on a "strong self" (p. 94), which Western psychotherapy views as a desirable goal of development. However, among Asian cultures a strong self is often considered a sign of arrested development, and the transcendence of selfhood may be more desirable.

Gardiner (1987) criticized self psychology theorists for ignoring gender as an important developmental variable. Layton (1990) went further in charging that Kohut's conception of the self was sexist. However, Gardiner (1987) also stated that in many other ways self psychology is compatible with feminist theory. For example, it values empathy and interpersonal relatedness over rational insight and autonomy. Lang (1990) and Gardiner (1987) agreed that the methods of self psychology, especially its use of the empathic mode, could be important for developing a deeper understanding of women, their needs, and their experiences.

Self psychology is most suited to clinical social work services with clients having primary or secondary disorders of the self. The former category includes those clients with narcissistic, borderline, or avoidant personality disorders (American Psychiatric Association, 2000), whereas the latter category includes all clients experiencing a reduction in their psychological and/or social functioning. Self psychology may be less useful for treatment of clients who are actively psychotic. Although certain elements of self psychology—especially the emphasis on empathic responsiveness—may be applicable to any kind of clinical social work, the theory as a whole is not suited to practice situations limited to providing concrete services or making referrals.

CASE EXAMPLE

Margaret F., a 39-year-old White female, self-referred to an outpatient mental health center because of trouble managing stress associated with her marriage and other sources. She decided to seek professional help 2 weeks after she asked her husband, Thomas, for some support and he responded by getting angry. Margaret had been married for 2 years to Thomas, age 44, but they had no plans to have children. According to Margaret, Thomas believed that people should deal with stress on their own, and not rely on others. Margaret recently began a job directing a small child welfare organization, her first job in 5 years. She felt underpaid, so she was continuing to look for a better-paying job.

Margaret had a previous marriage to David for 15 years, ending 2 years ago in a difficult divorce in which she lost custody of their two daughters (current ages 7 and 11). She identified her drinking binges during the last couple of years of the marriage as the reason why David won custody of the children. However, she reported that David abused alcohol and drugs too. She felt that her attorney did not represent her well. The divorce decree allowed her to see the children two weekends every month and for 6 weeks during the summer. Because David always refused to help her, for each visit Margaret drove more than 2 hours each way to pick up and return the children. Margaret reported that Thomas had two previous marriages that both ended in divorce. He had one son who was living on his own. Margaret grew up on a farm in rural Illinois. When she was 13 years old her parents divorced, but they both remarried sometime later. She was the oldest of three sisters, in addition to having a half brother and a stepbrother. Her relationships with both full sisters were strained.

Near the end of the first session, the social worker, Charles D., reflected that Margaret wanted support badly and that her life sounded very scattered. He told her that it would be difficult to work on improving her marital relationship in individual therapy, and recommended couples treatment for this purpose. However, Margaret did not want couples treatment because she wanted to work on "her part" in the marital problems. Charles honored her request for individual therapy, and suggested meeting 9 more times, for a total of 10 sessions. They contracted to work on the obstacles that Margaret put in the way of getting the support she wanted.

In the second session, Margaret talked easily and freely. When Charles asked Margaret about sources of support in her life other than her husband, she identified her stepmother and a couple of women friends. However, she complained of having little time to do anything socially with them. During the session, Charles sometimes found it hard to get a word in edgewise. Although it was not yet clear, he wondered if this pattern might reflect a mirroring transference in which Margaret just wanted to be heard. During this session he also learned that her refusal to engage in marital therapy was related to a theme of not being heard or understood. She and David had engaged in marital counseling, but she felt that the therapist sided with her ex-husband and blamed her for everything. At the end of the session, Charles gave Margaret the following homework assignment: She was to make a list of specific situations she would like help in changing. They would prioritize them in the next session.

At the beginning of the third session, Charles asked Margaret about the previous week's assignment. She said that although she did it, she forgot to bring it with her. Attempting to recall the list, she talked about two types of situations that she found difficult. The first one involved a coworker who seemed hypersensitive and critical. The second one involved her husband, who made it hard for her to express her own needs and stand up for herself. Charles asked what got in the way of her speaking up more with her husband. It did not take Margaret long to identify that she was afraid—afraid of being alone. Talking about being alone made her think about not being able to make ends meet financially. Coming close to tears, Margaret recalled the poverty of her family of origin, which led to strong memories of being treated unfairly by her mother. She felt that her mother's unwillingness to spend money to buy her new clothes like other children had expressed a lack of support and understanding. Focusing on feelings was uncomfortable for Margaret. For homework, Charles asked her to continue paying attention to her feelings. She agreed, but then asked if they could shift back to a more cognitive focus afterward. Charles thought that working on a more cognitive level probably allowed Margaret to avoid some of the potent issues preventing her from getting on with her life.

Charles asked about the homework assignment at the beginning of the fourth session. Margaret reported that she did focus on her feelings during the week. She also quit her job, and her husband supported her doing so. It turned out that he was supportive to her, though inconsistently. Margaret also talked about problems with her mother. She always experienced her mother as lacking interest in, or understanding of, her feelings. Margaret voiced concerns that she was "too needy." Charles responded that this was not possible, because her needs were what they were. He added that the problem was not her needs, but whether other people were meeting them.

In the sixth session, Margaret spent much of the session talking about her mother. She reported calling her mother to say that she was not angry with her anymore, adding that she was letting go of all her anger. Considering the strong feelings that Margaret had expressed about her mother in previous sessions, Charles thought this conversation had an unreal quality to it. He responded that it was not clear to him how Margaret could "let it go," and asked her to explain it to him. She said that she had been angry her whole life and was tired of it. The anger was not good for her. Charles asked her to tell him about it. As she talked about her anger it became clear that behind it was the fear that her mother would again betray her.

Charles clarified that Margaret had certainly expressed anger at her mother over the years, but added that she had not expressed the feelings that lay behind it. He said that when she was able to do so, and resolve the issue, she would naturally move beyond the feeling of anger. He asked if this made sense to her, and she said that it did. Charles said that in order for Margaret and her mother to have a relationship of any kind, Margaret would have to set the parameters. She would have to define the kinds of interactions they would have, and the ways in which her mother would have to treat her. Although this made sense to Margaret, she said that it sounded difficult. Charles reminded her that they had only four more sessions, and it would be good to see her accomplish this change before their work ended.

At the beginning of the seventh session, Margaret reported that she called her mother and told her what she expects if they are to have any kind of relationship. She said that although the conversation felt good she was aware that her mother could betray her again. Margaret also talked about some recent conflicts with her husband regarding finances. Charles commented that perhaps the couple needed to work out a budget and an agreement on handling their finances.

Margaret spent most of the eighth session talking about David. She said that he "ranted and raved" on the phone after their older daughter visited her. She stood her ground with him on several areas of disagreement. She reported that this was not the first time she had done so, but it was the first time that she did not feel guilty about it. Charles drew parallels between Margaret's relationships with David, her mother, and Thomas, in which she had ignored her own feelings and needs out of fear of being betrayed. In order to be treated better, she would need to verbalize how she felt and what she wanted.

In the ninth session, Margaret reported that her mother followed through on some things that she had asked her to do regarding the children. Instead of feeling pleased, Margaret felt hurt and angry because her mother did not do everything that she asked. Charles supported these feelings as understandable, but he also encouraged Margaret to give her mother positive feedback for following through partly. He said that it seemed any attention to her needs by her mother made her more aware of what she did not get over the years. Perhaps she used anger to insulate herself from feeling hurt and disappointed. Margaret thought this made sense. Charles encouraged her to keep asking her mother for what she wanted, to keep paying attention to her own feelings, and to try not to remain stuck in her angry/defensive posture. Near the end of the session, Margaret talked about having some positive interactions with her husband.

In the tenth session, Margaret said that she spent a 4-day weekend with her mother, sister, and daughters. She felt emotionally and physically depleted from the long weekend. She tried to explain to her sister how she felt about their mother, but her sister did not understand. Margaret made a point to thank her mother for helping with the children, and asked her to go a step further. Because her mother did not respond, it was not clear if she would follow through. Charles told Margaret that it sounded like her family did not support her feelings or respond to her needs for attention or confirmation regarding her unique worth, which left her feeling disappointed, hurt, and angry. He told her that these needs were normal, and so were the feelings of disappointment, hurt, and anger. He encouraged her to keep trying to get the kind of understanding she wanted and deserved from her family, while realizing that she might not always get it. He also encouraged her to develop other sources of support, including her husband. Margaret said that she had accomplished the goal that she set at the outset of treatment. She thought that learning about her fear, and how her feelings were important and valid, was the most valuable lesson that she learned. However, she identified reaching an agreement with her husband about their finances and the possibility of her oldest daughter coming to live with her as challenges yet to be faced.

SUMMARY

Disorders of the self may be some of the most common problems encountered in clinical practice today (Cushman, 1995; Martin, 1993), and self psychology is uniquely relevant for understanding and treating them. Although self psychology originated as a form of psychoanalysis, the above case illustrates one way in which it may be applied to short-term social work practice. Its focus on subjective experience helps clients to feel understood, and it may help to reduce the potential for treatment biases according to ethnicity, gender, sexual orientation, and other aspects of client diversity. However, the literature on the use of self psychology in clinical work with ethnic minorities, gay, lesbian, bisexual, and transgender clients, or children remains limited. Few articles describe short-term applications of self psychology, and none report on its effectiveness in treatment. These are important areas for continued development.

REFERENCES

American Psychiatric Association. (2000). *Diagnostic and statistical manual of mental disorders, DSM–IV–TR* (4th ed.). Washington, DC: Author.

Bacal, H. A. (1985). Optimal responsiveness and the therapeutic process. In A. Goldberg (Ed.), *Progress in self psychology* (Vol. 1, pp. 202–227). New York: Guilford Press.

Bacal, H. A., & Newman, K. M. (1990). *Theories of object relations: Bridges to self psychology.* New York: Columbia University Press.

Basch, M. F. (1988). *Understanding psychotherapy: The science behind the art.* New York: Basic Books.

Basch, M. F. (1995). *Doing brief psychotherapy.* New York: Basic Books.

Brown, J. (2004). Shame and domestic violence: Treatment perspectives for perpetrators from self psychology and affect theory. *Sexual and Relationship Therapy, 19,* 39–56.

Chenot, D. K. (1998). Mutual values: Self psychology, intersubjectivity, and social work. *Clinical Social Work Journal, 26,* 297–311.

Chernus, L. A. (1988). Why Kohut endures. *Clinical Social Work Journal, 16,* 336–354.

Chernus, L. A. (2005). Psychotherapy with alcoholic patients: A self psychological approach. *Smith College Studies in Social Work, 75*(3), 63–92.

Cushman, P. (1995). *Constructing the self, constructing America: A cultural history of psychotherapy.* Reading, MA: Addison-Wesley.

Elson, M. (1986). *Self psychology in clinical social work.* New York: W. W. Norton.

Elson, M. (Ed.). (1987). *The Kohut seminars on self psychology and psychotherapy with adolescents and young adults.* New York: W. W. Norton.

Fosshage, J. L. (1998). Self psychology and its contributions to psychoanalysis: An overview. *Journal of Analytic Social Work, 5*(2), 1–17.

Gardiner, J. K. (1987). Self psychology as feminist theory. *Signs: Journal of Women in Culture and Society, 12,* 761–780.

Gardner, J. R. (1991). The application of self psychology to brief psychotherapy. *Psychoanalytic Psychology, 8,* 477–500.

Gardner, J. R. (1995). Supervision of trainees: Tending the professional self. *Clinical Social Work Journal, 23,* 271–286.

Goldmeier, J., & Fandetti, D. V. (1991). Self psychology in child welfare practice. *Child Welfare, 70,* 559–570.

Goldmeier, J., & Fandetti, D. V. (1992). Self psychology in clinical intervention with the elderly. *Families in Society, 73,* 214–221.

Goldstein, E. G. (1997). To tell or not to tell: The disclosure of events in the therapist's life to the patient. *Clinical Social Work Journal, 25,* 41–58.

Hartmann, H. (1939). *Ego psychology and the problem of adaptation.* New York: International Universities Press.

Harwood, I. H. (1998). Advances in group psychotherapy and self psychology: An intersubjective approach. In I. H. Harwood & M. Pines (Eds.), *Self experiences in group: Intersubjective and self psychological pathways to human understanding* (pp. 30–46). London: Jessica Kingsley.

Harwood, I. H., & Pines, M. (1998). *Self experiences in group: Intersubjective and self psychological pathways to human understanding.* London: Jessica Kingsley.

Jenkins, S. (2002). The interpretive process with a phobic young woman. In A. Goldberg (Ed.), *Postmodern self psychology: Progress in self psychology* (Vol. 18, pp. 77–86). Hillsdale, NJ: Analytic Press.

Kohut, H. (1971). *The analysis of the self.* New York: International Universities Press.

Kohut, H. (1977). *The restoration of the self.* New York: International Universities Press.

Kohut, H. (1978). Introspection, empathy and psychoanalysis: An examination of the relationship between mode of observation and theory. In P. Ornstein (Ed.), *The search for the self: Selected writings of Heinz Kohut, 1950–1978* (Vol. 1, pp. 205–232). New York: International Universities Press. (Original work published 1959)

Kohut, H. (1984). *How does analysis cure?* New York: International Universities Press.

Kohut, H., & Wolf, E. S. (1978). Disorders of the self and their treatment. *International Journal of Psychoanalysis, 59,* 413–425.

Koppel, M. S. (2004). Self psychology and end of life pastoral care. *Pastoral Psychology, 53,* 139–152.

Lang, J. A. (1990). Self psychology and the understanding and treatment of women. *Review of Psychiatry, 9,* 384–402.

Layton, L. (1990). A deconstruction of Kohut's concept of the self. *Contemporary Psychoanalysis, 26,* 420–429.

Lazarus, L. W. (1991). Elderly. In H. Jackson (Ed.), *Using self psychology in psychotherapy* (pp. 135–149). Northvale, NJ: Jason Aronson.

Lessem, P. A. (2005). *Self psychology: An introduction.* New York: Jason Aronson.

Livingston, M. S. (1999). Vulnerability, tenderness, and the experience of selfobject relationship: A self psychological view of deepening curative process in group psychotherapy. *International Journal of Group Psychotherapy, 49,* 19–40.

Martin, J. I. (1993). Self psychology and cognitive treatment: An integration. *Clinical Social Work Journal, 21,* 385–394.

Martin, J. I., & Knox, J. (1995). HIV risk behavior in gay men with unstable self esteem. *Journal of Gay & Lesbian Social Services, 2*(2), 21–41.

Martin, J. I., & Knox, J. (1997). Self-esteem instability and its implications for HIV prevention among gay men. *Health & Social Work, 22,* 264–273.

Miller, J. P. (1996). *Using self psychology in child psychotherapy.* Northvale, NJ: Jason Aronson.

Mishne, J. M. (1993). *The evolution and application of clinical theory: Perspective from four psychologies.* New York: Free Press.

O'Connor, D. (1993). The impact of dementia: A self psychological perspective. *Journal of Gerontological Social Work, 20*(3–4), 113–128.

O'Dell, S. (2000). Psychotherapy with gay and lesbian families: Opportunities for cultural inclusion and clinical challenge. *Clinical Social Work Journal, 28,* 171–182.

Paradis, B. A. (1993). A self-psychological approach to the treatment of gay men with AIDS. *Clinical Social Work Journal, 21,* 405–416.

Phillips, S. B. (2005). The role of the bereavement group in the face of 9/11: A self psychology perspective. *International Journal of Group Psychotherapy, 55,* 507–525.

Pinsof, W. M. (1995). *Integrative problem-centered therapy.* New York: Basic Books.

Robinson, C. (1996). Alcoholics Anonymous as seen from the perspective of self psychology. *Smith College Studies in Social Work, 66,* 129–146.

Shapiro, E. (1991). Empathy and safety in group: A self psychological perspective. *Group, 15,* 219–224.

Shapiro, E. (1997). The twinship-alter ego experience in group. *Issues in Group Psychotherapy, 1,* 35–52.

Shreve, B. W., & Kunkel, M. A. (1991). Self psychology, shame, and adolescent suicide: Theoretical and practical considerations. *Journal of Counseling and Development, 69,* 305–311.

Solomon, M. F. (1988). Treatment of narcissistic vulnerability in marital therapy. In A. Goldberg (Ed.), *Learning from Kohut: Progress in self psychology* (Vol. 4, pp. 215–230). Hillsdale, NJ: Analytic Press.

Steele, S. (1998). Self beyond ego: A new perspective. *Journal of Humanistic Psychology, 38*(1), 93–100.

Stolorow, R. (1983). Self psychology: A structural psychology. In J. D. Lichtenberg & S. Kaplan (Eds.), *Reflections on self psychology* (pp. 287–296). Hillsdale, NJ: The Analytic Press.

Stolorow, R., Brandchaft, B., & Atwood, G. (1987). *Psychoanalytic treatment: An intersubjective approach.* Hillsdale, NJ: The Analytic Press.

Stone, W. N. (1992). The place of self psychology in group psychotherapy: A status report. *International Journal of Group Psychotherapy, 42,* 335–350.

Ungar, M. T., & Levene, J. E. (1994). Selfobject functions of the family: Implications for family therapy. *Clinical Social Work Journal, 22,* 303–316.

Winnicott, D. W. (1965). *The maturational processes and the facilitating environment: Studies in the theory of emotional development.* New York: International Universities Press.

Wolf, E. S. (1988). *Treating the self: Elements of clinical self psychology.* New York: Guilford Press.

Young, T. M. (1994). Environmental modification in clinical social work: A self-psychological perspective. *Social Service Review, 62,* 202–218.

Section B

Cognitive-Behavioral Theories

CHAPTER 9

Cognitive-Behavioral Theory and Treatment

Norman H. Cobb

One of the most exciting and beneficial evolutions in counseling theory and practice in the past 20 to 30 years has been the merger of significant portions of behavioral theory and cognitive theory. The benefit for professionals and clients is a variety of treatment methods called cognitive-behavioral therapies that have shown to be effective with an impressive list of client problems.

OVERVIEW OF COGNITIVE-BEHAVIORAL THEORY

For decades, cognitive theorists and behavioral theorists competed for influence in assessment and treatment in social work, psychology, counseling, and other helping professions. Cognitive and behavioral practitioners understood common disorders according to their respective theories. For example, cognitive theorists understood depression as the influence of negative, illogical, or self-destructive beliefs. Behavioral theorists understood depression as the result of a high rate of punishers and a low rate of reinforcers in the client's environment. Both cognitive and behavioral approaches acquired significant research support with clinical populations (Chambless & Ollendick, 2001).

Over the years, however, many professionals became more and more aware that their clients suffered from a combination of factors—some attributable to irrational beliefs, some resulting from aversive and negative environments. Additionally, clients with differing levels of severity of symptoms required more of either cognitive or behavioral methods

(Jacobson et al., 1996; Martell, Addis, & Jacobson, 2001). For example, in the early phase of treatment, severely depressed clients are unable to use the cognitive directives and require more behavioral interventions. Later, as the severity subsides, cognitive interventions become more effective.

As a result, more and more mental health issues and problems in living have benefited from the combination of cognitive and behavioral approaches. Cognitive-behavioral treatments have demonstrated effectiveness with a variety of disorders such as major depression, phobias, posttraumatic stress disorder, sexual disorders, and thought disorders, as well as in couple, family, and group counseling (refer to O'Hare, 2005, for a good review of evidence-based practices for social workers).

HISTORICAL DEVELOPMENT

Both the behavioral and cognitive traditions have their own array of famous theorists and models. In the behavioral tradition, Pavlov (1927) demonstrated that, through association in time and space, the sound of a bell could have the effect of cuing a dog to produce a biological reaction of salivation—classical conditioning/learning. B. F. Skinner (1953, 1974) documented that when behavior occurs, whatever follows it (the consequences of behavior) can either increase or decrease the frequency, duration, or intensity of the behavior—operant conditioning/learning.

Albert Bandura (1969), a behaviorist, explored the role of cognition, and he posited the prospect that people also learn vicariously, without having to directly experience stimulus-response conditioning such as the positive or negative consequences of behavior. He asserted that merely by watching, hearing, or reading about behavior, people capture cognitive images of behavior and, in their thoughts, they replay or rehearse the behavior. Furthermore, they expect to receive reinforcement in the future if and when they perform the behavior. Bandura's consideration of cognitive mediation in behavioral learning led to developments in social learning theory and pointed the field of behavior theory toward a merger with cognitive theory.

In the cognitive tradition, Albert Ellis (1977) contended that irrational beliefs lead people to display dysfunctional behavior, and he developed rational emotive therapy, which focused on challenging and changing irrational or illogical beliefs. Aaron Beck's (1967, 1976; Beck, Rush, Shaw, & Emery, 1979) research led him to believe that depression was a product of people's beliefs about their own defectiveness, helplessness, hopelessness, and/or insurmountable problems, and he developed his cognitive therapy for depression.

From the behavioral and the cognitive perspectives, theorists increasingly conceptualized two types of behavior—overt behavior and covert behavior. Overt behavior is composed of observable outward actions such as walking, speaking, and waving at someone to get their attention. Covert behavior is composed of behaviors that are performed in people's thoughts or cognitions. Covert behaviors include thoughts, perceptions, feelings, attributions of causality, and so forth. Most important, however, is the understanding that both overt and covert behaviors are learned through classical and operant principles and vicariously through modeling. For example, infants make sounds that remotely resemble words, and their parents get excited and loudly proclaim some version of "Our baby's talking!" Although infants are too young to be cognitively processing these events in any formal way, they are certainly stimulated by the experience. If the stimulation is pleasant and not aversive or scary, infants will soon repeat the sounds or similar versions of them. After a while, parents will give less attention to less meaningful (or understandable) words and more attention to relevant words that are similar to "Mama!" or "Papa!" Gradually, words are learned through reinforcement and the behavioral shaping process, and children's language skills emerge to be remarkably like those of their parents.

More recently, an additional theoretical development that has contributed to the cognitive-behavioral evolution is the constructivist perspective (Granvold, 1999; Neimeyer, 1993; see chapter 16), which asserts that people generate their own cognitive patterns and their own sense of reality. Constructivist theory suggests that people embellish historical events and relationships and create their own life perspectives. In essence, their learning histories become the grist for their views of their world.

The historical merger between cognitive and behavior theories and the evolution of cognitive-behavioral theory and treatment has been enormously helpful. This merger has enabled us to understand various ways that positive and troublesome behaviors, both overt and covert, are acquired and potentially changeable.

CENTRAL THEORETICAL CONSTRUCTS

Both behavioral and cognitive theories have constructs that address the acquisition, expression, and modification of overt or covert behavior. In the following pages, a discussion of the theoretical constructs of cognitive and behavioral theory will illustrate the ways in which all human beings—our clients, friends, coworkers, partners, children, and so forth—can unlearn problematic thoughts and behaviors and learn more adaptive thoughts and behaviors. It should be cautioned that learned behaviors that are deeply integrated into people's habits, perceptions, perceived emotional reactions, and so forth, may resist extinction or change. Still, even behaviors that are a function of biological processes (e.g., genetics, drug use, brain chemistry) may be altered or at least managed by coping strategies, cognitive restructuring, and learning alternative behavioral patterns. The following briefly details the fundamental principles in each theory.

Behavioral Theory

Learning is a central theme in behavioral theory. Three general paradigms are included in the behavioral learning process: classical conditioning/learning, operant conditioning/learning, and social learning theory. Each of these paradigms is discussed below.

Classical Conditioning/Learning

Pavlov (1927) was well aware of the biological connection between the smell of dog food and the dog's response of salivation. He discovered, however, that after a short time of pairing the ringing of a bell (originally a neutral stimulus) with the smell of dog food (an unconditioned/unlearned stimulus), he could make the dog salivate just by ringing the bell (the bell became a conditioned/learned stimulus; see Figure 9.1).

Human beings also learn through this familiar process. For example, prospective parents may purchase a small baby blanket in anticipation of their new infant. In the beginning, the blanket has no more meaning to

Smell of Dog Food   Salivation
UCS   UCR
Unconditioned (Unlearned)   Unconditioned (Unlearned)
Stimulus   Response

When an originally neutral stimulus, such as a ringing bell, is paired with a UCS (such as dog food), the bell becomes a conditioned stimulus (CS) that evokes a conditioned response (CR).

Ringing Bell   Salivation
CS   CR
Conditioned (Learned)   Conditioned (Learned)
Stimulus   Response

FIGURE 9.1   Classical conditioning.

the child than did the new bell to Pavlov's dog. However, if the parents use the baby blanket when the baby is feeding and feeling comfort from the milk, the blanket may take on magical qualities. After a few weeks of association of the milk/comfort and the blanket, the blanket may become a significant source of comfort to the child. As a result, the parents will be surprised to find that the child will not want to be separated from the "blankie" because of the comfort that it provides.

Unfortunately, classical learning does not always produce good learning. For example, the natural arousal produced by loud sounds can be associated with nonthreatening objects. If an unsuspecting toddler is playing near the family car and another child honks the car's horn, the toddler will most likely be frightened by the loud sound (a natural response). In classical conditioning fashion, the loud noise may become associated with the car. If the pairing of the loud sound and the car is sufficiently strong or repeated, the child may develop an aversion to the car. When the parents say, "Let's go for a ride!" the young child may exhibit some type of fear response. As in this example, some phobias can be acquired (learned) through this process.

Operant Conditioning/Learning

Skinner (1953, 1974) described an "operant" as a behavior that affects or is affected by the environment. Therefore, what follows the behavior, the consequence, either increases, maintains, or decreases the frequency, duration, or intensity of the behavior. Five behavioral principles describe operant learning mechanisms: positive reinforcement, negative reinforcement, punishment, extinction, and response cost. The following two sections briefly explore ways that the frequency, duration, or intensity of behaviors can be increased or decreased by operant conditioning principles.

Increasing behavior. The frequency, duration, or intensity of behavior can be increased through positive reinforcement or negative reinforcement. Positive reinforcement is a process, mechanism, or procedure where a behavior (R) is followed by a positive stimulus (S^+), such that the subsequent frequency, duration, or intensity of behavior increases (see Figure 9.2).

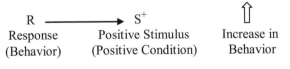

FIGURE 9.2   Positive reinforcement.

FIGURE 9.3   Negative reinforcement.

Negative reinforcement is a process, mechanism, or procedure where a behavior (R) is followed by the termination of a negative or aversive stimulus (S⁻), such that the subsequent frequency, duration, or intensity of behavior increases (see Figure 9.3).

In both positive and negative reinforcement, the stimuli are vitally important. For example, in positive reinforcement the stimuli must be of some value to the person who displays the behavior. For example, if your beloved gives you flowers and you respond with something that your beloved likes (e.g., a thank-you, a hug, a kiss), the frequency of "flower giving" is likely to increase. This is an example of positive reinforcement; however, if the frequency of the behavior does not increase or at least maintain the current rate, something else is happening. The stimulus (your response to the flowers) is of no value to the gift-giver, or he or she did not realize the connection. For example, if your response was sufficiently delayed or other things intervened (an argument, problem with the kids or work, etc.), your beloved may have missed the connection between the giving of the flowers and your response.

With negative reinforcement, the behavior terminates an aversive condition. For example, in the evening, you walk into a dark room and turn on the light. The "light turning on" behavior terminates the darkness (an aversive condition). After a few episodes of walking into the dark bedroom and turning on the light, you might be surprised to walk into the room in the middle of the day and, without thinking, turn on the light. You might suspect that you have "lost your mind," but in reality your light-turning-on behavior has become habituated through negative reinforcement! Other examples include putting on your seatbelt to terminate the aversive dinging sound in your car or putting on sunglasses to dim the bright sunlight.

Decreasing behavior. Punishment, extinction, and response cost decrease the frequency, duration, or intensity of behavior. As mentioned earlier, the characteristics of the stimuli that follow the behavior are all important.

Punishment is a process, mechanism, or procedure where a behavior (R) is followed by a negative or an aversive stimulus (S⁻), such that the subsequent frequency, duration, or intensity of behavior decreases (see Figure 9.4). To use an earlier example, your beloved gives you flowers;

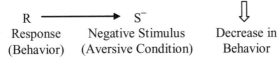

FIGURE 9.4   Punishment.

however, you are an ardent conservationist, and you reply, "I do not know why a responsible adult would kill a living organism to give it as some sacrificial expression of love." Now, unless your beloved is a slow learner, you have received your last gift of cut flowers.

Extinction is a process, mechanism, or procedure where a behavior (R) is no longer followed by a previously reinforcing stimulus (S+), such that the subsequent frequency, duration, or intensity of behavior decreases (see Figure 9.5). The best example is in the area of parent training: Parents are trained to extinguish their children's tantrums (when they are not destructive or harmful) by ignoring the tantrums.

Response cost is a process, mechanism, or procedure where a behavior (R) terminates a positive condition (S+), such that the subsequent frequency, duration, or intensity of behavior decreases (see Figure 9.6). For example, as an adolescent, you recently received your driver's license, and you asked to use the family car. Your parent reluctantly agreed, but because you were new to the driving role, your parent requested that you be home by 10 p.m. While you were gone, you had such a wonderful time and you could not imagine that your parent would mind if you were "a little late." When you returned home an hour and a half late, however, you were met by an anxious parent who said that you were now prohibited from driving the car. In operant learning terms, your lateness (R) resulted in the suspension of your driving privileges (S+), and subsequently, if the frequency of your coming home late decreased, response cost would have occurred.

Social Learning Theory (Vicarious Learning)

Albert Bandura (1969, 1977, 1978) recognized how people observe (or hear or read about) behavior and then perform the behavior much later,

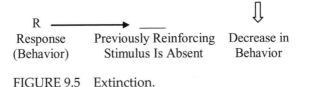

FIGURE 9.5   Extinction.

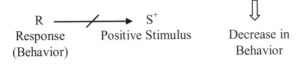

FIGURE 9.6   Response cost.

after several days or months have passed. Bandura called this vicarious learning through the process of modeling. In essence, people learned the behavior but withheld its enactment in their cognitive schema. They may have even played it repeatedly in their thoughts as if they were rehearsing the behavior. Later, they enacted the behavior with some expectation that they would receive a similar reinforcement to that received by the original model of the behavior (called expectancy of reinforcement).

In reality, we learn a great deal of our behavior through modeling. For example, if you have spent much time watching children and their parents, you have no doubt marveled how children mimic the facial expressions, hand gestures, and language patterns of their parents. Their parents have modeled the behavior for their children.

In clinical settings, clients report behaviors that are remarkably like the behaviors of their parents. For example, one man reported symptoms of dysthymia, a less severe, yet long-term version of major depression. When asked about his family, he described how his parents liked to stay at home, never got excited about much, seldom displayed emotion, and did not go out with friends because "they preferred to stay home at night and on the weekends." He remembered how his dad did not take a promotion at work, because he felt inadequate to handle the responsibilities. His mother talked about how life "used to be better." They modeled a life of little emotion, few outside activities, and employment that required little social interaction. He described himself as a "nice guy" who loved his couch and did not have much interest in outside activities. His wife said that she "knew how he was" before they married, but that she thought she could make him more social and feel better about himself. Although biological factors may play a role in some mood disorders, patterns of behavior and personality styles are easily modeled by parents and other important persons.

In a more positive vein, children learn many survival skills through modeling. For example, parents can easily demonstrate to children how to walk up to the street curb and look to the left and look to the right. Children will mimic parents' behavior, but further modeling is required to ensure sufficient survival skills. Parents must go the extra step to model for children how to watch for oncoming cars and learn the cognitive skill of estimating the rate of travel of oncoming cars and when it is safe to cross the street.

Cognitive Theory

Ellis's (1973, 1994) ABC model is a good example of how cognitive theory understands human functioning. In this model, A is an activating event from the environment (or a recalled memory). B refers to the beliefs (or covert behaviors), which can be rational or irrational, that people use to make sense of the activating event. C is the behavioral or cognitive/emotional consequence of the interaction of activating events and beliefs.

Covert behaviors are learned in the same manner as overt behaviors. Thus, beliefs, emotions, perceptions, attributions, and so forth, are acquired directly through classical conditioning, operant conditioning, and/or modeling (vicarious learning). For example, adolescent females experience a higher rate of depression than do males, and social and environmental reinforcers and punishers contribute significantly. When female and male high school students develop physically, they receive remarkably different reactions (activating events) from their peers, parents, and society. Males may be praised (reinforced) for gaining weight and looking bigger and tougher, more like a "real man." On the other hand, society puts so much emphasis on females' bodies that females may be rejected, criticized, or even blamed (all forms of punishment) for having body parts that are "too big" or "too small." They get the message that body shape is more important than good grades, sense of humor, or personality. This can have the unfortunate consequence of adolescent females developing negative beliefs about their self-worth. If this happens, environmental stimuli or activating events, such as interpersonal interactions, are filtered through increasingly negative beliefs about self-worth, and over time the consequence can be depression.

Beck's (1967, 1976; Beck et al., 1979) theory of depression underscored the impact of beliefs on people's mood. He found that depressed clients reported high rates of self-critical, judgmental beliefs. They reported feelings of helplessness and hopelessness and of being victims. As Beck and other cognitive theorists came to realize, people process information through a filter of their own thoughts and beliefs. Using a work setting example, when people hold the belief that they "don't measure up," evaluative comments from their bosses may be interpreted more harshly or more personally than intended. Similarly, depressed clients may interpret coworkers' compliments as fake or insincere. Clients can become despondent, even suicidal, because they believe that change is impossible and their life is hopeless. Beck et al. (1979) called such problematic beliefs "cognitive errors." They identified a number of common cognitive errors that lead to feelings of depression, including overgeneralizing, taking excessive responsibility, and dichotomous (right/wrong) thinking.

Cognitive theorists have shown how information processing affects people's judgments. For example, self-esteem (good or bad) has long been considered an important variable that influences behavior. The cognitive-behavioral perspective of self-esteem is practical and treatable. Self-esteem is construed as a belief (covert behavior) that is the product of a person's judgment about how he or she compares to others, either overall or with regard to specific abilities. For example, professionals who are required to take licensing exams frequently report that they "don't do well on tests." They are making the judgment that compared to "normal" test-takers (other recent graduates or other people in their profession whom they admire and respect), they will do much worse on the licensing exam. As a result, they feel inferior, and unfortunately, their belief may impact their performance on the exam. As a consequence, if they do poorly on the exam, they may have "proof" that they were right (and oddly enough, if they do well on the exam, they may attribute it to luck). If their poor self-comparison generalizes to other areas of their professional life, the feelings of low self-esteem may increase. The treatment of problematic covert behavior such as low self-esteem requires an analysis of the components of the client's judgment. Thus, depending on the person's beliefs, the intervention might focus on raising the person's assessment of his or her own testing ability, or the focus might be on lowering the unrealistic assumption about other people's abilities. Also, clients could be encouraged to take advantage of study aids (books, workshops, etc.) to raise their perceived level of competence.

Constructivism has received an increasing amount of attention among cognitive-behavioral theorists. Clearly, people construct their own sense of reality in numerous ways. For example, one person may apply one set of information-processing rules to one situation but not to another, and as a result, one's view of an event, other people, or oneself will vary from situation to situation and differ from other observers' views. Similarly, people interweave logical judgments, illogical beliefs, and individualized wishes, and create new beliefs, new ideas, and new versions of the present or the past. As a result, people generate an endless array of hypotheses about the world, and this underscores the rich diversity among individuals. The constructivist view should remind social workers that clinical assessment is a process of discovering the specific qualities of individuals, and treatments must be individualized to clients' unique behaviors and cognitions.

PHASES OF HELPING

Four phases map out a sequence for addressing clients' problems. They are engagement, assessment, intervention, and evaluation and termination.

Engagement

Cognitive-behavioral therapies endorse warmth, genuineness, and empathy as core ingredients in therapeutic communication. Warmth is communicated through a combination of gestures, tone of voice, facial expressions, and so forth, that convey a caring and sociable attitude. Professional warmth gives a sense of acceptance and concern for clients, but without the trappings of a personal friendship. Genuineness refers to helpers' communications that are open, spontaneous, and not defensive, thus allowing clients to experience the genuine communicator as upfront and straightforward (Egan, 2007). Finally, empathy requires workers to consider how clients might feel about particular events, and in response, communicate compassion and concern for the emotional impact of the situation on clients.

Engagement with clients is enhanced by viewing clients' problems from the perspective of learning. Clients are empowered by the perspective that if behavior (overt or covert) is learned, it can be unlearned, or if behaviors were never learned, they can be taught. Clients are delighted to hear that they are not defective, crazy, or "bad seeds," but rather their learned behaviors are not working for them, and/or they are not getting the results they want. This perspective is underscored by workers' acceptance of clients as human beings who have concerns about problem behaviors.

Assessment

The assessment process identifies problem areas and associated behaviors that need to be increased or decreased (in frequency, duration, or intensity) and/or learned and carried out. By focusing on behavior, clients can readily answer, "What happened?" "Who did what?" and "What happened next?" Many clients are less equipped to tell us how they are feeling, and even less capable of answering "Why?" With adolescents in particular, questions about "What happened?" or "Who did what" are less threatening than "Why did you do what you did?"

Assessment is a stage to determine what needs to change, but it is also a process that continues throughout the relationship between workers and clients. By assessing behaviors that work and behaviors that do not work, workers can plan fairly precise intervention methods to make changes. Also, identified behaviors allow for clear objectives by which the end product of treatment can be evaluated. Whether workers employ specific behavioral goals or single-subject design methods to track behavior change over time, identified behaviors (both overt and covert) can be used to verify treatment success or lead to strategic changes in the intervention plan.

Behavioral observation is one of the primary tools of assessment, and if properly conducted, it has high validity. Clients or observers can keep count of the frequency, duration, or intensity of behaviors. The observation serves as the baseline for future comparisons to determine change. For example, at a parent–child center, two sons were concerned about their mother's cussing, and their mother wanted them to clean up their rooms. All three agreed to the following assessment assignment: The boys would count the number of times their mother cussed in the morning and the evening. In turn, the mother counted the number the days when clothes were left on the floor of the bedroom or bathroom. She also counted the number of times she observed the boys taking dishes to the kitchen, cleaning the bathroom sink, and so forth. Although the task was intended to be for assessment purposes, the simple act of observing and being observed led to significant changes and agreements for future change.

Some problems, such as covert behaviors, are not as easily observed. For example, thoughts and feelings of depression are common mental health concerns. Depression, however, is a construct that takes on different forms with particular clients. Internal states of anger, sadness, feelings of lethargy, and so forth, are only measurable indirectly.

Rapid assessment instruments (RAIs) and self-anchored rating scales (also called individualized scales) enable clients to report covert behavior (Bloom, Fischer, & Orme, 2006). One of the most widely used RAIs is the Beck Depression Inventory (BDI; Beck, Ward, Mendelson, Mock, & Erbaugh, 1961). With this instrument, clients' responses to 21 questions result in a summary score that indicates the level of depression. The BDI is only one of dozens of RAIs for depression. Fischer and Corcoran (2007) compiled a two-volume set of RAIs most commonly used by social workers. They include measures for children, families, adults, and couples, and cover a wide variety of problems of social work clients.

The self-anchored rating scale allows clients to create their own scales. For example, a worker could have a client label a 5-point scale to indicate level of happiness (rather than level of depression, which is negatively focused). One client was encouraged to come up with her own label for "1" to indicate unhappy, and she chose "Feel like hell." For "5" she chose "Skipping down the street." Her "3" became "Just-so-so."

Regardless of the label choices, the process of having the client label the points on a scale creates a sense of ownership of the scale and a subtle, yet effective, motivation to actually use the scale at home and report the results to the social worker.

One additional element can help clients use self-anchored scales (or RAIs given to clients as homework). Workers can help clients select cues in the environment that will signal them to complete their scales. For example, a client asserted that she was angry "all the time." She was asked to keep a log of her anger and the situational contexts at three times during the day—morning, afternoon, and evening. Rather than using meal times as a reminder (which people sometime skip), the client decided to tape one copy of the scale to her bathroom mirror where she brushed her hair each morning, one copy in her computer calendar at work, and another copy on her alarm clock, which she set each evening. The cues successfully reminded her to mark her scale, and later, the information helped her understand the differential roles that her work, her teenage daughter, and her husband played in her levels of anger.

In addition to RAIs and self-anchored rating scales, clients can keep journals of their thoughts and behaviors during the day. The journal allows clients to record feelings or important events from the day. One strategy to ensure that clients record information in their journals daily is to have them put the journal on their bed pillow.

The observations, RAIs, scales, and journals enable clients and their social workers to pinpoint specific overt behavioral patterns and/or cognitions that, if changed, would significantly resolve their problems. Higher degrees of specificity enable more precise and, therefore, more effective methods of treatment.

Intervention

In the cognitive-behavioral approach, clients are not passive recipients of a magical therapy process. Instead, they must be involved in learning about and changing behavior and cognitions. Clients are usually very responsive to being educated about the cognitive-behavioral model of human functioning. In the cognitive-behavioral chapter of the first edition of this text, Regehr (2001) said, "Understanding . . . the theory empowers the client to engage fully in the process of determining targets of intervention and cognitive and behavioral prescriptions" (p. 171).

In a largely behavioral process, clinicians, clients, caregivers, and others can make reinforcers or punishers readily available in the environment and literally change how people behave and interact. In the cognitive mode, thoughts are viewed as covert behaviors that can be learned or unlearned. Information processing can be enhanced through an examination of the illogical beliefs or cognitive errors that drive actions. Because clients are seen as unique individuals, their specific, idiosyncratic beliefs, perspectives, and behaviors must be addressed in any intervention plan.

The following are brief descriptions of specific interventions that illustrate the range of cognitive-behavioral treatments. Most of the interventions reviewed incorporate a combination of cognitive and behavioral elements, and show that overt and covert behaviors rarely change independent of one another.

Systematic Desensitization and Flooding

Systematic desensitization (Wolpe, 1990) and flooding (Barlow & Brown, 1996) are behavioral approaches commonly used to treat phobias. They are similar in that each exposes clients to their feared objects (in vivo or through imagination) and clinicians help clients stay below their thresholds of panic and escape.

The first step in systematic desensitization is to help clients create hierarchies of fear-arousing situations or conditions. Although the feared object (e.g., snakes, airplanes) may be the same for different clients, the specific reasons or triggers for the fears are the result of the unique learning history of individual clients.

In the next step, clinicians teach or instruct clients to relax. Deep-muscle relaxation (Jacobsen, 1938; Bernstein & Borkovec, 1973) is an effective method to teach relaxation, but other methods are also effective (Madders, 1997).

In the third step, either in real-life situations (in vivo) or through imagined situations, clinicians gradually expose clients to increasingly fearful situations according to their fear hierarchies. As long as clients maintain levels of fear below their escape or panic threshold, clinicians can move on to scenarios of increased fear. The purpose is to expose clients to higher levels of fear without panic or escape, and therefore, enable them to become desensitized to feared objects or situations.

The technique called flooding also aims to desensitize clients to the feared object; however, rather than gradually exposing clients to a hierarchy of fears, they are given maximum exposure to their feared object. The maximum exposure takes place with the clinician talking the client through the experience. The purpose is to allow clients to experience the feared object without any of the feared or imagined consequences.

Cognitive restructuring is often used with systematic desensitization and flooding to help clients stay relatively relaxed. For example, clients who fear dogs can be exposed to dogs while the clinician reassures the client by saying such things as the following: "Dogs are living creatures just like us." "Dogs' saliva has fewer bacteria than humans' saliva." "Look how cute she is; she is so gentle." "As human beings, we are so big; we'll have to be careful to not scare her." "I'll bet she's afraid of us."

Behavioral Activation

One of the tenets of the behavioral theory of depression is that mood is dependent on the relative balance of reinforcers and punishers in people's lives. For example, people's moods are high when the level of reinforcers (e.g., good times, happy simulating events, pleasurable activities) is high and the level of punishers is low. Depression results when punishers significantly outweigh reinforcers. The cognitive perspective takes this situation a step further and emphasizes the connection between pleasurable, happy times and positive thoughts and emotional responses. Behavioral activation is a process of helping clients recall or recognize events or activities that bring pleasure and then motivating them to engage in those activities. The purpose is to increase the presence of positive reinforcers and reduce the incidence of punishers (Martell et al., 2001).

Contingency Management Techniques

Methods that focus on altering the consequences (both positive and negative) of behavior have wide applicability. Parents can ignore irritating, yet nondestructive behaviors in their children, and give positive attention, praise, or rewards for good behavior. The lack of attention to negative behavior initiates extinction, and the positive attention to good behavior reinforces the competing behavior. For example, children can be taught to play calmly with the family dog by praising them for gently petting the dog. A key element is to remember that behavior is "functional," meaning that behavior that receives reinforcement (e.g., praise, compliments, smiles) continues or increases; however, behavior that is punished or receives no attention decreases in frequency, duration, or intensity. The Premack Principle (Premack, 1965), whereby a high-probability (i.e., highly desirable) behavior is used to reinforce the performance of a lower probability behavior, demonstrates a type of contingency management. Barth (1986) referred to this principle as "Grand Ma's Rule" and used the example of a grandparent saying to a child, "As soon as you put your toys in the toy box, we can have a dish of ice cream." The assumption is, of course, that putting toys in a toy box is a low-frequency behavior, and eating a dish of ice cream is a high-probability behavior.

Response Prevention

In the past, the treatment for compulsive behavior prescribed a gradual decrease in the frequency of compulsive actions. For example, a client with a compulsion for checking that the stove was turned off was directed to gradually decrease the number of times he or she checked the stove daily. More recently, research discovered that attempts at gradual response reduction may inadvertently maintain compulsive behavior (O'Hare, 2005). Even though a client might reduce the number of times he or she checked the stove daily, the behavior could not be extinguished because checking the stove reduced anxiety and this reinforced the behavior. Therefore, any compulsive response maintained the connection between the obsessive worry and the compulsive behavior.

Therapy now focuses on helping clients to completely stop their compulsive behavior—response prevention. Toward this end, clients and workers first determine the events or thoughts that trigger obsessive thoughts. Then, these triggers are placed in a hierarchy of least to most intense. In a process similar to systematic desensitization, clients are exposed to the least intense triggers (imagined or real) until their level of anxiety gradually subsides. The decline in anxiety can be accelerated with relaxation, deep breathing, or reassuring comments from the clinician. The next intense trigger is presented until anxiety begins to decline, and so forth. In line with the behavioral principle of extinction, when clients no longer receive any benefit from the compulsive behavior, it declines in frequency or intensity.

Self-Monitoring

Self-assessment skills are useful for numerous situations and treatment interventions because self-awareness may often lead to change. The overall purpose of self-monitoring is to help clients recognize or be more aware of covert and overt behaviors. Journals or diaries enable clients to record their thoughts, feelings, and overt behavior. They become aware of critical self-statements, rational or irrational beliefs, and the circumstances that are associated with problematic behavior (e.g., the times when, or places where, they get angry).

Psychoeducation

For many client problems (e.g., parenting, obesity, medication management), simple skills training is very effective for facilitating change. The steps generally include the following: self-monitoring the behavior to be changed, setting realistic goals, developing a plan to change behavior, teaching ways to identify antecedents for distress and develop ways to control situations, identifying consequences of behaviors, teaching self-care skills (relaxation, increase in pleasant activities, control of negative thinking or social skills), and developing an emergency plan if problems develop (Craighead, Craighead, Kazdin, & Mahoney, 1994).

For example, parent training often incorporates skills to handle tantrums, reward good behavior, and provide alternatives to physical punishment. With overeating, clients can be taught to identify places or situations where overeating is probable, set specific meal times, remove foods from the house that encourage between-meal eating (and replace them with low-calorie foods), and get loved ones to cooperate with eating plans.

Anxiety and Stress Management

Interventions to control stress and anxiety include deep-breathing methods, self-talk (self-statements that are idiosyncratic to the client and produce a calming affect), cognitive distraction (where clients visualize positive and appealing scenes from their memory or imagination), and progressive muscle relaxation. As effective as progressive muscle relaxation is for inducing people's general state of relaxation, a word of caution is necessary. When clients are in heightened states of anxiety, their anxiety is maintained by their thoughts, which can occur and increase much faster than their ability to relax physiologically. Thus, in such situations, positive or protective thoughts or memories are more therapeutic.

Cognitive Restructuring

Clients' negative or destructive beliefs about themselves can be enormously troublesome. People tend to interpret actions and life events according to their negative views of themselves or others. Helping clients examine their beliefs and test their validity can enable clients to replace them with more realistic or more functional thoughts. For example, in Ellis's (1994) rational emotive behavior therapy (REBT), the worker's first task is to identify the irrational beliefs that are linked to the client's problem. This might involve pointing out to or convincing the client that he or she has an "all-or-nothing" belief (e.g., "I must be perfect every time and everywhere"). The worker would then actively dispute and refute the belief by pointing out its irrational aspects. This might involve assigning homework to refute the irrational belief. Finally, the worker would help the client to develop more rational beliefs and might assign homework to practice and reinforce such rational thinking.

Beck's (1967, 1976; Beck et al., 1979) cognitive therapy is also focused on cognitive restructuring and has many similarities to Ellis's REBT. In Beck's model, however, more reliance is placed on evidence from behavioral experiments and less emphasis on philosophical challenges to cognitive assumptions. Beck used three basic questions in his approach to cognitive restructuring: "What's the evidence?" "What's another way of looking at it?" and "So what if it happens?"

Self-Talk and Coping Statements

Most people are familiar with the old children's book where a train struggles to reach the top of the hill by saying, "I think I can, I think I can." Adults and children can be taught self-statements that guide their behavior or encourage a sense of competence or courage. The following example is an illustration of helping a mother address her children's fear of the dark and of going to sleep. A worker at a parenting center coached a mother to go through the following bedtime routine. In the evening, right before bedtime, she and the children were to sit on the floor outside their bedroom, and she was to hold up a book and say, "This book was written by a child expert who knows everything about kids." After thumbing through the pages, she was to pretend to read and say, "Oh, yes, the author wants me to read a special sentence, and you are supposed to repeat it after me." After the children agreed, she pretended to read and said, "Witches and ghosts (she paused for the children to repeat the words) are only real (pause) on TV and in the movies (pause). In my bed, I'm safe (pause)." Next, she said that the book directed her to repeat the phrase, but this time, the children were to whisper the sentence. She whispered, "Witches and ghosts (pause) are only real (pause) . . . " and so forth. Finally, she was to instruct the children to say the words inside their heads, and she again whispered the special sentence. Finally, she told them that the expert in the book said that at any time, if they felt afraid or worried, they could say the sentence to themselves and feel safe. At the next session with the social worker, she reported complete success.

Self-talk and coping statements can be used by everyone to benefit from self-encouragement or reassurance. Some clients who are afraid of public speaking are surprised to hear that famous public speakers are nervous before presentations, and they use self-statements to remember their speeches and reassure themselves. Test-takers may find comfort by reassuring themselves that they are not expected to know everything, and they know enough to do well on the test.

Summary

The interventions reviewed represent a sampling of cognitive-behavioral interventions; however, the list is not exhaustive. A wide variety of methods fit under the cognitive-behavioral rubric because of their assumptions about behavioral learning and change. Table 9.1 contains a list of common client problems and references to effective cognitive-behavioral interventions.

Evaluation and Termination

Evaluation is an ongoing process in cognitive-behavioral therapy. Progress toward the specific overt or covert behavioral goals, established early

TABLE 9.1   References for Cognitive-Behavioral Treatment of Selected Client Problems

Client Problem	Reference
Anxiety Disorders	
Obsessive-compulsive disorder	Abramowitz, Brigidi, & Roche (2001); Franklin & Foa (2002)
Panic and phobic disorders	Antony & Swinson (2000) Barlow & Craske (2000) Barlow, Raffe, & Cohn (2002)
Posttraumatic stress disorder	Boudewyns & Hyer (1990) Foa, Keane, & Friedman (2000) Mulick & Naugle (2004) Routhbaum, Meadows, Resick, & Foy (2000)
Medical Conditions	Giarratano (2004)
Mood Disorders	
Bipolar disorder	Reilly-Harrington & Knauz (2005)
Depression	Beck, Rush, Shaw, & Emery (1979) Kratochvil et al. (2005)
Schizophrenia	Huxley, Randall, & Sederer (2000) Mueser et al. (1999) Tarrier et al. (1999) Warman & Beck (2003)
Substance Abuse	Abbott, Weller, Delaney, & Moore (1998) Kaminer, Burleson, & Goldberger (2002) Miller, Meyers, & Hiller-Sturmhofel (1999)

in treatment, is reviewed continuously. Through behavioral observation, self-anchored rating scales, or journals, clients are largely responsible for providing the evaluative data to assess progress toward goals. Over time, the worker's clinical role may change from teacher to coach and supporter. The worker may also assess progress using single-subject or single-case methods to show clients how their behaviors have changed over time.

As clients become increasingly self-reliant over the course of therapy, termination is gradual. Termination becomes a time to celebrate the acquisition of new skills and to plan for ways to maintain changes following treatment. Clients are encouraged to continue to work on skills and reward themselves in meaningful ways, but they are reassured that they may return for further help if the need arises.

CASE EXAMPLE

The following is an example of a cognitive-behavioral intervention to effectively treat depression. The reader will notice different emphases on cognitive or behavioral issues in the various phases of the treatment. The combination is effective and can be tailored to the particular characteristics of clients (Craighead et al., 1994).

Mary is an adolescent female who recently graduated from college. During portions of her senior year, she experienced periods of depression. She was tired and lacked interest in some of her favorite activities. Her friends could seldom get her to go out, but when she did, she had to push herself to be friendly. Some of their old jokes seemed boring or even odd. When she was at home, she preferred to stay in her room and sleep. With her roommate, she preferred to watch TV and not interact.

The social worker began by helping her make the connection between her thoughts and her mood. She had Mary remember a time when one of her friends said or did something funny. During the discussion, the social worker pointed out that the memory seemed to affect her mood and made her feel happy. Similarly, she asked her to think about something that made her feel sad. They discussed how someone said something mean or rude to her that made her feel bad or sad. Together, they concluded that critical statements, or jokes at her expense, really bothered her. The worker proposed that her thoughts about the happy memory made her feel happy, and the memory of the critical remarks made her sad. The worker proposed the rationale that her thoughts determine her mood.

In the next step, the social worker asked Mary to self-monitor her behavior by keeping a journal of her thoughts and ideas that make her feel bad and the thoughts that make her feel good. They decided that every night before she went to sleep, Mary would write her thoughts in her journal.

In the next step, the worker asked Mary to list what she liked to do for fun and relaxation. The list included reading, playing with her cat, taking long baths, and going for walks. Mary stated that she had not taken the time to read or soak in the bathtub for a long time. The worker and Mary spent the next 15 minutes planning how she could find 30 minutes a day to read. Additionally, taking care of herself meant that in the next 7 days, she would take two long, hot baths.

At their next meeting, Mary forgot to bring the journal, but she talked about how the experience of keeping the journal helped her become more aware of the many negative or critical things about herself that she said inside her head. Mary was surprised at how this affected her. They began to list the comments and evaluate the extent to which they were true or false. Sometimes they were able to surmise that the comments were made by people who were not very happy themselves, or perhaps the person was simply being mean and critical.

Mary mentioned how she thought that she did not look very good. The social worker used humor, directed at herself, to illustrate how parts of her own body did not match up to society's advertising image of a perfect "10." She also laughed and said that while parts of her own body were not perfect, other parts were fantastic! The humor and phrase "Parts of me are fantastic" became an inside joke between them and a reassuring self-statement for Mary.

At the next meeting, Mary brought her journal, and she and the worker used three questions to evaluate the thoughts recorded in her journal: What evidence do you have for that belief? Is there an alternative explanation? What are the real implications for this belief? Together, they reframed and refocused most of Mary's worries and talked about some of Mary's assumptions about life and relationships. Some myths in Mary's thinking were exposed and some lack of fairness in society was put in proper perspective (reframed) or even made fun of. In the end, they constructed a plan for Mary to read, take baths, and pay attention to her self-care. They devised and rehearsed a strategy where she would evaluate other people's comments, decide if they had anything of value for her, and readily attribute the comments to the other person's personality or biases.

Two final notes are necessary. First, the combination of therapy and medication is often necessary for clients with depression. In this particular case, the social worker believed that antidepressants were not needed to raise her mood to facilitate counseling; however, a thorough medical/psychiatric examination should always be considered. When medications are appropriate, they increase clients' ability to make use of therapeutic interventions like the one above.

Second, the severity of depression should determine the emphasis placed on cognitive or behavioral approaches to treatment. When clients' depression is severe, behavioral treatment methods, such as behavioral activation, are required to raise clients' mood sufficiently for them to take advantage of the cognitive aspect of treatment.

APPLICATION TO COUPLES/FAMILIES AND GROUPS

Couple/Family Treatment

The cognitive-behavioral model can be very effective in work with couples because it accounts for individually learned behaviors, logical and illogical processing of information, and idiosyncratic constructions of reality. Epstein and Baucom (2003) have a fully developed treatment plan using cognitive-behavioral methods. One aspect of their interventions focuses on increasing the frequency of positive behaviors in couples' exchanges. The interventions are designed to increase the positive interactions through awareness and reinforcement. For example, in the "Caring Days" exercise (Stuart, 1980), each partner makes a list of behaviors (e.g., "Give me a hug," "Call me at work," "Say, 'Thank you' ") that, if enacted by the partner, would make the other partner feel loved and cared for. After the partners share their lists, they are invited in the following week to consider doing some of the requested behaviors. Later, the couple discusses the assignment to determine what worked.

Couples can also be coached to recognize automatic thoughts that occur in their day-to-day interactions. Gottman's (1999) research found that negative comments have far greater impact than positive comments. In his approach, couples are taught to recognize caustic or contemptuous words and phrases and eliminate them from their interactions. Additionally, couples are encouraged to consider "positive override"—a style of attributing their partner's aversive or negative behavior to accidents or temporary mistakes rather than to personality or character defects.

In family therapy, the cognitive-behavioral perspective helps family members identify their roles in the maintenance of beliefs and behavioral patterns. They are reminded that beliefs and actions continue if they are occasionally reinforced. For example, children learn to tantrum, and they use tantrums to get what they want. Parents are instructed that if the tantrum behavior is not destructive or dangerous, they should ignore the tantrum until extinction occurs.

Family members are taught that in troubled families, partners, as well as children, get more attention for negative behavior than they get for positive behavior. They are encouraged to watch for good behavior and give immediate and positive attention for the good behavior. Additionally, they are instructed to shape behavior by giving positive attention to versions of behavior that are fairly close to the fully formed behavior. Furthermore, they are encouraged, through cognitive restructuring, to develop a nonblaming attitude, where they do not take personally the difficulties of their children or their mates (Alexander & Parsons, 1982). For example, adolescents learn to avoid the axiom "It's all my parents' fault," and adults learn, "I am not totally responsible for all my children's mistakes" (Ellis, 1994).

Families are taught behavioral contracting where every member of the family accepts specific roles and behaviors (Falloon, 1991). The family devises a specific plan to celebrate when everyone meets most of the terms of the contract. For example, in one family, the family determined the specific duties for each family member for each evening. The children accepted their assigned tasks, and the adolescents felt empowered when they negotiated their duties. They also planned that if 80% of the tasks were completed by Friday evening, the whole family would celebrate with "Pizza Night." If the goal was not met, the meal would be sandwiches. One parent was in charge of keeping everyone aware of their tasks and keeping a chart of their completion. During the week, the parent updated the whole family on the progress toward the 80% criterion. When Friday evening arrived, the family celebrated with pizza or accepted the consequences of not meeting the goal.

Group Treatment

The power of a single therapist is multiplied as members in group therapy participate and support each other to make changes. Individual members can model for others a willingness to accept influence from the therapist (and the therapeutic modality) and one another. They can demonstrate courage to admit past problems and take on new behaviors. Group members can also coach each other on more effective ways to think and process information more logically. They may be more effective than the group worker in questioning the beliefs and assumptions of other group members.

Women's groups have a good history in creating and maintaining change. Women are socialized to emphasize the importance of relationships, which can translate into a willingness to accept change and experience group support.

One successful group work approach with which the author is familiar is for mothers who are recently divorced. The group focuses on the importance of having a structured evening routine and bedtime so that children feel a strong sense of security and mothers have some time for themselves. The structure provides some predictability of reinforcers, such as mother's attention to each of the children, evening baths, and so forth. Schedules are developed to give the mothers some private, personal time at the end of the evening. The schedule consists of an outline of tasks with specific times so that, in succession, all the children complete their homework, take baths, and get in bed by specified times. Each child is rewarded with 5 minutes of uninterrupted time with the mother at the child's bed. The mothers are rewarded for keeping the schedule because, when the children are in bed, they have a period of time for themselves to straighten up the house and do some type of self-care such as soak in the tub, read a book, or watch a favorite television show. The women in the group are reassured that keeping the schedule every evening might not always be possible, but regardless of what happens on any given night, they should be proud of their efforts, and the next evening will be another opportunity to try it again. The group setting allows the mothers to problem-solve different ways to create and carry out the schedule. As a result mothers feel empowered and supported to be successful.

COMPATIBILITY WITH THE GENERALIST-ECLECTIC FRAMEWORK

Cognitive-behavioral therapy and the generalist-eclectic framework are very compatible. Both emphasize the role of the social environment in shaping and maintaining individuals' behavior. In both approaches, clients are seen as collaborators throughout the helping process and everyone focuses on clients' strengths, concerns, and empowerment. Also, both approaches are open to incorporating a wide range of interventions from other treatment models. Some types of cognitive-behavioral therapy might be more structured and prescriptive than the generalist-eclectic approach, and the artistic, intuitive aspects of practice are less emphasized.

CRITIQUE OF COGNITIVE-BEHAVIORAL THERAPY

Strengths

Clients are attracted to cognitive-behavioral methods because of the commonsense perspective that both overt and covert behaviors are learned and can be unlearned. Typically, when clients come for treatment, they describe their problems from victim perspectives. They were victims of abusive or thoughtless parents or partners. Perhaps they are plagued by depression, fears, fate, "the nerves," bad bosses, unfair practices of others, and so forth. Through the assessment process and the focus on behaviors and thoughts, clients can begin to see that all of these issues are part of their learning histories and that some of their successes and failures are attributable to previously learned behaviors and thoughts. They become aware of how past experiences have led not only to poor coping skills, helplessness, or hopelessness, but also to survival and coping skills. Clients understand and appreciate the focus on learning new, more productive behaviors and ways of thinking. The cognitive-behavioral model works with all ages and can be tailored to the developmental level of the client. For example, children respond best to reinforcement, punishment, and extinction, whereas adolescents and adults often learn best through instruction, modeling, and cognitive interventions.

A major strength of cognitive-behavioral treatment is that a wide variety of interventions have been validated empirically for a range of client problems. The efficacy of cognitive-behavioral treatments has been established in controlled research projects, and its effectiveness has been documented in numerous clinical studies (Beck & Hollon, 2004; Chambless & Hollon, 1998; Chambless & Ollendick, 2001; Jacobson & Hollon, 1996; Lohr, 2003; Norcross, Beutler, & Levant, 2006).

Limitations

As mentioned earlier, the cognitive component of cognitive-behavioral treatment is not appropriate for some severe problems (e.g., severe depression, psychosis). Clients with severe problems often do respond, however, to behavioral interventions such as skills training. Still, even though behavior is learned, some long-standing, habituated behaviors resist change. Some behaviors are considered ingrained in the personality and behavioral repertoires of individuals and are resistant to change. Similarly, some anxiety-driven behaviors are difficult to extinguish because of the perceived level of threat to the individual. Also, clients who wish to explore life concerns in a philosophical, existential manner may not be suited to cognitive-behavioral treatment.

SUMMARY

Cognitive and behavioral theories and interventions have merged, and the result is a robust theoretical perspective of human behavior and a set of powerful, empirically validated interventions that address a variety of social work clients' problems. In this theoretical perspective, thoughts, cognitions, feelings, moods, and actions are conceptualized as covert and overt behaviors that are learned through the processes of classical and operant conditioning or vicariously learned through modeling. When social workers hear their clients talk about vague feelings and moods, they can direct their inquiry to the beliefs that trigger and maintain them. When clients display problematic behavior, they can look for the environmental contingencies (or clients' covert behaviors) that reinforce and maintain behavior.

Some cognitive-behavioral interventions focus on reinforcing positive behavior or reducing negative behavior with some version of punishment, extinction, or the reinforcement of alternative, competing behavior. Other interventions focus on helping clients to evaluate the validity of their personal beliefs and change their beliefs and internal dialogue through learned cognitive skills. Clients understand the focus on behavior and change. It makes sense to them, and therefore, they are more willing to cooperate. They understand how thoughts (covert behaviors) influence behavior and how overt behaviors are maintained through actual (or anticipated) reinforcement.

The continuing development and empirical validation of cognitive-behavioral interventions is exciting. The future challenge lies in the necessity that trained social workers adapt cognitive-behavioral interventions to fit the particular characteristics of their clients. The *science* embedded in the theory and interventions requires the *art* of caring and talented social workers.

REFERENCES

Abbott, P. J., Weller, S. B., Delaney, H. D., & Moore, B. A. (1998). Community reinforcement approach in the treatment of opiate addicts. *American Journal of Drug and Alcohol Abuse, 24,* 17–30.

Abramowitz, J. S., Brigidi, B. D., & Roche, K. R. (2001). Cognitive-behavioral therapy for obsessive-compulsive disorder: A review of the treatment literature. *Research on Social Work Practice, 11,* 357–372.

Alexander, J. F., & Parsons, B. V. (1982). *Functional family therapy.* Pacific Grove, CA: Brooks/Cole.

Antony, M. M., & Swinson, R. P. (2000). *Phobic disorders and panic in adults: A guide to assessment and treatment.* Washington, DC: American Psychological Association.

Bandura, A. (1969). *Principles of behavior modification.* New York: Holt, Rinehart and Winston.

Bandura, A. (1977). *Social learning theory.* Englewood Cliffs, NJ: Prentice Hall.

Bandura, A. (1978). Reflections on self-efficacy. *Advances in Behavior Research and Therapy, 1,* 237–269.

Barlow, D. H., & Brown, T. A. (1996). Psychological treatments for panic disorder and panic disorder with agoraphobia. In M. R. Mavissakalian & R. F. Prien (Eds.), *Long-term treatments of anxiety disorders* (pp. 221–240). Washington, DC: American Psychiatric Press.

Barlow, D. H., & Craske, M. G. (2000). *Mastery of your anxiety and panic: Client workbook for anxiety and panic.* San Antonio, TX: Graywind Psychological Corporation.

Barlow, D. H., Raffe, S. D., & Cohn, E. M. (2002). Psychosocial treatments for panic disorders, phobias, and generalized anxiety disorder. In P. E. Nathan & J. M. Gorman (Eds.), *A guide to treatments that work* (2nd ed., pp. 301–335). New York: Oxford University Press.

Barth, R. (1986). *Treatment of children and adolescents.* San Francisco: Jossey-Bass.

Beck, A. T. (1967). *Depression: Clinical, experimental, and theoretical aspects.* New York: Harper & Row.

Beck, A. T. (1976). *Cognitive therapy and the emotional disorders.* New York: International Universities Press.

Beck, A. T., & Hollon, S. D. (2004). Cognitive and cognitive-behavioral therapies. In M. J. Lambert (Ed.), *Bergin and Garfield's handbook of psychotherapy and behavior change* (5th ed., pp. 447–492). New York: Wiley.

Beck, A. T., Rush, A. J., Shaw, F. B., & Emery, G. (1979). *The cognitive therapy of depression.* New York: Guilford Press.

Beck, A. T., Ward, C. H., Mendelson, M., Mock, J., & Erbaugh, J. (1961). An inventory for measuring depression. *Archives of General Psychiatry, 4,* 561–571.

Bernstein, D., & Borkovec, T. (1973). *Progressive relaxation training: A manual for the helping professions.* Champaign, IL: Research Press.

Bloom, M., Fischer, J., & Orme, J. G. (2006). *Evaluating practice: Guidelines for the accountable professional* (5th ed.). Boston: Allyn & Bacon.

Boudewyns, P. A., & Hyer, L. (1990). Physiological response to combat memories and preliminary treatment outcome in Vietnam veteran PTSD patients treated with direct therapeutic exposure. *Behavior Therapy, 21,* 63–87.

Chambless, D. L., & Hollon, S. D. (1998). Defining empirically supported therapies. *Journal of Consulting and Clinical Psychology, 66,* 7–18.

Chambless, D. L., & Ollendick, T. H. (2001). Empirically supported psychological interventions: Controversies and evidence. *Annual Review of Psychology, 52,* 685–716.

Craighead, L. W., Craighead, W. E., Kazdin, A. E., & Mahoney, M. J. (1994). *Cognitive and behavioral interventions: An empirical approach to mental health problems.* Boston: Allyn & Bacon.

Egan, G. (2007). *The skilled helper: A problem-management and opportunity-development approach to helping* (7th ed.). Belmont, CA: Thomson Brooks/Cole.

Ellis, A. (1973). *Humanistic psychotherapy: The rational-emotive approach.* New York: McGraw-Hill.

Ellis, A. (1977). Rational-emotive therapy: Research data that supports the clinical and personality hypotheses of RET and other modes of cognitive-behavior therapy. *The Counseling Psychologist, 7*(1), 2–42.

Ellis, A. (1994). *Reason and emotion in psychotherapy: A comprehensive method for treating human disturbances* (Rev. ed.). New York: Birch Lane.

Epstein, N. E., & Baucom, D. H. (2003). *Enhanced cognitive-behavioral therapy for couples: A contextual approach.* Washington, DC: American Psychological Association.

Falloon, I. R. H. (1991). Behavioral family therapy. In A. S. Gurman & D. P. Kniskern (Eds.), *Handbook of family therapy* (2nd ed., pp. 65–95). New York: Brunner/Mazel.

Fischer, J., & Corcoran, K. (2007). *Measures for clinical practice and research.* New York: Oxford University Press.

Foa, E. B., Keane, T. M., & Friedman, M. J. (2000). *Effective treatments for PTSD: Practice guidelines from the International Society for Traumatic Stress Studies.* New York: Guilford Press.

Franklin, M. E., & Foa, E. B. (2002). Cognitive-behavioral treatments for obsessive-compulsive disorder. In P. E. Nathan & J. M. Gorman (Eds.), *A guide to treatments that work* (2nd ed., pp. 367–386). New York: Oxford University Press.

Giarratano, L. (2004). *Cognitive behavioral therapy strategies for use in general practice: Effective psychological strategies for medical practitioners.* Mascot, Australia: Talomin Books.

Gottman, J. M. (1999). *The marriage clinic: A scientifically based marital therapy.* New York: W. W. Norton.

Granvold, D. (1999). Integrating cognitive and constructive psychotherapies: A cognitive perspective. In T. B. Northcut & N. R. Heller (Eds.), *Enhancing psychodynamic therapy with cognitive-behavioral techniques* (pp. 53–93). Northvale, NJ: Jason Aronson.

Huxley, N. A., Randall, M., & Sederer, L. (2000). Psychosocial treatments in schizophrenia: A review of the past 20 years. *Journal of Nervous and Mental Disease, 188,* 187–201.

Jacobsen, E. (1938). *Progressive muscle relaxation.* Chicago: University of Chicago Press.

Jacobson, N. S., Dobson, K. S., Truax, P. A., Addis, M. E., Koerner, K., & Gollan, J. K. (1996). A component analysis of cognitive-behavioral treatment for depression. *Journal of Consulting and Clinical Psychology, 64,* 295–304.

Jacobson, N. S., & Hollon, S. D. (1996). Cognitive-behavior therapy versus pharmacotherapy: Now that the jury's returned its verdict, it's time to present the rest of the evidence. *Journal of Consulting and Clinical Psychology, 64,* 74–80.

Kaminer, Y., Burleson, J. A., & Goldberger, R. (2002). Cognitive-behavioral coping skills and psychoeducation therapies for adolescent substance abuse. *Journal of Nervous and Mental Disease, 190,* 737–745.

Kratochvil, C. J., Simons, A., Vitiello, B., Walkup, J., Emslie, G., Rosenberg, D., & March, J. S. (2005). A multisite psychotherapy and medication trial for depressed adolescents: Background and benefits. *Cognitive and Behavioral Practice, 12,* 159–165.

Lohr, J. M. (2003). *Science and pseudoscience in clinical psychology.* New York: Guilford Press.

Madders, J. (1997). *The stress and relaxation handbook: A practical guide to self-help techniques.* London: Vermilion.

Martell, C. R., Addis, M. E., & Jacobson, N. S. (2001). *Depression in context: Strategies for guided action.* New York: W. W. Norton.

Miller, W. R., Meyers, R. J., & Hiller-Sturmhofel, S. (1999). The community-reinforcement approach. *Alcohol Research and Health, 23,* 116–120.

Mueser, K. T., Rosenberg, S. D., Drake, R. E., Miles, K. M., Wolford, G., Vidaver, R., & Carrieri, K. (1999). Conduct disorder, antisocial personality disorder and substance use disorders in schizophrenia and major affective disorders. *Journal of Studies on Alcohol, 60*(2), 278–284.

Mulick, P. S., & Naugle, A. E. (2004). Behavioral activation for comorbid PTSD and major depression: A case study. *Cognitive and Behavioral Practice, 11,* 378–387.

Neimeyer, R. A. (1993). Constructivism and the cognitive psychotherapies: Some conceptual and strategic contrasts. *Journal of Cognitive Psychotherapy, 7,* 159–171.

Norcross, J. C., Beutler, L. E., & Levant, R. F. (Eds.). (2006). *Evidence-based practices in mental health: Debate and dialogue on the fundamental questions.* Washington, DC: American Psychological Association.

O'Hare, T. (2005). *Evidence-based practices for social workers: An interdisciplinary approach.* Chicago: Lyceum Books.

Pavlov, I. P. (1927). *Conditioned reflexes.* Oxford, England: Oxford University Press.

Premack, D. (1965). Reinforcement theory. In D. Levin (Ed.), *Nebraska symposium on motivation: 1965* (pp. 123–180). Lincoln: University of Nebraska Press.

Regehr, C. (2001). Cognitive-behavioral theory. In P. Lehmann & N. Coady (Eds.), *Theoretical perspectives for direct social work practice: A generalist-eclectic approach* (pp. 165–182). New York: Springer Publishing Company.

Reilly-Harrington, N. A., & Knauz, R. O. (2005). Cognitive-behavioral therapy for rapid cycling bipolar disorders. *Cognitive and Behavioral Practice, 12,* 66–75.

Routhbaum, B. O., Meadows, E. A., Resick, P., & Foy, D. W. (2000). Cognitive-behavioral therapy. In E. B. Foa, T. M. Keane, & M. J. Fredman (Eds.), *Effective treatments for PTSD: Practice guidelines from the International Society for Traumatic Stress* (pp. 60–83). New York: Guilford Press.

Skinner, B. F. (1953). *Science and human behavior.* New York: Macmillan.

Skinner, B. F. (1974). *About behaviorism.* New York: Knopf.

Stuart, R. B. (1980). *Helping couples change: A social learning approach to marital therapy.* Champaign, IL: Research Press.

Tarrier, N., Wittkowski, A., Kinney, C., McCarthy, E., Morris, J., & Humphreys, L. (1999). Durability of the effects of cognitive-behavioral therapy in the treatment of chronic schizophrenia: 12-month follow-up. *British Journal of Psychiatry, 174,* 500–504.

Warman, D. M., & Beck, A. T. (2003). Cognitive-behavioral therapy for schizophrenia: An overview of treatment. *Cognitive and Behavioral Practice, 10,* 248–254.

Wolpe, J. (1990). *The practice of behavior therapy* (4th ed.). Elmsford, NY: Pergamon Press.

CHAPTER 10

The Crisis Intervention Model

Karen S. Knox and Albert R. Roberts

Crisis intervention is one of the practice models that is essential for competent social work practice. Social workers must be prepared to handle acute crises of various types and causes, because clients typically are experiencing difficulties or obstacles in effectively resolving such crises without intervention. Social work practitioners working in the fields of suicide prevention, gerontology, hospice care, medical/health care, child abuse, family violence, criminal justice, sexual assault, school-based services, mental health services, and family counseling all need to be knowledgeable about and skilled in dealing with crises, which result from an acute stressor, a pileup of stressors, or a traumatic event.

This chapter presents an overview of the historical development of crisis intervention and its contributions to generalist social work practice. Thus, we link the past to the present in order to better prepare social workers for practice in the 21st century. The basic assumptions and theoretical constructs of crisis theory are explained to elucidate the major tenets and goals of crisis intervention. Descriptions of the levels and stages of crises, different practice models, intervention strategies, and evaluation methods are provided.

OVERVIEW OF CRISIS INTERVENTION

Case Illustrations of Crisis Reactions

Sexual Assault

Mary was a college freshman when she was raped. She was walking to her car from the library when she was attacked from behind. She recalled her reactions a week later:

I was sort of in shock and numb. It was something you don't expect to happen. I had terrifying nightmares. But it could have been much worse. He held a knife to my throat while raping me and I thought he was going to kill me afterwards. I'm so glad to be alive. (Roberts, 2005b, p. 8)

Sudden Death

Expecting his wife home from work soon, Jeff begins to cook dinner to make up for a little argument they had at breakfast over paying the bills on time. The phone rings and Jeff is informed that his wife has been admitted to the hospital for a gunshot wound. When he arrives at the hospital, he learns that one of her coworkers shot and killed the office manager and four other coworkers. Jeff waits for his wife to come out of surgery, but she dies on the operating table. He never gets to talk to her, to apologize for the argument, or tell her he loves her.

Spousal Abuse

Judy has been married to Ray for 6 years and they have two children. The battering started when she was pregnant with their first child. The beatings were worse when Ray had been drinking, and as his drinking increased, so did the abuse. The final straw was a violent attack when Ray punched her in the face several times and threatened to kill her. The next day, Judy purchased a handgun, but as she was driving home, she decided she needed help. She called the battered women's shelter and said, "I'm afraid I'm going to kill my husband." The crisis worker immediately realized the volatility and dangerousness of the situation and gave Judy directions to the shelter outreach office (Roberts, 2005b, p. 8).

These case illustrations highlight the crises reactions of violent crime victims in the aftermath of traumatic victimization. Some crises situations are personal or family incidents, while others can be triggered by a sudden, community-wide traumatic event, such as a natural disaster, terrorist attack, or industrial accident. Victims of violent crimes usually experience a series of physiological and psychological reactions. Some common symptoms and reactions include intense fears, heightened anxiety, hypervigilance and startle reactions, intrusive thoughts and flashbacks, despair and hopelessness, irritability, terror, sleep disturbances, shock and numbness, extreme distrust of others, and shattered assumptions that the community where they reside is safe (Roberts, 2005b).

BASIC PRINCIPLES IN CRISIS INTERVENTION

Persons experiencing traumatic events usually can benefit from rapid assessment and crisis intervention. Crisis counseling shares many principles and strategies with brief, time-limited, task-centered, and solution-focused practice models. Crisis intervention is one of the action-oriented models that are present-focused, with the target(s) for intervention being specific to the hazardous event, situation, or problem that precipitated the state of crisis. Therefore, this model focuses on problems in the here and now and addresses past history and psychopathology only as they are relevant to the current conditions.

Crisis theory postulates that most crisis situations are limited to a period of 4–6 weeks (Hepworth, Rooney, & Larsen, 2006; Parad & Parad, 2006; Roberts, 2005b). Crisis intervention is time limited in that the goal is to help the client mobilize needed support, resources, and adaptive coping skills to resolve or minimize the disequilibrium experienced by the precipitating event. Once the client has returned to her or his precrisis level of functioning and homeostasis, any further supportive or supplemental services are usually referred out to appropriate community agencies and service providers.

For example, a sexual assault victim may receive emergency crisis intervention services from several crisis intervention programs over a period of time. Crisis counselors and victim advocates employed by a victim-witness assistance program may work with the client through the initial investigation and rape exam. Hospital emergency room social workers also may provide crisis stabilization and crisis counseling during the medical examination, and rape crisis programs typically have emergency response services for rapid intervention at the hospital and afterward. Most rape crisis centers provide short-term individual counseling services and time-limited (6–12 week) groups. The client should have stabilized and returned to a level of adequate functioning within this time frame. Any longer term treatment needs would then be referred to other public or private sector services.

Time frames for crisis intervention vary depending on several factors, including the agency mission and services, the client's needs and resources, and the type of crisis or trauma. Crisis intervention can be as brief as one client contact, which is typical with 24-hour suicide prevention or crisis hotlines. Some crisis situations may require several contacts over a few days of brief treatment, while others may provide ongoing and follow-up services for up to 10–12 weeks. Additional crisis intervention services may be needed in the future. With the example of a sexual assault survivor, another critical time for crisis reactions is experienced when any court proceedings are conducted. This may require client involvement or court testimony that triggers memories and feelings about the rape, which can produce crisis reactions and revictimization.

The immediacy and action orientation of crisis intervention require a high level of activity and skill on the part of the social worker. They also require a mutual contracting process between the client and the social worker, but the time frame for assessment and contracting must be brief by necessity. People experiencing trauma and crisis need immediate relief and assistance, and the helping process must be adapted to meet those needs as efficiently and effectively as possible.

Therefore, some of the tools and techniques used in the assessment and contracting phases, such as intake forms, social history gathering, engagement of the client, and intervention planning, must be used in ways or formats that differ from longer term practice models. The assessment, contracting, and intervention stages may need to be completed and implemented at the very first client contact. Clients in an active state of crisis are more amenable to the helping process, and this can facilitate completion of such tasks within the rapid response time frame.

With a rape survivor, the investigation and medical needs must be assessed and intervention initiated immediately. After this, safety issues are addressed. The victim may not feel safe at home if the rape occurred there or there is concern that the offender would not be arrested and could find the person there. Crisis intervention counseling would be implemented simultaneously while addressing these other needs, with the police and/ or hospital social worker providing multiple crisis services during this first contact. This process could take several hours, depending on the response time by law enforcement and medical professionals, as well as the client's coping skills and resources. The crisis social worker would need to follow through until the client had stabilized or had been contacted by another collateral provider of crisis services.

The social worker must be knowledgeable about the appropriate strategies, resources, and other collateral services to initiate timely intervention strategies and meet the goals of treatment. Specialized knowledge about specific types of crises, traumatic incidents, or client populations may be necessary for effective intervention planning. For example, crisis intervention with victims of family violence requires education and training on the dynamics and cycle of battering and abuse, familiarity with the community agencies providing services to this client population, and knowledge about the legal options available to victims. Similarly, social workers dealing with bereavement and loss in hospice settings need to be knowledgeable about the grief process, medical terminology, specific health problems or conditions, and support services for family survivors. Due to the diversity of crisis situations and events, the basic models and skills of crisis intervention must be supplemented by continued professional education and experience with specialized client populations or types of trauma encountered in generalist practice.

Another characteristic of crisis intervention models is the use of tasks as a primary change effort. Concrete, basic needs services such as emergency safety, medical needs, food, clothing, and shelter are the first priority in crisis intervention. Mobilizing needed resources may require more direct activity by the social worker in advocating, networking, and brokering for clients, who may not have the knowledge, skills, or capacity to follow through with referrals and collateral contacts at the time of active crisis.

Of course, the emotional and psychological trauma experienced by the client and significant others are important considerations for intervention. Ventilation of feelings and reactions to the crisis are essential to the healing process, and the practice skills of reflective communication, active listening, and establishing rapport are essential in developing a relationship and providing supportive counseling for the client. The social worker may find that intervention strategies and activities must target all levels of practice simultaneously to be effective in meeting the goals of treatment.

HISTORICAL DEVELOPMENT

Although crisis intervention has developed into a cohesive treatment model only in the past 50 years, human beings have been dealing with crises since antiquity. In ancient Greece, the word *crisis* came from two root words—one meaning "decision" and the other meaning "turning point." Similarly, the two symbols in Chinese language for *crisis* represent danger and opportunity. These definitions imply that crisis can be both a time for growth and impetus for change, as well as an obstacle and risk for harm and unhealthy reactions (Roberts, 1995; Sheafor & Horejsi, 2006).

Historically, family and religious systems helped people in crisis. The roots of crisis intervention developed in the 1940s and 1950s from several sources, including physicians, psychologists, psychiatrists, sociologists, social work, and the military. Much of the work was done by multidisciplinary teams involving these disciplines in various settings, such as public health agencies, hospitals, family counseling centers, and disaster response programs.

One of the pioneers in crisis intervention was Dr. Eric Lindemann, who was associated with the Harvard School of Public Health and Massachusetts General Hospital. His pioneering study on loss and bereavement with 101 survivors and family members of the victims of the Coconut Grove nightclub fire in Boston was one of the first efforts to develop a more systematic way of helping people in crisis (Lindemann, 1944). From his research, theories of the grief process and typical reactions to crisis were developed. He also concluded that the duration and severity of grief reactions appeared to be dependent on the success with which the bereaved person mourns and grieves the loss and changes, and readjusts to life without the deceased loved one (Roberts, 2005b).

Other developments in psychiatry in the 1940s and 1950s contributed to the knowledge and research base of crisis intervention. From ego psychology, Erikson's (1950) stages of human development included key psychosocial crises that had to be resolved over the course of life. He postulated that crisis and major life transitions are normal in human and social development and can help individuals develop coping skills to successfully resolve both maturational and situational crises.

Suicide prevention services were another type of community-based mental health program that developed to respond to those in crisis. Much of the pioneering work was done at the Los Angeles Suicide Prevention Center in the late 1950s and 1960s (Dublin, 1963; Farberow & Schneidman, 1961; Roberts, 1975; Schneidman, Farberow, & Litman, 1970). As the suicide prevention movement developed, the Center for Studies of Suicide Prevention (now defunct) was established in 1966, and by 1972, almost 200 such programs had been established across the country (Roberts, 2005b).

The Victim Witness Assistance Act of 1982 and the Victims of Crime Act of 1984 established federal funding and state block grants for crisis intervention programs and victim advocacy services in the criminal justice system. These comprehensive programs are located at police departments, prosecutors' offices, and not-for-profit agencies. Victim advocates focus on helping crime victims and family members with court-related advocacy, medical and mental health issues, and financial assistance (Roberts, 1990). States and local communities have been able to develop family violence, sexual assault, and victim services programs as a result of this federal assistance. As a result, thousands of statewide, county, and city victim service and domestic violence programs expanded to help individuals resolve particular crime-related problems and crises (Roberts, 1990, 1997).

For the past 2 decades, the focus for research and development of crisis intervention services and skills has been on specialized client populations and groups, such as victims and survivors of sexual assault, child abuse, domestic violence, and violent crime. The effectiveness of crisis intervention programs in various community-based social service, law enforcement, and mental health agencies has been another focus of research and program evaluation (Boscarino, Adams, & Figley, 2005; Cohen, 2003; Dziegielewski & Powers, 2005; Nunno, Holden, & Leidy, 2003; Roberts & Everly, 2006). There has been a proliferation of journal articles and books dealing specifically with crisis intervention models, skills, and intervention strategies for particular client groups, including school-based programs, working with sexual assault and incest survivors, substance abuse, emergency services for disaster victims, family violence, and crisis intervention in health and mental health settings (Bowie, 2003; Jimerson, Brock, & Pelcher, 2005; Knox & Roberts, 2005a; Knox & Roberts, 2005b; Roberts & Yeager, 2005).

The nature of crisis intervention has changed dramatically since the Oklahoma City Federal Building bombing on April 19, 1995, and the terrorist attacks on the World Trade Center, the Pentagon, and United Airlines Flight 93 on September 11, 2001. We live in an era in which sudden, unpredictable crises and traumatic events are brought into our homes by the media (Roberts, 2005a). Millions of people are affected, either directly or indirectly. The flooding, widespread destruction of property, and evacuation of thousands of people from Hurricanes Katrina and Rita in 2005 serves as another wake-up call for all communities and crisis professionals to expand and coordinate interagency crisis response teams, programs, and resources. Recent research studies evaluating the effectiveness of the crisis responses to these recent disasters and terrorist attacks may serve as guideposts for more effective macro-level crisis intervention planning (Castellano, 2003; Dziegielewski & Sumner, 2002; Kaul, 2002; Underwood & Kalafat, 2002). The suddenness and severity of these recent national disasters and terrorist attacks that affect large numbers of people prove that it is imperative that all emergency services personnel and crisis workers be trained to respond immediately at both the micro and macro levels of practice (Roberts, 2005a).

THEORETICAL BASE AND CENTRAL CONSTRUCTS

The major tenets of crisis intervention derived originally from ego psychology and ecological systems theory. Central ideas borrowed from ego psychology include life developmental stages, psychosocial crises, coping skills, and defense mechanisms. From the systems/ecological perspective, concepts such as homeostasis, disequilibrium, and interdependence are basic principles of crisis intervention.

Cognitive-behavioral models, such as reality therapy, rational emotive behavior therapy, and neurolinguistic programming, share many characteristics with the basic assumptions and techniques of crisis intervention. These are all action-oriented models with a present focus and time-limited treatment. The cognitive-behavioral principle that an individual's perceptions and cognitions affect his or her beliefs, feelings, and behaviors in an interactive way is essential to crisis theory. The critical incident or precipitating event has to be perceived as a crisis by the client. Individuals involved in the same crisis situation may have very different perceptions, feelings, reactions, and coping skills (Datillo & Freeman 2000; Roberts, 2005b).

Two other newer practice models have contributed to or been included as part of a repertoire of techniques used in crisis intervention. The solution-focused model has been used in crisis intervention with diverse client populations and is particularly suited to managed care policies, which have institutionalized time-limited treatment in most public sector agencies, such as mental health clinics, medical or hospital settings, employee assistance programs, and health maintenance organizations (Dziegielewski, 1996; Greene, Lee, Trask, & Rheinscheld, 2005; Polk, 1996; Yeager, 2002; Yeager & Gregoire, 2005).

Another model that has been used in crisis intervention is eye movement desensitization and reprocessing, which was developed by Francine Shapiro (1995, 2001). This model is also time limited and espouses that if trauma can produce immediate symptomologies, then healing can also be accomplished in the same time frame by using this model's techniques. This approach has been used and researched with clients who suffer from posttraumatic stress disorder, such as military war veterans, community disaster victims, and sexual assault and incest survivors (Edmond, Sloan, & McCarty, 2004; Macklin et al., 2000; Marcus, Marquis, & Sakai, 2004; Roberts, 2005a; Silver, Rogers, Knipe, & Colelli, 2005).

Crisis intervention theories and models have evolved over the past 4 decades to incorporate a wide variety of techniques and skills from many different theoretical approaches. This is important in order to intervene with diverse client populations in various crisis situations and settings. However, the basic principles and assumptions of crisis theory provide a foundation knowledge base from which more specialized strategies and techniques can be learned and developed. Two other important concepts in crisis intervention—levels of crises and stages in crisis—are discussed next.

Levels of Crises

A classification paradigm developed by Burgess and Roberts (2005) for assessing emotional stress and acute crisis episodes identifies seven main levels of crises along a stress-crisis continuum. While each crisis and each individual's subjective experience to a crisis is unique, this stress-crisis continuum can be used in assessment and intervention planning to determine the level of care and most effective treatment modalities. It is important to note that the type of crisis services and the need for more intensive intervention may be necessary as the level of crisis increases along the continuum. An excellent source of information on appropriate, effective crisis intervention methods and techniques for the different types and levels of crises along the stress-crisis continuum is Roberts's (2005c) *Crisis Intervention Handbook: Assessment, Treatment, and Research.*

Level 1: Somatic Distress

This level of crisis results from biomedical causes and minor psychiatric symptoms that cause stress and disequilibrium in the individual's life. Other situational problems, such as health problems, relationship conflicts, work-related stressors, and chemical dependency issues would also be included in this level.

Level 2: Transitional Stress Crisis

This involves stressful events that are an expected part of the life span development. These crises are normal life tasks or activities that can be very stressful, such as premature birth, bankruptcy, divorce, and relocation. The individual may have little or no control over the situation and is unable to cope effectively.

Level 3: Traumatic Stress Crisis

These situations are unexpected, accidental, and outside the individual's locus of control. These crises can be life threatening and overwhelming. They include disasters, crime victimization, family violence, child abuse, and sexual assault.

Level 4: Family Crisis

This relates to developmental tasks and issues associated with interpersonal and family relationships that are unresolved and harmful psychologically, emotionally, and physically to those involved. Examples of this level of crisis are child abuse, family violence, homelessness, and parental kidnapping.

Level 5: Serious Mental Illness

This stems from a preexisting psychopathology, such as schizophrenia, dementia, or major depression, that can cause severe difficulties in adaptation for both the affected individual and the members of his or her family/support system.

Level 6: Psychiatric Emergencies

These are situations in which general functioning has been severely impaired, such as the acute onset of a major mental illness, a drug overdose, or suicide attempts. The individual has a loss of personal control and there is a threat of or actual harm to self and/or others.

Level 7: Catastrophic Crisis

This level of crisis involves two or more level 3 traumatic crises in combination with level 4, 5, or, 6 stressors. The nature, duration, and intensity of these stressful crisis situations and events and personal losses can be extremely difficult to accept and resolve. Examples of this level of crisis are losing all family members in a disaster or multiple homicides.

Stages of Crisis

The stages of crisis are similar to those of the grief process. These stages do not always follow a linear process—individuals can skip stages, can get stuck in a stage, or can move back and forth through successive stages. Although there are many theoretical frameworks for crisis intervention, most of them include the following four stages:

Outcry

This stage includes the initial reactions after the crisis event, which are reflexive, emotional, and behavioral in nature. These reactions can vary greatly and can include panic, fainting, screaming, shock, anger, defensiveness, moaning, flat affect, crying, hysteria, and hyperventilation, depending on the situation and the individual.

Denial or Intrusiveness

Outcry can lead to denial, which is blocking of the impacts of the crisis through emotional numbing, dissociation, cognitive distortion, or minimizing. Outcry can also lead to intrusiveness, which includes the involuntary flooding of thoughts and feelings about the crisis event or trauma, such as flashbacks, nightmares, automatic thoughts, and preoccupation with what has happened.

Working Through

This stage is the recovery or healing process in which the thoughts, feelings, and images of the crisis are expressed, acknowledged, explored, and reprocessed through adaptive, healthy coping skills and strategies. Otherwise, the individual may experience blockage or stagnation and may develop unhealthy defense mechanisms to avoid working through the impacts, issues, and emotions associated with the crisis.

Completion or Resolution

This final stage may take months or years to achieve, and some individuals may never complete the process. The individual's recovery leads to integration of the crisis event, reorganization of her or his life, and adaptation and resolution of the trauma in positive meanings of growth, change, or service to others in crisis. Many crisis survivors reach out through volunteer work and service organizations to support and help others who suffer similar traumas. For example, Compassionate Friends offers support groups and counseling services to parents and family who have lost a child through death.

PHASES OF HELPING

The phases of helping in various models of crisis intervention are similar to each other and to the phases of the problem-solving process (Hepworth, Rooney, & Larsen, 2006; Parad & Parad, 2006; Westefeld & Heckman-Stone, 2003). This chapter focuses on the ACT model (assessment, crisis intervention, and trauma treatment service), which is a conceptual three-stage framework and intervention model (Roberts, 2005a; see Figure 10.1). This model integrates various assessment and triage protocols with three primary crisis intervention strategies: the seven-stage crisis intervention model, critical incident stress management, and the 10-step acute traumatic stress management protocol. Each of these primary crisis intervention strategies will be discussed after a brief review of the ACT model.

The ACT model can be used with a broad range of crises and can facilitate the psychosocial/lethality assessment and helping process for effective crisis intervention across diverse types of clients and trauma situations. It is the only model that focuses explicitly on the need to assess lethality, particularly when clients present because of a life-threatening, dangerous, or violent precipitating crisis (Roberts, 1996, 2005a).

The A in the ACT model refers to triage, crisis, lethality, and trauma assessment and referral to appropriate community resources (Roberts, 2005a). The primary goal in conducting an assessment is to gather information that can be helpful in resolving the crisis. The assessment process should provide a step-by-step method of exploring, identifying, describing, measuring, and diagnosing health and mental health concerns, environmental conditions, strengths, resilience and protective factors, lifestyle factors, and current level of functioning (Roberts, 2005a). Appropriate triage and trauma assessment is critical to effective crisis intervention and treatment planning.

A	Assessment/appraisal of immediate medical needs, threats to public safety and property damage
	Triage assessment, crisis assessment, trauma assessment, and the biopsychosocial and cultural assessment protocols
C	Connecting to support groups, the delivery of disaster relief and social services, and critical incident stress debriefing (Mitchell & Everly, 1993)
	Crisis intervention (Knox and Roberts 2005a seven-stage model) implemented through a strengths perspective and coping skills bolstered
T	Traumatic stress reactions and posttraumatic stress disorders
	Ten-step acute trauma and stress management protocol (Lerner & Shelton, 2001), trauma treatment plans, and recovery strategies implemented

FIGURE 10.1   The ACT model.

The C in the ACT model refers to the crisis intervention treatment plan and services that are provided on the scene, through short-term treatment, or by referral to other community agencies. Types of services in this phase would include immediate crisis intervention; the delivery of basic needs and disaster relief; referral to appropriate community social services, medical facilities, and mental health agencies; and critical incident stress debriefing with survivors and first responders. The stages of crisis intervention are described more completely using Roberts's (2005a) seven-stage crisis intervention model (see below).

The T in the ACT model refers to the need for follow-up services to address any symptoms of posttraumatic stress disorder (PTSD) and to provide stress management services to prevent burnout for crisis responders. The secondary traumatization of first responders is addressed in this phase to deal effectively with their traumatic stress reactions and to implement recovery strategies.

Seven-Stage Crisis Intervention Model

Roberts's (2005a) seven-stage crisis intervention model can be used with a broad range of crises and can facilitate the assessment and helping process for effective crisis intervention across diverse types of clients and trauma situations (see Figure 10.2). This model is useful to delineate the specific tasks and strategies necessary for effective crisis intervention. The model adapts easily to the different levels of crises and to different time frames for intervention. All of these stages can be completed within one contact if necessary, and in many crisis situations, that may be all the time that is available.

Stage 1: Plan and Conduct a Crisis Assessment

Assessment in this model is ongoing and critical to effective intervention at all stages, beginning with an assessment of the lethality and safety issues for the client. With depressed or suicidal clients, it is critical to assess the risk for attempts, plans, or means to harm oneself at the current time, as well as any previous history of suicidal ideations or attempts. With victims of rape, family violence, child abuse, or assault, it is important to assess if the client is in any current danger and to consider future safety concerns in treatment planning. In addition to determining lethality and the need for emergency intervention, it is crucial to maintain active communication with the client, either by phone or in person, while emergency procedures are being initiated (Roberts, 1998, 2005b).

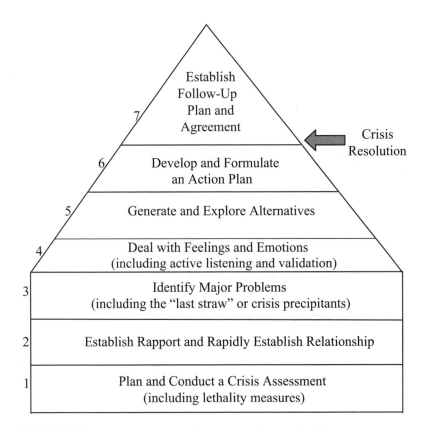

FIGURE 10.2   Seven-stage crisis intervention model.

To plan and conduct a thorough assessment, the crisis worker also needs to evaluate the severity of the crisis, the client's current emotional state, the client's immediate psychosocial needs, and the level of the client's current coping skills and resources. In the initial contact, assessment of the client's past or precrisis level of functioning and coping skills is useful; however, past history should not be a focus of assessment, unless related directly to the immediate traumatic event.

The goals of this stage are assessing and identifying critical areas of intervention, while also recognizing the hazardous event or trauma and acknowledging what has happened. At the same time, the crisis survivor becomes aware of his or her state of vulnerability and initial reactions to the crisis event. It is important that the crisis worker begin to establish a relationship based on respect for and acceptance of the client, while also offering support, empathy, reassurance, and reinforcement that the client has survived and that help is available. In crisis intervention, stages 1 and 2 may occur simultaneously; however, the most important goal in stage 1 is to obtain information to determine whether the client is in imminent danger (Roberts, 2005b).

Stage 2: Establish Rapport and Rapidly Establish Relationship

Stage 2 involves the initial contact between the crisis worker and the client, with the main tasks of establishing rapport and conveying genuine respect for and acceptance of the client (Roberts, 2005b). Survivors of trauma may question their own safety and vulnerability, and trust may be difficult for them to establish at this time. Therefore, active listening and empathic communication skills are essential to establishing rapport and engagement with the client. Even though the need for rapid engagement is essential, the crisis worker should try to let the client set the pace of treatment (Roberts, 2000). Many crisis victims feel out of control or powerless and should not be confronted or encouraged into action until they have stabilized and dealt with the initial trauma reactions.

Trauma survivors may require a positive future orientation, with an understanding that they can overcome current problems and with hope that change can occur (Roberts, 1996). During this stage, clients need unconditional support, positive regard, concern, and genuineness. Empathic communication skills such as minimal encouragers, reflection of thoughts and feelings, and active listening can reassure the client and help establish trust and rapport with the client. The crisis worker needs to be attentive to the tone and level of the verbal communications to help the client calm down or de-escalate from the initial trauma reactions.

The crisis worker must also pay attention to his or her body language and facial expressions, because trauma survivors may have been violated physically and may be hypersensitive to physical space and body movements, which can frighten or startle the survivor. Facial expressions can be difficult to monitor due to their automatic nature, but this is especially important when working with disaster or trauma victims when physical damage and destruction are evident.

Being observant of the survivor's physical and facial reactions can provide cues to the worker's level of engagement with the client, as well as a gauge to the client's current emotional state. It is also important to remember that delayed reactions or flat affect are common with trauma victims and to not assume that these types of reactions mean that the survivor is not in crisis.

Stage 3: Identify the Major Problems

The crisis worker should help the client prioritize the most important problems or impacts by identifying these problems in terms of how they affect the survivor's current status. Encouraging the client to ventilate about the precipitating event can lead to problem identification, and some clients have an overwhelming need to talk about the specifics of the trauma situation. This process enables the client to figure out the sequence and context of the event, which can facilitate emotional ventilation, while providing information to assess and identify major problems for work.

Other crisis clients may be in denial or unable to verbalize their needs and feelings, so information may need to be obtained from collateral sources or significant others. It is essential to use a systems framework during the assessment and identification of problems stages, because crisis situations may impact at all levels of practice. Family members and significant others may be important to intervention planning in supportive roles or to ensure the client's safety. However, they may be experiencing their own reactions to the crisis situation, and this should be taken into consideration in contracting and implementing the intervention plan.

The crisis worker must ensure that the client system is not overwhelmed during this stage, and the focus should be on the most immediate and important problems needing intervention at this time. The first priority in this stage is meeting the basic needs of emotional and physical health and safety. After these have stabilized, other problems for work can then be addressed (Roberts, 1998). In some cases, it can also be useful to identify the precipitating event or last straw that led the client to seek help now and to briefly explore any previous attempts or coping strategies to deal with the problem. The focus must clearly be on the present crisis, and any exploration of past problems or issues must be done rapidly and only to aid in intervention planning (Roberts, 2005b).

Stage 4: Deal With Feelings and Emotions

The primary tasks for the client in this stage include ventilation and exploration of his or her feelings and emotions about the crisis, which can be extremely therapeutic. The primary technique used by the crisis worker is active listening, which involves listening in an accepting and supportive way, in as private and safe a setting as possible (Roberts, 2005b). It is critical that the crisis worker demonstrate empathy and an anchored understanding of the survivor's experience, so that her or his symptoms and reactions are normalized and can be viewed as functional strategies for survival (Roberts & Dziegielewski, 1995). Many victims blame themselves, and it is important to help the client accept that being a victim is not one's fault. Validation and reassurance are especially useful in this stage, because survivors may be experiencing confusing and conflicting feelings.

Many clients follow the grief process when expressing and ventilating their emotions. First, survivors may be in denial about the extent of their emotional reactions and may try to avoid dealing with them in hopes that they will subside. They may be in shock and not be able to access their feelings immediately. However, significant delays in expression and ventilation of feelings can be harmful to the client in processing and resolving the trauma.

Some clients will express anger and rage about the situation and its effects, which can be healthy, as long as the client does not escalate out of control. Helping the client calm down or attending to physiological reactions such as hyperventilation are important activities for the crisis worker in this situation. Other clients may express their grief and sadness by crying or moaning, and the crisis worker needs to allow time and space for this reaction, without pressuring the client to move along too quickly. Catharsis and ventilation are critical to healthy coping, and throughout this process, the crisis worker must recognize and support the client's courage in facing and dealing with these emotional reactions and issues.

The crisis worker must also be self-aware of his or her own emotional reactions and level of comfort in helping the client through this stage. It is important for crisis workers to attend to their own self-care needs to avoid burnout and emotional fatigue. Secondary traumatization effects can be experienced by first interveners, and critical incident stress management interventions are necessary for their psychological health and safety (Kaul & Welzant, 2005).

Stage 5: Generate and Explore Alternatives

In this stage, effective crisis workers help clients recognize and explore a variety of alternatives for restoring a precrisis level of functioning. Such alternatives include (a) using support systems, such as people or resources that can be helpful to the client in meeting needs and resolving problems in living as a result of the crisis; (b) developing coping skills, which are behaviors or strategies that promote adaptive responses and resolution of the crisis; and (c) increasing positive and constructive thinking patterns to reduce the client's levels of anxiety and stress.

The crisis worker can facilitate healthy coping skills by identifying client strengths and resources. Many crisis survivors feel they do not have a lot of choices, and the crisis worker needs to be familiar with both formal and informal community services to provide referrals. For example, working with a battered woman often requires relocation to a safe place for her and her children. The client may not have the personal resources or financial ability to move out of the home, and the crisis worker needs to be informed about the possible alternatives, which could include a shelter program, a protective order, or other emergency housing services.

It is important to help the client generate and explore previously untried coping methods in a collaborative way, and it is equally important to examine and evaluate the potential consequences of and the client's feelings about those alternatives (Roberts, 2005b). The crisis worker may need to be more active, directive, and confrontational in this stage if the client has unrealistic expectations or inappropriate coping skills and strategies. Clients are still distressed and in disequilibrium at this stage, and professional expertise and guidance could be necessary to produce positive, realistic alternatives for the client.

Stage 6: Develop and Formulate an Action Plan

The success of any intervention plan depends on the client's level of involvement, participation, and commitment. The crisis worker must help the client look at both the short-term and long-range impacts in planning intervention. The main goals are to help the client achieve an appropriate level of functioning and maintain adaptive coping skills and resources. It is important to have a manageable treatment plan, so the client can follow through and be successful. Do not overwhelm the client with too many tasks or strategies, which may set the client up for failure (Roberts, 1996, 2000).

The client must also feel a sense of ownership in the treatment plan, so that the client can increase the level of control and autonomy in his or her life and not become dependent on other support persons or resources. Obtaining a commitment from the client to follow through with the action plan and any referrals is an important activity for the crisis worker that can be maximized by using a mutual process in intervention planning. Ongoing assessment and evaluation are essential to determine whether the intervention plan is appropriate and effective in minimizing or resolving the client's identified problems. During this stage, the client should be processing and reintegrating the crisis impacts to achieve homeostasis and equilibrium in his or her life.

The action plan should include attention to the four central tasks of crisis intervention (Slaikeu, 1984): (a) physical survival (maintaining physical health through adaptive coping skills and taking care of oneself through proper nutrition, exercise, sleep, and relaxation); (b) expression of feelings (appropriate emotional expression/ventilation and understanding how emotional reactions affect one's physiological and psychological well-being); (c) cognitive mastery (developing a reality-based understanding of the crisis event by addressing any unfinished business, irrational thoughts, or fears and by adjusting one's self-image/concept in regard to the crisis event and its impacts); and (d) behavioral and interpersonal adjustments (adapting to changes in daily life activities, goals, or relationships due to the crisis event, and minimizing any long-term negative effects in these areas for the future).

Termination should begin when the client has achieved the goals of the action plan, or has been referred for additional services through other treatment providers. Many survivors may need longer term therapeutic help in working toward final crisis resolution, and referrals for individual, family, or group therapy should be considered at this stage.

Stage 7: Establish Follow-Up Plan and Agreement

It is hoped that the sixth stage has resulted in significant changes and resolution for the client with regard to his or her postcrisis level of functioning and coping. This last stage should help determine whether these results have been maintained, or if further work remains to be done. Typically, follow-up contacts should be done within 4 to 6 weeks after termination. It is important to remember that final crisis resolution may take many months or years to achieve, and survivors should be aware that certain events, places, or dates could trigger emotional and physical reactions to the previous trauma. For example, a critical time is at the first anniversary of a crisis event, when clients may reexperience old fears, reactions, or thoughts. This is a normal part of the recovery process, and clients should be prepared to have contingency plans or supportive help through these difficult periods.

Critical Incident Stress Debriefing and Management

Critical incident stress debriefing is used for frontline crisis workers who are exposed to gruesome and life-threatening situations. Suicides, homicides, natural disasters, terrorist attacks, and hostage situations are examples of critical incidents that can cause secondary traumatization effects for first responders. The utilization of critical incident stress debriefing techniques allows crisis workers the opportunity to discuss the traumatic event, promote group cohesion, and educate first responders on stress reactions and coping techniques (Eaton & Roberts, 2002; Roberts, 2005a).

Critical incident debriefing typically occurs between 24 and 72 hours after the traumatic incident and can be done individually or with a group of first responders. Debriefing entails activities that let first responders ventilate their feelings and emotional reactions to the crisis and its impacts. Debriefing meetings should also encourage the first responders to be supportive and not be critical of each other.

The 10-Step Acute Traumatic Stress Management Protocol

The following are Lerner and Shelton's (2001) 10 stages of acute stress management, which provide useful guidelines for critical incident stress debriefing for first responders:

1. assess for danger/safety for self and others;
2. consider the physical and perceptual mechanism of injury;
3. evaluate the level of responsiveness;
4. address medical needs;
5. observe and identify each individual's signs of traumatic stress;
6. introduce yourself, state your role, and begin to develop a relationship;
7. ground the individual by allowing him or her to tell his or her story;
8. provide support through active and empathic listening;
9. normalize, validate, and educate; and
10. bring the person to the present, describe future events, and provide referrals.

APPLICATION TO FAMILY AND GROUP WORK

Roberts's (2005a, 2005b) seven-stage crisis intervention model is applicable to family and group crisis intervention, although there are certain considerations in relation to these levels of practice. "It has been said, only partly facetiously, that families are either part of the problem or part of the solution" (Golan, 1978, p. 110). Certain crisis situations, such as shifts in family structure and developmental changes, can affect family members differently, so the crisis worker may have to assess who in the family is experiencing crisis and who in the family will be participating in treatment. Other crisis events, such as child abuse, family violence, or criminal offenses, involve demands from community agencies that a family member change certain behaviors or ways of coping. Then there are traumatic situations that may affect all family members involved in the critical incident, such as disasters, accidents, and death.

During assessment, the family structure, dynamics, relationships, communication patterns, and support systems need to be evaluated as to potential strengths and areas in need of treatment. How the crisis impacts on the family system as a whole and on the individuals, the amount of family cooperation, and consideration of the family's support system in terms of local community resources are also important in assessment and intervention planning.

Group crisis work is used with clients experiencing similar types of trauma, such as sexual assault and child abuse survivors, individuals in community or institutional disasters, persons with chemical dependency, and individuals dealing with loss and bereavement. Having the support of and interaction with others who have shared similar crisis events are important benefits of group therapy. Group members can learn from each other about ways to cope and go on with their lives.

As in families, group members may have different reactions, experiences, feelings, and coping skills, so intervention has to be directed at the individual level, as well as with the group as a working system. The need for individual treatment in addition to group work should be part of the assessment and action plan. Self-help and time-limited groups are also excellent resources for longer term crisis- or grief-resolution work.

COMPATIBILITY WITH A GENERALIST-ECLECTIC FRAMEWORK

Crisis intervention has many things in common with a generalist-eclectic framework for direct social work practice. First, it is grounded in an eclectic orientation and theory base. This approach has incorporated the basic principles and perspectives from systems theory, ego psychology (including life cycle/human development theory), and cognitive-behavioral theories into a holistic framework for crisis intervention with diverse client populations and types of crises. Most crisis workers recognize that (a) there is no single theory that explains all clinical phenomena, (b) different treatment approaches work well with different clients, and

(c) different combinations of approaches may be used with the same client (Parad & Parad, 1990, 2006).

Second, crisis intervention places an emphasis on client strengths and empowerment. A strengths approach is inherent in the crisis intervention strategy of building on the client's own coping skills and natural support system. Client empowerment is a natural outcome of this approach, because the focus in crisis work is to provide the support and resources for clients to resolve any negative impacts through their own growth and development and not to become dependent on others in their social environment to meet those needs.

Third, crisis intervention emphasizes holistic assessment within an ecosystems perspective. Crisis intervention must address the biological, psychological, and environmental damage and trauma from both a macrosystemic and individual perspective to be effective (Burgess & Roberts, 2000, 2005). This is particularly true for catastrophic events. Current electronic media technology and its instant coverage of disasters have brought these events into our homes, and coverage of traumatic events has had ripple effects in the global community. This has helped to develop awareness of the importance of having large teams of experts in a variety of human and environmental specialties trained and available as rapid response teams to restore equilibrium to the total ecosystems environment in the event of catastrophes.

CRITIQUE OF CRISIS INTERVENTION

One of the strengths of crisis intervention is its effectiveness across diverse types of crises and client populations. However, although there is research and literature on specialized clients/crises, there is not much literature on cultural, gender, or age differences among crisis client populations (for exceptions, see Congress, 2000; Cornelius, Simpson, & Ting, 2003; Dykeman, 2005; Stone & Conley, 2004). It is important that crisis workers be culturally competent and tailor crisis intervention practices to differing ethnic and racial groups.

Another strength is the time-limited nature of crisis intervention that makes it conducive to the current realities of managed care and can permit crisis programs to reach larger numbers of clients for brief treatment. However, one of the drawbacks is that crisis workers usually do not see the end results of the initial interventions they have provided, and it may seem like a Band-Aid approach. While crisis resolution may take much longer than the 4- to 6-week time frame of most crisis services, professionals must realize that a small amount of help at this critical time in a person's life can make a great difference in the long-term effects that might be experienced otherwise.

CASE EXAMPLE

Maria is a sexual assault victim who has just called 911 to report a rape by an intruder in her home. As police officers rush to the scene, the police victim services counselors are requested as part of a team approach. When the police arrive, they begin the investigative work, and the victim services counselors begin the crisis intervention. The police get an initial report from Maria and request backup at the scene to search for the suspect. They ask her if she is willing to go to the hospital for a rape exam to gather physical evidence. Maria is experiencing initial postcrisis reactions, and the victim services counselors ask if they can speak with her. At this point, the focus of crisis intervention is to evaluate her medical and physical needs and to explain the investigative process to her so she can understand what is going on.

Maria is worried about leaving her home unattended and has questions about what will happen at the hospital and how much this will cost her, because she has no health insurance. She is concerned about telling her boyfriend, who is at work, and wants to call her parents. At the same time, she is remembering details about the rape and is experiencing shock and trauma reactions that are frightening and confusing. As the victim services counselors help her to calm down and focus on her immediate needs, they reassure her that they will be there to support her during the investigation and medical exam, will help her contact her loved ones, and will assist in making other necessary arrangements.

When they arrive at the hospital, the emergency room social worker is there to help during the medical exam and to answer the many medical and financial questions that worry Maria. While the victim services counselors contact her loved ones, they also telephone a rape crisis worker to assist with the case. After the police finish their initial report, they leave the hospital and tell Maria that an investigator will be contacting her soon to take a formal statement. Maria has a lot of questions about this, which the victim services counselors explain. They also offer supportive services during the investigation and legal proceedings.

After the medical exam, the rape crisis worker has arrived, along with Maria's family members. Plans are made for her to go to her parents' home, because she is too frightened to return to her own home. The victim services counselors then return to their duties, and the rape crisis worker accompanies Maria and her parents. Maria is concerned about how her boyfriend will react, and the rape crisis worker lets her ventilate her feelings and concerns about the sexual assault and its impacts on her and her loved ones.

The rape crisis worker helps Maria develop a plan of how to tell her boyfriend about the rape. They also explore her immediate needs and any changes in her daily routine, such as whether she will go to work tomorrow, when she will return home, and what will happen if the police arrest a suspect. The volunteer also lets Maria know that counseling services are available at the rape crisis center, and that the volunteer will follow up with her tomorrow to see how she is doing and what she needs.

Maria's case will also be followed up by the police victim services counselors and by the victim-witness advocates in the court system when (and if) the case goes to trial. During this time frame, which can sometimes last over a year, support services will be provided through individual and group counseling at the rape crisis center. In this type of continuum of care, the different crisis programs and counselors are responsible for various aspects of the case to ensure that the survivor receives crisis intervention services as needed.

SUMMARY

Crisis intervention is an eclectic approach that is effective across diverse types of crises, client populations, and settings. It is essential that social workers in generalist practice be knowledgeable and trained in basic crisis intervention skills to meet the needs of their clients. Research studies, journal articles, and textbooks on both basic and specialized crisis intervention skills and models are available in a variety of disciplines and treatment areas (e.g., Allen, Burt, & Bryan, 2002; Cohen, 2003; Datillo & Freeman 2000; France, 2002; Greenstone & Leviton, 2002; Hatou & Seishin, 2004; Hillman, 2002). This chapter has provided an overview of the principles, theoretical constructs, and basic intervention skills in crisis intervention. Crisis work can be both demanding and difficult, but its rewards can be immediate and long-lasting for both clients and social workers.

REFERENCES

Allen, M., Burt, K., & Bryan, E. (2002). School counselors' preparation for and participation in crisis intervention. *Professional School Counseling, 6*, 96–102.

Boscarino, J. A., Adams, R. E., & Figley, C. R. (2005). A prospective cohort study of the effectiveness of employer-sponsored crisis interventions after a major disaster. *International Journal of Emergency Mental Health, 7*, 9–22.

Bowie, S. L. (2003). Post-disaster crisis intervention with older adults in public housing communities. *Crisis Intervention and Time-Limited Treatment, 6*, 171–184.

Burgess, A. W., & Roberts, A. R. (2000). Crisis intervention with persons diagnosed with clinical disorders on the stress-crisis continuum: A managed care perspective. In A. R. Roberts (Ed.), *Crisis intervention handbook: Assessment, treatment, and research* (pp. 56–76). New York: Oxford University Press.

Burgess, A. W., & Roberts, A. R. (2005). Crisis intervention with persons diagnosed with clinical disorders on the stress-crisis continuum. In A. R. Roberts (Ed.), *Crisis intervention handbook: Assessment, treatment, and research* (3rd ed., pp. 120–140). New York: Oxford University Press.

Castellano, C. (2003). Large group crisis intervention for law enforcement in response to the September 11 World Trade Center mass disaster. *International Journal of Emergency Mental Health, 5,* 210–215.

Cohen, J. (2003). Crisis intervention and trauma: New approaches to evidence-based practice. *American Journal of Psychotherapy, 57,* 421–423.

Congress, E. P. (2000). Crisis intervention with culturally diverse families. In A. R. Roberts (Ed.), *Crisis intervention handbook: Assessment, treatment, and research* (pp. 430–449). New York: Oxford University Press.

Cornelius, L. J., Simpson, G. M., & Ting, L. (2003). Reach out and I'll be there: Mental health crisis intervention and mobile outreach services to urban African Americans. *Health & Social Work, 28,* 74–78.

Datillo, F. M., & Freeman, A. (2000). *Cognitive-behavioral strategies in crisis intervention.* New York: Guilford Press.

Dublin, L. (1963). *Suicide: A sociological and statistical study.* New York: Ronald Press.

Dykeman, B. F. (2005). Cultural limitations of crisis intervention. *Journal of Instructional Psychology, 32,* 45–48.

Dziegielewski, S. F. (1996). Managed care principles: The need for social work in the health care system. *Crisis Intervention and Time-Limited Treatment, 3,* 97–112.

Dziegielewski, S. F., & Powers, G. T. (2005). Designs and procedures for evaluating crisis intervention. In A. R. Roberts (Ed.), *Crisis intervention handbook: Assessment, treatment, and research* (3rd ed., pp. 742–773). New York: Oxford University Press.

Dziegielewski, S. F., & Sumner, K. (2002). An examination of the American response to terrorism: Handling the aftermath through crisis intervention. *Brief Treatment and Crisis Intervention, 2,* 287–300.

Eaton, Y., & Roberts, A. R. (2002). Frontline crisis intervention: Step-by-step practice guidelines with case applications. In A. R. Roberts & G. J. Greene (Eds.), *Social workers' desk reference* (pp. 89–96). New York: Oxford University Press.

Edmond, T., Sloan, L., & McCarty, D. (2004). Sexual abuse survivors' perceptions of the effectiveness of EMDR and eclectic therapy. *Research on Social Work Practice, 14,* 259–272.

Erikson, E. (1950). *Childhood and society.* New York: W. W. Norton.

Farberow, N., & Scheidman, E. (1961). *The cry for help.* New York: McGraw-Hill.

France, K. (2002). *Crisis intervention: A handbook of immediate person-to-person help.* Springfield, IL: Charles C Thomas.

Golan, N. (1978). *Treatment in crisis situations.* New York: Free Press.

Greene, G. J., Lee, M. L., Trask, R., & Rheinscheld, J. (2005). How to work with client strengths in crisis intervention: A solution-focused approach. In A. R. Roberts (Ed.), *Crisis intervention handbook: Assessment, treatment, and research* (3rd ed., pp. 64–89). New York: Oxford University Press.

Greenstone, J. L., & Leviton, S. C. (2002). *Elements of crisis intervention: Crises and how to respond to them.* Pacific Grove, CA: Brooks/Cole.

Hatou, K., & Seishin, I. (2004). Crisis intervention in psychiatry and the role of mental clinic. *Clinical Psychiatry, 46,* 585–590.

Hepworth, D. H., Rooney, R. H., & Larsen, J. A. (2006). *Direct social work practice: Theory and skills* (7th ed.). Pacific Grove, CA: Brooks/Cole.

Hillman, J. L. (2002). *Crisis intervention and trauma: New approaches to evidence-based practice.* New York: Springer.

Jimerson, S. R., Brock, S. E., & Pelcher, S. W. (2005). An integrated model of school crisis preparedness and intervention: A shared foundation to facilitate international crisis intervention. *School Psychology International, 26,* 275–296.

Kaul, R. E. (2002). A social worker's account of 31 days responding to the Pentagon disaster: Crisis intervention training and self-care practices. *Brief Treatment and Crisis Intervention, 2,* 33–37.

Kaul, R. E., & Welzant, V. (2005). Disaster mental health: A discussion of best practices as applied after the pentagon attack. In A. R. Roberts (Ed.), *Crisis intervention handbook: Assessment, treatment, and research* (3rd ed., pp. 200–220). New York: Oxford University Press.

Knox, K. S., & Roberts, A. R. (2005a). Crisis intervention and crisis team models in schools. *Children and Schools, 27,* 93–100.

Knox, K. S., & Roberts, A. R. (2005b). Crisis intervention with stalking victims. In A. R. Roberts (Ed.), *Crisis intervention handbook: Assessment, treatment, and research* (3rd ed., pp. 483–498). New York: Oxford University Press.

Lerner, M. D., & Shelton, R. D. (2001). *Acute traumatic stress management: Addressing emergent psychological needs during traumatic events.* Commack, NY: American Academy of Experts in Traumatic Stress.

Lindemann, E. (1944). Symptomology and management of acute grief. *American Journal of Psychiatry, 101,* 141–147.

Macklin, M., Metzger, L. J., Lasko, N. B., Berry, N. J., Orr, S. P., & Pitman, R. K. (2000). Five-year follow-up study of eye movement desensitization and reprocessing therapy for combat-related posttraumatic stress disorder. *Comprehensive Psychiatry, 41,* 24–27.

Marcus, S., Marquis, P., & Sakai, C. (2004). Three and 6-month follow-up of EMDR treatment of PTSD in an HMO setting. *International Journal of Stress Management, 11,* 195–208.

Mitchell, J., & Everly, G. (1993). *Critical-incident stress debriefing: An operations manual for the prevention of traumatic stress among disaster workers.* Ellicott City, MD: Chevron.

Nunno, M. A., Holden, M. J., & Leidy, B. (2003). Evaluating and monitoring the impact of a crisis intervention system on a residential child care facility. *Children and Youth Services Review, 25,* 295–315.

Parad, H. J., & Parad, L. G. (1990). *Crisis intervention book 2: The practitioner's sourcebook for brief therapy.* Milwaukee, WI: Family Service America.

Parad, H. J., & Parad, L. G. (2006). *Crisis intervention book 2: The practitioner's sourcebook for brief therapy* (2nd ed.). Tucson, AZ: Fenestra Books.

Polk, G. (1996). Treatment of problem drinking behavior using solution-focused therapy: A single-subject design. *Crisis Intervention and Time-Limited Treatment, 3,* 13–24.

Roberts, A. R. (1975). Self-destruction by one's own hands. In A. R. Roberts (Ed.) *Self-destructive behaviors* (pp. 3–31). Springfield, IL: Charles C Thomas.

Roberts, A. R. (1990). *Helping crime victims: Research, policy, and practice.* Thousand Oaks, CA: Sage.

Roberts, A. R. (1995). Crisis intervention units and centers in the United States: A national survey. In A. R. Roberts (Ed.), *Crisis intervention and time-limited cognitive treatment* (pp. 54–70). Thousand Oaks, CA: Sage.

Roberts, A. R. (1996). Epidemiology and definitions of acute crisis in American society. In A. R. Roberts (Ed.), *Crisis management and brief treatment: Theory, technique, and applications* (pp. 16–33). Chicago: Nelson-Hall.

Roberts, A. R. (1997). *Social work in juvenile and criminal justice settings.* Springfield, IL: Charles C Thomas.

Roberts, A. R. (1998). *Battered women and their families: Intervention strategies and treatment programs.* New York: Springer Publishing Company.

Roberts, A. R. (2000). An overview of crisis theory and crisis intervention. In A. R. Roberts (Ed.), *Crisis intervention handbook: Assessment, treatment, and research* (pp. 3–30). New York: Oxford University Press.

Roberts, A. R. (2005a). The ACT model: Assessment, crisis intervention, and trauma treatment in the aftermath of community disaster and terrorism attacks. In A. R. Roberts (Ed.), *Crisis intervention handbook: Assessment, treatment, and research* (3rd ed., pp. 143–170). New York: Oxford University Press.

Roberts, A. R. (2005b). Bridging the past and present to the future of crisis intervention and crisis management. In A. R. Roberts (Ed.), *Crisis intervention handbook: Assessment, treatment, and research* (3rd ed., pp. 3–34). New York: Oxford University Press.

Roberts, A. R. (2005c). *Crisis intervention handbook: Assessment, treatment, and research* (3rd ed.). New York: Oxford University Press.

Roberts, A. R., & Dziegielewski, S. F. (1995). Foundation skills and applications of crisis intervention and cognitive therapy. In A. R. Roberts (Ed.), *Crisis intervention and time-limited cognitive treatment* (pp. 3–27). Thousand Oaks, CA: Sage.

Roberts, A. R., & Everly, G. S. (2006). A meta-analysis of 36 crisis intervention studies. *Brief Treatment and Crisis Intervention, 6*, 10–21.

Roberts, A. R., & Yeager, K. R. (2005). Lethality assessment and crisis intervention with persons presenting with suicidal ideation. In A. R. Roberts (Ed.), *Crisis intervention handbook: Assessment, treatment, and research* (3rd ed., pp. 35–63). New York: Oxford University Press.

Schneidman, E., Faberow, N., & Litman, R. (1970). *The psychology of suicide.* New York: Science House.

Shapiro, F. (1995). *Eye movement desensitization and reprocessing: Basic principles, protocols, and procedures.* New York: Guilford Press.

Shapiro, F. (2001). *Eye movement desensitization and reprocessing (EMDR): Basic principles, protocols, and procedures* (2nd ed.). New York: Guilford Press.

Sheafor, B. W., & Horejsi, C. R. (2006). *Techniques and guidelines for social work practice* (7th ed.). Boston: Pearson.

Silver, S. M., Rogers, S., Knipe, J., & Colelli, G. (2005). EMDR therapy following the 9/11 terrorist attacks: A community-based intervention project. *International Journal of Stress Management, 12*, 29–42.

Slaikeu, K. (1984). *Crisis intervention: A handbook for practice and research.* Boston: Allyn & Bacon.

Stone, D. A., & Conley, J. A. (2004). A partnership between Roberts' crisis intervention model and the multicultural competencies. *Brief Treatment and Crisis Intervention, 4*, 365–375.

Underwood, M. M., & Kalafat, J. (2002). Crisis intervention in a new context: New Jersey post-September 11, 2001. *Brief Treatment and Crisis Intervention, 2*, 75–83.

Westefeld, J. S., & Heckman-Stone, C. (2003). The integrated problem-solving model of crisis intervention: Overviews and application. *Counseling Psychologist, 31*, 221–239.

Yeager, K. R. (2002). Crisis intervention with mentally ill chemical abusers: Application of brief solution-focused therapy and strengths perspective. *Brief Treatment and Crisis Intervention, 2*, 197–216.

Yeager, K. R., & Gregoire, T. K. (2005). Crisis intervention application of solution-focused therapy in addictions. In A. R. Roberts (Ed.), *Crisis intervention handbook: Assessment, treatment, and research* (3rd ed., pp. 566–601). New York: Oxford University Press.

CHAPTER 11

The Task-Centered Model

Blanca M. Ramos and Eleanor Reardon Tolson

The task-centered model (TC) was developed by social work educators and intended for work with social work clients including, but not limited to, those who are central to the profession's mission: the disadvantaged and disenfranchised. TC is a present-oriented, time-limited problem-solving approach that helps clients to solve their problems as they define them. Changes in problems are secured by developing and implementing tasks. Task work is accomplished through specific, structured intervention activities called the Task Planning and Implementation Sequence. Respect for clients' rights to be self-determining is emphasized in TC.

TC is an empirical approach to practice. This means that it was developed from research findings about practice, constructed with concepts that are measurable, and includes procedures for evaluating outcomes on an ongoing basis. It has been tested and found effective (see Historical Development, below).

TC can provide a structure for generalist practice that is both integrated and eclectic. This capacity results from the fact that TC is not attached to any particular theory of behavior. When explanations of behavior or alternative interventions are needed, it is possible to incorporate a wide variety of perspectives without losing the structure for intervention that the model provides. TC has been used at all system levels, including individuals, families, groups, organizations, and communities, and incorporates a strategy, work with collaterals, that makes it possible to include other systems in the intervention process.

TC has been used successfully in most settings where social workers practice, including child welfare, public social services, school social

275

work, corrections, medical settings, industrial settings, geriatric settings, family service, and mental health (Hepworth, Rooney, Rooney, Strom-Gottfried, & Larsen, 2006; Reid, 1996). TC has also been used in case management (Naleppa & Reid, 1998, 2000) and in supervision and staff development (Caspi & Reid, 1998).

HISTORICAL DEVELOPMENT

TC was developed in the early 1970s by Reid and Epstein (1972) and has evolved considerably throughout the years with adherents worldwide contributing to its expansion (e.g., Kilgore 1995; Lo, 2005; Pomeroy, Rubin, & Walker, 1995; Reid & Ramos, 2002; Rooney, 1992). One of the models for social work practice that was influential in its development was Perlman's (1957) *Social Casework: A Problem-Solving Process*, which articulated the problem-solving paradigm. Studt's (1968) concept of tasks in treatment also made an important contribution. Equally influential were the research findings about practice that were being generated at that time. The findings pertained to the use of time limits, the dropout rate, and the timing of change. It was found that time-limited treatment was at least as effective as treatment of indefinite length (Reid & Shyne, 1969). Research has consistently supported this finding over time, and in some instances has shown that time-limited treatment is more effective (Gurman & Kniskern, 1981; Johnson & Gelso, 1982; Koss & Shiang, 1994; Luborsky, Singer, & Luborsky, 1975; Wells, 1994; Wells & Gianetti, 1990). The literature on dropouts found that a substantial number of clients terminated treatment prematurely (Beck & Jones, 1973; Garfield, 1994; Lake & Levinger, 1960; Levinger, 1960; Meltzoff & Kornreich, 1970; Silverman, 1970). It was and is believed that a major cause of dropout is a lack of congruence between client and worker about the focus of treatment (Strean, 1968). Additionally, it was found that a substantial amount of change occurred early in contact (Meltzoff & Kornreich, 1970; Orlinsky & Howard, 1986; Presley, 1987; Strupp, Fox, & Lessler, 1969).

TC can be seen as the result of integrating these influences. The work of Perlman and Studt is apparent in the concepts of target problems and tasks. The empirical findings led to the incorporation of time limits and the insistence that clients determine the focus of treatment or target problem.

During the past 3 decades, TC has been continually tested and refined. It has been the subject of more than 50 published studies and doctoral dissertations, and findings have been consistently positive. Many of these studies have been controlled group experiments (Alley & Brown, 2002; Caspi, in press; Caspi & Reid, 2002; Gibbons, Bow, & Butler, 1985; Gibbons, Butler, Urwin, & Gibbons, 1978; Kane, 2001; Kinnevy, Healey,

Pollio, & North, 1999; Naleppa & Reid, 1998; Newcome, 1985; Pomeroy, Rubin, & Walker, 1995; Reid, 1975, 1978; Reid & Bailey-Dempsey,
1995; Reid, Epstein, Brown, Tolson, & Rooney, 1980; Viggiani, 1996).

In addition to demonstrating the effectiveness of the approach, the
studies have contributed to the development of the model. Perhaps the
most important contribution of the research is the Task Planning and
Implementation Sequence (TPIS). TPIS is a series of activities that are undertaken in the process of developing tasks. The research made it possible
to identify the activities and, later, to test the effectiveness of them (Reid,
1978). Research has also helped us understand what makes TC effective
(Reid, 1997). Changes in target problems are associated with the amount
of time spent on them. Task accomplishments are correlated with the degree of client commitment to doing the task and task preparation.

The possibility of using TC as a base for generalist practice has been
explored (Tolson, Reid, & Garvin, 1994, 2003). It appears that the basic
framework of TC can be adapted for work across system levels, including
families, groups, organizations, and communities. A meta-analysis found
a greater average effect size for TC as compared to other generalist approaches (Gorey, Thyer, & Pawluck, 1998).

THEORETICAL CONSTRUCTS

As previously observed, TC is fundamentally an empirical approach to
practice. This means that "one gives primacy to research-based theories
and interventions but still maintains a skeptical attitude toward all theories and interventions" (Reid, 1992, p. 7). As a result, the theoretical
base of TC is deliberately modest. The assumptions in this theoretical
base pertain to the nature of problems, the nature of people, the source
of motivation, and the source of change.

TC is intended to ameliorate psychosocial problems or problems
in living. Problems are seen as inevitable and resulting from unsatisfied
wants. Wants are shaped by belief systems, which include expectations,
appraisals, and values. Unmet wants occur when life experiences fall
short of expectations or are deemed deficient, unpleasant, unsatisfying,
or unworthy (Reid, 1992). Unmet wants are the source for motivation.
To capture this motivation, it is imperative that the clients determine the
focus of treatment, which in TC is labeled the target problem. Problems
are embedded in a context. The context can be the source of the unmet
want, an obstacle to satisfying it, or a resource for alleviating it.

Human beings are seen as active problem-solvers who are capable
of making rational choices about their wants and needs and participating
in change efforts. Clients are people whose independent problem-solving

efforts have been unsuccessful. The objective of intervention is to assist the clients' efforts.

Action—in particular, client action—is believed to be the most efficient source of change and, frequently, the predecessor to attitudinal or emotional change. Furthermore, action and the ensuing feedback are critical sources of perceived self-efficacy that determine the amount and persistence of efforts an individual will expend (Bandura, 1986). Thus, successful action enhances self-efficacy, which, in turn, supports further action. This belief is manifest in the use of tasks, which are actions that clients carry out for the purpose of reducing target problems.

Although the foregoing beliefs and assumptions provide a theoretical base for TC, it must be emphasized that TC is an open and flexible framework for practice. This means that other theories and interventions can and should be incorporated as the need for them arises. In fact, it is expected that the model and its theoretical underpinnings will change as knowledge is generated. Other sources should be selected and chosen on the basis of their relevance to the situation and the extent to which they are supported by empirical research. There is one vital caveat to borrowing from theories of human behavior: They should not be used to formulate the target problems (Reid, 1992). Rather, the problem should be used to scan different theories for determining the usefulness of them.

PHASES OF HELPING

The phases of helping in TC are usually identified as initial, middle, and termination. The initial phase activities include explaining role, purpose, and treatment procedures; obtaining necessary information; identifying, prioritizing, and specifying the target problems; identifying goals; setting time limits; contracting; and assessing. All of these activities must be accomplished to some extent before any intervention can occur. The middle phase consists of employing TPIS. TPIS is composed of a number of subactivities, which are described in the section on intervention. The last phase is termination. Relationship or rapport is seen as ongoing. Space limitations dictate a succinct summary of TC. Detailed descriptions of the procedures can be found in Reid (1992) and Tolson, Reid, and Garvin (2003).

Initial Phase

Engagement

Engagement in TC is three-pronged: developing a relationship with clients, introducing them to the problem-solving process, and connecting with them through a mutual commitment to resolve client-defined problems. The view of relationship in TC is consonant with the research on the topic, which finds that it is a mediating variable. This means that a good relationship is necessary but not sufficient to secure change (Lambert, Dejulio, & Stein, 1978; Mitchell, Bozarth, & Krauft, 1977; Orlinsky & Howard, 1986; Parloff, Waskow, & Wolfe, 1978; Patterson, 1984). Qualities stressed include warmth, empathy, genuineness, nonjudgmental acceptance, and respect for the client's right to self-determination. A relationship is developed as one engages in problem-solving; however, with children, some time usually has to be allotted for them to become familiar with the worker before problem-solving efforts begin.

Introduction to work is based on role induction or client preparation, the importance of which has been validated (Acosta, Yamamoto, Evans, Skilbeck, 1983; Sloane, Cristol, Pepernik, & Staples, 1970; Zwick & Attkisson, 1984). It includes explaining the social worker's role (name, title, name and purpose of agency, worker's purpose within the agency, the source and reason for referral when the client is not voluntary) and treatment procedures. In TC the important issues to explain in this early stage are that the focus will be determined by the client and that work will be time limited. Emphasis is placed on these two issues because they appear to enhance motivation, especially for nonvoluntary clients. The use of client preparation in TC is not limited to the initial session. We have found that repeating explanations is often sufficient to restart work that has bogged down.

Data Collection and Assessment

The most important activity in TC is the identification of target problems. Target problems are the aspects of the clients' lives that they most want changed. In TC it is imperative that clients choose the target problems. This does not mean that the client must be the one to identify the problem or that the worker should refrain from mentioning potential target problems. It does mean that the final choice of the focus of treatment will be determined by the client.

Identifying target problems includes two steps. First, all problems are listed. This list is usually generated by asking the client what aspects of his or her life the client would like to be different. In some cases, the client does not readily identify problems, and it is necessary to engage in a problem search that consists of reviewing the various arenas (work, school, personal relationships, health, mood, etc.) of the client's life. The client is encouraged to identify an inclusive list of concerns. Second, the client is asked to prioritize these potential problems. Usually no more than three target problems are worked on simultaneously. Problems include feelings, behaviors, attitudes, circumstances (including resource deficiencies), relationships, and skill deficits.

Data collection and assessment center on the target problems and entail detailed exploration. The goal of data collection is to develop a "problem specification." Problem specification consists of two activities: describing the manifestations of the problems and determining the frequency, duration, or severity of them. This process will be described using two different types of problems: depression and housing.

The manifestations of depression for a particular client might include crying spells, inability to sleep, and inability to perform daily chores. Manifestations are elicited by exploring how the client experiences the problem, and these will differ across clients with the same target problem. The next step concerns making the manifestations measurable so that change can be monitored. We want to know how many times the client cries each day or each week and how many hours per night he or she sleeps. Performance of chores can be indicated by the percent of chores completed or the time spent performing them on either a daily or a weekly basis.

A problem specification for acquiring resources is somewhat different. The manifestations are the characteristics that describe adequate resource provision for the particular client. Manifestations for a housing problem might pertain to the number of bedrooms, geographical location, and cost. In this case, manifestations are measured in terms of whether or not the desired characteristics have been obtained.

Problem specification enables the worker to individualize treatment by focusing on the particular manifestations of the problem as the client experiences it and to monitor changes as they occur over time. Monitoring change is necessary for making treatment decisions, as well as for assessing outcome. Problem specification is one of the unique strengths of TC, because it makes practice evaluation part of treatment.

During the process of exploring potential target problems and developing the problem specifications(s), the worker will usually learn a great deal about the context of the problem. An ecosystems framework is used for organizing this information and identifying gaps. The nature and impact of micro-, mezzo-, and macro-level systems are considered. This systemic assessment often influences decisions about how problems are to be solved and sometimes suggests modifications in the target problems. Frequently, it identifies important collaterals—people who are personally or professionally related to the client in the problem areas. Collaterals are representatives of other systems and are frequently involved, provided the client gives permission. The importance of collaterals is the linkage they provide for affecting other systems.

Goals, Time Limits, and Contracts

Establishing goals, setting time limits, and contracting occur before intervention. In TC, goals are determined by the client, but the worker helps to make them measurable. Thus, if the client's goal is to "feel better," the worker would help him or her to define "feeling better." A useful way to do this is to refer to the manifestations of the problem that were identified in the problem specification. Using the specification previously described, the worker would ask the client to identify the number of crying spells, chores, and hours of sleep that are desired. When the goal is long-term, the client is asked to identify conditions that indicate that it will be accomplished. The conditions for the goal of graduating from college, for example, may include passing all courses with a particular grade point average.

Time limits usually range from 6 to 12 sessions but can be as brief as 1 session. When more time is needed, contract extensions are considered, provided there is evidence that the client is working to resolve the problem. Contracts in TC are usually verbal. They include a list of the target problems and goals, the number and frequency of sessions, the participants, and fees, if applicable.

Middle Phase: The Use of Task Planning and Implementation Sequence (TPIS) in Intervention

TPIS is the intervention in TC. It consists of a number of activities that are employed in developing tasks. A task is an action performed for the purpose of reducing target problems. Optimally, tasks should be performed by the client outside the session. This allows clients to take action on their own behalf in the real-life settings in which problems occur. However, experience with TC suggests the need for two other types of tasks: practitioner and in-session tasks. Occasionally, cases will require that the practitioner perform tasks, particularly when the client cannot perform a task or when asking the client to perform it will result in delay or hardship. In-session tasks are most frequently used in work with families and groups (Tolson, Reid, & Garvin, 2003).

TPIS consists of the following activities: generating task alternatives, eliciting agreement to perform the task, planning the details of implementation, establishing the rationale and incentive for performing the task, simulating the task, identifying obstacles to task performance, summarizing the tasks, and reviewing task accomplishment and problem change. Each of these activities is briefly described. Although work will always begin with generating task alternatives, the sequence in which the activities are accomplished is variable.

Generating task alternatives consists of brainstorming with the client the possible actions that could be taken to alleviate the target problem. It is important to suggest alternatives and to encourage the client to do so (see Reid, 2000, for tasks for particular problems). The more alternatives, the better. Worker and client consider the advantages and disadvantages of the alternatives, and the client is asked to select the preferred one(s). The client is also asked whether he or she is willing to attempt the task. As with target problems, the client has the last word in choosing tasks.

After a task is chosen, the ways in which it will be implemented are planned. Decisions have to be made about when it is to be done, how often, for how long, where, with whom, under what circumstances, and in what manner. In addition to the common factors that must be planned, many tasks will require decisions about unique details. These are identified by thinking through what will be required to perform the task successfully. Careful planning is particularly important with tasks that are expected to be performed only once, such as asking for a raise at work. Some of the unique details might be identified when the client and worker begin to consider the obstacles that might be encountered. In this activity, potential hurdles are identified and ways to surmount them are planned. Although it is important to identify and plan for likely obstacles, it is also important to avoid raising unlikely concerns. Clients need to believe that they can do the tasks even if the tasks are challenging.

Establishing rationale refers to making sure that the client is aware of what is to be gained by performing the task. Incentives refer to concrete rewards that the client will receive for performing the task. They can be provided by the client, the worker, or collaterals. Incentives are particularly important when the task is difficult. The client whose task is to ask for a raise might plan to treat himself or herself to a nice dinner following task implementation, for example.

Simulation and guided practice involve rehearsing the task. These activities provide an opportunity for the client to practice the task and for the worker to provide feedback. Summarizing is done to ensure that the client knows what tasks are to be performed before the next session. Often clients are asked to provide the summary. When it is likely that some tasks might be forgotten, a task review schedule is provided (Rooney, 1981).

Problem and task reviews occur at the beginning of every session once task work has begun. The object is to learn the extent to which the tasks were implemented and the extent to which the target problems have changed. The problem specification developed during the initial phase can serve as a guide for problem review. Both task accomplishment and problem change can be rated on a 4-point scale. The client is praised when tasks are implemented. When they are not implemented or do not have the intended effect on problems, tasks are revised based on the obstacles that have been identified during the review. If tasks consistently are not performed, the target problems are reevaluated to check that they are conditions that the client indeed wants to change.

At each session, the client is reminded of the number of sessions that have occurred and the number that remain. Time limits can be extended when the client has been performing tasks and it is likely that problem resolution can be reached in a specified period of time.

Termination

Termination in TC is usually limited to one session. Brevity is possible because clients are reminded of the time limits in each interview. During the last session, the worker and the client engage in a final problem review, make plans for maintaining or enhancing gains, review the problem-solving process, and discuss their reactions to separation. Praise for the client's accomplishments is offered liberally.

APPLICATION TO FAMILY AND GROUP WORK

Family Work

Family work in TC consists of consulting with more than one family member for the purpose of resolving problems. It is not required to see all or most family members, although it is often helpful to see the entire family once; nor is it required to see family members together for all sessions. Because the most important activity for enhancing and maintaining motivation is the accurate identification of target problems that are meaningful to family members, care is taken to secure everyone's opinion about what they would like to see changed. Each family member is asked to share concerns. Generally, the lists of problems will differ, which makes prioritizing critically important, because each member has to believe that he or she has something to gain. In some cases, the family, when asked as a group which problems are most important, will readily reach agreement. When there are disagreements, a useful procedure to facilitate prioritization is to consider, as each problem is described, whether it is shared, reciprocal, or individual. Shared concerns are those that are experienced by more than one member. Reciprocal concerns require a change in another person in the family. Individual concerns primarily affect only one member. When families do not readily agree on priorities, the worker can suggest a priority on shared problems and pairs of reciprocal problems. For example, if the parents are complaining about homework completion and the teenager is complaining about curfew, prioritizing both these problems will enable the participants to consider trade-offs (later curfew for more homework) during the intervention phase and will give everyone a stake in successful problem resolution.

Group Work

Group work consists of working with more than one unrelated person who may share some problem area. TC group work can be used with either natural groups (e.g., several tenants in a housing project) or formed groups. Unlike the situation with families, the members will share an area of concern, such as problems in getting needed repairs to apartments or developing satisfying relationships. Group members are seen together for all treatment sessions, but the group sessions might be supplemented by individual sessions for members who need additional help. The unique challenges in group work entail developing a group culture that supports the members in their problem-solving efforts and using the model efficiently so that all members can progress.

The extent to which the individual concerns are related to the overall purpose of the group will affect progress and the attractiveness of the group to the members. Thus, individual pretreatment sessions to assess whether the person wants to participate in group work and in this particular group are strongly recommended. To expedite work and encourage participation throughout the stages of group development, members are taught the activities as they are encountered. In the initial phase, for example, members are taught to help one another identify target problems. When the members understand what is to be accomplished, they can be divided into subgroups or consulting pairs to work on a particular activity. Members who fall behind the progress of the group can be helped with individual sessions. An alternative is to pair a member who is making rapid progress with one who is struggling. Throughout the process, the worker is teaching the group members to give and receive feedback, to talk and listen to one another, to relate empathically, and to use the problem-solving method.

COMPATIBILITY WITH THE GENERALIST-ECLECTIC FRAMEWORK

Problem-Solving Structure and Theoretical Openness

TC is a structure for generalist-eclectic practice. Two of the defining characteristics of generalist approaches, a problem-solving structure and theoretical openness, have been part of TC since its inception. It is a flexible, structured problem-solving approach in that it comprises a specific set of procedures that are expected to alleviate problems and to be adapted according to the needs of the client and the situation. Flexibility derives from the fact that it is not attached to a particular theory of behavior but can be shaped to include understandings from many theories, as well as interventions from other approaches. TC functions like our spines: sufficiently structured to keep us upright but sufficiently flexible to allow us to bend. Interventions from many different theories have been incorporated into TC on a case-by-case basis, including behavioral and cognitive-behavioral therapies, family systems therapies, bibliotherapy, narrative therapies, and crisis intervention strategies. Interventions borrowed from other approaches are usually incorporated as tasks. Approaches that are incompatible with TC are those in which clients do not choose the focus of intervention, those in which long-term treatment is required, and those, like many educational approaches, that do not individualize intervention.

Holistic Assessment and Multisystem Focus

Two other characteristics common to generalist approaches, holistic assessment and applicability to work with all levels of systems, evolved over time in TC. The concept of context as a hierarchy of multiple open systems that guides a holistic assessment of problems emerged in the mid-1980s (Reid, 1985). The use of this concept is continuing to be refined (Kirst-Ashman & Hull, 1995; Miley, O'Melia, & DuBois, 2004). The applications to work with other systems emerged as social workers experimented with using the model with families, groups, communities, and organizations. These efforts have been synthesized by Tolson and colleagues (2003).

Empowerment, Diversity, and the Strengths Perspective

TC also embraces the generalist-eclectic framework's commitment to empowerment and the strengths perspective, which emphasize clients' abilities and ensure an active participation in treatment. TC is also consistent with this framework's concern for those who are disadvantaged and disenfranchised, including racial and ethnocultural groups. It should be noted that such emphases extend beyond and predate generalist practice. They are central to the mission of social work and distinguish it from other helping professions. The extent to which TC reflects this mission can be seen by examining the strategies of empowerment and the populations that have been served with TC.

The techniques common to empowerment approaches include (a) accepting the client's definition of the problem; (b) identifying and building upon existing strengths; (c) engaging in a power analysis of the client's situation; (d) teaching specific skills; and (e) mobilizing resources and advocating for clients (Gutierrez, 1990). The first technique is, in fact, the golden rule of TC. Recognizing and building on strengths are implicit in that the client's judgment is trusted and tasks are developed that utilize strengths. Furthermore, care is taken to develop tasks that are likely to enhance self-efficacy. Skills are frequently taught either because a skill deficit is the target problem or because they are necessary to successful task completion.

Mobilizing resources and advocating are aspects of practitioner tasks. At this time, TC does not include engaging the client in a power analysis, although engaging the client in a contextual analysis sometimes illuminates power dynamics. The many settings in which TC has been used successfully disproportionately serve poor and racial and ethnocultural diverse populations. In addition, clients from these groups are disproportionately represented in the controlled studies of the effectiveness of TC.

Several authors conclude that TC can be readily applicable in practice with racially and ethnically diverse clients as some of its intervention activities provide mechanisms to identify and address issues of powerlessness, injustice, and oppression (Boyd-Franklin, 1989; Devore & Schlesinger, 1999; Lum, 1996; Ramos & Garvin, 2003). For example, Devore and Schlesinger (1999) referred to the main principles of TC as a "major thrust in ethnic sensitive practice" (p. 121). Also, contextualizing problems helps identify and address environmental challenges associated with poverty, racism, prejudice, and discrimination. Further, the feelings of empowerment drawn from task mastery are especially significant for clients who have experienced unequal treatment and limited access to resources (Ramos & Garvin, 2003).

TC has been successfully used cross-culturally and translated into several languages including Dutch, French, German, and Spanish (e.g., Benbenishty, 1988; Benbenishty, Ben-Zaken, & Yekel, 1991; Chou, 1992; Gibbons, 1991; Harris & Franklin, 2003; Lo, 2005; Nguyen, 1999; Nofz, 1988; Reid & Ramos, 2002). Clearly, most of its components and principles are cross-culturally applicable. For example, the notion that problems are client-determined accommodates the influences of different worldviews on problem definitions. Also, its short-term nature can be appealing cross-culturally, although the specific reasons for this preference may vary across groups. Other TC components such as its highly structured procedural format and future-oriented stance, which may not be suitable in work with some ethnocultural groups, can be easily modified (Ramos & Garvin, 2003). For a more detailed description of the use of TC cross-culturally, see Tolson and colleagues (2003).

Therapeutic Relationship

Similar to the generalist-eclectic framework and traditional social work practice, TC holds that the development of a good working relationship with the client is critically important. It should be noted, however, that TC eschews the phrase "therapeutic relationship," because it can be interpreted to mean that the relationship is the cause of change, a belief espoused in psychotherapy models in the past. Rather, as previously described, the relationship is viewed as necessary but not sufficient to cause change. This is consistent with research on the topic. The kind of relationship that is sought in TC is highly collaborative. Workers and clients participate in the decisions that are made as partners, with the worker contributing knowledge and assuming the responsibility for keeping the process moving and the client holding the power to choose the focus of treatment and the course of action.

Although the views of generalist-eclectic practice developed by the editors of this book and those of TC are consistent on the applied level, there may be some differences in philosophy. The driving ambition in TC is to develop a model that is effective, as demonstrated by scientific methods, in alleviating psychosocial problems. This purpose has implications for the use of knowledge and the generation of it.

CRITIQUE OF TC

The research regarding the effectiveness of TC has been referred to in preceding sections. The model has been found to be effective with a wide variety of challenging problems and populations. The controlled studies previously cited, for example, included "psychiatric patients, distressed marital couples, sick elderly patients, families seeking to regain their children from foster care, school children with academic and behavioral problems, sexual offenders, and delinquents in a residential center" (Reid, 1996, p. 635). The studies also included environmentally at-risk youth, persons with diabetes, families involved with the child protection system, and family members of persons with AIDS (Alley & Brown, 2002; Kane, 2001; Kinnevy, Healey, Pollio, & North, 1999; Pomeroy, Rubin, & Walker, 1995).

Based on the evidence, TC is an attractive "first-line" approach in most situations for several reasons (Tolson, 1988). First, it is likely to be effective. Second, ineffectiveness will be quickly apparent by means of problem reviews. Third, it is easier and more efficient to shift from TC to less structured and lengthier approaches than it is to shift to TC. Starting with a straightforward time-limited approach is appealing to most clients, and, when results are unsatisfactory, clients generally are willing to participate in other approaches to alleviate the identified problems.

There are some clients for whom TC is not a good first choice. For example, mandated clients who do not want help and who are unable to identify any aspects of their lives that they wish to change are not appropriate (it is usually possible, however, to identify target problems with mandated clients). Clients who wish to explore existential concerns or who seek ongoing support of a general nature are not well served by TC. Finally, clients who do not choose or are not ready to take action to solve problems may prefer other approaches. This will be evident when tasks are reviewed.

The array of problems that has been addressed by TC has expanded. As a result, it seems premature to eliminate the application of TC to any particular problems. However, applications of TC in six problem areas have been delineated: family problems, emotional distress, problem drinking, and problems of clients with chronic mental illness, health related problems, and inadequate resources (Reid, 1992). More recently, TC has been applied in the areas of gambling, developmental disabilities, foster care, date rape, and homelessness (Reid, 2000).

TC should not be the first choice when there is an alternative approach that has demonstrated effectiveness for a particular problem. For example, a child with obsessive-compulsive disorder (OCD) probably will be best served by the cognitive-behavioral approach of March and Mulle (1997). It is entirely possible to integrate the procedures of this approach into the task activity of TC, however, if doing so seems desirable. Because there are no comparative studies of TC and cognitive-behavioral work with children with OCD, the choice will depend on situational factors, including which approach is likely to be appealing to the client.

CASE ILLUSTRATION

Mrs. Carter, a 40-year-old African American widow, has 10 children. Of her 10 children (ages 2 to 15) 9 were placed in foster homes a year before TC was employed to help her (Rooney, 1981). Public assistance has been providing support for the past 15 years. The reason for the removal of the children is disputed. The client reports that she had agreed to place the children temporarily while she was in the hospital for surgery, whereas others report that the hospitalization was for alcoholism. Mrs. Carter has changed her mind about both the hospitalization and temporary placement, but the child welfare agency went to court to obtain temporary custody, citing the truancy and hygiene of the children, the client's alcoholism, and her inability to supervise her children.

Work involves a number of collaterals, including three public assistance (PA) workers, two child welfare workers, the landlord, individuals connected with Alcoholics Anonymous (AA), various foster parents, school personnel, the juvenile court judge and various court officials (including several public defenders and prosecutors), and representatives of the public housing authority. Complicating the situation is the fact that the relationships between some of the collaterals and Mrs. Carter are poor, and she has to persuade them that she is cooperative and responsible.

At the first, brief meeting, Mrs. Carter, although inebriated and sometimes incoherent, clearly states her concern: She wants her children returned. Mr. Rooney, the social worker, is employed by a private agency that has been subcontracted to serve some of the child welfare clientele. During the second session, work begins on the conditions specified by the court for Mrs. Carter to regain custody of her children. The issues to be addressed included inadequate housing (her two pieces of furniture did not include a stove or refrigerator, and there was no hot water), her drinking problem, the children's school attendance, and an unkempt home. Correcting these conditions becomes the focus of treatment. Major obstacles are encountered in eradicating these conditions. For example, attempts to make the current apartment adequate fail when the landlord refuses to make the necessary improvements, instructs the tenants to send their rent to the gas company, and threatens Mrs. Carter with eviction. Securing new housing is complicated: Mrs. Carter lacks funds. PA workers have to approve the new housing. Moving to a new area means the case will have to be transferred to another PA office and the transfer will take 12 weeks. Another target problem identified by Mrs. Carter: She has not seen her youngest children for 2 months.

The following excerpt is a portion of the discussion about seeing the children. Development of a task, consideration of an obstacle, and planning one of the details is included.

MRS. CARTER: *I wish you'd ask them [i.e., child welfare] [to let her see her children].*

MR. ROONEY: *I would suggest this time—have you talked to her [a child welfare worker] on the phone yet?*

MRS. CARTER: *Nope. I never talked to nobody on the phone.*

MR. ROONEY: *Well, sooner or later you're going to have to start dealing with her more often, because you know she's got to get to know you better. Right now, she doesn't know much about you and she doesn't trust you very much, and you don't trust her. What I would suggest is . . .*

MRS. CARTER: *Well, I don't care nothing about her, period! I don't like her.*

MR. ROONEY: *She doesn't like you either.*

MRS. CARTER: *She doesn't have anything to do with my kids; she's supposed to bring them in.*

MR. ROONEY: *That's right; you have that right, so I would suggest that you—I can give you her number—you call her.*

MRS. CARTER: *I got her number.*

MR. ROONEY: *Ask her when it can be done—and I'll call her later.*

MRS. CARTER: *Okay.*

MR. ROONEY: *—to follow up. But she needs to hear from you first, I think.*

In the next excerpt, Mrs. Carter reflects movingly on her problems with alcohol. She shares her decision to attend AA meetings, a task Mr. Rooney had suggested previously.

MRS. CARTER: *Doctor told me last year that I had to stop drinking. And I never did take him in my mind, you know.*

MR. ROONEY: *That contributes to it [problem of high blood pressure], doesn't it?*

MRS. CARTER: *Yeah. All that whiskey and wine and stuff. It runs your blood pressure up. See, I always did have trouble with my blood pressure; I started as a kid. And then when I started getting drunk, falling out and, you know, on the street and things, wind up in the hospital you didn't know that, did you? (Laughs) Yeah, I did that a couple times last year. Got drunk and fell out on the sidewalk and wind up in the hospital.*

MR. ROONEY: *All I remember is the first time I met you, you were in pretty bad shape.*

MRS. CARTER: *(Laughs) Yeah, doctor said if I didn't stop it, I would wind up with sclerosis of the liver. The only reason that mine affects me so bad when I start it I don't—I stop eating. I don't have no appetite to eat. I just have an appetite to stay drunk.*

MR. ROONEY: *What about now?*

MRS. CARTER: *I don't want to drink because I might not survive next time I fall out. And I want my kids back. So I put myself to a test. I don't think it's always going to be easy, but—I guess I'm going through another phase.*

MR. ROONEY: *A good phase.*

MRS. CARTER: *Yup. I don't want no more. 'Cause he even told me, the doctor said you can drink some, but I don't want to drink no more, period. Alcohol has caused me everything bad that has happened to me in my life. Caused me to be drunk, get my TV stole out of here, my radio.*

MR. ROONEY: *People take advantage of you?*

MRS. CARTER. *Of course.*

MR. ROONEY: *You see, that's the thing; I think that PA doesn't know . . . they have been here but once in 5 months and they don't know that you haven't been acting like the person they knew before.*

MRS. CARTER: *I know that.*

MR. ROONEY: *So what they've been trying to say to me and to you is, why should we make any special efforts for somebody who is going to, you know, not be able to hold up?*

MRS. CARTER: *They say once you do something, you always have to do it, but that's wrong. A person can change if he really wants to . . . see, I've been so weak all my life 'til I just can't stand to hurt nobody. I would let them hurt me and then I go and get drunk and forget about it, but you don't forget about it. You forget about it while you're drunk 'cause you don't know nothing else, and when you're real drunk, you're out.*

MR. ROONEY: *And then?*

MRS. CARTER: *When you get sober, it's the same thing.*

The original contract with Mrs. Carter was for 12 weeks. In fact, several 12-week extensions occurred and 55 sessions were held over a period of 14 months. The length of time consumed was largely because of the slowness of the bureaucratic agencies involved. Contract extensions had to be approved by the public child welfare agency. Extensions were normally difficult to obtain, but the careful documentation of task accomplishments was persuasive. At the end of the contract, which occurred because Mr. Rooney was leaving the area, four of Mrs. Carter's children were in her custody. They were attending school regularly and progressing satisfactorily. The cleanliness of the apartment was vastly improved. Mrs. Carter was to petition for the return of the remaining children when she was able to provide beds for them. At termination, she had saved enough money to purchase two more beds, and a petition hearing was scheduled for the following month. Work with Mrs. Carter demonstrates the usefulness of TC in some of the most challenging circumstances. It can be seen that mandated clients are not necessarily unmotivated, provided efforts are addressed to their concerns. The work also reveals a flexible use of time limits and a collaborative relationship with a client who was rightfully suspicious of professionals.

SUMMARY

Although the research supporting TC is more extensive than that of other approaches to the practice of social work, more is needed. There is a need to test the model with more systems, problems, and populations. More comparative studies are needed, as well as ones that examine long-term effectiveness. Finally, testing the relative effectiveness of separate parts of the model might identify the elements that are vital for success. There are some specific components of TC that merit additional empirical attention. All generalist approaches would benefit from more empirical information about the use of collaterals and practitioner tasks because it would enhance our ability to include the context or environment in our intervention efforts. Studies of the associations between relationship variables and outcomes would permit more specificity in the delineation of the types of relationships that are desired and the ways to achieve them. This is an ambitious agenda, and everyone is invited to participate.

REFERENCES

Acosta, F. X., Yamamoto, J., Evans, L. A., & Skilbeck, W. M. (1983). Preparing low-income Hispanic, Black, and White patients for psychotherapy: Evaluation of a new orientation program. *Journal of Clinical Psychology, 39,* 872–877.

Alley, G. R., & Brown, L. B. (2002). A diabetes problem-solving support group: Issues, process, and preliminary outcomes. *Social Work in Health Care, 36,* 1–9.

Bandura, A. (1986). *Social foundations of thought and action: A social cognitive theory.* Englewood Cliffs, NJ: Prentice Hall.

Beck, D. F., & Jones, M. A. (1973). *Progress on family problems: A nationwide study of clients' and counselors' views on family agency service.* New York: Family Service Agency of America.

Benbenishty, R. (1988). Assessment of task-centered interventions with families in Israel. *Journal of Social Service Research, 11,* 19–43.

Benbenishty, R., Ben-Zaken, A., & Yekel, H. (1991). Monitoring interventions with young Israeli families. *The British Journal of Social Work, 21,* 143–155.

Boyd-Franklin, N. (1989). Major family approaches and their relevance to the treatment of Black families. In N. Boyd-Franklin (Ed.), *Black families in therapy: A multisystems approach* (pp. 121–132). New York: Guilford Press.

Caspi, J. (in press). An empirically developed model for treating sibling aggression. *Research on Social Work Practice.*

Caspi, J., & Reid W. J. (1998). The task-centered model for field instruction: An innovative approach. *Journal of Social Work Education, 34,* 55–70.

Caspi, J., & Reid, W. J. (2002). *Educational supervision in social work: A task-centered model for field instruction and staff development.* New York: Columbia University Press.

Chou, Y. (1992). *Developing and testing an intervention program for assisting Chinese families in Taiwan who have a member with developmental disabilities.* Unpublished doctoral dissertation, University of Minnesota, Twin Cities.

Devore, W., & Schlesinger, E. (1999). *Ethnic-sensitive social work practice* (5th ed.). Boston: Allyn & Bacon.

Garfield, S. L. (1994). Research on client variables in psychotherapy. In A. E. Bergin & S. L. Garfield (Eds.), *Handbook of psychotherapy and behavior change* (4th ed., pp. 190–228). New York: Wiley.

Gibbons, J. (1991). Children in need and their families: Outcomes of referral to social services. *British Journal of Social Work, 21,* 217–227.

Gibbons, J., Bow, I., & Butler, J. (1985). Task-centered social work after parasuicide. In M. Goldberg, J. Gibbons, & I. Sinclair (Eds.), *Problems, tasks, and outcomes: The evaluation of task-centered casework in three settings* (pp. 169–257). Boston: Allen & Unwin.

Gibbons, J. S., Butler, J., Urwin, P., & Gibbons, J. L. (1978). Evaluation of a social work service for self-poisoning parents. *British Journal of Psychiatry, 133,* 111–118.

Gorey, K. M., Thyer, B. A., & Pawluck, D. E. (1998). Differential effectiveness of prevalent social work practice models: A meta-analysis. *Social Work, 43,* 269–278.

Gurman, A. S., & Kniskern, D. P. (1981). Family therapy outcome research: Knowns and unknowns. In A. S. Gurman & D. P. Kniskern (Eds.), *Handbook of family therapy* (pp. 742–775). New York: Brunner/Mazel.

Gutierrez, L. M. (1990). Working with women of color: An empowerment perspective. *Social Work, 35,* 1499–1553.

Harris, M., & Franklin, C. (2003). Effects of a cognitive-behavioral, school-based, group intervention with Mexican American pregnant and parenting adolescents. *Social Work Research, 27,* 74–84.

Hepworth, D., Rooney, R., Rooney, G., Strom-Gottfried, K., & Larsen, J. (2006). *Direct social work practice: Theory and skills* (7th ed.). Belmont, CA: Thomson.

Johnson, D. H., & Gelso, C. J. (1982). The effectiveness of time limits in counseling and psychotherapy: A critical review. *Counseling Psychologist, 9,* 70–83.

Kane, D. (2001). *Child welfare: Innovations in practice task-centered and mediation strategies.* Unpublished doctoral dissertation, University of Chicago.

Kilgore, D. K. (1995). *Task-centered group treatment of sex offenders: A developmental study.* Unpublished doctoral dissertation, State University of New York, Albany.

Kinnevy, S. C., Healey, B. P., Pollio, D. E., & North, C. S. (1999). Bicycle WORKS: Task-centered group work with high-risk youth. *Social Work With Groups, 22,* 33–47.

Kirst-Ashman, K. K., & Hull, G. H. (1995). *Understanding generalist practice.* Chicago: Nelson-Hall.

Koss, M. P., & Shiang, J. (1994). Research on brief psychotherapy. In A. E. Bergin & S. L. Garfield (Eds.), *Handbook of psychotherapy and behavior change* (4th ed., pp. 664–700). New York: Wiley.

Lake, M., & Levinger, G. (1960). Continuance beyond application interviews at a child guidance clinic. *Social Casework, 41,* 303–309.

Lambert, M. J., Dejulio, S. S., & Stein, D. M. (1978). Therapist interpersonal skills: Process, outcome, methodological considerations, and recommendations for future research. *Psychological Bulletin, 85,* 467–489.

Levinger, G. (1960). Continuance in casework and other helping relationships: A review of current research. *Social Work, 5,* 40–51.

Lo, T. W. (2005). Task-centered group work: Reflections on practice. *International Social Work, 48,* 455–465.

Luborsky, L., Singer, B., & Luborsky, L. (1975). Comparative studies of psychotherapies: Is it true that "Everyone has won and all must have prizes"? *Archives of General Psychiatry, 32,* 995–1008.

Lum, D. (1996). *Social work practice and people of color: A process-stage approach* (3rd ed). Pacific Grove, CA: Brooks/Cole.

March, J. S., & Mulle, K. (1997). *OCD in children and adolescents: A cognitive-behavioral treatment manual.* New York: Guilford Press.

Meltzoff, J., & Kornreich, M. (1970). *Research in psychotherapy.* New York: Atherton.

Miley, K. K., O'Melia, M., & DuBois, B. L. (2004). *Generalist social work practice: An empowering approach* (4th ed.). Boston: Allyn & Bacon.

Mitchell, K. M., Bozarth, J. D., & Krauft, C. C. (1977). A reappraisal of the therapeutic effectiveness of accurate empathy, nonpossessive warmth, and genuineness. In A. S. Gurman & A. Razin (Eds.), *Effective psychotherapy* (pp. 482–502). Oxford, England: Pergamon Press.

Naleppa, M. J., & Reid, W. J. (1998). Task-centered case management for the elderly: Developing a practice model. *Research on Social Work Practice, 8,* 63–84.

Naleppa, M. J., & Reid, W. J. (2000). Integrating case management and brief treatment strategies: A hospital-based geriatric program. *Health & Social Work, 31*, 1–23.

Newcome, K. (1985). Task-centered group work with the chronically mentally ill in day treatment. In A. E. Fortune (Ed.), *Task-centered practice with families and groups* (pp. 78–91). New York: Springer.

Nguyen, W. (1999). Using a task-centered approach with Vietnamese families. In K. S. Ng, (Ed.), *Counseling Asian families from a systems perspective* (pp. 55–62). Alexandria, VA: American Counseling Association.

Nofz, M. P. (1988). Alcohol abuse and culturally marginal American Indians. *Social Casework, 69*, 67–73.

Orlinsky, D. E., & Howard, K. I. (1986). Process outcome in psychotherapy. In S. L. Garfield & A. E. Bergin (Eds.), *Handbook of psychotherapy and behavior change* (3rd ed., pp. 311–381). New York: Wiley.

Parloff, M. B., Waskow, I. E., & Wolfe, B. E. (1978). Research on therapist variables in relation to process and outcome. In S. L. Garfield & A. E. Bergin (Eds.), *Handbook of psychotherapy and behavior change* (pp. 233–282). New York: Wiley.

Patterson, C. H. (1984). Empathy, warmth, and genuineness in psychotherapy: A review of reviews. *Psychotherapy: Theory, Research, and Practice, 21*, 431–438.

Perlman, H. H. (1957). *Social casework: A problem-solving process.* Chicago: University of Chicago Press.

Pomeroy, E. C., Rubin, A., & Walker, R. J. (1995). Effectiveness of a psychoeducational and task-centered group intervention of family members of people with AIDS. *Social Work Research, 19*, 129–152.

Presley, J. H. (1987). The clinical dropout: A view from the client's perspective. *Social Casework, 68*, 603–608.

Ramos, B. M., & Garvin, C. (2003). Task-centered treatment with culturally diverse populations. In E. R. Tolson, W. J. Reid, & C. D. Garvin (Eds.), *Generalist practice: A task-centered approach* (2nd ed., pp. 441–463). New York: Columbia University Press.

Reid, W. J. (1975). An experimental test of a task-centered approach. *Social Work, 20*, 3–9.

Reid, W. J. (1978). *The task-centered system.* New York: Columbia University Press.

Reid, W. J. (1985). *Family problem solving.* New York: Columbia University Press.

Reid, W. J. (1992). *Task strategies: An empirical approach to social work practice.* New York: Columbia University Press.

Reid, W. J. (1996). Task-centered social work. In F. J. Turner (Ed.), *Social work treatment: Interlocking theoretical approaches* (4th ed., pp. 617–640). New York: Free Press.

Reid, W. J. (1997). Research on task-centered practice. *Social Work Research, 21*, 132–137.

Reid, W. J. (2000). *The task planner.* New York: Columbia University Press.

Reid, W. J., & Bailey-Dempsey, C. (1995). The effects of monetary incentives on school performance. *Families in Society, 76*, 331–340.

Reid, W. J., & Epstein, L. (Eds.). (1972). *Task-centered casework.* New York: Columbia University Press.

Reid, W. J., Epstein, L., Brown, L., Tolson, E. R., & Rooney, R. H. (1980). Task-centered school social work. *Social Work in Education, 2*, 7–24.

Reid, W. J., & Ramos, B. (2002). Intervención "centrada en la tarea," un modelo de práctica de trabajo social (The task-centered model of social work practice). *Revista de Treball Social, 168*, 6–22.

Reid, W. J., & Shyne, A. W. (1969). *Brief and extended casework.* New York: Columbia University Press.

Rooney, R. H. (1981). A task-centered reunification model for foster care. In A. A. Malluccio & P. Sinanoglu (Eds.), *The challenge of partnership: Working with biological parents of children in foster care* (pp. 135–150). New York: Child Welfare League of America Press.

Rooney, R. H. (1992). *Strategies for work with involuntary clients.* New York: Columbia University Press.

Silverman, P. R. (1970). A reexamination of the intake procedure. *Social Casework, 51,* 625–634.

Sloane, R. B., Cristol, A. H., Pepernik, C., & Staples, F. R. (1970). Role preparation and expectation of improvement in psychotherapy. *Journal of Nervous and Mental Disease, 150,* 18–26.

Strean, H. S. (1968). Some reactions of case workers to the war on poverty. *Journal of Contemporary Psychotherapy, 1,* 43–48.

Strupp, H. H., Fox, R. E., & Lessler, K. (1969). *Patients view their psychotherapy.* Baltimore: Johns Hopkins University Press.

Studt, E. (1968). Social work theory and implications for the practice of methods. *Social Work Education Reporter, 16,* 22–46.

Tolson, E. R. (1988). *The metamodel and clinical social work.* New York: Columbia University Press.

Tolson, E. R., Reid, W. J., & Garvin, C. D. (1994). *Generalist practice: A task-centered approach.* New York: Columbia University Press.

Tolson, E. R., Reid, W. J., & Garvin, C. D. (2003). *Generalist practice: A task-centered approach* (2nd ed.). New York: Columbia University Press.

Viggiani, P. (1996). *Social worker-teacher collaboration: Intervention design and development.* Unpublished doctoral dissertation, State University of New York, Albany.

Wells, R. (1994). *Planned short-term treatment* (2nd ed.). New York: Free Press.

Wells, R., & Gianetti, V. (Eds.). (1990). *Handbook of brief psychotherapies.* New York: Plenum Press.

Zwick, R., & Attkisson, C. C. (1984). The use of reception checks in client pretherapy orientation research. *Journal of Clinical Psychology, 40,* 446–452.

Section C

Humanistic and Feminist Theories

CHAPTER 12

Client-Centered Theory

Michael Rothery and Leslie Tutty

Developed by the psychologist Carl Rogers over a long career that ended with his death in 1987, client-centered (also referred to as nondirective and person-centered) therapy has been a major force in clinical psychology, and a counterweight to the deterministic behaviorism that Rogers rejected. Rogers is seen by many as one of the foundational thinkers in the development of humanistic psychology, even as one of the most generally influential psychologists of the 20th century. His client-centered theory was a radical innovation for psychology; for social work it was more a valuable refinement and reaffirmation of familiar principles, but it has nevertheless had a significant and beneficial impact on social work practice and education.

In developing this model, Rogers considered he had identified the *necessary* and *sufficient* conditions that lead to people changing. This is not a modest claim: The suggestion is that if one wants to be an effective helper, client-centered principles are something one must learn (they are necessary), and nothing else is required (they are sufficient).

The theory guiding this therapeutic method is a theory of *process*. As such, the approach is firmly aligned with the belief that we do not help our clients through an expertise with theories of personality, knowledge of family dysfunction, or a deep appreciation for critical ecological systems theory. Rather, we they assist people's growth by providing a particular kind of relationship, through communications that have specific qualities.

According to client-centered theory, those essential qualities are the Rogerian *core conditions*: congruence, acceptance, and empathy. (As one would expect, terminology has varied over time and from one writer to

299

another. Nuances that might distinguish *congruence* from *genuineness* or *authenticity* and similar semantic fine points are not important at this juncture.) When those interpersonal conditions are sufficiently available to us from our friends, loved ones, or social workers, we have what we need to grow personally, just as we grow physically when we have enough food and other necessities. Understanding more exactly what those essential relational conditions are and how we can learn to make them present in our work was Rogers's main mission in life.

This is a deceptively simple general idea possessing considerable explanatory force. Also, it fits easily with social work's historic principles. Indeed, relationship has always been critical in social workers' eyes, identified as both the context and the means for facilitating change (Biestek, 1957; Coady, 1999; Perlman, 1957, 1979). Indeed, in a book that is rightly regarded as a classic on the topic, Biestek (1957) argued that the emphasis on relationship is so important that it serves to define us:

> This is one principal difference between social work and some of the other professions. In surgery, dentistry, and law, for example, a good interpersonal relationship is desirable for the *perfection* of the service, but it is not necessary for the *essence* of the service. The surgeon may not have a good bedside manner; the dentist may be inconsiderate of the patient's feelings; the lawyer may be cold and overly businesslike. But if the surgeon operates successfully, if the dentist heals the ailing tooth, and if the lawyer wins the case, they have performed the essential service requested. Not so the caseworker. A good relationship is necessary not only for the perfection, but also for the essence, of the casework service in every setting. (p. 19)

For better and for worse we constantly affect one another's experience, through "the rich interplay of one human mind with another" (Garrett, Mangold, & Zaki, 1982, p. 4). Being thoroughly socially embedded as we are (see chapter 4), this mutual influence is simply a fact of life, and Rogers wanted to understand how to harness its power in the service of client growth.

OVERVIEW OF THEORY

Understanding of Human Problems

Though his theory is heavily weighted toward process, Rogers did suggest a basic psychological dynamic for understanding how we become distressed. Human problems, he thought, can generally be understood as reflecting a state of incongruence. People experience pain when they perceive themselves falling significantly short of what, ideally, they wish to be. One of his interpreters explains this aspect of Rogers's theory:

> The client's self-image is contradicted by his life experience; thus . . . two levels of self-being are . . . constituted: one involving the . . . idealized self; the other touching on and flowing from, the actual experience of self-in-process. . . . Determined to defend his self-concept . . . the client is unable to admit into clear awareness those experiences that would interfere with his sense of self-worth. (Barton, 1980, p. 169)

However, Rogers argued vehemently that beyond this it is counterproductive to approach clients with preconceptions in the form of theories of personality, or psychopathology, or anything else that might work against our openness to the uniqueness of people and their situations:

> The more I have observed therapists, and the more closely I have studied [the] research . . . the more I am forced to the conclusion that . . . diagnostic knowledge is not essential to psychotherapy. It may even be that its defense as a necessary prelude to psychotherapy is simply a protective alternative to the admission that it is, for the most part, a colossal waste of time. (Rogers, 1957, pp. 101–102)

It is therefore fair to say that Rogers and his followers did not pursue a highly developed understanding of human problems. Instead, they worked to illuminate the interpersonal processes that represent a context within which healing naturally occurs.

Conception of Therapeutic Intervention

The conditions that enable us to develop in self-actualizing ways are universal, Rogers believed. Good clinical social work or psychology are based on the same core elements as good parenting, good teaching, or the friendships that help us thrive. When we provide clinical social work services, therefore, we are paid to offer our clients the same growth-enhancing interpersonal experiences that more fortunate people receive freely from friends and loved ones. To the extent that our clients may be especially estranged from themselves, they require us to provide those conditions in a skilled, well-attuned way, but there is nothing that distinguishes their needs from everyone else's in any formal sense.

Client-centered tenets about intervention and change have an apparent simplicity that can easily result in misunderstanding:

Very early in my work . . . I discovered that simply listening to my client, very attentively, was an important way of being helpful. . . . Later a social worker, who had a background of Rankian training, helped me to learn that the most effective approach was to listen for the feelings. . . . I believe she was the one who suggested that the best response was to "reflect" these feelings back to the client—"reflect" becoming in time a word that made me cringe. But at that time, it improved my work as therapist, and I was grateful.

But this tendency to focus on the therapist's responses had appalling consequences. . . . The whole approach came, in a few years, to be known as a technique. "Nondirective therapy," it was said, "is the technique of reflecting the client's feelings." Or an even worse caricature was simply that "in nondirective therapy you repeat the last words the client has said." (Rogers, 1980, pp. 137–139)

The process of change, in the client-centered view, is at once simple and complex. Simply put, people are naturally inclined toward growth, and given the right conditions they will come to know themselves more fully, heal old wounds, and develop greater authenticity and congruence. They will become more knowledgeable and honest, first in relation to themselves, and then in relation to others.

As we have noted, the right conditions that facilitate such growth are relationships with particular characteristics: congruence, acceptance, and empathy. If we are honest, accepting, and understanding, our clients will benefit from their relationship with us. The apparent simplicity of this prescription belies the subtlety of the processes it describes, however—hence Rogers's concern about being so easily misunderstood. We will have more to say about the complexity of the core conditions below, in the section on central theoretical constructs.

HISTORICAL DEVELOPMENT

Precursors and Original Development

Mary Richmond (1899) can be credited with early efforts to understand relationship and its critical importance: "Friendly visiting means intimate . . . knowledge of and sympathy with a . . . family's joys, sorrows, opinions, feelings. . . . The visitor that has this is unlikely to blunder . . . [although] without it he is almost certain . . . to blunder seriously" (p. 180). This assertion is only marginally more cautious than Rogers's claims about necessity and sufficiency, and it represents an appreciation of the importance of empathic understanding that predates client-centered theory by a half century.

Richmond was a committed empiricist, convinced that careful case records in which services and their outcomes were documented would lead to an improved and scientific understanding of the helping process. In 1922, she wrote a short book reflecting on the essential nature of direct practice ("social case work"), in which she reported the results of her intensive analysis of six varied and well-documented cases.

A striking feature of Richmond's (1922) conclusions is the extent to which she attributed effectiveness of service with qualitative aspects of how workers *related* to their clients. More specifically, she identified a capacity for honesty, affectionate acceptance, and "imaginative sympathy" (p. 37) as critical factors in relationships that support change. When Rogers came to emphasize congruence, acceptance, and empathy in his own analysis of the effectiveness of psychotherapy, the language had changed, but the fundamental insight had not. It is also notable that in each case one of these conditions is paramount—Richmond's *imaginative sympathy* and Rogers's *empathy* are understood to be the dimension that encourages growth more than any other.

Since Richmond's early introduction of concepts such as *friendly visiting* and *sympathy*, social workers have striven for greater clarity in describing what it is about some relationships that makes them powerful tools for change. Different terms have been invoked in this effort to understand, such as *empathy* (Shaw, as cited in Biestek, 1957), *rapport* and *emotional bridging* (LeRoy, as cited in Biestek, 1957), some aspects of *transference* (Taft, as cited in Biestek, 1957; see also Garrett, Mangold, & Zaki, 1982, which addresses the phenomenon without using the term), *engagement* (Smalley, 1967), and the *therapeutic alliance* (Coady, 1999).

As social work grew it incorporated ideas from different disciplines, such as psychiatry and psychology, and our long-standing fascination with Freudian and related psychodynamic theories is a case in point—most observers see this development, in hindsight, as at least somewhat problematic. Like behaviorism in American psychology, Freud's theory was highly deterministic—it was this that caused Mary Richmond among others to worry about its implications for a field that had always been heavily committed to important social values.

Freudian theory also discouraged our traditional emphasis on relationship as the context and means for change:

> Although Freud paid some attention to the therapeutic relationship, he saw the development of insight and rationality, acquired through the analyst's interpretations, as the curative element in psychoanalysis. . . . Within psychoanalysis, of course, there has always been an interpersonal school, identified mostly with Sullivan and his followers, but until recently this school remained outside the mainstream of psychoanalytic theory. (Saari, 2002, p. 125)

One of Freud's early disciples was Otto Rank, who paid a heavy professional and personal cost for breaking with orthodox Freudian beliefs

(Lieberman, 1985). In contrast with Freud's determinism, Rank ascribed critical importance to *creativity* and *will* (Menaker, 1982)—concepts that did not fit comfortably with the narrowly scientific worldview predominant at the time. Rank also insisted that the heart of helping was not in diagnoses, interpretations, and rationalistic analyses, but in relationship (Menaker, 1982; Rank, 1964, 1989; Taft, 1958; see also Becker, 1973, 1975 for a more general, deep appreciation of Rank's thought).

Jessie Taft was the dean of the Philadelphia School of Social Work from 1934 to 1950. A friend of and collaborator with Rank, she wrote his biography (Taft, 1958) and translated some of his work into English, and it was she who brought him to the United States to share his ideas with American professionals. At the time, Carl Rogers was working with social workers in Philadelphia:

> From 1928 through 1939, Carl Rogers served as a therapist at the Society for Prevention of Cruelty to Children, in Rochester, New York. . . . On his staff at the Rochester clinic were a number of social workers trained at the University of Pennsylvania's School of Social Work . . . where Otto Rank had been lecturing since 1926. (Kramer, 1995, p. 58)

The helping method identified with the University of Pennsylvania, the *Functional* school of social work, drew heavily on Rank's ideas and made relationship a pivotal issue in its understanding of change—a sharp difference from the competing *Diagnostic* school, which remained more committed to orthodox Freudianism. Early in his career, Carl Rogers was a colleague of social workers imbued with functional thinking; it is likely through their influence that he came to meet Rank:

> In June, 1936, intrigued by social workers who were telling him that *"relationship therapy"*—not "interpretive therapy"—was the emphasis of the Philadelphia School, Carl Rogers invited Otto Rank to Rochester to conduct a 3-day seminar on his new, post-Freudian practice of therapy. (Kramer, 1995, p. 59)

This meeting was a turning point for Rogers, shaping his thinking for the rest of his life (Kramer, 1995). Rogers, in turn, did much to clarify conceptually what the elements of a helpful relationship are, and initiated a research program to measure those elements and their effects. The outcome was the client-centered school of counseling.

Otto Rank and Carl Rogers, then, are two prominent theorists whose thought imbues the client-centered framework. The complementarity of their ideas and values is remarkable, given their differences in background. Rank was very much a product of European culture and education. Rogers, in contrast, was thoroughly American (Van Belle, 1980), the son of "a narrowly fundamentalist religious home" (Rogers, 1980, p. 27) and a graduate of universities in Wisconsin and New York.

Each man made an important mark by rebelling against his earlier training, looking for a way out of the limitations he experienced in the doctrines of the day. Rank replaced the rigid determinism of Freud's thinking with a theory that celebrated the human capacity for creativity and choice (Menaker, 1982). Rogers rejected the deterministic, objective psychology that prevailed when he was starting out, offering in its place a humanistic "home-grown brand of existential philosophy" (Rogers, 1980, p. 39). In fact, calling his work "client-centered" and "nondirective" constitutes an important philosophical position on Rogers's part—a commitment to the belief that the resources for healing and growth are to be found primarily in the client, not in the theories and techniques of the helper.

Later Developments and Current Status

Few scholars have had the impact that Rogers enjoyed in his field. In the half century since he began publishing his ideas, he has stimulated an enormous response in terms of ongoing theory development and research. A perusal of influential journals such as *The Journal of Counseling Psychology* will verify that literally thousands of academic, research, and professional careers are rooted solidly in his work.

The client-centered model as Rogers formulated it has not gone unchallenged, and we will indicate where problems lie toward the end of this chapter. However, it is remarkable, given the energy that has gone into its development, to note how the foundation Rogers laid—the concepts that are the primary focus of this chapter—remain essentially unaltered.

Much effort has gone into developing ways of measuring the core conditions (Truax & Carkhuff, 1967, are a prominent example). This has contributed to some refinement of concepts, with terms like *self-disclosure* and *immediacy* serving to focus on the specifics of what Rogers described under the more general processes of congruence and empathy. Other conditions presented appear to be actual additions to the repertoire, such as *confrontation* and *concreteness* (Carkhuff, 1987; Truax, 1963; Truax & Carkhuff, 1964).

The effort to translate Rogers's general process conditions into operational behaviors has resulted in extensive catalogues of specific counseling skills (e.g., Ivey, 1988), and the application of these in education, industry, and other organizational domains has absorbed considerable interest and energy—as has their application cross-culturally (Sue, Ivey, & Pedersen, 1996).

Beyond these generalities, the scope of this chapter prevents our doing justice to the vast body of work that has grown out of client-centered theory. The extent to which derivatives of the basic model diverge from their roots varies; however, none challenges it in any fundamental way, and most pay frank homage to Rogers as the germinal thinker on whose shoulders they stand.

CENTRAL THEORETICAL CONSTRUCTS

We have noted a seeming simplicity about the basic client-centered formula for change. Drawing on Rank and other humanistic influences, Rogers came to the view that everyone has a creative capacity to make choices and is motivated to grow. These naturally present capacities and inclinations can be blocked or distorted by experience, with psychological pain as a consequence. However, in the context of a sufficiently nurturing relationship, the client will rediscover them and return to a healthy, self-actualizing path.

Congruence, acceptance (or unconditional positive regard), and empathy characterize the relational context that promotes such results. Although other ingredients have been recommended as client-centered thinking has evolved, these remain primary and, as we have emphasized, need to be understood as complex processes.

Congruence

Congruence is interpersonal genuineness, honesty, and directness. The social worker who is self-aware, comfortable with herself or himself, and able to find ways to relate to clients that do not disguise who he or she is, is relating congruently. What is meant, however, is far from simple encouragement to give free expression to whatever one thinks and feels. Congruence means that "the feelings the therapist is experiencing are available to him, available to his awareness, and he is able to live these feelings, be them, and able to communicate them if appropriate" (Rogers, 1961, p. 61; see also Rogers, 1980, p. 115).

Garrett et al.'s (1982) view of the requirements of social work interviewing is similarly demanding: "An interviewer's attention must continuously be directed in two ways: toward himself as well as toward his client" (p. 6). Both Garrett and her colleagues and Rogers (1961), therefore, described a disciplined effort to develop self-awareness and comfort with oneself. Further, congruence implies the ability to use that awareness in the service of the client, sharing aspects of our experience as it is *appropriate* to do so; that is, in a manner that is sensitively attuned to client needs and readiness.

Acceptance

The second condition that we provide clients in creating a context for growth is acceptance, or "unconditional positive regard," which "involves the therapist's genuine willingness for the client to be whatever feeling is going on in him at that moment . . . [and requires] that the therapist cares for the client in a non-possessive way . . . in a total rather than a conditional way . . . and without reservations, without evaluations" (Rogers, 1961, p. 62). Thus, we work to establish with our clients a positive attitude about them as people unaffected by our reactions to how they feel or what they may have done. This implies the belief that we can (and must) cultivate a capacity for interpersonal generosity, based on a differentiated understanding of others as a complex mix of characteristics and potentials. Further, we can discipline ourselves so that client behaviors, characteristics, or experiences that distress us do not undermine this capacity. There is something about each client that we value with no strings attached—and we need to be able to communicate that effectively.

Empathy

The third and preeminent element in a relational context for growth is empathy. Again, Rogers took considerable pains to be clear that he did not see empathy as achievable in a formulaic, superficial fashion—the caricature being an expression of soulful concern and the words "I *know* how you feel!" Empathic understanding is never so simple:

> [Empathy] means that the therapist senses accurately the feelings and personal meanings that the client is experiencing and communicates this understanding to the client. When functioning best, the therapist is so much inside the private world of the other that he or she can clarify not only the meanings of which the client is aware but even those just below the level of awareness. This kind of sensitive, active listening is exceedingly rare in our lives, . . . yet [it] is one of the most potent forces for change that I know. (Rogers, 1980, p. 116)

These definitions and elaborations remain consistent in Rogers's writing over time (compare with Rogers, 1959), and there are a number of elements in them that we would highlight. First, there is a role for intelligence, insight, training, and experience: The social worker should grasp *accurately* and *sensitively* the emotional content and meanings implied in what the client is saying.

Second, empathy as Rogers defines it is not simply understanding feelings: He is inclined to emphasize emotions, but also returns constantly to words like "experiencing" and "meaning." Thus, the point of empathic understanding is to communicate awareness of both the emotional and narrative aspects of what the client presents. Perhaps the word "experiencing" is attractive because it addresses both feelings about events and the meanings attributed to them—aspects that are always so interdependent that the wisdom of separating them is questionable.

A third point is that empathy implies a strong psychological attunement by the worker to the experience of the client, but not a loss of boundaries. The therapist "can grasp the moment-to-moment experiencing which occurs in the inner world of the client as the client sees it and feels it, *without losing the separateness of his own identity* [italics added]" (Rogers, 1961, pp. 62–63). This is a clarification about which he was consistent:

> It means to sense the hurt or the pleasure of another as he senses it and to perceive the causes thereof as he perceives them but without ever losing the recognition that it is *as if* I were hurt or pleased and so forth. If this "as if" quality is lost then the state is one of identification. (Rogers, 1959, pp. 210–211)

Although empathy as a concept stresses engagement, clients are served best if we are fully able to step back, understanding their experience but also inviting new perspectives and options.

Why is empathy considered to be such a powerful precondition for growth? Rogers explains this by suggesting several benefits that accrue when we experience an empathic relationship:

1. Empathy "dissolves alienation" (Rogers, 1980, p. 151). Clients often feel alone in their problems, and an empathic relationship with a clinical social worker is a powerful antidote: "If someone else knows what I am talking about, what I mean, then to this degree I am not so strange, or alien, or set apart. I make sense to another human being" (Rogers, 1980, p. 151).
2. Empathic understanding has the effect of communicating to people that they are valued, and is therefore useful for repairing damaged self-esteem. It is Rogers's contention that empathy is not possible without caring, and the experience of being cared about encourages a sense of self-value.

3. Because empathy is nonjudgmental, "always free of any evaluative or diagnostic quality" (Rogers, 1980, p. 154), being empathically treated encourages self-acceptance. Aspects of ourselves from which we recoil are less corrosive to our self-esteem if we see that another person can hear about them without becoming threatened or angry—and may regard them as normal, even admirable, rather than as cause for shame and self-denigration.

4. When people receive empathic responses to their troubles, they are encouraged to self-explore, increasing their awareness and developing a richer experience of themselves. This is beneficial in and of itself, because a broader self-understanding exposes more options regarding how we can respond to situations. Further, when painful aspects of our experience are "fully accepted and accurately labeled in awareness" (Rogers, 1980, p. 158), we are able to respond more creatively to those issues.

PHASES OF HELPING

Four phases of helping characterize generalist social work practice: engagement, data collection and assessment, planning/contracting and intervention, and evaluation and termination. What can we suggest the contribution of client-centered theory is to facilitating this process?

Respecting *engagement* the argument is simple. Relating honestly, respectfully, and empathically should speed the development of trust and openness. However, it may be that client-centered theory, interestingly, puts too much responsibility for such relationships on the worker. Recent research and theory emphasizes that predispositions of the client are powerful as well; however skilled we may be, we still depend on our clients to respond positively if an effective helping alliance is to be formed (Coady, 1999; Miller, Duncan, & Hubble, 1997).

With respect to *assessment* it is our view that the client-centered approach offers critical process skills. However, we would also argue that social workers require more of a framework to enable decisions regarding the kinds of data that are to be collected. With an abused spouse, we are trained to explore safety issues, for example, even if these do not automatically emerge in our interview. Similarly, if we suspect child maltreatment, addictions, suicidal tendencies, a significant lack of supports and resources, or any of a host of potentially relevant matters, we are trained to invite discussion of those, and this training is a good thing. This does not deny the risk of forming premature hypotheses about what is important and ceasing to listen carefully to the client—Rogers's thinking and approach are very useful protections against this possibility.

With respect to *planning/contracting and intervention*, client-centered theory does not offer as much direction as social workers and their clients may require. The assumptions that appropriate goals and plans will emerge if clients have the opportunity to explore their experience and that workers' congruence, acceptance, and empathy will be sufficient to enable clients to achieve their goals are sometimes valid, but by no means always.

The client-centered model is not prescriptive with respect to the length of treatment, and the timing of termination is likely similar to what we see with other models. What the client-centered model offers regarding *termination and evaluation* is, again, its understanding of process. In terminating, the opportunity for clients to reflect on their experience with the social worker and what it has meant to them are obviously very important, and an effective helping relationship is a context designed to encourage that. With respect to evaluation, the model suggests very good criteria for assessing the helping process, these being the core conditions and client-self exploration. Properly speaking, these are process rather than outcome variables; whereas outcomes independent of process have also been assessed in some client-centered research, the measures employed are familiar in research on other models as well. With respect to helping particular clients evaluate the success of their work, the model offers a process that facilitates that, but does not suggest independent criteria for assessing the merits of goals achieved. Because it is not a domain-specific model, this is appropriate—outcomes to be evaluated will vary across people and client populations.

APPLICATION TO FAMILY AND GROUP WORK

If the basic thesis of client-centered theory is true, it should apply equally whether work is being conducted with an individual, family, group, or other social system. It was, in fact, Rogers's (1980) position that communicational processes favoring the core conditions would make many diverse social settings more nurturing and supportive of learning and growth. He was a leader in the encounter group movement as it developed, and he suggested applications of his work in educational settings, families, and organizations of various sizes and diverse purposes.

The direct evidence for the impact of client-centered methods in groups is not strong, perhaps due to significant methodological difficulties. To the extent that modeling takes place and group members learn effective communication skills that they can use in their efforts to support and help one another, it seems logical to think this would be beneficial. In family work, there is evidence enough to convince some reviewers that the core conditions do contribute significantly to positive outcomes (Gurman, Kniskern, & Pinsof, 1986; Nichols & Schwartz, 2004; Sexton, Alexander, & Mease, 2004).

COMPATIBILITY WITH A GENERALIST-ECLECTIC FRAMEWORK

Though Rogers was suspicious about explanatory theory, the process orientation of the client-centered model invites eclecticism. Practitioners who consider themselves Rogerians freely incorporate concepts from schools of thought as diverse as behaviorism and psychodynamic theory (a point we will return to below, in our case discussion).

Social workers who practice from a generalist-eclectic framework commonly recognize the contribution of client-centered thinking to their work. A powerful emphasis on the importance of relationship is one shared commitment; the deep respect in client-centered theory for the competency, personal power, and motivation toward health in the client is another commonality.

Rogers's insistence on the central importance of attunement to clients' experience has obvious relevance to work in situations where diversity is a factor. The process of achieving and communicating shared understanding across disparate frames of reference is considered part of all helping, so it is no surprise that this knowledge has been applied in work with diverse cultural groups (Rogers, 1980).

For similar reasons, the theory prescribes a process that will be helpful in work with people who are different from the social worker in terms of age or gender. However, it does not offer knowledge of general themes associated with gender or the life cycle—or a systematic understanding of social systems. Familiarity with such knowledge is important to generalist-eclectic workers, and will need to be acquired from sources other than the client-centered literature, if holistic assessments and effective use of life cycle theories are to be achieved.

CRITIQUE: THE STRENGTHS AND LIMITATIONS OF THE MODEL

Several decades after Rogers began publishing and researching his work, there is no reason to question its profound impact on social work and other helping professions. The critical significance of relationship to the helping enterprise is now widely accepted as proven. Further, there is little dispute about the relevance to helping of the core conditions; while there are ongoing discussions about how they might best be defined and measured, there is a rather impressive consensus as to their basic credibility and importance.

There are, however, qualifications to suggest in relation to this theory. In part, these derive from Rogers's insistence that the core conditions are all there is, that they are the *necessary* and *sufficient* conditions for positive change. In social work practice (and, it turns out, in other disciplines as well), they are not always necessary and they are often not sufficient (Miller et al., 1997).

Like all of us, Rogers brought to his work certain professional and cultural assumptions. He grew up imbued with the values of American pragmatism and the Protestant belief in individual salvation. This history sets a context within which he developed an approach to helping that stresses (sometimes to the exclusion of all else) the need to assist clients in discovering the personal strengths and resources they possess so that they can apply them effectively in their lives. In his later years, Rogers worked for the development of better social conditions and more humane communities. However, it is still true that his theory could encourage an emphasis on the person of the client and a lack of attention to deprivations or sources of oppression in clients' environments.

Working as they do with very difficult situations, social workers will easily recognize that a client who is hungry or is being brutalized by an abusive parent or partner will not necessarily have as a priority the need to explore the meanings of those experiences. Relief or protection from extremely damaging circumstances can come with concrete interventions rather than an intense helping relationship—and it may be that this is all that is required. Even when a helping relationship and the opportunity to self-explore are useful in important ways (as they must be in most cases), they will often not be *sufficient*.

Another general concern to be raised is that the client-centered model can be utopian, and this entails risks. This is not a necessary outcome of absorbing the theory, but a possible one to be guarded against—one that can be a more general problem with the humanistic approaches overall. If the goal of intervention is to help clients achieve congruence, or complete harmony within themselves, the goal is an ideal that is never fully reached. If the helper's responsibility is to strive for complete attunement with the experience of another, it is a foregone conclusion that we will always fall short.

We are likely to be more comfortable, honest, and competent in our work if we remember that our interventions are intended to ameliorate problems and achieve modest objectives. Self-actualization, personal congruence, authenticity, and other forms of salvation are not disparaged as goals, but they are lifelong pursuits and require guidance and supports different from what social workers normally offer.

Given an adequate degree of realistic modesty, there are compelling reasons for social workers to learn and continually practice the approach to relating that Rogers and his colleagues have described for us. This, however, is not all we need to know.

CASE EXAMPLE

Dave is a young adult (25 years old), married, successful in his job, and prone to depression. He has been seen at a mental health clinic on an outpatient basis—the transcript begins about 20 minutes into the eighth interview. His childhood history involves treatment that he describes as "sadistic" and "terroristic" on the part of an alcoholic father. Events that he recalls certainly justify those labels.

Dave has maintained relationships with his family of origin, because there is much in it that he values. However, he acknowledges that he is especially likely to become depressed before and after visits to his parents. This is what he is discussing at the point the transcript begins:

DAVE: *I don't know why I get so down . . . into such a state. I want to see them, or I wouldn't go. But I think about walking through that door and it's hard. And thinking about being in a room with him [referring to his father] is just really awful.*

SOCIAL WORKER: *It sounds like you feel in a painful kind of bind about visiting them. Is part of that awful feeling the sense that you are . . . somehow feel trapped?*

DAVE: *Yeah! Like I have to go . . . I want to go . . . but also like I just want to get away from there.*

SOCIAL WORKER: *There's important stuff you need from your family, but you feel frightened when you go there.*

DAVE: *I can't stop myself from thinking about him taking his belt off (long pause) and yelling at me . . . screaming, really . . . about what he was going to do to me with it . . .*

SOCIAL WORKER: *So it makes sense that you're afraid. Going home triggers really painful memories, awful memories . . . memories that get you feeling small again, and maybe helpless.*

DAVE: *Helpless, yes, but . . . It's not as if I think he can treat me like that now. It's more like . . . (Long pause of 30 seconds or more) . . . it's more just that he did those things to me. Why me? How could he do that? I was just a kid.*

SOCIAL WORKER: *I think you've just asked a question that is really painful for you—Why me? How could he do that? (Dave nods.)—do you have an answer, or even part of an answer?*

DAVE: *I sort of see him standing over me, whipping off his belt, waving it around. . . . And he looks really angry. (A long pause, and efforts to maintain composure) . . . But he also looks weird . . . I don't know . . . like this feels good to him or something . . .*

SOCIAL WORKER: *I imagine it would be especially hard . . . almost impossible to think that.*

DAVE: *He is scaring the shit out of me, and he thinks it's fun. . . . The son-of-a-bitch is getting off on . . . (haltingly) on making me so scared . . . and like there's nothing I can do.*

SOCIAL WORKER: *Is there a feeling humiliation in this? (Dave nods.) And that you're alone? (Dave nods again, fighting tears.)*

DAVE: *You know, I was just a kid . . . but at that time I was always thinking about running away . . . even going off to die somewhere.*

SOCIAL WORKER: *You were that desperate . . . so much so that you weren't sure you could go on. But you did. Part of you wanted to hang in.*

DAVE: *I guess so . . . I'm not sure about that one. I mean, if I'm so weak, so unimportant that he could do that to me and have fun while he was at it, what does that make me?*

SOCIAL WORKER: *Another painful, important question . . .*

DAVE: *It's like he really did prove I'm a piece of crap.*

SOCIAL WORKER: *That he could treat you that way convinced you, as a kid, that there was something terribly wrong with you . . .*

DAVE: *. . . Instead of something being wrong with his head. (Long pause) You know . . . when I'm talking to you here, I can see that it doesn't make sense to sort of sell out or walk out on myself because of him . . . of what he did. But it's really hard to hang on . . . I don't know how to hang on to that. He kind of haunts me . . . this picture of him is there, and I can't shake it.*

SOCIAL WORKER: *You learned to see yourself as weak and alone, and now you sound really unsure about whether you can feel any other way.*

DAVE: *I've done a lot, but I still can't ever push him away for long. I let him back, and I feel like crap.*

SOCIAL WORKER: *The thought that he could cause you such pain and enjoy it seems very powerful to you. (Dave nods.) I'm trying to imagine what that might mean to a ten-year-old boy. What did it mean to you then . . . or now?*

DAVE: *If I mattered a damn . . . if there was anything about me to . . . (The tape is indistinct here, and Dave is swallowing his words: the gist is "anything about me to care for.") . . . he would never have treated me like that.*

SOCIAL WORKER: *Like you said, it's not that he can treat you like he did when you were a kid anymore. But he still has a terrible power over you—you let him tell you who you are. And you lose touch with how tough you've been, and how much you've accomplished.*

DAVE: *He is very powerful. . . . Funny thing, he's an old guy now, and he really can't hurt me. But he still seems so . . .*

SOCIAL WORKER: *What's real now is not the same as when you were ten. But it seems that what was real then is what keeps you stuck.*

DAVE: *You know, I'm trying to picture him as he is now, and I can't. I was there on the weekend, and I don't think I looked at him once, really. I can't explain it . . . I just point my eyes to other places than where he is. Or if I do have to look his way, there's a kind of tension in my brain, and I don't really see him.*

The interview then focused on Dave exploring ways he was still caught up in the past, and how this meant he has an imperfect view of his present reality—with its happy marriage, successful career, and his ability to protect himself from mistreatment. It ended with a plan that was quite simple, but also very impactful, which was that he would spend time during a visit home allowing himself to see his father, taking note in small steps of how this man looked in the present, as contrasted to the past. Learning to see, appreciate, and trust his own power was facilitated by taking the important first step of differentiating a past in which he truly was helpless from a present in which he possessed considerable strength.

An appreciation of relationship is not unique to client-centered intervention, and other models have been strongly influenced by Rogers's work. This said, it is suggested that there are important features in this transcript that illustrate how client-centered intervention is distinguished from other approaches.

It would be easy for a theoretically predisposed interviewer to be more directive in guiding this discourse. For example, a psychodynamically oriented social worker might be very tempted to focus in detail on Dave's experience with his father, with more exploration of the fears associated with that childhood reality. Was he in fact afraid that his father would kill him? Did he feel abandoned by his mother? How might his distrust of his father affect the present helping relationship?

Existentialists from some of the more tough-minded schools might begin to develop themes around how Dave relinquishes personal power to his father—how this is a choice to continue permitting his father to dictate how he regards himself and how he feels. His reluctance to grow up, accepting responsibility for his life in the here and now, might become a major focus.

A cognitive-behaviorist social worker might pick up on Dave's characterization of himself as a "piece of crap" and the image of his father as being all-powerful, labeling these as pernicious and irrational beliefs, leading inexorably to depressed feelings. The focus of the interview might be directed toward strategies for blocking such thoughts, replacing them with an internal dialogue that is more nurturing and self-respectful.

We recognize that by being brief we can easily do a disservice to the models we have identified, and that is not the point. Each perspective has validity, and each has proven useful with some clients under some circumstances. Dave might well benefit from any one or all of them, skillfully applied.

What client-centered social workers strive for, however, is a noninterpretive and nondirective style of working. The social worker in the transcript is aware of the various theoretical possibilities, but chooses to set them aside in an effort to listen to how Dave is uniquely experiencing his situation. Faith is placed in *Dave* to figure out what is going on and where hope for improvement lies, rather than in the theories the social worker respects or the interventive techniques they prescribe. The goal is not to come up with an interpretation and plan on Dave's behalf; rather, it is to provide a relationship within which he develops his own awareness of himself, his situation, and his options.

Trusting our clients and the helping process in this way is a difficult discipline. In our view, it is further complicated by the belief that we do not really approach problems in a state of theoretical innocence. We cannot function (professionally or otherwise) without cognitive maps, and when client-centered practitioners imply that any theory at all is dangerous, we would suggest another viewpoint.

The social worker in the preceding transcript, for example, allows a number of beliefs to affect the questions posed and responses offered. Her experience working with clients with a history of trauma inevitably informs her work. She is sensitive to the importance of traumatic memories. She understands that when abuse is perpetrated sadistically, this has a special meaning for victims. She knows how important differentiating the past from the present can be for such clients.

A second reading of the transcript will show that knowledge, training, and experience are influencing what the social worker does. However, to the extent that client-centered principles are honored in this brief vignette, the worker's predispositions are utilized with tentativeness and care, and are not allowed to result in Dave's experience going unheard. Whereas theory can be a barrier to empathy, it can also (properly used) increase the depth and efficiency with which we become attuned to critical aspects of our clients' experience.

SUMMARY

The relationship that social workers offer their clients has always been considered the sine qua non of our helping enterprise, to the extent that we may treat it overly reverentially (cf. Perlman, 1979). If we can accept a more modest position, recognizing that not all clients need a profound experience in relation to us, and that in many other cases this may not be enough, then that is progress (however disillusioning).

Modifications of the Rogerian point of view will likely be a matter of continuing to recognize its contribution and importance while adding caveats and qualifications. The relationship conditions offered by the social worker *do* help create a context for change. So too, however, do other factors (Coady, 1999; Duncan, Solovey, & Rusk, 1992; Miller et al., 1997). These include the social worker's techniques, extra-therapeutic or environmental factors, and predispositions on the part of the client. Continuing to capitalize on the legacy Rogers left us will (somewhat ironically) be a matter of building a more differentiated appreciation of our clients' needs and circumstances, and a refined ability to tailor the relationship we offer to those realities. Perhaps, though it reintroduces the need for analytical thinking about clients, something that Rogers distrusted, it is a direction more congruent with his basic agenda than may seem, on the surface, to be the case.

Interest in extending Rogers's premises continues in our professional literatures. For example, the question of how such Rogerian concepts as acceptance and empathy are connected to compassion (an obvious social work concern) is attracting interest (Berlin, 2005; Nussbaum, 2001; Rothery, 1999). In psychodynamic psychology, attachment theory and self psychology have come to ascribe basic importance to attunement and empathy as necessary experiences for human flourishing—a significant change from its traditional priorities (Saari, 2002).

As we have turned to qualitative research methods as alternatives to positivistic science, we have had to consider how disciplined communication can address such maters as subjective (and intersubjective) experience. Phenomenological researchers are especially involved in questions about the "rich interplay of one human mind with another" (Garrett et al., 1982, p. 4), and with the interpretive aspect of our efforts to understand each other well (see Kögler, 1996, for an assessment of developments in this large and complex field). These are matters on which Rogers and his followers have much to say.

With spirituality emerging as an issue that clinicians need to address more effectively (especially in an increasingly culturally diverse world), it is noted that relationality is discussed in theology with the same interest it receives from secular helpers. In this regard, we note that Rogers seems to have seen spiritual implications in his work, and to have pursued them in discussions with prominent religious thinkers like Martin Buber, Rollo May, and Paul Tillich (Anderson & Cissna, 1997; Kirschenbaum & Henderson, 1989). Again, scholars who are engaged with the most current issues affecting social work practice and its future can continue to look back to the work of Rogers (and Richmond among many others) for important insights.

Increasingly, Rogers's central concerns appear in contexts far beyond clinical psychology. A further interesting example is how aspects of critical social theory have shown an interest in how our ability to communicate well interacts with our responsibilities as citizens (Habermas, 1984). Also, there is a necessary moral dimension in how we treat one another, and the importance of congruence, acceptance, and empathy to the ethical demands of everyday life is highly relevant (Bly, 1996). At a more abstract level, social work's commitment to the values of social justice promotes a concern with the politics of recognition (see Fraser, 1996, and McLaughlin, 2006); far from being a simple clinical technique, empathic relating is seen to be the vehicle for necessary human rights to recognition and validation.

Such extensions of his work would not likely surprise Rogers himself, because he never thought the importance of his core conditions was restricted to their use in professional helping relationships. Rather, he was clear that because his concern was for the quality of our relating, his work has implications that extend to all aspects of human life. On this point as on many others, history may well be proving him correct.

REFERENCES

Anderson, R., & Cissna, K. N. (1997). *The Martin Buber–Carl Rogers dialogue: A new transcript with commentary.* New York: State University of New York Press.

Barton, A. (1980). *Three worlds of therapy: An existential-phenomenological study of the therapies of Freud, Jung, and Rogers.* Palo Alto, CA: National Press Books.

Becker, E. (1973). *The denial of death*. New York: Free Press.

Becker, E. (1975). *Escape from evil*. New York: Free Press.

Berlin, S. (2005). The value of acceptance in social work direct practice: A historical and contemporary view. *Social Service Review, 79*, 482–510.

Biestek, F. (1957). *The casework relationship*. Chicago: Loyola University Press.

Bly, C. (1996). *Changing the bully who rules the world: Reading and thinking about ethics*. Minneapolis, MN: Milkweed.

Carkhuff, R. (1987). *The art of helping* (6th ed.). Amherst, MA: Human Resource Development Press.

Coady, N. (1999). The helping relationship. In F. Turner (Ed.), *Social work practice: A Canadian perspective* (pp. 58–72). Scarborough, Ontario, Canada: Prentice Hall Allyn & Bacon Canada.

Duncan, B., Solovey, A., & Rusk, G. (1992). *Changing the rules: A client-directed approach to psychotherapy*. New York: Guilford Press.

Fraser, N. (1996). *Social justice in the age of identity politics: Redistribution, recognition, participation*. Retrieved June 22, 2006, from http://www.tannerlectures.utah.edu/lectures/Fraser98.pdf

Garrett, A., Mangold, M., & Zaki, E. (1982). *Interviewing: Its principles and methods* (3rd ed.). New York: Family Service Association of America.

Gurman, A. S., Kniskern, D. P., & Pinsof, W. (1986). Research on marital and family therapies. In S. L. Garfield & A. E. Bergin (Eds.), *Handbook of psychotherapy and behavior change* (3rd ed., pp. 565–624). New York: Wiley.

Habermas, J. (1984). *The theory of communicative action* (T. McCarthy, Trans.). Cambridge, England: Polity.

Ivey, A. (1988). *Intentional interviewing and counseling: Facilitating client development* (2nd ed.). Pacific Grove, CA: Brooks/Cole.

Kirschenbaum, H., & Henderson, V. L. (Eds.). (1989). *Carl Rogers: Dialogues*. Boston: Houghton Mifflin.

Kögler, H. H. (1996). *The power of dialogue: Critical hermeneutics after Gadamer and Foucault* (P. Hendrickson, Trans.). Cambridge, MA: The MIT Press.

Kramer, R. (1995). The birth of client-centered therapy: Carl Rogers, Otto Rank, and "the beyond." *Journal of Humanistic Psychology, 35*(4), 54–110.

Lieberman, J. E. (1985). *Acts of will: The life and work of Otto Rank*. New York: Free Press.

McLaughlin, A. M. (2006). Liberal interpretations of social justice for social work. *Currents: New scholarship in the human services*. Retrieved October 23, 2006, from http://fsw.ucalgary.ca/currents

Menaker, E. (1982). *Otto Rank: A rediscovered legacy*. New York: Columbia University Press.

Miller, S. D., Duncan, B. L., & Hubble, M. A. (1997). *Escape from Babel: Toward a unifying language for psychotherapy practice*. New York: W. W. Norton.

Nichols, M. P., & Schwartz, R. C. (2004). *Family therapy: Concepts and methods* (6th ed.). New York: Pearson.

Nussbaum, M. (2001). *Upheavals of thought: The intelligence of emotions*. Cambridge, England: Cambridge University Press.

Perlman, H. H. (1957). *Social casework: A problem-solving process*. Chicago: University of Chicago Press.

Perlman, H. H. (1979). *Relationship: The heart of helping people*. Chicago: University of Chicago Press.

Rank, O. (1964). *Truth and reality* (J. Taft, Trans.). New York: Knopf.

Rank, O. (1989). *Art and artist: Creative urge and personality development*. New York: W. W. Norton.

Richmond, M. (1899). *Friendly visiting among the poor.* New York: Macmillan.

Richmond, M. (1922). *What is social case work?* New York: Russell Sage.

Rogers, C. (1957). The necessary and sufficient conditions of therapeutic personality change. *Journal of Consulting Psychology, 21,* 95–103.

Rogers, C. (1959). A theory of therapy, personality, and interpersonal relationships as developed in the client-centered framework. In S. Koch (Ed.), *Psychology: A study of a science* (Vol. 3, pp. 184–256). New York: McGraw-Hill.

Rogers, C. (1961). *On becoming a person: A therapist's view of psychotherapy.* New York: Houghton Mifflin.

Rogers, C. (1980). *A way of being.* New York: Houghton Mifflin.

Rothery, M. (1999). Antisocial personality disorders. In F. J. Turner (Ed.), *Adult psychopathology: A social work perspective* (2nd ed., pp. 457–474). New York: Free Press.

Saari, C. (2002). *The environment.* New York: Columbia University Press.

Sexton, T. L., Alexander, J. F., & Mease, A. L. (2004). Levels of evidence for the models and mechanisms of therapeutic change in family and couple therapy. In M. J. Lambert (Ed.), *Bergin and Garfield's handbook of psychotherapy and behavior change* (5th ed., pp. 590–646). New York: Wiley.

Smalley, R. (1967). *Theory for social work practice.* New York: Columbia University Press.

Sue, D., Ivey, A., & Pedersen, P. (1996). *A theory of multicultural counseling and therapy.* Pacific Grove, CA: Brooks/Cole.

Taft, J. (1958). *Otto Rank.* New York: The Julian Press.

Truax, C. (1963). Effective ingredients in psychotherapy: An approach to unraveling the patient-therapist interaction. *Journal of Counseling Psychology, 10,* 256–263.

Truax, C., & Carkhuff, R. (1964). Concreteness: A neglected variable in research in psychotherapy. *Journal of Clinical Psychology, 20,* 364–367.

Truax, C., & Carkhuff, R. (1967). *Toward effective counseling and psychotherapy: Training and practice.* Chicago: Aldine de Gruyter.

Van Belle, H. (1980). *Basic intent and therapeutic approach of Carl R. Rogers: A study of his view of man in relation to his view of therapy, personality, and interpersonal relations.* Toronto, Ontario, Canada: Wedge Publishing Foundation.

CHAPTER 13

Existential Theory

Elizabeth Randall

Existential theory is conceptually rooted in a philosophical movement that has indelibly influenced social work practice in a variety of ways, yet these influences are often subtle and elusive of precise definition. In clinical practice, for instance, there is no single, preeminent model of existentially informed therapy; rather, as expressed by Cooper (2003), existential therapy is "best understood as a rich tapestry of intersecting therapeutic practices, all of which orientate themselves around a shared concern: human lived-existence" (p. 1). Similarly, Walsh and McElwain (2001) have concluded, it is probably better "to speak of existential psychotherapies rather than of a single existential psychotherapy" (p. 254). Nor are the influences of existential thought on direct practice limited to the arena of psychotherapy alone, a point to which we will return later in this chapter. Meanwhile, as challenging as it may be to nail down a precise definition either of existentialism itself or of existential therapy, we will try to identify some of the commonalities upon which most existential writers and practitioners would probably agree.

AN OVERVIEW OF EXISTENTIALISM

Existential Philosophy

The term "existential" could be construed as a conceptual melding of the words "exist" and "essential," suggesting that while we live, the bald fact of our *existence* is the *essential* "given" of human experience; and that all else is subject to question and interpretation. This implies that any *meaning* or *purpose* behind our existence is unknowable, and must be chosen afresh by each person, from a dizzying array of competing possibilities, through a responsible process of reflection and careful consideration. "Who am I?" and "Why am I here?" are questions that humans have faced since language began. Because humankind craves a sense of purpose and direction, the necessity of grappling with these inscrutable mysteries is considered, within existential thought, to be essential. A wellspring of uncertainty and anxiety can plague a person who has not done his or her life's "existential homework," potentially leading to the painful erosion of inner peace and harmony, or a life of unfulfilled possibility.

A central idea of existential theory, then, is that of the inherent tension arising from mankind's desire for meaning and purpose where none is given by the infinite and indifferent universe in which we find ourselves (Yalom, 1980). Related to this are the ideas that mankind possesses free will and is responsible at all times for choosing a way of being in the world and a course of action. However, any celebration of mankind's freedom to choose and act is also tempered within existential thought by a recognition of the significant limits on human possibility, such as bodily constraints, the circumstances of one's birth, the cultural and historical context of one's place and era, and the inescapable finitude of the life course. Also implicit in the majority of existential thought is a recognition of the mutual incompatibility of various possible human goals and aspirations, such that all choices must inevitably involve loss of that which was not chosen. This necessity gives rise to the expression *existential dilemma*, which involves a dawning realization that the choice of a certain path or object may occasion the sharp pain of parting from all others, even if the choice itself is a joyous one.

Authenticity is another central existential value. Most proponents seek always to strip away "the veils of illusion" (Mihaly, 1993) created by denial, wishful thinking, and a variety of other psychological and social pressures, in order to base the hard choices that must be made, if one is to live more authentically, on a clear-eyed understanding of what *is*, rather than what *could* have or *should* have been had the world been more perfect.

Existential Therapy

Like existential philosophy, existential therapy is best understood as a collectivity of helping modalities, each with considerable conceptual and philosophical compatibility yet also numerous points of divergence. As a rule, existential psychotherapies are more readily identified by their orientation toward *desirable goals* than by particularly well-defined technical or procedural guidelines. In other words, they tend to defy standardization and to elude what the contemporary field of behavioral health refers to as "manualization" (Cooper, 2003).

In general, however, most existential therapies are dialogic ("talking cure") processes of open-ended, intermediate length, designed to assist people in achieving greater and more lucid understanding of both the potentialities and the limitations of their lives in order to help them choose or create a life course that is more intentional, more congruent with their natures, and more likely to be need-satisfying (Bugental, 1981; Lantz, 2001b; van Deurzen, 2002). These therapies are hardly on speaking terms with the medical model of behavioral health, and are neither interested in nor geared toward the alleviation of any certain psychological symptoms (although this will often occur more or less spontaneously in a successful course of treatment). In terms of their use of self, most existential therapists value a high degree of authenticity and genuineness in their relationships with clients, which are often more emotionally intimate and reciprocal in nature than would be expected or desired in other practice models. Past, present, and future are all considered within the course of therapy, but the preponderance of the work is focused on the present, in a mode of phenomenological inquiry and exploration.

HISTORICAL DEVELOPMENT

Precursors

As noted above, existential therapy is conceptually rooted in the philosophical movement of existentialism, originating with the work of Soren Kierkegaard, a 19th-century Danish philosopher who argued against conformity in religious doctrine and urged folk to honor their own subjective truths and personal pathways to the divine (Kierkegaard, 1844/1980a, 1849/1980b). Important philosophical contributions were added to existential thought by the German philosophers Friedrich Nietzsche (1844–1900), Martin Buber (1878–1965), and especially Martin Heidegger (1889–1976), who cast additional light on awareness of death as a major source of existential anxiety (Heidegger, 1926/1962). The 20th-century existential literary movement, represented most notably by the French writers Jean-Paul Sartre (1905–1980) and Albert Camus (1913–1960), expanded upon the existential paradox of freedom in the absence of meaning and the necessity of choosing (Camus, 1942/1955; Sartre, 1943/1958).

Existentially informed psychotherapy is a 20th-century development. One of its earliest forms is generally credited to the Swiss psychiatrist Ludwig Binswanger (1881–1966) who, in the 1930s, introduced *daseinanalysis*, or the exploration of one's "being-in-the-world," as a therapeutic pursuit (Binswanger, 1963). Another influential figure was the Austrian psychiatrist Victor Frankl (1905–1997), who developed *logotherapy* (from the Greek word *logos*, or meaning), a treatment approach focused on helping clients discover meaning and purpose for living (Frankl, 1986). Frankl, a Holocaust survivor, is noted for his observation that holding onto some form of meaning was often a key to survival in the desperate world of the concentration camps.

Later Developments and Current Status

In this country, a major contribution to the field came in 1980 with the publication of Irvin Yalom's seminal text, *Existential Psychotherapy*, which articulated treatment as a process of helping clients come to terms with the "ultimate concerns" that inevitably accompany human experience. Rollo May (1958a, 1958b) and James Bugental (1981) were also important contributors, and collectively the work of these major authors (and others of similar theoretical orientation) is generally referred to as the existential-humanistic approach. Presently, the Existential-Humanistic Institute, home to a faculty largely comprised of students of Yalom, Bugental, and May, is an American center for research and training in this tradition. In Europe, contemporary existential therapies are fostered by the Society for Existential Analysis, founded by Emmy van Deurzen.

Past and Current Connections to Social Work

Two important contributors to existential thought in social work practice have been Donald Krill (1978, 1988) and Jim Lantz (1993, 1994, 2004b). Donald Krill published the first text dedicated solely to existential social work and is, according to Lantz (2001b), "the pioneer existential social work practitioner who has most actively introduced the philosophy of existentialism into our profession" (p. 247). Krill's work, however, is often quite abstract and far-flung in its exploration of the links between existential philosophy and direct practice, and his text is replete with literary allusions and references to history and mythology. These stylistic elements of his work create high levels of intellectual engagement but may not have contributed as much to the development of a process-oriented understanding of existentially informed practice as a more applied expository style might have done. Jim Lantz (2001b) also justifiably credited himself with "consistently and systematically introducing existentialism into the fields of family social work and family psychotherapy over the past thirty years" (p. 247). Other social work authors who have contributed to the literature on existential social work include Goldstein (1984), Brown and Romanchuk (1994), and Randall (2001).

CENTRAL THEORETICAL CONSTRUCTS

Irvin Yalom is generally recognized as the single most influential contemporary existential therapist (Cooper, 2003), and his description of four *ultimate concerns*, or ineluctable givens of human existence, has profoundly shaped much of existential clinical practice. According to Yalom (1980), these four ultimate concerns are *meaninglessness, death, isolation*, and *freedom*. The work of therapy is that of helping clients improve their conscious awareness of these inevitable parameters of life, to come to terms (if not peace) with them, and to decide how best to live their lives, given these irreducible conditions of the experience of humanness.

Meaninglessness

According to Yalom (1980), "Therapists . . . must be attuned to meaning, they must think about the overall focus and direction of the patient's life. Is the patient in any way reaching beyond himself or herself, beyond the humdrum daily routine of staying alive?" (p. 471). In his view, the antidote to meaninglessness is often found in creative engagement with others, with causes, with the arts, or with any significant entity beyond the self:

> I have treated many young adults who were immersed in a California singles' life style which is characterized to a large degree by sensuality, sexual clamor, and pursuit of prestige and materialistic goals. In my work I have become aware that therapy is rarely successful unless I help the patient focus on something beyond these pursuits. (p. 471)

Other existentially influenced models such as logotherapy, however, may take a more faith-based approach to the quest for meaning and posit that meaning is not something to be chosen or created, but rather, to be *discovered*:

> Logotherapists believe that each individual's existence is ascribed a super- or ultimate-meaning: a unique calling that only they have the ability, and responsibility, to fulfill. Furthermore, logotherapists believe there is only one true meaning to each situation an individual encounters, and it is the responsibility of each individual to decipher what this true meaning is, before that situation and its potentiality is lost forever. (Cooper, 2003, p. 54; also see Frankl, 1986, 2000)

In this model, then, the discovery of meaning takes precedence over freedom, and assumes a moral character, as being of "good conscience" is considered to depend on having discovered one's intended purpose in life at each crossroad in life, and answering its call (Fabry, 1980).

Contemporary practitioners of Binswanger's (1963) *daseinanalysis* tend to take a less deterministic outlook and strive to help clients achieve greater openness to possibility and the freedom to interpret the world outside the constraints engendered by the "shoulds and oughts" of societal or familial expectations. In this model, "openness" (i.e., to possibility) is seen as an intrinsically meaningful value, and "closedness" as a source of symptoms or distress. This model is among the most client centered, least directive of the existential therapies, and is consistent with a certain Rogerian optimism that clients will grow and thrive in meaningful ways in the absence of culturally or interpersonally dictated sources of conditionality (Boss, 1963).

Death

Death anxiety and denial of death awareness are powerful forces in the psyche, yet ironically little recognized or discussed at the conscious level. According to Yalom (1980),

> We exist now, but one day we shall cease to be. Death will come, and there is no escape from it. It is a terrible truth, and we respond to it with mortal terror. . . . A core existential conflict is the tension between the awareness of the inevitability of death and the wish to continue to be. (p. 8)

Yalom (1980) wrote of a sense of *specialness* as a common defense against death awareness, which is described as an irrational belief that the natural laws of finitude as a condition of life somehow do not apply to oneself. Another common defense against death anxiety, in Yalom's view, is a "belief in the existence of an ultimate rescuer" (p. 141), which if taken to an extreme, can lead to passivity and unwillingness to accept personal responsibility for one's actions or one's life trajectory.

A case illustration, to be discussed in more detail later in the chapter, provides an example of a client whose defenses against death anxiety weakened during a peak experience, leading to an emotional crisis. A young adult woman, engaged to a concert violinist, was invited to sit quietly in a concert hall as her fiancé's symphony practiced to record a major work. At first she was moved to joy by the music. As she listened, however, her mood began to shift inexplicably, and she found herself increasingly restless, upset, and unable to control sudden bitter tears, which forced her to tiptoe out and return home to "pull herself together," where she remained, agitated and sleepless, for much of her weekend.

Clinical exploration of this incident revealed important insights. Listening to the music, she had been awed by the recognition that her fiancé was taking part in the creation of a work of transcendent beauty, which could live on as part of the symphony's recorded archive beyond his own life. She was happy for him, yet sitting apart in the back of the concert hall, she had begun to feel personally diminished by her own role as a passive witness and was uneasily aware of having no similar legacy accomplishment to distinguish her own life, and hence no comparable "symbolic immortality." She realized that the disturbance in her mood throughout the weekend was related to this unanticipated encounter with the ultimate concerns of meaninglessness and death awareness. Similarly, an outsized or driven desire on the part of any client for fame and recognition, such as having monuments, buildings, or foundations named after oneself, or even an unusually urgent wish for offspring to carry on one's name or tradition in an inflexible way, might be viewed by the existentially sensitive clinician as a possible indicator of unresolved existential anxieties.

Isolation

An existential stance acknowledges that no person can ever completely share or express his or her inner experiences, nor totally comprehend those of another. Yet a deep desire for escape from isolation via merger or seamless absorption into the identity of a loved one is very common, potentially leading to great damage to one's relationship with oneself. A goal of existential therapy is to help clients appreciate that while deep connections are both necessary and life enhancing, they are not the totality of experience; and that all relationships, however centrally important to an individual, are ultimately bounded and time limited.

May and Yalom (1995) spoke of profound deficits on the part of many clients to articulate their own wishes and desires. They noted that these clients "have enormous social difficulties because they have no opinions, no inclinations, no desires of their own" (p. 280). Yet the only relationship guaranteed to be lifelong is with oneself, and this is not to be sacrificed for the sake of merger with significant others, regardless of their perceived importance within the current emotional sphere. This existential honoring of an appropriate amount of "truth-to-self" is shared to a greater or lesser extent by all major schools of contemporary existential therapy (Cooper, 2003; Spinelli, 1996; van Deurzen, 2002).

Freedom

Freedom, in existential thought, can be both a blessing and a curse, as people in modern societies may revel in the globalization of opportunity and the unprecedented availability of novel experiences, yet feel over-whelmed and immobilized by the sheer scope of possibility, and end up abdicating responsibility for choosing at all. Danger to self-actualization also exists in choosing impulsively or cavalierly, or on the basis of very limited (or very inaccurate) self-understanding. Another goal of existential psychotherapy is that of assisting clients to make optimal use of the personal freedoms available to them, given the holistic context of their lives and relationships.

Two conceptual corollaries of freedom in Yalom's (1980) model are *will* and *responsibility*, which he described as follows: "To be aware of *responsibility* for one's situation is to enter the vestibule of action or, in the therapy situation, of change. *Willing* represents the passage from responsibility to action" (p. 274). Thus, adaptive and creative exercise of freedom is also dependent upon an application of both responsibility and will in a given life situation, and the existentially sensitive clinician seeks to assist clients toward the realization of these accomplishments. According to May and Yalom (1995), "The therapist's task is not to *create* will but instead to *disencumber* it" (p. 280).

PHASES OF HELPING

Because the existential therapies are renowned for their relative lack of a precise structure and their de-emphasis on technique (Corey, 2005; van Deurzen, 2002), a description of the phases of the helping process may not be as exacting as one might expect in a discussion of another modality. Nevertheless, the existential therapies are highly planful in their own way and are as committed to client change and to forward therapeutic momentum as any other model.

Engagement

As with all effective forms of therapy, a therapeutic alliance based on trust and authenticity is essential. However, this relationship may be uniquely and reciprocally intimate in some forms of existential therapy. Yalom's recent work (2003) described an essentially no-limits approach to matters of self-disclosure and the appropriateness of openly answering any personal questions that clients may pose. Additionally, he favored an active, mutually confiding *process exploration* (in the here and now) of the relationship between client and therapist as it unfolds and deepens. Corey (2005) noted that the particular salience of the therapeutic alliance in existential therapy harks back to Martin Buber's conceptualization of the authentic, fully present "I/Thou" relationship: "The relationship essential for connecting the self to the spirit and, in so doing, to achieve true dialog" (p. 148). The centricity of the alliance as a therapeutic factor is also affirmed by other contemporary existential clinicians, such as Ernesto Spinelli, of the British tradition of existential analysis, who is critical of power imbalances in client–therapist relationships and holds that the client's authentic experience of the therapist himself or herself matters more than the content of their dialogue (Spinelli, 1997).

For social work, however, these views, if taken too far, might present a conflict with the constraints against dual relationships found in the social work Code of Ethics (National Association of Social Workers, 1999). This risk could be especially problematic for clients whose age or cultural orientation might predispose them to difficulty conceptualizing a relationship of unique intimacy that is nevertheless professional and completely nonsocial outside of the therapy hour. Having no frame of reference from prior experience for such a relationship, some clients might experience a therapeutic climate with this unprecedented degree of intimacy to be tantamount to an invitation into the social realm, or even into surrogate kinship. This in turn might lead the client to feelings of deep disappointment or betrayal when faced with any subsequent need on the part of the therapist to maintain appropriate physical and temporal boundaries. It is also essential for social workers to self-reflect very carefully and to seek attentive supervision if they encounter any doubts within themselves about whose needs are primarily being met in clinical situations characterized by unusually high levels of therapist transparency and self-disclosure.

Data Collection and Assessment

Rooted as they are in a philosophical movement rather than a scientific or positivistic orientation, the existential therapies are primarily qualitative and experiential rather than empirical or data-driven in their approach to assessment. Clients' concerns are explored primarily through a process of phenomenological reflection, as the therapist encourages them to get in touch with their worldview and feelings and to identify their sources for important values and life choices. Are the voices that dictate their assumptions and rule their behavior authentically their own, or perhaps inherited or internalized scripts, with origins in conventional wisdom, of questionable validity in the clients' private minds? Of all possible systems of meaning that the clients have encountered, are those that presently guide their life course truly the most excellent? Or, can they imagine any better? Open expression of hopes, wishes, and aspirations may also be actively encouraged, no matter how seemingly implausible at the outset.

Quantitative assessment of symptoms for purposes of measuring change via single-system designs is not valued, and would likely be met with considerable skepticism by many existential therapists, who would view these activities as possible indicators of biomedical reductionism. Existential therapists would also tend to be relatively disinterested in psychoactive medication monitoring as a routine clinical undertaking, not seeing this activity as a crucial feature of their therapeutic contract with most clients. They might also wonder whether excessive dependency upon medication might serve as a way of distancing oneself from a certain amount of personal responsibility for holistic emotional well-being, in some client situations.

Contracting

For therapists who work from an existential frame of reference, an explicit contracting protocol may often be viewed as excessively directive and controlling, especially where such procedures are particularly formulaic. According to van Deurzen (1997), therapy is more a collaborative venture with the potential to be transforming for both participants rather than a process of client enlightenment in the hands of a more experienced or wiser therapist. Many would tend to assume that a contract for the work exists so long as the client continues to keep his or her appointments and to participate meaningfully, both within and between sessions.

Intervention

The middle or working phase of existential therapy can be far-reaching and highly variable depending on the needs of the individual client. In general, however, as client and therapist meet and converse together, "clients get a better idea of what kind of life they consider worthy to live and develop a clearer sense of their internal valuing process" (Corey, 2005, p. 150). Yalom's work guides clients to confront the four ultimate concerns in a more fully conscious way. For instance, he might touch on existential issues around meaning and isolation by encouraging clients to ask themselves such questions as "If I continue on a similar course throughout my life, will I end consumed by guilt over my own unrealized potentialities?" or "Are my own loving feelings and actions equal in power to my longings for love?" Similarly, on the issue of freedom, Bugental (1981) suggested that therapists who remain attuned to the right opportunities emerging from the dialogue can help clients select more effective uses of their freedom, to act in more mindful and deliberate (rather than compulsive) ways, to slow down if they so desire, to pursue an interest long denied, and to generally (as it were) "seize the day." In some cases, clients may also achieve radical acceptance (Brach, 2003) of some irremediable life limitation through existentially influenced therapy.

Special mention may be made of Yalom's (1980) emphasis on therapeutic confrontation of *death anxiety*. He described the poignant reengagement with life often seen among cancer survivors and others who have had near-death experiences and suggests that any who consciously seek to break through their own denial of death may reap benefits of similar revitalization in their present lives. Although his work is much more conceptual than technique-based in most areas, he does include discussion of specific techniques for confronting and combating death anxiety, both one's own and that of clients, and interested readers are referred to his text for these suggestions, which have also been discussed by Cooper (2003).

Termination

The literature on the existential therapies is rich with narratives of presenting problems and concerns that clients bring into treatment (or discover along the way). Many process commentaries and anecdotal accounts of client changes and growth are also on record (Cooper, 2003; Corey, 2005; Imes, Clance, Gailis, & Atkeson, 2002; Lantz, 2001b; May & Yalom, 1995; Randall, 2001; van Deurzen, 1997, 2002; Yalom, 1980). For the most part, however, not much is said regarding any particular phases or stages of treatment. Similarly, relatively little is said about termination, such as specific guidelines for promoting maintenance and generalization of change or for establishing closure. When existential therapies were newer and perhaps undergoing growth pangs several decades ago, this relative lack of planfulness regarding termination may sometimes have been problematic. According to Yalom (1980),

> One situation where the patient's and the therapist's wills are certain to clash is the termination of therapy. Some patients choose to terminate precipitously; while others refuse to terminate and, if necessary, cling to their symptoms and resist the therapist's efforts to bring therapy to a conclusion. (p. 297)

Yalom's thinking on the issue has evolved, however, and more recently he has suggested that readiness for termination is usually at hand when meetings between the client and therapist begin to seem relatively tranquil and the tone becomes closer to one of cordiality than challenge, and when no new ground has been discovered for several sessions in a row (I. Yalom, personal communication, December 2005). Most existential therapists would probably agree in spirit with this point of view.

Lantz (2001b) was among the few writers who delineated an existential therapy model according to specific stages, and his final, or *redirection*, stage of treatment included themes of affirmation and celebration:

> In the redirection stage, the clients are getting ready for termination. In this stage, they demonstrate readiness to continue to search actively for, discover, and honor meaning without the social worker's assistance. The redirection stage includes celebration. The client and the social worker celebrate the client's growth, then terminate the treatment relationship. The termination is an affirmation, by both the social worker and the client, of the client's ability to continue to grow. (p. 250)

Evaluation

In the arena of outcomes assessment, the existential therapies continue to lag somewhat behind the times. With their emphasis on inner states of being, subjectivity, and phenomenology, these models are not always on comfortable terms with the epistemological assumptions behind the principles of evidence-based practice: "Symptomatic relief or behavioral change may be quantified with reasonable precision. But more ambitious therapies, which seek to affect deeper layers of the individual's mode of being in the world, defy quantification" (May & Yalom, 1995, p. 285). Cooper (2003) sounded a similar note in posing the question "How, for instance, can one put a score to the 'I-Thou-ness' of a therapeutic relationship?" (p. 148). However, Cooper (2003) also went on to suggest that qualitative research methods offer the best way to bridge the void between existential therapies and evidence-based practice: "Indeed, many of the newly-emerging research methodologies—such as Kvale's (1996) qualitative interviewing approach—are entirely consistent with an existential outlook" (p. 148).

The use of single-system designs is another highly promising (but underutilized) way to improve the evidence basis for the existential therapies in the social sciences, and even "I-Thou-ness" could be measured quantitatively through the use of a well-designed, individualized rating scale (Bloom, Fischer, & Orme, 2006). To date, however, there is a very limited amount of quantitative research on outcomes and effectiveness of the existential therapies (Walsh & McElwain, 2001).

APPLICATION TO FAMILY AND GROUP WORK

Social work scholar Jim Lantz was among the most prolific of contributors to the literature on the application of existential thought to family practice (Lantz, 1993, 2001a, 2001b, 2004b; Lantz & Harper-Dorton, 1996). Lantz (2001b) saw existential family therapy as the treatment of choice when "client symptoms are a signal pointing out meaning disruption problems in the client's total social network as a whole, or when the social worker hopes to mobilize social support and network resources for the client's struggle to grow" (p. 250). Goals and desired outcomes are similar to those of individual treatment, but with a committed couple or family as the client system to be engaged in the therapeutic work. Like the individual models, his method of existential family social work places central importance on the quality of the worker/family therapeutic alliance: "In existential family psychotherapy, it is believed that the therapist's capacity and ability to allow the self to be touched by the client's problems and pain is the basic and most important ingredient in the treatment process" (Lantz, 2004b, p. 169).

Irvin Yalom has been a key proponent of existentially congruent group work. He has commented in particular on the fruitfulness of clients' exploration of issues of isolation versus connectedness in the group setting. The group can serve as a unique interpersonal laboratory where clients glean crucial feedback about the effect they typically have on others. It can also serve as a setting in which to experiment with new interpersonal behaviors, if clients begin to realize that elements of their present style of interaction have some unintended social consequences and that certain modifications would lead to happier relationships. May and Yalom (1995) also commented on the usefulness of the existential therapy group as a vehicle for increasing client acceptance of personal responsibility:

> This is one of the most fascinating aspects of group therapy: all members are "born" simultaneously. Each starts out on an equal footing. Each gradually scoops out and shapes a particular life space in the group. Thus, each person is responsible for the interpersonal position he scoops out for himself in the group (and in life). The therapeutic work in the group then not only allows individuals to change their way of relating to one another but also brings home to them in a powerful way the extent to which they have created their own life predicament—clearly an existential therapeutic mechanism. (p. 286)

A number of specialized group applications have also been described, such as existential group therapy for cancer survivors (Kissane, 2004), existential group treatment for battered women (Weingourt, 1985), and existential group therapy for persons in later life confronting death anxiety (Garrow & Walker, 2001). Existential practice principles appear to lend themselves in a therapeutically significant way to a variety of group settings where client encounters with ultimate concerns are natural and expectable.

COMPATIBILITY WITH THE GENERALIST-ECLECTIC FRAMEWORK

Five major elements of a generalist-eclectic framework for practice have been identified in the approach to practice described in this text, and existential theory is highly congruent or conceptually compatible with several of these, although perhaps less so with others. Each of these will briefly be considered in turn.

Person-in-Environment Perspective/Ecological Systems Theory

Existential theory is congruent with this perspective in that most practitioners would recognize such biologically deterministic elements of life as niche, boundedness, finitude, and the instinctual inevitability of interrelatedness among human beings. These concepts are attuned to the ecosystemic point of view.

Emphasis on Therapeutic Relationship

Existential theory excels in this regard and is as attuned to the necessity of a working relationship of mutuality and respectfulness as any model of direct practice, and probably considerably more so than many.

Flexible Use of Problem-Solving

A problem-solving approach is not exactly anathema to an existential stance but may often be so topical and pragmatic as to be somewhat apart from its central concerns. For instance, a worker using a problem-solving approach might help a young adult decide how best to gain conversational skill and comfort with social dialogue in order to make friends, while an existential therapist might be more apt to encourage the client to ponder the core value-based and behavioral characteristics of satisfying friendships in general. In addition, some existential therapists would tend to view problem-solving methodologies as excessively deterministic and directive.

Attention to Issues of Diversity and Empowerment

In many significant ways existential treatment can be highly empowering, as well as uniquely liberating. However, existential theory may not always achieve complete recognition and acceptance of a culturally appropriate, sociocentric value orientation as a basis for selecting one's destiny or life course (Landrine, 1992). From a social work perspective, a given individual may experience inner peace and serenity most fully by honoring prescribed, culturally sanctioned role expectations (such as familial or spousal roles), rather than assuming a more individualistic stance and seeking meaning or fulfillment primarily through individual self-actualization (Maslow, 1998). For instance, a woman from a highly patriarchal Asian culture might at first appear passive within her marriage. Yet from a social work perspective, it could mean a lack of respect for cultural diversity to interpret her stance as a failure of existential *responsibility assumption* (Yalom, 1980). Other risks arising from the existential emphasis on personal responsibility are those of overlooking issues of distributive justice and oppression, the need for advocacy, and the necessity of selecting macrosystemic entities or forces as targets for change where appropriate.

Eclecticism

A social worker need not labor to view every client situation and interaction as existentially significant or momentous. Rather, an existentially informed approach would allow the worker to assess and proceed in treatment from the perspective of one or several theories or methodologies, while at the same time remaining attuned to existentially relevant issues, if and when they arise.

For instance, a high school graduate working in the hospitality industry might present with issues of low self-worth and dysthymia, suggesting a cognitive-behavioral course of treatment. This approach might help the client reduce self-doubts about her competence and value in her present job, leading to modest improvement in her mood. At the same time, the worker might sense an inner struggle as the client attempted to reconcile a partially suppressed, private judgment of the relative meaninglessness of her work with the simple need to make a living. These issues might be explored in a purposeful yet relatively unstructured way from an existential perspective, ultimately yielding a significant increase in the client's motivation to reinvent herself in a new and more ego-syntonic vocational capacity, even if this meant tackling the necessity of further education. This work might then turn from a primarily existential approach to a problem-solving approach to help the client make plans to fulfill this commitment to herself and a more rewarding future.

Yalom (1980) has described several particular existential ideas or values that have been highly regarded as helpful and curative by therapy clients:

1. recognizing that life is at times unfair and unjust;
2. recognizing that ultimately there is no escape from some of life's pain and from death;
3. recognizing that no matter how close I get to other people, I must still face life alone;
4. facing the basic issues of my life and death, and thus living my life more honestly and being less caught up in trivialities; and,
5. learning that I must take ultimate responsibility for the way I live my life no matter how much guidance and support I get from others. (p. 265)

These ideas are highly congruent with the central premises of several other widely used treatment modalities, such as reality therapy (Glasser, 2000) and rational emotive behavior therapy (Ellis, 2001), which also promote clear-eyed recognition of "what *is*" in preference over preoccupation with what "ought to be" or what "should have been." However, rich opportunities for exploration and application of these existential values abound in much of social work practice, even beyond the psychotherapy office, such as in the fields of medical social work, school social work, and forensic or correctional social work, to suggest just a few. The present author has observed this brief summary of existential values being used as a source of guidance for clients in inpatient aftercare groups, hospice settings, assertiveness training, a divorce support group, and several life skills training groups, suggesting that existential thought has contributed to the professional eclecticism of social workers in a wide variety of practice settings.

CRITIQUE OF EXISTENTIAL THEORY

General Strengths and Weaknesses

One of the great strengths of existential theory in social work practice is its sensitivity to issues of deep significance for the quality of human lives that other models or theories, with their attention focused on issues of more immediate topical relevance, may overlook. For instance, Randall (2001) recently described the use of existential therapy with a client presenting with panic disorder, who experienced full remission of symptoms in 10 sessions, following a deteriorating course during a psychopharmacological intervention spanning several years. The outcome of this case was attributed to "a triumph of meaning over matter" (p. 266).

However, several weaknesses or limitations may also exist for most existentially attuned forms of psychotherapy. The first of these is a relative lack of empirical support (Walsh & McElwain, 2001). Much of the evidence in support of the effectiveness of these therapy models, while interesting, possessing considerable face validity, and emotionally compelling, is nevertheless anecdotal in nature.

Another serious limitation is the relative lack of philosophical and conceptual compatibility between existentially influenced practice and the managed care environment, with its emphasis on standardization of procedures, brevity, efficiency, and symptom reduction as a primary goal of treatment (Davis & Meiers, 2001). This is not to say that there is no place or use for the existentially congruent therapies within the managed care environment, yet these two systems of care operate from very distinct and disparate value orientations. While compromise or the identification of a middle ground should be possible, little specific guidance is presently available in the human services literature for clinicians who might be inclined to work in a way that does justice to both. For social workers, local peer consultation or support group meetings, or a local NASW chapter meeting, might represent a forum for sharing ideas on professional issues such as this.

Populations Most Suited

Adult psychotherapy patients, especially those who are especially introspective in nature and who may be particularly psychologically minded, are among the most obviously well suited customers for existential therapy. Individual, group, and family practice settings may all be amenable to existential influences. Additionally, any clients who have recently been touched (or shaken) by death awareness may benefit, such as in medical settings or within later life service settings (Brown & Romanchuk, 1994). Reports of significantly helpful contributions of existential thought to treatment settings for substance abuse clients (Scher et al., 1973), veterans (Lantz, 1990), sexual abuse survivors (Fisher, 2005), and conduct-challenged youth (Carlson, 2003) are also available in the literature.

Populations Least Suited

Existential concepts are not especially applicable to therapeutic services for children, owing to the legal and developmental limits they face with regard to freedom and personal responsibility, and also to their relative lack of life experience. Also, the higher-than-average degree of abstraction contained within much of existential thought may limit the usefulness of this approach for persons of significantly limited intellectual capacity.

The philosophical underpinnings of the approach are Western and relatively individualistic. This may suggest a need for the existential therapist to make adjustments within his or her own mind for clients whose culture values the greater good of other social systems such as families, communities, or small groups over and above individual needs. Existential thought is not, however, inherently incompatible with religious thought, and there are schools of existential thought fully integrated into particular faith traditions such as Christianity.

CASE ILLUSTRATION

Let us return to the case of the young woman engaged to the concert violinist, described earlier in the chapter, as an example of existential therapy in social work practice. This client ("Anna") was seen for about 26 weeks (more or less weekly) of outpatient treatment in the adult services unit of a community mental health center by a master's level social worker with mental health training.

Anna's presenting problems were low self-esteem, emotional insecurity, and dysthymia. A recent college graduate who had done well in school, she now found herself feeling underemployed in a retail position, and socially rather lonely (isolation), as well as troubled by a vague sense of being "adrift in the world" (meaninglessness). She cared a great deal for her fiancé ("Bern") but worried that they seemed to be so different: He was considerably more socially gregarious than she, more lighthearted rather than serious-minded, and neither particularly practical nor ambitious. She ruminated about their possible incompatibility. Equally problematic for her was his circle of friendships and interests, which included the outdoors, several sports, woodworking, socializing, musical pursuits, and parties. She complained that he was a bit flighty and "spread himself too thin," but she also admitted in therapy to some degree of jealousy, and had tried throughout their dating relationship to "lay a guilt trip" on him to get him to spend less time in these various pursuits and more quiet, companionable time with "just the two of us."

The crisis in the concert hall took place in about the fifth week of treatment. This incident helped Anna to realize that her distress permeated all levels of her psyche and was as much related to her own inability to pinpoint what her own life was "about" as it was to her complaints about Bern or her wish for more friends of her own. She had a dream in which she saw a grave marker with a "smiley face" on it, a symbol that had always seemed irritatingly vacant and fatuous to her, and she took this dream to symbolize a fear that, in the event of her own untimely demise (death anxiety), this symbol would have to serve as her epitaph, there being none more suitable to take its place. Yet being employed, unmarried, and childless (at least for now), Anna had almost unlimited freedom, and much of the remaining work was devoted to an exploration of how best to use it. Among her choices were to rekindle and strengthen friendships with several women, which had suffered from inattention during the early, heady days of her romance with Bern, and to join a choral society ("If you can't beat 'em, join 'em," she said). She realized that she yearned for a career rather than "just a job," and she undertook to complete a battery of vocational aptitude and preference testing in order to learn more about how to find a niche for herself in the world of work that would mean a happier fit with her personality and temperament. She also took up several "outdoorsy" pursuits such as hiking and camping in order to be able to join Bern in these activities, and she reported that these had become her passions as much as his, and that sharing these enthusiasms had made them both feel closer.

Upon conclusion of treatment, Anna was filling out applications for admission to a graduate program in library and information science, was less preoccupied with and dependent upon her fiancé, was entertaining and socializing more, and was getting along considerably better with Bern. She still had an inner sense of emotional insecurity but was cautiously optimistic that the combination of more maturity and additional experiences of social and vocational success in the future would cause this feeling to fade away. She was looking forward to a future that was beginning to seem full of possibility rather than "drifty." Best of all, she said, "The less I need from my friends, the more I get."

SUMMARY

Existential theory and the related therapies have an established place in the contemporary world of social work practice, and their unique contributions have been reported in an ever-growing body of professional literature. Proponents of this theory nevertheless face challenges that may hamper further dissemination and acceptance of these methods, particularly in the United States, in the area of congruence or compatibility with managed behavioral health care. The relative lack of empirical evidence in support of their effectiveness is one possible obstacle. Another is the dearth of information on the usefulness of an existential stance within a brief, time-limited treatment model, the darling of managed care.

The present author remembers two cases in particular from practice in which clients achieved powerful insights leading to significant life course alterations, once in a single session, and once in two sessions, and so believes that these principles can be highly relevant even to the briefest of practice encounters. Several published works have also offered conceptualizations of brief existential treatment models (Bugental, 1995;

Strasser & Strasser, 1997). Yet on the whole, the literature on brief existential therapies is significantly underdeveloped, and additional contributions could be very beneficial.

In summary, existential theory is a conceptually rich and deeply humanistic source of potential guidance for social work practice that has evolved greatly since its 20th-century debut. Yet clinical social work settings have greatly evolved as well in the ensuing decades, creating ongoing challenges for each to respect the value orientation and priorities of the other, if their association is to remain fruitful on behalf of clients. Several clients have commented on the existential approach in precisely the same terms: "This is truly wise." The present author hopes this wisdom will continue to evolve in creative ways that social work practice will be able to harvest and apply in practice-congruent ways for decades more to come and beyond.

REFERENCES

Binswanger, L. (1963). *Being-in-the-world: Selected papers of Ludwig Binswanger* (J. Needleman, Trans.). London: Condor.

Bloom, M., Fischer, J., & Orme, J. G. (2006). *Evaluating practice: Guidelines for the accountable professional* (5th ed.). Boston: Allyn & Bacon.

Boss, M. (1963). *Psychoanalysis and daseinanalysis*. New York: Basic Books.

Brach, T. (2003). *Radical acceptance*. New York: Bantam.

Brown, J. A., & Romanchuk, B. J. (1994). Existential social work practice with the aged: Theory and practice. *Journal of Gerontological Social Work, 23*, 49–65.

Bugental, J. (1981). *The search for authenticity: An existential-analytic approach to psychotherapy* (Rev. ed.). New York: Holt, Rinehart and Winston.

Bugental, J. (1995). Preliminary sketches for a short-term existential-humanistic therapy. In K. J. Schneider & R. May (Eds.), *The psychology of existence: An integrative, clinical perspective* (pp. 261–264). New York: McGraw-Hill.

Camus, A. (1955). *The myth of Sisyphus* (J. O'Brien, Trans.). London: Penguin. (Original work published 1942)

Carlson, L. A. (2003). Existential theory: Helping school counselors attend to youth at risk for violence. *Professional School Counseling, 6*, 310–316.

Cooper, M. (2003). *Existential therapies*. Thousand Oaks, CA: Sage.

Corey, G. (2005). *Theory and practice of counseling and psychotherapy* (7th ed.). Belmont, CA: Brooks/Cole.

Davis, S. R., & Meiers, S. (2001). *The elements of managed care*. Belmont, CA: Brooks/Cole.

Ellis, A. (2001). *Overcoming destructive beliefs, feelings, and behaviors: New directions for rational emotive behavior therapy*. Amherst, NY: Prometheus Books.

Fabry, J. (1980). *The pursuit of meaning: Victor Frankl, logotherapy, and life*. San Francisco: Harper & Row.

Fisher, G. (2005). Existential therapy with adult survivors of sexual abuse. *Journal of Humanistic Psychology, 45*, 10–40.

Frankl, V. (1986). *The doctor and the soul: From psychotherapy to logotherapy* (3rd ed.) (R. Winston & C. Winston, Trans.). New York: Vintage Books.

Frankl, V. (2000). *Recollections: An autobiography* (J. Fabry & J. Fabry, Trans.). Cambridge, MA: Perseus Books.

Garrow, S., & Walker, J. A. (2001). Existential group therapy and death anxiety. *Adultspan: Theory, Research, and Practice, 3,* 77–88.

Glasser, W. (2000). *Counseling with choice theory: The new reality therapy.* New York: HarperCollins.

Goldstein, H. (1984). *Creative change: A cognitive humanistic approach to social work practice.* New York: Methuen.

Heidegger, M. (1962). *Being and time* (J. Macquarrie & E. Robinson, Trans.). Oxford, England: Blackwell. (Original work published 1926)

Imes, S., Clance, P. R., Gailis, A. T., & Atkeson, E. (2002). Mind's response to the body's betrayal: Gestalt/existential therapy for clients with chronic or life-threatening illnesses. *Journal of Clinical Psychology/In Session: Psychotherapy in Practice, 58,* 1361–1373.

Kierkegaard, S. (1980a). *The concept of anxiety: A simple psychologically orienting deliberation on the dogmatic issue of original sin: Vol. 8* (R. Thomte, Trans.). Princeton, NJ: Princeton University Press. (Original work published 1844)

Kierkegaard, S. (1980b). *The sickness unto death: A Christian psychological exposition for upbuilding and awakening: Vol. 19* (H. V. Hong & E. H. Hong, Trans.). Princeton, NJ: Princeton University Press. (Original work published 1849)

Kissane, D. W. (2004). Effect of cognitive-existential group therapy on survival in early-stage breast cancer. *Journal of Clinical Oncology, 22,* 4255–4260.

Krill, D. (1978). *Existential social work.* New York: Free Press.

Krill, D. (1988). Existential social work. In R. Dorfman (Ed.), *Paradigms of clinical social work* (pp. 295–316). New York: Brunner/Mazel.

Kvale, S. (1996). *InterViews: An introduction to qualitative interviewing.* Thousand Oaks, CA: Sage.

Landrine, H. (1992). Clinical implications of cultural differences: The referential vs. the indexical self. *Clinical Psychology Review, 12,* 401–415.

Lantz, J. (1990). Existential social work with Vietnam veterans. *Journal of Independent Social Work, 5,* 39–52.

Lantz, J. (1993). *Existential family therapy: Using the concepts of Victor Frankl.* Northvale, NJ: Jason Aronson.

Lantz, J. (1994). Marcel's availability in existential psychotherapy with couples and families. *Contemporary Family Therapy, 16,* 489–501.

Lantz, J. (2001a). Depression, existential family therapy, and Viktor Frankl's dimensional ontology. *Contemporary Family Therapy, 23,* 19–32.

Lantz, J. (2001b). Existential theory. In P. Lehmann & N. Coady (Eds.), *Theoretical perspectives for direct social work practice: A generalist-eclectic approach* (pp. 240–254). New York: Springer Publishing Company.

Lantz, J. (2004a). Research and evaluation issues in existential psychotherapy. *Journal of Contemporary Psychotherapy, 34,* 331–340.

Lantz, J. (2004b). World view concepts in existential family therapy. *Contemporary Family Therapy, 26,* 165–177.

Lantz, J., & Harper-Dorton, K. (1996). *Cross-cultural practice: Social work with diverse populations.* Chicago: Lyceum Books.

Maslow, A. H. (1998). *Toward a psychology of being* (3rd ed.). New York: Wiley.

May, R. (1958a). Contributions of existential psychotherapy. In R. May, E. Angel, & H. F. Ellenberger (Eds.), *Existence: A new dimension in psychiatry and psychology* (pp. 37–91). New York: Basic Books.

May, R. (1958b). The origins and significance of the existential movement in psychology. In R. May, E. Angel, & H. F. Ellenberger (Eds.), *Existence: A new dimension in psychiatry and psychology* (pp. 3–36). New York: Basic Books.

May, R., & Yalom, I. (1995). Existential psychotherapy. In R. J. Corsini & D. Wedding (Eds.), *Current psychotherapies* (5th ed., pp. 262–292). Itasca, IL: Peacock.

Mihaly, C. (1993). *The evolving self: A psychology for the third millennium.* New York: HarperCollins.

National Association of Social Workers. (1999). *Code of ethics.* Washington, DC: NASW Press.

Randall, E. J. (2001). Existential therapy of panic disorder: A single-system study. *Clinical Social Work Journal, 29,* 259–267.

Sartre, J.-P. (1958). *Being and nothingness: An essay on phenomenological ontology* (H. Barnes, Trans.). London: Routledge. (Original work published 1943)

Scher, J., Leavitt, A., Rothman, R., Kaplan, J., Weinstein, J., & Weisfeld, G. (1973). Professionally directed existential group therapy in methadone maintenance rehabilitation. *Proceedings, National Conference on Methadone Treatment, 2,* 1191–1202.

Spinelli, E. (1996). The vagaries of the self: An essay in response to Emmy van Deurzen-Smith's "The survival of the self" and Mick Cooper's "Modes of existence: Towards a phenomenological polypsychism." *Journal of the Society for Existential Analysis, 7,* 57–68.

Spinelli, E. (1997). *Tales of unknowing: The existential-phenomenological approach to counseling and psychotherapy.* London: Gerald Duckworth, Ltd.

Strasser, F., & Strasser, A. (1997). *Existential time-limited therapy: The wheel of existence.* New York: Wiley.

van Deurzen, E. (1997). *Everyday mysteries: Existential dimensions of psychotherapy.* London: Routledge.

van Deurzen, E. (2002). *Existential counseling and psychotherapy in practice* (2nd ed.). London: Sage.

Walsh, R. A., & McElwain, B. (2001). Existential psychotherapies. In D. J. Cain & J. Seeman (Eds.), *Humanistic psychotherapies: Handbook of research and practice* (pp. 253–278). Washington, DC: American Psychological Association.

Weingourt, R. (1985). Never to be alone: Existential therapy with battered women. *Journal of Psychosocial Nursing and Mental Health Services, 23,* 24–29.

Yalom, I. (1980). *Existential psychotherapy.* New York: Basic Books.

Yalom, I. (2003). *The gift of therapy: An open letter to a new generation of therapists and their patients.* New York: HarperCollins.

CHAPTER 14

Feminist Theories

Christine Flynn Saulnier

The greatest challenge of this chapter is to choose among the various theories, approaches, and perspectives that come under the label of feminist theory. It is not possible to sum up the whole of feminism with a set of common ideas; there are too many fundamental contradictions among the theories to attempt any such reduction.

I limited the number of theories discussed in this chapter to those that I think are most likely to be useful to direct service social work practitioners. The most helpful theories are those that guide social workers in operationalizing the profession's commitment to social and economic justice. I briefly discuss liberal, socialist, lesbian, radical, and womanist theories: liberal feminism because of its wide use more than its potential for serving the needs of social and economic justice; socialist and lesbian feminist theories because of their power to challenge fundamental beliefs about issues that are often discussed but seldom addressed in American social work (i.e., economic class and sexual orientation hierarchies as two of the foundations upon which our culture is built); and radical feminist and womanist theories because they best synthesize the interaction of psychological and sociological phenomena.

Those who seek a firm grounding in feminist social work have additional reading to do—beyond the thumbnail sketches of the theories presented in this chapter, and beyond the limited number of feminist theories reviewed here. The primary sources cited in this chapter provide a next step for continuing study.

AN OVERVIEW OF FEMINIST THEORY

Understanding of Human Problems

For this overview, analyzing the varied experiences of people from a political perspective that holds a sex-based analysis as one of the key analytical lenses constitutes a feminist approach. Another way of saying this is that within feminist theoretical analyses, many distresses experienced by women—and some of those experienced by men—can best be understood in terms of sex-based and gender-based social and structural restrictions, constrictions, and resource deficits, as these limitations interact with various other structural and interpersonal constraints.

For example, child care arrangements, built primarily to meet the needs of middle-class White women (Grahame, 2003), continue to be woefully inadequate and unaffordable in the United States, but without a feminist perspective, a working-class or poor mother who uses substandard or no care while she works is likely to be held individually responsible for child neglect (Henderson, Tickamyer, & Tadlock, 2005). Social and legal systems deal with her as though it is her personal inadequacy as a mother, rather than American child care policy, grounded in a sex-based social structure, that is at fault. If she also happens to be lesbian, a woman of color, an immigrant, or otherwise outside the mainstream, her child care arrangements might be seen as indicative of how difficult it is for members of her population to function as fit mothers. Often, a flurry of analyses will attempt to explain how she is disadvantaged by her beliefs and practices, making her culturally or constitutionally less likely to comprehend the necessity for child protection guidelines. This is the antithesis of feminist analysis.

Feminist theories, first of all, explain and suggest directions for change in social and environmental factors that create or contribute to dilemmas and problems experienced by women. Second, they explain and propose interventions for women's intrapersonal and interpersonal concerns. Third, feminist theories provide a perspective for evaluating social and environmental experiences of groups and individuals, regardless of sex or gender. The emphasis placed on each of these three areas, along with the centrality of additional factors that influence marginalization, oppression, and unwarranted constraints, depends on which feminist theory is used.

Conception of Therapeutic Intervention

Most feminist theories call for multilevel interventions. Depending on which theory is used and which feminist social worker is practicing, intervention might be primarily at a macro level and might only secondarily include micro-level interventions. The opposite may also be true, however. Many feminist social workers intervene almost entirely with individuals, families, and small groups, but few feminist practitioners would suggest that intervening on only one level is adequate. Most feminists would agree on the need for policy change but would disagree about how fundamental the change in our social fabric needs to be (Saulnier, 1996).

The utility of psychotherapy is hotly debated. It is not that feminists would necessarily dismiss empirical evidence that the goals of psychotherapy are often met (L. S. Brown, 2006). Rather, some would argue that the goals of psychotherapy—individual change in behavior and self-perception—distract feminist social workers, community members, and service users from social justice work. Psychotherapy may even be in direct conflict with social justice work if women are encouraged to cope with, instead of change, injustice (Arches, 1984; Kitzinger & Perkins, 1993). Other feminist theorists and practitioners would argue that for women to engage fruitfully in social change, healing at the individual level is often a prerequisite, and the task is best undertaken within a feminist framework (hooks, 1993; E. A. Lewis & Kissman, 1989; Roberts, Jackson, & Carlton-LaNey, 2000; Roche & Wood, 2005). Still other social workers argue that individual and social change must proceed simultaneously (N. Farwell, 2004; Weiner, 1998).

HISTORICAL DEVELOPMENT: FEMINIST THEORIES AND SOCIAL WORK CONNECTIONS

Feminist theories vary, their historical development differs, and the relationship between feminism and social work has been mixed. Some branches of feminist thought are inextricably bound to the sociopolitical climate of the historical period in which they arose. For example, it is hard to imagine how the tenets of lesbian feminism could have emerged prior to the naming and marginalization of lesbianism. On the other hand, most of the tenets of womanism—considered a late-20th-century theoretical phenomenon—have been clearly identified in both the thinking and the activism of mid-19th-century African American women.

The profession of social work is more than 100 years old. The history of feminist social work practice is equally long (Saulnier, 1996; Weil, 1986; Wetzel, 1976; Wise, 1988). Although not all social workers have been open to feminist thought (Abramovitz, 1978), many social work practitioners have worked within feminist frameworks (Abbott, 1994; G. Lewis, 1996). For example, in 1917, feminist social workers were working to eliminate the incongruity of having laws against public drunkenness but no economic or legal recourse for women living with heavy drinking, violent husbands (Woods, 1917). During the same era, Jane Addams was working diligently for women's suffrage (Meigs, 1979). Sophonisba Breckinridge advocated women's rights in the 1930s and 1940s from her prominent position at the School of Social Service Administration, University of Chicago. Addie Hinton campaigned for peace and for racial justice (Chandler, 2005). Over the last few decades feminist social work theory and practice have gained increasing academic recognition. Since 1986, *Affilia*, a major scholarly journal in social work, has published writings devoted to the theories and practice of feminist social work.

Despite significant feminist social work activities, it should be noted that discrimination against women within the profession of social work has been well documented (Dattalo, 2006; Gibelman & Schervish, 1993; Kravetz, 1976), social work practices have often reflected the antiwoman biases of the larger society (Krane, 1990; Kravetz, 1976; Stout & Kelly, 1990), and social work responses to feminist critiques of society and the profession have not always been positive (Abramovitz, 1978). Some social workers have supported public policies that uphold patriarchal control within and outside of families (Abramovitz, 1978); other social workers have written detailed accounts of welfare reform that explicitly dismiss the relationship between women's sociopolitical roles and the antiwoman stance of welfare policies (Kost & Munger, 1996).

FEMINIST THEORIES AND THEIR THEORETICAL CONSTRUCTS

Liberal Feminism

Liberal philosophy, on which liberal feminism is based, describes society as being composed of separate individuals, each competing for a fair share of resources. Liberalism's dedication to individual liberty demands freedom from interference by the state (Donovan, 1985). Of key importance to liberal feminism is that a dividing line is drawn between the public realm, which the state is expected to regulate, and the private realm, which is expected to be free from state control (Jaggar, 1983). The traditional liberal values of independence (vs. interdependence), equality of opportunity (vs. equality of outcome), and individualism (vs. collectivism) are so ingrained in Western society that they are accepted as standard social functioning, rather than viewed as a particular ideology. These traditional liberal values are central to liberal feminist thought. Liberal feminists point out that society violates the value of equal rights in its treatment of women, primarily by restricting women as a group, rather than treating women as individuals (Jaggar, 1983). They argue that women should have the same rights as men, but they often fail to examine the de facto inequality in distribution of men's rights by race, socioeconomic, and other factors (Richards, 2006).

Liberal feminists contest such public issues as women's lack of political equality and lack of access to certain social services needed to ensure equality between the sexes. Battles for equal education, equal employment opportunities, and equal pay for equal work have been the hallmark of liberal feminism. Often inequality is seen as being exacerbated, if not caused, by women's lack of training in the skills thought to enable men's success; for example, assertiveness. Rather than train women to dismantle structural supports of power imbalances, liberal feminists are more likely to examine interpersonal interactions and encourage women to behave more like those men who are successful in their careers. That is, liberal feminists work within the structure of mainstream society to integrate women into that structure (Moore, 1993), often using a model of individual rather than structural deficit (Gorey, Daly, Richter, Gleason, & McCallum, 2002).

Socialist Feminism

Socialist feminism draws on the theories of Karl Marx to explain how economic or material conditions form the root of culture, social organization, and consciousness itself. Oppression of women is said to be based in the private property system that exists within capitalist social and economic structures. Although socialist feminism draws on Marx's analysis of property relations, modes of production, and changes in material relations across history, it focuses primarily on a feminist-based class analysis as the central theorizing structure (Burnham & Louie, 1985). Theoretically, socialist feminists seek to end women's oppression, in part by eliminating capitalism (Moore, 1993). A socialist economic and social system is seen as insufficient to eliminate patriarchal structures and sexual division of labor, however. The latter would require a feminist revolution in addition to a socialist one (Burnham & Louie, 1985).

More pragmatically, socialist feminists focus attention on women's role in the wage labor force, often using the labor movement as a base from which to promote more equitable redistribution of resources. They focus on organizing women as women to eliminate gender-specific aspects of oppression, such as the problems of sexual abuse, insufficient child care, and constraints on reproductive rights (Burnham & Louie, 1985). Socialist feminists draw attention to apparently sex-neutral labor issues; for example, job protection, pointing out the overrepresentation of women among temporary workers and the underrepresentation of women among the workers whose jobs have been protected against contracting out. They demonstrate that these and other policies, such as privatization of social security, have a greater negative impact on women workers than on men and reinforce sexual division of labor (Creese, 1996; Estes, 2004). The analysis also focuses on how women's labor is controlled by men both in the family and in the workplace and on the enormous economic cost to women—during the work years, after divorce, and in retirement—of sporadic employment patterns and low wages (Catlett & McKenry, 1996; Estes, 2004; Thorne, 1983). Despite considerable disagreement over whether capitalism and patriarchy are separate systems (dual systems theorists include Hartmann, 1981, and Mitchell, 1971) or a single entity (unified systems theorists include Al-Hibri, 1981, and Young, 1981), socialist feminists tend to address the connections among family, employment, and social issues along both sex and class lines (Poster, 1995).

Socialist feminists have tended to work at macro levels, addressing policy (Abramovitz, 1988, 1991; Holmstrom, 2003) and organizing needs (Weil, 1986). Increasingly they focus on how racism intersects with sex and class (Naples & Dobson, 2001). In each case, they have worked toward finding collective means for solving both individual and community problems (Weil, 1986). Socialist feminists have been at the forefront of addressing the sex and economic bases of caregiving (Fredriksen, 1996; Langan, 1992). In this arena, direct practice social workers are often involved.

Lesbian Feminism

Lesbian feminism is a political perspective critical of heterosexual institutions (Smith, as cited in M. Farwell, 1992) and supportive of women's identification with women. Some argue it is only coincidentally related to sexual orientation. Charlotte Bunch's (1987) distinction is often quoted in this regard:

> A lesbian is a woman whose sexual/affectional preference is for women, and who has thereby rejected the female role on some level, but she may or may not embrace a lesbian-feminist political analysis. A woman-identified woman is a feminist who adopts a lesbian-feminist ideology and enacts that understanding in her life, whether she is a lesbian sexually or not. (p. 198)

Heterosexuality is defined by feminist theorists as both a political and a personal institution in which some members of society are given privileges that are withheld from others, based on sex, gender, and sexual orientation. Gender assignments are made in this sociopolitical context with neither gender nor sexual orientation being free from social constraint. The relationship between the prescribed social roles and stigmatization of lesbians is clear (Stevens, 1995), but the implications extend beyond the place of lesbians in society. Once gender identities and sexual orientation are exposed as socially rather than naturally created, the rationale for lesbian subordination is lost. Thus, the arbitrariness of exclusive organization of sexuality, romance, love, and marriage around the heterosexual imperative is also exposed (Calhoun, 1994). That is, lesbian feminism questions the necessity for heterosexuality as a basis on which to organize society. The invisibility and active suppression of lesbianism is seen as a gauge of how threatening lesbianism is to the ideology of gender assignments, male superiority, and female dependence.

Social service and health systems have all but ignored lesbians. The result is twofold: Lesbians' needs are unmet, and strictures on acceptable diversity are shored up as all women—regardless of sexual orientation—receive a forceful message about who are and what is tolerable. That is, health and social service systems powerfully reinforce the social order that privileges, or even requires, heterosexuality. The silence about lesbians and lesbianism that theorists analyzed in the 1970s (Rich, 1979) is still reflected at macro and micro levels in health and mental health care delivery (Saulnier, 2002; Saulnier & Wheeler, 2000; Stevens, 1995). Heterosexuality is still thought of as the natural condition and is still strongly associated with positive attitudes toward sex-based hierarchies (Kane & Schippers, 1996).

Radical Feminism

Radical feminists argue that individual women's experiences of injustice and the miseries that women think of as personal problems are actually political issues, grounded in power imbalances. Often using the slogan "The personal is political," they argue that separating public from private issues masks the reality of male power, a system of domination that operates similarly in interdependent public and private spheres. Radical feminists hold that public-private divisions isolate and depoliticize women's experience of oppression (Nes & Iadicola, 1989; Parker, 2003; Roth, 2004). Sexism is described as a social system consisting of "law, tradition, economics, education, organized religion, science, language, the mass media, sexual morality, child rearing, the domestic division of labor, and everyday social interaction" (Willis, 1989, p. x), the purpose of which is to give men power over women. The pervasiveness of sexism necessitates fundamental social change.

Radical feminists characterize society as patriarchal. By this they mean that, historically, families have been organized according to male lines of inheritance and dependence, and also that society has been constructed in a way that accrues a disproportionate share of power to men. The patriarchal structure privileges men through the complex political manipulation of individual identity, social interactions, and structural systems of power. Formal structures such as legal systems create and reinforce the sexual hierarchy, and virtually all human interactions are permeated by male privilege (Eisenstein, 1981; N. Farwell, 2004). Patriarchy, although varied in its manifestations, is described as a cultural universal, with all institutions reinforcing that social order (Nes & Iadicola, 1989).

Radical feminism's psychological analysis of male supremacy has two main themes: (a) Women are damaged psychologically by the internalization of oppressive patriarchal messages (Atwood, 2001; Echols, 1989), and (b) psychological control of women is a significant component of patriarchal systems (Donovan, 1985). Rigid sex role prescriptions not only distort people, they also lead to sex-based oppression. The psychology of sex-role conditioning accounts for women's apparent complicity with patriarchy (Echols, 1989). Radical feminists study the prevalence of violence against women, define it as political in nature, and point out that it is men who tend to abuse women and that battering is usually woman abuse.

Because of the comprehensiveness of their demand for change, radical feminists have had an uneasy relationship with health and mental health service providers and have preferred to develop new women-focused services rather than adapt existing services to meet women's needs (Koedt, Levine, & Rapone, 1973). A prime example is the virtual revolution in women's services, with the Boston Women's Health Book Collective often credited as the inspiration for women taking health care into their own hands (Tuana, 2006), although radical women's health activists in Black communities sought community rather than women's health services (Nelson, 2005).

Womanism

In addition to contributing significantly to the development of all of the divisions of feminist theory discussed here, African American writers and theorists developed another branch of feminist theory, often referred to as womanism (Alexander-Floyd & Simian, 2006; Collins, 1990; Davis, 1989; Giddings, 1988; hooks, 1984; Joseph & Lewis, 1981; Lorde, 1990). Womanism starts with the perspective of Black women and centers on a complex matrix of oppressions. Womanists argue that additive models of oppression—in which oppressive systems are seen as parallel and only occasionally intersecting—hide from view, and therefore from change, interlocking systems. Because of categorical thinking, it is difficult to conceive of race, sex, and class as a single consciousness with a single struggle needed to overcome them (E. B. Brown, 1990). Womanists argue, however, that it is necessary to examine all these aspects so that neither race, nor sex, nor class is hidden or discounted (Christian, 1985). That means we cannot dismantle one system of domination, then move on to the next, without understanding their intersections and interdependencies. Working from an assumption of interlocking systems is a paradigmatic shift away from focusing on separate, interacting systems. It is a move toward an inclusive view of mutually dependent, oppressive systems (Collins, 1990). Rather than posing race and gender as contradictory opposites, where a woman is expected to identify either as Black or as a woman, womanism allows for a unified whole (E. B. Brown, 1990; Ogunyemi, 1985). (Note the title of the widely read anthology *All the Women Are White, All the Blacks Are Men, But Some of Us Are Brave*, by Hull, Scott, & Smith, 1982.)

Both action and articulation are emphasized in womanist theory (Lorde, 1984). Womanism uses racial consciousness to underscore the positive aspects of African American life (Ogunyemi, 1985). But womanism does not focus solely on a social agenda. Self-healing is among the goals (E. B. Brown, 1990). To survive, despite racist and sexist valuations, Black women need to define themselves quite differently from the way they are viewed by those in power. Although mainstream social work does not use a womanist framework for service organization or delivery, individual social workers have (Carlton-LaNey, 1997), and social and health care services have sometimes been designed within a womanist framework (E. B. Brown, 1990; Comas-Diaz, 1994; Giddings, 1988). This framework takes into consideration the importance of a multifaceted sociopolitical analysis, the need for individual healing, and the importance of placing high value on racial consciousness. It is likely that many, though not all, African American women will come to social workers with a strong racial and feminist consciousness (Wilcox, 1997) and will be interested in working within a womanist framework.

Recent Formulations

To some extent, feminist theories sound more similar than in prior years in that nearly all theorists and many activists acknowledge the need to address sex, race/ethnic, class, sexual orientation, and sometimes religious biases; often the analyses, if not the work, focus on both structural and personal levels. However, emphasis continues to vary, so that current thinking that grows out of womanism continues to emphasize if not prioritize racism (Alexander-Floyd & Simien, 2006; Neville & Hamer, 2001). Theorists with a grounding in socialist feminism continue to center economic analyses (Naples & Dobson, 2001), and radical feminists continue to begin with sexism (L. S. Brown, 2006; Parker, 2003). With increased attention to globalization, and more focused work with immigrant women who come from Asia, the Middle East, Africa, the Caribbean, and other parts of the world, feminist theorists and social work practitioners continue to critique the limitations of individualism (versus collectivism) and independence (versus interdependence) found in liberal feminist theories (Patterson, 2003), finding the structural approaches such as radical, womanist, and socialist or materialist theories more useful. What remains unchanged, however, is that even those feminist therapists who continue to advocate political consciousness raising as a form of therapy (e.g., L. S. Brown, 2006) rarely go the next step, which is encouraging service users to engage in social change efforts as part of the therapeutic process.

DESCRIPTIONS OF PHASES OF HELPING

In the following discussion of the application of feminism in direct practice, I will stress the commonalities across branches of feminist theory.

Engagement

Feminist practitioners work to enable women to empower themselves as individuals and collectively. Feminists seek to minimize power differentials between service users and social workers, but they do not pretend that they have equal power with all the people who seek their services. Such a masking of power is dishonest and does not work (Baines, 1997). A feminist approach means engaging a person in a manner that conveys a genuine respect for the individual's perspective. Social workers bring valuable skills and knowledge to an exchange, but these are no more valuable than the knowledge that service users bring about themselves and their circumstances.

Data Collection and Assessment

Gathering data on a micro level only is a diminishing truncation of feminist social work. Data concerning family, friends, and neighborhood and other potential social supports are important sources of information about strengths, circumstances, and perceptions. This information is necessary but not sufficient. In addition to examining individual circumstances, the influence of a person's membership in a particular socioeconomic class, ethnic group, racial category, and so on, should be considered. This too is necessary but still incomplete. Social workers using feminist theories will gather information about populations who have comparable strengths, experience similar challenges, and are affected by the same type of sociopolitical circumstances. Without this final step, it is not possible to determine whether planning and intervention should be focused on micro and/or macro levels.

Assessment starts with the service user. The person seeking help provides the most important assessment of assets, hindrances, concerns, and problems. Although it may be tempting in some situations (e.g., when working with people who have chronic mental illness or alcohol problems) to assume a social work practitioner has clearer insight into circumstances and needs, it is vital to recognize that this is a deficit approach that defines service users as less expert on their own lives than professionals.

Feminist assessment centers the perspective of the service user or community member. Skilled feminist assessment requires the ability to draw out information from another's perspective. The knowledge and skills the practitioner brings to bear are important. They are the reason people accept assistance from social workers, but it is the analysis of the service user or community member that must be the basis from which we form a picture of the whole person in context.

Planning/Contracting and Intervention

Feminist planning/contracting means that both the worker and the service user have goals to accomplish. Meetings with service users help ground feminist social workers in the direction in which social justice work needs to proceed. One way of looking at the implications of feminist theories is that it is quite difficult to do feminist or womanist interventions. Intervention at a single level is insufficient in most cases, yet the circumstances in which many social workers find themselves require just that sort of truncation of social work intervention. Another way of viewing feminist intervention is that it is simply good social work to help service users meet basic needs, give service users the specific help they ask for, demystify the work we do, and teach skills. Changing the world is our job as social workers. Some service users will want to join social workers in the effort, some will do it on their own, and some will not want any part of it. Often this is because they are too busy trying to stay alive or because they are tired from the effort and need to back away for a while.

Feminist social workers need to be aware that a focus on process that is important to many people from middle-class backgrounds may be of no interest to people from working-class or poor backgrounds (Baines, 1997). It may be challenging for people who have been trained to use process as the primary method of intervention to put aside their predilection in favor of service user/community member preferences, but self-determination requires it.

Evaluation and Termination

As with any social work intervention, the work with the individual is complete when the service user no longer needs a social worker. Determination of when that time has arrived and measures of outcome depend heavily on the service user's goals. Progress toward goals, satisfaction with social work help, and decrease in problems should all be evaluated regularly and systematically to ensure that the intervention helps rather than hinders.

A key component is service user feedback. If process and outcomes are measured only at the individual level, however, social work will have fallen short. Social justice is a larger concept than what can be measured at the micro level. Social work practice using feminist theory also will examine social structures, organizations, and communities for improvement, with careful attention to systems of oppression, particularly sex-based oppression. For example, are more women's jobs being protected from contracting out (Creese, 1996)? Are the staff's negative attitudes toward women interfering with people getting high-quality services (Beckman & Mays, 1985)? Are intake forms heterosexist (Saulnier & Wheeler, 2000)? Do social policies require and reinforce a specific family form (Grahame, 2003)? Has progress been made toward providing an adequate amount of high-quality, low-cost child care in the community (Bergmann, 1997)? More comprehensive forms of feminism such as womanism and radical feminism seem particularly pertinent and successful in addressing larger social justice issues (Gorey et al., 2002).

APPLICATION TO FAMILY AND GROUP WORK

Family Therapy

Family therapy theories have been widely critiqued for their sexism (Whipple, 1996), as has family therapy practice (Werner Wilson, Price, Zimmerman, & Murphy, 1997; Wright & Fish, 1997), although many family therapists practice from a feminist perspective (Dankoski, Penn, Carlson, & Hecker, 1998; Goodrich, Rampage, Ellman, & Halstead, 1988) and feminist family therapy is being developed more extensively

(Akamatsu, Basham, & Olson, 1996; Goodrich & Silverstein, 2005). Yet preference for patriarchy continues to guide some education programs and some practitioners of family therapy (Goodrich & Silverstein, 2005; Ivey, 1996). For example, one self-labeled feminist family therapist (Erickson, 1996) argued that women and men are "naturally dependent" upon each other. Such feminist family therapists should avoid working with lesbians, women who choose to be single, those struggling with sexual orientation, and any other people who find the heterosexual imperative distasteful. Attitudes and beliefs contrary to feminist perspectives are often more subtle. In one published case study (Goodrich et al., 1988), several clinicians, while acknowledging that the notion of fusion in lesbian relationships often reflects homophobia, had treatment goals of separation and individuation, and took an anthropologic view of the lesbian foursome they chose for an illustration of feminist family therapy with lesbians.

More recently, family therapists, in general, have incorporated feminist ideas into their practice, including a critique of gender-role constraints. Incorporating feminist behaviors into practice seems to be more common among those who specifically identify themselves as feminists, however (Dankoski et al., 1998; Goodrich & Silverstein, 2005). Feminist family therapy acknowledges the changes in family forms over time and across cultures. It also takes into account our developing knowledge of the limitations of family therapy; for example, there are good reasons and good evidence that family treatment is not the treatment of choice for battered women (Nappi et al., 2004; L. E. Walker, 1995).

Group Work

Group work is common to most approaches to feminist practice (Saulnier, 1996, 2000). The groups include consciousness-raising groups, women's self-help groups, feminist therapy groups, and woman-specific skill-building groups, where women are trained in such skills as assertiveness. Through these groups, feminists counter the sex biases that have been identified in traditional groups (Black, 2003a; L. Walker, 1987). As far back as 1958, researchers confirmed that women's verbal inhibition, willingness to be interrupted, and commitment to defending their ideas were all influenced by the sex composition of a group (Tuddenham, MacBride, & Zahn, 1958). Additionally, feminists defined the confrontation, conflict, and competition that they perceived to be common in traditional groups as inappropriate male-identified approaches to group work (Hagen, 1983).

One form of group work, called the structural approach (Wood & Middleman, 1991), fits especially well with a feminist framework.

It focuses on the uneven distribution of resources among people and works toward redress by means of advocacy, consciousness raising, and training clients how to negotiate systems and how to alter social arrangements. Members are encouraged to provide mutual support while using community resources to effect political change.

Social workers have noted the parallels between feminist theory and the social action components of group work (Garvin, 1991; E. Lewis, 1992; Saulnier, 2000, 2003). Personal experience as the basis for political analysis and the potential for groups to make social change are the most obvious ways in which feminism and social group work overlap (Home, 1991; Lee, 1994; Pack Brown, Whittington Clark, & Parker, 1998; Saulnier, 2000). Garvin and Reed (1995) pointed out their shared historical roots, including simultaneous attention to social change and individual growth (Coyle, as cited in Garvin, 1991). Kravetz (1987) noted the importance of consciousness-raising groups as a mental health resource for women. She contrasted the goals of traditional psychotherapy—changing "deviant, sick, or maladaptive" aspects of an individual and helping women to adjust—with consciousness raising's call for change in both structural-social and personal-interpersonal processes. In consciousness raising, women examine personal problems in sociopolitical context, and change is assumed to be needed in both social policy and personal attitudes and behavior. Kravetz (1987) stressed the need to counteract the internalization of cultural messages that support powerlessness and devalue women, and she argued that women's groups, particularly consciousness-raising groups, can alter internalized views, thereby challenging "one of the most basic ways that oppression is maintained" (p. 64).

Cox (1991) argued that the tendency to focus either on personal or on political aspects of a problem was misguided because a single focus contributes insufficiently to empowerment of group members, particularly their ability to change their environment. She argued that social workers should promote multifaceted groups. In her own work, Cox encouraged group members to intervene at both personal and political levels. She reported that group members succeeded in changing both their consciousness (e.g., courage, sense of power, and knowledge of bureaucratic functions) and their environments (e.g., increased safety, improved food stamp policy, and increased hours of service availability at a facility used by participants). Social work practitioners have noted bidirectional skill development, indicating that women who were empowered as individuals were better equipped to undertake collective group action. By the same token, members developed personal skills and increased confidence when they were engaged in social action leading to more tangible outcomes, such as policy change and resource development (Regan & Lee, 1992).

COMPATIBILITY WITH THE GENERALIST-ECLECTIC FRAMEWORK

Attention to Holistic Assessment and Use of Systems and Life Cycle Theories

Systems perspectives have been used by feminists, including feminist family therapists, for a long time (Featherstone, 1996). Feminism is a systems perspective, to a large extent. With the possible exception of liberal feminism, a multilevel or holistic assessment would be essential in social work practice guided by feminist theory.

Historically, life cycle theories, although not necessarily incompatible with feminism, tended not to be used by feminists because they have often used a deficit model to discuss single-parent families, women who are alone, and women and children's adjustment to divorce (Candib, 1989), but feminist life cycle analyses have been developed more recently (Zaytoun, 2006). Family life cycle theories are often fraught with male, White, and heterosexual biases (Rice, 1994). There are notable exceptions (Dutton Douglas & Walker, 1988; Green, 2003; Kissman, 1991; Mirkin, 1994) in which women's development across the life cycle is centered rather than marginalized. The most prominent example is the work of the Stone Center (Jordan, Kaplan, Miller, Stiver, & Surrey, 1991), where theories of women's development are created within an explicitly feminist framework.

Emphasis on Therapeutic Relationship and Fit With Strengths Perspective

A strengths-based perspective is often used by feminist practitioners, including feminist group workers (Black, 2003b; Pollio, McDonald, & North, 1996). Feminist emphasis on the therapeutic relationship varies. Although it is the primary intervention used by many feminist social workers, others argue that the focus on developing a therapeutic relationship is sometimes outside the interests of people who seek their services, and that the focus on relationship building and process may be class based (Baines, 1997). The relationship focus may mask a clinician's desire for a client to adopt his or her worldview, rather than engage in open dialogue about the social, and often political, forces impinging on a service user's life (Kitzinger & Perkins, 1993).

Attention to Issues of Diversity and Empowerment

Feminist theories have improved in their attention to diversity, although it would be a mistake to assume that the media portrayal of feminism as developed and supported only, or primarily, by White middle-class women is accurate. African American women, Latinas, American Indian women, Asian American women, and working-class women from many backgrounds have all been committed to feminism, under many names, for many decades (Saulnier, 1996). This said, it is also true that there has been considerable racism, classism, and heterosexism in various theoretical and activist camps of feminism. There is still much room for improvement (Richards, 2006), but many feminists have grown by exposure to multiple perspectives on women's issues, and it is much less common to see feminist theorizing or practice that fails to take diversity into account. Empowerment is what feminism is about; however, the goal of empowerment varies from intrapsychic change to social action (Cox, 1991) and tends to depend on which feminist theory is used.

Generalist Versus Specialist Practice

Feminist theories support the generalist framework. The author's perspective is that specialization limits effectiveness except under particular circumstances. Those circumstances include work that is done in conjunction with other practitioners who are intervening across multiple levels, for example, as part of a task force or coalition of individuals or organizations committed to feminist/womanist social work practice. Specialists may work toward a particular goal, each using a specific method of intervention. To be compatible with feminist theories, however, the work would have to be integrated, so that positive change occurred at multiple levels (Goodkind, 2005).

Eclecticism

Given the pervasiveness of oppression of women and the negative effects on one person of diminishing another, theories that guide our understanding and dismantling of oppression can guide all our social work practice. This generalizability holds for feminist theories, as well as others that promote social justice. This does not preclude, however, the use of other theories. Depending on the branch of feminism, feminist practice can be consistent with other theories. For example, radical feminist consciousness raising could draw on cognitive theories, or liberal feminist assertiveness training might mesh well with cognitive-behavioral approaches. Also, as mentioned previously, some feminist practitioners incorporate family therapy models into their practice.

A larger question for feminist practitioners is how to choose which feminist theory will guide their work. On the surface, it might seem that social workers should choose a feminist theory based on which systems of oppression impinge on the people with whom they are working at the time. It makes sense that the problem to be solved is the best guide to choice of theory. Some theories apply better than others to particular populations and problems. For example, given liberal feminism's concern with the glass ceiling, it would not be the best approach for women who are concerned more with the income floor. In this case, a theory that centers on class struggles would be more appropriate.

The problem in choosing which feminist theory to use is complicated by the inescapable reality that theories are value-laden. Some of us value pervasive structural change and see social justice as possible only in the context of profound redistribution of power and resources. Others value stability, predictability, and incremental change. Some theories question the very foundations of American society; for example, the heterosexual nuclear family structure upon which many social policies and services are built. For some social workers, the fundamental shake-up recommended by these theories is precisely what is needed. For others, that is taking self-definition and social justice too far, too fast. Practitioners must decide what is most in-line with their reading of the code of ethics and with social work values.

CRITIQUE OF THE THEORIES

As a whole, the major strengths of feminist theories are that they (a) explain sex-based disparities, (b) guide social workers in their efforts to dismantle structural and interpersonal restrictions and constrictions, and (c) provide an analytic lens for evaluating the various forms of oppression experienced by women. Because of feminist theories and the ways that the women's movement has used them, more services are available that meet women's needs. Some common criticisms of feminist theories include the narrowness of some branches, the limited populations to whom some branches may apply, and the lack of political viability of the more comprehensive theories.

CASE EXAMPLE

Following the example of a woman in search of child care that was introduced at the beginning of the chapter, traditional intervention might focus on helping the woman improve her ability to recognize the need for adequate supervision of her child and the need to work harder to locate and keep quality child care. Perhaps she would be referred to a child care registry for news of an opening and to county offices for a voucher to cover the cost of child care during her work hours. For an immigrant woman, her extended family may be seen as responsible for providing child care (Grahame, 2003). A woman may be offered counseling to help her value herself and her child and to strengthen her inner resources so she can better meet the challenges of parenting. She would not be encouraged to see herself as one of many, perhaps a class of, people who are held personally responsible for failures in social policies and social systems.

Feminist social work would approach the problem differently, although many of the concrete services would still be offered. First, the problem would be contextualized, and the woman would be encouraged to see the problem as a generalized need, rather than her deficit. Next, she would be supported in her struggle to provide for herself and her family. Together, she and the social worker would identify concrete needs, goals, and specific resources available. They would determine which services the woman herself should pursue and which would require advocacy or other social work intervention.

The social worker might also inform the woman of community efforts to make child care more available to low-income women, if such efforts existed. This would be in the form of information giving, not pressure to take on activism as yet another duty. However, if the woman's circumstances and interests allowed (and child care was available), the worker might help her devise ways she could contribute to the effort. If not, the social worker would still contribute in some way to the efforts of the community to provide for its children.

SUMMARY

Most feminist theories suggest ways to help eliminate misperceptions, sexual inequalities, restrictions, and oppression faced by women—goals that many writers have pointed out are shared by social workers (see review by Dore, 1994)—but the goals of each branch of feminism vary according to the perspective on the forces that impede women. If backlash is any measure of how threatened patriarchal structures are by feminist analysis and intervention, the false memory syndrome campaign of the 1990s and an examination of violence against women as a measure of backlash suggest that feminists hit a nerve (Martin, Vieraitis, & Britto, 2006; Park, 1997). It is important to maintain feminist theory as a crucial approach to social work and to not let feminism slip into gender studies. Research suggests that training in gender issues without a specifically feminist perspective does not reduce sexism in clinical decision making (Leslie & Clossick, 1996).

REFERENCES

Abbott, A. A. (1994). A feminist approach to substance abuse treatment and service delivery. *Social Work in Health Care, 19*(3/4), 67–83.

Abramovitz, M. (1978). Social work and women's liberation: A mixed response. *Catalyst* (U.S.), *1*(3), 91–103.

Abramovitz, M. (1988). *Regulating the lives of women.* Boston: South End Press.

Abramovitz, M. (1991). Poor women in a bind: Social reproduction without social supports. *Affilia, 7*(2), 23–43.

Akamatsu, N. N., Basham, K., & Olson, M. (1996). Teaching a feminist family therapy. In K. Weingarten & M. Bograd (Eds.), *Reflections on feminist family therapy training* (pp. 21–36). New York: Haworth Press.

Alexander-Floyd, N., & Simian, E. M. (2006). Revisiting "What's in a Name?" Exploring the contours of Africana womanist thought. *Frontiers, 27*(1), 67–89.

Al-Hibri, A. (1981). Capitalism is an advanced state of patriarchy: But Marxism is not feminism. In L. Sargent (Ed.), *Women and revolution: A discussion of the unhappy marriage of Marxism and feminism* (pp. 165–194). Boston: South End Press.

Arches, J. (1984). Women and mental health: One step forward, one step back? *Catalyst* (U.S.), *4*(16), 43–57.

Atwood, N. (2001). Gender bias in families and its clinical implications for women. *Social Work, 46,* 23–36.

Baines, D. (1997). Feminist social work in the inner city: The challenges of race, class, and gender. *Affilia, 12,* 297–317.

Beckman, L. J., & Mays, V. M. (1985). Educating community gatekeepers about alcohol abuse in women: Changing attitudes, knowledge, and referral practices. *Journal of Drug Education, 15,* 289–309.

Bergmann, B. R. (1997). Government support for families with children in the United States and France. *Feminist Economics, 3,* 85–94.

Black, C. (2003a). Creating curative communities: Feminist group work with women with eating issues. *Australian Social Work, 56,* 127–140.

Black, C. (2003b). Translating principles into practice: Implementing the feminist and strengths perspectives in work with battered women. *Affilia, 18,* 332–349.

Brown, E. B. (1990). Womanist consciousness: Maggie Lenna Walker and the Independent Order of St. Luke. In E. DuBois & V. Ruiz (Eds.), *Unequal sisters* (pp. 208–223). New York: Routledge.

Brown, L. S. (2006). Still subversive after all these years: The relevance of feminist therapy in the age of evidence-based practice. *Psychology of Women Quarterly, 30,* 15–24.

Bunch, C. (1987). *Passionate politics: Feminist theory in action.* New York: St. Martin's Press.

Burnham, L., & Louie, M. (1985). The impossible marriage: A Marxist critique of socialist feminism. *Line of March, 17,* 1–128.

Calhoun, C. (1994). Separating lesbian theory from feminist theory. *Ethics, 104,* 558–581.

Candib, L. M. (1989). Point and counterpoint: Family life cycle theory: A feminist critique. *Family Systems Medicine, 7,* 473–487.

Carlton-LaNey, I. (1997). Elizabeth Ross Haynes: An African American reformer of womanist consciousness, 1908–1940. *Social Work, 42,* 573–584.

Catlett, B. S., & McKenry, P. (1996). Implications of feminist scholarship for the study of women's post-divorce economic disadvantage. *Family Relations, 45,* 91–97.

Chandler, S. (2005). Addie Hunton and the construction of an African American female peace perspective. *Affilia, 20,* 270–283.

Christian, B. (1985). *Black feminist criticism: Perspectives on Black women writers*. New York: Pergamon Press.

Collins, P. H. (1990). *Black feminist thought: Knowledge, consciousness, and the politics of empowerment*. Boston: Unwin Hyman.

Comas-Diaz, L. (1994). An integrative approach. In L. Comas-Diaz & B. Greene (Eds.), *Women of color: Integrating ethnic and gender identities in psychotherapy* (pp. 287–318). New York: Guilford Press.

Cox, E. O. (1991). The critical role of social action in empowerment-oriented groups. *Social Work With Groups, 14*(3/4), 77–90.

Creese, G. (1996). Gendering collective bargaining: From men's rights to women's issues. *The Canadian Review of Sociology and Anthropology, 33*, 437–456.

Dankoski, M. E., Penn, C. D., Carlson, T. D., & Hecker, L. L. (1998). What's in a name? A study of family therapists' use and acceptance of the feminist perspective. *American Journal of Family Therapy, 44*, 368–376.

Dattalo, P. (2006). *2005–2006 academic year salary survey*. Alexandria, VA: National Association of Deans and Directors of Social Work.

Davis, A. (1989). *Women, culture, and politics*. New York: Random House.

Donovan, J. (1985). *Feminist theory: The intellectual traditions of American feminism*. New York: Ungar.

Dore, M. M. (1994). Feminist pedagogy and the teaching of social work practice. *Journal of Social Work Education, 30*, 97–106.

Dutton Douglas, M. A., & Walker, L. E. A. (Eds.). (1988). *Feminist psychotherapies: Integration of therapeutic and feminist systems*. Norwood, NJ: Ablex.

Echols, A. (1989). *Daring to be bad: Radical feminism in America, 1967–1975*. Minneapolis: University of Minnesota Press.

Eisenstein, Z. R. (1981). *The radical future of liberal feminism*. New York: Longman.

Erickson, B. M. (1996). Ethical considerations when feminist family therapists treat men. *Journal of Family Psychotherapy, 7*(2), 1–19.

Estes, C. L. (2004). Social Security privatization and older women: A feminist political economy perspective. *Journal of Aging Studies, 18*, 9–26.

Farwell, M. (1992). The lesbian literary imagination. In S. Wolfe & J. Penelope (Eds.), *Sexual practice, textual theory: Lesbian cultural criticism* (pp. 66–84). Cambridge, MA: Blackwell.

Farwell, N. (2004). War rape: New conceptualizations and responses. *Affilia, 19*, 389–403.

Featherstone, V. (1996). A feminist critique of family therapy. *Counseling Psychology Quarterly, 9*, 15–23.

Fredriksen, K. I. (1996). Gender differences in employment and the informal care of adults. *Journal of Women and Aging, 8*(2), 35–53.

Garvin, C. D. (1991). Barriers to effective social action. *Social Work With Groups, 14*(3/4), 65–76.

Garvin, C. D., & Reed, B. G. (1995). Sources and visions for feminist group work: Reflective process, social justice, diversity, and connection. In N. Van Den Bergh (Ed.), *Feminist practice in the 21st century* (pp. 41–67). Washington, DC: NASW Press.

Gibelman, M., & Schervish, P. H. (1993). The glass ceiling in social work: Is it shatterproof? *Affilia, 8*, 442–455.

Giddings, P. (1988). *When and where I enter*. New York: Bantam.

Goodkind, S. (2005). Gender-specific services in the juvenile justice system: A critical examination. *Affilia, 20*, 52–70.

Goodrich, T. J., Rampage, C., Ellman, B., & Halstead, K. (1988). *Feminist family therapy: A casebook*. New York: W. W. Norton.

Goodrich, T. J., & Silverstein, L. B. (2005). Now you see it, now you don't: Feminist training in family therapy. *Family Process, 44,* 267–281.

Gorey K., Daly, C., Richter, N., Gleason, D., & McCallum, M. J. (2002). The effectiveness of feminist social work methods: An integrative review. *Journal of Social Service Research, 29*(1), 37–55.

Grahame, K. M. (2003) "For the family": Asian immigrant women's triple day. *Journal of Sociology and Social Welfare, 30*(1), 65–90.

Green, S. (2003). *The psychological development of girls and women: Rethinking change in time.* New York: Routledge.

Hagen, B. H. (1983). Managing conflict in all-women groups. *Social Work With Groups, 6*(3/4), 95–104.

Hartmann, H. (1981). The unhappy marriage of Marxism and feminism: Towards a more progressive union. In L. Sargent (Ed.), *Women and revolution: A discussion of the unhappy marriage of Marxism and feminism* (pp. 1–42). Boston: South End Press.

Henderson, D. A., Tickamyer, A. R., & Tadlock, B. L. (2005). The impact of welfare reform on the parenting role of women in rural communities. *Journal of Children & Poverty, 11,*131–147.

Holmstrom, N. (2003). The socialist feminist project. *Monthly Review, 54*(10), 38–48.

Home, A. (1991). Responding to domestic violence: A comparison of social workers' and police officers' interventions. *Social Work and Social Sciences Review, 3,*150–162.

hooks, b. (1984). *Feminist theory from margin to center.* Boston: South End Press.

hooks, b. (1993). *Sisters of the yam: Black women and self-recovery.* Toronto, Ontario, Canada: Between the Lines.

Hull, G. T., Scott, P. B., & Smith, B. (Eds.). (1982). *All the women are White, all the Blacks are men, but some of us are brave.* New York: The Feminist Press.

Ivey, D. C. (1996). Family history and gender roles: Critical factors in practitioners' views of family interactions. *Contemporary Family Therapy, 18,* 425–445.

Jaggar, A. M. (1983). *Feminist politics and human nature.* Totowa, NJ: Rowman & Littlefield.

Jordan, J., Kaplan, A., Miller, J. B., Stiver, I., & Surrey, J. (1991). *Women's growth in connection: Writings from the Stone Center.* New York: Guilford Press.

Joseph, G., & Lewis, J. (1981). *Common differences: Conflicts in Black and White feminist perspectives.* Boston: South End Press.

Kane, E., & Schippers, M. (1996). Men's and women's beliefs about gender and sexuality. *Gender and Society, 10,* 650–665.

Kissman, K. (1991). Feminist-based social work with single-parent families. *Families in Society, 72,* 23–28.

Kitzinger, C., & Perkins, R. (1993). *Changing our minds: Lesbian feminism and psychology.* New York: New York University Press.

Koedt, A., Levine, E., & Rapone, A. (Eds.). (1973). *Radical feminism.* New York: Quadrangle Books.

Kost, K., & Munger, F. (1996). Fooling all of the people some of the time: 1990s welfare reform and the exploitation of American values. *Virginia Journal of Law and Social Policy, 4,* 3–126.

Krane, J. (1990). Patriarchal biases in the conceptualization of child sexual abuse: A review and critique of literature from a radical feminist perspective. *Canadian Social Work Review, 7,* 183–196.

Kravetz, D. (1976). Sexism in a woman's profession. *Social Work, 21,* 421–427.

Kravetz, D. (1987). Benefits of consciousness-raising groups for women. In C. Brody (Ed.), *Women's therapy groups: Paradigms of feminist treatment* (pp. 55–66). New York: Springer Publishing Company.

Langan, M. (1992). Who cares? Women in the mixed economy of care. In M. Langan & L. Day (Eds.), *Women, oppression, and social work* (pp. 67–91). New York: Routledge.

Lee, J. A. B. (1994). No place to go: Homeless women. In A. Gitterman & L. Shulman (Eds.), *Mutual aid groups, vulnerable populations, and the life cycle* (2nd ed., pp. 297–313). New York: Columbia University Press.

Leslie, L., & Clossick, M. (1996). Sexism in family therapy: Does training in gender make a difference? *Journal of Marital and Family Therapy, 22,* 252–269.

Lewis, E. (1992). Regaining promise: Feminist perspectives for social group work practice. *Social Work With Groups, 15*(2), 271–284.

Lewis, E. A., & Kissman, K. (1989). Factors linking ethnic-sensitive and feminist social work practice with African-American women. *Arete, 14*(2), 23–31.

Lewis, G. (1996). Situated voices: "Black women's experience" and social work. *Feminist Review, 53,* 24–56.

Lorde, A. (1984). *Sister outsider.* Freedom, CA: Crossing Press.

Lorde, A. (1990). I am your sister: Black women organizing across sexualities. In G. Anzaldua (Ed.), *Making face, making soul* (pp. 321–325). San Francisco: Aunt Lute Books.

Martin, K., Vieraitis, L. M., & Britto, S. (2006). Gender equality and women's absolute status: A test of the feminist models of rape. *Violence Against Women, 12,* 321–339.

Meigs, C. (1979). *Jane Addams: Pioneer for social justice.* Boston: Little, Brown.

Mirkin, M. P. (1994). *Women in context: Toward a feminist reconstruction of psychotherapy.* New York: Guilford Press.

Mitchell, J. (1971). *Woman's estate.* New York: Pantheon Books.

Moore, C. T. (1993). *Subject: soc.feminism terminologies.* Retrieved December 12, 2006 from www.cis.ohio-state.edu/hypertext/faq/usenet/feminism/terms/faq.html

Naples, N., & Dobson, M. (2001). Feminists and the welfare state: Aboriginal health care workers and U.S. community workers of color. *NWSA Journal, 13*(3), 116–137.

Nappi, T., Seligson Sillman, J., Brockmeyer, D., Rand, L., Aviva Lee-Parritz, A., Welch, C., et al. (2004). *Domestic violence: A guide to screening and intervention.* Retrieved Jaunary 8, 2007, from www.brighamandwomens.org/communityprograms/Passage wayScreening.pdf

Nelson, J. (2005). "Hold your head up and stick out your chin": Community health and women's health in Mound Bayou, Mississippi. *NWSA Journal, 17*(1), 99–118.

Nes, J. A., & Iadicola, P. (1989). Toward a definition of feminist social work: A comparison of liberal, radical, and socialist models. *Social Work, 34,* 12–21.

Neville, H., & Hamer, J. (2001). "We make freedom": An exploration of revolutionary Black feminism. *Journal of Black Studies, 31,* 437–461.

Ogunyemi, C. (1985). Womanism: The dynamics of the contemporary Black female novel in English. *Signs, 11,* 63–80.

Pack Brown, S. P., Whittington Clark, L. E., & Parker, W. M. (1998). *Images of me: A guide to group work with African-American women.* Boston: Allyn & Bacon.

Park, S. (1997). False memory syndrome: A feminist philosophical approach. *Hypatia, 12*(2), 1–50.

Parker, L. (2003). A social justice model for clinical social work practice. *Affilia, 18,* 272–288.

Patterson, F. (2003). Heeding new voices: Gender-related herstories of Asian and Caribbean-born elderly women. *Affilia, 18,* 68–79.

Pollio, D. E., McDonald, S. M., & North, C. S. (1996). Combining a strengths-based approach and feminist theory in group work with persons "on the streets." *Social Work With Groups, 19,* 5–20.

Poster, W. (1995). The challenges and promises of class and racial diversity in the women's movement. *Gender and Society, 9,* 650–679.

Regan, S., & Lee, G. (1992). The interplay among social group work, community work, and social action. *Social Work With Groups, 15,* 35–50.

Rice, J. K. (1994). Reconsidering research on divorce, family life cycle, and the meaning of family. *Psychology of Women Quarterly, 18,* 559–584.

Rich, A. (1979). *On lies, secrets, and silence.* New York: W. W. Norton.

Richards, P. (2006). The politics of difference and women's rights: Lessons from Pobladoras and Mapuche women in Chile. *Social Politics: International Studies in Gender, State, & Society, 13,* 1–29.

Roberts, A., Jackson, M. S., & Carlton-LaNey, I. (2000). Revisiting the need for feminism and Afrocentric theory when treating African-American substance abusers. *Journal of Drug Issues, 30,* 901–918.

Roche, S., & Wood, G. G. (2005). A narrative principle for feminist social work with survivors of male violence. *Affilia, 20,* 465–475.

Roth, B. (2004). *Separate roads to feminism: Black, Chicana, and White feminist movements in America's second wave.* Cambridge, England: Cambridge University Press.

Saulnier, C. F. (1996). *Feminist theories and social work: Approaches and applications.* Binghamton, NY: Haworth Press.

Saulnier, C. F. (2000). Incorporating feminist theory into social work: Group work practice examples. *Social Work With Groups, 23*(1), 5–29.

Saulnier, C. F. (2002). Deciding who to see: Lesbians discuss their preferences in physical and mental health care providers. *Social Work, 47,* 355–365.

Saulnier, C. F. (2003). Goal setting process: Supporting choice in a feminist group for women with alcohol problems. *Social Work With Groups, 26*(1), 47–68.

Saulnier, C. F., & Wheeler, E. (2000). Social action research: Influencing providers and recipients of health and mental health care for lesbians. *Affilia, 15,* 409–433.

Stevens, P. (1995). Structural and interpersonal impact of heterosexual assumptions on lesbian health care clients. *Nursing Research, 44,* 25–30.

Stout, K. D., & Kelly, M. J. (1990). Differential treatment based on sex. *Affilia, 5*(2), 60–71.

Thorne, B. (1983). Feminist rethinking of the family: An overview. In B. Thorne & M. Yalom (Eds.), *Rethinking the family: Some feminist questions* (pp. 1–24). New York: Longman.

Tuana, N. (2006). The speculum of ignorance: The women's health movement and epistemologies of ignorance. *Hypatia, 21*(3), 1–19.

Tuddenham, R., MacBride, D., & Zahn, V. (1958). The influence of the sex composition of the group upon yielding to a distorted norm. *Journal of Psychology, 46,* 243–251.

Walker, L. (1987). Women's groups are different. In C. Brody (Ed.), *Women's therapy groups: Paradigms of feminist treatment* (pp. 3–12). New York: Springer Publishing Company.

Walker, L. E. (1995). Current perspectives on men who batter women: Implications for intervention and treatment to stop violence against women. *Journal of Family Psychology, 9,* 264–271.

Weil, M. (1986). Women, community, and organizing. In N. Van Den Bergh & L. Cooper (Eds.), *Feminist visions for social work* (pp. 187–210). Silver Spring, MD: NASW Press.

Weiner, K. M. (1998). Tools for change: Methods of incorporating political/social action into the therapy session. *Women & Therapy, 21,* 113–123.

Werner Wilson, R. J., Price, S. J., Zimmerman, T. S., & Murphy, M. J. (1997). Client gender as a process variable in marriage and family therapy: Are women clients interrupted more than men clients? *Journal of Family Psychology, 11,* 373–377.

Wetzel, J. W. (1976). Interaction of feminism and social work in America. *Social Casework*, *57*, 227–236.

Whipple, V. (1996). Developing an identity as a feminist family therapist: Implications for training. *Journal of Marital and Family Therapy*, *22*, 381–396.

Wilcox, C. (1997). Racial and gender consciousness among African-American women: Sources and consequences. *Women and Politics*, *17*(1), 73–93.

Willis, E. (1989). Foreword. In A. Echols (Ed.), *Daring to be bad: Radical feminism in America 1967–1975* (pp. vii–xv). Minneapolis: University of Minnesota Press.

Wise, S. (1988). Doing feminist social work: An annotated bibliography and an introductory essay. *Studies in Sexual Politics*, *21*, 71.

Wood, G., & Middleman, R. (1991). Advocacy and social action: Key elements in the structural approach to direct practice in social work. *Social Work With Groups*, *14*(3/4), 53–63.

Woods, A. (1917). Family life and alcoholism. *Proceedings of the National Conference of Social Work*, *44*, 491–494.

Wright, C. I., & Fish, L. S. (1997). Feminist family therapy. The battle against subtle sexism. *Contemporary Family Therapy*, *29*, 341–350.

Young, I. (1981). Beyond the unhappy marriage: A critique of the dual systems theory. In L. Sargent (Ed.), *Women and revolution: A discussion of the unhappy marriage of Marxism and feminism* (pp. 43–70). Boston: South End Press.

Zaytoun, K. (2006). Theorizing at the borders: Considering social location in rethinking self and psychological development. *NWSA Journal*, *18*(2), 52–72.

Section D
Postmodern Theories

CHAPTER 15

Narrative Therapies

Rudy Buckman, Delane Kinney, and Ann Reese

What better way to start a chapter on narrative therapies than to recount a good story. This story is about three old umpires sitting around talking baseball when they are asked how they made their calls. The first umpire, naively possessing great faith in objectivity and his ability to perceive reality as it is, states, "I calls 'em as they are!" The second umpire, well aware of the difficulties of objectivity and the vagaries of perception, states, "I calls 'em as I sees 'em." The third umpire, believing that reality is socially constructed through language, states, "Until I calls 'em, they ain't."

Hopefully, this story provides a simple example of the difficulty in knowing what we know. The first umpire, believing in objectivity, claims to perceive realty as it is. The second umpire, while recognizing that perceptual errors can make objectivity difficult, believes that perceptual errors can be corrected and reality known with a high probability of accuracy. Together, the first two umpires represent the philosophical assumptions of modernism and its faith in the efficacy of the scientific method to cleanse or correct human observation, so that a universal/singular reality or truth can be revealed. In contrast, the third umpire represents a postmodern perspective; a perspective that emphasizes that reality is socially constructed (i.e., constructed among groups of human beings) through a system of signs (language).

Narrative therapies (collaborative language systems and narrative deconstruction), influenced by postmodernism, emphasize the social construction of knowledge and the power of language to construct multiple realities through language (social constructionism). Consequently, this chapter will explore the philosophical assumptions and therapeutic implications of both modernism and postmodernism. This exploration, while drawing contrasts between the two, is not intended as a dismissal

369

of modernism or as a modernism versus postmodernism battle with a winner and a loser. Aware of the dangers of constructing these types of linguistic battles, Watzlawick (1984) warned, "The reality thus constructed reverberates from the violent clash of these opposites. No matter how long and how furious the struggle has been raging, neither side seems capable of gaining the upper hand" (p. 169). Therefore, the authors advocate a both/and approach of embracing multiple perspectives, which allows one to both appreciate modernism as a partial approach to knowledge (Hoshmand & Polkinghorne, 1992) and avoid the hegemony of one perspective over another.

Although "narrative therapy" has come to be identified with the therapeutic approach of White and Epston (1990), we also consider the collaborative language systems (CLS) therapy of Anderson and Goolishian (1988, 1992) to be a co-emerging branch of narrative therapy (Neimeyer, 1995; Smith & Nylund, 1997). Both have been influenced by the philosophical assumptions of postmodernism and have similarities in their therapeutic approach; however, there are important differences between the two. Recognizing the influence of hermeneutics (Gadamer, 1975; Heidegger, 1926/1962) on CLS and the influence of deconstruction (Derrida, 1981; Foucault, 1979, 1980) on White and Epston's therapeutic approach, Neimeyer (1995) referred to CLS as a therapy of conversational elaboration and to White and Epston's (1990) approach as a therapy of narrative deconstruction. Continuing this dialogue of differences, Monk (2003) described CLS therapists as conversational partners and narrative deconstruction therapists as sociopolitical activists. Finding these distinctions helpful, we will not only discuss their similarities but also their differences throughout the chapter.

OVERVIEW OF NARRATIVE THEORIES

Modernist approaches typically emphasize assessment, diagnosis, treatment, and prognosis of human problems from the perspective of the therapist. Because the perspective of the therapist is based upon knowledge that has been scientifically cleansed of subjectivity and has received the official stamp of validity by the professional community, it is considered superior to the client's perspective (Varela, 1979).

In privileging the therapist's knowledge and perspective over the client's knowledge and perspective, a hierarchy of power is created. The therapist, sitting at the apex of this hierarchy of power/knowledge, may be seduced into adopting a detached "gaze." Similar to a scientist identifying and categorizing an organism through a microscope, a detached "gaze" tends to view other human beings and their problems as specimens to be identified and categorized. In describing this superior detached "gaze," Griffith and Griffith (1994) wrote, "The neuropsychiatrist meets the patient with an objectifying gaze, in the style of an internist with a patient on an examining table," and, "the psychoanalyst meets the patient with a studied gaze like a wise elder who has learned over the years the hidden secrets of life" (pp. 22–23). Once the problem is diagnosed, modernist approaches to therapy usually require the therapist to act upon or treat the underlying damage or problem (White & Epston, 1990).

Narrative approaches challenge this hierarchy of power/knowledge, which empowers professionals to marginalize others' descriptions by imposing their allegedly objective knowledge. Narrative therapists attempt to flatten the hierarchy by positioning themselves more as co-travelers or conversational partners who are willing to learn from others. Rather than diagnostic categories that measure deviance from scientifically derived norms of behavior, narrative therapists view problems as being socially constructed via language. As Efran and Fauber (1995) explained,

> Problems are not just sets of circumstances, as objectivists would have everyone believe. They are appraisals—in words and symbols—of what should and should not be, what might or might not happen, what is fair or unfair, lucky or unlucky, malleable or fixed. (p. 279)

As these words and symbols are woven into stories, there exists the possibility of making meaning from life experiences that are helpful or problematic. Problematic stories about self, others, life, and so forth, entrap the person in a journey filled with emotional pain and difficult relationships. Like a cyberspace nightmare that has no off switch, problem-saturated stories entrap people within a linguistic virtual reality that blinds them to stories of their competence, strength, and ability to cope. Bruner (as cited in Held, 1995) captured this idea well when he wrote, "With repetition, stories harden into reality, sometimes trapping the storytellers within the boundaries that the storytellers themselves have helped to create" (p. 108). Consequently, therapy from a narrative perspective emphasizes an elaboration of constraining monologues to liberating dialogues and/or the deconstruction or rewriting of problem-saturated stories to stories of courage, strength, and competence.

Collaborative Language Systems Therapy

Anderson and Goolishian (1988) described CLS or conversational elaboration as the process of creating a safe space in which people can "participate in a conversation that continually loosens up, rather than constricts and closes down" (p. 381). This is facilitated by a therapist posture that emphasizes collaboration, openness, and curiosity (not knowing). CLS therapists are not intentionally trying to rewrite stories or externalize problems as narrative deconstruction therapists might; however, they do value elaborating dialogues from stuck monologues to more liberating dialogues. Questions from a position of curiosity, which invite the client to entertain a variety of perspectives, assist in this conversational elaboration. This conversational elaboration from the said or known to the unsaid or unknown provides "the development, through dialogue, of new themes and narratives and, actually, the creation of new histories" (Anderson & Goolishian, 1988, p. 380).

Narrative Deconstruction Therapy

Narrative deconstruction emphasizes deconstruction and power in therapy. White (1991) defined deconstruction as

> procedures that subvert taken-for-granted realities and practices; those so-called "truths" that are split off from the conditions and the context of their production, those disembodied ways of speaking that hide their biases and prejudices, and those familiar practices of self and of relationships that are subjugating of person's lives. (p. 27)

These practices include questions that invite clients to consider how certain narratives shape their lives, questions that invite clients to examine times when they were able to refuse living by problem-saturated narratives, and separating the problem from the person (externalizing). Modernist theories typically place pathology "inside" clients, which White and Epston (1990) considered to be a potentially harmful cultural tradition. Externalizing is a countercultural practice that protests this tradition and is a way to invite clients to deconstruct and reauthor problem-saturated stories into stories of competence and courage.

HISTORICAL DEVELOPMENTS AND PHILOSOPHICAL ASSUMPTIONS OF THE POSTMODERN PERSPECTIVE

Postmodernism, as its name implies, developed after and in response to the philosophical assumptions of modernism. Modernism, influenced by Descartes' (1968) separation of subject/object, mind/body, and epistemology/ontology, constructs the view that a singular mechanistic world of objects (including humans) can be objectively analyzed and universal principles/laws of cause-effect established. By separating subject from object, Descartes created two independent realms of existence; however, this disunion means subjects can neither analyze nor know objects. To bridge this disunion, he created a disembodied mind (i.e., a nonphysical mind uncontaminated by the body's subjectivity) that is capable of objectively analyzing the realm of objects (nature). Consequently, knowledge and language are believed to accurately reflect or correspond to nature as it is (Rorty, 1979). Any distortions in the reflection of the mind's mirror or logical inconsistencies of language are thought to be correctable through the empirical methods of science. Once corrected, scientific knowledge deservedly takes its place at the apex of the knowledge hierarchy, where it becomes the standard against which all other knowledge is measured. Descartes (as cited in Robbins, 2005), in describing the purpose of his scientific method, wrote that scientists could make themselves "the masters and possessors of nature" (p. 115). As the masters and possessors of nature, humans are conceptualized as discrete beings, separated from community and nature; essentially aliens who analyze nature from a distance.

In becoming bewitched by Descartes' image of the objective study of and mastery over nature (Shotter, 2005), modernism made numerous philosophical assumptions about the nature of mind, reality, and knowledge (Slife, 1993). Specifically, the assumptions of modernism maintain that (a) Reality exists independent of an observer; (b) immaculate perception or objectivity is possible; any error in the objective reflection of reality is cleansed from data by the self-correcting process of science; (c) the resulting scientific truth is universal and more legitimate than knowledge not subjected to this cleansing process; (d) universal laws of human behavior enable one to understand, predict, and control all humans regardless of culture or historical time; and (e) those who possess this scientific knowledge have a role of expert in society (Cushman, 1990; Gergen, 1991; Hoshmand & Polkinghorne, 1992; Toulmin, 1990).

During the second half of the 20th century, modernism's optimistic agenda of human progress through an accumulation of objective data about the natural world was eroded by several postmodern critiques. These critiques focused on objectivity, the relationship of power and knowledge, and the appropriateness of using the scientific method to study humans. Early critiques by linguistic philosophy (Heidegger, 1926/1962; Rorty, 1979; Wittgenstein, 1927/1953) and poststructural literary theory (Derrida, 1981; Foucault, 1979, 1980; Gadamer, 1975) focused on modernism's ideology of objectivity. In contrast to modernism, both of these critiques emphasize that because subjects and objects are inextricably linked, knowledge is a construction imposed on reality by the subject. Therefore, neither knowledge nor language captures the essence of and accurately reflects reality. Instead, critiques of modernism argue that we exist and live our lives within linguistic maps of socially constructed symbols and meaning. In other words, just as a map only symbolizes a territory, one should not mistake a socially constructed map for reality.

Although language does not mirror or reflect reality as it is, it does provide a system of signs or maps for making meaning of our experiences. Wittgenstein (1927/1953) referred to these maps as "language games," which are developed within a social context. Consequently, language is useful for sharing meaning within the social context of our lives; however, what is communicated? For example, can one interpret the "real" meaning of words or does meaning depend upon the interpretive "language games" of the culture? For example, Gergen (1991) wrote,

> Her boss approached her with a steady gaze and ready smile. How is the reader to interpret the line? What is the author's intent? For a teenager subcommunity obsessed with romance, the "steady gaze" and "ready smile" are obvious signals of a budding love affair, so clearly the author intends to write about love. In contrast, a business executive might assume the author was describing a popular managerial style. If the reader were a feminist, however, the "steady gaze" and "ready smile" might reveal the nuances of sexual harassment. And for a Marxist, the author might be describing the seductive exploitation of the working class. In effect, each reader incorporates the author into his or her own perspective. (pp. 104–105)

Gergen's example illustrates the difficulty of determining the "true" meaning of a text (words or actions) and how meaning is constructed according to the perspective of particular groups (teens, executives, feminists, Marxists). However, how does a perspective gain an allegiance or acceptance over other perspectives? Who decides which perspective is the most "real" or "accurate"?

In attempting to answer these questions, Derrida (1981) examined how power and knowledge are interrelated. He was interested in how certain perspectives gain allegiance and acceptance as more "true" or "accurate," while others are excluded or marginalized. For example, in patriarchic societies the male perspective is privileged and the female perspective is marginalized (Hare-Mustin & Marecek, 1990). Privileging the male perspective is based on men's greater social power and influence over language, which is rooted in a history of having privileged access to education and positions of authority in social institutions. Consequently, as Hare-Mustin and Marecek (1990) pointed out, "The arbiters of language usage are primarily men, from Samuel Johnson and Noah Webster to H. L. Mencken and Strunk and White" (p. 26).

Foucault (1979, 1980), a major influence on the narrative therapy of White and Epston (1990), also examined how power influences which knowledge is privileged and which is marginalized. He considered power and knowledge to be inseparable, expressing this by placing the terms together as *power/knowledge.* In doing this, Foucault was drawing attention to the power of this "true" knowledge to constitute or shape our lives and the fact that we all are operating within this sociopolitical field of *power/knowledge.* He was particularly concerned with hierarchies of knowledge that place objective reality discourses (modernism) above alternative discourses.

Another historical influence on narrative therapy, especially collaborative language systems, has been the work of Heidegger (1926/1962), who proposed that hermeneutics, rather than science, is the appropriate method for studying human action. Hermeneutics comes from the Greek term *Hermeneutikos,* meaning interpretation, and is a field of study that focuses on the social generation of meanings (Neimeyer & Mahoney, 1995). In studying human actions, hermeneutics attempts to do so as free as possible from prior theoretical assumptions and studies human action as though it has a semantic and "textual" structure. Heidegger (1926/1962) described this mode of engaging the world as ready-to-hand.

In the ready-to-hand mode of engagement, our immediate experience of the world is studied—our relationships to practical everyday projects, to others, and to our pasts and futures. These relationships are characterized by a belief that we are simultaneously both the knower and the known. Like shaking your own hand, one is simultaneously the subject and the object, the narrator and the narrated. This mode of engagement is thought to provide the most direct access to human phenomena and is Heidegger's way of describing human beings (Packer, 1985). In contrast, the present-at-hand mode of engagement describes methods of inquiry based on the detachment of self from the ongoing practical activity in the world. In detaching ourselves from the world, the world becomes an object of study—something that requires a more general or abstract method of analysis such as that proposed by modernism. Heidegger (1926/1962) objected to this separation of subject-object, which he believed forms the foundation to Western philosophy and science and legitimizes the belief that humans can describe the world from a godlike position outside creation.

CENTRAL THEORETICAL CONSTRUCTS

Freedman and Combs (1996) distill the essential ideas of narrative theory down to four constructs: (a) Realities are socially constructed, (b) language constructs realities, (c) realities are organized and maintained through narrative, and (d) there are no essential truths.

Realities Are Socially Constructed

A social constructionist approach assumes that all knowledge is created in community through discourse. Simply put, we develop our self-image and our view of others through the particular context of our relationships. Certainly that belief is similar to many other prevailing notions in psychotherapy; however, the narrative metaphor takes the idea of social construction of meaning as the springboard of therapeutic practice. If ideas, perceptions, and beliefs that support problems are constructed, that means they are malleable. We may not be able to change the events of history, but we can change the interpretation or meanings associated with events.

Language Constructs Realities

Creatively using language, discourse, or conversation is the art of both branches of narrative therapy. In the narrative deconstruction approach, emphasis is placed on deconstructing problematic or oppressive meanings so that new, more empowering stories can emerge.

For example, in the treatment of individuals who have experienced sexual abuse, clinicians often see people who present with life stories and self-views that are filled with shame, guilt, and secrecy. Because all sexually abused people do not develop these problematic stories, therapists recognize the importance of meanings and how these are storied within the client's context. Largely it is the relationship context of the abuse that creates problematic stories. If a child is abused and the important people in that child's life blame, ignore, or otherwise respond in a nonsupportive way, it is likely that the child will develop subsequent problems. On the other hand, if children are immediately supported by their relational contexts, it is quite possible that no problems will develop. In fact, it is even possible that a child could emerge from such a trauma with an enhanced sense of self; that is, as a person who had the strength to tell the truth within a caring, protective support system.

In the conversational elaboration approach, the basic premise is that human systems are language-generating and meaning-generating systems. As such, communication is seen as defining rather than as being a product of sociocultural systems. The therapeutic system itself is seen as a linguistic system that has become organized around a "problem." Because the problem is socially created in language, it is also resolved in language. "The therapeutic system is a problem-organizing, problem-dis-solving system" (Anderson & Goolishian, 1988, p. 372). Therapy, then, is a conversational elaboration where new ideas emerge and new meanings are generated. Both branches of narrative rely heavily on the conversational artistry of the therapist; however, CLS allows for more drift in the conversation in order to make a wide path for new possibilities. Although neither CLS nor narrative deconstruction views language as neutral, narrative deconstruction is much more concerned with the sociopolitical foundations and consequences of language.

Realities Are Organized and Maintained Through Narratives

We are born into cultural, contextual stories, and we take on personal stories through our lived experience. Therefore, new and preferred stories of self must extend beyond the therapy hour by being lived and circulated within the client's community. In subscribing to this view, Epston and White are interested in bringing forth the stories of unique outcomes into a relational context. White (1995) said, "If stories that we have about lives are negotiated and distributed within communities of persons, then it makes a great deal of sense to engage communities of persons in the re-negotiation of identity" (p. 26). Questions such as "Who from your past would not be surprised to know that you have overcome this difficulty?" or "What difference do you think this accomplishment will make in the eyes of your classmates?" or "If your (deceased) mother were here now, what qualities in you do you think she would recognize that helped you overcome your fears?" assist in broadening and strengthening successes by moving them into a social rather than intrapsychic realm. Client victories can be reinforced by literally including family, friends, and colleagues in the conversation.

There Are No Essential Truths

Being born at a certain time as male/female; within a particular region, family, socioeconomic level; and learning a particular language, religion, cultural values, and so on, shapes one's meanings and stories. Consequently, meanings and stories are not neutral, and the narrative work of Epston and White does not assume that one story/meaning is as good as another. They are not moral relativists and in fact are quite concerned about the real effects of these meanings. White (1995) said that "any constructionist position . . . [cannot] escape a confrontation with questions of values and personal ethics" (p. 14). What is valued and privileged are culture, gender, and class specific. Whatever is privileged in the dominant culture, and whatever sexism, classism, racism, and heterosexism exists in the culture, shapes our language. Because therapists, like fish, live in the waters of their culture, they are often inducted into therapeutic practices that inadvertently collude with oppressive cultural practices. White (1995) said,

> There has been a general challenge to some of the practices of power that have incited persons to measure their lives, relationships, families, and so on, against some notion of how they should be, and some challenges over the extent to which therapists have gone about trying to fashion persons and relationships to fit with the 'ideal' frames that support these notions. (p. 19)

CLS therapy, however, is not necessarily concerned with dismantling oppressive social structures that promote problems nor is it so energetically directed at competency or empowerment. CLS certainly rests on the same foundation, which recognizes that language constructs knowledge, and knowledge is power, but it is relatively apolitical.

PHASES OF HELPING

Conversational Artistry: Guiding Practices

Many therapies that have been influenced by the theory of modernism are often described in terms of having a beginning, middle, and end of the therapeutic process. Typically, from this perspective, the stages of engagement, assessment, treatment, evaluation, and termination are emphasized. From a postmodern perspective, however, narrative therapists are more interested in an ongoing collaborative conversational process of learning about clients' stories than interpreting, intervening, or imposing therapists' views or theories on them. The therapeutic process initially begins with the first telephone contact from the client, and the process of collaborating with and learning about the client continues throughout therapy. The sessions, therefore, may appear similar with little distinction between beginning, middle, and end of therapy. "They move from part to whole to part again, thus remaining within the circle. In this process, new meaning emerges for both therapist and client" (Anderson & Goolishian, 1992, p. 30). Therefore, narrative therapies de-emphasize making distinctions between stages of therapy and, with their emphasis on therapy as a collaborative process, philosophically disagree with intervention as a scientific prescription. Despite these concerns, the following sections will discuss how narrative therapies might generally fit into traditional phases of helping schema and how narrative deconstruction and CLS differ in their approaches to intervention.

Engagement

The Initial Phone Call

Therapy begins before the client enters the therapist's office. Usually much thought has been given to the idea of therapy, and significant others may have influenced the client's decision to consider counseling. So, when a narrative therapist receives an initial phone call from a new client, it is important to remember that the therapeutic conversation has begun; it is an opportunity to begin understanding preexisting stories. Learning how the client decided to seek counseling, who (if anyone) influenced the decision, and generally what are the client's concerns are important questions to consider during the first call. This early collaboration is helpful in sorting out who should attend the sessions, what the focus should be, and when therapy will end.

The Initial Meeting

Creating a respectful (nonjudgmental) and safe place that invites open conversation, reflection, and understanding is essential in beginning (and throughout) the process of therapy. A therapeutic context is based upon an awareness and spirit of "how we are with people, what we ask, how we ask it, how our bodies are when we ask, the physical space in which we ask, the spirit with which we ask, and the form of the actual questions asked—all these invite some response and discourage others" (Roth, 1998, p. 1). What we say and how we say it must be genuine, and we must maintain an awareness that we can participate in creating new options or we can do harm. Constant awareness of the effect we are having is crucial in setting a scene that promotes opening space as opposed to closing space.

Much significance is placed on taking the therapeutic process slowly toward a co-understanding of the client's view. The therapist listens carefully and respectfully and never understands too quickly, as this could limit conversational elaboration. There is great respectfulness for clients, their pace, their use of language, and the meaning given to the words/stories. Also, "the therapist keeps inquiry within the parameters of the problems as described by the clients" (Anderson & Goolishian, 1988, p. 382). Expertise is in conversation and opening space toward new possibilities.

In the initial meeting, central themes are established and discussed. These themes are woven throughout the therapy so the entire process should feel connected. Some useful questions to help establish central themes and focus are (a) What is the concern that brings you here? (b) How is it affecting you and others? (c) What has been helpful with this situation? (d) What has not been helpful? (e) How long has it been a concern? (f) What are your ideas about how the difficulties began? and (g) How do you hope the situation changes?

Multiple Helpers: Getting Others on the Treatment Team

Many clients are involved in multiple systems: their families, friends, colleagues, neighbors, agency representatives, church members, organizations, and so forth. Consequently, from the beginning we are interested in learning about what systems are involved and who are the people in conversation about the problem or difficulty. Those who are in language about the situation/problem are members of the "problem-determined system" (Anderson, Goolishian, & Winderman, 1986), as are the client and therapist. Often, if mutually agreed upon, these members are invited into the therapeutic process (i.e., the therapy room, telephone conversations, or meetings at home/office/agency of others).

It is helpful to remember that all involved have useful information and strengths and we assume they are doing their best for the client: "Given the context from which they view the problem, neither the family nor the helping agents have to be thought of as wrong, crazy, or unhelpful" (Levin, Raser, Niles, & Reese, 1986, p. 64). Narrative therapists are curious about what others believe the problem is, their ideas about what may be making the situation better or worse, what solutions have been attempted and by whom, the degree to which the attempted solutions were useful, who is most concerned, and where and when the situation improves.

It is important to be aware of whether there is a referring agency or person involved (e.g., child protective services, court, or church). The agency often holds more power than the client and may have specific goals for treatment. For example, if a child protective service has custody of a client's children and the client hopes for their return, it is critical that the therapist and client include the referring person in the process. Again, this decision is always made in collaboration with the client. Through conversation an understanding develops as to what the agency and the client hope is accomplished in therapy. Omitting this important person could unintentionally do harm.

Data Collection and Assessment: Ongoing Conversations

Often traditional therapies focus on completing extensive information gathering, assessments, individual histories, social studies, scales, and genograms. Many therapists, in this process, are encouraged to seek the "truth" about the situation or uncover clues concerning the origin of the problem, and the pathology within the client. These static or convergent assessments and diagnosing tools are used to make and confirm a diagnosis and design a therapeutic plan utilizing appropriate interventions. While narrative therapists do find some of this information useful, they are generally more interested in an interactional relationship where the therapist and client together develop an understanding of the situation, how it is of concern, and how the client hopes the situation will change.

As narrative therapists we are in the position of being learners about the lives of our clients. They teach us about themselves—their concerns and hopes. Together, the narrative therapist and client define the problem to be addressed. We learn about our clients and their concerns through a process of recursive or divergent assessment where our questions are designed to generate new meaning, open space, and highlight change. These recursive assessment questions and the themes that have been generated in the conversation between client and therapist recur from session to session.

Planning/Contracting and Intervention: An Overview

Narrative therapy is about conversation, dialogue, and mutually rewritten stories. It is not about intervening on people. *Interventions* and *strategies* are terms that imply power and private knowledge held by the therapist, to be imposed on the client. The postmodern perspective, having shifted from scientific explanations and prescriptions to collaborative public conversation, suggests we not be expert technicians who design interventions to cure people:

> Therapy is now being seen as conversation, not as intervention. The focus of therapy is increasingly on the storied basis of human life and the social construction of meaning. Within these parameters the expertise of the therapist is no longer that of the skilled technician powerfully intervening in the family feedback system. (Goolishian & Anderson, 1992, p. 13)

Therapy is not done to the client but with the client.

Some questions toward cocreating a therapeutic focus might be (a) What do you hope to accomplish by coming to therapy? (b) How would you know if you got what you came here for? (c) What would that accomplishment look like in your life, to you, to others? and (d) If the process were successful how would I know or what might I see?

Questions are the hallmark of both narrative approaches: deconstruction narrative and conversational elaboration. Neither approach is interventionist, but both emphasize skill in the use of questions in therapy. Although we are not experts on our clients' lives, we do have expertise in the use of questions and guiding the process.

> The therapeutic or conversational question is the primary tool that the therapist uses to express this expertise. It is the means through which the therapist remains on the road to understanding. Therapeutic questions always stem from a need to know more about what has just been said. (Anderson & Goolishian, 1992, p. 32)

Countless possibilities are born from questions, offering opportunities for new narratives to be created between therapist and client. The goal of questioning is not to interrogate or gather information toward diagnosis.

Intervention: Narrative Deconstruction Therapy

White and Epston (1990) indicate that people usually enter therapy dominated by "problem-saturated stories." Consequently, clients believe that the problem captures their identity ("I am manic-depressive" or "She is enuretic"). These problem-saturated stories blind clients to times when they were able to influence the problem. White and Epston (1990) describe the deconstruction of problem-saturated stories and the "bringing forth" of more empowering narratives as externalizing conversations. According to Paré and Lysack (2004), "Externalizing can be understood as a speech genre which furnishes a scaffolding for constructing meaning, and . . . this practice promotes a move from monologue to dialogue in relation to problem existence" (p. 6). The process of externalizing is characterized by relative influence questioning that (a) maps the influence of the problem on a person's life, (b) maps the influence of the person on the life of the problem, and (c) objectifies or personifies the problem.

Mapping the Influence of the Problem on the Person

This process begins with questions that bring forth the oppressive internalized views of self such as "How did the abuse talk you into seeing yourself as a bad person?" One would also map the influence of the problem in various arenas of a person's life. For example, the therapist might ask such questions as "How does the temper affect your relationship with your wife?" "In what way does shame influence your relationship with God?" and "How does disrespect shape your teacher's view of you?" Thus, by developing an understanding of how problems influence important aspects of the client's life (e.g., relationship with self, God, lover, friend, family, work, future), the therapist develops a broader understanding of how a problem shapes a person's life.

Unique Outcomes: Mapping the Influence of the Person on the Problem

This phase of questioning focuses on bringing forth times or experiences in which the client was able to influence the problem. Because the dominant or problem-saturated story is an account of how the problem influences the client's life, these questions highlight the client's ability to face and alter the problem's influence on his or her life. Because "life is multi-storied, not single-storied" (White, 1995, p. 27), the therapist's task is to bring forth stories that re-author a person's life. These stories of strength, small victories, and accomplishments, which have gone unnoticed, are called "unique outcomes." Examples of unique outcome questions might be "How were you able to overcome the fears and join into the conversation?" "How did you not give in to temptation when everyone else at the party was drinking?" and "What did you do to keep the temper from getting the best of you when your boss was yelling at you?" Such questions highlight times when a client exercises personal agency and is not completely controlled by the problem. As clients recognize stories and claim responsibility for these unique outcomes, they tend to feel more empowered.

Externalizing Problems and Internalizing Responsibility

Michael White (1984), in his now familiar paper describing the treatment of pseudo-encopresis or "Sneaky Poo," was the first to use externalization. Influenced by Foucault's (1979, 1980) critique of modernism, White and Epston (1990) challenged modernism's "truth" that the site of pathology is a person who can be diagnosed and categorized according to accepted norms. They defined externalization as

> an approach that encourages persons to objectify and, at times, personify the problem that they experience as oppressive. In this process, the problem becomes a separate entity and thus external to the person or relationship that was ascribed the problem. Those problems that are considered to be inherent, as well as those relatively fixed qualities that are attributed to persons and to relationship, are rendered less fixed and less restricting. (p. 38)

In separating the problem from the person, they constructed an alternative discursive option; the person is not the problem, the problem is the problem. This discursive option encourages clients to separate their own identities from the problem (i.e., from being the problem to facing the problem), which reduces the power of the problem to immobilize clients with feelings of self-blame and shame. As clients are freed from these painful emotions, they become mobilized to face the problem. In facing the problem, clients are encouraged to explore the many ways they inadvertently provide "life support" to the problem, including thoughts, feelings, and behaviors that were intended to solve the problem but in actuality keep the problem alive. Gradually, as clients develop an understanding of how they inadvertently contribute to keeping problems alive, they also experiment with ways of removing "life support" from the problem. Consequently, as clients learn and practice these important lessons, they assume and internalize more responsibility for their own lives (Tomm, 1989).

Consistent with Foucault's (1979, 1980) critique, externalization privileged the oppression/liberation metaphor (Durrant, 1989; White, 1984, 1988; White & Epston, 1990). Typically, this metaphor constructs a discourse in which the problem is personified as an oppressive character who dominates the lives of clients. The goal of therapy is for clients to resist being dominated by the problem and to liberate their lives from the problem's oppression. For example, White (1984) externalized a child's encopresis and renamed the problem "Sneaky Poo," a sneaky character who was skilled in dominating the lives of both the child and his family. Eventually, this different way of talking about the problem enabled the child and his family to liberate their lives from the domination of this sneaky, dirty character.

The oppression/liberation metaphor, while widespread and useful, also has inherent dangers and limitations (Freeman, Epston, & Lobovits, 1997; Freeman & Lobovits, 1993; Paré & Lysack, 2004; Roth & Epston, 1996; Stacy, 1997; Tomm, 1993; Wagner, McGovern, & Buckman, 2003). First, this metaphor promoted an adversarial posture toward problems. In doing so, it emphasized a patriarchic and culturally bound view that problem-solving is a matter of having power over problems. Second, having only one discursive option (oppression/liberation) inherently constrains the therapist to one taken-for-granted "truth"; once constrained, the therapist may inadvertently become monologic and unresponsive to the client's preferred descriptions and meanings (Paré & Lysack, 2004). Third, the idea that problems are to be resisted is not culturally resonant worldwide. Tomm, Suzuki, and Suzuki (1990) noted this limitation of the oppression/liberation metaphor when they described how some cultures (e.g., Japanese culture) emphasize compromise and peaceful coexistence with problems. Others (Freeman et al., 1997) who are critical of adversarial metaphors have proposed metaphors that emphasize "power in relation to the problem" (p. 67); clients use their power to change their relationship to the problem.

In developing these alternative metaphors that are sensitive to both the clients' preferred descriptions and their cultures, these therapists are trying to create a dialogic space that is relationally responsive (Shotter, 2000, 2005). This represents a way of being responsive to both the client's preferred meanings and the therapist's expertise in bringing forth something new in the conversation. Rather than warring against problems, they prefer following Maturana's path of loving by "opening oneself to the existence of the other" (Freedman & Combs, 1996, p. 271).

In this spirit, Wagner et al. (2003) presented additional discursive options that emphasized becoming open to the externalized other. For example, problems might be thought of as helpers/guides or as passports to creativity, spirituality, or humor. These discursive options are developed through such questions as "In your spiritual tradition, what ideas support the notion that problems might help your spiritual development?" and "What angel, silver lining, or lesson do you believe is hidden in this problem?" In conclusion, Freedman and Combs (1996) wisely cautioned therapists to think of externalization as an "attitude." They say that "when people approach externalization as a technique or linguistic trick, it can come off as shallow, forced, and not especially helpful" (p. 47).

Intervention in CLS Therapy

Not Knowing and Curiosity

The cornerstone of CLS is the stance of not knowing (Anderson & Goolishian, 1992). Anderson and Goolishian (1992) explained that the not-knowing position is vital to facilitating the elaboration of dialogue. However, labeling this stance "not knowing" inadvertently created an unproductive debate that was characterized by an either-or construction of knowing versus not knowing. As Watzlawick (1984) warned, this either-or construction resulted in a violent clash of opposites and overshadowed Anderson and Goolishian's explanations of the not-knowing stance. In this clash of knowing versus not knowing, knowing becomes defined as the therapist's theoretical preunderstanding (e.g., psychological theories, *DSM–IV*), which is imposed upon the client's experiences. Consequently, the knowing stance undermines collaboration and curiosity, while also entitling the therapist to unilaterally guide the therapy.

Unfortunately, in this either-or construction, not knowing becomes the extinction of self through having no knowledge or by being neutral. Because the not knowing stance privileges the client's knowledge over the therapist's and entitles the client to guide therapy, collaboration and curiosity are again undermined. Hopefully, our description of self-reflexivity, which emphasizes the interrelationship of knowing and not knowing (both-and), will enable a new dialogue that does not inherently lead to a clash of opposites (knowing vs. not knowing).

A Reflexive Stance/Self-Reflective Habits of Mind

Gadamer (1975), in describing the hermeneutically trained mind, stressed the importance of being sensitive to a text's quality of newness by consciously assimilating one's own biases. The both-and stance of self-reflexivity (knowing and not knowing) recognizes that it is impossible to become a blank slate or neutral within any situation. Each person has a vast amount of knowledge shaped by educational background, gender, ethnic group, race, socioeconomic status, religion, and so on, that affects how one makes meaning and constructs a reality. CLS therapists, mindful of self-reflexivity, recognize that being unaware of preunderstandings can entrap one within a self-fulfilling prophecy, leading to certainty and arrogance. However, by being aware that knowledge or preunderstandings shape one's constructions of reality, the therapist is more able to invite alternative or more useful meanings. In doing so, the self-reflexive therapist is less likely to constrict the ongoing conversation and more likely to nurture an attitude of curiosity and openness to knowing more about the client's story.

Therapists with this attitude of curiosity and openness express themselves through questions and listening "in such a way that their pre-experience does not close them to the full meaning of the client's descriptions of their experiences" (Anderson & Goolishian, 1992, p. 30). Through questions and listening in this way, the client is invited to participate in a conversation characterized by collaboration, curiosity, and respect.

Anderson and Goolishian (1992) have described the spirit of a therapeutic conversation:

> A therapeutic conversation is no more than a slowly evolving and detailed, concrete, individual life story stimulated by the therapist's position of not knowing [self-reflexivity] and the therapist's curiosity to learn. It is this curiosity and not knowing [self-reflexivity] that opens conversational space and thus increases the potential of the narrative development of new agency and personal freedom. (p. 38)

Just as narrative therapists engage in externalizing conversations to create space where clients can "adopt a reflexive stance and exercise enhanced choices for action" (Paré & Lysack, 2004, p. 7), narrative therapists must also engage in practices that assist their own self-reflexivity. As Hoshmand and Polkinghorne (1992) pointed out, "Approaches aimed at the development of reflective habits of mind should be central to our professional training. Professional wisdom should include the ability to evaluate and critique one's own understanding and actions" (p. 62). Narrative therapists' ability to look at their own looking and to be aware of the dominant culture's influence on their worldview is integral to their practice. Freedman and Combs (1996) and Roth (1998) have suggested useful questions in promoting self-reflection. To aid the reader in developing reflective habits of mind, the authors offer the following sets of questions:

1. What are my theoretical preunderstandings or assumptions about my role as a therapist? About my client? What effect will

these assumptions have on me and on my client? Are these useful or helpful in our relationship? Are there other views that may be more useful/helpful? Do I value my client's perspective as much as my own?

2. How is my own experience with the dominant culture shaping my views about gender, class, ethnicity, religion, and sexual orientation? What assumptions about gender, ethnicity, sexual orientation, and so forth, are influencing my descriptions of this client or situation? How do I need to change myself to create new possibilities?

3. Does my model promote clinical practices that bring forth my preferred self as well as what I want for my client? How are my client and I working together to assume the direction of therapy? What reality are my questions bringing forth in this relationship? Am I fixed in my view of this person/problem or am I entertaining multiple views?

Evaluation and Termination: No More Complaints or New Preferred Identities

As the late Harry Goolishian often said, therapy ends when clients no longer complain about what originally brought them into therapy. This could mean many things. Possibly the problem has been dissolved and no longer exists, or new ways of viewing the problem have emerged. For example, clients may perceive their responses to the situation differently or view themselves differently and in a more accepting light. Also, others may no longer complain about the situation. There are infinite reasons clients may no longer feel as oppressed by an issue. As the concerns are reduced, the client and therapist together decide whether to continue sessions, end the process, or take a vacation from therapy.

Although the notion of termination is not explicitly described in narrative deconstruction therapy, typically the latter phase of therapy focuses on taking new preferred stories and identities into the client's own communities. The new preferred stories and identities are like a rich tapestry of action and meaning; a tapestry that has been woven from externalizing conversations, scaffolding questions about the landscape of action (e.g., How did you do that?) and about the landscape of consciousness (e.g., What does it say about you that you were able to take this new step?). As clients practice performing these new actions and meanings, they begin to experience less problem domination and more personal agency. To solidify the potential of these gains, Gerhart and Tuttle (2003) suggested that the therapist's task is to help the client "to create supportive input from chosen audience and other witnesses"

(p. 224). This can be done in a variety of ways, including through such activities as inviting supportive friends and family into sessions and through letters and certificates.

APPLICATION TO FAMILY AND GROUP WORK

Narrative approaches, emphasizing the social construction of knowledge, power, language, and multiple realities, are well suited to working with individuals, families, and groups within a variety of therapy contexts. For example, narrative deconstruction approaches have been developed to address specific populations and/or problems including eating disorders (Epston & Maisel, 2000; Madigan, 1996; Maisel, Epston, & Borden, 2004), addiction (Diamond, 2000), children and their families (Buckman, 1997; Buckman & Reese, 1999; Freeman et al., 1997; Smith & Nylund, 1997; White & Morgan, 2006), somatic problems and illnesses (Griffith & Griffith, 1994; Weingarten, 1997), school problems (Winslade & Monk, 1999), couples (Freedman & Coombs, 2002), violent and abusive men (Jenkins, 1990), pediatric psychology (Suberri, 2004), and conflict resolution (Winslade & Monk, 2000).

Likewise, CLS has developed discursive practices suited for various populations and problems, including children (Anderson, 2000; Anderson & Levin, 1997; Raser, 1999), adolescents (Biever, McKenzie, North, & Gonzalez, 1995), couples (Anderson, Carleton, & Swim, 1998), families (Anderson, 2001), schools (Swim, 1995), and sexual abuse (Reichelt, Tjersland, Gulbrandsen, Jensen, & Mossige, 2004; Tschudi & Reichelt, 2004). Of particular note is Seikkula et al.'s (Seikkula, 2002; Seikkula, Alakare, & Aaltonen, 2001a, 2001b; Seikkula & Olson, 2003) highly successful open dialogue treatment developed for working with psychosis.

One example of a group application of narrative approaches is the Teaching Empowerment through Active Means (TEAM) program (Redivo & Buckman, 2004). This group model blends concepts from experiential, social skills and process-oriented group approaches to bring to life stories of competency and resiliency. A unique aspect of this program is its ongoing research component that embraces methodological pluralism, which provides quantitative and qualitative information for continuous program development.

Another example of narrative group work is the Vancouver Anti-anorexia/Anti-bulimia League. Through social action this group externalizes and fights against social messages that support eating disorders; for example, by painting "FEED ME" on billboards of emaciated models. Within group meetings they support and witness each other's success in resisting unrealistic social pressures to stay thin.

Taking a visually creative and unique approach to group work, Wagner (2004, 2006) has produced two videos that can be used with groups. The first one, which can be used with teens, parents, and school counselors, depicts interviews demonstrating how four common problems (stress, peer pressure, anger, and giving up) take over the lives of teens. The second one, which can be used with clients or professionals, depicts the reading of a poem by chronic pain clients and is designed to open viewers to compassion and dialogue about chronic pain.

COMPATIBILITY WITH THE GENERALIST-ECLECTIC FRAMEWORK

Although there are differences, we believe there is a great deal of compatibility between narrative therapy and the generalist-eclectic framework for direct social work practice. The following addresses the compatibility of narrative therapy with selected components of the generalist-eclectic framework.

Use of Problem-Solving Process

Narrative therapy does not conceptualize therapy as a progression through stages of a problem-solving process. Adherence to an abstract professional schema of how therapy should unfold, such as the problem-solving process, would seem to undermine the collaboration between therapist and client. Most narrative therapists are more interested in collaborating with their clients to open space toward a new view of the problem. With this broader view, the client then may feel more able to manage the situation. Rather than "solving" problems in therapy, the process is viewed as "dissolving" problems. When the conversation about the concern or problem ends, the therapeutic relationship also dissolves.

Emphasis on a Good Worker-Client Relationship

Many of the preferred or valued ways of thinking and languaging about the worker-client relationship in narrative approaches to therapy are consistent with those in the generalist-eclectic framework. For example, narrative therapists prefer thinking of themselves as having expertise as "conversational artists," who, through collaboration and respect, open themselves to the uniqueness of another human being. By valuing and respecting the uniqueness, strengths, and competence of each person, a safe place is created that encourages the sharing of multiple perspectives.

Emphasis on Holistic, Multilevel Assessment

Although assessment has a different meaning in narrative therapy than in the generalist-eclectic perspective, there are similarities. Narrative therapists focus on exploring how the client's ever-changing self-stories affect the client's life, which entails a broad exploration of various client life domains. For example, in externalizing discourses we are interested in how a problem affects family relationships, intimate relationships, friendships, work, school, leisure time, spiritual issues, and physical well-being, as well as how it may affect one's view of self. Equally important is assessing how the client and others have prevented the problem from dominating various life domains. Not only do narrative therapists map the effects of the problem in many domains of the client's life but they also seek the views of multiple people in the problem-organized system. Also, particularly in the narrative deconstruction approach, importance is placed on issues of culture, diversity, and oppression. Thus, similar to the generalist-eclectic perspective, narrative therapies seek to develop a broad understanding of client's lives.

Beyond the more specific focus on self-stories, other differences between narrative and generalist-eclectic perspectives are apparent with regard to assessment. In narrative therapy, assessment is viewed as an ongoing, self-reflexive process. Throughout the process of therapy, narrative therapists not only assess changes in their clients' views but also in their own internal dialogues. They question whether their inner conversations generate unhelpful views of clients that lead to a closing of space or helpful views that allow them to open space therapeutically. Also, despite the strengths focus of the generalist-eclectic perspective, narrative approaches place more emphasis on identifying how a problem does not dominate the clients' lives.

Flexible Use of a Variety of Theories and Techniques

In a general sense, narrative therapies share with the generalist-eclectic perspective this emphasis on a flexible use of a variety of theories and techniques. Because postmodernism values multiple perspectives, any attempt toward hegemony of one approach would be distrusted. Although narrative approaches do not endorse an eclectic amalgamation of theories, they are supportive of greater dialogue across arbitrarily constructed knowledge boundaries. Therefore, postmodernism encourages therapists to be "multilingual" and able to discuss issues from a variety of perspectives. By being knowledgeable and fluent in a variety of professional theories and approaches, a narrative therapist may be less likely to become stuck in a less useful viewpoint. In other words, narrative therapists would never "marry" or become devoted to a theory and its techniques. Doing so could seduce therapists into too much certainty and reduce their flexibility and curiosity about the client's theory of the problem.

CRITIQUE

In challenging modernism's hegemony, postmodernism and narrative therapies have had no shortage of critics. Salvador Minuchin (1991), the father of structural family therapy, criticized narrative approaches for emphasizing the social construction of reality. Especially in contexts of poverty and harsh conditions of life, he is concerned that the focus of narrative therapists on narratives would interfere with helping clients cope with the "reality" of social injustices. For example, in describing a woman living in poverty, he made the point that her reality "is not a construct; it is a stubbornly concrete world" (p. 50). He seems to believe that only realists who believe in an objective reality are equipped to help clients cope with "real" problems; however, narrative therapists, well aware of the tendency of narratives to harden into reality, would be just as concerned as Minuchin about helping this woman find and navigate programs that could assist her with food, medical services, housing, and so forth. Narrative therapists would not assume that poverty unilaterally has the power to cause this woman to have an invariant experience that is shared by each and every person who lives in poverty. Efran and Fauber (1995) wrote,

> Thus, there are as many different poverties as there are individuals who consider themselves poor. Even in the meanest of ghettos, it would not take long to find people who are deeply fulfilled, lead meaningful lives, and have a clear vision for their children and for the future. Alternatively, a visit to an affluent community will quickly turn up many lost souls, leading "lives of quiet desperation" amid an overabundance of creature comforts and venture capital. (p. 287)

Barbara Held (1995) also offered a critique of postmodern theory in psychotherapy. While not totally negative about the ascent of postmodern therapies, she criticized therapists for uncritically accepting postmodern ideas and practicing narrative therapies without evidence of their efficacy. She criticized postmodernism and narrative therapies for their "antirealist" perspective that "a theory, construct, or narrative always intervenes, or mediates, between the knower and the known" (p. 7). Consequently, she recommended a modest realism and claimed it is "essential for the scientific or any other rational enterprise, including psychotherapy, that we be capable in many circumstances of attaining a reality that is independent of the knower and the knower's subjectivity" (p. 6). Without this capability, many believe it is impossible to scientifically study psychological disorders as well-defined entities that can be alleviated through standardized treatments.

This is a serious critique in the context of widespread efforts to restrict therapy to techniques that have been empirically supported

(Norcross, 2001) and manualized to ensure they produce replicable results by other therapists (Bryceland & Stam, 2005). Because postmodern therapies do not share the same philosophical assumptions and empirical research methods as modernism, they are in danger of becoming disenfranchised from reimbursement and managed care systems (Busch, Strong, & Lock, 2004). Postmodern researchers and therapists have countered that the empirically supported treatment (EST) movement is too restrictive because it does not allow for (a) methodological pluralism in research, (b) tailoring therapy to the individual rather than diagnostic categories, (c) a focus on contextual factors rather than the individual as site of pathology, or (d) a focus on meanings rather than observable behaviors.

Critics of the EST movement also point out that it ignores 30 years of research indicating that therapies using different techniques are equally effective (Ahn & Wampold, 2001; Luborsky, 2001; Luborsky, McClellan, Diguer, Woody, & Seligman, 1997; Luborsky, Singer, & Luborsky, 1975; Wampold et al., 1997). Furthermore, Lambert and Barley (2001), in a review of therapy outcome research, found that specific therapy techniques accounted for only about 15% of the outcome variance, while relationship and common factors of different therapy approaches accounted for 30%, client qualities and extratherapeutic change accounted for 40%, and expectancy/placebo effect accounted for 15%. Even more challenging to the EST movement are the findings that strict adherence to therapy manuals may actually lead to less favorable outcome results. For example, studies of short-term psychodynamic (Henry, Strupp, Butler, Schacht, & Binder, 1993) and cognitive (Castonguay, Goldfried, Wiser, Raue, & Hayes, 1996) therapies found that therapists who were most conscientious and rigorous in following their treatment manuals were associated with less favorable outcomes and with difficulties in forming and maintaining a therapeutic alliance with clients.

Additionally, postmodern practitioners have been critical of the EST movement's implication that approaches that are not dominated by modernism and objective/empirical research methods are unethical (Bryceland & Stam, 2005). Although practitioners of postmodern therapies believe a therapist should be knowledgeable of outcome studies and empirical research methods, they are concerned that being an informed and competent therapist should not be equated with adherence to a list of empirically supported techniques.

CASE EXAMPLE OF NARRATIVE DECONSTRUCTION

At age 10, Jana kept secret that Jim, a 16-year-old male, coerced her into having sex on several occasions by telling her he would not like her if she refused. Although the secret was painful, his moving away from the neighborhood brought some relief. Later, however, he moved back to the neighborhood and all of her pain and fear returned. Jana revealed the situation to her mother, and her mother notified the police and child protective services (CPS). CPS referred them to our agency.

During an externalizing conversation, Jana, her mother, and we talked about how the abuse and secrets had affected their relationship, Jana's friendships, schoolwork, view of herself, and so forth. The themes of self-hatred and fear kept coming up, and so we asked Jana, "How have you kept fear and self-hatred from completely messing up your life?" and "What or who has helped you in not letting the self-hatred and fear mess up your life?" She told a story about a time she wrote a note to a friend about how "deprest" she felt and the friend wrote back that Jana needed to "heal her brain." As Jana continued the story, she put a hand on each side of her head and stated, "It's like ever since then I've been healing my brain."

Because many children's preferred way of communicating is through their imaginations and play, we often use drawing, singing, sculpting in clay, and role playing to encourage the objectification or personification of problems (Buckman, 1997). We asked Jana to draw a picture of her brain, and she drew a brain divided in two parts. The left side was colored pink and contained an "A," the words "best friends," and "Good job Jana." The right side contained a girl's face and a boy's face, which she indicated was Jim, and vertical black wavy lines surrounding the two. Using this drawing to objectify her problem seemed to allow her to think about and consider her situation from a safer distance. Consequently, she seemed to have an easier time engaging questions such as "How have good friends, good grades, and doing a good job helped heal this side of the brain?" "Do you have to cut this side out (side with her and Jim) to heal this brain or can you grow the healing side enough so it heals the whole brain?" "Are there things you'd like to add to the healing that would help this brain heal even more?" and "Does this side (her and Jim) ever try to convince the healing side that it's your fault?"

This drawing and others, in conjunction with curious questions, created an environment of playful seriousness where multiple viewpoints and alternative meanings could more easily be explored. Gradually, stories of Jana's courage in preventing her whole brain from being destroyed by the abuse and of ways to continue the healing of her brain began to take form. The drawings were also helpful in working with Jana's mother and CPS. Her mother would listen intently as Jana talked about her drawings and how Jana had become vulnerable to Jim's interpersonal coercion. Consequently, her mother was able to drop a great deal of her anger and blame of Jana and adopt a more compassionate/supportive attitude. The drawings and resulting conversations with the CPS worker enabled the worker to use similar language with Jana and her mother; for example, she would discuss "brain healing" and relationship healing with them during home visits.

CASE EXAMPLE OF CONVERSATIONAL ELABORATION

Franky, age 12, was referred for therapy by his teacher, who was concerned because he was distracted in class and he was becoming interested in gangs. The teacher became worried about gang involvement because of the baggy pants Franky wore daily to school. He had been suspended several times for wearing them. Because this was an inner-city school with significant neighborhood gang activity, these concerns were taken seriously. The mother's primary concern was that Franky maintain good grades. She did not share the teacher's view that Franky was in gangs but voiced hope in Franky's education being his ticket out of poverty.

We began slowly in our work with Franky, and he told us about his friends and favorite school subjects. In response to broad questions, he discussed his teacher's concern about gang affiliation. Although he thought this was funny and denied any gang involvement, he was worried about being perceived as "crazy" and being "sent away to a home." After explaining our role was not to send him away, he felt more comfortable talking to us. He agreed that distraction was a difficulty for him in class. He also voiced that his mother thought therapy sessions would improve his grades. Franky wore the baggy pants to the first session and most subsequent meetings.

In the second meeting Franky taught us that besides improving his grades he wanted to ease his mother's and teacher's worries. This opened up space for conversation about how to help his mom and teacher not worry. His primary concern, of which his teacher was unaware, was the sadness he was feeling over the recent death of his father. The majority of dialogue concerned this profound loss, how he was coping, and how he kept his father alive in his life at home and school. From this point on Franky brought photos of his father to sessions and began keeping photos in his notebook. He used them for guidance and would consult his father about how to handle tough situations.

Franky quickly taught us, once he had disclosed his loss, that the primary way of comforting himself was by wearing his father's pants. With this revelation, the baggy pants, symbolizing gang affiliation, suddenly "dis-solved" into the comforting presence of his father. This transformation in meaning allowed everyone in Franky's life to reconsider his or her own views and practices around him. The teacher no longer reprimanded him for wearing the baggy pants, his distractibility and grades improved, his sadness lightened, and his teacher and mother worried less.

A commitment to collaboration, curiosity, respect, and opening space to multiple views enabled us to avoid privileging the teacher's concerns about gangs or the mother's concerns about grades. Limiting therapy to these concerns and our preconceived ideas about gang styles could have limited conversations and closed space. By staying open to different voices we were able to open space and collaborate with Franky. Franky's baggy pants became a reminder to be wary of tightly fitting or constraining ideas.

SUMMARY

In this chapter, we have presented two co-emerging narrative therapies: CLS therapy and narrative deconstruction therapy, both of which have been heavily influenced by postmodernism. Both approaches emphasize that humans, through social linguistic interactions, develop stories about self, others, and life. These stories are problematic when they entrap a person, family, or group to a journey filled with pain and prevent the development of competence and strength to address the challenges of life. Both approaches envision therapy as a process of curiosity, collaboration, and respect. The narrative deconstruction approach emphasizes deconstruction of narratives through the process of externalization and questions that invite clients to examine how stories not only shape their lives but also how they have refused to be dominated by problem-saturated narratives. The narrative deconstruction approach also focuses on the relationship of power/knowledge and the use of power to privilege some perspectives while marginalizing others. CLS therapy, influenced by hermeneutics, emphasizes the "not-knowing" (self-reflexive) posture of the therapist and the development of new stories that are more liberating and supportive of competence and strength. It is our sincere hope that readers will use this chapter to encourage and support their ability to provide respectful, collaborative, and competency-based therapy.

REFERENCES

Ahn, H., & Wampold, B. E. (2001). Where o where are the specific ingredients? A meta-analysis of component studies in counseling and psychotherapy. *Journal of Counseling Psychology, 48,* 251–257.

Anderson, H. (2000). Reflections on collaborating beyond the family system. In C. E. Bailey (Ed.), *Children in therapy: Using the family as a resource* (pp. 46–72). New York: W. W. Norton.

Anderson, H. (2001). Dreams now and then, collaborative language systems: Conversations about a family's struggles. In S. McDaniel, D. D. Lusterman, & C. Philpot (Eds.), *Integrating family therapy casebook* (pp. 111–125). Washington, DC: American Psychological Association.

Anderson, H., Carleton, D., & Swim, S. (1998). A postmodern perspective on relational intimacy: A collaborative conversation and relationship with a couple. In J. Carlson & L. Sperry (Eds.), *The intimate couple* (pp. 186–207). New York: Brunner/Mazel.

Anderson, H., & Goolishian, H. (1988). Human systems as linguistic systems: Preliminary and evolving ideas about the implications for clinical theory. *Family Process, 27,* 371–393.

Anderson, H., & Goolishian, H. (1992). The client is the expert: A not-knowing approach to therapy. In S. McNamee & K. Gergen (Eds.), *Therapy as social construction* (pp. 25–39). Newbury Park, CA: Sage.

Anderson, H., Goolishian, H., & Winderman, L. (1986). Problem-determined systems: Toward transformation in family therapy. *Journal of Strategic and Systemic Therapies, 5,* 1–13.

Anderson, H., & Levin, S. (1997). Collaborative conversations with children: Country clothes and city clothes. In N. Nylund & C. Smith (Eds.), *Narrative therapy with children and adolescents* (pp. 255–281). New York: Guilford Press.

Biever, J. L., McKenzie, K., North, M. W., & Gonzalez, R. C. (1995). Stories and solutions in counseling with adolescents. *Adolescence, 30,* 491–499.

Bryceland, C., & Stam, H. (2005). Empirical validation and professional codes of ethics: Description or prescription? *Journal of Constructivistic Psychology, 18,* 131–155.

Buckman, R. (1997). Using art to externalize and tame tempers. In T. Nelson & T. Trepper (Eds.), *101 interventions in family therapy* (Vol. 2, pp. 436–439). New York: Haworth.

Buckman, R., & Reese, A. (1999). Therapeutic loving: Opening space for children and their families. *Journal of Systemic Therapies, 18*(2), 5–19.

Busch, R., Strong, T., & Lock, A. (2004). *Evaluation and the challenges of evaluating narrative therapy.* Unpublished manuscript.

Castonguay, L. G., Goldfried, M. R., Wiser, S. L., Raue, P. J., & Hayes, A. M. (1996). Predicting the effect of cognitive therapy for depression: A study of unique and common factors. *Journal of Consulting and Clinical Psychology, 64,* 497–504.

Cushman, P. (1990). Why the self is empty: Toward a historically situated psychology. *American Psychologist, 45,* 599–611.

Derrida, J. (1981). *Positions* (A. Bass, Trans.). Chicago: University of Chicago Press.

Descartes, R. (1968). *Discourse on method and other writings* (F. E. Sutcliffe, Trans.). Marmondsworth, England: Penguin.

Diamond, J. (2000). *Narrative means to sober ends: Treating addiction and its aftermath.* New York: Guilford Press.

Durrant, M. (1989, Autumn). Temper taming: An approach to children's temper problems—revisited. *Dulwich Centre Newsletter,* 61–62.

Efran, J., & Fauber, R. (1995). Radical constructivism: Questions and answers. In R. A. Neimeyer & M. J. Mahoney (Eds.), *Constructivism in psychotherapy* (pp. 275–304). Washington, DC: American Psychological Association.

Epston, D., & Maisel, R. (2000). *Archive of resistance: Anti-anorexia/anti-bulimia.* Retrieved April 20, 2006, from http://www.narrativeapproaches.com/antianorexia%20folder/anti_anorexia_index.htm

Foucault, M. (1979). *Discipline and punish: The birth of the prison.* Middlesex, England: Peregrine.

Foucault, M. (1980). *Power/knowledge: Selected interviews and other writings.* New York: Pantheon Books.

Freedman, J., & Combs, G. (1996). *Narrative therapy: The social construction of preferred realities.* New York: W. W. Norton.

Freedman, J., & Combs, G. (2002). Narrative couple therapy. In A. S. Gurman & N. S. Jacobson (Eds.), *Clinical handbook of couple therapy* (3rd ed., pp. 308–334). New York: Guilford Press.

Freeman, J., Epston, D., & Lobovits, D. (1997). *Playful approaches to serious problems.* New York: W. W. Norton.

Freeman, J., & Lobovits, D. (1993). The turtle with wings. In S. Friedman (Ed.), *The new language of change: Constructive collaboration in psychotherapy* (pp. 185–225). New York: Guilford Press.

Gadamer, H. (1975). *Truth and method* (D. Linge, Trans.). Berkeley: University of California Press.

Gergen, K. (1991). *The saturated self: Dilemmas of identity in contemporary life.* New York: Basic Books.

Gerhart, D., & Tuttle, A. (2003). *Theory-based planning for marriage and family therapists.* Pacific Grove, CA: Brooks/Cole.

Goolishian, H., & Anderson, H. (1992). Strategy and intervention versus nonintervention: A matter of theory. *Journal of Marital and Family Therapy, 18,* 5–15.

Griffith, J., & Griffith, M. (1994). *The body speaks: Therapeutic dialogues for mind-body problems.* New York: Basic Books.

Hare-Mustin, R., & Marecek, J. (1990). Gender and the meaning of difference: Postmodernism and psychology. In R. Hare-Mustin & J. Marecek (Eds.), *Making a difference: Psychology and the construction of gender* (pp. 22–64). New Haven, CT: Yale University Press.

Heidegger, M. (1962). *Being and time* (J. Macquarrie & E. Robinson, Trans.). New York: Harper & Row. (Original work published 1926)

Held, B. S. (1995). *Back to reality: A critique of postmodern theory in psychotherapy.* New York: W. W. Norton.

Henry, W. P., Strupp, H. H., Butler, S. F., Schacht, T. E., & Binder, J. L. (1993). Effects of training in time-limited dynamic psychotherapy: Changes in therapist behavior. *Journal of Consulting and Clinical Psychology, 61,* 434–440.

Hoshmand, L., & Polkinghorne, D. (1992). Redefining the science-practice relationship and professional training. *American Psychologist, 47,* 55–66.

Jenkins, A. (1990). *Invitations to responsibility: The therapeutic engagement of men who are violent.* Adelaide, Australia: Dulwich Centre Publications.

Lambert, M. J., & Barley, D. E. (2001). Research summary on the therapeutic relationship and psychotherapy outcome. *Psychotherapy: Theory, Research, Practice, Training, 38,* 357–361.

Levin, S., Raser, J., Niles, C., & Reese, A. (1986). Beyond family systems—toward problem systems: Some clinical implications. *Journal of Strategic and Systemic Therapies, 5,* 62–69.

Luborsky, L. (2001). The meaning of empirically supported treatment research for psychoanalytic and other long-term therapies. *Psychoanalytic Dialogues, 11,* 583–604.

Luborsky, L., McClellan, A. T., Diguer, L., Woody, G., & Seligman, D. A. (1997). The psychotherapist matters: Comparison of outcome across twenty-two therapists and seven patient samples. *Clinical Psychology: Science and Practice, 4,* 53–65.

Luborsky, L., Singer, B., & Luborsky, L. (1975). Comparative studies of psychotherapies: Is it true that "Everyone has won and all must have prizes"? *Archives of General Psychiatry, 32,* 995–1008.

Maisel, R., Epston, D., & Borden, A. (2004). *Biting the hand that starves you: Inspiring resistance to anorexia/bulimia.* New York: W. W. Norton.

Minuchin, S. (1991). The seductions of constructivism: Renaming power won't make it disappear. *The Family Therapy Networker, 15*(5), 47–50.

Monk, G. (2003). *Sociopolitical activist or conversational partner?* Retrieved February 15, 2006, from http://www.foucault/info/weblog/000045.html

Neimeyer, R. A. (1995). Constructivist psychotherapies: Features, foundations, and future directions. In R. A. Neimeyer & M. J. Mahoney (Eds.), *Constructivism in psychotherapy* (pp. 11–38). Washington, DC: American Psychological Association.

Neimeyer, R. A., & Mahoney, M. J. (1995). *Constructivism in psychotherapy.* Washington, DC: American Psychological Association.

Norcross, J. C. (2001). Purposes, processes, and products of the Task Force of Empirically Supported Therapy Relationships. *Psychotherapy: Theory, Research, Practice, Training, 38,* 345–356.

Packer, M. (1985). Hermeneutic inquiry in the study of human conduct. *American Psychologist, 40,* 1081–1093.

Paré, D., & Lysack, M. (2004). The willow and the oak: From monologue to dialogue in the scaffolding of therapeutic conversations. *Journal of Systemic Therapies, 23*(1), 6–20.

Raser, J. (1999). *Raising children you can live with: A guide for frustrated parents* (2nd ed.). Houston, TX: Bayou.

Redivo, M., & Buckman, R. (2004). T.E.A.M. Program. *Journal of Systemic Therapies, 23*(4), 52–66.

Reichelt, S., Tjersland, O. A., Gulbrandsen, W., Jensen, T. K., & Mossige, S. (2004). From the system of sexual abuse to the system of suspicion. *Journal of Systemic Therapies, 23*(1), 67–82.

Robbins, B. D. (2005, Summer). New organs of perception: Goethean science as a cultural therapeutics. *Janus Head, 8*(1). Retrieved February 15, 2006, from http://www.janushead.org/8–1/Robbins.pdf

Rorty, R. (1979). *Philosophy and the mirror of nature.* Princeton, NJ: Princeton University Press.

Roth, S. (1998). *Questions & ways of being in therapeutic conversation (stance and focus of attention).* Unpublished manuscript.

Roth, S., & Epston, D. (1996). Consulting the problem about the problematic relationship: An exercise for experiencing a relationship with an externalized problem. In M. F. Hoyt (Ed.), *Constructive therapies* (Vol. 2, pp. 148–162). New York: Guilford Press.

Seikkula, J. (2002). Open dialogue with good and poor outcomes for psychotic crises: Examples from families with violence. *Journal of Marital and Family Therapy, 28,* 263–274.

Seikkula, J., Alakare, B., & Aaltonen, J. (2001a). Open dialogue in psychosis I: An introduction and case illustration. *Journal of Constructivist Psychology, 14,* 247–266.

Seikkula, J., Alakare, B., & Aaltonen, J. (2001b). Open dialogue in psychosis II: A comparison of good and poor outcome. *Journal of Constructivist Psychology, 14,* 267–284.

Seikkula, J., & Olson, M. (2003). The open dialogue approach to acute psychosis: Its poetics and micropolitics. *Family Process, 42,* 403–418.

Shotter, J. (2000). Seeing historically: Goethe and Vygotsky's "enabling theory-method." *Culture and Psychology, 6,* 233–252.

Shotter, J. (2005, Summer). Goethe and the refiguring of intellectual inquiry: From "aboutness"—thinking to "withness"—thinking in everyday life. *Janus Head, 8*(1). Retrieved February 22, 2006, from http://www.janushead.org/8–1/Shotter.pdf

Slife, B. (1993). *Time and psychological explanation.* New York: SUNY Press.

Smith, C., & Nylund, N. (1997). *Narrative therapies with children and adolescents.* New York: Guilford Press.

Stacy, K. (1997). Alternative metaphors for externalizing conversations. *Gecko, 1,* 29–51.

Suberri, K. (2004). Pediatric psychology with a postmodern twist. *Journal of Systemic Therapies, 23*(1), 21–37.

Swim, S. (1995). Reflective and collaborative voices in the school. In S. Friedman (Ed.), *The reflecting team in action* (pp. 100–118). New York: Guilford Press.

Tomm, K. (1989). Externalising the problem and internalising personal agency. *Journal of Strategic and Systemic Therapies, 8*(1), 54–59.

Tomm, K. (1993). The courage to protest a commentary on Michael White's work. In S. Gilligan & R. Price (Eds.), *Therapeutic conversations* (pp. 62–80). New York: W. W. Norton.

Tomm, K., Suzuki, K., & Suzuki, K. (1990). Kan-no-mushi: An inner externalization that enables compromise? *The Australian and New Zealand Journal of Family Therapy, 11*(2), 104–106.

Toulmin, S. (1990). *Cosmopolis: The hidden agenda of modernity.* New York: Free Press.

Tschudi, F., & Reichelt, S. (2004). Conferencing when therapy is stuck. *Journal of Systemic Therapies, 23*(1), 38–52.

Varela, F. (1979). *Principles of biological autonomy.* New York: Elsevier North-Holland.

Wagner, V. (Producer). (2004). *Problems talk: Kids talk back* [Video]. (Available from Grand Rapids Community College Media Center, 143 Bostwick Avenue NE, Grand Rapids, MI 49503–3295.)

Wagner, V. (Producer). (2006). *The pain scale* [Video]. (Available from Too Reelistic Productions, 858 Pinecrest Avenue SE, East Grand Rapids, MI 49506.)

Wagner, V., McGovern, T., & Buckman, R. (2003, August). *Dilemmas, conundrums, and other beasts of burden.* Workshop presented at the Narrative & Community Work Conference, Chicago.

Wampold, B. E., Mondin, G. W., Moody, M., Stich, F., Benson, K., & Ahn, H. (1997). A meta-analysis of outcome studies comparing bona fide psychotherapies: Empirically, "all must have prizes." *Psychological Bulletin, 122,* 203–215.

Watzlawick, P. (Ed.) (1984). *The invented reality: How do we know what we believe we know?* New York: W. W. Norton.

Weingarten, K. (1997). A narrative approach to understand the illness experience of a mother and daughter. *Families, Systems, and Health, 15*(1), 41–54.

White, M. (1984). Pseudo-encopresis: From avalanche to victory, from vicious to virtuous cycles. *Family Systems Medicine, 2*(2), 150–160.

White, M. (1988, Summer). The externalizing of the problem and the re-authoring of lives and relationships. *Dulwich Centre Newsletter,* 3–20.

White, M. (1991). Deconstruction and therapy. *Dulwich Centre Newsletter, 3,* 21–40.

White, M. (1995). *Re-authoring lives: Interviews & essays.* Adelaide, Australia: Dulwich Centre Publications.

White, M., & Epston, D. (1990). *Narrative means to therapeutic ends.* New York: W. W. Norton.

White, M., & Morgan, A. (2006). *Narrative therapy with children and their families.* Adelaide, Australia: Dulwich Centre Publications.

Winslade, J., & Monk, G. (1999). *Narrative counseling in schools: Powerful and brief.* Thousand Oaks, CA: Corwin Press.

Winslade, J., & Monk, G. (2000). *Narrative mediation: A new approach to conflict resolution.* San Francisco: Jossey-Bass.

Wittgenstein, L. (1953). *Philosophical investigations* (G. Anscombe, Trans.). New York: Macmillan. (Original work published 1927)

CHAPTER 16

Constructivist Theory and Practice

Donald K. Granvold

Social workers and other mental health professionals are increasingly embracing constructivism and other postmodern therapies both philosophically and methodologically. Constructivism represents the first major "evolution" within the cognitive revolution of the 1960s and 1970s. Constructivism has been described as more a philosophical context of practice than a technique (W. T. Anderson, 1990). As will be evident in this chapter, however, there are rich and varied practice implications to be drawn from the constructive school of thought. Currently, constructivism is one of the most exciting, provocative developments in psychological thought. The scholar/practitioner who is open to postmodern thinking will find the movement to be ripe with possibilities.

Although this chapter does not specifically address social constructionism, this parallel movement shares many philosophical and practice similarities with constructivism. (For information on social constructionism see chapter 15, as well as H. Anderson, 1997; Burr, 1995; Combs & Freedman, 1990; Efran, Lukens, & Lukens, 1990; Franklin, 1998; Gergen, 1985, 1991, 1994; Goolishian & Anderson, 1987; Hoyt, 1994, 1996; Watzlawick, 1984; White & Epston, 1990).[1]

AN OVERVIEW OF CONSTRUCTIVISM

Constructivist approaches to psychotherapy are comprised of a fuzzy set of principles and practices that are dissonant in many ways with modern psychology both philosophically and methodologically (R. A. Neimeyer

& Raskin, 2000b). Although distinguishably postmodern, there are many varieties of constructivism reflecting differences in semantics and terminology, conceptual variability, and methodological biases (Mahoney, 2003; R. A. Neimeyer & Raskin, 2001; Raskin, 2002). Hence, a succinct definition of constructivism is no less formidable to attempt than to define other psychotherapeutic approaches such as behaviorism, cognitivism, or psychoanalytic psychotherapy. Entire books have been devoted to the definition of constructivism and its psychotherapeutic applications (cf. Franklin & Nurius, 1998; Guidano, 1987, 1991b; Guidano & Liotti, 1983; Kuehlwein & Rosen, 1993; Mahoney, 1991, 1995a, 2003; Martin, 1994; G. J. Neimeyer, 1993; R. A. Neimeyer & Mahoney, 1995; R. A. Neimeyer & Raskin, 2000a; Raskin & Bridges, 2002, in press; Rosen & Kuehlwein, 1996; Sexton & Griffin, 1997). Although narrow consensus does not exist, common features can be heard among the diverse voices.

Constructivist psychotherapy is based on the premise that humans attach unique meanings to life experience. These constructions are formulated individually or are co-constructed interpersonally. The view that a fixed, external reality exists from which absolute, immutable meanings are drawn is rejected. Individual mental health is, in large part, a product of the individual's capacity to generate multiple meanings for the same event. The dichotomous approach to meaning making, driven by logical positivism, would have the individual replacing irrational thoughts (constructions) with rational ones. The constructive approach is based on no such dichotomy, but rather encourages the development of multiple meanings with attention devoted to various consequences, both active and potential, of each meaning.

It is assumed that people are active participants in meaning making. "Reality" is subjective, the cocreation of the individual and the stimulus condition. Meanings are socially embedded and are constructed out of life experience. "Reality" is dynamic, rather than a static condition. Consequently, while some meanings are rather inexorable over time, other meanings are highly subject to reconstruction. The passage of time, altered circumstances, and selfhood changes have tremendous potential impact on meaning reconstruction. Socialization promotes the tendency in people to form rather restrictive, often singular views of complex life events, circumstances, and processes. Furthermore, negative constructions often prevail over more positive meanings. These simplistic, absolutistic, and negative biases in human meaning making are readily challengeable psychotherapeutically.

HISTORICAL DEVELOPMENT

The cognitive revolution began in the mid-1950s with the pioneering works of George Kelly (1955) and Albert Ellis (1955, 1958, 1962), followed shortly thereafter by Aaron T. Beck (1963, 1967, 1976). When the cognitivists entered the debate, the behaviorists and psychodynamicists were in a fervent struggle for psychotherapeutic supremacy. By the mid- to late 1970s the cognitive revolution was mounting full strength, and by the mid-1980s the revolution could be considered a success—a majority of the behaviorists and a substantial number of psychodynamicists recognized the legitimate strength of cognitive intervention and began to align themselves with the movement.

The cognitive revolution initially was predominated by a logical positivist view of human functioning in which individuals were appraised as evidencing "rational" or "irrational" cognitive functioning. Logical positivism emphasizes a scientific view of reality in which factual knowledge is connected with experience in such a way that direct or indirect confirmation is possible. Therapists assisted their clients in determining the faulty thoughts, beliefs, and/or information processing considered to be etiologically accountable for their emotional responses, maladaptive behaviors, and other consequential cognitive responses.

Constructivism evolved from traditional cognitivism as scholar/clinicians began challenging the logical positivist philosophy undergirding established cognitive treatment procedures. The most notable pioneers in the movement include Michael Mahoney (1980, 1985, 1991, 2003) and Vittorio Guidano (1987, 1991b; Guidano & Liotti, 1983), followed soon by Robert Neimeyer (1987, 1993a, 1993b). This development began in the early 1980s in concert with the postmodernism movement under way in the intellectual world including art, philosophy, and the humanities. Postmodernity challenges the belief in obdurate truths and universal models in favor of multiple perspectives, contradiction, and change. Postmodern thought holds that reality is subjective and that language constitutes the structures of social reality (Kvale, 1992; Maturana & Varela, 1987). Both constructivism and social constructionism represent developing clinical perspectives from postmodern consciousness.

THE PHILOSOPHICAL FOUNDATIONS
OF CONSTRUCTIVISM

Constructivist Ontology

Although constructivism is a fairly recent development, its philosophical roots can be traced to the works of Vico, Kant, and Vaihinger, and more recently to the writings of Hayek (Mahoney, 1991, 1995b). Consistent with the views of these learned scholars, constructivists consider humans to be active participants in the creation of their own reality. This ontological position stands in contrast to realism and objectivism, which contend that a fixed, verifiable, external reality exists. The implications of such a fixed, absolutistic view are that it is possible to achieve a "reality check" and that "truth" exists objectively. R. A. Neimeyer (1993a) noted that, according to this correspondence theory of truth, "the validity of one's belief systems is determined by their degree of 'match' with the real world, or at least with the 'facts' as provided by one's senses" (p. 222).

The constructivist view is that "reality" is a cocreation between the individual and the external stimuli to which he or she is responding. The human mind is not a tabula rasa, but rather each individual's meaning structures are uniquely and independently forged. Prior experiences, images, sensations, conceptualizations, and associations mutually interact and collectively operate to effect each individual's unique brand of meaning making. "Reality," thus, is highly influenced by idiosyncratic human mentation. Based on this understanding of human functioning, constructivists abandon validity in favor of *viability*. Here, the viability of any construction (conceptualized personal reality) "is a function of its consequences for the individual or group that provisionally adopts it (cf. von Glasersfeld, 1984), as well as its overall coherence with the larger system of personally or socially held beliefs into which it is incorporated (R. A. Neimeyer & Harter, 1988)" (R. A. Neimeyer, 1993a, p. 222). Human mentation necessarily results in the development of unique meanings for each individual.

Constructivist Epistemology

The constructivist view of human knowing (epistemology) is based on a motor theory of the mind. That is, the mind has the capacity to create meanings beyond the mere information processing of sensory data. This proactive and generative feature of human mentation is a cardinal principle of constructivism. The locus of reality and knowledge development is *within* the individual. Furthermore, not only is the mind considered to be proactive and generative, but human systems are considered to be *autopoietic*—self-organizing and active in determining their own evolution (Maturana & Varela, 1980). This motor theory view of the mind stands in contrast to sensory theories that assert that information from the external world flows inward through the senses to the mind, where it is maintained. Popper (1972) referred to this view as the "bucket theory of the mind." Behaviorism and information-processing models are examples of psychological approaches based on this sensory theory.

Constructivist epistemology further holds that knowledge processing is performed at both tacit and explicit levels. In this two-level model, unconscious processes are accorded a central role in the formulation of cognitive structures necessary for ordering everyday experience. The contention is that there can be no meaning independent of an abstract order and that to perceive particulars requires abstract ordering.

It is particularly noteworthy that these tacit ordering rules are considered to govern the individual's conscious processes and operate to constrain the individual's sense of self and the world. In this central/ peripheral knowledge-processing duality, core or nuclear processes are change resistant. It is theorized that the self-system "protects" core ordering processes in order to preserve the integrity of the system (Mahoney, Miller, & Arciero, 1995). Change in these core ordering processes, or *second-order change* as described by Watzlawick, Weakland, and Fisch (1974), involves system *perturbation*—challenge, disorganization, and distress—leading to emerging complexity and differentiation. Humans evolve through an ongoing recursion of perturbation and adaptation. Although core structures must be relatively stable and change resistant in order to maintain the integrity of the self-system, it is necessary that they be challenged in order to promote the very changes that keep the individual alive as an adapting, evolving self.

CENTRAL THEORETICAL CONSTRUCTS AND THERAPEUTIC PROCESSES

Constructivists hold that human evolution inherently involves disorder. Disorder is not construed as pathology or the enemy of mental health or personal well-being (Mahoney, 2003). To the contrary, complex, human living systems maintain their "aliveness" and progression through the experience of personal disorganization with its concomitant emotional expressions. In short, constructivists do not share the assumptions upon which the pathology perspective is based. Correspondingly, diagnostic labeling is approached with caution and skepticism due to its characteristic negative, deficit meanings (descriptions of negative traits, behaviors, and cognitive and emotive functioning) and the implication that an external, knowledgeable expert can possibly narrowly classify another human being. For most constructivists, the *Diagnostic and Statistical Manual of Mental Disorders (DSM)* represents an invented model of abnormality in which mental disorders are viewed as naturally occurring, objective entities (Raskin & Lewandowski, 2000). Exception is taken with the use of such psychiatric nosology in which clients are objectified and their complexities of self obviated.

The constructivist's normalization (depathologization) of human disturbance and distress has remarkable clinical conceptualization and intervention implications. Drawing on individual uniqueness and human creative potential, "problems" are construed as opportunities for constructive change. An empowerment agenda is sought in which the client gains greater agency over internal discovery and differentiation, interpersonal relationships and satisfaction, and the achievement of life goals. Treatment is ideally focused on the client's core meaning structures (self-schemas) and overall evolutionary objectives.

Goal of Therapy: Focus on Process Versus Problem Resolution

Constructivists lean toward process-focused treatment goals rather than problem resolution. Conceptualizing the human condition from a systems and developmental theory perspective, "problems" and other forms of human discomfort may be considered to be disequilibriating perturbations to the individual self-system. A problem is conceptualized as a discrepancy between a client's current capacity and the developmental challenges being experienced. A perturbation is an opportunity to explore new meanings and to consider creative change possibilities. Ongoing evolution and higher order differentiation of self derive from the process of adaptation and change (preferably proactive).

Intervention tends to emphasize a variety of historical, developmental (e.g., attachment), and self-organizational (self-identity) themes. The cognitive focus is on defining the client's meanings and meaning-making patterns, followed by the elaboration of these meanings toward more viable representations of experience (Lyddon, 1990).

For example, a client who presents with nonendogenous clinical depression and is free of suicidal risk may adopt the perspective through constructivist treatment that the depression exists as a catalyst for change in one or more key areas of life (including self-identity). To consider the depression a "problem" to be eliminated or remarkably reduced could interfere with the preferable, albeit painful, change process. By taking a problem focus and treating the depression, the client could experience short-term relief but sustain long-term untoward or negative consequences for failing to make effective change in self, his or her social relationships, or life circumstances. This is not to say that treating the depression could *not* effect profound and pervasive change in the individual, but rather the likelihood of such change is considered to be greater through constructivist means.

Unconscious Processes

The complexity of human cognitive functioning necessarily relies on abstract operations. Unconscious processes are considered to have a strong influence on cognitive, emotional, and behavioral functioning. They are accorded a central role in the ordering of everyday experience (Guidano, 1988; Mahoney, 1991). As noted earlier, core ordering processes are critical to the integrity of the human system; therefore, it is theorized that they are heavily protected against challenge. Even though they may promote disadvantageous outcomes for the individual, they remain relatively immutable. Their change resistance prevents the human system from becoming highly unstable. The abstract ordering capabilities of these deep structures are considered to govern the individual's conscious processes and operate to constrain the individual's sense of self and the world. The therapeutic challenge is to access and produce modification in the core meanings operating to negatively influence the client's sense of self, interpersonal interactions, and view of the world and his or her self-actualization possibilities.

Emotions as Change Agents

In the cognitive-behavioral tradition, therapists have applied methods to control, alter, or terminate emotions considered to be maladaptive in effect: anxiety, anger, worry, guilt, sorrow, sadness, and the like. Such emotions have typically been labeled "negative" and they have tended to be conceptualized as intrusive, maladaptive, debilitating, and generally unpleasant to experience. Constructivists contend that meaningful change inherently involves experiencing intense emotions, and, therefore, measures to limit or eliminate emotive responses may actually inhibit the change process. In postmodern psychotherapy practice, emotions should neither be labeled as negative nor should they be therapeutically targeted for extreme limitation or eradication. Although deep depression, feelings of loss, aloneness, anxiety, fear, and the like, may be uncomfortable, untoward, or subjectively undesirable, there is potential utility in these feelings.

For example, in the postdivorce recovery period, oftentimes intense anger is helpful in the process of letting go of the ex-mate. The process of deattachment is advanced by the realization, experiencing, and expression of emotions such as anger, hurt, resentment, and loathing. Emotions are emotions, the effects of which may be immediately unappealing to the client while holding the promise of long-term gain. The disclaimer appropriate to this discussion is that extreme emotions associated with suicidal ideation/planning or homicidal ideation/planning obligate the therapist to take steps to protect the client from acting on these urges. Hospitalization for protection and medication for control may be desirable options under these circumstances.

Constructivists encourage clients to explore, experience, and express their emotions through the use of experiential treatment procedures. Disequilibrium resulting from emotional intensity is considered to be a viable means of accessing core beliefs and state-dependent cognitions (Greenberg & Safran, 1987; Lyddon, 1990; Safran & Greenberg, 1991a). Methods to access affective states and stimulate emotional arousal include guided discovery, imagery, imaginary dialogues (empty-chair technique), and therapeutic rituals.

Selfhood Processes

Constructivist conceptualizations reflect a view of self as an evolutionary, epistemological, self-organizing, autopoietic (self-producing or self-renewing) system rather than as a fixed entity (Arciero & Guidano, 2000; Guidano, 1987, 1991b, 1995a; Guidano & Liotti, 1983; Kegan, 1982; Mahoney, 1991; Maturana & Varela, 1987; R. A. Neimeyer, 2000). The self is not singular or fixed, but rather is a multifaceted and ever-changing "system" of identity meanings. Selfhood is a process reflecting a history of development and accumulated meanings forged through tacit and explicit cognitive operations (Guidano, 1988). The beliefs, memories, and patterns of processing information that make up the individual's core sense of self provide "a set of basic expectations that direct the individual's patterns of self-perception and self-evaluation" (Guidano, 1988, p. 317). During childhood, these core ordering structures (Mahoney, 1991) or deep cognitive structures (Guidano, 1987) "develop into highly stable and enduring themes" and "are elaborated upon throughout an individual's lifetime," ultimately serving as "templates for the processing of later experience" (Young, 1990, p. 9). For many, early experiences result in the development of maladaptive schemas. These self-schemas tend to be highly change resistant, self-perpetuating, are activated by events in the environment, and lead to psychological distress (McGinn & Young, 1996; Young, 1990).

   Nurius and Berlin (1994) noted that because schemas are seldom "purged" from our memory system, we have ever-increasing sets of self-conceptions. Due to cognitive limitations, only a partial set of self-schemas can be activated at a given time. The activated "self" is the one that "reflects meaningful links between the demands of the situation and self-conceptions related to those cues" (p. 255). Thus, the socially embedded nature of self-schemas plays a powerful role in the activation of one set of self-conceptions over another. From the above conceptualization, it can be concluded that multiple "possible" selves exist among stored schemas (Markus & Nurius, 1986). One's "active" sense of self is *never* a complete representation of one's being. Furthermore, one's sets of self-conceptualizations are continuously expanding as the experience of life is translated into selfhood development.

Activity

Humans are active participants in their own evolution, not merely "passive pawns in life" (Mahoney & Granvold, 2005, p. 75). Individuals are seen as ripe with potential to assume a proactive role in their experiencing of life. The past may be revisited and given new meaning through the application of current perspectives and preferential ways of construing past "realities." Life in the moment reflects the meeting of external demands and human choice. While not within total human control, individual agency is a powerful influence on the meaning and experience of life in the moment. As with the past and the present, constructive focus on the future is biased with hope, possibilities, and rejuvenation. Constructive conceptualizations of human change emphasize client awareness and expression of creative potential, self-efficacy, and activity. Life and psychotherapy are about possibilities—those "realized" but perhaps lacking form, recognition, or acknowledgment and possible futures with the potential for achievement, revitalization, and revisioning of self and life experience.

Strengths and Possibilities Vis-à-Vis Pathology

The pathology conceptualization of mental health so central to the dominant models of psychotherapy practice reflects views of the human condition that constructivists eschew. The pathology model objectifies human functioning, reducing to a diagnostic label human adaptation, coping, and evolution (Leitner & Faidley, 2002). *The necessary unrest that characterizes humans when they are confronted with loss, exposed to trauma, or challenged with personal or interpersonal crisis, is construed as dysfunction, disability, and disorder.*

In contrast to such conceptualizations, constructivists maintain that human change and adaptation are inherently emotionally provocative processes. Under extreme challenge, people draw upon their human resources to cope and ultimately to adjust, develop, and psychologically evolve. The focus on individual limitation, liability, flaw, incapacity, and shortcoming produces a remarkable negative bias, one of deviance, debilitation, and disorder. Furthermore, labeling people as "disordered" promotes an artificial division between normal and abnormal experiencing of life.

Addressing the undesirable consequences associated with conceptualizing human functioning in terms of mental disorder, Gergen and McNamee (2000) encouraged in both therapy and diagnosis a "move from disciplinary determination to dialogues of difference" (p. 336). They cited several undesirable consequences of diagnostic categorization, including stigmatization; locus of blame on the individual vis-à-vis other contributions to the condition; promotion of client dependency upon mental health professionals to the exclusion of family, social, and spiritual support in many cases; and disempowerment of the individual. In concert with many other voices (T. Anderson, 1995; Elkaim, 1990; Leitner & Faidley, 2002; Raskin & Lewandowski, 2000; Saleebey, 2006; Seikkula et al., 1995; Szasz, 2002), Gergen and McNamee promoted a transformative dialogue in which a multiplicity of meanings is sought to better understand human experiencing and to facilitate human change.

Rather than emphasizing what is "wrong" with the individual, constructive practice wisdom would have us look for client strengths. The identification of and placement of emphasis on client strengths, resiliency, coping capacities, and interpersonal and social resources hold rich promise for meeting the challenges of human adaptation and change. Saleebey (2006) stated that to practice from a strengths perspective means that everything you do as a practitioner

> will be predicated, in some way, on helping to discover and embellish, explore and exploit clients' strengths and resources in the service of assisting them to achieve their goals, realize their dreams, and shed the irons of their own inhibitions and misgivings, and society's domination. (p. 1)

Clients are to be viewed as ripe with the capacity to draw on personal, interpersonal, and socio-environmental resources in accommodating past and present losses, disappointments, and regrets. The future is an expression of human resiliency, regenerative potential, realized human resources and activity.

Constructive psychotherapy is about possibilities, a stance that emphasizes the present and future. McNamee (2002) posed the question "What would happen if therapists were to shift the psychotherapeutic conversation from the realm of charting the history of a problem to the realm of future images?" (p. 164). It is my belief that such a shift coupled with an emphasis on personal, interpersonal, and socio-environmental assets will erode the power of negativity, doubt, hopelessness, despair, and inactivity.

PHASES OF HELPING

The relationship between client and therapist is recognized as the most meaningful ingredient in the helping process. Constructivists assume a non-authoritarian role with their clients for the most part. Knowledge-based authority is recognized, but information is shared in a nonabsolutistic and nonauthoritarian manner (Granvold, 1996a; Szasz, 2002). Research findings, clinical conceptualizations and interpretations, approaches to change, and the like, are not presented as absolute, inexorable, or inviolate but rather as understandings, perspectives, or one of several ways to construe experience. Clients' meaning constructions are given paramount importance. It is the therapist's task to access those meanings as opposed to telling the clients what they are experiencing and why.

Engagement

The engagement process involves a determination of the client's purposes for seeking treatment, expectations of the therapeutic relationship and the treatment process, and motivation for change. Initial attention is given to structuring the roles of client and therapist. Role structuring requires gaining answers to many questions from the client, as well as imparting information as a means of clarifying the treatment process. Ultimately, the effective engagement of the client is accomplished by joining the client's unique meaning-making processes through mutual inquiry. Achieving this end and progressing to the elaboration of client constructions relies heavily on the use of the Socratic method (Beck & Emery, 1985; Beck, Rush, Shaw, & Emery, 1979; Ellis, 1994; Granvold, 1994). The therapist assumes an active role in the process of illuminating deeply held, often "inarticulate constructions" considered highly operative in the client's life experience (R. A. Neimeyer, 1995b).

On the basis of therapist behavior, the client should become aware early on that a collaborative relationship is being promoted and that the client retains ultimate control over access to his or her constructions. It is the client's awareness of this potential and his or her trust in the therapist that will allow access to and constructive elaboration of these constructs toward the client's greater well-being. This critical awareness and the outcomes identified above represent the operations of constructivist engagement of the client in treatment.

Assessment

Consistent with the reciprocal determinism model of human functioning (Bandura, 1978), assessment should include consideration of social/environmental forces, overt behavior, and internal dispositions. Although all of these phenomena are considered to be active components in determining behavior, constructivists consider cognitive functioning to be highly influential in the maintenance and modification of human disturbance and dysfunction. Hence, the primary focus is on meaning-making activity.

The assessment of meaning making is focused on (a) peripherally held beliefs, views, and conceptualizations; (b) relationships between and among constructs; and (c) core ordering processes or tacitly held constructs (about self, others, and the experience of life). Surface-held cognitions are much easier to access and are considered to be much less influential in their impact on functioning than core meaning structures. They may, however, serve as a point of entry to the process of excavating for core schemas. Furthermore, isolating surface constructs may allow for meaningful cognitive elaboration important to desired, more immediate behavioral and emotional activation.

In contrast to assessment procedures in the tradition of many therapies where the objective is to proceed unobtrusively, constructivist assessment is inherently change stimulating. Constructivist assessment involves the client in the discovery of meanings, an enterprise that cannot be pursued passively. There are no constructivist standardized tests that are "objectively" administered and interpreted, resulting in a static "expert opinion" of the client by the therapist. Should a constructivist use psychological test results, single responses, response "patterns," and composite results, this data would be utilized to access peripherally held cognitions and ideally to provide preliminary direction to the discovery of core meaning structures. (See the following for additional information on constructivist assessment: Feixas, 1995; Mahoney, 1991, 2003; G. J. Neimeyer, 1993; G. J. Neimeyer, Hagans, & Anderson, 1998; G. J. Neimeyer & R. A. Neimeyer, 1981; Safran, Vallis, Segal, & Shaw, 1986.)

Planning/Contracting and Intervention

Although constructivist treatment is looser in form than orthodox cognitive intervention, the therapist sets an agenda with the client and exercises an active role in guiding the course of treatment. Early in treatment, attention is focused on defining goals. Presenting problems set the direction in treatment. They may serve as incremental steps in a more grand developmental undertaking, or alternatively, the *process* utilized in the treatment of these dilemmas may become the client's blueprint for future self-directed or therapist-guided personal development. In either case, once treatment goals are identified, client and the therapist engage collaboratively in planning a change strategy. The negotiation of a therapeutic contract may be done more or less formally. The contract involves agreement on the goals, methods, and course of treatment (scheduling, frequency rate, payment, etc.). Although the contract may be maintained tacitly, prudent practice standards call for the consummation of a written contract (signed by both client and therapist) as soon as clinically feasible in which treatment goals and indicators of progress and outcomes are set forth (Bernstein & Hartsell, 1998; Houston-Vega, Nuehring, & Daguio, 1997).

Consistent with the multiplicity of constructivism, there is no narrowly formulated treatment technology for universal application to clients. To the contrary, there has been resistance to the development of a proliferation of techniques (Guidano, 1991b; Mahoney, 1986, 1991; Rosen, 1993). Despite the reluctance to promote treatment technologies, this section on intervention would be incomplete without the inclusion of a listing of intervention options that constructivists have used to promote change. The following is a sampling of techniques: cognitive elaboration (Granvold, 1996b; Mahoney, 1991, 2003; G. J. Neimeyer, 1993; R. A. Neimeyer, 1993d, 1996); movieola (Guidano, 1991a, 1995b); stream of consciousness, journaling, life review, mirror time, bibliotherapy (Mahoney, 1991, 2003); repertory grid, downward arrow, laddering, the "bow tie" technique (G. J. Neimeyer, 1993); narrative writing (Freedman & Combs, 1996; Goncalves, 1995; Hoyt, 1998; White & Epston, 1990); externalizing the problem (White & Epston, 1990); symptom prescription (Watzlawick, 1984); enactments (role plays, empty-chair technique; Greenberg & Safran, 1987; Safran & Greenberg, 1991b); imagery and guided discovery (Safran & Segal, 1990); embodiment exercises (promoting sensory and physical awareness; Mahoney, 1991, 2003); and therapeutic rituals (Mahoney, 1991, 2003; R. A. Neimeyer, 1993a). The clinical example at the end of this chapter will give the reader insight into cognitive elaboration, an intervention method frequently used by constructivists to facilitate client meaning constructions that promote client well-being, interpersonal satisfaction, and personal development.

Evaluation

The most profound question with regard to evaluation is "What are the specific, salient indicators of change?" For those wedded to an empirical practice model, change is reflected in measurable outcome criteria, such as scores on standardized psychological tests, and records of discrete cognitive or overt behavior. Constructivists tend to consider such quantitative measurement to be reductionistic and an inadequate means to explain the complexities and idiosyncratic nature of the human experience. Daniels and White (1997) contended that to understand therapeutic change, therapists must understand "what 'change' means *to the actual people who are undergoing counseling*, rather than looking at the nature of change merely through the perspectival lens of a particular psychological theory" (p. 177). In an effort to seek this understanding, constructivists have shifted focus from outcome research to an exploration of the process of psychotherapeutic change. Questions are being asked about what kinds of intervention strategies at what moments in therapy produce what effects (Greenberg, 1986, 1992; Martin, 1994; R. A. Neimeyer, 1995a; Rennie, 1995; Rice & Greenberg, 1984; Toukmanian & Rennie, 1992). The conduct of process research takes many forms, including the "change events" perspective in which observable markers of change within therapy are delineated and analyzed, and narrative research focused on such phenomena as retrospective client or therapist accounts of their intentions at specified points in the narrative (Rennie, 1992; Rennie & Toukmanian, 1992).

Termination

Termination of the change effort is a collaborative process, as are all other aspects of constructivist treatment. Determining timely termination is ideally associated with the achievement of client-generated outcomes. Exceptions to this protocol are those circumstances in which treatment has been mandated for clients exhibiting socially irresponsible, unethical, or unlawful behavior. In those situations, termination decision making is biased toward the therapist. Despite the client's inclination to terminate, the therapist may sustain treatment until treatment goals have been satisfactorily achieved in his or her judgment. With voluntary clients, termination is sought as the client exercises a desire for time-out following incremental change or upon satisfactory completion of the change effort. The decision to terminate is preferably jointly made by client and therapist. As the final session approaches, relapse prevention strategies (preferably infused throughout treatment) are addressed specifically (Granvold & Wodarski, 1994; Greenwald, 1987; Laws, 1989; Marlatt & Gordon, 1985; Segal, Williams, & Teasdale, 2002; Wilson, 1992).

APPLICATION TO FAMILY AND GROUP WORK

Constructivist practice methods have been applied with couples, families, and groups. The constructivist (and social constructionist) conceptualization of couples and families as social systems, along with the emphasis on development from infancy across the life span, are highly relevant in the assessment and treatment of family system dilemmas. Constructivists focus on the possibilities for mutual (couple) or collective (family) enhancement, enrichment, and achievement through the promotion of the synergistic constructive potential of the family system. Creative avenues for systemic change are sought for the benefit of family members individually and interpersonally.

Constructivist approaches to treatment are also suitable for group treatment. The group has been advanced as a valuable context in which to develop an awareness of constructivist thinking for the promotion of individual change and to learn of group processes (Brower, 1998). Group members' unique perceptions and cognitive elaborations may provide meaningful inroads into rigid, narrow, or judgmental thinking on the part of group members. The established advantages of group process are as highly relevant for constructivist psychotherapy as for other interventions.

COMPATIBILITY WITH GENERALIST-ECLECTIC FRAMEWORK

Constructivist treatment is highly compatible with a generalist-eclectic social work practice perspective. Constructivism emphasizes the client's strengths and possibilities (Saleebey, 2006). A collaborative relationship is sought with the client in which the therapist assumes a nonauthoritarian, albeit knowledgeable, stance. Although the primary focus of constructivist assessment and intervention is on the meaning-making process (internal dispositions), in the social work tradition, environmental conditions and social factors are considered in the promotion of the client's immediate goals and ultimate personal development. Constructivist conceptualizations of human functioning and human change processes embrace *reciprocal determinism* (Bandura, 1985)—the model that contends that behavior, cognition, and personal factors (emotion, motivation, physiology, and physical factors) and social/environmental factors are interactive, overlapping, and mutually influential. Intervention strategies often target change in several areas, and methods are varied, flexible, and adjustable as treatment proceeds. Unlike "manualized" treatment protocols, intervention is uniquely tailored to the client. There is a priority on the therapeutic relationship in recognition of the powerful role relationship factors play in efficacious treatment.

Constructivist voices are highly evident in the psychotherapy integration movement (Granvold, 1999; Greenberg, 2002; Mahoney, 1991, 1995c; R. A. Neimeyer, 1993c, 1995a; Safran & Messer, 1997). This movement honors contributions of various schools of psychotherapy in the formulation of potentially viable theories of human behavior and human change processes. Change is considered possible through multiple avenues, and the cross-fertilization of schools of thought is believed to be worthy of active and ongoing consideration.

CRITIQUE OF CONSTRUCTIVIST PRACTICE

Constructivism is not a closely bound construction of postulates and techniques. Consistent with the essence of postmodernism, there are as many forms of constructivism as there are constructivists. Within the movement, internal tensions exist around issues such as (a) the *centrality of the self*, ranging from an "evolving self" to a self-less psychology; (b) the *locus of meaning*—more internally generated versus socially constructed languaging; (c) acceptance or rejection of *ontological realism* and the degree of importance placed on ontology; (d) the *therapist's degree of directiveness* and vigor in promoting therapeutic change; and (e) the endorsement of empirical versus qualitative process *research* (R. A. Neimeyer, 1995a). There is such diversity within constructivism that specifying the defining features is somewhat problematic. The metatheoretical assumptions and theoretical developments discussed above represent interrelated conceptualizations more or less reflected in the theoretical bases and clinical interventions of constructivists. The range of diversity that constructivism allows is at once creditworthy in terms of therapeutic freedom, flexibility, and creativity, and simultaneously poses challenges to those interested in learning the praxis of constructivism. From student to experienced practitioner, the "how-to"s are fuzzy.

Constructivism is clearly far more highly developed philosophically than methodologically. Temptation exists to develop definitive treatment manuals outlining and demonstrating constructivist practice. There is a strong bias within the movement against "technologizing" constructivist practice (Guidano, 1991b; Mahoney, 1986, 1991; Rosen, 1993). The explication of practice methodologies, however, may serve to clarify, inform, expand, and refine the spiny constructions of human change processes. The positive potential of clear, demonstrative treatment exemplars presented in the form of *a* way, vis-à-vis *the* way, to intervene with clients merits strong consideration.

Many constructivists have criticized current psychological research, identifying an incompatibility with constructivist epistemology (Arvay, 2002; Denzin & Lincoln, 2000; Hoskins, 2002). "New paradigm research" (Denzin & Lincoln, 2000) that embraces the following perspectives is called for: (a) there are no obdurate or universal truths; (b) knowledge is a co-construction of the individual and a stimulus condition; (c) knowledge is socially imbedded, discursive, and dialogical; (d) knowledge is historically influenced; (e) knowledge is contextual, multiple, and dynamic; and (f) empirical knowledge cannot be reached free of influence from the researcher (Arvay, 2002; Hoskins, 2002; Kelly, 1955; Mahoney, 1991; Maturana & Varela, 1987). Research findings, empirical data, and psychological theories may be useful clinically, but not as prescriptive evidence of what *is* (or is *wrong*). Rather, such information may be presented as stimuli for subjective inquiry and possibly ultimate meaning making. Research findings may be used as organizing themes that both shape the therapist's conceptualizations of, and conjecture regarding, a given category of human experience (e.g., loss), and thus may provide a framework or context for inquiry. The therapist's ways of exploring subjective meanings are through avenues that likely have been drawn from empirical research.

For example, a line of questioning regarding parallel parenting expectations of a divorced parent may be drawn from empirical research on postdivorce parenthood. Furthermore, specific subjective meanings expressed by a client make sense to the therapist based upon a cognitive structural meaning matrix into which the content is integrated. This meaning matrix is, for the critically informed therapist, likely infused with empirical knowledge. The use of research in the manner noted above may have a remarkable impact on practice. Although there is great need to develop more viable constructivist research methodologies, there is apparent value in the use of empirical research in clinical practice.

Constructivism has come under sharp criticism for the appearance of failing to hold people accountable for cruel, unfair, abusive, socially insensitive, selfish, and irresponsible conduct (see Held, 1995; Pittman, 1992). Bandura (1986, 1996) noted that, despite our commitment to idiosyncratic meanings, therapists must be wary of client "mechanisms of moral disengagement" that serve to obscure or minimize the client's agentive role in irresponsible and unconscionable conduct. When clients evidence socially irresponsible, unethical, or illegal behavior and maintain corresponding beliefs, attitudes, and viewpoints supportive of such behavior, the therapist must assume the role of agent of social responsibility (Granvold, 1996a). Social workers in particular, but helping professionals from all disciplines, come into contact with clients whose behavior fits the above criteria. It is consistent with the *intent* of constructivist philosophy and praxis for therapists to promote client self-regulatory processes (self-monitoring, self-evaluation, and self-sanction) and humane conduct, and when there is evidence of client despicable or unconscionable behavior, to challenge the mechanisms of moral disengagement such as denial, gross distortions and misattributions, and rationalization. Constructivism does not endorse an "anything goes" solipsism in which personal meanings are maintained independent of a social order. Constructivists are charged with the dual responsibility to facilitate personal development and well-being and to guide clients in making choices that satisfy and uphold moral standards. Where there is bona fide evidence that the client has failed to self-govern in a socially conscionable manner, the therapist is to intervene to establish or restore the mechanisms of humane agency.

CASE EXAMPLE

Constructivist treatment methods invite clients to explore, examine, appraise, experience, define, and redefine themselves, their life experiences, and their directions in life both inside and outside the session (Mahoney,

1991). In the example that follows, I have tried to explicate the use of cognitive elaboration to promote this process in some measure.

Blake presented for therapy approximately one year after the death of his only son. Throughout the preceding year, Blake had been experiencing intense grief and severe depression. Despite his emotional state, he continued his senior management position but reported the ability to perform his responsibilities only minimally. His marital relationship with Jeana (his second wife and not the mother of his deceased son) was suffering from his "protracted" grief. Blake explained that he and his 28-year-old son, James, were to have gone hunting together last year on the weekend that James was killed in an auto accident. Blake and Jeana were scheduled to take a weeklong trip beginning the weekend following the hunting trip. Blake (who has cancer in remission) withdrew from the trip with his son on the advice of his physician. The doctor believed that Blake needed to rest prior to his vacation based upon symptomatic evidence. Blake maintained that he was responsible for his son's death because he withdrew from the hunting trip.

The first session was devoted to understanding his views of what happened and empathizing with Blake's pain. No effort was made to involve him in construct elaboration while attempting to empathetically join him. In the second session, I decided to seek a better understanding of the consequences (viability) of his constructs surrounding his son's death and to promote an elaboration of constructs.

BLAKE: *I was perfectly aware of James's drinking problem. If I had gone hunting with him I am convinced that he would be alive today.*

DON: *I see, Blake. So, you feel responsible for his death—that had you been with him, you could have prevented the accident from happening.*

BLAKE: *Yes. It's my fault.*

DON: *Blake, when you think "It's my fault," what thoughts and images cross your mind?*

BLAKE: *Oh God . . . I feel a terrible feeling in the pit of my stomach. I hear myself saying things like, "Why didn't you go with him?" "You knew that this might happen!"*

DON: *You have a sick feeling in your stomach and you sound critical of yourself. What other feelings can you identify as you concentrate on "It's my fault"?*

BLAKE: *I feel overwhelming loss, regret, pain, and helplessness. It's depressing; the whole bundle is depressing.*

DON: *So you experience many intense feelings, and they've lasted for approximately a year now; is that correct, Blake?*

BLAKE: *Yes, that's right.*

DON: *How would you say that these feelings have served you, Blake?*

BLAKE: *I'm not sure that I understand what you mean.*

DON: *Can you think of any benefits you have derived from feeling this array of feelings?*

BLAKE: *I guess that they are just part of my grief.*

DON: *Yes, I believe that they are an important part of your grief, and also grieving is a very important part of dealing with loss—especially one as great as the loss of your son. (Pause) Blake, while these emotional reactions and their effects are to be expected as part of grieving, do you have any thoughts about how you might reduce the intensity of your grieving at this time?*

BLAKE: *If you are getting at "Have I grieved long enough?" I really don't know. I do know that I think I need to perform better at work like I used to, and my relationship with Jeana is suffering from my depression. I don't want to lose her. I really don't know, though, how I can get a better handle on my feelings.*

DON: *Blake, in a sense, I believe that you're saying that your grieving has fit your views of proper or acceptable grieving. You appear to be saying now, however, that change needs to happen so that the grief doesn't create other problems for you. And furthermore, you are uncertain how to go about change. Have I fairly accurately captured your views?*

BLAKE: *That's it. You pretty much understand the situation I think.*

DON: *Blake, perhaps you can continue to honor the memory of James, accept that you could likely have prevented his death had you gone with him that weekend, and yet, modify your grieving so that other problems don't get created in the process.*

BLAKE: *That's sounds good to me and I think that's really why I'm here.*

DON: *And I am really pleased that you are here, Blake. . . . Since focusing specifically on blaming yourself for James's death appears to result in other problems, suppose you expand your thoughts about James's death in addition to "It's my fault." What other thoughts do you have about James's life or his premature death?*

BLAKE: *Well, not to be too hard on the kid, but he did have a drinking problem and, ultimately, I guess that you could say he was responsible for the accident that took his life. He was drunk!*

DON: *Yes, I agree with you that James was responsible for his drinking and the accident. It is somewhat a question of when does a parent quit protecting his child. Blake, can you function with both of these beliefs, "It's my fault" and "James was responsible for his drinking"?*

BLAKE: *Even though they seem contradictory, I think I can.*

DON: *So it is possible to maintain multiple views or beliefs about a situation.*

BLAKE: *Yes, I think it is.*

Blake continued to elaborate the meanings of his son's life and ultimate death through this session and several subsequent sessions. My role was to prompt the generation of a variety of meanings through Socratic questioning and to guide Blake in appraising the various meanings in terms of their consequences. For example, Blake concluded that James's death would have been a "waste" if he did not do something in James's name that would have a positive impact on the problem of drinking and driving in our society. That meaning-making process resulted in Blake's active involvement in and financial support of Mothers Against Drunk Driving (MADD). Blake also reconciled that had the roles been reversed and *he* was killed under the same circumstances as was James, he would want James to enjoy happiness and joy in life despite the loss. This role reversal contemplation was particularly significant to Blake. Further elaborations included the following: Depression will not bring James back; Had I prevented the accident that night, it would not have ensured that James would not have a fatal accident on another occasion; Focusing on self-blame is likely to bring many unwanted consequences, including poor work performance, marital unhappiness, and potentially an end to the remission state of my cancer; and I can focus on James's *life* through more active devotion of time and energy to my grandson (James's only child). Blake construed his active relationship with his grandson as both "standing in" for James and being grandpa. He vowed to make certain that his grandson would "know" his father through pictures, stories, and personal accounts.

Blake arrived at the above elaborations and many more. He learned to appraise meanings in terms of their various consequences, and he attempted to translate the meanings into more productive (by his definition) actions. The elaboration of meanings, rather than the restructuring of the belief that "It's my fault," allowed Blake to hold on to an important, and in some ways viable, view of self-responsibility for the tragic death of his only son. Challenging that belief would have been, I believe, less effective than allowing it to stand as one of many meanings in the matrix of constructs surrounding Blake's loss. The emotions that comprise grief will be lifelong visitors in Blake's experiencing of life. He accepted this as both normal and reasonable and remained committed to making "use" of his grief for the benefit of himself and others.

SUMMARY

Constructivist philosophical and metatheoretical assumptions are a challenge to the theories that undergird many currently popular interventions. The view that distress and disorder are inherent and necessary in the enterprise of human change is at odds with the pathology and mental illness models that predominate. Constructivist ontology and epistemology represent a marked departure from well-established rationalist and empiricist perspectives. Criticism, challenge, and resistance notwithstanding, the strength of constructivism can be expected to mount as a result of internal and external developments. From within, theoretical sophistication and experientially grounded practice applications are ongoing. The broader context of these developments is the postmodernism movement, which is continuing to shape our intellectual culture across disciplines. The critical helping professional in evolution may well find constructivism to be viable in addressing some of the deficiencies that characterize many contemporary forms of intervention.

NOTE

1. The revised version of this chapter is dedicated to the memory of my colleague and friend, Michael J. Mahoney, PhD (1946–2006). Michael passed away unexpectedly on May 31, 2006. At the time of his death, Michael was professor of holistic counseling at Salve Regina University. He was the most influential person in the advancement of the constructivist movement worldwide. Michael was a lifelong student of philosophy, a prolific author, and visionary in his thoughts about human change. He was on the cutting edge of contemporary psychological thought, a central figure in the cognitive revolution, and the leader of the evolution in cognitive thought known as constructivism. Michael was kind, caring, thoughtful, gentle, humble, and respectful. He was brilliant, a critical thinker, and one who preferred to discover and emphasize similarities when he encountered differences. He was a man of many interests and passions. Weight lifting was among his passions, and at the time of his death he was a current National Champion Weight Lifter.

In the first edition of this volume, I dedicated this chapter to the memory of Vittorio Guidano, MD (1944–1999). Michael and Vittorio were best friends. Although they lived in different continents, the evolutions of their thoughts about human behavior and the processes of human change were incredibly coincident. Beyond their respect for one another's ideas, they loved each other as brothers. This chapter evidences the remarkable influence each had on constructivist theory and practice. I feel incredibly fortunate to have known both Michael and Vittorio. The passing of each was premature and untimely. They left a work that will continue to enlighten students of constructivism at all levels and provide unending thrust to the constructivism movement. Until we meet again, ciao i miei amici, ciao.

REFERENCES

Anderson, H. (1997). *Conversation, language, and possibilities.* New York: Basic Books.

Anderson, T. (1995). Reflecting processes; acts of informing and forming: You can borrow my eyes, but you must not take them away from me! In S. Friedman (Ed.), *The reflecting team in action* (pp. 11–37). New York: Guilford Press.

Anderson, W. T. (1990). *Reality isn't what it used to be.* San Francisco: Harper & Row.

Arciero, G., & Guidano, V. F. (2000). Experience, explanation, and the quest for coherence. In R. A. Neimeyer & J. D. Raskin (Eds.), *Constructions of disorder: Meaning-making frameworks for psychotherapy* (pp. 91–118). Washington, DC: American Psychological Association.

Arvay, M. J. (2002). Putting the heart back into constructivist research. In J. D. Raskin & S. K. Bridges (Eds.), *Studies in meaning: Exploring constructivist psychology* (pp. 201–223). New York: Pace University Press.

Bandura, A. (1978). The self system in reciprocal determinism. *American Psychologist, 33,* 344–358.

Bandura, A. (1985). Model of causality in social learning theory. In M. J. Mahoney & A. Freeman (Eds.), *Cognition and psychotherapy* (pp. 81–99). New York: Plenum Press.

Bandura, A. (1986). *Social foundations of thought and action: A social cognitive theory.* Englewood Cliffs, NJ: Prentice Hall.

Bandura, A. (1996). Reflections on human agency: Part 1. *Constructive Change, 1*(2), 3–12.

Beck, A. T. (1963). Thinking and depression. *Archives of General Psychiatry, 9,* 324–333.

Beck, A. T. (1967). *Depression: Clinical, experimental, and theoretical aspects.* New York: Harper & Row.

Beck, A. T. (1976). *Cognitive therapy and the emotional disorders.* New York: International Universities Press.

Beck, A. T., & Emery, G. (1985). *Anxiety disorders and phobias.* New York: Basic Books.

Beck, A. T., Rush, A. J., Shaw, B. F., & Emery, G. (1979). *Cognitive therapy of depression.* New York: Guilford Press.

Bernstein, B. E., & Hartsell, T. L. (1998). *The portable lawyer for mental health professionals.* New York: Wiley.

Brower, A. M. (1998). Group development as constructed social reality revisited: The constructivism of small groups. In C. Franklin & P. S. Nurius (Eds.), *Constructivism in practice: Methods and challenges* (pp. 203–214). Milwaukee, WI: Families International.

Burr, V. (1995). *An introduction to social constructionism.* London: Routledge.

Combs, G., & Freedman, J. (1990). *Symbol, story, and ceremony: Using metaphor in individual and family therapy.* New York: W. W. Norton.

Daniels, M. H., & White, L. J. (1997). Applying second-generation cognitive science toward assessing therapeutic change. In T. L. Sexton & B. L. Griffin (Eds.), *Constructivist thinking in counseling practice, research, and training* (pp. 174–187). New York: Teachers College Press.

Denzin, N. K., & Lincoln, Y. S. (2000). *Handbook of qualitative research* (2nd ed.). Thousand Oaks, CA: Sage.

Efran, J. S., Lukens, M. D., & Lukens, R. J. (1990). *Language, structure, and change: Frameworks of meaning in psychotherapy.* New York: W. W. Norton.

Elkaim, M. (1990). *If you love me, don't love me.* New York: Basic Books.

Ellis, A. (1955). New approaches to psychotherapy techniques. *Journal of Clinical Psychology* (Monograph Suppl. 2).

Ellis, A. (1958). Rational psychotherapy. *Journal of General Psychology, 59,* 35–49.

Ellis, A. (1962). *Reason and emotion in psychotherapy.* New York: Lyle Stuart.

Ellis, A. (1994). *Reason and emotion in psychotherapy: A comprehensive method for treating human disturbances* (Rev. ed.). New York: Birch Lane Press.

Feixas, G. (1995). Personal constructs in systemic practice. In R. A. Neimeyer & M. J. Mahoney (Eds.), *Constructivism in psychotherapy* (pp. 305–337). Washington, DC: American Psychological Association.

Franklin, C. (1998). Distinctions between social constructionism and cognitive constructivism: Practice applications. In C. Franklin & P. S. Nurius (Eds.), *Constructivism in practice: Methods and challenges* (pp. 57–94). Milwaukee, WI: Families International.

Franklin, C., & Nurius, P. S. (Eds.). (1998). *Constructivism in practice: Methods and challenges.* Milwaukee, WI: Families International.

Freedman, J., & Combs, G. (1996). *Narrative therapy: The social construction of preferred realities.* New York: W. W. Norton.

Gergen, K. (1985). The social constructionist movement in modern psychology. *American Psychologist, 40,* 266–275.

Gergen, K. (1991). *The saturated self.* New York: Basic Books.

Gergen, K. (1994). *Realities and relationships.* Cambridge, MA: Harvard University Press.

Gergen, K. J., & McNamee, S. (2000). From disordering discourse to transformative dialogue. In R. A. Neimeyer & J. D. Raskin (Eds.), *Constructions of disorder: Meaning-making frameworks for psychotherapy* (pp. 333–349). Washington, DC: American Psychological Association.

Goncalves, O. F. (1995). Hermeneutics, constructivism, and cognitive-behavioral therapies: From the object to the project. In R. A. Neimeyer & M. J. Mahoney (Eds.), *Constructivism in psychotherapy* (pp. 195–230). Washington, DC: American Psychological Association.

Goolishian, H., & Anderson, H. (1987). Language systems and therapy: An evolving idea. *Psychotherapy, 24,* 529–538.

Granvold, D. K. (1994). Concepts and methods of cognitive treatment. In D. K. Granvold (Ed.), *Cognitive and behavioral treatment: Methods and applications* (pp. 3–31). Pacific Grove, CA: Brooks/Cole.

Granvold, D. K. (1996a). Challenging roles of the constructive therapist: Expert and agent of social responsibility. *Constructivism in the Human Sciences, 1,* 16–21.

Granvold, D. K. (1996b). Constructivist psychotherapy. *Families in Society, 77,* 345–359.

Granvold, D. K. (1999). Integrating cognitive and constructive psychotherapies: A cognitive perspective. In T. B. Northcut & N. R. Heller (Eds.), *Enhancing psychodynamic therapy with cognitive-behavioral techniques* (pp. 53–93). Northvale, NJ: Jason Aronson.

Granvold, D. K., & Wodarski, J. S. (1994). Cognitive and behavioral treatment: Clinical issues, transfer of training, and relapse prevention. In D. K. Granvold (Ed.), *Cognitive and behavioral treatment: Methods and applications* (pp. 353–375). Pacific Grove, CA: Brooks/Cole.

Greenberg, L. S. (1986). Research strategies. In L. S. Greenberg & W. M. Pinsof (Eds.), *The psychotherapeutic process: A research handbook* (pp. 707–734). New York: Guilford Press.

Greenberg, L. S. (1992). Task analysis. In S. G. Toukmanian & D. L. Rennie (Eds.), *Psychotherapy process research* (pp. 22–50). Newbury Park, CA: Sage.

Greenberg, L. S. (2002). Integrating an emotion-focused approach to treatment into psychotherapy integration. *Journal of Psychotherapy Integration, 12,* 154–189.

Greenberg, L. S., & Safran, J. D. (1987). Emotion in psychotherapy. *American Psychologist, 44,* 19–29.

Greenwald, M. A. (1987). Programming treatment generalization. In L. Michelson & L. M. Ascher (Eds.), *Anxiety and stress disorders* (pp. 583–616). New York: Guilford Press.

Guidano, V. F. (1987). *Complexity of the self.* New York: Guilford Press.

Guidano, V. F. (1988). A systems, process-oriented approach to cognitive therapy. In K. S. Dobson (Ed.), *Handbook of cognitive-behavioral therapies* (pp. 307–354). New York: Guilford Press.

Guidano, V. F. (1991a). Affective change events in a cognitive therapy system approach. In J. D. Safran & L. S. Greenberg (Eds.), *Emotion, psychotherapy, & change* (pp. 50–79). New York: Guilford Press.

Guidano, V. F. (1991b). *The self in process.* New York: Guilford Press.

Guidano, V. F. (1995a). Constructivist psychotherapy: A theoretical framework. In R. A. Neimeyer & M. J. Mahoney (Eds.), *Constructivism in psychotherapy* (pp. 93–108). Washington, DC: American Psychological Association.

Guidano, V. F. (1995b). Self-observation in constructivist psychotherapy. In R. A. Neimeyer & M. J. Mahoney (Eds.), *Constructivism in psychotherapy* (pp. 155–191). Washington, DC: American Psychological Association.

Guidano, V. F., & Liotti, G. A. (1983). *Cognitive processes and emotional disorders.* New York: Guilford Press.

Held, B. S. (1995). *Back to reality: A critique of postmodern theory in psychotherapy.* New York: W. W. Norton.

Hoskins, M. (2002). Towards new methodologies for constructivist research: Synthesizing knowledges for relational inquiry. In J. D. Raskin & S. K. Bridges (Eds.), *Studies in meaning: Exploring constructivist psychology* (pp. 201–223). New York: Pace University Press.

Houston-Vega, M. K., Nuehring, E. M., & Daguio, E. R. (1997). *Prudent practice: A guide for managing malpractice risk.* Washington, DC: NASW Press.

Hoyt, M. F. (Ed.). (1994). *Constructive therapies.* New York: Guilford Press.

Hoyt, M. F. (Ed.). (1996). *Constructive therapies: Vol. 2.* New York: Guilford Press.

Hoyt, M. F. (Ed.). (1998). *The handbook of constructive therapies.* San Francisco: Jossey-Bass.

Kegan, R. (1982). *The evolving self.* Cambridge, MA: Harvard University Press.

Kelly, G. A. (1955). *The psychology of personal constructs.* New York: W. W. Norton.

Kuehlwein, K. T., & Rosen, H. (Eds.). (1993). *Cognitive therapies in action: Evolving innovative practice.* San Francisco: Jossey-Bass.

Kvale, S. (1992). Introduction: From the archaeology of the psyche to the architecture of cultural landscapes. In S. Kvale (Ed.), *Psychology and postmodernism* (pp. 1–16). London: Sage.

Laws, D. R. (Ed.). (1989). *Relapse prevention with sex offenders.* New York: Guilford Press.

Leitner, L. M., & Faidley, A. J. (2002). Disorder, diagnoses, and the struggles of humanness. In J. D. Raskin & S. K. Bridges (Eds.), *Studies in meaning: Exploring constructivist psychology* (pp. 99–121). New York: Pace University Press.

Lyddon, W. J. (1990). First- and second-order change: Implications for rationalist and constructivist cognitive therapies. *Journal of Counseling and Development, 69,* 122–127.

Mahoney, M. J. (1980). *Psychotherapy process: Current issues and future directions*. New York: Plenum Press.

Mahoney, M. J. (1985). Psychotherapy and human change processes. In M. J. Mahoney & A. Freeman (Eds.), *Cognition and psychotherapy* (pp. 3–48). New York: Plenum Press.

Mahoney, M. J. (1986). The tyranny of technique. *Counseling and Values, 30,* 169–174.

Mahoney, M. J. (1991). *Human change processes: The scientific foundations of psychotherapy*. New York: Basic Books.

Mahoney, M. J. (Ed.). (1995a). *Cognitive and constructive psychotherapies: Theory, research, and practice*. New York: Springer Publishing Company.

Mahoney, M. J. (1995b). Continuing evolution of the cognitive sciences and psychotherapies. In R. A. Neimeyer & M. J. Mahoney (Eds.), *Constructivism in psychotherapy* (pp. 39–67). Washington DC: American Psychological Association.

Mahoney, M. J. (1995c). Theoretical developments in the cognitive psychotherapies. In M. J. Mahoney (Ed.), *Cognitive and constructive psychotherapies: Theory, research, and practice* (pp. 3–19). New York: Springer Publishing Company.

Mahoney, M. J. (2003). *Constructive psychotherapy: A practical guide*. New York: Guilford Press.

Mahoney, M. J., & Granvold, D. K. (2005). Constructivism and psychotherapy. *World Psychiatry, 4*(2), 74–77.

Mahoney, M. J., Miller, H. M., & Arciero, G. (1995). Constructive metatheory and the nature of mental representation. In M. J. Mahoney (Ed.), *Cognitive and constructive psychotherapies: Theory, research, and practice* (pp. 103–120). New York: Springer Publishing Company.

Markus, H., & Nurius, P. S. (1986). Possible selves. *American Psychologist, 41,* 954–969.

Marlatt, G. A., & Gordon, J. R. (Eds.). (1985). *Relapse prevention: Maintenance strategies in the treatment of addictive behaviors*. New York: Guilford Press.

Martin, J. (1994). *The construction and understanding of psychotherapeutic change: Conversations, memories, and theories*. New York: Teachers College Press.

Maturana, H., & Varela, F. J. (1980). *Autopoiesis and cognition*. Boston: Reidel.

Maturana, H., & Varela, F. J. (1987). *The tree of knowledge: The biological roots of human understanding*. Boston: New Science Library.

McGinn, L. K., & Young, J. E. (1996). Schema-focused therapy. In P. M. Salkovskis (Ed.), *Frontiers of cognitive therapy* (pp. 182–207). New York: Guilford Press.

McNamee, S. (2002). The social construction of disorder: From pathology to potential. In J. D. Raskin & S. K. Bridges (Eds.), *Studies in meaning: Exploring constructivist psychology* (pp. 143–168). New York: Pace University Press.

Neimeyer, G. J. (Ed.). (1993). *Constructivist assessment: A casebook*. Newbury Park, CA: Sage.

Neimeyer, G. J., Hagans, C. L., & Anderson, R. (1998). Intervening in meaning: Application of constructivist assessment. In C. Franklin & P. S. Nurius (Eds.), *Constructivism in practice: Methods and challenges* (pp. 115–137). Milwaukee, WI: Families International.

Neimeyer, G. J., & Neimeyer, R. A. (1981). Personal construct perspectives on cognitive assessment. In T. V. Merluzzi, C. R. Glass, & M. Genest (Eds.), *Cognitive assessment* (pp. 188–232). New York: Guilford Press.

Neimeyer, R. A. (1987). An orientation to personal construct therapy. In R. A. Neimeyer & G. J. Neimeyer (Eds.), *Personal construct therapy casebook* (pp. 3–19). New York: Springer.

Neimeyer, R. A. (1993a). An appraisal of constructivist psychotherapies: Some conceptual and strategic contrasts. *Journal of Consulting and Clinical Psychology, 61,* 221–234.

Neimeyer, R. A. (1993b). Constructivism and the cognitive psychotherapies: Some conceptual and strategic contrasts. *Journal of Cognitive Psychotherapy, 7,* 159–171.

Neimeyer, R. A. (1993c). Constructivism and the problem of psychotherapy integration. *Journal of Psychotherapy Integration, 3,* 133–157.

Neimeyer, R. A. (1993d). Constructivist psychotherapy. In K. T. Kuehlwein & H. Rosen (Eds.), *Cognitive therapies in action: Evolving innovative practice* (pp. 268–300). San Francisco: Jossey-Bass.

Neimeyer, R. A. (1995a). Constructivist psychotherapies: Features, foundations, and future directions. In R. A. Neimeyer & M. J. Mahoney, (Eds.), *Constructivism in psychotherapy* (pp. 11–38). Washington, DC: American Psychological Association.

Neimeyer, R. A. (1995b). An invitation to constructivist psychotherapies. In R. A. Neimeyer & M. J. Mahoney (Eds.), *Constructivism in psychotherapy* (pp. 1–8). Washington, DC: American Psychological Association.

Neimeyer, R. A. (1996). Process interventions for the constructivist psychotherapist. In H. Rosen & K. T. Kuehlwein (Eds.), *Constructing realities: Meaning-making perspectives for psychotherapists* (pp. 371–411). San Francisco: Jossey-Bass.

Neimeyer, R. A. (2000). Narrative disruptions in the construction of the self. In R. A. Neimeyer & J. D. Raskin (Eds.), *Constructions of disorder: Meaning-making frameworks for psychotherapy* (pp. 207–242). Washington, DC: American Psychological Association.

Neimeyer, R. A., & Mahoney, M. J. (Eds.). (1995). *Constructivism in psychotherapy.* Washington, DC: American Psychological Association.

Neimeyer, R. A., & Raskin, J. D. (Eds.). (2000a). *Constructions of disorder: Meaning-making frameworks for psychotherapy.* Washington, DC: American Psychological Association.

Neimeyer, R. A., & Raskin, J. D. (2000b). On practicing postmodern therapy in modern times. In R. A. Neimeyer & J. D. Raskin (Eds.), *Constructions of disorder: Meaning-making frameworks for psychotherapy* (pp. 3–14). Washington, DC: American Psychological Association.

Neimeyer, R. A., & Raskin, J. D. (2001). Varieties of constructivism in psychotherapy. In K. S. Dobson (Ed.), *Handbook of cognitive-behavioral therapies* (2nd ed., pp. 393–430). New York: Guilford Press.

Nurius, P. S., & Berlin, S. B. (1994). Treatment of negative self-concept and depression. In D. K. Granvold (Ed.), *Cognitive and behavioral treatment: Methods and applications* (pp. 249–271). Pacific Grove, CA: Brooks/Cole.

Pittman, F. (1992). It's not my fault. *Family Therapy Networker, 16*(1), 56–63.

Popper, K. R. (1972). *Objective knowledge: An evolutionary approach.* London: Oxford University Press.

Raskin, J. D. (2002). Constructivism in psychology: Personal construct psychology, radical constructivism, and social constructionism. In J. D. Raskin & S. K. Bridges (Eds.), *Studies in meaning: Exploring constructivist psychology* (pp. 1–25). New York: Pace University Press.

Raskin, J. D., & Bridges, S. K. (Eds.). (2002). *Studies in meaning: Exploring constructivist psychology.* New York: Pace University Press.

Raskin, J. D., & Bridges, S. K. (Eds.). (in press). *Studies in meaning 3: Constructivist therapy in the "real" world.* New York: Pace University Press.

Raskin, J. D., & Lewandowski, A. M. (2000). The construction of disorder as human enterprise. In R. A. Neimeyer & J. D. Raskin (Eds.), *Constructions of disorder: Meaning-making frameworks for psychotherapy* (pp. 15–40). Washington, DC: American Psychological Association.

Rennie, D. L. (1992). Qualitative analysis of the client's experience of psychotherapy. In S. G. Toukmanian & D. L. Rennie (Eds.), *Psychotherapy process research* (pp. 211–233). Newbury Park, CA: Sage.

Rennie, D. L. (1995). Strategic choices in a qualitative approach to psychotherapy process research. In L. T. Hoshmand & J. Martin (Eds.), *Research as praxis* (pp. 198–220). New York: Teachers College Press.

Rennie, D. L., & Toukmanian, S. G. (1992). Explanation in psychotherapy process research. In S. G. Toukmanian & D. L. Rennie (Eds.), *Psychotherapy process research* (pp. 234–251). Newbury Park, CA: Sage.

Rice, L. N., & Greenberg, L. S. (1984). *Patterns of change.* New York: Guilford Press.

Rosen, H. (1993). Developing themes in the field of cognitive therapy. In K. T. Kuehlwein & H. Rosen (Eds.), *Cognitive therapies in action: Evolving innovative practice* (pp. 403–434). San Francisco: Jossey-Bass.

Rosen, H., & Kuehlwein, K. T. (Eds.). (1996). *Constructing realities: Meaning-making perspectives for psychotherapists.* San Francisco: Jossey-Bass.

Safran, J. D., & Greenberg, L. S. (1991a). Emotion in human functioning: Theory and therapeutic implications. In J. D. Safran & L. S. Greenberg (Eds.), *Emotion, psychotherapy, & change* (pp. 3–15). New York: Guilford Press.

Safran, J. D., & Greenberg, L. S. (Eds.). (1991b). *Emotion, psychotherapy, & change.* New York: Guilford Press.

Safran, J. D., & Messer, S. B. (1997). Psychotherapy integration: A postmodern critique. *Clinical Psychology: Science and Practice, 4,* 140–152.

Safran, J. D., & Segal, Z. V. (1990). *Interpersonal process in cognitive therapy.* New York: Basic Books.

Safran, J. D., Vallis, T. M., Segal, Z. V., & Shaw, B. F. (1986). Assessment of core cognitive processes in cognitive therapy. *Cognitive Therapy and Research, 10,* 509–526.

Saleebey, D. (2006). *The strengths perspective in social work practice* (4th ed.). New York: Allyn & Bacon.

Segal, Z. V., Williams, J. M. G., & Teasdale, J. D. (2002) *Mindfulness-based cognitive therapy for depression.* New York: Guilford Press.

Seikkula, J., Aaltonen, J., Alakara, B., Haarakangas, K., Keranen, J., & Sutela, M. (1995). Treating psychosis by means of open dialogue. In S. Friedman (Ed.), *The reflecting team in action* (pp. 62–80). New York: Guilford Press.

Sexton, T. L., & Griffin, B. L. (Eds.). (1997). *Constructivist thinking in counseling practice, research, and training.* New York: Teachers College Press.

Szasz, T. (2002). "Diagnosing" behavior: Cui bono? In J. D. Raskin & S. K. Bridges (Eds.), *Studies in meaning: Exploring constructivist psychology* (pp. 169–179). New York: Pace University Press.

Toukmanian, S. G., & Rennie, D. L. (1992). *Psychotherapy process research: Paradigmatic and narrative approaches.* Newbury Park, CA: Sage.

Watzlawick, P. (Ed.). (1984). *The invented reality: How do we know what we believe we know?* New York: W. W. Norton.

Watzlawick, P., Weakland, J. H., & Fisch, R. (1974). *Change: Principles of problem formulation and problem resolution.* New York: W. W. Norton.

White, M., & Epston, D. (1990). *Narrative means to therapeutic ends.* New York: W. W. Norton.

Wilson, P. H. (Ed.). (1992). *Principles and practices of relapse prevention.* New York: Guilford Press.

Young, J. (1990). *Cognitive therapy for personality disorders: A schema-focused approach.* Sarasota, FL: Professional Resource.

CHAPTER 17

Solution-Focused Therapy

Jacqueline Corcoran

Solution-focused therapy is a relatively new treatment approach with a unique focus, not on problems, but rather on solutions to problems and the strengths clients invariably possess. After providing a brief overview of solution-focused practice, this chapter will discuss the historical development behind the model's formulation by de Shazer (1985, 1988, 1994) and associates (de Shazer et al., 1986) and the phases of the helping process, including some of the key theoretical constructs. After a detailed explanation of the model, its compatibility with a generalist-eclectic framework will be discussed, along with a critique of the model. Finally, a case example of solution-focused therapy with a young woman suffering from social anxiety will be presented.

OVERVIEW OF SOLUTION-FOCUSED PRACTICE

In solution-focused therapy, clients are viewed as having the necessary strengths and capacities to solve their own problems (De Jong & Berg, 2002). Because individuals are unique and have the right to determine what it is they want, the task of the practitioner is to identify strengths and amplify them so that clients can apply these "solutions." Given the lack of emphasis on problems, history-taking and discussion of how symptoms manifest themselves is not detailed. Nor is there a need to understand how the problem began, because this knowledge may offer little in terms of how to solve the problem. In general, the past is de-emphasized other than times when "exceptions" to problems occurred.

The model orients instead toward the future when the problem will no longer be a problem. To this end, practitioners assist clients in eliciting exceptions, times when the problem is either not a problem or is lessened in terms of duration, severity, frequency, or intensity (O'Hanlon & Weiner-Davis, 1989).

The construction of solutions from exceptions is considered easier and ultimately more successful than stopping or changing existing problem behavior. When exceptions are identified, the practitioner explores with clients the strengths and resources that were utilized. These resources are enlarged upon through the use of questions presupposing that positive change will occur (e.g., "When you are doing better, what will be happening?" "When our work here is successful, what will be different?"), because changes in language are assumed to lead to changes in perception. When clients view themselves as resourceful and capable, they are empowered toward future positive behavior. Behavioral, as well as perceptual, change is implicated because the approach is focused on concrete, specific behaviors that are achievable within a brief time period. The view is that change in specific areas can "snowball" into bigger changes due to the systems orientation assumed to be present: Change in one part of the system can lead to change in other parts of the system (O'Hanlon & Weiner-Davis, 1989).

The systemic basis of solution-focused therapy also means that the context of a particular behavior is more influential than innate individual characteristics. In this model, the individual is depathologized; instead, the emphasis is on situational aspects—the who, what, where, when, and how of a particular behavior (Durrant, 1995).

HISTORICAL DEVELOPMENT

Although some of the key figures associated with solution-focused therapy are social workers (e.g., Insoo Kim Berg and Michelle Weiner-Davis), the model has arisen out of the field of family therapy, with Mental Research Institute (MRI) brief therapy as a specific influence (de Shazer et al., 1986). An essential family therapy concept involves a systemic notion of causality, that a change in one part of a routine sequence will result in further change for the system. In both MRI and solution-focused approaches, the pattern around a problem is altered as opposed to discovering its underlying cause (O'Hanlon & Weiner-Davis, 1989). Where the models depart is that MRI brief therapy focuses on problems, whereas solution-focused therapy emphasizes solutions to problems.

Another major influence on solution-focused therapy has been the work of the psychiatrist Milton Erickson (O'Hanlon & Weiner-Davis,

1989). Erickson believed that individuals have the strengths and resources to solve their own problems and that the practitioner's job is to uncover these resources and activate them for the client. For Erickson, many times an activation of these resources involves an amplification of symptomatic behavior through the use of paradoxical directives (e.g., prescribing symptoms). Unlike MRI brief therapy, which also employs paradoxical interventions on a routine basis, solution-focused therapy relies on paradox only as a last resort when other, more direct attempts to elicit positive behavior in the client have failed.

A further theoretical influence on solution-focused therapy is social constructivism, the view that knowledge about reality is constructed from social interactions (Berg & De Jong, 1996). In other words, reality is relative to the social context. Therefore, the concept of the "expert" practitioner, who categorizes, diagnoses, and solves client problems objectively, is viewed with skepticism. Sharing perceptions with others through language and engaging in conversational dialogues is the medium by which reality is shaped (de Shazer, 1994). Thus, the solution-focused practitioner uses language and questioning to influence the way clients view their problems, the potential for solutions, and the expectancy for change (Berg & De Jong, 1996).

PHASES OF HELPING

The phases of helping in solution-focused therapy can be described as (a) engagement, (b) assessment, (c) goal-setting, (d) intervention, and (e) termination. However, it must be noted that phases are typically not as discrete as they are in a generalist-eclectic framework. Indeed, engagement occurs concurrent to helping the client formulate treatment goals, with questions such as "What needs to happen so that you won't have to come back to see me?" Discussion of goals leads to exception-finding, identification of times when movement toward treatment goals already happens. Evaluation in the solution-focused model most commonly involves noting progress on solution-focused scales; however, solution-focused scales are also used for goal-setting, task construction, and exception-finding. In addition, termination is a focus from the beginning of treatment, because goal-setting and solution-finding orient the client toward change in a brief time period (De Jong & Berg, 2002).

Engagement

The practitioner gains cooperation of the client in finding solutions by "joining" with the client as the initial phase of engagement. "Joining" is the clinician's task of establishing a positive, mutually cooperative relationship (Berg, 1994). The worker should convey acceptance of the client's positions and perspectives rather than becoming invested in who is "right" and who is "wrong." These strategies are seen as counterproductive in that defensive clients are less amenable to working with the practitioner and to change (Cade & O'Hanlon, 1993).

Strategies for enhancement of joining involve recognition of idiosyncratic phrasing the client uses and adopting this language (Berg, 1994; O'Hanlon & Weiner-Davis, 1989). For example, a person may describe anxiety as problems with their "nerves." The assumption is that clients feel understood when their language is used by the worker. Additionally, the use of client language means less reliance on clinical terms, which may be viewed as pathologizing.

As well as using language idiosyncratic to the client, the worker should also be vigilant for any strengths and resources to compliment, recognizing that every problem behavior contains within it an inherent strength (O'Hanlon & Weiner-Davis, 1989). For example, a child whom a parent describes as "hyperactive" could be viewed as "energetic" and "high-spirited." Through reframing, the client is given credit for positive aspects of his or her behavior, and the joining process is enhanced.

A related intervention, normalizing, involves depathologizing people's concerns. For example, a parent objecting to his or her teenager's dress style can be told that a normal process of adolescence involves finding an identity, and this may include experimentation with different styles. The objective is to help people view themselves as struggling with ordinary life difficulties rather than overwhelming problems that cannot be solved. Normalizing thus makes more manageable problems previously viewed as insurmountable. Further, normalizing "de-escalates" the tendency of some problems to exacerbate beyond their original nature. In the previous example, if a parent continually argues with a child about dress style and attempts to control the behavior, conflict might take hold of the relationship and the child may become increasingly rebellious. However, if the parent views experimentation as a normal part of identity development, he or she may be better able to see this as fairly harmless.

Assessment

Assessment involves determining the client's relationship to the helping process, finding strengths, and inquiring about pretreatment changes. There are three main client relationships in the solution-focused model: the customer, the complainant, and the visitor (De Jong & Berg, 2002). Most traditional treatment models assume the presence of a "customer," a person who comes in voluntarily to make changes in his or her life.

The second type of client is the complainant. Complainants ostensibly come to the helping process voluntarily to change, but it soon becomes apparent that they want someone or something else outside of themselves to change. These clients tend to blame other people, events, and circumstances for their problems. The third type of client, the visitor, is directed or mandated to visit a practitioner by another person or entity invested in the client's change. The visitor, therefore, is a nonvoluntary participant in treatment whose main goal is ending contact with the helping system.

The person presenting with the visitor or the complainant relationship to the helping process is often difficult to engage, because these clients are not interested in change for themselves (Berg, 1994). In the solution-focused model, strategies are used with both client types. For example, visitors can be engaged toward the goal of getting the mandating body "off their backs" ("Whose idea was it that you come to see me?" "What would they say you need to do so you don't need to come here anymore?") and change can be directed toward that end. Complainants can be engaged through the use of "coping questions," which are designed to elicit the resources people use to cope with difficult circumstances ("This sounds very hard. How do you manage? How do you have the strength to go on?"). An additional intervention with complainants is to emphasize the context for behavior ("What are you doing when he is behaving?"), which orients individuals to their own personal agency in the situation.

A key part of assessment in solution-focused therapy is for the social worker to be vigilant for strengths clients display outside the problem area, such as in their employment, schooling, hobbies, and relationships (see Bertolino & O'Hanlon, 2002). For example, potential strengths to exploit could involve patience, energy, communication skills, organizational ability, the ability to delay gratification, managerial skills, attention to detail, and so forth. Here, the intent is to help clients see themselves as resourceful, as such a person will be presumably more hopeful about the future and his or her own abilities to confront problems, and to build upon existing strengths in order to solve presenting problems.

Another aspect of assessment involves inquiry about pretreatment changes; that is, asking clients what kind of changes they have noticed between the time they first scheduled their appointment and the first session. Drawing clients' attention to pretreatment changes might bolster client motivation to stay in treatment (Allgood, Parham, Salts, & Smith, 1995). Furthermore, attention to pretreatment change might have a snowball effect in that small changes lead to bigger changes. For example, if someone feels more hope for the future as a result of scheduling an appointment, he or she might be more prone to see people as helpful and react to them in kind.

Goal-Setting

In the solution-focused model, emphasis is on well-formulated goals that are achievable within a brief time frame. Although goal-setting is discussed as a discrete phase of helping, it is more accurate to view discussion of goal formulation as starting as soon as the client comes in contact with the practitioner: "What will be different about your life when you don't need to come here anymore?" The presuppositional phrasing of this question is presumed to affect the way clients view their problems and the potential for change (Cade & O'Hanlon, 1993) and underlies all solution-focused questioning. Further, expectancy for change is conveyed by using words such as "when" and "will." Examples of such questioning include "*When* you are sober, what *will* you be saying/doing?" The use of definitive phrasing to convey an expectancy for change is consistent with the solution-focused orientation toward the future. People who have experienced a negative and stressful past may easily project this past into the future and assume their lives will always be the same. Use of the miracle question and scaling questions are ways to help clients envision a more hopeful future.

The Miracle Question

In the miracle question, clients are asked to conjure up a detailed view of a future without the problem: "Let's say that while you're sleeping, a miracle occurs, and the problem you came here with is solved. What will let you know the next morning that a miracle happened?" (de Shazer, 1988). Specifics are elicited about this no-problem experience so that clients may develop a vision of a more hopeful and satisfying future. Sometimes asking clients to envision a brighter future may help them be clearer on what they want or to see a path to problem-solving. By discussing the future in a positive light, hope can be generated, and change can be enacted in the present by the recognition of both strengths to cope with obstacles and signs of possibilities for change (Cade & O'Hanlon, 1993; see also Corcoran, 2005, for a list of other future-oriented change techniques).

Scaling Questions

After clients are encouraged to expand their futures and the possibilities, the practitioner helps the client develop concrete, behaviorally specific goals that can be achieved in a brief time frame (De Jong & Berg, 2002). Clients typically begin to discuss their goals in abstract and non-sensory-based language: "I will feel better." The task of the clinician is to encourage and develop observable correlates of these states (Cade & O'Hanlon, 1993).

For example, rather than "not feeling depressed," goals might involve "getting to work on time," "calling friends," and "doing volunteer work." As this example illustrates, goals should involve the presence of positive behaviors rather than the absence of negatives (De Jong & Berg, 2002).

A useful technique for making concrete even the most abstract of goals involves scaling questions (Berg, 1994; Berg & Miller, 1992). Scaling questions involve asking clients to rank order themselves on a scale from 1 to 10, with "1" representing "the problem" and "10" representing "when the problem is no longer a problem." The practitioner then develops with the client specific behavioral indicators of the "10" position.

Scales offer a number of advantages (Cade & O'Hanlon, 1993). First, a rank ordering will enable clients to realize they have already made some progress toward their goals ("You're already at a five? You're halfway! What have you done to get to that point?"). Any progress made can then be the basis for exception-finding. (Exception-finding will be covered in more detail in the following section.) Scales can also be used to guide task-setting ("What will you need to do to move up to a six?"). Clients identify specific behaviors that will help them move up one rank order on the scale. Finally, scales can be used to track progress over time.

Scales can further be used as a basis for the exploration of "relationship questions" (Berg, 1994). Relationship questions help clients understand the context of situations and the part they themselves play in interactions. Typical questions include "Where do you think your partner would rank you?" or "Where would your teacher put you?" Further questioning can help the client identify the steps necessary to take so that other key people will recognize progress: "What would she say you need to do to move up a number?" When more than one person is present in the session, relationship questions can be used to stimulate interaction, helping family members clarify their expectations of each other. Relationship questions also enable clients to become more adept at taking on the perspective of others. This ability opens up new meanings and possibilities for client change as they reflect on how they might act differently (Berg & De Jong, 1996).

Intervention

The major intervention of solution-focused practice is identifying exceptions, times when the problem is not a problem or when the client solved similar problems in the past (Bertolino & O'Hanlon, 2002). Exceptions provide a blueprint for individuals to solve their problems in their own unique way. Exceptions assist people to access and expand upon the resources and strengths they already own, which is seen as easier than teaching them entirely new behaviors. Exception-finding also reduces the way people often view problems as all-encompassing and unchangeable. When people realize there are exceptions, problems are viewed as much more manageable.

Once exceptions are identified, the social worker helps the client deconstruct the contextual details of the exception through the following types of investigative questions: who ("Who was there? What did they do? How was that helpful?"), what ("What did you do differently? What's different about those times?"), where ("Where does the exception occur? How does that contribute to the outcome?"), when ("When is the problem a little better? At what times of the day and what days? Before or after?"), and how ("How did you get that to happen? How are you managing to do this?"; Bertolino & O'Hanlon, 2002). People come to see, through such inquiry, that behaviors are the result of certain situations and personal choices rather than ingrained personality traits.

A further way to find and build on exceptions involves an intervention borrowed from narrative therapy, called "externalizing the problem" (White & Epston, 1990). Externalizing the problem involves making a linguistic distinction between the person and the problem by personifying the problem as an external entity (i.e., "the anger," "the arguing," "the urge to use"). In this way, a problem that is considered inherent or fixed can be viewed as less stable and less rigid. Because problems are no longer viewed as innate, pathological qualities, people are more able to generate options.

Externalizing also has the benefit of freeing up people to take a lighter approach to "serious" problems, particularly when problems are named in a humorous vein; for instance, "Sneaky Poo" for encopresis (White, 1984). A final benefit of externalizing is that it can act as a bridge between talk about problems and talk about solutions (Dyes & Neville, 2000). People are empowered to "fight against" these problems through the use of "relative influence questions" (White & Epston, 1990), which ask clients to determine the extent of their influence over their problems, as well as the influence of the problem over them: "When are you able to stand up to the anger and not let it tell you what to do?" "When can you resist the urge to smoke/shoot up?" "When are you able to overcome the temptation to just stay in bed instead of getting your kids ready for school?" "What percentage of the time do you have control over the craving to see him again." In this way, clients discover exceptions by identifying times when they are able to exert control over their problems.

A final way to help clients discover exceptions is to prescribe the "first formula task" for homework after the first session, which is to have them notice the things happening in their lives that they would like to have continue to happen (de Shazer, 1985). The purpose of the task is to have clients focus on what is already working for them. Adams, Piercy, and Jurich

(1991) compared the use of the solution-focused "first formula task" and a task focusing on details of the problem. The authors found that the solution-focused task resulted in greater improvement on presenting problems and clearer formulation of treatment goals. Other solution-focused homework tasks are detailed in Corcoran (2005).

Termination

Because change is oriented toward a brief time frame in the solution-focused model, work is oriented toward termination at the beginning of treatment. Questions include "What needs to happen so you don't need to come back to see me?" "What will be different when our work here has been successful?" (Berg, 1994). Once clients have maintained changes on the small concrete goals they have set, the practitioner and client start to discuss plans for termination, as it is assumed that achievement of these small changes will lead to further positive change in the client's life. Termination is geared toward helping clients identify strategies so that change will be maintained and the momentum developed will further cause change to occur.

Although the practitioner does not want to imply that relapse is inevitable, the client must be prepared with strategies to enact if temptation presents itself or if the client begins to slip into old behaviors. Therefore, it is during termination that possibility rather than definitive phrasing is used. For example, "What *would* be the first thing you'd notice *if* you started to find things slipping back?" "What *could* you do to prevent things from getting any further?" "*If* you have the urge to drink again, what *could* you do to make sure you didn't use?" might be typical inquiries to elicit strategies to use if there is a return to old behavior.

Termination also involves building on the changes that have occurred, with the hope they will continue into the future. Selekman (1995, 1997) has proposed a number of such questions, including "With all the changes you are making, what will I see if I was a fly on your wall 6 months from now?" or "With all the changes you are making, what will you be telling me if I run into you at the convenience store 6 months from now?" Questions are phrased to set up the expectation that change will continue to happen.

APPLICATION TO FAMILY AND GROUP WORK

Family Work

Because of the emphasis on the context of the relationship for behavior change, solution-focused therapy works well with couples and families, and, in fact, the model emerged from the family therapy field. Solution-focused questions are asked of family members so they can understand the way their behavior influences others ("What are you doing when he is behaving?"). The solution-focused orientation also redirects the blaming and attacking stance of family members into requests for the presence of positive behaviors ("What would you like her to be doing?"). Then the focus turns to times when the hoped-for behavior already occurs and what is different about the context, particularly the responses of other family members, during these nonproblem times. This focus presumably leads to a more positive view of other family members, which, in turn, leads to more positive behaviors.

Solution-focused therapy also poses advantages for family work because it addresses the various types of relationships that present to the change process. There are strategies for complainants, typically parents who bring their children to treatment. Coping questions elicit the resources parents employ to deal with difficult circumstances. Parents are asked to consider how their own behavior impacts their children's. Focus on when their children display appropriate behavior cultivates in parents a more positive view of their children and encourages future positive behavior. Solution-focused questioning further engages children, who usually represent the visitor type of relationship, in developing treatment goals and in taking responsibility for the work in the helping process.

Group Work

Since the last edition of this book, much has been written on solution-focused group work, typically clinically focused articles on how to apply the model with various populations and problems (e.g., Burns & Hulusi, 2005; Lange, 2001). A solution-focused approach alone or in combination with another model can offer advantages for group therapy. First, the goal-oriented and short-term nature of solution-focused therapy is adaptable to either closed-ended groups of a brief nature (for example, Selekman, 1995) or open-ended groups (for example, Corcoran, 1997, describes an open-ended, revolving membership group with juvenile offenders).

Solution-focused therapy can empower clients who might otherwise find a group too problem focused or complaint driven. A solution-focused model can also build on the strengths of individuals in groups, offering inspiration and solutions to problems.

In addition, a solution-focused approach can be advantageous for nonvoluntary populations in group work, such as those who have been involved in criminal offending or substance use. As mentioned, nonvoluntary populations can be difficult to engage in traditional treatment models, but solution-focused therapy has many strategies so that the nonvoluntary client is responsible for the work in treatment ("Whose idea was it that you come to group?" "What does your probation officer/ the court need to see to know you don't need to come here anymore?" "What would they say you're doing differently?" and "What would they say is the next step you should take?"). By eliciting answers to these types of questions, nonvoluntary clients can be engaged in their main objective: to get the referral source "off their backs," so they no longer have to attend treatment (Berg, 1994).

COMPATIBILITY WITH THE GENERALIST-ECLECTIC FRAMEWORK

Solution-focused therapy shares many similarities with a generalist-eclectic framework. Although solution-focused therapy is classified as a "therapy" approach, it is actually applicable to the wide range of settings and problems with which direct practice social workers are involved, such as crisis intervention (Greene, Lee, Trask, & Rheinscheld, 1996) and child protective services (Berg, 1994; Berg & Kelly, 2000; Corcoran, 1999; Corcoran & Franklin, 1998). Solution-focused and social work practice share a systemic view, acknowledging the importance of context rather than an emphasis on individual pathology. Although both solution-focused therapy and social work address the key influence of the immediate relationship context, social work also emphasizes systems, ecological, and broader environmental levels. In both perspectives, a systemic notion of change is promoted in recognition that a small change in one part of the system can produce change in another part of the system.

However, solution-focused therapy departs from a generalist-eclectic framework in eschewing a holistic assessment of the various system levels, along with information-gathering about the problem and history-taking. Although the generalist-eclectic framework espouses an emphasis on health, normality, and client strengths, in actuality "assessment" implies the diagnosis of a problem. The practitioner has to decide on the client's problem so that it can be solved. Hence, the assumption is that a logical link exists between the problem and the solution (De Jong & Berg, 2002). In contrast, solution-focused therapy does not emphasize the problem; nor does it assume that an understanding of a problem leads to its solution. In this approach, treatment begins with an exploration of strengths and how to target these strengths toward positive change.

Although both solution-focused therapy and a general-eclectic framework speak of a collaborative relationship between practitioner and client, the solution-focused approach concretely puts this into practice.

First, there are specific techniques to assist in joining, such as normalizing and reframing, and specific interventions depending on the client type involved. The spirit of collaboration is also seen in clients being given respect for their unique worldviews and being allowed to determine their own treatment goals. Respect is further conveyed for people's individual strengths and resources, with the assumption that people are capable of solving their own problems. The task of the practitioner is to help clients identify their resources and then enlarge upon them. This approach is in contrast to a view of an "expert" practitioner who possess specialized knowledge on life cycle theories or minority populations. In these approaches, specialized knowledge is applied to client problems and a diagnosis is made. It appears, therefore, that although a collaborative process is touted in a generalist-eclectic framework, "expert" knowledge is still required.

Although eclecticism is not as central a feature in solution-focused therapy as it is in the generalist-eclectic framework, allowance is made for the use of other models and theories if these fit with the client's needs and goals. For example, Bertolino and O'Hanlon (2002) discussed medication as one possible solution for people with mental disorders. Cognitive and behavioral approaches are particularly compatible with solution-focused therapy, as they are directed toward both cognitive and behavioral change. Cognitive interventions can, for example, be used to help clients identify the resources they use that are cognitive in nature. "What were you thinking about yourself/the other person when you were able to do that?" "What were you telling yourself?" The use of cognitively based questions can help people develop further resources for coping.

Behavioral change techniques may also be used to supplement solution-focused therapy, specifically the use of behavioral rehearsal and feedback. Rehearsing behaviors through the use of role plays in session, for example, may be helpful so that clients are cued as to how they demonstrated exceptions in certain situations. In addition, clients may have to practice a situation successfully before they are able to implement the new pattern of behavior in future settings. These suggestions show that solution-focused therapy might benefit from cognitive-behavioral interventions in helping clients discover resources (cognitive coping) or those that allow them to practice new situations (rehearsal and feedback) or focus on reinforcement of positive behaviors.

CRITIQUE OF SOLUTION-FOCUSED PRACTICE

Strengths

A main strength of solution-focused practice is its compatibility with social work values, including the importance of context for behavior, a systemic perspective, client self-determination, a focus on strengths and resources of the individual, and applicability to a range of social work settings and problems. The focus on strengths is a particularly unique orientation, because many other practice models are pathologizing (De Jong & Berg, 2002). The focus on client resources and what the client is doing right empowers and offers hope to people who are often beleaguered by the time they come to a social worker for assistance. Solution-focused questioning offers a concrete way to implement these values in social work practice.

In addition, social workers intervene with many nonvoluntary populations, such as those in child welfare, criminal offending, and substance use settings, to name a few. As discussed, there are many strategies to engage the person who has a visitor relationship to the change process. In solution-focused therapy, the work of treatment is placed on the client rather than the practitioner. Clients have to decide on their own goals and clarify what they want in concrete terms. Practitioner collaboration helps clients discover and build on the resources they employ during nonproblem times. Through this process, clients are empowered to help themselves.

Limitations

Despite an increase in the number of studies since the last volume of this book, empirical evidence still lags far behind anecdotal reports of effectiveness, which are numerous. Indeed, a systematic review of solution-focused therapy (Corcoran & Pillai, in press) identified only 10 studies that meet the criteria for empirical evidence (group designs and statistics necessary to calculate an effect size). The solution-focused research was difficult to synthesize because of the different populations and problem areas that were examined, so effect sizes were tabulated. Using this method only 4 of the 10 studies indicated a moderate to high effect.

Methodological limitations are present even in these 10 studies. For instance, only 5 involved randomization to treatment conditions, and some only used nonstandardized measures. In addition, basic information, such as a description of the psychometric work of measures and treatment fidelity, is often missing. Finally, the studies are, for the most part, inadequately powered, having too small a sample size to detect differences, if they do exist, between the treatment and comparison/control conditions.

Possible reasons can be put forward for the lack of empirical research and its poor quality. The major explanation involves the constructivist origins of solution-focused therapy. These origins do not fit within the positivist framework that gives rise to quantitative procedures and treatment outcome studies. A second reason is that many measures tend to be problem focused in nature and contradict the strengths orientation of solution-focused therapy. Third, the brief focus of solution-focused therapy, which can involve even only one session, makes it difficult to collect pretest and posttest measurement instruments after a certain standard length of time. Because of the lack of empirical evidence, it is unknown to which problem areas or populations solution-focused therapy is ideally suited.

Another potential limitation of solution-focused therapy involves the assumption that clients have the necessary resources and strengths to solve their own problems. Sometimes clients may have deficits in their knowledge or skills; if the social worker has information that may assist the client with a certain deficit, then it appears that it would be unethical to hold back this knowledge and rely on only what the client brings. It seems that a "balanced" approach, both working with skills and deficits and risk and protection, is needed to optimally help clients (McMillen, Morris, & Sherraden, 2004).

Solution-focused therapy has also been critiqued for its emphasis on behavior and perception rather than feelings. Lipchick (2002) argued that feelings, behaviors, and cognitions are linked, and feelings cannot be ignored, as they are an inextricable facet of human existence. If feelings are ignored, they may cloud people's ability to remember the exceptions to their problems or to imagine a future without the problem. She suggested that the role of feelings can be integrated into solution-focused work. For example, exceptions can center around times individuals felt better and what was different about their behaviors and cognitions when they felt this way.

Solution-focused therapy has been critiqued from a feminist perspective. Dermer, Hemesath, and Russell (1998) commended the model for its emphasis on competence and strengths, but decried the lack of sensitivity to gender and power differentials.

Another critique that may be leveled at solution-focused therapy has to do with the limited attention paid to client diversity. Social work professes a commitment to "cultural competence" and "culturally sensitive" interventions. The solution-focused position on diversity is that although practitioners may have knowledge of and experience with a particular population, they do not know a particular individual with a unique history, traits, strengths, and limitations. To make assumptions about that person due to cultural membership verges on stereotyping. Instead the client is considered the expert; practitioners should respectfully inquire about clients' worldview and distinctive ways of solving problems (De Jong & Berg, 2002). Although social workers will not argue with the idea of treating people as individuals, one of the requirements put forth by the National Association of Social Workers (1999) and the Council on Social Work Education (2004) is that social workers have a knowledge base on diverse groups and be able to deliver services that are congruent with these populations.

CASE EXAMPLE

A 25-year-old woman, Sarah Matthews (fictitious name), presented in treatment because she had never had a serious boyfriend, much less a date, due to her extreme anxiety and discomfort when speaking to men. Sarah coped with this anxiety by avoiding contacts with men. When contact was inevitable, her heart would pound, and she would blush, stammer, and mumble. Sarah related she had been sexually abused as a child (a one-time incident when she was 5 years old) by a teenage uncle. Sarah had never told anyone before about the abuse and was adamant about not discussing it any further in therapy. She said she only wanted to tackle the social anxiety.

The first intervention with Sarah was the construction of a *solution-focused scale*. Sarah was asked specific behaviors that would indicate she was at a "10," *when she did not need to come to therapy anymore.* She described that she would be able to speak to men in casual social contact and to feel comfortable in social and work situations that might include men. Sarah's description entailed *a behaviorally specific goal that was achievable within a brief time period.* She did not, for instance, state that she wanted to be able to date men or have a boyfriend. These objectives might have been possible only after she had been able to meet her more immediate goal, as small change can snowball into bigger changes.

Sarah was then asked to rank herself on the solution-focused scale. Sarah placed herself at a "2" because she was able to speak to one man at her workplace. Sarah was *complimented*; she had made some progress toward her goal. Inquiry about the *exceptions* that had occurred to get her to this point was explored. Sarah said that the exception involved a delivery man who came out weekly to her work setting. Her job as office manager was to get him to sign for the order he delivered. She said at first she had avoided him, conveniently being "way too busy" when he came by, forcing a coworker to get him to sign. However, her coworker's job duties then changed and Sarah had no choice but to have contact with him. She said she would experience extreme dread at the prospect of him coming to the office. When he would make his weekly visit, she described that she would shake and sweat, avoid eye contact, and mutter enough of a response to get the job done. After 4 months of this, she said she was finally at the point where she no longer dreaded his visits and could respond to him very brusquely with one-word answers, but at least she was no longer submerged with anxiety. When asked about the *resources* she had employed to get to this point, she said that becoming familiar with him and seeing him joke around with her coworkers had helped. She was asked how she could apply the resources she had employed in the past to current situations that were bothering her. She identified that the exception involved exposing herself to contact with a man over time, which allowed her to eventually perceive him as safe. She denied that there were any other men with whom she had contact on a regular or, even an occasional, basis.

When asked how she could make more of that happen in her life, she stated she had considered joining a church social club. She was *complimented* for coming up with such a creative solution and was asked how she could go about joining such a group. She said she had attended a couple of different churches in the area and had found one with which she felt comfortable and that this church offered a singles group. It was agreed that the task for the following week, which would get her to a "3," would involve calling about meeting times for the singles group.

Sarah came in to the session the next time, smiling and pleased. She reported that not only had she called about the singles group, she had also attended a meeting on Friday night. She was asked again about the *resources* she had used to do this. How had she been able to face her fears and get herself to this group? She said she was just at the point where she was sick of having her life so curtailed. She said she wanted a husband and children one day, so she needed to get past this problem if she was to achieve this. She reported that the group comprised both young women and men and that everyone was very welcoming and accepting; she only felt minor anxiety in the presence of so many men. When asked how she had been able to do this, she said that getting the courage up to call and then to attend the meeting had been the hard part. She further stated that she had been able to summon up the courage because she was so motivated to deal with this problem. She said that scheduling a therapy appointment had also meant she was serious about tackling her problem. For Sarah, calling about a therapy appointment seemed to comprise *pretreatment change*. It appeared as if taking such a positive step toward action motivated her to make further changes. As a result of these changes, Sarah ranked herself at a "5" on the solution-focused scale.

As sessions progressed, she ranked herself at a "7," an "8," a "9," and a "10," respectively. She was able to make these changes by attending the singles group meetings on a regular basis, as well as other social events connected with the group. Through hearing people talk about their issues, Sarah learned that even the male members were no different from herself in having problems and difficulties with which they struggled. Over time, Sarah became comfortable with relating to men on a social basis with none of her earlier anxiety symptoms.

SUMMARY

This case example illustrates how the solution-focused model can be used to identify and enlarge upon people's strengths in order to facilitate change. The present chapter has also suggested that solution-focused therapy can be used in combination with other helping models when the practitioner is faced with certain client problems. However, further empirical work is needed to establish how effective solution-focused therapy is both alone and in combination with other models for different populations and in different problem areas.

REFERENCES

Adams, J., Piercy, F., & Jurich, J. (1991). Effects of solution-focused therapy's "formula first session task" on compliance and outcome in family therapy. *Journal of Marital and Family Therapy, 17,* 277–290.

Allgood, S., Parham, K., Salts, C., & Smith, T. (1995). The association between pretreatment change and unplanned termination in family therapy. *The American Journal of Family Therapy, 23,* 195–202.

Berg, I. K. (1994). *Family-based services: A solution-focused approach.* New York: W. W. Norton.

Berg, I. K., & De Jong, P. (1996). Solution-building conversations: Co-constructing a sense of competence with clients. *Families in Society, 77,* 376–391.

Berg, I. K., & Kelly, S. (2000). *Building solutions in child protection.* New York: W. W. Norton.

Berg, I. K., & Miller, S. (1992). *Working with the problem drinker.* New York: W. W. Norton.

Bertolino, B., & O'Hanlon, B. (2002). *Collaborative, competency-based counseling and therapy.* Boston: Allyn & Bacon.

Burns, K., & Hulusi, H. (2005). Bridging the gap between a learning support centre and school: A solution-focused group approach. *Educational Psychology in Practice, 21,* 123–130.

Cade, B., & O'Hanlon, W. H. (1993). *A brief guide to brief therapy.* New York: W. W. Norton.

Corcoran, J. (1997). A solution-oriented approach to working with juvenile offenders. *Child and Adolescent Social Work Journal, 14,* 277–288.

Corcoran, J. (1999). Solution-focused interviewing with child protective services clients. *Child Welfare, 78*(4), 461–479.

Corcoran, J. (2005). *Building strengths and skills: A collaborative approach to working with clients.* New York: Oxford University Press.

Corcoran, J., & Franklin, C. (1998). A solution-focused approach to physical abuse. *Journal of Family Psychotherapy, 9*(1), 69–73.

Corcoran, J., & Pillai, V. (in press). Solution-focused therapy: A systematic review of the published studies. *Research on Social Work Practice.*

Council on Social Work Education. (2004). *Curriculum policy statement for master's degree programs in social work education.* Alexandria, VA: Author.

De Jong, P., & Berg, I. K. (2002). *Interviewing for solutions* (2nd ed.). Pacific Grove, CA: Brooks/Cole.

Dermer, S., Hemesath, C., & Russell, C. (1998). A feminist critique of solution-focused therapy. *The American Journal of Family Therapy, 26,* 239–250.

de Shazer, S. (1985). *Keys to solutions in brief therapy.* New York: W. W. Norton.

de Shazer, S. (1988). *Clues: Investigating solutions in brief therapy.* New York: W. W. Norton.

de Shazer, S. (1994). *Words were originally magic.* New York: W. W. Norton.

de Shazer, S., Berg, I. K., Lipchick, E., Nunnally, E., Molnar, A., Gingerich, W., et al. (1986). Brief therapy: Focused solution development. *Family Process, 25,* 207–221.

Durrant, M. (1995). *Creative strategies for school problems: Solutions for psychologists and teachers.* New York: W. W. Norton.

Dyes, M. A., & Neville, K. E. (2000). Taming trouble and other tales: Using externalized characters in solution-focused therapy. *Journal of Systematic Therapies, 19*(1), 74–81.

Greene, G. J., Lee, M. L., Trask, R., & Rheinscheld, J. (1996). Client strengths and crisis intervention: A solution-focused approach. *Crisis Intervention, 3,* 43–63.

Lange, S. (2001). Solution-focused psychotherapy for incarcerated fathers. *Journal of Family Psychotherapy, 12,* 1–20.

Lipchick, E. (2002). *Beyond technique in solution-focused therapy: Working with emotions and the therapeutic relationship.* New York: Guilford Press.

McMillen, J., Morris, L., & Sherraden, M. (2004). Ending social work's grudge match: Problems versus strengths. *Families in Society, 85,* 317–325.

National Association of Social Workers. (1999). *Code of ethics.* Washington, DC: NASW Press.

O'Hanlon, W. H., & Weiner-Davis, M. (1989). *In search of solutions: A new direction in psychotherapy.* New York: W. W. Norton.

Selekman, A. (1995). *Pathways to change: Brief therapy solutions with difficult adolescents.* New York: Guilford Press.

Selekman, A. (1997). *Solution-focused therapy with children.* New York: Guilford Press.

White, M. (1984). Pseudo-encopresis: From avalanche to victory, from vicious to virtuous cycles. *Family Systems Medicine, 2*(2), 150–160.

White, M., & Epston, D. (1990). *Narrative means to therapeutic ends.* New York: W. W. Norton.

PART IV

Service Models for High-Risk Populations

CHAPTER 18

Wraparound in Services to Children and Families

Theresa J. Early

Wraparound is both a philosophy and a service approach that is intended to integrate various formal services and informal supports needed to care for children with problems that affect several areas of functioning. Typically, the children have multiple needs across a number of domains, and their families need support from agencies and the community in order to enable the children to remain in the home and community settings. A system-spanning team guides and coordinates services and resources; the team includes the youth, parents, other relatives, other support people (such as a scout leader or mentor), and professionals. Youth served through a wraparound approach may have serious emotional and behavioral disorders, involvement with juvenile justice, school problems, and/or other serious difficulties.

This chapter will introduce the wraparound approach from historical and theoretical perspectives, describe and illustrate the phases of helping in this approach, and illuminate compatibility of this approach with the generalist-eclectic framework. Wraparound requires system modification and intervention as well as meaningful involvement of youth, family members, and natural supports. Although the system and community practice aspects are critical for the success of wraparound, this chapter's primary focus is on the direct service aspects of the approach, in keeping with the theme of the book. Finally, the chapter will close with a critique of the wraparound approach, highlighting issues of fidelity to the theoretical model and other concerns that are arising from research on attempts to implement the approach in urban and rural communities in the United States.

HISTORY OF WRAPAROUND

Many authors trace the beginning of the wraparound approach to various efforts to serve youth with serious emotional disorders in their communities. The Alaska Youth Initiative was one such effort, designed to return to the state youth who were placed in hospitals and residential treatment out-of-state in order to receive services (VanDenBerg, 1999). Kaleidoscope in Chicago initially developed group homes and later more community-based services. Information on the wraparound approach was shared through conferences and other venues, which led to similar approaches being initiated in other states that also were experiencing a great number of long-distance placements or excessive use of institutional placements for children with serious emotional and behavioral disorders.

On the federal level, the Child and Adolescent Service System Program (CASSP), sponsored by the National Institute of Mental Health (NIMH), was instrumental in facilitating dissemination of the approach through training, technical assistance, and funding. Lenore Behar, a researcher and administrator with the state department of mental health in North Carolina, is credited with first use of the term "wraparound" in a 1986 article in *Children Today* (Behar, as cited in VanDenBerg, 1999), in discussing the needs of a group of children for whom the state was court-ordered to develop individualized services.

Although wraparound emerged somewhat spontaneously in states from Illinois and Alaska to Vermont and North Carolina, it is very much a part of the "systems of care" movement initiated by CASSP. The philosophy and goals of wraparound mirror the system of care principles put forth on behalf of CASSP by Stroul and Friedman (1986), which called for services to be community based, family focused, child centered, and culturally competent.

A little more than a decade after the publication of the systems of care monograph and considerable investment in statewide or community system of care grants, the federally funded Comprehensive Community Mental Health Services for Children and Their Families Program published the first volumes in the *Promising Practices* initiative. Volume IV of this series (Burns & Goldman, 1999) is devoted to wraparound and includes a consensus definition of wraparound and its values, essential elements, and requirements for practice (Burns & Goldman, 1999). According to this group, "Wraparound is a philosophy of care that includes a definable planning process involving the child and family that results in a unique set of community services and natural supports individualized for that child and family to achieve a positive set of outcomes" (Goldman, 1999, p. 28). Essential elements of wraparound are described as follows:

1. the services are community based, intended to serve youth in their homes and in their home communities;
2. services are individualized, built on strengths and to meet needs in all life domains;
3. services are culturally competent, using strengths of the youth's culture and community;
4. family members are full and active partners in planning and providing care;
5. the process is team-driven and based on consensus and partnership;
6. the approaches used are flexible (in setting, location, time, and services) and require adequate and flexible funding;
7. the service plans include a balance of formal services and informal supports, with gradual replacement of formal services with informal, natural supports;
8. the agencies and the team make unconditional commitment to serve youth and families; there is no rejection of youth or families. If necessary, services and supports are changed or redesigned to meet the needs of the child and family who would otherwise be rejected;
9. the service plans are developed and implemented based on a collaborative process between agencies, the community, and the neighborhood; resources of the whole community are involved in plan design/implementation;
10. the outcomes must be specified, measured, and monitored for child/family level goals as well as program/system level—desired outcomes have to do with success, safety and permanence in home, school, and community settings. (Goldman, 1999)

At the point in time of release of this monograph, at least 43 U.S. states and territories had implemented wraparound initiatives of some kind (Faw, 1999). These initiatives were sometimes called by other names, such as "Individualized and Tailored Care," "Family Support Services," "Person-Centered Planning," "Intensive Family Based Treatment," or "Children's Systems of Care" (Faw, 1999, p. 80). Although various social services sectors were involved in the wraparound initiatives, mental health was most frequently the lead agency either alone or in combination with other agencies. Child welfare, juvenile justice, education, other community agencies and parent advocacy groups, substance abuse, developmental disabilities, and public health were involved in at least some of the initiatives (Faw, 1999).

The primacy of mental health agencies in leadership of wraparound efforts is most likely because the approach originated in relation to children's mental health services and because some of the major funding streams for development are the Center for Mental Health Services' programs to develop systems of care. The extensive involvement of other child-serving agencies is a testament both to the systems of care movement as well as evidence of the level of mental health problems experienced by youth served in other systems such as child welfare and juvenile justice.

The essential elements of wraparound, as described above, have been further explored through extensive case studies of six youth and their families who have received wraparound services in Rhode Island; North Dakota; Seattle, Washington; Ohio; Vermont; and Milwaukee, Wisconsin (Kendziora, Bruns, Osher, Pacchiano, & Mejia, 2001). The insights from this volume will be highlighted in describing the wraparound practice in the sections to follow.

PHASES OF HELPING

Some of the key distinguishing features of the wraparound approach are that there is not a single service provider but rather a team; "services" may include informal supports that are suggested or arranged by the team; youth and family members are on equal footing with professionals in planning services and specifying goals; and, rather than a youth needing to fit into the constraints of the service system, services may be modified to meet a youth's needs.

Clearly, workers who are involved with wraparound will go about their work differently than they might in a more traditional service not only because the services are different but because the philosophy of service is different. Wraparound teams are comprised of people representing organizations, families, and community groups. Goldman (1999) recommended the team consist of 4 to 10 people in addition to the child and immediate family members, and that the team represent a blend of formal and informal resources, with professionals comprising no more than half of the team membership. The team leader, who is usually a professional, may be called a resource coordinator or care coordinator. In keeping with the broad emphasis on resources (formal services, informal supports, community strengths), we will refer to this staff person as a resource coordinator and consider how the resource coordinator and other team members interact with youth and their families in the wraparound process.

Engagement

Engagement in wraparound begins with a referral to the wraparound coordinating group. This might be a county-wide child and family council, a mental health council, or a consortium of child and family agencies. The resource coordinator would arrange to meet with the youth and family in order to begin a relationship-building process as well as an assessment process. Because the wraparound approach is based on a strengths perspective toward youth and families, it is important for the resource coordinator to engage the youth and family members as collaborators in a strengths assessment.

As described previously, it is not only the resource coordinator who needs to develop a relationship with the youth and family, but all of the other team members as well. Some of the team members will have pre-existing relationships with the youth and family, of course, because some of them will already be acting as supports either through a formal role such as a case manager or an informal role such as a family friend. Initially, all of the team members, the youth, and the family need to become familiar with one another. Relationship building focuses on youth and family strengths. As Kendziora and colleagues (2001) observed, there is a "fundamental incompatibility between developing a caring relationship with a child and family and then continuing to focus on what is wrong with the situation and the people involved" (p. 134).

Assessment

In the wraparound approach, the resource coordinator has primary responsibility for conducting the strengths and needs assessment. "Strengths, potential resources, values, preferences, perspectives, and issues are determined before identifying needs" (Goldman, 1999, p. 33).

Assessment of clients often means discovering their problems. In a strengths-based intervention such as wraparound, however, assessment seeks to uncover positive aspects of the youth and family, such as "survival skills, abilities, knowledge, resources, and desires that can be used in some way to help meet client goals" (Early & GlenMaye, 2000, p. 119). During the past 20 years, various authors have conceptualized strengths assessment, some focusing on aspects such as cognitive function, attitudinal and behavioral components (Dunst, Trivette, & Mott, 1994), as well as family functions, subsystems, culture, and life cycle (Ronnau & Poertner, 1993). Cowger and Snively (2002) focused on strengths and deficits at both the client and environmental levels.

In addition to articulating the content of a strengths assessment, several authors also have described important elements of the *process* of a strengths assessment. Interviewing is important as a vehicle to obtain information and build relationships, as well as an opportunity to begin to build the confidence of the youth and family that they can change their situation. Pointing out strengths (Ronnau & Poertner, 1993), focusing on solutions (Early & Newsome, 2004), and eliciting motivation (Prochaska, 1994) are all interview techniques that acknowledge client strengths. Focusing on solutions assumes the youth and family already are taking helpful actions and uses questioning to uncover these efforts. The family's current effort to solve the problem is a strength, as is the ability to articulate a vision of the future when the problem is no longer present (De Jong & Miller, 1995). Motivational interviewing, based on a transtheoretical model of readiness to change (Prochaska, 1994), can help identify client strengths in preparing for change. If the youth and family already are thinking about making changes that will improve the situation at home or at school, even if they are not yet able to implement change on their own, the cognitive shift that will enable change has begun to occur.

In sum, assessment for practice with families from a strengths perspective is "focusing on identifying what the client is doing to make things better, what works, what will facilitate the continuation of desired behaviors and situations. Primary focus of assessment is on what [the] client is doing 'right' in relation to goals and vision" (Early & GlenMaye, 2000, p. 124). Many wraparound teams use various means to explore areas such as "living situation, educational and vocational needs, safety and legal issues, medical and health needs, cultural and spiritual needs, and recreational needs" (Kendziora et al., 2001, p. 134).

Along with interviewing as a key to strengths assessment, paper-and-pencil instruments, checklists, and timelines may also be useful, both for documenting strengths as well as for later measuring change as an outcome of the wraparound process. For instance, a recent study (Bruns, Suter, Force, & Burchard, 2005) documented the wraparound process as being effective in improving youth scores on the Behavioral and Emotional Rating Scale (BERS; Epstein & Sharma, 1998), a strengths-based measure. The following section presents a summary of measurement instruments, including the BERS, that could be used to document youth and family strengths. For a fuller presentation of this material with examples of using some of the instruments, as well as information on additional instruments that measure problems as well as strengths, see Early (2001) and Early and Newsome (2004).

Strengths-Based Measures for Children

Many instruments exist to measure children's behavioral and emotional problems; however, there are fewer instruments that provide a focus on positive functioning. Three such recently developed measures are reviewed briefly below.

The Behavioral and Emotional Rating Scale (BERS; Epstein & Sharma, 1998) measures children's behavioral and emotional strengths from the perspective of parent, teacher, or other caregiver. The respondent rates the relative presence or absence of 52 behavioral items for the child. The scores include an overall Strengths Quotient and five subscales: Interpersonal Strengths, Family Involvement, Intrapersonal Strengths, School Functioning, and Affective Strengths. Interpersonal Strengths represents the child's ability to control his or her emotions or behavior in social situations. Family Involvement reflects a child's participation in and relationship with his or her family. Intrapersonal Strengths captures a child's perception of his/her competence and accomplishments. School Functioning is a measure of the child's school competence and classroom performance. Affective Strengths measures the extent to which a child accepts affection and expresses feelings.

The School Success Profile (SSP; Bowen & Richman, 1997) is a questionnaire developed from a risk and resilience perspective. The authors drew on the school success literature, as well as an ecological perspective of risk and protective factors, in order to identify a variety of challenges faced by youth. As published, the SSP is for use with middle and high school students and is written at the fourth-grade level. The 220 items operationalize protective and risk factors in the areas of neighborhood, school, friends, and family. The measure is written in English- and Spanish-language versions. Scoring results in two profiles, Social Environment and Individual Adaptation, and a number of subdimensions. The School Success Profile is unique in its ecological approach, tapping youth perspectives on their social environments as well as their own competencies.

The Social Skills Rating System (SSRS; Gresham & Elliott, 1990) is a checklist that evaluates the presence of specific, prosocial behaviors in the areas of cooperation, assertion, responsibility, empathy, and self-control. Versions for different respondents and different age groups each contain about 50 items. In addition to social skills subscales and a total social skills score, scoring yields internalizing and externalizing problems scores and a total problems score. The SSRS is particularly suited to intervention planning for school settings. It identifies both presence and significance of behaviors for the rater (parent, teacher, or student) and is sensitive to positive changes in the identified behaviors.

Strengths-Based Measures for Families

The wraparound approach has youth and family goals that are similar to the early intervention field, which has produced useful materials for guiding strengths-based practice with families (Dunst, Trivette & Deal, 1994). The first three measures reviewed below are from the early intervention field.

The Family Resource Scale (FRS; Dunst & Leet, 1994) measures tangible and intangible resources considered important for families with young children. A parent or other adult family member completes the instrument, indicating the extent to which 30 resources are adequately met for the family. The scale items represent a hierarchy of needs for both internal and external supports, such as food, shelter, financial resources, transportation, time to be with family and friends, toys for the children, and vacation/leisure.

As part of a strengths assessment, the Family Resource Scale could be used to identify areas in which the family is successfully meeting needs. The Family Resource Scale also could be used to quickly identify areas for intervention targets or goals, as well as to measure outcomes when program goals include families being able to meet their needs.

The Family Functioning Style Scale (FFSS; Trivette, Dunst, Deal, Hamby, & Sexton, 1994) is intended to measure family strengths. Twenty-six items reflect the extent to which the family is characterized by different strengths and capabilities, from the perspective of one or more family members, in the areas of Interactional Patterns, Family Values, Coping Strategies, Family Commitment, and Resource Mobilization.

The Family Support Scale (FSS; Dunst, Trivette, & Hamby, 1994) is a measure of social support for families from sources ranging from extended family members to professionals and other service providers. The 18 items are designed to assess the degree to which potential sources of social support have been helpful to families. As with all of the measures from Dunst, Trivette, and Deal (1994), the perspective that is obtained is that of a parent or other adult family caregiver. The Family Support Scale captures not only information about what sources of support the family has available, but also how helpful they have been. This is particularly useful because of the critical difference between the size of a social network and the value of its support to an individual or family. The sources of social support measured are Informal Kinship, Spouse/Partner Support, Social Organization, Formal Kinship, and Professional Services. The FSS could be used to begin a conversation with family members to identify ways to increase the support available to the family.

The Family Empowerment Scale (FES; Koren, DeChillo, & Friesen, 1992) was developed specifically for families with children with emotional disorders. A program goal of empowerment is consistent with the wraparound approach. The FES consists of 34 items designed to reflect three levels of empowerment (family, service system, community/

political) in statements about personal attitudes, knowledge, and behaviors. Examples of the statements rated include "I feel my family life is under control," "I make sure that professionals understand my opinions about what services my child needs," and "I know the steps to take when I am concerned my child is receiving poor services."

Planning/Contracting and Implementation

"The best resource coordinators are those with flexible, open views of what children and families need and how those needs can be met to achieve positive outcomes" (Goldman, 1999, p. 33). As should be obvious from the previous section, there are a number of resources to collect information on strengths and needs, broadly considered, of children and families who might be served in the wraparound approach. Planning and contracting will use this information, and the resource coordinator will be instrumental in the planning/contracting process. However, responsibility for planning and contracting will also be shared among members of the wraparound team. Planning/contracting relies on mobilizing resources to improve the youth's and family's situation (Saleebey, 1997): "These resources may include adults in a child's life who can help the child develop social competence, skills of various family members that enable family needs to be met, and relationships with extended family or friends that provide positive role models" (Early & GlenMaye, 2000, p. 123).

Planning as a group is challenging. Further, the situations and service systems involved are challenging. Kendziora and colleagues (2001) described reframing and brainstorming as effective strategies to deal with the challenges of the service system: "When teams were challenged about the plausibility of meeting the child's and family's needs in the community, they responded by reframing the challenge . . . to ask what a more restrictive placement might give the child and then brainstormed ways to create those components in the community, in the school, and in the home" (p. 133).

Recognizing the challenges in involving all team members in the planning process, Walker and Schutte (2005) have developed a model of effectiveness for teamwork in wraparound in order to maximize creativity and individualization of the plan. The model describes interrelated sets of activities that focus on "broadening perspectives" and "generating options": "A team is more likely to develop an individualized plan that effectively responds to a family's needs when the team adheres to a high quality, inclusive planning process, using practices that also promote team collaborativeness and the values of wraparound" (Walker & Schutte, 2005, p. 252). Broadening perspectives, according to Walker and

Schutte, comes through intentional strategies to hear diverse perspective on the issue at hand. A facilitated round-robin approach to hear from every team member is one such strategy. It is important that options not be evaluated until everyone has had input. Generating options through brainstorming should be given enough time so that a number of different ideas are generated. The number of ideas generated is proportional to the quality of ideas generated (i.e., the more the better), and ideas generated later are often better than initial suggestions (Walker & Schutte, 2005). Further, generating multiple solutions is useful in that if the first option tried is not successful, the team may be able to move fairly seamlessly to "plan B."

A unique aspect of the wraparound approach is that it is "family driven" (Kendziora et al., 2001). "When parents already have strong advocacy skills, establishing a family lead in decision making often occurs both naturally and quickly. For others, encouragement was ongoing, since the family required more time to feel secure in developing plans of care" (Kendziora et al., 2001, p. 136). Spending sufficient time on generating options provides for greater opportunity to actually elicit the perspectives of family members and members of the family's informal support system and to affirm the value of these contributions. A further benefit of having generated a number of options to choose from is that there is a greater likelihood that the family can choose strategies that not only meet team goals but also mesh with the family's culture and valued home and community roles (Walker & Schutte, 2005). Finally, through engaging in a process to develop multiple solutions, the team may develop greater insight into the situation and thus a better match between goals adopted and strategies pursued. Without this process, the team described by Kendziora and colleagues (2001) would not have been able to reframe the "need" for residential placement into strategies that provided support and safety at home and school.

The wraparound planning approach is collaborative among all the team members. This requires that team members have similar understandings of the goals for the wraparound team and that movement toward goals is monitored on an ongoing basis. In this way, strategies may be modified if they are ineffective:

> Within the wraparound context . . . practices related to defining goals, acquiring feedback on progress toward goals, and revising plans based on feedback . . . can contribute to perceptions of team collaborativeness by enhancing perceptions of collective efficacy, increasing commitment to team decisions, *maintaining the family's perspective as a shared reference point* [italics added], and increasing the likelihood that disagreements will be managed in a constructive, non-conflictual manner. (Walker & Schutte, 2005, p. 254)

Contracting requires specifying step-by-step, concrete, measurable goals and objectives that include time frames, standards for measurement, and clear delineation of responsibility. Goals should be positively stated if at all possible. Care plan goals need to clearly specify the outcomes intended for youth and families, and these should reflect desired changes in behavior, affective state, environment, status, and/or knowledge. For instance, youth served in wraparound often need to *learn* to manage their impulses or behavior and then to *practice* those strategies in specific settings such as school. In addition, the youth may need the support of a formal service provider to learn how to manage behavior or to implement the strategies. If drawing helps a youth manage anxiety in the classroom, and unmanaged anxiety contributes to the youth hitting other classmates, then the youth needs to learn to ask to draw for a specified period of time, and the teacher needs to be aware of the appropriateness of the request and agree to honor it. If the youth is allowed to draw but it does not help the situation (i.e., he hits the classmate anyway), another contingency should be in place to remove the youth from the situation with something else to help him regain control. If these graduated contingencies are not in place, the situation may escalate to suspension or expulsion, but with the plans to help the youth manage his own behavior, he may have short periods directed at activity other than schoolwork in order to remain in the classroom and resume schoolwork when he can.

Implementation of the plan is highly dependent on the elements of the plan, with shared responsibilities for implementation clearly spelled out. Verbally "walking through" the plan with all team members should be a part of the team meeting, to ensure that everybody knows what they are supposed to do and so that any gaps in the plan are identified and filled.

Evaluation and Termination

Evaluation of the plan and the services is ongoing and should be a part of every team meeting. Specifying outcome-oriented goals for the youth and family with time frames of expectations for achievement will facilitate ongoing and periodic evaluation. Goal attainment is cause for celebration of success and progress. When goals are met, the planning process should identify further goals if needed. When goals are evaluated and found not to be met, the planning process should be used to determine whether to try to remove barriers to goal attainment, whether new goals should be negotiated, or whether more time is needed to attain the original goals.

Termination should be worked toward through gradual shifting to more informal and less formal supports. Given that youth served through a wraparound approach likely have a number of challenges across different areas of their lives, there may be long-term, continuing need for formal support, and ideally this should be available. However, even if long-term, community-based services are available to a youth and family, experience indicates that youth and families may choose to drop out of services without formal termination. Therefore, wraparound plans should always emphasize considerable informal supports from the very beginning of services, as families may be less likely to separate from these, even if they discontinue other services.

COMPATIBILITY WITH THE GENERALIST-ECLECTIC FRAMEWORK

Wraparound is highly compatible with the generalist-eclectic framework for direct social work practice that is described in earlier chapters of this text. The wraparound approach does not seem to have been developed from a particular theory base but rather a value base, and the value base is particularly aligned with the elements of the generalist-eclectic framework.

Attention to Holistic Assessment and Use of Systems and Life Cycle Theories

Wraparound relies to a great extent on systems theory for its emphasis on planning through a team process and involving various aspects of a child's and family's natural supports as well as formal services. This is in recognition of the various systems and subsystems that exist in the community that can be mobilized for family support. It is also in recognition that many problems are best thought of as systems problems rather than individual ones. Strategies to secure needed support from a system (e.g., a teacher agreeing to a behavior management plan that is unorthodox) are common in wraparound. The theory of change for wraparound includes the assumption that "effective wraparound programs change the surrounding environment for the child and thus foster lasting changes that occur in individuals, families, and communities" (Burns, Schoenwald, Burchard, Faw, & Santos, 2000, p. 296).

Emphasis on Therapeutic Relationship and Fit With the Strengths Perspective

Wraparound, as demonstrated herein, is highly compatible with the strengths perspective. In identifying and building on strengths, soliciting the child's and family's vision in goal-setting, and fashioning interventions out of both formal services and extensive informal resources, the two approaches are synonymous.

The wraparound approach also emphasizes a therapeutic relationship, although perhaps to less an extent with any particular individual than other treatment models because of the primacy of the team in the intervention. Thus, change is seen to be influenced less by one therapeutic relationship and more by a supportive team and network of service and supports. That the relationship with families is a working partnership is of paramount importance.

Attention to Issues of Diversity and Empowerment

The wraparound approach is intended to be culturally competent, by definition. The assessment and planning methods emphasize identifying strengths of the youth's culture and asking about aspects of culture that should be considered in developing supports. There are examples in the literature of wraparound plans that incorporate cultural practices (e.g., Kendziora et al., 2001). Although this is the ideal, it is unclear from the research published what the diversity actually is of youth and families served. Cultural competence is a significant challenge for mental health and social services in general. As one of the staff interviewed for the *Promising Practices* monograph stated, "[Being culturally competent] simply means not assuming anything. Not assuming that I know a person's experiences . . ." (Kendziora et al., 2001, p. 135).

As to empowerment, the wraparound approach is potentially quite empowering for both youth and families, with its emphasis on meaningful participation of the youth and family. Youth and their families can learn about resources and the problem-solving process, as well as develop supports apart from the formal service system. Further, the input of youth and families into goals and strategies is privileged in the wraparound process. For this reason, the Family Empowerment Scale (Koren et al., 1992) may be an important instrument to use in evaluating the effectiveness of implementation. Again, although empowerment is the ideal, there may be significant challenges in achieving this aim.

CASE EXAMPLE

Several extensive case examples may be found in the *Promising Practices* volumes cited (e.g., Burns & Goldman, 1999; Kendziora et al., 2001). However, a brief example here will highlight some of the critical issues that have been identified in relation to the generalist-eclectic framework.

The Youth and His Family

Brad is the 14-year-old adopted son of the Matthews family. The family consists of mom Barbara, a school teacher; dad Dave, an administrator for the local electric utility; brother Steve, 16, biological son of Barbara and Dave; and sister Katie, 21, biological daughter of Barbara and Dave, who attends college in a town 15 miles from the family home. Brad has lived with the Matthews family since he was a 6-month-old foster child, removed from his mother's custody because of her extensive cocaine use both prior to and after his birth. He was formally adopted by Barbara and Dave at the age of 5. Since the family moved to Texas from their previous home in the Midwest shortly after the adoption, Brad has had no contact with his birth family.

Brad has always been "a handful," as Dave and Barbara would put it, getting kicked out of every day care center in town before entering kindergarten, flashing his sweet smile as he dunked the family cat in the toilet after catching its fur on fire with a cigarette lighter he found outside. Brad makes friends easily, but also loses them easily when he is mean to them. More than one school psychologist has recommended residential treatment for Brad, but Dave and Barbara have always been committed to keeping Brad at home if at all possible. Although he is of normal intelligence, he has grades of C and D in most of his classes this year.

A recent incident, which has resulted in Brad's referral to the county wraparound initiative, suggests that there may be serious safety concerns with Brad remaining at home. Katie is so mad at Brad that she refuses to speak to him when she comes home for family meals or to do laundry. After all, his behavior has been extremely disrespectful to her parents—and they're not really his parents. Steve is a standout two-sport athlete (basketball and track) and one of the most popular juniors at the high school. He feels torn between loyalty to his big sister, Katie, and to the little brother whom he has always tried to stick up for.

Two weeks ago, Brad was having a tough time at school. He had a biology project he was supposed to work on and he just did not feel like it, so he took off during the school day with some older boys who had a car and a six-pack of beer. They were picked up by the local police when the car was seen racing other cars out on the highway. Dave had to leave work to go to juvenile court to pick Brad up. Brad was already under juvenile court supervision for petty theft, so eloping from school and underage drinking were likely to result in a more serious penalty.

Things were quiet for a few days. Brad went to school, apparently behaved fairly well (Dave and Barbara did not get any phone calls from the principal, at any rate), came home when he was supposed to, and was pretty cooperative around the house. Then, one morning at school, he went to the nurse's office, saying that he was sick and needed to go home. The nurse took his temperature, which showed he had a slight fever, so she called his father, who picked him up at school to take him home. The family rule is that if one is too sick to be at school or work, he or she needs to be in bed, so Dave made up a bed for Brad in the living room recliner so he could watch television and still be "in bed." Dave went back to work but then returned home at noon to check on Brad and give him lunch. As Dave left for work, he instructed Brad to stay put until his mother came home after school. At about 4:15, Dave received a panicked phone call from Barbara—she could not find her keys and was stranded at school. The day was pretty well shot anyway for Dave, having already been home twice, so he took an extra set of keys to Barbara and then followed her home. When they got half a block from the house, they could see the pickup truck Dave uses for hauling and chores, in mud up to its front axle in the vacant lot beside their house. It had apparently been driven through the front yard several times, based on the 6-inch-deep ruts in the grass. Two peach trees seemed to have been run over as well. They found Brad in the house calmly playing a video game—and Barbara's keys in the truck ignition. Brad had apparently taken them after Barbara parked the car at school that morning. Just about that time, a police car arrived, having been alerted by a neighbor to the pickup truck driving through lawns. Brad claimed he had been inside since his father brought him home, but his mud-caked shoes and muddy footprints indicated otherwise.

The Referral

Based on the escalating involvement in legal issues and safety concerns, Brad's juvenile probation supervision worker (Julie Lewis) referred him to the Family First wraparound initiative. The resource coordinator assigned to coordinate Brad's team, Bill Butler, contacted Mr. and Mrs. Matthews to set up a visit with the family in their home.

Strengths Assessment

When Bill arrived at the Matthews home for the visit, the first thing he saw was two teenagers shooting baskets in the driveway. The smaller of the two boys called out that he had been fouled on a shot. When the larger boy lofted a shot over him, the smaller boy grabbed the basketball and threw it over the house. Bill said to himself, "Hello, Brad," and made a mental note to ask about basketball as a hobby.

Mrs. Matthews invited Bill into the living room. Soon they were joined by Mr. Matthews and the boys, who Bill learned were Steve and

Brad. Mr. Matthews explained that their daughter, Katie, was running late but would join them shortly. Bill began to explain wraparound and the assessment process: "We're going to try to do several things this evening to start this process. One thing is that I want to hear from all of you about how you want things to be at home and at school, especially where Brad is concerned. The other is that I want to learn about people or groups you all are involved with. For wraparound to work, we need a team, which will include all of us and others who you think of who can help."

Brad interrupted, "Help with what?"

"Well, Brad, seems like there have been a few times recently that you've gotten into trouble, and Ms. Lewis thought it might be a good idea to have a team of people get together to see how we might help you with staying out of trouble," Bill responded.

"You mean like watching me all the time?" Brad asked.

"Not necessarily—do you think that would help?" Bill asked, and Brad quickly responded, "NO!" "Okay," Bill said, making a note on his papers, "no need to watch Brad all the time." Then still addressing Brad, "If that wouldn't help, what do you think might help? That's what we want to figure out."

Bill then explained that he was going to ask a lot of questions about various aspects of the family—both big and little things, from how they get routine things done to what some of their favorite things are to do as a family. Bill encouraged everyone to think about things that were important to the family, what they were good at, what they enjoyed.

Mrs. Matthews said that education is important to the family—Katie had just started college and they were saving to be able to help all of the kids complete their education. Mr. Matthews agreed, education is important, but it's also important that the kids learn the value of work, so Steve is going to be getting a part-time job after track season is over. Steve said his grades are important and so are sports—he hopes he might go to college on an athletic scholarship. Brad said school's really not that important to him, except that it's where he can meet girls. "Friends and relationships are important, aren't they?" Bill responded. "What do you like to do with your friends, Brad?" This elicited a discussion about hiking in the area and good places to ride mountain bikes. "And even if school's not that important to you, what subjects are you good in?" Bill asked. Brad responded that he does not like most of the subjects but he has a pretty cool teacher for speech and drama. He said that just making speeches is boring, but being in a play would be alright.

Through the strengths assessment, Bill learned not only of Brad's potential interest in drama, but also the importance of education, work, and church to the family. Mrs. Matthews's younger sister lived nearby and the two families spend time together on weekends sometimes and especially at holidays. Interestingly, even though Katie was having problems with Brad, her boyfriend of 3 years spends some time playing video games with Brad. Brad is also particularly close to the "adopted" grandparents of the family, Bennie, a retired coworker of Mr. Matthews, and Bennie's wife. Bennie had to retire from the electric company 3 years ago when he was blinded in an accident. Since Bennie recovered from his physical injuries, Brad has learned how to guide Bennie while walking.

The Wraparound Team

Bill turned the discussion to the wraparound team. Ms. Lewis would be a member, as would Bill. Mrs. Matthews nominated the school counselor, who also is a family friend and, of course, Bennie. There was also the therapist that Brad had recently begun to see at the mental health center. Mr. Matthews nominated Rita, Mrs. Matthews's sister. When asked who he would like to nominate, Brad picked Mr. Ramirez, the speech and drama teacher, and Katie's boyfriend.

The Plan

The initial plan arrived at by the wraparound team focused on three issues: as a consequence of the various legal issues, community service involvement and greater supervision of Brad's time when he is out of school; and improving Brad's grades so that he can participate in the next school play (short term) and take driver's education (longer term). Brad says that he knows he needs to do something to keep from messing up when he has "bad" impulses, so he is going to try to talk to Mr. Ramirez before he acts on a bad impulse at school (such as to elope), or Bennie before he acts on a bad impulse at home. For the community service, Brad is going to volunteer with a group that is turning an abandoned railroad into a hiking and biking trail. Katie's boyfriend is a crew leader in the group and has agreed to sponsor Brad and report back to the team and juvenile court supervision about Brad's participation. Because he wants to get his driving learner's permit when he is 15, Brad will be able to enroll in driver's education in the summer, provided he has final grades of at least C in all his classes. In the meantime, Brad needs a C average in the next grading period to be able to audition for the school play.

Successes and Challenges in Implementing the Plan

As is to be expected, there were both aspects of the plan that worked well and additional problems encountered. Overall, the intervention led to significant improvement for Brad and his family.

Brad was able to improve his grades enough to audition for the school play. Although he did not get a speaking role, he was involved in running the sound and light equipment for rehearsals and performances. Consistent supervision of Brad's out-of-school time continued to be a challenge for the family, even though there were afternoons and some weekends spent working on the hiking and biking trail project. Brad continued to test limits, as most teenagers do, and continued to get caught. After sneaking out of the house one night after everyone was in bed, Brad was returned home in the back of a police cruiser. A consequence for this adventure was a 6-month delay in driver education and the learner's permit. A subsequent positive event was that Brad was asked to cut the ribbon opening the first 2-mile section of the trail and lead a bike ride on it for local dignitaries. Brad was very proud of the pictures of this event that were in the paper and presented framed prints of them to the wraparound team members. A new goal that the team is working toward is a part-time job for Brad, in a continued effort to structure his time and present more opportunities for taking responsibility in age-appropriate ways.

CRITIQUE OF THE WRAPAROUND APPROACH

The state wraparound survey (Faw, 1999) indicated that some states and localities are implementing similar approaches with different names (e.g., Intensive Home-Base Services). It is understandable and not particularly problematic that there are other similar approaches with different names. It is troubling, however, that some states or localities may be implementing something called "wraparound" that is missing one or many of the required elements. For instance, some sites call a service wraparound that is little more than case management, absent the significant involvement of family and informal supports in planning and implementation. At times, there are difficulties in arranging informal supports. In a federally funded demonstration project, for instance, the process of gaining approval for providers of formal services was extensive, and gaining approval for informal providers required several steps beyond that (Bickman, Smith, Lambert, & Andrade, 2003). Analysis of service utilization in this comparison study determined that the wraparound demonstration "did in fact use *more* [italics added] 'Wraparound' services" than the treatment as usual comparison (Bickman et al., 2003, p. 146), but still relatively few informal supports. There is also evidence that the lead agency involved in wraparound may have an influence on the type of individuals included on the team as well as on the areas addressed, with education-based teams more likely to include parents and teachers and community service-based teams more likely to include family advocates and informal supports (Nordness, 2005).

The research base on wraparound, although increasing, is limited, in part because of the concern about exactly what is being implemented. This is referred to as "fidelity," two measures of which have been developed and used in research. The Wraparound Observation Form (Nordness & Epstein, 2003) and the Wraparound Fidelity Index (Bruns, Burchard, Suter, Leverentz-Brady, & Force, 2004) have both been used in attempts to document the extent to which actual implementation of wraparound corresponds with important elements of the conceptual model described earlier. Studies are finding less adherence than desired in the area of involving informal supports (Bruns et al., 2005). The field awaits research that connects implementation to outcomes. To date, much of the research on wraparound is descriptive. Many researchers point out the need for more controlled studies to determine in a more definitive way whether wraparound works as intended.

Finally, although system-level concerns are largely beyond the scope of this chapter and volume, it should be noted that a fundamental tenet of wraparound is that there be availability of adequate and flexible funding, ideally at the control of the wraparound team. Research awaits as to the extent to which such flexibility is achieved in practice.

SUMMARY

This chapter has outlined the direct practice aspects of wraparound, a team approach that integrates formal services and informal supports in the care of children and adolescents at-risk of out-of-home placement because of multiple challenges. The case example illustrated assessment and planning, demonstrating how natural supports may be amplified through the team process. Wraparound has a value base rather than theory base and is consistent with most aspects of the generalist-eclectic approach. Strengths of wraparound include its flexibility to address a variety of presenting problems and clients involved with various systems. However, a potential weakness is a tendency for the term wraparound to be used to refer to services that are actually missing important elements or in systems where adequate services are lacking. Thus, the research community is rightly focusing on two important areas: developing tools to document fidelity with the wraparound model and studies of effectiveness.

REFERENCES

Bickman, L., Smith, C. M., Lambert, E. W., & Andrade, A. R. (2003). Evaluation of a congressionally mandated wraparound demonstration. *Journal of Child and Family Studies, 12,* 135–156.

Bowen, G., & Richman, J. (1997). *School Success Profile*. Chapel Hill: Jordan Institute for Families, School of Social Work, The University of North Carolina at Chapel Hill.

Bruns, E. J., Burchard, J. D., Suter, J. C., Leverentz-Brady, K., & Force, M. M. (2004). Assessing fidelity to a community-based treatment for youth: The Wraparound Fidelity Index. *Journal of Emotional and Behavioral Disorders, 12*, 79–89.

Bruns, E. J., Suter, J. C., Force, M. M., & Burchard, J. D. (2005). Adherence to wraparound principles and association with outcomes. *Journal of Child and Family Studies, 14*, 521–534.

Burns, B. J., & Goldman, S. K. (Eds.). (1999). *Systems of care: Promising practices in children's mental health, 1998 series: Vol. IV. Promising practices in wraparound for children with serious emotional disturbance and their families*. Washington, DC: Center for Effective Collaboration and Practice, American Institutes for Research.

Burns, B. J., Schoenwald, S. K., Burchard, J. D., Faw, L., & Santos, A. B. (2000). Comprehensive community-based interventions for youth with severe emotional disorders: Multisystemic therapy and the wraparound process. *Journal of Child and Family Studies, 9*, 283–314.

Cowger, C. D., & Snively, C. A. (2002). Assessing client strengths. In D. Saleebey (Ed.), *The strengths perspective in social work practice* (3rd ed.; pp. 106–123). Boston: Allyn & Bacon.

De Jong, P., & Miller, S. D. (1995). How to interview for client strengths. *Social Work, 40*, 729–736.

Dunst, C. J., & Leet, H. E. (1994). Measuring the adequacy of resources in households with young children. In C. J. Dunst, C. M. Trivette, & A. G. Deal (Eds.), *Supporting and strengthening families: Methods, strategies and practices* (pp. 105–114). Cambridge, MA: Brookline Books.

Dunst, C. J., Trivette, C. M., & Deal, A. G. (Eds.). (1994). *Supporting and strengthening families: Methods, strategies and practices*. Cambridge, MA: Brookline Books.

Dunst, C. J., Trivette, C. M., & Hamby, D. W. (1994). Measuring social support in families with young children with disabilities. In C. J. Dunst, C. M. Trivette, & A. G. Deal (Eds.), *Supporting and strengthening families: Methods, strategies and practices* (pp. 152–160). Cambridge, MA: Brookline Books.

Dunst, C. J., Trivette, C. M., & Mott, D. W. (1994). Strengths-based family-centered intervention practices. In C. J. Dunst, C. M. Trivette, & A. G. Deal (Eds.), *Supporting and strengthening families: Methods, strategies and practices* (pp. 115–131). Cambridge, MA: Brookline Books.

Early, T. J. (2001). Measures for practice with families from a strengths perspective. *Families in Society, 82*, 225–232.

Early, T. J., & GlenMaye, L. F. (2000). Valuing families: Social work practice with families from a strengths perspective. *Social Work, 45*, 118–130.

Early, T. J., & Newsome, W. S. (2004). Using measures for assessment and accountability in practice with families from a strengths perspective. In J. Corcoran (Ed.), *Building strengths and skills: A collaborative approach to working with clients* (pp. 359–393). New York: Oxford University Press.

Epstein, M. H., & Sharma, J. (1998). *Behavioral and Emotional Rating Scale: A strengths-based approach to assessment*. Austin, TX: PRO-ED.

Faw, L. (1999). The State Wraparound Survey. In B. J. Burns & S. K. Goldman (Eds.), *Systems of care: Promising practices in children's mental health, 1998 series: Vol. IV. Promising practices in wraparound for children with serious emotional disturbance and their families* (pp. 79–93). Washington, DC: Center for Effective Collaboration and Practice, American Institutes for Research.

Goldman, S. (1999). The conceptual framework for wraparound: Definition, values, essential elements, and requirements for practice. In B. J. Burns & S. K. Goldman (Eds.), *Systems of care: Promising practices in children's mental health, 1998 series: Vol. IV. Promising practices in wraparound for children with serious emotional disturbance and their families* (pp. 27–34). Washington, DC: Center for Effective Collaboration and Practice, American Institutes for Research.

Gresham, F., & Elliot, S. (1990). *Social Skills Rating System.* Circle Pines, MN: American Guidance Service.

Kendziora, K., Bruns, E., Osher, D., Pacchiano, D., & Mejia, B. (2001). *Systems of care: Promising practices in children's mental health, 2001 series: Vol. I. Wraparound: Stories from the field.* Washington, DC: Center for Effective Collaboration and Practice, American Institutes for Research.

Koren, P. E., DeChillo, N., & Friesen, B. J. (1992). Measuring empowerment in families whose children have emotional disabilities: A brief questionnaire. *Rehabilitation Psychology, 37,* 305–321.

Nordness, P. D. (2005). A comparison of school-based and community-based adherence to wraparound during family planning meetings. *Education and Treatment of Children, 28,* 308–320.

Nordness, P. D., & Epstein, M. H. (2003). Reliability of the Wraparound Observation Form Second Version: An instrument to assess the fidelity of wraparound approach. *Mental Health Services Research, 5,* 89–96.

Prochaska, J. O. (1994). Strong and weak principles for progressing from precontemplation to action on the basis of twelve problem behaviors. *Health Psychology, 13,* 47–51.

Ronnau, J., & Poertner, J. (1993). Identification and use of strengths: A family system approach. *Children Today, 22,* 20–23.

Saleebey, D. (1997). The strengths approach to practice. In D. Saleebey (Ed.), *The strengths perspective in social work practice* (2nd ed.; pp. 49–57). White Plains, NY: Longman.

Stroul, B. A., & Friedman, R. M. (1986). *A system of care for children and youth with severe emotional disturbances* (Rev. ed.). Washington, DC: Georgetown University Child Development Center, CASSP Technical Assistance Center.

Trivette, C. M., Dunst, C. J., Deal, A. G., Hamby, D. W., & Sexton, D. (1994). Assessing family strengths and capabilities. In C. J. Dunst, C. M. Trivette, & A. G. Deal (Eds.), *Supporting and strengthening families: Methods, strategies and practices* (pp. 132–139). Cambridge, MA: Brookline Books.

VanDenBerg, J. (1999). History of the wraparound process. In B. J. Burns & S. K. Goldman (Eds.), *Systems of care: Promising practices in children's mental health, 1998 series: Vol. IV. Promising practices in wraparound for children with serious emotional disturbance and their families* (pp. 19–26). Washington, DC: Center for Effective Collaboration and Practice, American Institutes for Research.

Walker, J. S., & Schutte, K. (2005). Quality and individualization in wraparound team planning. *Journal of Child and Family Studies, 14,* 251–267.

CHAPTER 19

Family Preservation Services

Scottye J. Cash

Family preservation services (FPS), as originally designed, focus on short-term, intensive, in-home services to families to help avoid the unnecessary placement of children in out-of-home care (Kinney, Haapala, & Booth, 1991). Although FPS have been used predominantly with child welfare clients, these services have been adapted for use with families in the juvenile justice system (i.e., multisystemic therapy [MST]; Henggeler & Borduin, 1995) and with families who have children with mental health needs (e.g., Seelig, Goldman-Hall, & Jerrell, 1992). This chapter provides an introduction to the characteristics and principles of FPS (based on Kinney et al., 1991), a brief history on the creation and evolution of FPS, an overview of the phases of helping within FPS, consideration of the congruence of FPS with the generalist-eclectic approach, and a critique of FPS. The chapter concludes with a case example to illustrate how FPS were used with a family in need of these services.

CHARACTERISTICS AND PRINCIPLES OF FAMILY PRESERVATION SERVICES

Family preservation services (FPS) were developed in the late 1970s and early 1980s as a response to the ever-growing number of children who were being placed in foster care with little hope of ever being reunified with their families (Lindsey, 1994). The Homebuilders program (Kinney et al., 1991) and other FPS programs were developed with the basic premise of doing whatever it takes to avoid *unnecessary* out-of-home placements of children. The term "unnecessary" provides a unique distinction that should be recognized, but is often overlooked, when critiquing the model. FPS are not for every family; there are simply some families whose risks and stressors are so great that leaving the child in the home is not a viable option. The safety of the child must be of primary concern and should not be minimized or ignored in an effort to keep a family together. As Kinney and colleagues (1991) said, "Some placements will always be necessary because some families will never be able to raise their own children safely and productively" (p. 9). Another important issue to note is that FPS programs were designed to prevent out-of-home placement for those children who were at *imminent risk* of placement. Imminent risk has been difficult to operationalize and consequently measure in a reliable and valid way. Without a reliable and valid measure of imminent risk, identifying appropriate families for FPS programs has been difficult.

The term "family preservation" can be described as both a philosophy and as a set of practice guidelines (Ronnau & Sallee, 1995). Berry (1997) wrote,

> As a *philosophy*, it explicates a values base. . . . Family preservation as a philosophy espouses varied definitions of family; diversity and uniqueness among families and communities; and the beliefs that families are the experts on their own lives and that family preservation work is a partnership involving the worker. (p. 72)

The practice guidelines of FPS focus specifically on the techniques, skills, and intervention methods used. Services are typically provided in the home rather than in an office or agency setting. Also, services involve the entire family rather than focusing only on specific individuals in the family. Some family preservation models are crisis oriented, with workers being available to help families 24 hours a day, 7 days a week. This level of involvement requires a shift in practice logistics. Family preservation services were designed to be intensive (approximately 10 hours a week) and short term (lasting 4–8 weeks), and caseworkers carry a caseload of two to three clients at one time (Berry, 1997; Kinney et al., 1991; Schuerman, Rzepnicki, & Littell, 1994). Finally, FPS seek to connect families to support systems in their larger community environment. These community connections are intended to serve as additional resources and continued sources of support once FPS cease.

Certain principles and values of FPS differentiate them from traditional child welfare services. The following principles and values underlie the Homebuilders model (Kinney et al., 1991) and are an integral part of the family preservation model.

1. *It is the worker's job to instill hope.* Many clients who come to the attention of FPS have been involved in the social service system for long periods of time. Many of these clients have experienced multiple stressors and losses and have had negative experiences with professionals and the system. A sense of hopelessness is often the result for these clients. Consequently, this first principle is a major tenet of the model and guides workers to recognize and point out the family's strengths and resiliency. This might involve demonstrating to clients that they can have a more positive experience with the social service system and teaching them how to navigate and influence the system to better meet their needs. A corollary of this principle is that workers cannot know ahead of time if a family's situation is hopeless. Every family has strengths, and it is imperative that the family and worker create a partnership to help identify their strengths and learn how their strengths can help mitigate the family's stressors. The family's strengths may not be obviously present at the first meeting; however, once rapport is established, these strengths will more than likely become apparent.

2. *Clients are our colleagues and they should be given as much power as possible.* Kinney et al. (1991) contended that "clients will want to form partnerships with us if they perceive that we are trying to give them something rather than taking something away" (p. 63). Clients are more likely to "warm up to us and loosen up much faster if we show we are interested in and sincerely care about them" (p. 65). This principle highlights the importance of the clients' active participation in the helping process in terms of both providing information and active problem-solving. The ultimate goal is self-determination and empowerment: "Our job is to help clients take control of their lives rather than to take control of their lives for them. . . . That is the whole point: to empower them to handle their problems" (Kinney et al., 1991, p. 65). Clients should always be viewed as experts of their own lives. The "helper" meets the family without knowing the family's entire history, or having a clear understanding of the relational patterns present. Making assumptions based on information documented by others or early on in a case can be detrimental to building rapport and effectively working with the family. A corollary of this principle is that "not knowing can be valuable" (Kinney et al., 1991, p. 66). It is very important to be honest with clients and let them know that we may not know all of the answers. Given that each family presents with unique issues, strengths, and resources, solutions may not

be immediately evident; however, by partnering with the family and creating mutually agreed upon and achievable goals, the likelihood for success is increased.

3. *We can do harm.* It is important to remind ourselves that good intentions do not necessarily lead to good outcomes and we can do harm to clients. Gibbs and Gambrill (1999) argued that the "history of the helping professions demonstrates that caring is not enough to protect people from harmful practices and to ensure that they receive helpful services" (p. 5). Common mistakes in helping include offering the wrong types of services (e.g., offering psychological counseling when clients need material resources), withdrawing intervention too soon or continuing it too long, increasing client dependency, and overlooking client assets. These issues make it imperative to evaluate our practice on an ongoing basis so that we can understand when to stop a treatment that is not working and when to change the type of treatment being used (Berlin & Marsh, 1993; Bloom, Fisher, & Orme, 1999). Potentially helpful strategies include reading the literature to determine what has been found to be effective with certain populations or problems, looking at the logical relationship between needs and services, and keeping records of clients' goal achievements (i.e., outcomes) over time. Still, because every client is unique (with regard to culture, ethnicity, socioeconomic status, etc.) we need to factor in the unique characteristics and circumstances of each client in formulating our assessments and interventions. Furthermore, we need to check with clients regularly to be sure our services are helpful rather than harmful.

HISTORICAL DEVELOPMENT

Program History

The impetus for the development of FPS came from a number of demonstration projects in the 1970s that focused on some of the problems in the child welfare system (Lindsey, 1994). These problems included lack of permanent placement for children who had been removed from their homes, foster care drift (i.e., multiple foster care placements for a child without a plan for reunifying the child or terminating parental rights to free the child for adoption), and the absence of a tracking system to constantly monitor where children were placed and what the permanency plan and goals were (Lindsey, 1994). Overall, the demonstration projects found that when services were intensive, utilized cognitive-behavioral treatments, and involved biological families in the treatment, the children were more likely to be reunified with their biological family and the children experienced fewer placements (Lindsey, 1994).

These findings created the impetus for changing the way in which services were delivered and families were treated. The Homebuilders program (Kinney et al., 1991), one of the most widely known family preservation models, emerged in 1974 in Tacoma, Washington. Homebuilders quickly gained national and international attention because overwhelmingly positive outcomes were reported (it was claimed that 85%–95% of families were able to avoid the out-of-home placement of a child), service duration was significantly shorter, and the costs of providing Homebuilders services were significantly less expensive than out-of-home placement (Blythe, Salley, & Jayarante, 1994). Although Homebuilders programs were able to report very positive results, over time these results were questioned because the programs were not evaluated using rigorous research methods (Berry, 1997; Gelles, 1996; Schuerman et al., 1994). Few studies incorporated comparison or control groups, and many studies were one group, posttest only, with placement of the child as the only dependent variable. These limitations made it difficult to establish with any certainty that FPS were more effective than traditional child welfare services.

During the 1980s and 1990s family preservation programs proliferated throughout North America and Australia. Although many programs have claimed to follow the Homebuilders model, few have demonstrated treatment fidelity. Instead, agencies modified the Homebuilders model (e.g., by making services less intensive, longer in duration, and less family or home based; and having caseworkers carry larger caseloads) to meet their agency and client population's needs. Because of this treatment infidelity, it was no longer appropriate for agencies to claim success rates based on the findings from the original Homebuilders studies (Berry, 1997; Cash & Berry, 2002).

Policy History

The early research findings from the demonstration projects and the recognition that more effective and efficient services needed to be provided to this population led to the creation and implementation of new policies. The Adoption Assistance and Child Welfare Act was passed in 1980 and established a set of permanency priorities for children who were in the child welfare system. The permanency priorities were ordered as follows: (a) Children should be with their natural families; (b) when preservation of the family is not possible, the next alternative is for termination of parental rights and the adoption of children; (c) if adoption is not possible, legal guardianship by a foster or kinship care provider should be established for the child; and (d) if foster care is the only permanent solution available (i.e., this is commonly the case with older children or children with special needs), the placement should be long term and the child should not be moved from one placement to the next (Barth & Berry, 1987).

Although the permanency priorities were set by the federal government, monetary support to implement these new priorities was not provided. State and county child welfare agencies were left with a political impetus to keep a child with his or her family; however, the financial support was nonexistent or contradictory to the policy. For example, although FPS were considered less expensive compared to out-of-home placement, states received significant reimbursement from the federal government for each child in the foster care system. It was not until 1993, with the enactment of the Family Preservation and Family Support Act, that fiscal support was provided to create and maintain services that helped to keep the child with his or her natural family.

In 1997, the Adoption and Safe Families Act (ASFA) was enacted, whereby the priorities changed from family preservation to timely adoption of children. This policy shift created a complete readjustment in the child welfare system, especially for family preservation services. Parents' rights could now be terminated if the child had been in care 15 of the last 22 months, which was a reduction in time from the 18 of 22 months specified in earlier legislation. Since ASFA was implemented, family preservation services no longer receive the same type of attention or funding. As a result, the empirical exploration of family preservation services has almost ceased since ASFA was implemented. Much of the empirical knowledge base has now shifted to managed care in child welfare, adoption, and alternative response systems.

THEORETICAL FOUNDATIONS

FPS are based generally on an ecological model (Bronfenbrenner, 1979; Garbarino, 1991; Germain & Gitterman, 1980; Kemp, Whittaker, & Tracy, 1997; also see chapter 4) of human functioning and interaction. The ecological model provides a comprehensive way of understanding and helping families as it recognizes the interdependence between people and their environments. As Berry (1997) explained,

> There are layers of interaction within ever-widening circles of the environment, much like the layers of an onion, and effective social intervention (understanding and helping) will assess the contribution of each layer to a situation and attempt to bolster or influence each layer. (p. 52)

A distinguishing element of the ecological model is the focus on not only the individual and interpersonal factors in a family's situation but also aspects of the social and physical environment—and the adequacy (or "goodness of fit") of the links between the family and its environment. The ecological model is congruent with a strengths perspective (Cole, 1995; Saleebey, 1996; Weick & Saleebey, 1995), as it incorporates not only the risk factors present for each individual in the family and the family's environment, but also the strengths and resources. The ecological perspective posits that child maltreatment occurs when a family's stresses and demands outweigh their strengths and resources (Darmstadt, 1990; Fraser, 1997; Moncher, 1995; Thomlison, 1997). Whittaker, Schinke, and Gilchrist (1986) noted that the ecological model suggests that "effective service programs and policies for children, youths, and families will be those that attend to both skill acquisition and the provision of social support" (p. 492). Whittaker and colleagues' model, however, fails to highlight one key issue: Before families can learn new skills and use available social supports, they must first be able to meet their immediate, concrete needs (i.e., food, clothing, and shelter; Cash & Berry, 2002).

Social support theories (Whittaker et al., 1986) and stress and coping theories (Lazarus & Folkman, 1984; also see chapter 4) also inform the family preservation model. Research has established that parental stress and social isolation are key factors associated with child maltreatment and out-of-home placement (Coohey, 1996; Moncher, 1995; Thomlison, 1997). Social support and positive social networks have been found to be key mediating factors in a person's (or family's) ability to adapt in a positive way to stressful situations (Lovell & Richey, 1991). FPS endeavor to help families connect to sources of social support in their informal social networks not only to help them deal with their immediate concerns but also to create a safety net that they can rely on in times of crisis or need (Darmstadt, 1990; Lovell & Richey, 1991; Moncher, 1995).

FPS also draw on a wide variety of clinical theories and techniques. Cognitive-behavioral, client-centered, and crisis theories have been critical clinical components of most family preservation models. Lewis (1991) studied the theoretical perspectives of the Homebuilders model and found that there were nine core interventions used in most Homebuilders cases. Four of these "involved activities that tended to be used to establish and facilitate therapeutic relationships" (Lewis, 1991, p. 95), which is illustrative of the client-centered theory of practice. The other five core techniques were clarifying problems; setting treatment goals; reframing; using reinforcements; and identifying natural consequences, all of which illustrate techniques associated with cognitive-behavioral and crisis theories.

PHASES OF HELPING

The description of the steps in the helping process provided in this section is adapted from the Homebuilders model (Kinney et al., 1991). Although the Homebuilders model does not use the same terminology, the descriptions of the phases of helping in this model have been organized according to the stages in the problem-solving process (i.e., engagement, data collection and assessment, contracting and intervention, and evaluation and termination). Given the short-term and intensive nature of FPS, these stages of helping might possibly overlap and blend together more than one would find when using traditional counseling approaches.

Engagement

The engagement phase focuses on establishing trust and forming a partnership with the family. Engagement usually begins with the first phone call to the client, which Kinney et al. (1991) called "getting to know you: chitchat therapy on the phone" (p. 55). Kinney and colleagues suggested that during the initial phone calls, workers should try to avoid direct questioning and instead use their active listening skills to begin to understand clients' concerns. Active listening allows clients to talk about any feelings of anger or being pressured and to feel understood. The family preservation worker must always ensure that the child, who has been identified to be at risk, is safe and can remain safe in the current environment. If the worker does not think the child can remain safe, alternative arrangements need to be made to ensure the child's safety. These alternative arrangements will most often include out-of-home placement of a child in either an emergency shelter or with a relative or kin. Safety of the worker is also paramount, and talking on the phone is a safe way to first meet the family, discuss service options, and defuse negative emotions and expectations.

The first face-to-face meeting with the family usually takes place in the family's home, but if there are concerns about safety it is advisable to meet in a public environment, such as a restaurant. Workers should act as gracious guests in the family's home and should work to help family members feel at ease by relating to them in a person-to-person manner (e.g., using social chitchat) before moving into a helper–helpee mode of relating. The primary goal in the first meeting is to encourage clients to tell their stories and to begin gaining the family's trust.

In the engagement stage, it is necessary to develop a working partnership with the family. To do this, it is recommended that the social worker acknowledge that the family members are the experts of their own lives. Kinney et al. (1991) outlined beliefs necessary for achieving trust with families. These beliefs include the following: (a) There are many similarities between us and the clients we work with; (b) families are doing the best they can, and families have coped with difficult situations in the past; (c) families have optimism and inherent strengths; and (d) most of the time, family members really do care about each other.

Some child welfare clients have had previous experiences with the social service system—both positive and negative. Negative experiences with social service systems may make it difficult to initially engage the family. Clients may be distrusting of the agency and find it difficult to believe that a social worker views them positively and wants to form a working partnership with them. Workers can help this situation by focusing on ways to build trust and working to create an environment where the family will want to spend time with the worker and is willing to share thoughts and feelings that make them vulnerable. The cardinal rule in the Homebuilders model is "When in doubt, listen" (Kinney et al., 1991, p. 68; for further information on issues in and strategies for working with involuntary clients see Kinney et al., 1991, and Rooney, 1992).

Data Collection and Assessment

Data collection and assessment are intertwined with the engagement process. Active listening is the key to accurate data collection and assessment. Workers need to allow clients to tell their stories and to ensure that each family member is able to provide his or her own view. Kinney et al. (1991) described the essence of data collection and assessment as follows:

> The priority now is understanding, withholding judgments on the specifics, trying to feel compassion, and engaging with each family member. This is imperative. The more compassion family members can feel from us, the more they will trust us. The more they trust us, the more information they will give us. The more information we have, the better the assessment we can formulate. (p. 81)

In instances where there is family conflict, it may be necessary to talk with each family member individually.

There are a number of important principles to remember about the data collection and assessment phase in FPS. First, workers need to check in to see if they really understand what clients have told them. Second, assessments need to focus on strengths and abilities as well as problems and deficits. Third, assessment is not static but rather an ongoing process that follows the evolution of problems and strengths. Assessment should continue until there is resolution and the family's functioning is at a level where the child can remain safely in the home (in the Homebuilders model this means only that there is no longer a threat of placement; Kinney et al., 1991).

Kinney and colleagues (1991) suggested a number of strategies for ongoing data collection and assessment: (a) minimize blame and labeling, (b) help the family members to reach consensus about the facts (either by clarifying very specifically about the details in question or by finding very general statements that family members can agree on), (c) help family members to gradually interpret each other's behavior in less negative ways, and (d) define problems in terms of skill deficits, which avoids blaming individuals and implies hope about learning necessary skills. Kinney and colleagues recommended using natural observation and conversation rather than formal procedures and tests/instruments for assessment purposes. Pecora, Fraser, Nelson, McCrosky, and Meezan (1995) urged FPS workers to "consider the possibility of building an assessment protocol that combines demographic and clinical data with measurement of family and individual functioning" (p. 96). Pecora and colleagues (1995) and Berry (1997) provided a comprehensive list of measures that may be appropriate to use with a child welfare population. When using standardized assessments, it is still important to consult with the family about the practicality and meaningfulness of standardized tests. The assessment of family functioning should also be individualized and culturally sensitive, logically related to the family's goals, and descriptive enough to inform the service delivery.

Contracting and Intervention

After the assessment process, it is important to set goals that are directly related to the family's needs, and these goals should drive the choice of services or interventions provided to the family. A logic model is helpful in laying out the logical sequencing that shows the relationship between needs, goals, services, and outcomes (Cash & Berry, 2002, 2003; Pecora, Seelig, Zirps, & Davis, 1996; see Figure 19.1).

In order to find a starting point, it is necessary to prioritize the family's problems and goals. This contracting process involves a balance between letting the family members set their own priorities and ensuring that such priorities ensure child safety and do not contradict ethical standards. Workers need to help families be realistic about the number and the scope of goals (i.e., a small number of achievable goals) that they choose to focus on. It is necessary to prioritize goals so that families may achieve incremental success on one goal, especially at the beginning of a case. This initial success might increase the family's likelihood of achieving other goals. Once initial goals are set, workers may use goal

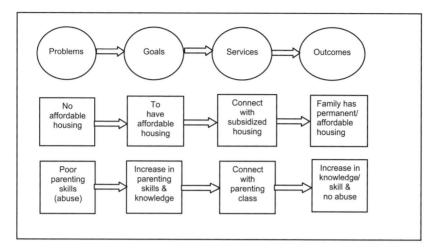

FIGURE 19.1   Logic model.

attainment scaling to measure goal achievement over time. Goal attainment scales can be used to specify behaviors or events that are related to potential outcome levels. A 3-point goal attainment scale (scores ranging from +1 to –1) would specify the *Best possible outcome/exceeds expectations (+1)*, *Expected outcome (0)*, and *Least favorable outcome (–1)*. Using this framework, the worker would identify one goal and then operationalize what each level of achievement would look like. For example, the worker and family may identify as a goal "to obtain housing." Using a 3-point goal attainment scale, the Best outcome (+1) might be "Family obtained permanent housing," the Expected outcome (0) might be "Family obtained temporary housing," and the Least favorable outcome (–1) might be "Family does not have sustainable housing." Every week, the worker reviews progress made toward each goal, records the score, and helps the family make necessary adjustments to the goals or the strategies to achieve them.

Intervention in FPS is driven by client self-determination. It involves not only helping clients to solve their particular problems but also teaching clients how to learn general problem-solving skills. Kinney and colleagues (1991) made the analogy that clients are "personal scientists . . . [who] learn to observe their problems and systematically vary ways of dealing with these problems until they come up with one that fits for them" (p. 93). They also specified three ways by which they teach clients: (a) direct instruction (e.g., teaching skills), (b) modeling (specific skills as well as productive attitudes), and (c) contingency management (i.e., rewarding positive behavior either informally or through a behavior management program).

Workers in FPS use many different strategies for working with a family and the problems the family is experiencing. For problems involving basic needs, workers may help a family obtain food, shelter, income assistance, employment, furniture, clothing, child care, and/or medical services. Workers also help clients develop skills (e.g., budgeting, housework, home repair) so that they can learn to meet their basic needs. Lewis (1991) suggested that providing clients with concrete services early in the helping process helps to engage the family and demonstrates to them the worker's commitment to helping. For intrapersonal problems, workers use cognitive, behavioral, and reflective listening/supportive strategies to help clients learn to manage and change their feelings. For interpersonal problems, workers may teach communication, assertiveness, problem-solving, and/or parenting skills. Berry (1997) argued that a focus "on modeling life skills, such as parenting skills, and teaching and practicing with family members the positive and constructive communication and negotiation skills . . . will contribute to a more positive and less abusive family environment" (p. 144).

Assigning homework is one way to help a family become actively involved in their change process and to remain focused on their goals even when the worker is not available. Workers may also help a family to develop and maintain daily routines with regard to getting up in the morning, cooking meals at specified times, and getting kids to bed on time. Kinney et al. (1991) contended that "the more family members are preoccupied with productive pursuits, the less time they will have for getting in trouble" (p. 74).

As previously emphasized, FPS are oriented, intensive, and short term. Crises do not always occur during regular business hours and cannot always be dealt with quickly. Workers must have a flexible schedule and a certain degree of openness when using this approach, as this crisis-oriented approach requires being available to a family 24 hours a day and 7 days a week.

Evaluation and Termination

Termination, when using FPS, usually occurs within a relatively short period of time (i.e., 4–8 weeks, depending on the model). In the Homebuilders model, services continue "only until the threat of out-of-home placement has been averted" (Kinney et al., 1991, p. 139). Determining when the threat of placement has been averted can be assessed through a combination of standardized instruments that measure change, risk assessment instruments that use posttests, and the worker's practice wisdom. Termination decisions are also influenced by periodic goal attainment scaling reviews. In the traditional Homebuilders model, if the family has problems that have not been resolved after the threat of placement has been averted, they are referred to other services in the community.

Termination is an ongoing process, and it should begin at the first session. Families should be informed during the engagement phase that services are time limited. Workers should "count down" with families to help them anticipate termination. Families can also be assisted to create problem-solving strategies to help them cope with problems that arise after FPS have ceased. One way to assist with this transition is for workers to identify and set up ancillary support services that the family can call upon when needed. To assist in the transition from an FPS model to community services, workers can serve as the bridge by introducing the family members to the community services workers so that when services are terminated, the family has an established network to provide necessary supports (formal and/or informal).

The last time a worker meets with a family, he or she may create a celebratory atmosphere by providing certificates of achievement, serving food, or creating unique ways to celebrate the family's successes. It is not unusual for workers to "to maintain minimal and informal contact with clients for years" (Kinney et al., 1991, p. 156).

COMPATIBILITY WITH THE GENERALIST-ECLECTIC FRAMEWORK

FPS are very compatible with the generalist-eclectic framework. The principles and values of family preservation practice are congruent with those of the profession of social work. These principles and values include a genuine respect for clients, a commitment to self-determination and empowerment, recognition of clients' strengths, a focus on creating partnerships with clients, and a person-in-environment perspective. It should be acknowledged that our profession's adherence to these principles and values has waxed and waned over the years, and at times we have become more closely aligned with psychiatry than the roots of social work (Specht & Courtney, 1994). FPS represent a move to reembrace traditional social work practice values and principles.

There are a number of other ways that the family preservation model is compatible with the generalist-eclectic framework. These include (a) commitment to holistic, multilevel assessment that is informed by ecological systems theory; (b) use of a problem-solving framework to help clients learn how to deal with current and subsequent problems; and (c) the flexible use of a wide variety of theories and techniques.

CRITIQUE OF FAMILY PRESERVATION SERVICES

The family preservation model has been scrutinized, and its use with child welfare families has created more heated debate than perhaps than any other approach to practice. The concerns and questions about FPS have centered around two issues: (a) the overall effectiveness of the model, and (b) the appropriateness of its use with families that are at high risk for child maltreatment.

Effectiveness of FPS

As mentioned earlier, although the results of early research on FPS were very positive (Fraser, Pecora, & Haapala, 1991), recent, more method-ologically rigorous studies of FPS have produced less positive results. Summary reviews of the research on FPS (Blythe et al., 1994; Rossi, 1992; Schuerman et al., 1994; Wells & Biegel, 1992) note the conflicting results of family preservation studies and conclude that there is a need for additional rigorous studies in order to determine the effectiveness of these services. One of the most rigorous studies of family preservation services was conducted by Schuerman and colleagues (1994). The evalu-ation of the Illinois Family First program has become widely recognized, as it was the "most scientifically credible evaluation of any family preser-vation program" (Epstein, 1997, p. 46) performed to date.

Schuerman and colleagues (1994) found no significant differences in outcomes with regard to rate or duration of child placement or sub-sequent reports of child maltreatment between families who received FPS and those who received traditional child welfare services. FPS fami-lies reported better family and child functioning, but this difference was not sustained over time. Clients who received FPS did, however, report more satisfaction with their services and had more positive views of the relationships with their workers. Despite their overall negative findings, Schuerman and colleagues noted study limitations, and were cautious about drawing firm conclusions. In particular, they pointed out that, as in many previous studies, the rates of placement and maltreatment were low for both the experimental (FPS) and control (traditional services) groups, and therefore, the probability of detecting differential effects was low.

The Families First (Schuerman et al., 1994) research has generated a number of debates in the field with regard to the effectiveness of FPS and directions for research. Courtney (1997) noted that "whereas the results of the Family First evaluation should temper uncritical enthusiasm for family preservation services, they should not be considered prima facie evidence that service approaches to preserving families are doomed to failure"

(p. 73). Furthermore, Nelson (1997) has argued that "the universally high satisfaction both families and workers express with the services" (p. 111) represents some evidence of effectiveness and that the negative finding to date with regard to more objective criteria "may represent a failure of the research to detect the successes of the program" (p. 105).

With regard to directions for research, a number of authors (e.g., Berry, 1997; Cash, 1998; Cash & Berry, 2002, 2003) have pointed out that, to date, family preservation studies have focused almost exclusively on outcomes and have ignored process variables. Neglecting process variables in the research has resulted in a dearth of information about the types of services provided, the characteristics of the target populations, and how such factors influence outcomes. The assessment of the overall effectiveness of FPS is particularly difficult because there is such a wide range of family preservation models that differ from one another in many important ways. In the Families First evaluation by Schuerman and colleagues (1994), tracking service provision was difficult, especially for the control group. Given this difficulty, service provision remained as a "black box" (Staff & Fein, 1994), and it was not possible to determine what services were actually provided and if services in each of the conditions were related to outcomes.

Littell (1997) reanalyzed the data from the Family First project, with a specific emphasis on the influence of duration, intensity, and breadth of services on outcomes. She found that duration of services had no effect on out-of-home placement or recurrence of maltreatment. These findings were consistent for the 3-, 6-, and 12-month follow-up times. Unexpectedly, intensity of services was related to an increase in out-of-home placements and recurrence of child maltreatment. This finding may be explained, however, by the fact that workers are more likely to have more intensive involvement with the most high-risk families. With regard to the breadth and type of services, families who received more concrete services were less likely to experience out-of-home placement (at 3 months only); however, there was no effect for receipt of concrete services on recurrence of abuse or neglect. Overall, Littell concluded that duration, intensity, and breadth of services had little effect on outcomes.

Cash and Berry (2002) examined the specific relationships between needs and services in a family preservation program. Based on a logic model analysis, Cash and Berry found that on the whole, services were related to the family's needs. There were, however, some discrepancies when the family was poor. Families in poverty were less likely to receive services that would assist the family with alleviating the stressors associated with being in poverty. These families tended to receive services that were more general in nature (i.e., parent training and clinical services) rather than services related to financial needs.

In the same family preservation evaluation, Cash and Berry (2003) also explored the relationship between family characteristics, services provided, and three different outcome criteria. Findings in this study showed that "differential service provision did not lead to good outcomes (variously defined) for the families" (p. 21) and that overall, family preservation services had minimal effects on outcome. Reflecting on these findings, the authors raised two issues. First, they suggested that family preservation programs should not be expected to produce "big changes" because "issues associated with poverty, health, employment, and social injustice have a greater impact than one program can be expected to overcome" (p. 22). Second, they raised the possibility that in terms of predictors of success, it might be better to focus on the rapport and relationship between the family and the caseworker than on service characteristics (e.g., type and duration of service).

The research on family preservation services needs to continue; however, due to the effect of ASFA, these evaluations have become almost nonexistent. Although research has shown that the early claims about the effectiveness of FPS may have been inflated, research results do not warrant an abandonment of the model. It is clear that families are more satisfied with the services and the workers' approach in this model when compared to traditional services. It is now a matter of determining if certain aspects of FPS are more effective with particular families and problems. Outcomes of different program types cannot be fully understood without attending to how types of services and family characteristics/needs may influence these outcomes. A "one size fits all" model will not work with these families and could further tax an already burdened child welfare system. If families' needs are not addressed while they are receiving child welfare services, a revolving door effect is created whereby families have multiple involvements with child welfare. Families do not have a fair chance to succeed if the agency that is responsible for helping them reach their goals provides services that are inconsistent with their needs. Furthermore, as Cash and Berry (2003) suggested, research might begin to focus on relationship factors as predictors of outcome in family preservation services.

Concerns About Placing Children at Unnecessary Risk

Gelles (1996) and McDonald (1994) contended that family preservation services place children at unnecessary risk. Gelles argued that assessment strategies and tools are not reliable and valid enough to warrant making decisions to keep a child in a home that may be dangerous. McDonald's critique of FPS offered a similar view; however, she went further in arguing that family preservation services may reward a family that does not deserve help. For example, she questioned why a family who has maltreated their child be rewarded with housecleaning and child care? McDonald's argument is clearly simplistic and does not take into account how the stressors of poverty and a lack of basic resources influence a family's ability to be successful in their own lives (Fraser, 1997). The system needs to ensure both that the child can remain safe and that families are given the opportunity to get help with their problems while, if at all possible, their children can remain at home. Additional research is needed to explore the types of services that are necessary to help different types of families while ensuring a safe environment for the child.

CASE EXAMPLE

The Norton family, consisting of father (Charles), mother (Crystal), and 5-year-old son (Jack), was referred to the state child protective services (CPS) department for child physical abuse. The intake worker documented from the referral that the father had hit his son with a belt numerous times and left bruises on his buttocks, upper legs, and lower back. After the call was processed by the intake unit, the referral was sent to the investigation unit. The investigation worker completed a safety and risk assessment, which included an examination of prior history with CPS; the parents' history; issues of substance use and abuse, domestic violence, and mental health; and the parents' and child's interactions and strengths. Once the risk assessment was completed it was determined that physical abuse did occur (i.e., the allegation was substantiated), and the investigation worker determined that the child was at imminent risk of being placed into foster care. The Norton family was presented with two options: participate in family preservation services or have the child placed in foster or kinship (if a family member was available) care. The parents indicated they did not want to have their child placed in foster care and hoped that by participating in family preservation services, they would be able to keep their family together.

The family preservation worker, Roberta, received the referral on a Thursday afternoon. That same afternoon, Roberta contacted (via the telephone) the mother, Crystal, to arrange a time to meet with the whole family. During the initial phone conversation, Roberta explained to Crystal the process involved when working with CPS. Roberta used this initial phone conversation to initiate the rapport-building process by actively listening and asking questions about the family's strengths and empathizing with their struggles and stresses. As time progressed, Crystal seemed to open up on the telephone and seemed more trusting than she did initially. Roberta asked Crystal when a good time would be for her to come over and meet the family; Crystal indicated they would all be home on Saturday.

Roberta arrived at the Norton's house at the agreed upon time. When Roberta arrived at the house, she noticed the screens on the windows were ripped and that the front steps to the house were somewhat dangerous (nails sticking out, old rotted boards, etc.). Roberta rang the doorbell and was promptly greeted at the door by Crystal. Upon entering the home, Crystal introduced Roberta to her husband, Charles, and their 5-year-old son, Jack. Roberta noted that Charles seemed suspicious of her, so she reviewed the purpose of family preservation services. Roberta decided to work on building rapport with Charles and began "chitchatting" with both Crystal and Charles about their week and what they enjoyed doing. Through this conversation Roberta discovered that they enjoyed camping, bowling, and playing ball in the front yard. Roberta also found out that Charles was a plumber by trade but also enjoyed painting and metal sculpting. Throughout the time that Roberta was at the house, Jack was watching cartoons; however, at times he would get loud and noisy and run around the house. Roberta noticed that Charles and Crystal would become anxious and annoyed by Jack's behavior and seemed tempted to yell at Jack.

During this visit, Roberta discussed with Crystal and Charles that she would be their partner during this process. Roberta discussed the report and substantiation of physical abuse with Crystal and Charles. Roberta gave them her cellular phone number, indicating that she would be available to the family 24 hours a day, 7 days a week. She asked that they call her if they ever felt like they were losing control with Jack or if there was an emergency. Roberta stressed that the key to achieving success with family preservation services was to create a contract stating they would work on the problems that brought them to the attention of the child welfare system and would agree to not physically abuse Jack. Before leaving the house, Roberta arranged another visit with the family on Monday morning.

On Monday morning, Roberta again came to the family's home. From her previous discussions with the family, she found out that they all love jelly-filled donuts, so, on her way to the house, she stopped by the local donut store and bought some. Everyone seemed pleased to see that she had remembered what they liked. While eating donuts at the dining room table, Roberta discussed the importance of setting goals. Together with Roberta, each family member (including Jack) worked together to develop several goals. For each goal listed, they outlined who was responsible for completing the goal and what steps were necessary to achieve the goal. For each goal, they noted what resources and strengths the family currently possessed that would help them achieve their goal.

The three goals that they created were (a) to maintain control (i.e., refrain from emotional and physical abuse) when Jack needed discipline, (b) to learn and utilize positive parenting skills, and (c) to better manage their finances and the upkeep of the home.

The first goal, to not physically or emotionally abuse Jack, was the primary goal, as this goal was needed in order to ensure that Jack would remain in a safe environment. The second goal, to learn and utilize positive parenting skills, would help with achieving the first goal. The third goal, creating a budget and fixing the broken screens and porch so that the home was physically safe, was important because if they could better meet their basic needs (their utilities had been shut off at times due to failure to pay bills) they would be more able to focus and work on the other goals. This final goal was also created to help the family feel better about themselves and their home, and to begin to feel more hopeful about their future.

During the second visit, each of the goals was broken down into smaller tasks with corresponding target dates. The first two goals were going to be accomplished through the parents attending a parent training class located in their neighborhood, and also through Roberta teaching and modeling positive parenting skills to the family in their own home. Roberta estimated that she would need to work with the family, in their home, for at least 8 hours a week. Roberta also offered to provide the family members with transportation (the family did not have a car) for grocery shopping and other errands.

The third goal would serve as a family project to be worked on during Roberta's visits. Roberta (through the agency's Concrete Services fund) would provide the necessary materials to fix the house and they would work on it together. If a particular part of the project was beyond their capabilities, Roberta was also allocated a limited amount of money to hire someone to complete the job.

The focus of subsequent visits by Roberta was dictated primarily by the needs and interests of the family. Roberta purchased board games that were appropriate for Jack, taking into consideration his age and developmental stage. The entire family played the games together, along with Roberta, so that she could model and coach Crystal and Charles how to interact in a more positive manner with Jack. Some visits focused on fix-it projects around the house whereas others focused on teaching parenting skills, budgeting, and learning to problem-solve when ongoing family issues arose. As time passed, Roberta became a trusted friend of the family and would help with meal preparation, dishes, or other house-work tasks. She would also stop by the house from time to time, bringing dinner, and would join the family for dinner. By developing this relation-ship with the family, she was able to integrate informal counseling and support into social/recreational and practical activities.

Crystal and Charles attended the parent training group. While at the group, they not only learned new skills but they also made several friends, thus increasing their social support system. They exchanged phone numbers with some of the group members so they could call during times of crisis. Roberta also referred Crystal to other community agencies and organizations in an effort to ensure that the family was able to meet their basic needs over time and to connect her with needed resources and other sources of formal and informal support.

Over the 6-week time period, the family made many gains in the areas of parenting, budgeting, and getting along with each other. They began to feel much better about themselves and their home. At times, the family still had its difficulties, and Roberta would go to the house to help mediate crisis situations. Over time, "unscheduled" visits decreased and Roberta was able to document that the family seemed to be doing better all around. Crystal and Charles indicated that they appreciated the services and did not feel that CPS was only there to "take away their child."

Roberta closed the Norton case approximately 7 weeks after the case was opened. She determined, based on her own observations as well as a formal assessment of risk (the Family Assessment Form; Meezan & McCroskey, 1996), that the risks and needs were reduced, and the strengths increased. The family worked hard during the time their case was open and achieved success, meeting all three of their goals. In addition, the parents created support systems, both formal and informal, that they could now rely upon in times of crisis or need. At a 6-month follow-up the family was still intact and no subsequent reports had been filed with the child welfare system.

SUMMARY

FPS are not a panacea for all of the problems that families face, but they are an important part of a continuum of child welfare and other social work services. Although the model is not without its flaws, the principles and values associated with the model are sound and congruent with those of the social work profession. The model is neither dogmatic nor static—it pushes the boundaries of traditional practice, encourages creativity and innovation, and continues to evolve.

REFERENCES

Barth, R., & Berry, M. (1987). Outcomes of child welfare services under permanency planning. *Social Service Review, 61,* 71–90.

Berlin, S., & Marsh, J. (1993). *Informing practice decisions*. New York: Macmillan.

Berry, M. (1997). *The family at risk: Issues and trends in family preservation services*. Columbia: University of South Carolina Press.

Bloom, M., Fischer, J., & Orme, J. G. (1999). *Evaluating practice: Guidelines for the accountable professional*. Boston: Allyn & Bacon.

Blythe, B. J., Salley, M. P., & Jayaratne, S. (1994). A review of intensive family preservation services research. *Social Work Research, 18*, 213–224.

Bronfenbrenner, U. (1979). *The ecology of human development: Experiments by nature and design*. Cambridge, MA: Harvard University Press.

Cash, S. J. (1998). *Family preservation services: Predicting service usage and subsequent outcomes*. Unpublished doctoral dissertation, University of Texas at Arlington.

Cash, S. J., & Berry, M. (2002). Family characteristics and child welfare services: Does assessment drive service provision? *Families in Society, 83*, 499–507.

Cash, S. J., & Berry, M. (2003). The impact of family preservation services on child and family well-being. *Journal of Social Service Research, 29*, 1–26.

Cole, E. S. (1995). Becoming family centered: Child welfare's challenge. *Families in Society, 76*, 163–172.

Coohey, C. (1996). Child maltreatment: Testing the social isolation hypothesis. *Child Abuse & Neglect, 20*, 241–254.

Courtney, M. E. (1997). Reconsidering family preservation: A review of Putting Families First. *Children and Youth Services Review, 19*, 61–76.

Darmstadt, G. L. (1990). Community-based child abuse prevention. *Social Work, 35*, 487–493.

Epstein, W. M. (1997). Social science, child welfare, and family preservation: A failure of rationality in public policy. *Children and Youth Services Review, 19*, 41–60.

Fraser, M. W. (1997). The ecology of childhood: A multisystems perspective. In M. W. Fraser (Ed.), *Risk and resilience in childhood: An ecological perspective* (pp. 1–9). Washington, DC: NASW Press.

Fraser, M. W., Pecora, P. J., & Haapala, D. A. (1991). *Families in crisis: The impact of intensive family preservation services*. Hawthorne, NY: Aldine de Gruyter.

Garbarino, J. (1991). *Children and families in the social environment* (2nd ed.). New York: Aldine de Gruyter.

Gelles, R. (1996). *The book of David*. New York: Basic Books.

Germain, C., & Gitterman, A. (1980). *The life model of social work practice*. New York: Columbia University Press.

Gibbs, L., & Gambrill, E. (1999). *Critical thinking for social workers: A workbook*. Thousand Oaks, CA: Pine Forge Press.

Henggeler, S. W., & Borduin, C. M. (1995). Multisystemic treatment of serious juvenile offenders and their families. In I. M. Schwartz & P. AuClaire (Eds.), *Home-based services for troubled children* (pp. 113–130). Lincoln: University of Nebraska Press.

Kemp. S. P., Whittaker, J. K., & Tracy, E. M. (1997). *Person-environment practice*. Hawthorne, NY: Aldine de Gruyter.

Kinney, J., Haapala, D., & Booth, C. (1991). *Keeping families together: The Homebuilders model*. New York: Aldine de Gruyter.

Lazarus, R. S., & Folkman, S. (1984). *Stress, appraisal, and coping*. New York: Springer Publishing Company.

Lewis, R. E. (1991). What are the characteristics of intensive family preservation services? In M. W. Fraser, P. J. Pecora, & D. A. Haapala (Eds.), *Families in crisis: The impact of intensive family preservation services* (pp. 93–107). Hawthorne, NY: Aldine de Gruyter.

Lindsey, D. (1994). *The welfare of children*. New York: Oxford University Press.

Littell, J. H. (1997). Effects of the duration, intensity, and breadth of family preservation services: A new analysis of data from the Illinois Family First Experiment. *Children and Youth Services Review, 19,* 17–40.

Lovell, M. L., & Richey, C. A. (1991). Implementing agency-based social-support skill training. *Families in Society, 72,* 563–573.

McDonald, H. (1994). The ideology of "Family Preservation." *Public Interest, 115,* 45–60.

Meezan W., & McCroskey, J. (1996, Winter). Improving family functioning through family preservation services: Results of the Los Angeles experiment. *Family Preservation Journal,* 9–29.

Moncher, F. J. (1995). Social isolation and child-abuse risk. *Families in Society, 76,* 421–433.

Nelson, K. E. (1997). Family preservation—What is it? *Children and Youth Services Review, 19,* 101–118.

Pecora, P. J., Fraser, M. W., Nelson, K. E., McCroskey, J., & Meezan, W. (1995). *Evaluating family-based services.* New York: Aldine de Gruyter.

Pecora, P. J., Seelig, W. R., Zirps, F. A., & Davis, S. M. (Eds.). (1996). *Quality improvement and evaluation in child and family services: Managing in the next century.* Washington, DC: CWLA Press.

Ronnau, J. P., & Sallee, A. L. (1995). *Theoretical framework for family preservation.* Las Cruces: Family Preservation Institute, New Mexico State University.

Rooney, R. H. (1992). *Strategies for work with involuntary clients.* New York: Columbia University Press.

Rossi, P. H. (1992). Assessing family preservation programs. *Children and Youth Services Review, 14,* 77–97.

Saleebey, D. (1996). The strengths perspective in social work practice: Extensions and cautions. *Social Work, 41,* 296–305.

Schuerman, J. R., Rzepnicki, T. L., & Littell, J. H. (1994). *Putting families first: An experiment in family preservation.* New York: Aldine de Gruyter.

Seelig, W. R., Goldman-Hall, B. J., & Jerrell, J. M. (1992). In-home treatment of families with seriously disturbed adolescents in crisis. *Family Process, 31,* 135–149.

Specht, H., & Courtney, M. (1994). *Unfaithful angels.* New York: Free Press.

Staff, I., & Fein, E. (1994). Inside the black box: An exploration of service delivery in a family reunification program. *Child Welfare, 73,* 195–211.

Thomlison, B. (1997). Risk and protective factors in child maltreatment. In M. W. Fraser (Ed.), *Risk and resilience in childhood: An ecological perspective* (pp. 50–72). Washington, DC: NASW Press.

Weick, A., & Saleebey, D. (1995). Supporting family strengths: Orienting policy and practice toward the 21st century. *Families in Society, 76,* 141–149.

Wells, K., & Biegel, D. E. (1992). Intensive family preservation services research: Current status and future agenda. *Social Work Research & Abstracts, 28,* 21–27.

Whittaker, J. K., Schinke, S. P., & Gilchrist, L. D. (1986). The ecological paradigm in child, youth, and family services: Implications for policy and practice. *Social Service Review, 60,* 483–503.

Interactive Trauma/ Grief-Focused Therapy With Children

Kathleen Nader and Christine Mello

Disasters, violence, and severe accidents may result in symptoms of post-traumatic stress disorder (PTSD), complex trauma or grief, comorbid disorders such as depression, and/or a number of adverse and prolonged effects (e.g., disturbed information processing, anguish, fear, distrust, and poor health; Nader, 1997a, in press). When unresolved posttraumatic symptoms such as reenactments, altered impulse control, and disturbed thought patterns result in violence (e.g., previously traumatized school snipers) or revictimization, they may perpetuate a cycle of trauma and violence (Nader, 1996a). In general, violence has increased following traumatic events that affect an entire population (e.g., after war or floods; Ibrahim, 1992; Kohly, 1994).

The treatment model discussed in this chapter, interactive trauma/ grief-focused therapy (IT/G-FT), represents an eclectic approach that draws on psychodynamic, cognitive-behavioral, and other theories. Although it has been used primarily after exposure to single incidents of trauma, it has been adapted for use after multiple traumas, such as repeated sexual abuse, and other severe traumas, such as torture or a massacre. In this chapter, the focus will be on the use of this treatment with youths traumatized by a discrete event (e.g., witness to suicide, violence, and natural disasters). Alterations in the method become necessary for complex trauma and for youths with damaged trust. In lieu of presenting a separate case example at the end of the chapter, the application of the treatment model is illustrated by references to case material throughout the chapter.

AN OVERVIEW OF THE MODEL

Understanding Traumatic Response

Psychic trauma occurs when an individual is exposed to an overwhelming event and is rendered helpless in the face of intolerable danger, anxiety, or instinctual arousal (Pynoos & Eth, 1986). The *Diagnostic and Statistical Manual of Mental Disorders* (*DSM–IV*; American Psychiatric Association [APA], 2000) describes the reexperiencing, avoidance, increased arousal, and distress or impairment in functioning of PTSD that may occur after exposure to these events. There is significant evidence that failure to resolve moderate to severe traumatic reactions may result in long-term consequences that interfere with the child's ability to function adequately (socially, academically, professionally, and personally; La Greca, Silverman, Vernberg, & Roberts, 2002; Wilson & Raphael, 1993). In addition, there is evidence that individuals who experience traumas are more likely to have children who experience traumas and are vulnerable to increased traumatic reactions (Danieli, 1998).

Although the more complicated reactions to traumatic experience— proposed as complex PTSD, disorders of extreme stress not otherwise specified, or developmental trauma for *DSM–V*—are most commonly associated with interpersonal, early, extreme, or prolonged stressors (APA, 2000; van der Kolk & Courtois, 2005), studies of adults who experienced childhood traumas suggest that a percentage of individuals exposed to a disaster, as well as those exposed to such traumas as ongoing abuse, suffer from complex traumatic reactions (van der Kolk, Roth, Pelcovitz, Sunday, & Spinazzola, 2005). According to Herman (1992), the approximately 27 symptoms of complex trauma are described in seven categories: (a) dysregulation of *affect and impulses*, (b) alterations in *attention and consciousness*, (c) alterations in *self-perception*, (d) distorted *perception of the perpetrator*, (e) alterations in *relationships with others*, (f) *somatization*, and (g) alterations in *systems of meaning or beliefs* (see also van der Kolk et al., 2005).

Conception of Therapeutic Intervention

The goals of IT/G-FT treatment for children traumatized by discrete events include both repair of the injured aspects of the child and recovery of healthy aspects that may have been eclipsed by traumatic response and changes (Nader, 1994). IT/G-FT incorporates review and reprocessing of the traumatic event, the emotions and perceptions linked to it, and the associated cognitive processes.

Effective individual intervention goals include (a) to hear everything, including the worst, and to help the child see more clearly and tolerate the minute details of the experience (Nader, 1994; Pynoos & Nader, 1993); (b) to recognize distortions, omissions, spatial misrepresentations, and distractions, along with their emotional meaning for the child (Nader, 1997c; Pynoos & Nader, 1989b; Terr, 1979, 1991); (c) to recognize and address the many intense impressions (e.g., multiple visual and perceptual experiences) before, during, and after a traumatic event (Nader, 1997c, in press; Pynoos & Nader, 1989b); (d) to discover the emotional meaning that becomes embedded in the details of the event (Nader & Pynoos, 1991; Pynoos & Nader, 1989b, 1993); (e) to correct underinflation or overinflation of important aspects of the event; (f) to identify fantasies/ desires or urges to act (Nader, 1994; Nader & Pynoos, 1993b; Pynoos & Eth, 1986; Pynoos & Nader, 1989b, 1993); (g) to facilitate facing emotional moments with the associated affect and reenter the fantasy/ moment with the child/adolescent resulting in release, reprocessing, and redefinition (Levy, 1938; Nader & Pynoos, 1991; Pynoos & Eth, 1986); (h) to provide a sense of resolution and reorientation so that a healthy ego is returned to a normal developmental path (Nader & Pynoos, 1991; Pynoos & Nader, 1993); and (i) to enhance recognition of the successful self through recognition of good choices, successful actions, right thinking, and personal strengths.

Of primary importance is uncovering the truth and examining it clearly without distortions engendered by fears, horrors, confusions, avoidances, and/or a sense of helplessness. The method includes a process of reviewing and reworking specific aspects of the event toward that end. This process is designed to elicit a thorough account from the child of his or her experience, including affective, sensory, and physiological experiences; sources of traumatic anxiety; traumatic reminders; early coping processes; and trauma-related life stresses.

The clinician's recognition of the following aspects of the traumatic situation is essential for effective intervention: the youth's personal presentation, including complex and simple PTSD and comorbid symptoms (Ford, Courtois, Steele, van der Hart, Nijenhuis, 2005; Nader, in press; van der Kolk & Courtois, 2005); all details of the event (Nader, 1994; Pynoos & Eth, 1986; Pynoos & Nader, 1989b); the phases of response (Nader 1994, 1997a, 1997c, in press); cultural differences (Marsella, Friedman, Gerrity, & Scurfield, 1996; Nader, Dubrow, & Stamm, 1999; Wilson & Tang, in press); the phase of the traumatic event (e.g., ongoing war or violence vs. the initial or later aftermath; Nader, 1997a); and the needs and recovery of others in the family or community (Nader, 1997c, in press; Nader & Pynoos, 1993b; Pynoos & Nader, 1988b).

For youths with *simple* PTSD, this treatment method is directive while observing the child/adolescent's timing and need for closure. The degree of directiveness is adjusted to the tolerance and needs of the child (Nader, 1994). Treatments for simple PTSD may not be applicable to complex trauma or to PTSD with comorbid disorders (Ford et al., 2005; van der Kolk et al., 2005). Some evidence suggests that successful intervention for complex traumatic reactions is sequenced and progressive (Ford et al., 2005). Symptom reduction, stabilization, and/or trust building precede the processing of traumatic memories and emotions and the subsequent life integration and rehabilitation. IT/G-FT may be less directive or intermittently directive and nondirective for youths with complex and/or severe traumatic reactions.

During sessions, in order to face fully and in detail each traumatic moment, the clinician must be unhindered by personal distractions (including *unresolved* traumas). For example, traumatized clinicians have become stalled or have over- or under-focused on aspects of trauma, thereby hindering a survivor's progress (Nader & Pynoos, 1993b). Trauma recovery is often characterized by progress and periodic exacerbation of symptoms. Each child establishes his or her own rhythms of review and focus on the issues of trauma and bereavement (Nader, 1994, 2002). Success in using this method requires a good sense of timing: knowing when to push the child or when to permit things to unfold. For example, in the case of Angie, described in Nader (1997c, 2002) and Box 1, the clinician recognized that Angie had both loving and angry feelings toward her dead sister. In the right way and at the appropriate moment, the clinician pushed Angie to express her anger and to demonstrate how she wanted to act on her concern for her sister. This freed her to honor both emotions fully on her own. The clinician assists the child through treatment sessions skillfully, in order to provide a sense of resolution, closure, and reorientation. Achieving the proper closure at the end of each session prevents leaving the child with renewed anxiety, disorientation, and an unnecessary avoidance of the therapeutic situation (Nader, 1994, 2002; Pynoos & Eth, 1986).

Because trauma may interrupt the development of biological, cognitive, social, and emotional knowledge, skills, and other resources, it can have a cascading and cumulative effect on a youth's life (Cicchetti, 2003; Ford, 2002; Geiger & Crick, 2001; Nader, in press; Price & Lento, 2001). To address the multiple and complicated effects of trauma, IT/G-FT also employs adjunctive treatments. These interventions may address specific symptoms such as trauma's injury to the developing brain and neurobiological systems, impaired self-systems (e.g., self- and other-awareness,

Box 1 Case of Angie (see Nader, 2002)

At the beginning of her diagnostic treatment session, Angie was asked to draw a picture of anything she wanted and to tell a story about it. She drew a girl with sad eyes standing at the edge of a hill holding two ropes. The girl was leaning as though she might fall. There was a great pink circle over her heart region.

In her story, Angie is the one holding the two ropes. She said that she needed to tie them together to make a jump rope. Angie elaborated that she was sliding over the edge of the hill and was holding onto the ropes.

Angie's sister was shot to death in a sniper attack. Before her death, her deceased sister received most of her parents' attention because the sister was naughty. Angie had mixed feelings toward her sister—anger and love. The shooting added to these mixed feelings. Angie was angry toward her sister because she did not run for safety. She was unable to reconcile or express the mixed feelings and had shown no signs of grieving. Angie indeed needed to "tie the two ropes together" so that she was free to grieve and to process her traumatic experience. During her session, Angie was assisted to express her anger at her sister for not running for safety. Using the toys in the therapy room, she then spontaneously enacted making two lines of mourners to approach what represented a reinforced casket. One line expressed their disapproval of the sister, the other expressed love and approval. Most of Angie's posttrauma behavioral problems relented after this treatment session.

---

self-control, self-esteem), and changed information processing (e.g., attributions of hostility, script-like self-attributions; Haine, Ayers, Sandler, Wolchik, & Weyer, 2003; Knox, 2004; Nader, in press; Perry, 2006). For example, these additional treatments may include specific repetitive rhythmic interventions, such as daily repetitions of specific music, massage, or dance, to repair altered brain development or neurochemistry in children (Field, Seligman, Scafidi, & Schanberg, 1996; Perry, 2006). Symptoms such as humiliation or shame, guilt, and rage have been shown to increase traumatic reactions and may require particular attention (Herman, 1992; Nader, in press; Tangney, 1996).

Theoretical Base

Therapeutic approaches to PTSD nearly all incorporate emotional and cognitive reprocessing of traumatic memories (Pynoos, Nader, & March, 1991). Bringing together the right brain hemisphere emotions and the left hemisphere cognitions related to the trauma helps the youth to reintegrate the experience and to produce a coherent narrative about it (Nader, in press; Siegel, 2003). The techniques of this treatment cross psychotherapeutic boundaries and include principles found in a number of clinical theories. For example, directed and spontaneous symbolic or actual reenactments of traumatic episodes may find their precursors in the psychodrama of Gestalt therapy or spontaneous play of play therapy (Amster, 1943; Axline, 1947; Webb, 2002); bringing subconscious traumatic impressions to clear consciousness and permitting the assignment of new meaning is found in the cathartic abreactions of psychoanalytic treatment, the hypnotic elicitation and reframing of Ericksonian therapies (Rossi, 1993), and Levy's abreactive therapy (Levy, 1938); and emphasis of intense traumatic moments prior to redefinition are similar to the review, flooding, redefining, and sometimes desensitization of cognitive-behavioral therapies (Cohen, 1999; Meadows & Foa, 1998).

CENTRAL PREMISES OF TREATMENT

Assisting Children's Accurate Traumatic Recall

Intense impressions, desires to act, imagined actions, and role identifications are deeply imprinted into children's traumatic memory representations and, if unresolved, can result in major changes in behavior and personality (Nader, 1997c). In remembering discrete traumatic events, children's recall is not organized as a single episode, but rather as multiple traumatic episodes within a single event (Pynoos & Nader, 1989a).

Children's memories are context-specific. When children have initial difficulty in accurate recall, rather than memory impairment, it may be because they lack an adequate retrieval strategy (Johnson & Foley, 1984). In the initial interview, the clinician can provide children with a strategy of recall that permits retrieval of accurate descriptions of subjective experiences (Nader, 1994). Prohibiting or misleading recall instructions may limit memory and thereby introduce distortions. Instructing a child to forget what happened or progressing only to a certain point in recalling an incident may restrict future memories (Pynoos & Nader, 1989a). Therefore, the initial interview and the clinician's ability to explore the traumatic experience thoroughly may be key to the overall intervention with traumatized children exposed to single events.

Each Individual's Experience Is Unique

Although there are similarities in response to traumatic events, experiences are different for each individual enduring these events. Each of the

200 people in the room where a tornado hit had a unique experience. Each individual brings to a traumatic experience different backgrounds, strengths, cognitive and personality styles, reactions to stress, and expectations that influence perceptions and reactions. For example, children who have been traumatized previously (e.g., those who have been abused or exposed to intermittent violence) often respond differently to the initial interview that is focused on a recent, single traumatic incident. Resistance and avoidance are more prominent; trust is more difficult. For these children, trust building may precede other trauma work, and treatment may be less directive or nondirective. It is essential to treat the individual in context. This means understanding the personal experience of trauma; the individual's culture and personality; and his or her family, school/job, and community needs.

This treatment recognizes the need for changing levels of numbing and periods of avoidance as ego strength and trust are restored. Treatment may become more directive as tolerance increases. Inasmuch as a child's personal rhythms and timing are respected, the clinician recognizes an individual readiness to regress, express traumatic emotions or desires, or engage in repetitive play of the trauma with appropriate interpretations or a silent therapeutic presence (Nader, 1997c). As ego strength returns, with direct focus, forgotten traumatic memories representing moments too horrible to recall initially are often recovered and thoroughly addressed. These moments may be addressed as they become relevant to recovery, or as they are identified by the child. Directing the focus of treatment to the full force of traumatic rage and/or helplessness may have to wait until some recovery has been accomplished (Nader, 1994). Over time, aspects of the trauma take on new meaning for the child as he or she enters a new developmental phase or as life and treatment unfold. These issues are then worked through in the context of this new meaning or reappraisal (Nader & Pynoos, 1991; Pynoos & Nader, 1993).

The Importance of Advocacy

In order to minimize secondary adversities and promote recovery, clinicians or their appointees act as advocates and enlist the support of family, friends, teachers, employers, and the community for the child or adolescent (Nader, 1994; Nader & Pynoos, 1993b). In the immediate aftermath of the event, children need protection from unnecessary reexposure to traumatic scenes (e.g., blood, bodies). Inappropriate media coverage or courtroom pictures that exhibit corpses or mutilated bodies may also have a harmful effect (Nader, Pynoos, Fairbanks, Al-Ajeel, & Al-Asfour, 1993). In enlisting the aid of the personal and community milieu, the therapist mobilizes people in the child's life to protect the child from clumsiness, confusion, lack of concentration, and/or compulsions that may lead to injury or hazard (Nader, 1994, 1997c). The importance of school, family, and peer support to youths' and adults' initial and ongoing posttrauma recovery has been well documented (Nader, Pynoos, Fairbanks, & Frederick, 1990; Pole, Best, Metzler, & Marmar, 2005; Udwin, Boyle, Yule, Bolton, & O'Ryan, 2000).

Doing No Harm

Appropriate training and supervision are essential to trauma interventions. Failure to understand trauma treatment (Nader & Pynoos, 1993b) or cultural customs can lead to mishap (e.g., misdirection of rage) and even death (e.g., murder or suicide; Nader, 1997a; Swiss & Giller, 1993). This understanding is crucial to assuring accurate assessment and protection of those affected by the event (Nader, 1997a, in press).

Understanding the interaction of trauma and grief reactions is essential to treatment and the prevention of harmful reactions and behaviors by the bereaved (Eth & Pynoos, 1985; Nader, 1997a, 1997b). This interaction includes but is not limited to the difficulty a youth may have grieving when thoughts of the deceased trigger trauma memories and symptoms (Cohen, Mannarino, Greenberg, Padlo, & Shipley, 2002; Nader, 1997b, in press).

In the course of successful treatment of trauma, intense traumatic emotions (e.g., rage and helplessness) and strong wishes to act (e.g., to fight, flee, or avenge) emerge. These emotions and desires must be dealt with appropriately within the session and in a manner that prevents their dangerous or harmful expression in the external world (Nader, 1997c). Moreover, abreactive experiences are not just giving permission or encouraging the expression of feelings. For example, there is the story of the rageful man who was taught in Gestalt treatment to bring his anger to the surface and beat on a mattress. Later, he beat an elderly woman to death when frustrated by her slowness. When traumatic emotions are reawakened, it is essential that there be some sense of resolution or closure. A school psychologist reported having read numerous articles on trauma/grief-focused therapy, but when she and her colleagues tried the techniques, students felt worse instead of better afterward. Reviewing an experience with a traumatized individual must be done skillfully and only when the goals of a session can be achieved (e.g., processing of traumatic thoughts and emotions, a new view of aspects of the experience, or repairing the self-concept). It may be important to reorient the youth to the present and to reinstate an attitude of coping before ending a session (Nader, in press).

HISTORICAL DEVELOPMENT

Original Development

This interactive trauma/grief-focused therapy began as a semistructured research interview. The interview included a draw-a-picture/tell-a-story method and a set of research questions developed by Drs. Ted Shapiro, Karen Gilmore, and Robert Pynoos (personal communications: K. Gilmore, August 1994; R. Pynoos, 1985; T. Shapiro, August 1994). This research interview initially was used at Payne Whitney Medical Center (Cornell University) with children whose parents had attempted suicide and later in Los Angeles as a diagnostic interview with children exposed to violence (Eth & Pynoos, 1985). The initial specialized interview for traumatized children, with innovations by Drs. Pynoos and Eth and additions by Dr. Nader, was first published in detail in 1986 (Pynoos & Eth, 1986). It has continued to evolve in its clinical diagnostic and therapeutic use in response to the needs of traumatized children (Nader, 1994, 1997c, 2002; Nader & Pynoos, 1991; Pynoos, 1993; Pynoos & Nader, 1993).

Later Developments and Current Status

This treatment has been used nationally and internationally (Goenjian et al., 1997; Nader, 1997c, 2002; Nader & Pynoos, 1993a) in (a) school or community settings following acts of violence and disasters resulting in multiple deaths and injuries (Nader, 1997c; Nader & Pynoos, 1993b; Nader et al., 1990) and (b) the aftermath of war (Nader et al., 1993). Adaptations are made depending on the circumstances of the precipitating event and the culture and community in which the treatment is used. When provided by Dr. Nader, training in the use of this specialized treatment involves didactic training sessions with opportunities for trainees to observe and to be observed in sessions with children. Continued training over time addresses the progression of treatment and provides continued feedback regarding the progress of the children and the progress of the clinician in applying this treatment.

PHASES OF HELPING

Engagement

For youths exposed to a traumatic event, a format that is essentially equal to that described in Pynoos and Eth (1986) is used both as a diagnostic and an initial treatment interview. Initial contact acknowledges that the interview is prompted by an actual event in the child's life. Rapport is important to the success of any treatment method. Its establishment varies by national and ethnic cultures (Nader, in press; Westermeyer, 1987; Wilson & Tang, in press). A youth's early and ongoing attachment style and his or her personality may also affect rapport, patterns of interaction, and needs in treatment (Hesse, Main, Abrams, & Rifkin, 2003; Nader, in press; Rothbaum, Rosen, Ujiie, & Uchida, 2002). One method of establishing rapport is to have the child draw a picture and tell a story about it. The interviewer's genuine interest in the picture and the youth's story have been observed to assist in establishing a comfortable relationship between the interviewer and the child (Nader, 1993). Moreover, the visual and perceptual episodes of children's experiences become embedded and transformed in their drawings and play (Nader, 1993; Nader & Pynoos, 1991; Pynoos & Eth, 1986; Pynoos & Nader, 1993). The child provides clues to important psychodynamic issues in initial drawings (see case of Angie, Box 1).

Assessment

The potential results of unresolved traumatic response underscore the need for accurate assessment (Wilson & Keane, 1997). Age-appropriate scales are currently available to assess exposure, PTSD, traumatic grief, associated and complex trauma symptoms, and coping, as well as child traits and circumstances (Nader, in press). Methods of personalized assessment as a supplement to standardized measures can be of assistance in measuring the progress of goals for the youth's individual treatment. Multiple issues affect the accuracy of both standardized and personalized assessments, including the selection and training of interviewers, interviewer style, trauma-intrinsic issues (e.g., briefing, phase of response), and child-intrinsic issues (e.g., culture, age; Nader, 1997a). For further information on instruments that directly measure childhood traumatic reactions, the reader is directed to Nader (1997a, 2004, in press) and Stamm (1996).

Preliminary briefing is an essential part of preparation for assessment with children following traumatic events. Knowing the details of the traumatic event enables the clinician to recognize aspects of symptomatic response and variables affecting response. For example, some traumatic reminders are event specific, such as the lasagna children were eating when the tornado hit or the white van that the bomber drove (Nader, 1997c).

Well-conducted assessment sessions have proven therapeutic (Nader et al., 1990). A child trauma reaction index has been used for periodic assessment (available from measures@twosuns.org). The initial clinical interview described above is both diagnostic and therapeutic. It permits assessment of specific traumatic moments, their effects, and grief. It provides a strategy of recall that helps enable future treatment, including delayed treatment. Done well, it provides the child with an initial sense of relief and often reinstates a sense of self-control. The initial interview can provide a measure of progress and recovery at specific checkpoints. Further information with regard to risk and protective factors can be assessed through interviews with parents and teachers and through school records (Nader, 1993, in press). In this treatment model, assessment is an ongoing process that is intertwined with intervention. Thus, many of the principles and techniques discussed in the next subsection on intervention relate to assessment as well.

Planning/Contracting and Intervention

The length of treatment for traumatized children varies depending on the length and severity of traumatic experiences and responses and other factors (e.g., personality, previous experience of trauma, emotional health, and family circumstances; Ford et al., 2005; Nader, 2002). Children who are mildly to moderately traumatized may benefit from 2 to 16 sessions. Moderately to severely traumatized children may need 1 or more years of treatment. Life events may prompt the need for additional sessions over the course of the child's development.

When there have been dual or multiple individual traumas or a trauma and a loss, attention to relevant aspects of each event may be necessary. Depending on the emotional impact of each event, some children may need to address a previous trauma before attending to the current event; others may be reminded over time of the previous trauma and undergo symptoms related to each. Additionally, issues that were of relevance in the earlier trauma or traumatic sequence (e.g., abandonment, betrayal, and victimization) are likely to appear as issues in the current trauma or traumatic episode (Nader, 1997c). Individuals with multiple traumas such as repeated abuse may have blended memories that solidify into a single script-like representation. Individual trauma incidents may lose their uniqueness and details may become blurred (Howe, 1997; Lindsay & Read, 1995; Terr, 1994).

Several principles and techniques (see below) are used to help children review, express, and resolve traumatic emotions and memory impressions. Using these techniques assumes a trusting relationship between the clinician and the child. Reworking traumatic memories may include reentering a moment or fantasy toward abreaction, redefinition, or completion of a desired act. The availability of a variety of toys, including those representative of aspects of the event, permits restoration of the anxiety-provoking situation in play and reentering the experience or fantasy associated with the event (Levy, 1938; Nader, 2002; Nader & Pynoos, 1991).

Orienting to the Trauma and Reorienting to the Present

At the beginning of treatment, the trauma survivor must be oriented to the trauma. Introducing oneself as a trauma therapist, at the first session, is the beginning of this process. Children who have been traumatized repeatedly or who become easily entranced with some aspect of a personal traumatic experience may need orientation away from the trauma (e.g., noticing the beautiful day/view/picture) at the beginning and end of the session. For these children, reorientation to the present may prevent mishap after the session.

Recognizing Clues to Content

Children's play, drawings, initial comments or verbalizations, and the reports of others give clues to the portion of the traumatic event that needs resolution during a session. A child may give clues to specific moments of importance by gesture or expression. For example, Sandy, a third-grade student who, 18 months after a tornado disaster, appeared to be functioning well, was asked to review again her experience just prior to the destruction and her injury. At one point, the clinician observed that Sandy kept her visual focus on the corner of the room. Attention to what she saw in a corner, where the trauma had occurred, revealed a continued deep sadness about her helplessness to move herself and friends to safety once the debris began to fly.

Information from teachers, parents, or friends may also suggest the traumatic content that has engaged the child's mind during the week. For example, when a boy who had been molested was heckled about his effeminate haircut, he flashed the other children to prove his manhood. In session, he dressed a female doll in clothes like his own. The session focused on his anger at and destruction of this helpless feminine/masculine form. He was not ready to focus on his molestation for many months afterward.

Using Play and Drawings

Play and drawings invariably signify in some way the child's unconscious preoccupation with memories of the trauma. The use of play and drawings in the assessment and treatment of trauma can (a) provide an opportunity for reexamination of an experience in order to give it new meaning, (b) indicate the child's processing and eventual resolution of traumatic elements, (c) allow the child an opportunity to be active in completing a desired or fantasized act within a safe therapeutic setting, (d) reveal the details of the event that remain in the child's active mind, (e) reveal elements of the child's continuing internal experience of the event, and (f) display the child's spatial representation of the event. Details revealed may become a part of review and re-review of aspects of the event (see below). Both play and drawings permit the interpretation or the linking of the play/drawings to aspects of the traumatic episode. The traumatic link is most often identified after completion of the story or segment of the play. If the drawings or play are interpreted or addressed too early, the child may stop (Nader, 2002; Nader & Pynoos, 1991). At times for some children, the clinician acts as a silent witness to spontaneous play (Gil, in press; Nader, 1997c). At such times, interpretation would interrupt play's therapeutic nature. This may be especially true with complex trauma.

Recognizing Symbolism

There is no standard symbolism for trauma. What are important are the child's own symbolism, history, and personal traumatic experience. After a traumatic death, children have often used balloons as a way to send a message (perhaps of love) to the deceased (Nader & Pynoos, 1991). For one child, recognizing that each of three different colored balloons represented a particular girl gave meaning to a series of pictures with colored balloons in them. Although it has been interpreted as a maternal figure, with individual traumatized children the sun has been used, for example, to represent father; deity; or the contrast of a beautiful, now empty, day against the gloom of sudden, tragic death. After seeing his mother stabbed with a barbecue fork, a boy included a two-pronged item in each of his drawings (e.g., adjacent buildings, unidentifiable objects, "sticks" on the ground, and pointed hills).

Working Through the Intensity of Traumatic Impressions

As a consequence of physiological (e.g., neurochemical) and psychological (e.g., horror) phenomena during traumatic events, multiple impressions register or imprint themselves with intensity and may become interlinked (Nader, 1997a). They include sensory impressions (e.g., touch, images, sounds, and smells), strong desires (e.g., to fight, flee, hide, rescue, or find), attempts to understand (e.g., feelings or actions of others; "Why me?"), senses of injustice (e.g., bad things happen to good people; bad people have success), senses of betrayal (e.g., the unwelcome actions of known others), rejection of self (e.g., disdain for the helpless or ineffectual self), and changes of focus (e.g., prominence of the ineffectual self or of negative events over positive). These deeply ingrained impressions, desires to act, imagined interventions, and role identifications become embedded in children's traumatic memory representations and will become evident over time in the course of treatment (Nader, in press). Even the smallest details may become carved solidly into a child's memory (Nader, 1997a, 1997c; Terr, 1991; see cases of Shanti and Hassan, Box 2).

Box 2 Cases of Shanti and Hassan

Shanti. During Hurricane Katrina, Shanti, age 8, and her little sister waited for hours in the attic with their mother before they were rescued. They were afraid of drowning and of snakes, alligators, and dead bodies that might be in the water. When the man in the boat rescued them, they saw babies and other dead bodies floating in the water. When they were in a higher and drier location, there were frightening sounds like gunfire and horrible smells because people tracked feces across the floor. The girls heard people talking about alligators eating people, bodies floating in the water, bacteria in the water, and disease. After they were relocated to Texas, whenever their mother took them for a bath in the tub, they would scream and fight to get away. Treatment began with family education about how to tell good water from unsafe water. They retold their story about their experiences. In directed and spontaneous play sessions, Shanti played out fearful waiting, rescue scenes, alligators and bodies in the water, and relief at arrival on dry ground. Later sessions included spontaneous play about the scary water versus the good water in the swimming pool and bathtub.

Hassan. Hassan and his friend, Asif, were 16 years old and working at World Trade Center (WTC) Building 7 when the planes crashed into the towers. Although he was one of the last out of his building, Asif was calmly walking blocks away before he turned to see a 50-story, massive dark cloud of glass and debris headed toward him. Asif had reached for his pendant with the Arabic prayer for safety but could not find it. He tripped and was assisted by a Hasidic Jewish man who handed him his dropped pendant and helped him up. The man spoke kindly, and they ran together to safety. Hassan, on the other hand, had completed a task before leaving and was a few minutes behind Asif. When the sky became dark and the great noise seemed to be rushing toward him, Hassan ran as fast as he could. He soon found that he could not breathe. He saw something fly by across the way and heard someone screaming. He was pushed through a doorway into shelter where he crouched behind a counter for safety. Later, Asif could not stop talking about how great it was that a Jewish man had helped him, a Pakistani boy—in the crisis the least likely person had helped him to safety. Hassan berated himself because Asif seemed to be doing well while he, Hassan, was having horrible nightmares and anxiety. When he was younger, he had occasionally dreamed that he was trying to get out of a ditch but could not make his legs move except very small amounts at a time. Now he dreamed this was happening while he tried to run down the street to get away from WTC flying debris. He dreamed of being hit by large objects, people screaming, and not being able to get to them to help. He would awaken coughing or would begin to cough at length when a little dust was kicked up. Hassan was a very conscientious boy before 9/11. Now conscientiously rushing to finish something was linked to great danger and fear. When focusing on segments of his experience in more detail, Hassan remembered seeing the man across the way when the metal hit him and the flash of red blood spurting. He remembered how time seemed to move slowly, worried thoughts during the long wait for water, and the chance to move to safety and aid.

Intensely imprinted traumatic wishes, urges, and emotions may remain in the psyche as strong urges to express that must be intensely expressed. Consequent repeated behaviors may endanger or frustrate. In the treatment session, these wishes, urges, and emotions can be expressed with intensity and without harm. Traumatically imprinted thoughts and images repeat themselves until they are properly processed or become suppressed, remaining influential in the child's life. This can result in an increase in arousal symptoms or in readiness to arousal (Nader & Fairbanks, 1994; van der Kolk & Sapporta, 1991) or in a variety of other troubles (Herman, 1992; Nader, 1996a, in press; Terr, 1991). Some of these unresolved thoughts and images, as well as many of the urges to act or desires that occur in the intensity of a traumatic moment, endure as compulsions to act. For example, memories of his mother's horror when as a young child a boy had fallen on his head resulted in repeated head banging in elementary school. He told the therapist that, although he did not know why, he had to show his mother that it did not hurt.

In treatment, a child's embedded impressions from various traumatic moments represent themselves in play or drawings. The playing out of these moments to the desired completion is facilitated. The therapist allows the denial in fantasy (e.g., healing the mutilated or shot father; stopping the harm to self or others) and addresses the feeling (e.g., "I'll bet you wish you could have patched up your father and that he could have talked to you like that"). These interpretations often lead to an expression of sadness, to a sense of relief, or to an examination of heretofore unstated feelings (e.g., self-blame), fantasies (e.g., jumping up and punching the assailant), or desires (e.g., to be protected from seeing the mutilation).

When children's impressions and desires to act during an event go unresolved, the result can be major changes in behavior and personality. For example, ongoing intervention fantasies include the child's fantasies during and after the event of preventing or stopping harm, of challenging the assailant, or of repairing damage. Lack of resolution of a revenge fantasy (see Nader & Pynoos, 1991; Pynoos & Eth, 1986), traumatically imprinted desire for retaliation, or identification with the aggressor, especially combined with posttrauma dysregulation of impulse control, may result in increased aggression or inhibition (Nader, 1997c; van der Kolk & Sapporta, 1991).

If, at the end of treatment, the clinician and the child have not uncovered and resolved specific traumatic moments or emotions, these emotions may translate into repeated complexes of behavior and emotions (attentional or attributional biases, behavioral patterns, life scripts, or dramas; see Nader, in press).

For example, unexpressed depression over not assisting an injured child across the room may result in the repeated need to rescue others, an ongoing depression over a sense of ineffectualness, or a sense of hurting others somehow. The cause of these scripts, patterns, or disorders, having been undiscovered in relation to the event, may remain unrecognized. A girl molested by her father and others until age 12 remembered only his rubbing against her body. Under stress she experienced tightness of throat, nausea, fatigue, a sense of aloneness, and feelings of being trapped and of being caretaker to everyone else. She did not remember the forced oral copulation until treatment sessions in her 50s (Nader, 1996b). Even unresolved curiosity may become a part of reenactments (e.g., curiosity about what death feels like; see Nader, 1994).

Recognizing Roles

Some intense impressions (e.g., desires to take action, understand, or change things) may result in assuming specific roles over time (Liotti, 2004; Loewenstein, 2004; Nader, 1997c, in press). Consequently, children may take one of several roles in their play and actions following traumatic events based on their experiences and what they witnessed during the event. These include most prominently aggressor, rescuer, or victim. They may include other roles dictated by the experience such as witness (or mobilized witness), assistant to the perpetrator, soother/calmer, aggravator, or searcher. The child may change role or identification over the course of treatment (in and out of session). Remaining in one of the roles without resolution may alter personality and/or life choices and lead to dangerous or troublesome behaviors (Nader, 1997a, 1997c; see example of Ralph in Nader, 1997c; Mathew in Nader, in press).

Understanding Developmental Differences

Children differ developmentally in the ways in which they approach and respond to danger (Eth & Pynoos, 1985; Nader, in press; Nader &

Pynoos, 1991; Pynoos & Nader, 1988a). Issues such as trust, protection, and ability to intervene change with age. For example, preschool children may look to external sources for protection. School-age children may become involved in fantasies of rescue and exile and may envision special powers to intervene or be rescued. Preteens may become more specific in the manner in which they would intervene, such as the 11-year-old boy who wished he had used his martial arts training to stop his mother's rapist and who proceeded to further perfect his martial arts skills (Pynoos & Nader, 1988a). Adolescents may be especially troubled by a sense of their own physical ineffectualness and vulnerability or their aggressive impulses. For example, a mature 12-year-old girl had a difficult time expressing, in play, her revenge fantasy toward a sniper who shot her in the neck, until the therapist helped her to understand that she would not really be hurting anyone.

Understanding Aspects of Rage

Anger is a part of the human biological process aimed at self-protection. It may be a response to threat or humiliation. Its purpose is to mobilize the individual. Successful anger is never unleashed upon another person. It is used to do something productive. For example, in the traumatic situation, it mobilizes self-protection, escape from danger, fending off the aggressor, protecting others, and making things right (e.g., calling medics, moving people out of harm's way). After a traumatic situation/experience, anger may facilitate good efforts, such as sticking with treatment, working toward the protection of others (e.g., court testimony), or a creative work (e.g., that informs others, honors the deceased, or shows strength of spirit).

When facilitating the expression of rage or anger, it may be important for children to know that you believe in their goodness and self-control. This can be done, for example, by acknowledging that the child would never really hurt anyone, and that hurting the doll/picture will not really hurt anyone. For some traumatized children, expression of rage (even in fantasy) has frightening implications for a morality challenged by recent events.

Recognizing Spontaneous and Ongoing Regression

Regression is common following traumatization and may be difficult to recognize (see 9/11 case examples, Box 3). Childlike behaviors are common under normal circumstances—for example, during playfulness, anger, or endearment. Moreover, regression may be as subtle as returning to an old desire for a person (e.g., old friend), place (e.g., a place representing happier times), or situation that signifies good feelings (e.g., a sense of safety). Regressions such as loss of academic or other personal skills may be complicated or exaggerated by other trauma symptoms (e.g., changed biochemistry, cognitive difficulties, lack of sleep, and/or preoccupations; Nader, 1999). Consequently, regression may be difficult to recognize. In children, it may be interpreted as defiance, laziness, sloppiness, or attention getting. It is important that clinicians, parents, and teachers learn to identify a child's specific regressive tendencies.

Box 3 Brief Case Examples of Reactions to 9/11

Following the September 11 terrorist attacks, a number of youths demonstrated regressed behaviors. After the attacks, 11-year-old Kiera's father was called up from the reserves and assigned to the World Trade Center. Kiera developed a sleep disturbance and became anxiously attached to her parents. She did not want to leave them to go to school.

Before he was born, Bobby's sister and parents had gone through a tornado that killed several of his sister's classmates when a school cafeteria wall collapsed. Bobby heard much about this incident in his childhood. At the age of 10, Bobby, who was somewhat anxiously attached to his parents before 9/11, became even more so afterward. He became less adept at things he had learned to do well and now needed retraining. He stubbornly insisted upon being near exit doors in the classroom and cafeteria. He wanted to know where his parents and other adults were at all times and did not want to sleep alone.

After 9/11, John, age 5, seemed to become aware of the dangers in the world. He too had separation difficulties. He refused to go into the school bathroom alone.

Reviewing and Re-Reviewing of Trauma

Over time the clinician and the child may go over a specific issue or trauma segment many times as it takes on new meaning in the course of development or treatment (Nader, 2002). Additionally, with progress, children may lose levels of their numbness and become more aware of the issues and aspects of a traumatic episode. Children may have partial amnesia for details that are regained in the process of review and re-review in a single session. Backing up and moving forward in slow motion allows the child to recapture details (Nader, 1997a) and the emotions that go with them (see example of Susan in Nader, 1997c, 2002). If done without skill, purpose, and good timing, this technique can distress and/or add to a tendency toward psychological numbing and avoidance. Timing is essential in recognizing how to go over and over in finer detail.

Recognizing Successes

When successes during a traumatic event are recognized, it can be emotionally freeing in a number of ways: (a) skills become more prominent, failures less prominent; (b) overall functioning may improve; and (c) some forms of guilt or self-recrimination may cease. For example, a boy in Kuwait watched as the Iraqi soldiers beat a man to death. He stood motionless behind a TV to save himself, yet felt like a failure and as if he had betrayed the man who was killed. In session, it was necessary to go over, in detail, his silent conversation with himself while the soldiers beat the man. This revealed a strong desire to help the man and an accurate assessment that both would die if he intervened. His analytic skills were noted. Relief was observable in the session, and afterward he was able to lift his head and gaze in his interactions with others.

Evaluation and Termination

In working with traumatized children, the therapist requires ample debriefing and sufficient self-care in order to perform effectively (Figley, 2002). Without this, the therapist may terminate cases prematurely. This can occur as a result of a reduction in thoroughness in discovering and exploring the child's individual emotion-laden moments and intense traumatic impressions (Nader, 1994).

One measure of recovery is whether the child can function without fear, has regained parts of lost self, and can experience joy. When directive methods are appropriate, during treatment it is important that clinicians be thorough in review and re-review in order to assess resolution and reorientation of all significant "moments" and impressions of traumatic experience. The semistructured interview or assessment measures used in the initial consultation can be readministered at intervals to assess progress. In the example of Sandy, cited earlier, it was in re-reviewing prior to termination that the clinician noted the child's fixed visual focus as a clue to the need to further resolve feelings of sadness and helplessness.

Other life issues, unresolved developmental issues, or a sense of success may bring trauma work to an apparent stopping point or diversion (Nader & Pynoos, 1991). Children and adults often save the deeper levels of some traumatic emotions (e.g., rage or helplessness) until other issues have been resolved in treatment. After significant improvement in their levels of functioning, they may wish to leave treatment prematurely both to avoid the intensity of the unresolved issues and because it no longer seems urgent to resolve anything. In the event that termination is premature, it is of help to prepare the child for the kinds of issues (e.g., unresolved anger) that may occur in the future and to leave the door open for return to treatment.

APPLICATION TO FAMILY AND GROUP WORK

Family and group work can provide important supplemental supports to this individual treatment method. Moreover, it is essential to work collaboratively with the child's family and school.

Family Work

Even if only one family member has been subjected to a trauma, the entire family is affected. Whole-family sessions generally are held to help families to understand the differences in their courses of recovery, to aid their abilities to help rather than hinder each other's recovery, and to address specific posttrauma family issues. For example, a mother and two young daughters entered treatment after the shooting death of the husband and father. Individual treatment addressed the personal traumatic and grief reactions of each family member; occasional family sessions permitted the discussion of, for example, why Sally became so upset when her mother wanted to visit the grave regularly. Sally was still contending with traumatic, intrusive images of her father's bloody body and was not yet ready to grieve. Her mother and sister had not seen the body (Pynoos & Nader, 1993). In cases such as this, when more than one family member is in treatment, weekly communication between clinicians is also essential.

Conjoint work has proved helpful to children and other family members when there has been intense worry about a family member during the traumatic event. After a sniper attack, a preschooler began checking on her brother in the night and became anxious when he was away from home. Another young girl was very angry with her brother, who had run for safety, leaving her behind. Joint sessions with the pairs of children allowed expressions of both anger and worry (Nader, 1997c).

Group Work

Group work is especially pertinent when a traumatic event has affected a group or community. When addressing the needs of a community following a catastrophic event, a comprehensive mental health program includes periodic groups for administrators, for school personnel, and for parents; individual treatment for identified adults and children; and small groups for grieving and for injured children. Cooperative efforts, at all phases of intervention, between clinicians and intervention teams are essential to prevent working at cross-purposes and divisiveness (Nader, 1997c; Nader & Pynoos, 1993b).

Although childhood traumatic response occurs primarily in relationship to exposure to traumatic phenomena regardless of adults' experiences, recovery of the adult community affects the recovery of children (see Nader, 1997a, 1997c). Initially after a traumatic event, a large group meeting for parents and school personnel generally includes the following: (a) discussion of the event and correcting rumors, (b) discussion of the adults' reactions to the event, (c) question-and-answer period about the children's reactions and discussion about the possible course of traumatic and grief reactions, (d) information about the psychological first aid that parents can provide, and (e) descriptions of planned services. Helping adults to discuss and understand their own reactions assists them in understanding their children's reactions (Nader, 1997c; Pynoos & Nader, 1988b).

When working with a school community, a classroom exercise and general discussion have been used to normalize the spectrum of the children's reactions, to screen for posttraumatic stress and other symptomatic reactions, and to address issues of dying and loss (Nader, 1997c; Pynoos & Nader, 1988b). These techniques in the group setting must be psychologically sound; for example, we do not engage children in their revenge fantasies in this group setting.

Child Groups

Group work can be helpful in addressing issues, such as injury or grief and loss, and in providing peer support and general coping strategies. For example, grief groups can help children establish a support system and permit open discussion of reactions and difficulties related to their losses. Children who previously have resolved their own grief reactions are assets to these groups.

Adult Groups

Periodic meetings with parents and teachers are important to a child's progress. We have conducted parent groups and periodic teacher groups when the event has affected a community. Parents may need assistance to adjust to regressions and other changes in the child and to establish a rhythm with the child that enhances recovery. For example, severely traumatized or retraumatized children may need to reestablish a sense of trust, especially toward adults. A child who trusts is often easier to like than a child who distrusts (Nader, 1997c). Distrustful behaviors may result in the discomfort, rejection, or annoyance of others. These reactions may contribute to or perpetuate the distrust.

Parents and teachers may need assistance in recognizing that some traumatized children's behaviors are both measures of self-protection and cautious attempts to regain love and trust. The distrustful and annoying conduct is the noise that covers an intense desire to be loved and protected, combined with an intense fear of continued betrayal and harm.

COMPATIBILITY WITH THE GENERALIST-ECLECTIC FRAMEWORK

Interactive trauma/grief-focused therapy is compatible with the main tenets of the generalist-eclectic framework for practice. First, it emphasizes the need to consider the child in context and to conduct a holistic assessment that considers factors such as family relationships, school adjustment, peer relationships, and culture. The model also promotes the use of environmental resources (e.g., support of family and school) in treatment. Second, this approach emphasizes the importance of a strong therapeutic relationship in order to enable children to work through the trauma. Third, with regard to a strengths perspective, the model focuses on successes and recognizes that high levels of personal strength can coexist with fragility in individuals who are moderately to severely traumatized. Fourth, the goal of the treatment is to replace a sense of helplessness with a sense of empowerment. Fifth, the model is eclectic and stresses flexibility in using techniques that fit the individual.

CRITIQUE OF THE MODEL

This treatment model has assisted children exposed to a variety of traumatic events and has been adapted for work with adults. Unaltered, the method works best with individuals who have been exposed to single or multiple discrete incidents of trauma and who have an ability to develop trust. There is statistical evidence of the effectiveness of the direct screening interview (Goenjian et al., 1997; Nader, 1997a; Nader et al., 1990) and of the treatment method (Nader, 1991). Preliminary findings suggest significant reduction in trauma symptoms and improved functioning after use of this method. Moreover, the reports of children and adults who have undergone treatment suggest improvement in the quality of life. For example, close adult friends have observed that children were happier after treatment than before the traumatic incident. Adults and adolescents have suggested the same results for themselves.

Like other methods, this treatment model requires knowledge of trauma, child development, and psychotherapeutic principles. Personal strength, courage, confidence, sensitivity, and skilled timing are essential to the trauma clinician. If a clinician has been exposed to a personal traumatic experience, any unresolved traumatic symptoms or themes may hinder the giving of treatment. For widespread traumatic events (e.g., war or disaster), mental health professionals must have addressed their own traumatic responses prior to assisting others.

This treatment method can be more difficult to apply when the trauma is in the distant past and its aspects are well buried and/or distorted. It may be more difficult to use this treatment with adults or adolescents who have adopted a successful and ingrained style of avoidance (e.g., use of drugs). Adaptations and preliminary interventions are essential when (a) symptoms such as aggression or suicidality need immediate attention, (b) the dysregulations and alterations common to complex traumatic reactions are present, and/or (c) trust has been impaired. When trust has been badly damaged, some individuals require trust building and slower paced treatment, perhaps less strongly directive in the beginning or during phases over the course of treatment. Complex trauma may require alternated directive and nondirective or simply nondirective play therapy methods in combination with other interventions.

SUMMARY

During traumatic events, multiple traumatic impressions become embedded in memory. If unresolved for children, these intense impressions may result in repeated patterns of thought, emotion, and/or behavior (e.g., traumatic reenactments, script-like behavioral patterns, attentional biases), disturbances in thought or conduct (e.g., disturbed morality, violence), or chronic mental disorders (e.g., major depression, PTSD). Interactive trauma/grief-focused therapy enables reprocessing and resolution of traumatic memory impressions and restoration of self-esteem, joy, and a normal developmental path.

REFERENCES

American Psychiatric Association. (2000). *Diagnostic and statistical manual of mental disorders, DSM–IV–TR* (4th ed.). Washington, DC: Author.

Amster, F. (1943). Differential use of play in treatment of young children. *American Journal of Orthopsychiatry, 13,* 62–68.

Axline, V. (1947). *Play therapy.* Boston: Houghton Mifflin.

Cicchetti, D. V. (2003). Neuroendocrine functioning in maltreated children. In D. Cicchetti & E. Walker (Eds.), *Neurodevelopmental mechanisms in psychopathology* (pp. 345–365). Cambridge, England: Cambridge University Press.

Cohen, J. A. (1999). *Treatment of traumatized children* (cassette recording; Trauma Therapy Audio Series). Thousand Oaks, CA: Sage.

Cohen, J. A., Mannarino, A. P., Greenberg, T., Padlo, S., & Shipley, C. (2002). Childhood traumatic grief: Concepts and controversies. *Trauma, Violence, & Abuse, 3,* 307–327.

Danieli, Y. (1998). *International handbook of multigenerational legacies of trauma*. New York: Plenum Press.

Eth, S., & Pynoos, R. S. (1985). Developmental perspectives on psychic trauma in children. In C. R. Figley (Ed.), *Trauma and its wake* (pp. 35–52). New York: Brunner/Mazel.

Field, T., Seligman, S., Scafidi, F., & Schanberg, S. (1996). Alleviating posttraumatic stress in children following Hurricane Andrew. *Journal of Applied Developmental Psychology, 17,* 37–50.

Figley, C. R. (2002). *Treating compassion fatigue*. New York: Routledge.

Ford, J. D. (2002). Traumatic victimization in childhood and persistent problems with oppositional-defiance. *Journal of Aggression, Maltreatment and Trauma, 6*(1), 25–58.

Ford, J. D., Courtois, C. A., Steele, K., van der Hart, O., & Nijenhuis, E. R. S. (2005). Treatment of complex posttraumatic self-dysregulation. *Journal of Traumatic Stress, 18,* 437–447.

Geiger, T. C., & Crick, N. R. (2001). A developmental psychopathology perspective on vulnerability to personality disorders. In R. E. Ingram & J. M. Price (Eds.), *Vulnerability to psychopathology: Risk across the lifespan* (pp. 57–102). New York: Guilford Press.

Gil, E. (in press). *Helping abused and traumatized children: Integrating directive and non-directive approaches*. New York: Guilford Press.

Goenjian, A., Karayan, I., Pynoos, R. S., Minassian, D., Najarian, L. M., Steinberg, A., et al. (1997). Outcome of psychotherapy among early adolescents after trauma. *American Journal of Psychiatry, 154,* 536–542.

Haine, R. A., Ayers, T. S., Sandler, I. N., Wolchik, S. A., & Weyer, J. L. (2003). Locus of control and self-esteem as stress-moderators or stress-mediators in parentally bereaved children. *Death Studies, 27,* 619–640.

Herman, J. L. (1992). Complex PTSD: A syndrome in survivors of prolonged and repeated trauma. *Journal of Social Issues, 40,* 33–50.

Hesse, E., Main, M., Abrams, K. Y., & Rifkin, A. (2003). Unresolved states regarding loss or abuse can have "second-generation" effects: Disorganization, role inversion, and frightening ideation in the offspring of traumatized, non-maltreating parents. In M. Solomon & D. J. Siegel (Eds.), *Healing trauma* (pp. 57–106). New York: W. W. Norton.

Howe, M. L. (1997). Children's memory for traumatic experiences. *Learning and Individual Differences, 9,* 153–174.

Ibrahim, Y. M. (1992, August 4). Iraqis left coarse scars on the psyche of Kuwait. *The New York Times,* p. A3.

Johnson, M. K., & Foley, M. A. (1984). Differentiating fact from fantasy: The reliability of children's memory. *Journal of Social Issues, 40,* 33–50.

Knox, J. (2004). *Reflective function, the mind as an internal object*. Manuscript submitted for publication.

Kohly, M. (1994). *Reported child abuse and neglect victims during the flood months of 1993*. St. Louis: Missouri Department of Social Services, Division of Family Services, Research and Development Unit.

La Greca, A. M., Silverman, W. K., Vernberg, E. M., & Roberts, M. C. (Eds.). (2002). *Helping children cope with disasters and terrorism*. Washington, DC: American Psychological Association.

Levy, D. M. (1938). Release therapy in young children. *Psychiatry, 1,* 387–390.

Lindsay, D. S., & Read, J. D. (1995). "Memory Work" and recovered memories of childhood sexual abuse: Scientific evidence and public, professional, and personal issues. *Psychology, Public Policy, and Law, 1,* 846–908.

Liotti, G. (2004). Trauma, dissociation, and disorganized attachment: Three strands of a single braid. *Psychotherapy: Theory, Research, Practice, Training, 41,* 472–486.

Loewenstein, R. J. (2004). Dissociation of the "bad" parent, preservation of the "good" parent. Commentary on "Cherchez la femme, cherchez la femme: A paradoxical response to trauma." *Psychiatry, 67,* 256–260.

Marsella, A. J., Friedman, M. J., Gerrity, E. T., & Scurfield, R. M. (Eds.). (1996). *Ethnocultural aspects of posttraumatic stress disorder: Issues, research, and clinical applications.* Washington, DC: American Psychological Association.

Meadows, E. A., & Foa, E. B. (1998). Intrusion, arousal, and avoidance: Sexual trauma survivors. In V. M. Follette, J. I. Ruzek, & F. R. Abueg (Eds.), *Cognitive-behavioral therapies for trauma* (pp. 100–123). New York: Guilford Press.

Nader, K. (1991, February 28). *Posttraumatic stress assessment following a tornado at a school.* Unpublished report to a school district.

Nader, K. (1993). *Childhood trauma: A manual and questionnaires.* Costa Mesa, CA: Two Suns.

Nader, K. (1994). Countertransference in treating trauma and victimization in childhood. In J. P. Wilson & J. Lindy (Eds.), *Countertransference in the treatment of posttraumatic stress disorder* (pp. 179–205). New York: Guilford Press.

Nader, K. (1996a). Children's exposure to traumatic experiences. In C. A. Corr & D. M. Corr (Eds.), *Handbook of childhood death and bereavement* (pp. 201–222). New York: Springer.

Nader, K. (1996b). Children's traumatic dreams. In D. Barrett (Ed.), *Trauma and dreams* (pp. 9–24). Cambridge, MA: Harvard University Press.

Nader, K. (1997a). Assessing traumatic experiences in children. In J. P. Wilson & T. Keane (Eds.), *Assessing psychological trauma and posttraumatic stress disorder* (pp. 291–348). New York: Guilford Press.

Nader, K. (1997b). Childhood traumatic loss: The interaction of trauma and grief. In C. R. Figley, B. E. Bride, & N. Mazza (Eds.), *Death and trauma: The traumatology of grieving* (pp. 17–41). London: Taylor & Francis.

Nader, K. (1997c). Treating traumatic grief in systems. In C. R. Figley, B. E. Bride, & N. Mazza (Eds.), *Death and trauma: The traumatology of surviving* (pp. 159–192). London: Taylor & Francis.

Nader, K. (1999). *Psychological first aid for trauma, grief, and traumatic grief* (3rd ed.). Austin, TX: Two Suns.

Nader, K. (2002). Treating children after violence in schools and communities. In N. B. Webb (Ed.), *Helping bereaved children* (2nd ed., pp. 214–244). New York: Guilford Press.

Nader, K. (2004). Assessing traumatic experiences in children and adolescents: Self-reports of DSM PTSD Criteria B-D symptoms. In J. P. Wilson & T. Keane (Eds.), *Assessing psychological trauma and posttraumatic stress disorder* (2nd ed., pp. 513–537). New York: Guilford Press.

Nader, K. (in press). *Understanding trauma in children and adolescents: The multiple facets of assessment.* New York: Routledge.

Nader, K., Dubrow, N., & Stamm, B. (Eds.). (1999). *Honoring differences: Cultural issues in the treatment of trauma and loss.* Philadelphia: Taylor & Francis.

Nader, K., & Fairbanks, L. (1994). The suppression of re-experiencing: Impulse control and somatic symptoms in children following traumatic exposure. *Anxiety, Stress and Coping: An International Journal, 7,* 229–239.

Nader, K., & Pynoos, R. S. (1991). Play and drawing as tools for interviewing traumatized children. In C. Schaefer, K. Gitlin, & A. Sandgrund (Eds.), *Play, diagnosis, and assessment* (pp. 375–389). New York: Wiley.

Nader, K., & Pynoos, R. S. (1993a). The children of Kuwait following the Gulf Crisis. In L. Lewis & N. Fox (Eds.), *Effects of war and violence on children* (pp. 181–195). Hillsdale, NJ: Lawrence Erlbaum.

Nader, K., & Pynoos, R. S. (1993b). School disaster: Planning and initial interventions. *Journal of Social Behavior and Personality, 8,* 299–320.

Nader, K., Pynoos, R. S., Fairbanks, L., Al-Ajeel, M., & Al-Asfour, A. (1993). A preliminary study of PTSD and grief among the children of Kuwait following the Gulf crisis. *British Journal of Clinical Psychology, 32,* 407–416.

Nader, K., Pynoos, R. S., Fairbanks, L., & Frederick, C. (1990). Children's PTSD reactions one year after a sniper attack at their school. *American Journal of Psychiatry, 147,* 1526–1530.

Perry, B. D. (2006). Applying principles of neurodevelopment to clinical work with maltreated and traumatized children. In N. B. Webb (Ed.), *Working with traumatized youth in child welfare* (pp. 27–52). New York: Guilford Press.

Pole, N., Best, S. R., Metzler, T., & Marmar, C. R. (2005). Why are Hispanics at greater risk for PTSD? *Cultural Diversity and Ethnic Minority Psychology, 11,* 144–161.

Price, J. M., & Lento, J. (2001). The nature of child and adolescent vulnerability. In R. E. Ingram & J. M. Price (Eds.), *Vulnerability to psychopathology: Risk across the lifespan* (pp. 20–38). New York: Guilford Press.

Pynoos, R. S. (1993). Traumatic stress and developmental psychopathology in children and adolescents. In J. M. Oldham, M. B. Riba, & A. Tasman (Eds.), *American Psychiatric Press review of psychiatry* (Vol. 12, pp. 205–238). Washington, DC: American Psychiatric Press.

Pynoos, R. S., & Eth, S. (1986). Witness to violence: The child interview. *Journal of the American Academy of Child Psychiatry, 25,* 306–319.

Pynoos, R. S., & Nader, K. (1988a). Children who witness the sexual assaults of their mothers. *Journal of the American Academy of Child and Adolescent Psychiatry, 27,* 567–572.

Pynoos, R. S., & Nader, K. (1988b). Psychological first aid and treatment approach for children exposed to community violence: Research implications. *Journal of Traumatic Stress, 1,* 445–473.

Pynoos, R. S., & Nader, K. (1989a). Children's memory and proximity to violence. *Journal of the American Academy of Child and Adolescent Psychiatry, 28,* 236– 241.

Pynoos, R. S., & Nader, K. (1989b). Prevention of psychiatric morbidity in children after disaster. In D. Schaffer, I. Philips, & N. B. Enzer (Eds.), *Prevention of mental disorders, alcohol, and other drug use in children and adolescents* (pp. 225–271). Rockville, MD: U.S. Department of Health and Human Services.

Pynoos, R. S., & Nader, K. (1993). Issues in the treatment of posttraumatic stress in children and adolescents. In J. P. Wilson & B. Raphael (Eds.), *International handbook of traumatic stress syndromes* (pp. 535–549). New York: Plenum Press.

Pynoos, R. S., Nader, K., & March, J. (1991). Posttraumatic stress disorder in children and adolescents. In J. Weiner (Ed.), *Comprehensive textbook of child and adolescent psychiatry* (pp. 339–348). Washington, DC: American Psychiatric Press.

Rossi, E. (1993). *The psychobiology of mind-body healing: New concepts of therapeutic hypnosis* (Rev. ed.). New York: W. W. Norton.

Rothbaum, F., Rosen, K., Ujiie, T., & Uchida, N. (2002). Family systems, theory, attachment theory, and culture. *Family Process, 41,* 328–350.

Siegel, D. J. (2003). An interpersonal neurobiology of psychotherapy: The developing mind and the resolution of trauma. In M. Soloman & D. J. Siegel (Eds.), *Healing trauma* (pp. 1–56). New York: W. W. Norton.

Stamm, B. H. (Ed.). (1996). *Measurement of stress, trauma, and adaptation.* Lutherville, MD: Sidran.

Swiss, S., & Giller, J. E. (1993). Rape as a crime of war: A medical perspective. *Journal of the American Medical Association, 270,* 612–615.

Tangney, J. P. (1996). Conceptual and methodological issues in the assessment of shame and guilt. *Behaviour Research and Therapy, 34,* 741–754.

Terr, L. (1979). Children of Chowchilla: Study of psychic trauma. *Psychoanalytic Study of the Child, 34,* 547–623.

Terr, L. (1991). Childhood traumas: An outline and overview. *American Journal of Psychiatry, 148,* 10–20.

Terr, L. (1994). *Unchained memories: True stories of traumatic memories, lost and found.* New York: Basic Books.

Udwin, O., Boyle, S., Yule, W., Bolton, D., & O'Ryan, D. (2000). Risk factors for long-term psychological effects of a disaster experienced in adolescence: Predictors of posttraumatic stress disorder. *Journal of Child Psychology and Psychiatry, 41,* 969–979.

van der Kolk, B., & Courtois, C. (2005). Editorial comments: Complex developmental trauma. *Journal of Traumatic Stress, 18,* 385–388.

van der Kolk, B., Roth, S., Pelcovitz, D., Sunday, S., & Spinazzola, J. (2005). Disorders of extreme stress: The empirical foundation for a complex adaptation to trauma. *Journal of Traumatic Stress, 18,* 389–399.

van der Kolk, B., & Sapporta, J. (1991). The biological response to psychic trauma: Mechanisms and treatment of intrusion and numbing. *Anxiety Research, 4,* 199–212.

Webb, N. B. (Ed.). (2002). *Helping bereaved children* (2nd ed.). New York: Guilford Press.

Westermeyer, J. (1987). Cultural factors in clinical assessment. *Journal of Consulting and Clinical Psychology, 55,* 471–478.

Wilson, J. P., & Keane, T. (Eds.). (1997). *Assessing psychological trauma and post-traumatic stress disorder.* New York: Guilford Press.

Wilson, J. P., & Raphael, B. (Eds.). (1993). *International handbook of traumatic stress syndromes.* New York: Plenum Press.

Wilson, J. P., & Tang, C. (in press). *The cross-cultural assessment of psychological trauma and PTSD.* New York: Springer.

PART V

Summary and Conclusion

CHAPTER 21

Revisiting the Generalist-Eclectic Approach

Nick Coady and Peter Lehmann

The first 3 chapters (Part I) of this book dealt with the major elements and basic principles of the generalist-eclectic approach to direct social work practice. Given the fact that the last 17 chapters have focused on various theoretical perspectives for direct practice, for purposes of review and integration it is important to revisit the generalist-eclectic approach in this final chapter.

In the first part of this chapter we review conceptualizations of levels of theory (high-, mid-, and low-level theory) and broad classes of mid-level practice theory (psychodynamic, cognitive-behavioral, humanistic, feminist, and postmodern) that were discussed in chapter 2 and revisit how these conceptualizations can facilitate an eclectic use of theory in practice. Second, the compatibility between the various mid-level practice theories reviewed in Part III (chapters 6–17) of the book and the generalist-eclectic approach is considered. The third part of the chapter revisits how the problem-solving model is a useful framework for integrating the eclectic use of theory with the artistic, intuitive-inductive elements of practice. Finally, some of the challenges to generalist-eclectic practice are identified and strategies for dealing with these challenges are suggested.

THE USEFULNESS OF CONCEPTUALIZING LEVELS AND CLASSES OF THEORY TO FACILITATE ECLECTICISM

Reflecting on the variety of theoretical perspectives that are represented by chapters in this book raises the potential for feeling confused and overwhelmed by the wide variety of views about the causes of human problems and ways of helping. This potential for *theoretical overload* becomes heightened when one considers that estimates of the overall number of theories for direct practice have ranged from 200 to 400 (Lambert, Bergin, & Garfield, 2004).

Given this confusing and overwhelming array of theories, many of which feature rather esoteric and mystifying language, one can understand why some practitioners eschew eclecticism because they prefer the simplicity, structure, and certainty that can be provided by a narrow allegiance to a single theoretical framework. As understandable as this may be, we are convinced of the arguments for eclecticism that were reviewed in the first chapter. In order to make eclecticism feasible, however, strategies for simplifying and demystifying the vast array of theoretical perspectives are necessary. It is our hope that the organization of this book reflects two helpful strategies in this regard: (a) differentiating among high-, mid-, and low-level theoretical perspectives, and (b) classifying the vast array of mid-level practice theories into like categories and providing general descriptions of the commonalities within each broad category.

Differentiating Among the Levels of Theory

A consideration of the differential function and usefulness of the various levels of theory can be a helpful first step in dealing with theoretical overload. Chapter 2 presented a discussion of three levels of theory for direct practice (see Figure 2.1 in chapter 2 for an overview). The chapters on theory in this book were grouped into three parts corresponding to the three levels of theory identified. Part II (chapters 4 and 5) of the book contained chapters on high-level or meta-theories (critical ecological systems and human development theories, respectively) that provide general ways of looking at and understanding a broad range of human behavior. These theories represent foundational knowledge for generalist-eclectic practice, and their main value is in providing broad, normative lenses for data collection and assessment. Although these high-level theories can also provide general ideas for intervention, they do not provide the guidelines or prescriptions for interventions that lower level theories do.

Part III (chapters 6–17) of the book was devoted to mid-level practice theories (the usefulness of the subclassifications of these theories will be considered later). In general, this level of theory provides more specific ways of understanding human behavior and at least some guidelines, if not prescriptions, for the change process. Historically, most of these theories have laid claim to being universally applicable to understanding and intervening with the entire range of human problems. A generalist-eclectic approach maintains, however, that each of these theories may be relevant for understanding and intervening with some clients' problems but not with others. Workers should use these theoretical perspectives tentatively in the data collection and assessment phases and take care not to force-fit clients' experience into theoretical boxes. These theories can be used individually or in combination to guide intervention, based on a determination of their relevance to the client's problem situation and their fit with client factors. For example, research suggests that clients who have an externalizing coping style (i.e., blaming others) tend to do better in a structured treatment approach such as cognitive-behavioral therapy (Schottenbauer, Glass, & Arnkoff, 2005).

Examples of low-level theories (i.e., wraparound services, family preservation services, and interactive trauma/grief-focused therapy with children) were provided in Part IV (chapters 18–20) of the book. These theories provide much more concrete understanding of and intervention guidelines for specific problems and populations. These models and therapies usually apply concepts and strategies from one or more of the mid-level theories to a specific client problem (e.g., grief, child abuse and neglect, addictions, psychiatric disorder). Thus, this level of theory can be viewed as a subset or derivative of the mid-level of theory. In many respects, low-level theory that incorporates concepts and strategies from a number of different mid-level theoretical perspectives can be viewed as a logical extension of the generalist-eclectic approach, as long as it is not rigidly prescriptive, it allows for individualized interventions based on holistic assessment, and it embraces basic social work values and principles.

For example, interactive trauma/grief-focused therapy (chapter 20) is consistent with a generalist-eclectic approach in that it not only incorporates therapeutic strategies from a number of theories (e.g., psychodynamic, cognitive-behavioral, humanistic/Gestalt) in the treatment of trauma, but it also values broad-based assessment, tailors intervention flexibly to individual clients, and recognizes the need for clinical judgment or a good sense of timing with regard to decisions about intervention.

The conceptualization of levels of theory is one way of bringing order to the overwhelming number of theoretical perspectives for practice. The three levels of theory can be viewed as complementing rather than competing with each other. High- and low-level theories can be construed as providing support to the use of mid-level theories. High-level theories provide a broad lens for viewing human behavior and ensure that a broad range of factors (e.g., biological, personal, interpersonal, environmental, and sociocultural) are considered in the effort to understand clients' problem situations. These theories ensure that the big, person-in-environment picture is considered in data collection and assessment, and they guard against the danger of tunnel vision or myopia that exists with mid- and low-level theories. On the other end of the spectrum, the type of in-depth knowledge that low-level theories provide about specific client problems can be seen as a valuable resource to support the use of more general, mid-level theory. For example, even if one is drawing eclectically from a range of mid-level theory in working with a client, if a specific clinical issue (e.g., grief or trauma) surfaces, it would be helpful to refer to low-level models (e.g., interactive trauma/grief-focused therapy) for more specific ideas for understanding and treating such issues.

Conceptualizing and Characterizing Classes of Practice Theory

A second useful way of simplifying and demystifying theoretical perspectives is to group the vast array of mid-level practice theories, models, and therapies into like groupings. In this book we have grouped mid-level clinical theories into one of five classifications: (a) psychodynamic, (b) cognitive-behavioral, (c) humanistic, (d) feminist, and (e) postmodern. Chapter 2 provided a discussion of the general characteristics of each of these five groupings of theory and presented a table (Table 2.1) that compared these groupings of theory on central issues (i.e., view of causation of human problems; goal of intervention; primary focus on past or present; primary focus on affect, cognition, or behavior; primary focus on specific symptoms or general growth/development; and degree of structure and directiveness).

We believe that this conceptualization and characterization of broad classes of practice theory helps to bring some order and clarity to the confusing array of theories within the field. Furthermore, this facilitates the identification of commonalities and differences among the five classes of theory, as well as the identification of their strengths and weaknesses. The discussion in chapter 2 identified ways in which this could facilitate the eclectic use of theory in practice. We acknowledge the danger of oversimplification in such broad classifications and general descriptions of theory, however, and we encourage students and practitioners to pursue a more in-depth understanding of a wide variety of theories.

THE COMPATIBILITY OF THE DIRECT PRACTICE THEORIES WITH THE GENERALIST-ECLECTIC APPROACH

Compatibility With Elements of the Generalist Perspective for Social Work

All of the chapters in Part III of this book included a brief discussion of the compatibility between the particular practice theory under consideration and at least some of the five elements of the generalist social work perspective that are central to our generalist-eclectic approach (as outlined in Table 1.1 in chapter 1). Although there were differences in emphasis noted by some authors, overall there was a strong endorsement of the importance of (a) a person-in-environment perspective that is informed by ecological systems theory; (b) the development of a good helping relationship that fosters empowerment; (c) the flexible use of a problem-solving process to provide structure and guidelines for practice; (d) a holistic, multilevel assessment that includes a focus on issues of diversity and oppression and on strengths; and (e) an eclectic use of other theories and techniques.

A cynic might wonder if authors felt compelled to endorse such principles, either to conform to the wishes of the editors or to the social work profession's commitment to the generalist perspective; however, we do not think that this was the case. Instead, it seems to us that this convergence in thinking reflects the relatively recent trend in the clinical field toward valuing these elements of the generalist social work perspective. We think that this is a major and healthy shift in thinking, because the historical legacy of the clinical field has been marked, to a large extent, by rigid adherence to single models of therapy that tended to have narrow, mostly psychological, views of human problems and noncollaborative, expert orientations.

It is particularly noteworthy that the older, more traditional theoretical perspectives (i.e., psychodynamic and cognitive-behavioral theories) have undergone significant changes in emphasis over the years. In general, psychodynamic theories have broadened their intrapsychic focus to include much greater consideration of environmental factors; have moved away from a rather distant, expert-oriented therapeutic stance toward a much more collaborative and empathic approach; and have become more open to the value and usefulness of other theories and their techniques. It should be noted, however, that we chose to include in this book the psychodynamic theories that had moved furthest in these directions. There are still psychodynamic theories that do not embrace these trends.

Similarly, cognitive-behavioral theories, particularly the more behaviorally oriented ones, have not always embraced generalist principles. Over time, these theories have broadened their focus of assessment beyond stimulus-response patterns to include cognitive and social factors; have embraced the importance of a good therapeutic relationship, at least as a facilitating factor for change; and have become more open to eclecticism. Again, for the cognitive-behavioral section of the book, we selected theories that were most compatible with the generalist approach. In particular, readers should be reminded that the task-centered and crisis intervention models have a strong connection to social work and are perhaps better conceptualized as atheoretical and eclectic models, respectively (see chapter 2 for fuller discussion of this point). There are still traditional behavioral theories that are not consistent with generalist principles.

Despite the overall compatibility between the variety of practice theories presented in this book and the elements of the generalist social work perspective that are central to our generalist-eclectic approach, it would be remiss to not make a closer examination of differences. The strongest contrast that we noted between an element of the generalist social work perspective and a theoretical perspective is solution-focused therapy's dismissal of the value of holistic assessment. In chapter 17, Corcoran states that "solution-focused therapy departs from a generalist-eclectic framework in eschewing a holistic assessment of the various system levels, along with information-gathering about the problem and history-taking" (p. 439). This and other conflicts between solution-focused therapy and mainstream social work principles have been noted by others (e.g., Stalker, Levene, & Coady, 1999). This suggests that social workers should be particularly mindful of following generalist social work principles when using solution-focused therapy as part of their eclectic approach.

Another difference that emerged between some theoretical perspectives and an element of the generalist perspective related to the use of a problem-solving process. Again, the strongest difference was with solution-focused therapy. Corcoran challenged any focus on problems or problem-solving as antithetical to a focus on strengths. We expressed our disagreement with this view in chapter 3 when we cited the argument by McMillen, Morris, and Sherraden (2004) that those who advocate for a strength focus versus a problem focus set up a false dichotomy. We agree with McMillen and colleagues' contention that "the best social work practice has always maintained a dual focus on both problems and capacity building" (p. 317).

There were more moderate challenges to the use of a problem-solving process expressed by other authors. Authors of the chapters on constructivist, narrative, and existential theories noted that the open, process-oriented nature of their approaches did not fit well with a structured, pragmatic, problem-solving focus. We understand this concern, but we think it is based on a misconception of our proposed use of a problem-solving process. We believe that problems can be defined in many different ways. Although identification of a specific, tangible problem may be the preferred approach of a cognitive behaviorist or a task-centered practitioner, our generalist-eclectic approach allows for a much broader conception of problems, including problem conceptions of an existential or postmodern nature. Also, we believe that the problem-solving process needs to be used flexibly, and that while it can offer guidelines for practice, these should not be construed as prescriptions or followed rigidly. Our valuing of artistic, intuitive-inductive practice processes attests to this and reflects openness to the less structured, more process-oriented theories. As Perlman (1957) argued 50 years ago about the problem-solving model, "In no sense is such a structure a stamped out routine. It is rather an underlying guide, a pattern for action which gives general form to the caseworker's inventiveness or creativity" (p. vi).

Some authors also noted differences between their and our understanding of the importance of the helping relationship. Saulnier (chapter 14) noted that although some feminist practitioners use relationship development as a primary intervention, others are skeptical of this. She explained that such skepticism relates to concerns that workers might use a focus on the helping relationship to get the client to adopt the worker's worldview instead of engaging in sociopolitical analysis of the client's life situation. Furthermore, Saulnier pointed out that some feminist workers believe a focus on the helping relationship may be class based and outside the interests of many marginalized clients.

We believe that such concerns are based on a conception of the helping relationship that is different from the one we promote. In our view, the former concern represents a misuse of the helping relationship because the focus should always be on understanding the client's worldview and the worker should consider macro as well as micro factors. With regard to the latter criticism, while we acknowledge that the influence of class and culture can result in preferences for different types of helping relationships, we contend that it is incumbent on workers to adapt their relationship style to client preference. There is no one ideal type of helping relationship, but all clients are likely to appreciate and benefit from a helping relationship in which they perceive the worker to be genuinely supportive, understanding, empathic, and trustworthy.

Ramos and Tolson (chapter 11) raised another issue in noting a difference between the task-centered and the generalist-eclectic view of the helping relationship. Although the task-centered model values the same type of helping relationship as our generalist-eclectic approach, it avoids the use of the term *therapeutic relationship* because this can imply that the relationship can be the cause of change. The task-centered model views a good helping relationship as necessary, but never sufficient to cause change, and Ramos and Tolson contend this understanding is consistent with research on the issue.

We agree that a good helping relationship is often not sufficient to cause change, but we maintain that it can contribute directly to change and that it is sometimes sufficient. A good helping relationship contributes directly to change by combating demoralization, instilling hope, and bolstering self-esteem. For some clients, particularly for those who have not been subjected to severe, long-standing stressors and who have supportive networks, this may be sufficient to restore their coping ability. We would also contend that our understanding of the impact of relationship factors is consistent with the research (see chapter 1 for a brief review of research on the importance of relationship and other common factors).

More generally, we should also note that, despite endorsement of the elements of the generalist perspective that are central to our generalist-eclectic approach, there are certainly differences in the degree to which various theories emphasize these elements. First, despite a commitment to a person-in-environment perspective and holistic assessment by all but one practice theory represented in the book (i.e., solution-focused therapy), specific practice theories, by definition, have more preconceptions and are less comprehensive than a generalist perspective. Every practice theory has preconceived ideas about the cause of human problems. For example, psychodynamic theories may give consideration to environmental and sociocultural factors in assessment, but focus is directed to intrapsychic and interpersonal issues. Thus, despite a commitment to broad-based assessment, the preconceptions that exist for all practice theories can function as blinders.

Second, most practice theories pay much less attention to issues of diversity and oppression than a generalist social work perspective. Of the practice theories reviewed in this book, only task-centered and feminist theories devote considerable attention to broad social issues (e.g., poverty). These same two theories, along with the social deconstruction variety of narrative therapy, are the only theories that focus considerably on issues of diversity and oppression.

Finally, despite an openness to eclecticism, by virtue of their primary theoretical orientation, all practice theories are less theoretically and technically "open" than the generalist-eclectic approach. Thus, despite the general compatibility between many theoretical perspectives and the generalist-eclectic approach, we believe that, when drawing on theories, clinical social workers need to consciously integrate the central principles and values of the generalist perspective of social work into their practice.

Compatibility With the Artistic, Intuitive-Inductive Elements of Practice

A key aspect of our generalist-eclectic framework is the endorsement of the artistic elements of direct practice. As explained in chapters 1 and 2, we believe that the importance of artistic, intuitive-inductive practice processes need to be recognized and integrated with an eclectic use of theory. We did not ask authors of the chapters on direct practice theories to

comment on the compatibility of their practice approach to our endorsement of the artistic, intuitive-inductive elements of practice. Thus, our
discussion of this issue is based on our understanding of the various
direct practice theories presented in Part III of the book.

In reviewing the direct practice theories, it seemed evident to us
that a few of these theories have a particular affinity with the artistic,
intuitive-inductive approach to practice. Most noteworthy in this regard
are client-centered theory (chapter 12), existential theory (chapter 13),
and the collaborative language systems variety of narrative therapy
(chapter 15). These approaches emphasize the importance of suspending
theoretical thinking, entering into the phenomenological world of clients,
building genuine and collaborative personal relationships with clients,
and developing felt understanding of clients' lives.

In chapter 12, Rothery and Tutty note the client-centered disdain
for "preconceptions in the form of theories of personality, or psychopathology, or anything else that might work against our openness to
the uniqueness of people and their situations" (p. 301). In chapter 13,
Randall explains that existential therapies "are more readily identified by
their orientation toward *desirable goals* than by particularly well-defined
technical or procedural guidelines" (p. 322) and that they "are renowned
for their relative lack of a precise structure and their de-emphasis on
technique" (p. 328). In discussing collaborative language systems therapy
in chapter 15, Buckman, Kinney, and Reese describe "a therapist posture
that emphasizes collaboration, openness, and curiosity (not knowing)"
(p. 372). Although each of these theories has somewhat different emphases, they share with each other, and with the intuitive-inductive approach
to practice, an emphasis on the artistic and humanistic elements of
practice.

Another model that has a somewhat different affinity to artistic
practice processes is the task-centered (TC) model. Although the TC
model is much more structured and less process-oriented than the three
theories discussed above, it also incorporates the recognition that theory
is not always used in practice. The TC literature does not refer to intuition or inductive theory building, but it does refer to the related idea of
commonsense reasoning: "When an explanation is required, we turn first
to explanations based on reasoning. When a theoretical explanation is
needed, we are free to apply the theory or combination of theories that
best explains the problem encountered" (Tolson, Reid, & Garvin, 2003,
p. 32). We see this type of atheoretical, commonsense reasoning as part
of the art of practice.

In highlighting the compatibility between particular theories and
artistic practice processes, this is not to say that the other theories reviewed
in the book do not also allow for artistic and humanistic factors. In fact,

we would suggest that most of the theories in Part III of the book, as well as the low-level practice models in Part IV, have significant artistic elements. With some exceptions, however, we would contend that because they are usually more process-oriented and less structured, the psychodynamic, humanistic, feminist, and postmodern theories are more compatible with artistic practice processes than the cognitive-behavioral models. We have noted, above, the exception of the emphasis on artistic elements of practice by the cognitive-behavioral TC model. An exception of the opposite kind is the postmodern solution-focused model being less compatible with artistic processes because of its prescriptive structure and emphasis on techniques.

REVISITING THE IMPORTANCE OF THE PROBLEM-SOLVING MODEL AS A FRAMEWORK FOR INTEGRATING THE ARTISTIC AND SCIENTIFIC APPROACHES TO PRACTICE

As discussed in chapter 3, the downside to both the artistic, intuitive-inductive approach to practice and a scientific orientation that emphasizes the eclectic use of theory is a lack of structure and guidelines for practice. Without some dependable structure and guidelines, both the artistic and the theoretically eclectic approaches to practice can lack focus and direction and become haphazard—which is the common criticism from those who advocate following a single model of therapy. We have argued that the problem-solving model provides such structure and guidelines for practice and thus facilitates the integration of the artistic and scientific approaches to practice.

The broad guidelines that are contained in the problem-solving model for each phase of practice (from engagement to termination) provide sufficient structure for the eclectic use of various theories, but because they are not rigidly prescriptive they also afford enough flexibility to allow for intuition and inductive reasoning. For instance, with regard to data collection and assessment, the general structure and guidelines of the problem-solving model remind practitioners to use a person-in-environment perspective and direct them to give consideration to a broad range of factors (micro and macro, stressors and strengths) in order to understand clients' life situations. The problem-solving guidelines in this phase of practice also direct practitioners to consider a broad range of theoretical perspectives to help make sense of clients' situations, including mid- and low-level practice theories, as well as high-level or meta-theories. Furthermore, the general nature and the flexibility of these problem-solving guidelines allow for practitioners to use their intuition and inductive reasoning to develop together with their clients an in-depth understanding of unique problem situations. Thus, as with other phases of the problem-solving process, the general guidelines of the data collection and assessment phase allow for a synthesis of an eclectic use of theory and intuitive-inductive processes.

CHALLENGES FOR GENERALIST-ECLECTIC DIRECT SOCIAL WORK PRACTICE

Given the fact that we have tried to extol the virtues of and argue persuasively for a generalist-eclectic approach to direct social work practice, we would be remiss if we did not consider some of the challenges that exist for this approach. Below, we discuss important challenges for research and for practice, as well as strategies for dealing with these challenges.

Challenges for Research

Although cumulative research on psychotherapy has found no significant differences in the effectiveness of the various theoretical approaches (the "equal outcomes" phenomenon), the research indicates clearly that psychotherapy is effective compared to nonintervention (Lambert, Bergin, & Garfield, 2004). Because single theory approaches have predominated historically in the helping professions, the cumulative research that has established the effectiveness of psychotherapy has been based primarily on single theory approaches. Due to the newness of the movement toward eclecticism in psychotherapy and to the preoccupation with theory development in this movement, until recently, research on eclectic models has been neglected. In 1997, Norcross noted, "The commitment to psychotherapy integration is largely philosophical rather than empirical in nature. The adequacy of various integrative and eclectic approaches remains to be proven" (p. 87).

Even before much research on eclectic therapies had been conducted, however, proponents of eclecticism argued for the probable effectiveness of such approaches. In 1992, Lambert argued,

> To the extent that eclectic therapies provide treatment that includes substantial overlap with traditional methods that have been developed and tested, they rest on a firm empirical base, and they should prove to be at least as effective as traditional school-based therapies. (p. 71)

In recent years, research on eclectic/integrative therapies has increased significantly. As reported in chapter 1, a recent review of such research

(Schottenbauer et al., 2005) found empirical support from randomized controlled studies for 20 such therapies. This accumulating body of research on eclectic/integrative therapies provides support for Lambert's (1992) prediction that eclectic therapies will prove to be at least as effective as single theory approaches. Still, research on eclectic approaches is in its early stages.

In chapter 1, we considered how the cumulative research findings of the equal outcomes of various types of therapy and the importance of factors that are common across therapies (e.g., relationship factors) provide indirect empirical support for the movement toward eclecticism. We also reviewed how, despite these research findings and the emerging direct empirical support for eclectic therapies, the empirically supported treatment (EST) movement in psychology has continued to push a research focus of establishing the effectiveness of single theory approaches with specific disorders. Furthermore, because EST research protocols that require the use of treatment manuals (in order to standardize treatment) and a focus on specific disorders with outcome measurements related to the disorder are best suited to cognitive-behavioral treatments, the vast majority of treatments that have achieved "empirically supported" status are cognitive-behavioral therapies (Messer, 2001).

Although some eclectic approaches have been supported by EST research, most eclectic approaches are ill-suited to the protocols of this research. In particular, the EST requirement for the development of standardized, manualized treatments for specific disorders does not fit well with the flexible, creative nature of most eclectic therapies. Because most eclectic therapies cannot and would not want to specify what therapists should do during therapy sessions, treatment manuals are not used, results of studies on eclectic therapy cannot be replicated (i.e., because what therapists do during treatment is not clearly defined or standardized), and eclectic therapies cannot achieve the status of an empirically supported therapy. For similar reasons, the same is true for most psychodynamic, humanistic, feminist, and postmodern therapies. This becomes especially problematic because ESTs have become required by some managed care and insurance companies and thus practitioners feel pressured to use ESTs (Wampold, 2001).

We will not repeat here our critique of the EST movement in chapter 1; however, among many other authors, we believe that the focus of EST research is misplaced and the interpretations of the results are misleading. As Lambert and Ogles (2004) have argued,

> Decades of research have not produced support for one superior treatment or set of techniques for specific disorders. . . . These findings . . . argue against the current trend of identifying empirically supported therapies that purport to be uniquely effective. (p. 167)

Nevertheless, the EST movement presents a serious challenge to establishing the credibility of eclectic therapies. The solution is not, however, to make eclectic therapies more standardized in order to fit EST research protocols. This could compromise the effectiveness of eclectic therapy, which we think depends in large part on the artistry of relationship development and reflection, and on the flexible, creative use of theory.

On an individual level, one response to counter the negative effects of the EST movement is to become familiar with the conceptual and empirical arguments against ESTs and to enter into the debate on the issues (e.g., in classroom, agency, or professional training settings). We refer readers to chapter 1 for a summary discussion of the issues and for references to more detailed arguments provided by authors such as Henry (1998), Messer (2001), Norcross (2001), and Wampold (2001). On the level of a program of research, another response to the EST challenge suggested by Wampold (2001) is to compare the effectiveness of ESTs and eclectic therapies in natural, clinical practice contexts. Such a comparison has never been conducted, and although many such studies would have to be conducted in order to come to any firm conclusions, on the basis of the cumulative results of psychotherapy research (i.e., the equal outcomes phenomenon and the importance of common factors) we would expect that eclectic therapies would prove to be at least as effective as ESTs. Once the claims about the superior effectiveness of ESTs are refuted empirically, clinical research could shift to more productive foci. As suggested in chapter 1, such foci include the therapeutic relationship (Norcross, 2001) and the qualities and actions of highly successful therapists (Lambert & Ogles, 2004; Wampold, 2001).

We would be remiss if we did not add some comments about the evidence-based practice (EBP) movement in social work (Gibbs & Gambrill, 2002; Howard, McMillen, & Pollio, 2003; Magill, 2006), which has connections to the EST movement in psychology. We see the EBP movement in social work as broader and, at its best, more flexible than the EST movement. Magill (2006) has explained that the goal of EBP "is not to standardize clinical practice to the extent that social workers merely deliver an intervention empirically tied to a specific diagnostic category" (p. 107). Similarly, Gibbs and Gambrill (2002) have argued that EBP's "consideration of client values and expectations as well as the extent to which research findings apply to a particular client shows that it is not a cookbook approach" (p. 459). Still, it is clear that EBP is based largely on a scientific understanding of practice, which assumes that the specific factors of theory and technique are the primary determinants of clinical effectiveness. Although we support the use of empirical knowledge in practice, as explained above, we think that research that identifies "empirically supported" theories or techniques is misleading and that there are more productive foci for research.

Challenges in Practice

A generalist-eclectic approach to practice does not provide the comfort and certainty for practitioners that following a single model of therapy can provide. Practitioners who adhere to one theoretical approach, particularly if it has a narrow focus and prescriptive guidelines, can gain comfort in "knowing" at the outset of counseling what the problem is and/or what they need to do to help ameliorate it. In generalist-eclectic practice, the emphasis on theoretical openness and broad-based assessment precludes this type of certainty. Furthermore, the emphasis on the artistic, intuitive-inductive elements of practice, as well as on collaboration and partnership with the client, involves giving up control and certainty in the helping process. Although the guidelines of the problem-solving model and understanding and/or techniques gleaned from a variety of theories provide helpful guidance for practice, a generalist-eclectic approach requires the practitioner to be creative and to find courage "in the face of the uncertain" (Papell & Skolnik, 1992, p. 22). This can be difficult, particularly for beginning practitioners who frequently yearn for "a 'secret handbook' of practical 'how-to-do-it' knowledge" (Mahoney, 1986, p. 169); however, it is our contention that clients respond better to this humble, open, and humane approach to practice than to theoretical certainty and prescriptive formulas.

Another obvious challenge in this approach to practice is that of becoming familiar with the wide variety of theories for direct practice. Although we have offered strategies for simplifying and demystifying the confusing array of clinical theories (i.e., conceptualizing levels and broad classes of theory, and identifying the general characteristics of classes of theory), there is no denying that developing in-depth knowledge and skill in a variety of theoretical approaches is a formidable task. This is particularly difficult given the unfortunate but continuing use of "idiosyncratic jargon" by many theoretical orientations (Goldfried & Castonguay, 1992). This not only makes learning different theories more difficult and intimidating but it also hinders the development of understanding about similarities across theories.

With regard to the latter issue, we support the long-range goal of translating theories into ordinary English in order to further demystification and to facilitate cross-theory dialogue (Goldfried & Castonguay, 1992). With regard to the more general difficulty of becoming a "master of all trades" (i.e., of all theories and techniques), we think that practitioners should construe this as a career-long goal, in the context of understanding that theoretical knowledge and technical expertise can never be complete and that artistic elements of practice such as interpersonal sensitivity and relationship skills are of prime importance to counseling effectiveness.

A third, general challenge to practicing from a generalist-eclectic orientation concerns the necessity of integrating a consideration of broader social issues, particularly issues of diversity and oppression, into both assessment and intervention. As noted earlier in this chapter, very few counseling theories pay much attention to these issues. Thus, from a generalist social work perspective there is a need to utilize other sources of knowledge about working with issues of diversity and oppression. In addition to the generalist social work literature, practitioners can draw from other broad frameworks for social work practice, such as empowerment practice (Gutierrez, Parsons, & Cox, 1998) and the strengths perspective (Saleebey, 2002), that pay special attention to these issues. In drawing from the empowerment and strengths models of practice, however, practitioners should be mindful of the "dichotomizing rhetoric" in these frameworks that pit their capacity focus against the problem focus of traditional direct social work practice (McMillen et al., 2004).

Managed Care

The major transformation in counseling services that has been brought about over the last 15 years by the managed care industry deserves special attention as a potential challenge to a generalist-eclectic approach to practice. We surmise that the managed care industry, which frequently limits counseling to as few as 5 or 10 sessions, might be skeptical of an approach to practice that values holistic assessment, the development of in-depth understanding within the context of a good therapeutic relationship, and intervention that draws on a range of theories and techniques. In fact, in advising practitioners how to present themselves to case managers within the managed care industry, Nichols and Schwartz (2004) suggested that "calling yourself 'eclectic' is more likely to sound fuzzy than flexible" (p. 87). We do not doubt that this type of pejorative thinking about eclecticism continues to exist, particularly with regard to brief treatment, and we see this is as a challenge that needs to be addressed.

Although we do have concerns about the rigid enforcement of short-term counseling limits, particularly for clients who have multiple, severe, and/or long-standing stressors, we believe that a generalist-eclectic approach to practice can be used effectively in the context of brief treatment and managed care. As discussed in chapter 3, holistic assessment does not usually involve a long, drawn-out process of data collection. Practitioners can learn to focus a broad lens rather quickly, and some holistic assessments (which are always tentative and subject to change) can be completed in single sessions. Similarly, the development of a strong therapeutic relationship does not usually require long periods of time; research has shown that alliances predictive of outcome are usually formed within the first few sessions (Horvath & Greenberg, 1994).

With regard to intervention, a generalist-eclectic approach to practice can be as focused and brief as necessary. Within a managed care context, practitioners and clients should plan and contract to focus on the most pressing problem that can be dealt with within the allotted time frame. From a generalist-eclectic perspective, however, practitioners working within the managed care industry would be obligated to attempt to secure longer term help for those clients who want and require it. This could involve lobbying a case manager for extending the counseling limits, contracting with the client to continue work together after the managed care session limits have been reached (and working out payment issues), or referring the client to other services.

There are two myths that can limit the managed care industry's openness to eclectic and other process-oriented therapeutic approaches and that therefore need to be challenged. First, as discussed above, is the myth that designated that "empirically supported treatments" are, by virtue of the designation, more effective than other therapeutic approaches. Clinicians and researchers who challenge the empirical basis of this contention need to continue to debate proponents of ESTs in professional arenas (e.g., in refereed publications and in professional associations) and to educate the managed care industry about this issue.

The second myth is that only therapeutic approaches that are self-labeled as "brief" are suitable for the parameters set by the managed care industry for treatment duration. In particular, brief solution-focused therapy's "promise of quick solutions has endeared it to the managed care industry. Indeed . . . many applicants for provider status call themselves 'solution-focused' regardless of whether or not they have any training in this approach" (Nichols & Schwartz, 2004, p. 312). There are, however, good reasons to believe that most models of therapy (whether single theory or eclectic) are adaptable to the treatment duration parameters of managed care. A review of studies that have examined length of treatment across settings and theoretical orientations has established that the median number of sessions was between five and eight (Garfield, 1994). Thus, traditional counseling approaches are often as brief as the so-called brief therapies. Even the psychodynamic school, which is traditionally the longest term approach to counseling, has developed brief treatment models that can fit the constraints of managed care (Koss & Shiang, 1994; Messer, 2001). Thus, the managed care industry needs to be educated to the fact that all theoretical orientations, including an eclectic orientation to the use of theory, are adaptable for brief treatment.

SUMMARY

In addition to providing a survey of contemporary theories for direct social work practice, this book represents an attempt to integrate a number of important and compatible ideas in the field of counseling into a broad framework for practice. To summarize, there are three important aspects to what we have called the generalist-eclectic approach to direct practice.

The first aspect is commitment to social work principles and values reflected by elements of the generalist perspective of social work practice. These elements include a person-in-environment perspective informed by ecological systems theory, an emphasis on a good helping relationship that fosters empowerment, the flexible use of a problem-solving process to guide practice, holistic assessment that includes a focus on issues of diversity and oppression and on strengths, and the flexible and eclectic use of a wide range of theory. The latter element is informed by theory and research in the broader movement toward eclecticism in the fields of counseling and psychotherapy. A second important aspect of our approach to practice is the valuing of the artistic elements of practice, or what we have called intuitive-inductive practice. This includes the recognition that much of the time practice does not involve the conscious application of theory and technique and that intuition, inductive reasoning, and creativity play important roles in practice. The third key aspect of our approach is the use of the problem-solving model of generalist practice to provide a flexible structure and general guidelines for practice in order to support the integration of the eclectic use of theory with the artistic elements of practice.

In conclusion, we wish to stress that the generalist-eclectic approach is not meant to represent yet another competing approach to or framework for direct social work practice. It is a way of conceptualizing practice that encourages flexibility in the use of multiple theories, perspectives, and ideas, while placing the principles and values central to the profession of social work at the forefront.

REFERENCES

Garfield, S. L. (1994). Research on client variables in psychotherapy. In A. E. Bergin & S. L. Garfield (Eds.), *Handbook of psychotherapy and behavior change* (4th ed., pp. 190–228). New York: Wiley.

Gibbs, L., & Gambrill, E. (2002). Evidence-based practice: Counterarguments to objections. *Research on Social Work Practice, 12,* 452–476.

Goldfried, M. R., & Castonguay, L. G. (1992). The future of psychotherapy integration. *Psychotherapy, 29,* 4–10.

Gutierrez, L. M., Parsons, R. J., & Cox, E. O. (1998). *Empowerment in social work practice: A sourcebook.* Pacific Grove, CA: Brooks/Cole.

Henry, W. P. (1998). Science, politics, and the politics of science: The use and misuse of empirically validated treatment research. *Psychotherapy Research, 8,* 126–140.

Horvath, A. O., & Greenberg, L. S. (1994). Introduction. In A. O. Horvath & L. S. Greenberg (Eds.), *The working alliance: Theory, research, and practice* (pp. 1–9). New York: Wiley.

Howard, M. O., McMillen, C. J., & Pollio, D. E. (2003). Teaching evidence-based practice: Toward a new paradigm for social work education. *Research on Social Work Practice, 13,* 234–259.

Koss, M. P., & Shiang, J. (1994). Research on brief psychotherapy. In A. E. Bergin & S. L. Garfield (Eds.), *Handbook of psychotherapy and behavior change* (4th ed., pp. 664–700). New York: Wiley.

Lambert, M. J. (1992). Psychotherapy outcome research: Implications for integrative and eclectic therapists. In J. C. Norcross & M. R. Goldfried (Eds.), *Handbook of psychotherapy integration* (pp. 94–129). New York: Basic Books.

Lambert, M. J., Bergin, A. E., & Garfield, S. L. (2004). Introduction and historical overview. In M. J. Lambert (Ed.), *Bergin and Garfield's handbook of psychotherapy and behavior change* (5th ed., pp. 3–15). New York: Wiley.

Lambert, M. J., & Ogles, B. M. (2004). The efficacy and effectiveness of psychotherapy. In M. J. Lambert (Ed.), *Bergin and Garfield's handbook of psychotherapy and behavior change* (5th ed., pp. 139–193). New York: Wiley.

Magill, M. (2006). The future of evidence in evidence-based practice: Who will answer the call for clinical relevance? *Journal of Social Work, 6,* 101–115.

Mahoney, M. J. (1986). The tyranny of technique. *Counseling and Values, 30,* 169–174.

McMillen, J. C., Morris, L., & Sherraden, M. (2004). Ending social work's grudge match: Problems versus strengths. *Families in Society, 85,* 317–325.

Messer, S. B. (2001). Empirically supported treatments: What's a nonbehaviorist to do? In B. D. Slife, R. N. Williams, & S. H. Barlow (Eds.), *Critical issues in psychotherapy: Translating new ideas into practice* (pp. 3–25). Thousand Oaks, CA: Sage.

Nichols, M. P., & Schwartz, R. C. (2004). *Family therapy: Concepts and methods* (6th ed.). Boston: Pearson.

Norcross, J. C. (1997). Emerging breakthroughs in psychotherapy integration: Three predictions and one fantasy. *Psychotherapy, 34,* 86–90.

Norcross, J. C. (2001). Purposes, process, and products of the Task Force on Empirically Supported Treatment Relationships. *Psychotherapy: Theory, Research, Practice, Training, 38,* 345–356.

Papell, C. P., & Skolnik, L. (1992). The reflective practitioner: A contemporary paradigm's relevance for social work education. *Journal of Social Work Education, 28,* 18–26.

Perlman, H. H. (1957). *Social casework: A problem-solving process.* Chicago: University of Chicago Press.

Saleebey, D. (2002). *The strengths perspective in social work practice* (3rd ed.). New York: Allyn & Bacon.

Schottenbauer, M. A., Glass, C. R., & Arnkoff, D. B. (2005). Outcome research on psychotherapy integration. In J. C. Norcross & M. R. Goldfried (Eds.), *Handbook of psychotherapy integration* (2nd ed., pp. 459–493). New York: Oxford University Press.

Stalker, C. A., Levene, J. E., & Coady, N. F. (1999). Solution-focused brief therapy—One model fits all? *Families in Society, 80,* 468–477.

Tolson, E. R., Reid, W. J., & Garvin, C. D. (2003). *Generalist practice: A task-centered approach* (2nd ed.). New York: Columbia University Press.

Wampold, B. E. (2001). *The great psychotherapy debate: Models, methods, and findings.* Mahwah, NJ: Lawrence Erlbaum.

Index

Cognitive Behavior Therapy in Clinical Social Work Practice

Tammie Ronen, PhD
Arthur Freeman, EdD, ABPP, Editors
Foreword by **Aaron T. Beck,** MD

"Few volumes on CT are as comprehensive as the volume that [Ronen and Freeman] have edited. It is the first volume of its kind for this important professional discipline and group. With this publication, CT has moved yet another step forward."

—From the foreword by **Aaron T. Beck**, MD
University Professor, University of Pennsylvania

Edited by a leading social work authority and a master CBT clinician, this first-of-its-kind handbook provides the foundations and training that social workers need to master cognitive behavior therapy.

From traditional techniques to new techniques such as mindfulness meditation and the use of DBT, the contributors ensure a thorough and up-to-date presentation of CBT. Covered are the most common disorders encountered when working with adults, children, families, and couples.

Written by social workers for social workers, this new focus on the foundations and applications of cognitive behavior therapy will help individuals, families, and groups lead happier, fulfilled, and more productive lives.

Contents (main headings):

- The Basic Foundation (Social Work, Cognitive Behavior Therapy, Evidence-Based Developmental Characteristics)
- Methods of Intervention: Theory and Techniques
- Focus on Children
- Focus on Couples and Families
- Focus on Adult and Problem Areas
- Directions for the Future

2006 · 656pp · hardcover · 978-0-8261-0215-7

11 West 42nd Street, New York, NY 10036-8002 • Fax: 212-941-7842
Order Toll-Free: 877-687-7476 • Order Online: www.springerpub.com